Voices from War

PROPERTY OF
CURRIE
DISTRICT
HISTORY
SOCIETY

The Author

Ian MacDougall left school at 15, worked for some years on newspapers, did National Service in the army, graduated from Edinburgh University, was a History teacher or lecturer for over twenty years, and is presently employed in local government. Secretary of the Scottish Labour History Society since its formation in 1961, he is also secretary of the Scottish Working People's History Trust. His other books include:

Minutes of Edinburgh Trades Council, 1859-1873 (ed.) (1969)
A Catalogue of some Labour Records in Scotland and some Scots Records outside Scotland (1978)
Essays in Scottish Labour History (ed.) (1978)
Militant Miners (1981)
Labour in Scotland: A Pictorial History from the Eighteenth Century to the Present Day (1985)
Voices from the Spanish Civil War (1986)
The Prisoners at Penicuik: French and other Prisoners-of-War 1803-1814 (1989)
Voices from the Hunger Marches (2 vols) (1990-91)
Hard Work, Ye Ken (1993)
Hoggie's Angels (1995)
Mungo Mackay and the Green Table (1995)

VOICES FROM WAR
AND SOME LABOUR STRUGGLES

*Personal Recollections of War in our Century
by Scottish Men and Women*

IAN MacDOUGALL

THE MERCAT PRESS
EDINBURGH

First published in 1995 by Mercat Press
at James Thin, 53 South Bridge, Edinburgh EH1 1YS

ISBN 1873644 450

Set in Bembo 10/12 pt
Printed in Great Britain by The Cromwell Press
Broughton Gifford, Wiltshire

CONTENTS

FOREWORD

by Emeritus Professor V G Kiernan

Oral history, the gathering of information about the past from memories of people still living, has become an important branch of modern history-writing. It is of course not altogether new; it has been practised here and there for long, for instance by biographers like that eminent Scotsman Boswell. Such memory-collecting is in one light a form of conservation; it can keep alive much of human experience otherwise doomed to disappear. Written records proliferate, libraries bulge, but there is still need for as much oral evidence as can be had, to fill gaps, or confirm or disprove ideas derived from printed records, all set down by fallible human hands.

Apart from this kind of utility, other people's recollections of things done or lived through can always make an appeal to our curiosity about our fellow-beings, whom modern styles of living are apt to remove to a further and further distance from us. More authentically than any novels or films, they give us glimpses of individuals who have been our unseen neighbours, and taken together help to clarify our picture of the community, the country, they and we have belonged to. They carry us into places and situations otherwise beyond our ken. One disagreeable instance to be found here is what used to be known to soldiers lodged in Edinburgh Castle before 1914 as the Rat Trap, because so horridly inhospitable; accommodation judged quite good enough, in the Land of Hope and Glory, for the Tommy Atkins whose bayonet propped up the glorious British Empire.

All history-writing demands patience and dedication, and history-gathering from the lips of men and women probably more than most. Ian MacDougall is ideally qualified to draw out confidences and encourage flows of memory from the recesses where it has lain concealed. Tape-recording is not mere mechanical work. But older people, such as the voices heard in this book belong to, often feel a growing need to tell their stories, if they can find a listener. They are lucky when they find one able to steer them away from what has been trivial in their lives to what can still have meaning for others. For some of these speakers it must have brought a kind of purgation of evil things lurking in their minds, as in the minds of millions of others fated to 'draw their breath with pain', as Hamlet says, in this in many ways evil age.

Ian MacDougall can be expected on arrival in heaven to ask first not for a harp but for means of jotting down whatever his fellow-guests, and the angels in charge of his sector, have to tell him. He is a veteran Oral Historian, with a reputation securely founded on several volumes of Scottish memories collected and edited. This new one, as he explains in his Introduction, has been put together over a period of three decades; most of the voices heard in it will be heard no more. A great part of his life has been devoted to learning or teaching history; he has changed to a new profession, as perhaps we should all do from time to time to keep our mental muscles from stiffening, but he is still as much attached to history as ever, and is contributing to its study in various ways. His latest work is focused on one of the ugliest, but one of the most important, things in all world history. What is war, why do human beings fight, how do they feel while fighting, and afterwards?

He has gone to much further trouble, and added greatly to the interest and helpfulness of these records, by supplying explanatory notes, including some necessary corrections. They can be relied on, like everything that he does, for conscientious accuracy, and will tell readers much else about twentieth-century Scotland. He has shown good judgement in deciding how to transpose the sounds of colloquial Scottish into Roman letters. Very many writers have faced this problem, and the great majority must have taken their cue from Walter Scott. Ian has followed a path of his own, and managed to keep his sentences from looking either too English or too mysterious. Whatever the claim of Lallans to be a language fit for a free Scotland to speak and write, it will be a pity if it ever ceases to be comprehensible to English readers as well. I was puzzled for a moment by 'We yaised tae go', and resolved to look up Scott and how he *used* to write this word.

Some of the names met with here are well-known, like that of Harry McShane, some records of whose long life have been garnered by other hunters, or put on paper by himself; and William Marwick, long a highly respected teacher of economic history at Edinburgh University; and Norman MacCaig the poet. Most, however, are names of people unheard of outside their own small corners, as the rank and file of humankind usually are. Not many of them possessed any diaries or letters to serve them as remembrancers, and in view of this it is surprising how much they were able to recall; though it may be that the habit of diary-keeping weakens the independent power of memory. Some of those who make their appearance had gone through what we conventionally call education. Others had to 'scramble themselves', in Jane Austen's phrase, into an education of sorts, as all women had to do in her day. And, after all, the part of any education that counts most is self-education.

Some names come from abroad. Scotland has been a great place for comings and goings, since long before the Scots arrived from Ulster to fight their long wars with the Picts, after which some of them returned to Ulster to help the English to conquer their distant relatives there, and many others later removed from Europe, leaving plenty of room at home for the reception of newcomers. There are Italian names in the list, one at least of them familiar to all dwellers in Edinburgh with an interest in Chianti or Valpolicella. One witness was recruited not in Scotland but in France, where Ian and his wife have been indefatigable cyclists and explorers. A shortage of women is to be regretted, though reasons for it are not hard to find. In the bad old days the fact of women being mostly cut off from civic activity and responsibility may well have dulled awareness among them of what was happening in the public arena. This was impressed on me one day when I was combing an Edinburgh street with a questionnaire about opinions on the war in Vietnam. An elderly woman told me that I must put my questions to her husband, it was *his* business to know about such things, not hers.

Variety of experience has been at least as great as of names, though there are recurrent notes to be heard. The period covered was dominated by two World Wars, two volcanoes glowering over the landscape. Nearer home the General Strike and the Hunger Marches cast other shadows over the pages. Scots through the centuries have been very often professional fighting-men, and often militants in less violent contests. My old Edinburgh friend Don Renton, who fought with the International Brigade in the Spanish Civil War, when I asked him what kinds of reading he liked best, in poetry for example, replied that what he liked best was writing that 'strikes the note of struggle' (in his mouth this word really ought to be written 'strrruggle'). In the light of some of this book's legacies, it would seem that all through at least the first half of this century a smouldering class struggle, a hidden guerrilla war, was going on.

Struggle for human rights was being waged on many fronts. Before 1914 soldiers in Ireland, one of them says, could be quite friendly with Irish folk, and sometimes fell in love with Irish girls, but they were so heavily indoctrinated and dragooned that they could feel no sympathy for Irish nationalists, or even for Scottish workers on strike. But during the Great War when conscription came in and a young Scot was court-martialled for refusing to serve, he was surprised at the end by the prosecuting officer shaking hands with him, and most of the soldiers he met with were sympathetic or even admiring. One Christmas Day on the Somme, when a company was going into action, a hated officer was shot in the back; all the men knew, none of them disapproved. An unheroic memory, supplied in written form by a volunteer who joined the International Brigade in 1937—when he got to Spain, Charlie Chaplin's *Modern Times* was being shown there—is of a night before battle when he lay 'stiff with cold and fear, wondering what the morning would bring', and had to buy some wine from a peasant to give him 'Dutch courage'.

All these testimonies, from swimmers saved by a zealous coastguard from sinking out of sight in the ocean of time, will be found well worth reading. Perhaps of them all the most striking, as well as one of the longest, and latest to be completed, is the narrative of the chequered career of Eddie Mathieson. The fortunes of war, in World War II, led him by way of a coffin-shaped cell in a military prison to a training course for commandoes. This was long and gruelling, but to his surprise left him with feelings of pride in his new uniform, and *esprit de corps*. 'Your own troop that you were in was the most important thing. It was your family really.' His new family carried him to India, where he found the army, because of arrogant behaviour in pre-war years, highly unpopular; and he was probably one of many whose eyes were opened by the spectacle of Indian poverty and wretchedness. 'I think my own political awareness, awareness of problems in society, was being aroused by what I saw and experienced in India.' In the Burmese jungle, beset by Japanese inhumanly brave and fiendishly cruel, he lived through things so appalling that half a century later he was still suffering from nightmares, like the 'terrible dreams' that shook Macbeth and Lady Macbeth. His final conclusion was that war is, and must be, both horrible and senseless.

Many hours and days must have been expended on the preparation of this book, and it can fairly look forward to having many readers. It has a serious part to play in times like ours, when collective memory, like other social links, is under heavy strain. In older, simpler epochs, events were fewer and more easily remembered, even if they took on little by little less realistic shapes, and might end as Border Ballads. Capitalist industrialism has had a blighting effect, as it has on all popular culture. Life is nomadic, mechanised, washed over by quickening tides of news and impressions from everywhere, each flood blotting out the one before. We have, most of us, desperately little knowledge even of the history we have lived through, and this is one reason why politicians find it so easy to pull the wool over our eyes. To learn something, at first hand, of even a few lives in our own nook of the world and our own century, ought to be one remedy, and make us eager to learn more.

Already four centuries ago when capitalism was getting under way, Shakespeare lamented that in his pell-mell era no one had time to think about anyone but himself, and worthy individuals, even great ones, were quickly forgotten. None of Ian's flock may have been 'great' in the ordinary sense, but many of them went through great enough trials and tribulations, and in spite of these had ideals and beliefs to which they clung. Scotland must often have seemed to its children a sad, haunted country. One youngster recorded here went to work in a coal mine not long after leaving school, and within three weeks the older miner he was working with was crushed to death by falling coal.

Still, there were always those who were ready to take up arms against a sea of troubles, in defence of themselves or their neighbours. The will to win, or to grow, has persisted through Scotland's rugged history, fashioning Scots into the 'dour' folk they have prided themselves on being. Virgil called his fellow-Romans, using the same word, *gens dura,* a tough lot. Part of their endowment has been a faculty of seeing a cheering side to life, even if—as everywhere in the Northern Continent to which Scotland belongs—it may have needed liberal aid from Bacchus to find it. A young member of a bomber crew in World War II found that the expectation of life in his job was reckoned at three or four missions, and some were killed on their first raid. It is one of the intriguing surprises which turn up everywhere in this book that he found relief by writing poems after each raid he got back alive from. In one way or another, happiness has kept breaking in.

These pages, left to us by as worthy a group of human beings as ever represented Scotland in Parliament, are an encouragement to think of this as a country still with a future, a time coming, if it is made to come, that will be better than any in its unquiet past. But readers of this Foreword will be turning over its pages impatiently to get at what is waiting for them. A small episode from my own past comes into my memory, from India a lifetime ago. I was standing at the front of a stage, in a college hall, introducing a Shakespeare play which was to be performed, and was still in the middle of my few words when the curtain behind me suddenly opened and the play began. Happy to be able this time to retire a little more gracefully, I leave readers to a feast that Shakespeare, as a student of human nature and the human condition, would have been likely to enjoy.

INTRODUCTION

These personal recollections by twenty-nine men and women of their experiences in war and, in some cases, labour struggles in the twentieth century have been recorded at various stages during the past thirty years. But it was only in the last few years that the idea presented itself of publishing as a book what until then had been randomly gathered oral history recordings.

The earliest recordings—by Harry McShane, Grace Kennedy, Robert Irvine, Allan Young, Charlie McPherson, and William Carey—were all made at an informal oral history seminar at Pollok Community Centre in Glasgow in September 1963. Chaired by Dr Fred Reid, the seminar was tape-recorded very much as a pioneering project in oral history by Jean McCrindle and me, inspired by the then recently formed Scottish Labour History Society. The most recent recording—by Eddie Mathieson—was made in January 1994. All the other recollections below were gathered at one time or another between those years. In some cases the recordings were part of a series of oral history seminars at Newbattle Abbey Adult Residential College, where from 1971 to 1984 I was lecturer in history and trade union studies. James Marchbank, Dominic Crolla and Mark Hurny wholly, and William H Marwick and Dr Eric F Dott partly, recorded their recollections there before an audience of students. Most of the recollections of Mr Marwick and Dr Dott and all those of all but two of the remaining eighteen interviewees I recorded in their own homes (or at that of John and Anne Steadman, in the case of Bill Hanlan, and mine in the case of Eddie Mathieson). The remaining two—J P M Millar and John Lochore sent me their written recollections. J P M Millar, who was general secretary from 1923 to 1964 of the National Council of Labour Colleges, lived at Dartmouth in Devon for many years before his death in 1989 and it never proved possible for me to interview him about his war experiences (apart from a brief recording made by telephone in 1983 for inclusion in a BBC Radio Scotland programme about conscientious objectors in 1914-18). John Lochore I met only in 1987, a year after I had had published a book of recollections by other Scots who like him had fought for the Republic in the Spanish Civil War. It was then, when he allowed me to record his recollections as a hunger marcher in 1936 immediately before he had gone to Spain, that he showed me his unpublished memoirs of his Spanish experiences, an edited version of which appears below. The differing circumstances in which these twenty-nine sets of recollections were gathered may help explain their varying length and detail. The veterans at Pollok Community Centre in 1963 were unavoidably limited to only a few minutes each. My interviews with Joseph Pia and Eddie Mathieson, on the other hand, lasted several hours on each of the occasions we met in 1992-3 and 1994 respectively. Most of the interviews with other veterans lasted a varying number of hours each.

The recollections taken as a whole cover the years from before 1914 until the present, but the great bulk of them deal with aspects of the First and Second World Wars. In most cases (the Pollok group were unavoidably one exception) an attempt has been made to set recollections of war in the context of peace-time conditions and personal experience: family, community, housing, education, employment or unemployment, political and trade union activity etc.

The order in which the recollections are presented is broadly chronological. First come accounts by five of eight men who fought in the 1914-18 War. Of the other three who fought then in the trenches, Major Dan Bonnar bears testimony further on about the conscientious objectors he recalls seeing in detention at Hamilton Barracks; and the two others, William Murray and Hugh McIntyre, most of whose recollections are about labour struggles between the two World Wars, follow later. Clydeside agitators, including Harry McShane, are followed by conscientious objectors of 1914-18, including Dr Eric F Dott, who found himself found himself at the age of eighteen among a host of fellow objectors in Dartmoor prison. In the later 1930s the experiences of John Lochore in the International Brigade in the Spanish Civil War may remind the reader how that war was indeed a prologue to, or rehearsal by the Fascist Powers for, the Second World War. Of the Second World War, or at least its opening stages, Mark and Irena Hurny provide personal accounts of what they experienced in Poland, as well as of their subsequent experiences in labour camps in the Soviet Union. Paul Dunand, a Parisian, recalls how and why at the age of eighteen he joined the French Resistance to the German occupation and his activity thereafter in the Maquis in or near the centre of France. Service in the navy (including escorting convoys to Russia), in Bomber Command, and with the commandos in Burma are recalled respectively by James K Annand, Bill King and Eddie Mathieson. Four conscientious objectors—Andrew Gilhooley, Fred Pitkeathly, Bill Prentice and Norman MacCaig—in recalling their various experiences enable some comparisons to be made with those of fellow objectors in the previous World War. Internment—one in Canada, one in the Isle of Man—for their Fascist affiliations or activities is the subject of the recollections by the two cousins Dominic Crolla and Joseph Pia, and the latter also presents a vivid sketch of the Italian community in Edinburgh before the Second World War.

Each of these twenty-nine men and women provide their testimony of what they saw, heard, and experienced. Their testimony is given in their own words. Their accounts are personal, often vivid, sometimes moving. There is no self-pity in their accounts, but there is a great deal of humour, resilience, and (though these veterans would disclaim it) courage. It is in the nature of such personal recollections that they cannot always be verified by contemporary documents or by published works, though an attempt has been made in the accompanying notes to explain references that may not be clear or self-evident, to correct any obvious slips of fact, and so far as possible to identify persons mentioned.

These recollections possess the characteristic strengths and weaknesses of oral history. As contributions to knowledge and understanding of the historical events they deal with they are at their best when they are recounting personal experience— that corner, as it were, of the campaign, battle or struggle in which the speaker was personally engaged. On the other hand, they are retrospective accounts, recalled after, even long after, the events they describe. 'I often wish I had kept a diary,' says Eddie Mathieson. 'You werenae allowed tae.' Except to some extent in the case of William H Marwick, who kept a diary or made rough notes during at least the earlier phases of his detention as a conscientious objector in 1916; James K Annand, from whom survive a 22-page letter he wrote to some former teaching colleagues in Edinburgh, covering his experiences between November 1941 and April 1942 while he was serving on HMS *Tartar*, and some notes written while he was on HM trawler *Bute* based in Iceland in 1942-44; and Bill King, who wrote poems about his experiences in Bomber Command, the recollections below are based on memory, not on diaries or letters or notes or other documents written at or soon after the times they deal with. They are therefore no doubt subject to those subtle, conscious or unconscious mouldings or adaptations of past experience that all of us are prone to make. Those shortcomings, actual or potential, must be recognised. That done, these recollections nevertheless remain gateways through which the reader may pass to a greater knowledge and a better understanding of at least some aspects of war and, to a lesser extent, labour struggles in the twentieth century. These twenty-six men and three women are informative and stimulating guides. None of them would claim to be providing comprehensive, systematic, balanced, scholarly accounts of the campaigns, battles, struggles or other experiences they recount.

Within one volume it would hardly be possible to include personal accounts of all or even most of the campaigns, battles or other aspects of war in the twentieth century in which people in Britain, let alone those of other countries, have been involved. The voices of submariners, war widows, tank crews, merchant navymen, service women, fighter pilots, firemen, evacuees, prisoners-of-war, land girls, civilian victims of bombing, and many other groups who experienced war this century are not heard here. It is particularly regrettable that a much higher proportion of women's voices is not included. Such omissions and imbalances were not deliberate. But these and any other shortcomings in the book are to be blamed on me alone.

In editing the recollections for publication a continuous attempt has been made to preserve and present the actual words used by these twenty-nine men and women. The main changes made have been the cutting out of repetitious or extraneous matter and the transposition of occasional sentences or paragraphs in order to present a coherent narrative. Most of the tapes and copies of the verbatim transcripts of the recordings have been deposited in the School of Scottish Studies at Edinburgh University and may be consulted there.

The bulk of these recollections has never been published or broadcast before. Hugh McIntyre's activities in the labour movement in the Vale of Leven were drawn on for a section of Stuart Macintyre's book *Little Moscows* (London, 1980). Harry McShane's autobiography *No Mean Fighter* (London, 1978), written jointly with Joan Smith, deals later and more comprehensively with some of the ground he covers below. James K Annand published several articles in Scots in the magazine *Lallans* about his wartime experiences in the navy. J P M Millar contributed a chapter about his experiences as a conscientious objector in the Great War to a long out of print book *We did not Fight,* published sixty years ago. He, William H Marwick, Dr Eric F Dott, Mrs Dorothy Wiltshire, and William Carey contributed some of their recollections to a BBC Radio Scotland programme broadcast in 1983 that I compiled on conscientious objectors in that war. Andrew Gilhooley, Fred Pitkeathly, Bill Prentice and Norman MacCaig contributed to a similar programme broadcast by BBC Radio Scotland in 1993 on conscientious objectors in the 1939-45 war. Some of Joseph Pia's recollections were the subject of a BBC Radio Scotland programme I compiled that was broadcast also in 1993.

My thanks are due to all those who have helped in the making of this book. These recollections would or might never have been recorded or published without the willing co-operation of the twenty-nine men and women concerned, most of whom are, alas, now dead. Their warmth and sincerity, honesty and frankness, friendliness and helpfulness, and, where the interviews took place in their homes, generous hospitality, as well as the trouble taken by those who were able to do so in checking and correcting their edited transcripts, leave me greatly in their debt. I am grateful also to several of them who loaned me photographs or documents. Councillor David Smith and Lloyd and Helen Olson helped arrange my interview with the latter's father, Peter Corstorphine; only Peter's advanced age prevented a further interview taking place. John and Anne Steadman arranged for me the interview with Bill Hanlan. To Jean McCrindle I am grateful for readily agreeing that the transcripts of the tapes of the seminar in 1963 at Pollok Community Centre be included in edited form in this volume. Mrs Irena Hurny not only helped with further information about the family, employment and other background of her late husband Mark, who sadly had passed away before we could meet again to expand on his recollections recorded some years earlier at Newbattle Abbey, but also herself agreed to be interviewed about her own experiences in the 1939-45 war. Paul Dunand, owner of a holiday cottage in his village of Tournon Saint Martin where my wife and I spent our summer holiday in 1991, took particular trouble in checking my transcript in French of his recollections; and I am no less grateful to my friend René Abraham of Saint Denis-sur-Sarthon for a preceding check of the typescript, and to Professor Sian Reynolds for likewise pointing out faults in my English translation of it. Any shortcomings that may remain in it are to be blamed on me alone. My thanks are due also to his widow Mrs Hazel Lochore and their son Mr John R Lochore, for giving me permission to include below a slightly edited version of the unpublished recollections of the late John Lochore of his experiences in the International Brigade in the Spanish Civil War. David Jackson Young, producer of the BBC Radio Scotland programmes I compiled about conscientious objectors in the 1939-45 war and the recollections of Joseph Pia, encouraged more perhaps than he realised the making of this book. I am also indebted to my friend and former tutor Victor Kiernan for agreeing to write the Foreword. The Mercat Press deserves praise for taking on such a bulky manuscript, and Allan Boyd, Tom Johnstone and Seán Costello thanks for their encouragement and their skill in shepherding it into print. For donations toward the cost of publication I am grateful to the Binks Trust, Scottish International Education Trust, and the Nancie Massey Charitable Trust. Above all my thanks are due to the unshakeable tolerance and helpfulness of my wife Sandra.

Ian MacDougall,
Edinburgh, August 1995

Some Relevant Events

1899-1902	Boer War
1900	Labour Party founded
1904	Russo-Japanese War begins. Anglo-French Entente Cordiale
1905	British and French army staff secret talks begin. Sinn Fein founded. Revolution in Russia
1906	Liberals' landslide win in general election
1907	Anglo-Russian Entente
1908	Bosnian crisis
1912	Anglo-French Naval Agreement
1912-13	Balkan wars
1913-14	Dublin strikes
1914	Assassination of Austrian Archduke Franz Ferdinand: First World War begins. Battles of the Marne and First Ypres. Formation of Union of Democratic Control and No-Conscription Fellowship
1915	U-boat warfare begins: *Lusitania* sunk. Dardanelles campaign. Italy enters the war as ally of Britain and France. Russia promised Black Sea Straits at end of war. Battles of Neuve Chapelle, Second Ypres, Aubers Ridge, Festubert and Loos. Poison gas first used on Western Front. Salonika campaign begins. Bulgaria enters war as ally of Germany and Austria-Hungary. Munitions Act passed. Shop stewards' movement begins. Rent strikes on Clyde
1916	Battles of Verdun, the Somme and Jutland. Military Service Acts impose conscription in Britain. Rumania enters war as ally of Britain, France and Russia but is overrun by German army
1917	Entry into war of United States of America as ally of Britain, France and Russia. Nivelle's offensive on the Aisne: French army mutinies. Pétain becomes commander-in-chief. Battles of Arras, Passchendaele (Third Ypres), Cambrai and Caporetto. Height of U-boat warfare. February/March and October/November Revolutions in Russia
1918	President Wilson issues his Fourteen Points. Treaty of Brest-Litovsk: Bolshevik Russia withdraws from the war. Big German offensive on Western Front. Battles of the Marne and Vittorio Veneto. Armistice, November 11, ends the war. Allies invade Bolshevik Russia. Anglo-

Irish war begins

1919 Treaty of Versailles. Mussolini forms Fascist Party. Abortive Communist (Spartakist) uprising in Germany. Formation of Third (Communist) International

1920 Beginning of inter-war recession. Formation of Communist Party of Great Britain. Hitler founds Nazi Party

1921 National lock-out of miners: savage wage reductions imposed. Anglo-Irish Treaty and formation of Irish Free State

1922 First national Hunger March to London. Civil war in Ireland. Mussolini comes to power in Italy

1923 France and Belgium occupy Ruhr. Hitler's Munich Putsch. Death of John Maclean. Formation of Fife miners' reform union

1924 First Labour government. J R Campbell case. Zinoviev or 'Red' letter. Dawes Plan regulates German war reparations. Death of Lenin

1925 Britain returns to Gold Standard. 'Red Friday' (31 July): government forced to subsidise miners' wages for nine months. Labour Party urges unions not to elect Communists as delegates to Labour conferences, and debars Communists from individual membership of Labour Party. Treaty of Locarno

1926 National lock-out of miners: General Strike. Miners' wages again reduced and hours increased. Fascist regime established in Portugal. Germany admitted to League of Nations

1927 Trade Disputes and Trade Unions Act. Stalin dominant in Soviet Union

1928 First national Scottish Hunger March to Edinburgh. Women enfranchised on same basis as men. First Five Year Plan launched in Soviet Union. Communist International and Party adopt 'Class against Class' policy. Kellogg Pact disavows use of force in international relations

1929 Second Labour government elected. Wall Street crash. Second National Hunger March to London. Trotsky deported from Soviet Union by Stalin

1930 Big rise in unemployment. Third National Hunger March to London, second to Edinburgh. Nazis greatly increase their support in Reichstag elections

1931 Fall of second Labour government. Reduction of unemployment benefit. Introduction of household Means Test. Gold Standard abandoned, pound devalued. Naval mutiny at Invergordon. Fall of monarchy and establishment of republic in Spain. Japanese invasion of Manchuria

1932 Over three million people unemployed. Fourth National Hunger March to London, third to Edinburgh. Independent Labour Party disaffiliates from Labour Party. Another big increase in Nazi vote in Reichstag elections

1933 Mass unemployment at its worst. Hitler and Nazis in power in Germany. Germany leaves League of Nations. Fourth national Scots

Hunger March to Edinburgh

1934 Socialist uprising in Austria crushed by Chancellor Dollfuss. Fascists or semi-Fascists march on Chamber of Deputies in Paris. Asturian uprising crushed by General Franco in Spain. Soviet Union joins League of Nations and presses for United Front against fascism. Ten-year non-aggression pact between Poland and Nazi Germany. Fifth national Hunger March to London. Peace Pledge Union formed

1935 Formation of German air force and conscription announced by Hitler. Abyssinia (Ethiopia) invaded by Mussolini: Hoare-Laval Pact. Soviet-French Treaty of mutual assistance. Peace Ballot. Anglo-German naval agreement allows Nazi Germany to build fleet to 35 per cent of strength of British navy. Rearmament begins in Britain. Labour again defeated in general election

1936 Nazi Germany repudiates Treaty of Locarno. Remilitarisation of Rhineland by Hitler. Popular Front governments formed in France and Spain. Spanish Civil War begins: formation of International Brigades. Moscow trials begun by Stalin. Last National Hunger march to London. Rome-Berlin Axis formed

1937 Chamberlain succeeds Baldwin as prime minister. Anti-Comintern Pact by Germany, Italy and Japan. Japan begins war on China. Hitler tells his generals his secret plans for launching war

1938 Anschluss: Austria annexed by Nazi Germany. Munich Crisis: Czechoslovakia betrayed by Britain and France. Withdrawal of International Brigades from Spain. End of Popular Front government in France. Last Scots National Hunger March to Edinburgh

1939 Franco overthrows Spanish Republic. Soviet Union proposes military alliance to Britain and France. Hitler takes Prague; Bohemia and Moravia become Nazi 'protectorates'. Mussolini seizes Albania. Britain introduces conscription. 'Pact of Steel' between Hitler and Mussolini. Hitler denounces Anglo-German naval agreement and his Non-Aggression Pact with Poland. Nazi-Soviet Non-Aggression Pact (23 August): Hitler invades Poland (1 September). Britain and France declare war on Nazi Germany: Second World War begins. Soviet Union enters Poland from east (17 September). 'Phoney War' in west. Russo-Finnish War begins. Neutrality Act repealed by United States government: war material supplied on a 'cash and carry' basis.

1940 Red Army occupies Lithuania, Latvia and Estonia. Nazi Germany invades Denmark and Norway, then Low Countries and France. Churchill replaces Chamberlain as prime minister. The 'Miracle of Dunkirk'. Mussolini enters the war as ally of Hitler. Home Guard formed. End of Third Republic in France. DeGaulle leaves France for London. Pétain becomes head of new Vichy French state. Battle of Britain. Blitz begins

1941 'Lease Lend' Act. Commando raid on Lofoten Islands. Hess lands in Scotland. Mussolini's army in Abyssinia surrenders. Hitler overruns

Balkans and Greece. Rommel's army lands in North Africa. HMS *Hood* and German battleship *Bismarck* sunk. Japanese attack Pearl Harbor: USA enters the war. Japanese invade Malaya and Philippines and seize Hong Kong

1942   Japanese invade Burma and capture Singapore and Java. Tokyo bombed by Americans. Battle of Midway. RAF 1,000 bomber raid on Cologne. Dieppe raid. Battle of El Alamein. Allied landings in North Africa. French fleet scuttled at Toulon. Germans overrun Unoccupied Zone in France. British offensive in the Arakan, Burma

1943   Germans at Stalingrad surrender. Germans driven out of North Africa. Allies land in Sicily then Italy. Mussolini overthrown. Japanese evacuate Guadalcanal. Red Army retakes Kiev. Battle of Atlantic won by Allies

1944   Siege of Leningrad raised. Battle of Cassino. Fall of Rome. D-Day: Allied landings in Normandy. Flying bomb and rocket attacks on London begin (13 June). Battles of Imphal and Kohima in Burma. Hitler survives bomb plot. Paris and Brussels liberated. Failure of the Warsaw Rising. Allied landings in south of France. Germans launch Ardennes offensive. Bulgaria, Rumania, Hungary and Finland driven out of the war. Americans land on Philippines

1945   Bombing of Dresden. Mandalay captured from Japanese. Yalta Conference. Red Army enters Warsaw. Death of President Roosevelt. Mussolini shot. Death of Hitler. Unconditional surrender of Nazi Germany. Labour win landslide victory in general election. Potsdam conference. Americans capture Iwo Jima and Okinawa. Atomic bombs dropped on Hiroshima and Nagasaki. Unconditional surrender of Japan. End of Second World War

1946   War Crimes Trials at Nuremberg pass sentences of death or imprisonment on Nazi leaders

Peter Corstorphine

Ah tried tae join the army in 1907 at Cockburn Street in Edinburgh. But they widnae have me because ah wis too small and too young: ah wid be between fourteen and fifteen.

Ah wis born in Edinburgh in 1892. Ma father was an auctioneer. It wis a good paid job at that time. But he wis a great whisky man. And as a consequence very little o' the money came intae the hoose. It wis all goin' on the evil spirit.

I had five brothers. I wis the youngest. We used tae lie in wir bed at night and listen till the auld hansom cab came up the street with the bells ringin' on the horse's neck. This wis Dad arrivin' home, wi' his splittit troosers and swallowtailed shirt, and his Gladstone collar, bowler and tie and rolled umbrella. Oh, he wis really a picture, there were no doubt about it. But whenever we saw him we used tae run oot the road and hide frae him. We didnae want tae be recognised!

Dad began as an upholsterer. But he became an auctioneer and he dealt in almost everything: jewellery, furniture—primarily furniture. He wis very good at the furniture for no other reason than, as ah say, he wis an upholsterer and he knew quite a lot about it.

But he even used tae go to the Bird Show when it used tae be held in the Waverley Market. He sold the birds there. He didnae ken a budgie frae a craw. But he could sell them. So that wis how he made his livin'.

He wis never ill in his life but eventually he took this illness and when he was walkin' across the kitchen a big lump o' blood came oot his throat and landed on the floor. So we sent for the doctor and he whipped him away tae the Infirmary and he was operated on. But he died in about five or six days. He wis only sixty-nine, quite a young man.

Ah went to North Merchiston primary school at the age o' six. Ah wis a long time o' gettin' tae school first but ah wis so good ah went from class tae class till ah had made up wi' the years that ah had lost. In fact, before ah wis twelve ah had got as high as ye could go in North Merchiston school.

The headmaster at that time was a man called Taylor—we used tae call him Danny Taylor—and he sent word round to ma father that ah wis ready for a higher grade o' education, and he said, 'You consider it.' But my father was one o' these bombastic men, when he wis talkin' down tae ye he said, 'Why not go to the higher grade school?' Ah says, 'Why not?' Ah says, 'Where ah'm ah gaun tae get sports clothes and ma uniform for the school?' Ah says, 'Will you buy it?' The answer was complete—he wouldnae do it.

So ah had started tae go wild by this time. Ah had struck the joinery master on the head wi' a bit o' wood, and wi' one thing and another they were on the point of havin' me put away. It wis near the end o' the session. Ah wis thirteen. Somebody— ah think it wis Cocky Turnbull, another master—suggested 'Why not jist let him go?' So ah went. That wis how ah stopped ma schoolin' at thirteen years of age. It either meant that or goin' where the bad boys go—the Industrial School.[1]

That wis about 1906, ah think. When ah left school ah started goin' messages. Ah went messages for nearly every baker's shop in Bruntsfield Place. Sometimes ah went tae a fruit shop and got a job for a week or two. But finally ah got a chunt wi' ma father and ah went tae be an apprentice plumber. Ah wid be between fourteen and fifteen.

As an apprentice ah started wi' 2/6d. The second year it went up to 3/6d. Third year to 4/6d. Ye started at six o'clock in the mornin' and ye finished at half-past five at night. On the Saturday you stopped at one o'clock. Ye had an hour for your dinner and half an hour for your breakfast.

Ah wis with Mackie and Simpson, quite a good sized firm. They employed about twelve plumbers. They were also gas-fitters, of course. They had a double quality there. Any amount o' them were just plumbers. But quite a number o' them were gas-fitters. Gas was jist comin' intae its own. There wis a' the auld gas mantle stuff and that.

Well, as ah said, ah tried tae join the army in 1907 at Cockburn Street. But they widnae have me because ah wis too small and too young. But they said they could put me on a trainin' course for six months if ah wished. But ah didnae want that. Once ah got away ah wanted tae stay away. That wis the whole circumstance.

What made me want tae join the army at that time wis merely the fact that there were no jobs goin' around, especially for the likes o' me. And workin' as an apprentice plumber ah wis gettin' about 3/6d. a week.

Ma mother used tae give me a sixpence pocket money. And life became very hard, especially when you got to the length of fifteen and sixteen. You were still only gettin' 4/6d. a week and you were gettin' very little pocket money. Ye couldnae even go tae the theatre. And the young lads at that time were a' beginnin' tae wear bowlers and what-have-you. I was goin' about like Coconut Tam.[2]

Now the army wis seven shillins a week and ye're all found, plus the fact that ye got your uniform and boots and everything. Ye were well fed and a good bed. What more did a fellow want ?

Ma brother Alex was already in the army. Ah wis very fond o' that brother. And funnily enough, he had been an apprentice plumber as well. He joined the army in 1908. That gave him two years' start on me.

Alex was in the Black Watch. That's why ah went tae join them. Ah joined them in Curragh camp in Ireland in 1910.

Then from Curragh camp the Black Watch went tae Limerick. Ah went tae a place called Tome, which wis jist outside Limerick. Ma brother had been courtin' this lassie before he left Ireland for India. Her name wis Katie McInerdie. So he handed her over tae me, ye see. She steyed in this place called Tome. And it wis a funny house: the fire was in the centre o' the floor. The chimney went right through the ceilin' and they burned peat.

Well, it wis there that I first found myself popular with the folk roond aboot. And I wis singin' all their Irish songs and what have you. They taught me a few. Quite definitely ah got on well with the local Irish people personally. I don't think they were really against the soldiers as such. They were against the uniform. If we decked wirselves in civvies I suppose we'd been all right. But whenever they saw the priest they beat it. They wouldnae go wi' ye, although some o' the girls used tae come tae the dancin'. We used tae have dancin' on a Friday. There were quite a few marriages between the British soldiers and the Irish girls. Ah had a wee pal Danny Gillies that got married there and he used tae go back every year.

There wis an awful lot o' incidents. When we were in Limerick we were very much on the alert for Sinn Feins. The Sinn Fein were organised at the back o' Limerick and right down as far as the Curragh camp. There were a big gang o' them there. They had all their windows painted wi' the Sinn Fein colours and all that kind o' thing. We darenae go out unless we were in threes or fours. We weren't made welcome in any place at all.[3]

In 1911 the railwaymen were on strike and we were bein' sent down—not a whole battalion but a contingent—to Dublin tae sort o' restore order or what have you. The engine driver and his mate decided that they werenae goin' tae help us. So they unlooped the engine and drove the engine away and left us lyin' at the sidin' in the train.

There wis no sympathy whatever, none, among the ordinary soldiers for the Irish nationalist movement. I don't think it wis patriotism as far as the soldier wis concerned. He's inculcated with his job. For instance, in 1921, when ah wis called up for the miners' strike, the first thing that the colonel of the regiment said to us as he formed us all—and we hadnae even got uniforms yet, we were in our civilian clothes—he says: 'Ye may be miners but whatever you are whenever you entered that door,' he says, 'you're a soldier and you're under military discipline.' That's the word ye got. This is inculcated intae the soldier all his life. So that's why so many o' them were unaffected by strikes or anything. They had no sympathy for the workin' classes. And that is applicable, ah think, throughout the world. The armies of all countries are the same.

From Limerick we came in 1911 to Edinburgh Castle. Conditions there were terrible, terrible. The only good point about it was you could see the city and a' that kind of thing. But we wis in the Rat Trap, facin' Castle Terrace, right above there, that was where ah wis. They called it the Rat Trap because there was no lavatory accommodation or anything like that. You had to go up the stair—and it wisnae a good stair. Ye were put doon the Rat Trap and that wis it. The wind yaised tae blaw through the flair—aw, terrible.

In ma barrack room alone there were thirty. We were fed in there. You had to have your room orderly that went and collected the food at the cookhouse, brought the food down tae ye, and then he had tae distribute it. We had tables and they were beautifully scrubbed. It wis us that scrubbed them, of course. Oh, it wis clean enough, the Rat Trap. But there was no privacy whatever: the only privacy ye had was when ye were in your bed.

The pay at that time was a shillin' a day for a private. And you could have as much as, oh, fourpence or fivepence taken off for barrack room damages—the likes of if a window was broken or somebody broke plates. This was all jist takin' money off ye for nothin'.

Ye got your first set o' uniforms free. That wis, you would get a kilt, a red tunic, a white buff and a khaki tunic, two pairs o' socks, two shirts, no underpants or anythin' like that. You weren't allowed to wear underpants at that time. You got two pairs o' shoes—we wore shoes at that time—and white spats and khaki spats and a set o' hose tops to pull up wi' your red garter. Everything after that you'd tae buy out o' your shillin' a day. It wasn't easy at all.

Ah remember we went tae a military funeral in Colinton. He was an old major or something but he wis a gey auld yin. Anyway we'd tae go there and it was a hot, blisterin' day. We were carryin' our rifles on our shoulder and the oil from the box gradually oozed its way up wi' the sun. Right down wir tunics we were all black when we got back. Now we all complained of course. We were told: 'You'll either clean it or buy a new one.' Well, there wis all sorts o' suggestions as to how we could take this oil oot. But it wis impossible because the stuff that they did give us eventually left this scar. It took away the oil but it left a scar right down the red tunic. A red tunic at that time cost you about thirteen shillins—a fortnight's wages: a lot o' money. The khaki wis cheaper but it wis pretty expensive an' all. Ah don't know about the white buff, it wis so easy marked. But it had a feature about it that you could clean it. We used tae go intae the beatin' board and rub it up wi' dry blanco and beat it in wi' your stick. That would cover up most marks.

The kilt was another point. A kilt would maybe cost ye about thirty shillins. Ye had tae be very careful wi' it. You looked efter your kilt.

Now I had joined the army thinkin' I would get free clothin' as well as a shillin' a day. But ah don't know if ah felt disillusioned about that. You hardly thought about it because ye were so careful wi' everything—aye, even socks. Ye'd get a pair o' socks for three ha'pence but nevertheless you looked after your socks. Ye had tae because if ye didn't some other body did: they would whip them away under your nose.

There wis quite a lot o' theft in the barrack room. They stole anythin' frae a wee cake o' soap, well worn too, at that. They'd pinch your washin' soap. You kept your own soap, your own teeth paste and all that kind o' thing.

Discipline was very tight. I got seven days confined to barracks. I was room orderly that day. In fact, when you were room orderly you were on for a week. And the fire wisnae goin' in this room. It wis a great big room: 34 people lived in it. Ah couldnae see anything tae blow the fire up wi'. Ah took what ah thought was an old dishcloot and ah put it round the fire. It blew up the fire right enough but it blew the dishcloot an' a'. And jist at that moment the colour sergeant he comes in. 'What's that?!' He wis a Fifer: Rab Bowden. Anyway—'That's a dishcloot!' Ah says, 'Aw, it's a dishcloot but it's a gey auld yin and a durty yin.' And that's what he charged me wi'—blowin' up the fire wi' a dishcloth. And ah got seven days confined to barracks. That meant all the menial jobs o' the day ye got. For instance, if there wis a big dinner in the officers' mess ye were sent ower there tae wash up a' the dishes and wash the pans. In fact, when they were runnin' short o' defaulters they made them! That was the kind o' situation we were in.

When ye were confined to barracks ye had tae answer three times a night. You can be in defaulters as long as you like as long as you answer your name. That wis the auld bugle call.

Half past five in the mornin' wis yer first reveille. That wis the bugle. The bagpipes played the second reveille: 'Hey, Johnnie Cope, are ye waukin' yet?' Lights out was at ten o'clock at night.

Ah widnae grumble too much about the food at Edinburgh Castle. It wis good enough but it wis rough. Ah widnae say ye got plenty of it.

Breakfast consisted generally of either a sausage—ye only got one sausage: one soldier, one sausage—or a bit o' bacon. But on the Friday ye always got a wee bit o' fish, sometimes saut fish.

This wis tae make ye buy beer. The canteen sold the beer. The canteen wis in where they sell postcards at the Castle now. Beer was three ha'pence a pint and ye could see the hops floatin' about on the top o' it. Oh, it wis terrible.

At the midday meal generally you got either stew or broth. Ye got broth, potatoes, and then the general fruit: prunes, rice and prunes. All good wholesome stuff.

There wis no evening meal. It wis a slice o' bread and jam. That wis a' ye got there.

There wis no supper. They yaised tae put on a big can o' soup, made wi' a' the rubbish that wis left the day before, or something like that. Ye jist went in and if ye wanted it ye took it, and if ye didn't ye jist left it.

Oh, ah wis aye stervin! Ah wis a hungry man, believe me.

The canteen sold food. Ye could get a plate o' mince and tatties for 4d. I think you could get a pie for 1d. and a cup o' tea for 1d., and so on. It wis quite reasonable there. So ah spent most o' ma money on food—bars o' chocolate, tae: ah wis a great chocolate eater at that time.

Ah made an allowance tae ma mother. Ah gave her 3d. a day out o' ma shillin' a day pey. That left me 9d. That went mostly on food. Ah didn't smoke and ah didn't drink at that time. Ah wisnae long till ah did, though!

Ye had tae buy yer own cleanin' materials—blanco and brasso and that other yellow stuff ye used tae use. Ye had tae buy a' that. And teethpaste, soap, washin' and shavin' soap.

Out o' ma shillin' a day ah never had a sausage left. Ah never saved any money at all before the war, not a penny, not a penny. But ah wis never in debt. Naebody wid trust ye wi' a sojer's pey. Ye never got a chance tae go in debt! Ah never borrowed money from other sojers. Ah made do.

When ah first joined the army it wis very hard trainin'. Ye had physical trainin' at seven o'clock in the mornin'. Ye got a cup o' hot tea without milk or sugar. It wis black. And that wis supposed tae make ye go. Well, ye did that. About eight o'clock in the mornin' ye finished. Then ye come in for yer breakfast. After that you'd go out and do some drill, real drill. And then after dinner you went out and did your bayonet fightin' and a' that kind o' rubbish. Sometimes you'd do a night drill an' a'—night exercises.

Ye did most o' yer trainin' on the esplanade at Edinburgh Castle. We did a lot o' it then. Ah fairly enjoyed that part o' the army life. In fact, ah enjoyed most of it. Ah wis very fond o' the army.

There wis any amount o' opportunity for sport. And if ye were any good at all they encouraged ye. Ah went in more or less for gymnastics and football. Ah played a good deal o' football. And ah tried a bit o' boxin'. Ah fought in the Synod Hall in Edinburgh but there again ma height was a great disadvantage. Ah'm five foot three and an eighth. At that time ah had tae fight featherweight, nine stone four. A man nine stone four could quite easy be six feet. Davie Livingstone, an old soldier, the chap that was aye coachin' me, tryin' his best for me, he says: 'Ye'll never be a boxer.' So that went by the board and ah concentrated on the gyms. And here again ah wis at a disadvantage, because all the installations such as the shelf or even the cross-bar, they were a' too high for me an' ah had tae get a bigger spring from the ground—and ah wisnae always good at it.

Now the relations between the other ranks and the officers before the war were, oh, very much apart, you were very much apart. They were a different class altogether. They could be comradely enough, ye know, but ta, ta a lot. Each rank wis segregated.

When ah joined the army in 1910 ah wis surrounded wi' old soldiers who had been in the Boer War—there wis Tim Fish, John Roberts, och, a whole lot o' them. They were good soldiers, good shots. But Haldane, who had become Minister o' War, got a bill passed through the House o' Commons sayin' that a soldier should be educated: as well as bein' a good soldier he had to be educated. And he built this argument on the South African War where there wis any amount o' instances where the troops had got lost by the simple fact that they couldn't map-read. Map-readin' can be difficult even if ye can read. But Haldane brought it through that a soldier had to have a third class certificate of education before he got his efficiency pay raised— and it was 6d. a day of an increase. He had to be a first-class shot, a third class certificate of education at the least, and of good behaviour before he got this profi- ciency of 6d. a day.[4]

Now these fellahs in the room where ah wis in the Rat Trap at the Castle, they had all been in the South African War and many o' them couldn't read or write. It became ma job then—ah took it on maself—tae try and teach them tae read and write. They preferred that tae goin' tae this military school where they would feel that they were completely out of place. Ah worked quite long hoors wi' them but always ah got their spare bread—or I might get tuppence or thruppence from each o' them at the end o' the week. So ah wis in the money, really. Ah spent it on food for maself.

Then in 1911 ah left Edinburgh Castle for India. Ah went out on the *Elephanta* troopship. Conditions on board were terrible, terrible. We were in hammocks. And you had to collect your hammock at six o'clock at night and bring it back at six o'clock in the mornin'. And it had all tae be beautifully folded so that it went intae the storeroom. I never used mine. Ah couldnae stand them. In fact, periodically ah fell out. I used tae go up and sleep on the floor. That saved me an awful lot o' bother, because there ah wis, ma hammock all ready tae hand in in the mornin'.

The food on board was terrible. We had jist the general run o' stews and what have you. Sometimes it wis sausages and you didn't know how long they'd kept them. Ah dinnae think there wis any freezers in them days. Oh, it wisnae very good.

And the heat inside—terrible, especially after we were gettin' into the hotter parts. We landed at Bombay.

I was very fond o' India and ah liked ma time there. Ah think the most that ah liked about it wis the fact that there wis a freedom about it, ye know. There wisnae sae many dress parades and a' that kind o' thing. And ye were allowed dog and stick walks. There wis a lot o' other good things, too, such as cheap fruit and a' that kind o' thing.

It wis taboo tae mingle wi' the ordinary Indian people. Ye werenae allowed tae mingle wi' them at all. That wis a rule, that wis regulations. Ah mean, they were a different people from us altogether and there wis no family. They wouldnae have ye in the family anyway. But there wis a case o' one soldier in ma regiment becomin' friendly wi' an Indian girl and gettin' married. That's the only one that ah know of. He brought her hame tae Edinburgh wi' him. He had tae ask permission to get married. If you wanted tae be taken on the strength of the regiment you had to ask the Colonel's permission tae get married. And he wis very loth tae give it in the case o' this particular fellow that ah'm talkin' aboot. But she wisnae totally black. The common word that wis used wis half-caste, Anglo-Indian, or somethin' like that.

There wis a class, a sort o' in-between class—ah forget what they called them—but they came tae the dances.[5] But generally speakin' the men were dancin' wi' men, ye know. That wis if ye werenae a boozer. If ye were a boozer then ye went tae the canteen tae drink or ye went tae the canteen tae eat tea and buns.

We were more or less confined to barracks. Well, in a city like Calcutta there wisnae any place for us tae go, bar the low places. But when they went there—'No Soldiers Allowed': notices all over the place. That didnae apply tae officers, of course.

The poverty in India was terrible, terrible. But we didnae pay much attention tae it. When you're young and that you don't think about these things at all. As a matter o' fact, ah concentrated on the gym nearly a' the time. And we had that game where ye jist bang the ball on a great big high wall. At nearly all the barracks at that time we had outside alleys. It wisnae squash at that time, we called it ball alley.

Ah wis in India when the Delhi Durbar took place. Ah wisn't at it. Ah wis in the plains o' Calcutta at that time. Those that were chosen tae go tae the Durbar were all the stalwarts of the regiment, ye know, the biggest and smartest lookin' men. They were all chosen. About 150 o' them went. And they all got a medal for that. They used tae call it the Blue Peter. It wis blue wi' a big rid stroke in it. We didnae go but we formed up when the king George V came tae visit Calcutta.[6]

Ma brother Alex wis there in India at that time. He wis a sergeant. He wis later appointed tae the Deputy Director o' Medical Services job—a sort o' secretary he wis, somethin' like that. And he wis alright. He mixed wi' the natives quite a lot. But ah didn't see much o' Alex when we were in India. Ah wis sent on duty tae pick up a prisoner in Lucknow prison. And that's where Alex wis stationed, at Lucknow, wi' the medical services. He had been in Calcutta tae until he went up there. In fact, Alex need never have gone tae the war in France at all. His job wis tae look after the families o' the army, which he could have done right tae the end of the war. But he thought he was missin' somethin', ye see.

Well, when the 1914 War broke oot we wis sent tae France. We got there in '14.[7] By this time it wis gettin' kind o' wet on the ground, and this is where the Germans decided tae dig in after the Battle of the Marne. They started tae dig in because of the mud. They couldnae get movin'—the big guns and what have you. They were all horse-drawn guns and the mud made it very difficult. And this was the beginnin' o' the trench warfare. So the British army and the French army, we started tae dig wirselves in too. By October they were dug in thick and the only fightin' that wis goin' on wis shellin' and grenades. They hadnae the up-to-date hand grenades they latterly had. In fact, the Germans' first grenades were a' hand-made. They were filled wi' gramophone needles and a' that kind of thing, it wis a' jist scrap. But as the system developed they were more professionally made, I suppose. Anyway one landed in between three of us. I can remember the two fellows that wis beside me—their names and everything and where they came from. Charlie Lamont wis one and Jimmy Skene wis the other, and they both came from Montrose. I got very little of it but they hustled me down anyway. It wis possible at that time tae get the men wounded down to the hospital, the clearance stations. Then you got from there to maybe the likes o' Boulogne, and from Boulogne across tae Blighty. And ah wis home by about the last day o' December in 1914. Ah wis home for Hogmanay.

So that wis one o' the stops in ma career as a fightin' man. Roughly three month ah wis at home in Scotland. They sent ye up tae Nigg from Perth. They had built huts up in Nigg. Ah wis gettin' ready tae pass for an instructor. Ah had been told that if ah got on the staff ah wouldn't go back to the war. But ah didnae get ma certificate. Ah hadnae time. As you can understand, the Regular army by this time wis gettin' gradually wiped out. There wis no Regular soldiers left and non-commissioned officers were very scarce. There wis no sign o' Kitchener's Army at that time. The Territorials and volunteers they had started tae come out. In fact, some o' them were out quite early—the London Scottish, for instance, from the Territorials. They were out very early. And the 8th Battalion o' the Black Watch from Dundee they were out early.[8]

But ye were re-trained and given new uniform and off ye went again out tae France. So there we were at Neuve Chapelle. That wis the 11th, 12th and 13th o' March 1915. Then there was another lull and both sides seemed tae be waitin' on dry weather comin' in before they could start their nonsense. So the next affray that ah wis in was on the 9th o' May, 1915: the Second Battle o' Ypres. The first Battle wis in 1914. Ma brother

Alex was ma platoon sergeant by this time and ah got in beside him.[9]

The engineers had built small ladders for us tae climb up and get over wir own trenches in the attack. We were supposed tae have attacked at ten minutes tae four in the mornin' but we didnae attack tae ten minutes tae four in the afternoon. And the Germans were leanin' ower their trenches waitin' on us.

At that time, too, the Germans had two huge battalions o' what they called the Kaiser's Bodyguard. They wore great big high brass helmets. This wis one o' the souvenirs that a' the soldiers tried tae pick up. So anyway tae show ye how disorganised we were: after we got out wir trenches ah wis over the top and runnin' towards the Germans. Ah widnae be more than 50 tae 60 yards frae them and ah flung masel' on ma belly, because ye could look up and see the brass helmets starin' ye in the face. And there ah wis, right in front, and nobody tae order ye what tae do or anything. But ah heard a screech. Ah wis sure it wis Alex, ma brother, ma platoon sergeant. Here he'd been killed.

So ah wis stuck out there till it became dark and then a message came out some way or another—ah can't remember how, but ah believe it wis a pickaxe handle flung out—to retire. And I turned round and made for wir own trenches—what I thought were wir own trenches anyway. And jist as I was gettin' over—about fifteen yards from gettin' in—ah got this bullet through the arm. So of course it birled me round. Ah dropped ma gun and ran towards wir own trenches. And that's how ah got away. Ah got in the trench. By that time the Germans were usin' shrapnel shells that burst in the air and came down.

Anyhow ah got away and somehow or other ah got down the length o' Albert. Then from Albert it wis quite easy, because there wis trains standin' tae take the wounded down to either Boulogne or Calais. Anyway I went to Boulogne. If you were a walkin' patient you were taken on right away tae the boat. When you got to the other side o' the Channel you were lined up: 'Where do you want to go, where do you want to go?' And ye'd tell them: 'I'd like tae go tae Edinburgh.' We a' finished up in London! We went tae London General Hospital in Whitechapel and from there ah wis sent to convalescent, to a house, The Goldings, at Hertford. There ah met the Queen Mother, when she was fifteen year old. She was a visitor tae this house. They were very good tae us. Each o' us had a room to ourselves. It wis a wonderful place. Then ah wanted tae get hame.

But ah got transferred tae a military place jist outside London. Then we were sent home tae Scotland. That wis about the end o' May. Ah still had ma arm in a bandage, of course. When we got tae Scotland ah reported at Perth Barracks. The doctor there sent me away convalescent again to Dunblane. That wis where ah met up wi' ma little girl again and we decided tae get mairried. So we got married and went wir honeymoon tae Dunblane. We were wi' a man that had a hen farm there and they took pity on us. They knew that sojers hadnae much money so they kept us for nothin' for a fortnight. We were fed like fightin' cocks, tae.

It wis after that that ah wis sent tae Aldershot tae complete ma trainin' as an instructor. Ah wis in a big gymnasium at Aldershot. Oh, there wis about a thousand instructors and would-be instructors at the one time. We were a' divided intae classes of twenty. And ah passed out there. I was a gymnastics, physical trainin' and bayonet fightin' instructor.

So that took me up tae Nigg again. By this time the New Army, Kitchener's Army, was bein' formed and the recruits were pilin' up and nobody tae instruct them. So that they were pleased tae see the like o' me comin' in there.

Bayonet fightin' became a very prominent part o' the trainin' because you hadn't long tae instruct the recruit in gymnastics. Gymnastics wis a secondary consideration. It involved parallel bars, horizontal bars and the rope and all that kind o' thing. Whereas the physical trainin' was all body work. But the bayonet fightin' was the crux. That had tae be perfected. No' that it wis very much used in the First World War after the trench warfare came along. There wis very little bayonet fightin'.

The Germans broke through again in '16.[10] Ma opinion wis there were no hopes o' me bein' sent out to the war, them bein' short o' instructors in Blighty. That's why ah sent for ma wife and ma wife came up tae Nigg tae stey wi' me. Then suddenly ah got the tip that ah wis bein' sent out tae France again. Meantime there wis another bombshell—the 1916 revolution in Dublin. Well, we were sent to that, instead o' France. I would rather ha' went tae France than that.

They sent the whole Black Watch. But we were just part. The King's Own Scottish Borderers were sent tae. But they were a' the trainin' battalions. The fightin' battalions of all these regiments were still in France. The like o' us, the 3rd Battalion o' the Black Watch up in Nigg, we were jist a trainin' battalion. But everybody was taken helter skelter, whether ye were young or old, and hummed over tae this revolution in Ireland. We went up the Liffey in a warship all ready tae jump ashore and go forrit immediately. But we never fired a shot in it. But the K.O.S.B.s did. They were involved in it very thickly and that's how they were never very popular in Dublin. Our officers insisted on the safety catches bein' on on our rifles all the time, whereas the K.O.S.B.s were lying there ready to fire. And that's exactly what happened. We seen the firing at the General Post Office. That's where we were stationed. But we were never engaged once, never fired a shot. That's why they returned us to the Curragh camp and got us embarked back to France.

Well, the like o' me and ma kind were sent back frae Dublin to Nigg, got ourselves ready again' and back to France. That's the way ah went all the time.

Ah landed in France for the third time in 1917. We were down below Peronne, ah cannae mind the name o' the place—was it Simcay? A name like that anyway. By this time ah had been sent tae join the 8th Battalion o' the Black Watch and they were lying in this place. Anyhow we were there till the 21st o' March, 1918.[11]

On the mornin' of the 21st of March 1918 ah wis standin' wi' the platoon sergeant and we had a whole lot o' tin cans tied on the barbed wire.[12] We had the wire pretty well advanced: possibly twenty yards o' wire before the trench, because we had been informed that the Germans were goin' tae attack. It wis tae be a real one—and it was and all.

Even wi' all our preparations they broke through wi' nae bother. We were retirin' for six days. And ah don't know how it stopped. But we stopped and it wis the first time we had had an hour's rest for six days. But it didnae last long. About the next day they started again. We were goin' back—some o' us runnin'. Somebody said that the German cavalry was out. Of course we were all past all the areas that had been entrenched.

I'm hoppin' down there anyway like mad and all of a sudden ah got a bullet through the thighs. There wis a khaki apron in front o' your kilt and there wis a wee pocket in it. I had a wee cigarette case in there wi' five cigarettes in it. That wis all that it wid hold. The bullet sliced the cigarettes and it stripped a place on my thighs. Jist missed old John Smith, ye know! The scar's still there on ma thighs. There wis a big Irish fellow came forward and he bundled a field dressin' on tae baith ma legs and tied a knot in it. 'There you are now, Jock,' he says. 'Look after yerself'—and left me. So ah got up on ma feet and found ah could stand all right. 'I'll soon be all right', I said—and down the road.

As we got down a bit the British officers were standin' there on horseback, revolvers in their hands. 'Get in there! Get in there!' They were tryin' tae re-form the runaway soldiers. So ah jist lifted ma kilt and showed them ma two wounds. I had two great big pads right ower ma thighs. So they looks at me and says: 'Make your own way, make your own way!' So ah made it all right. It wis a good job ah had a guid Scotch heid on me. Ah got right down tae the Albert road. So ye'll ken how far back we were. There used tae be a crucifix on the top o' the church at Albert. And they said that if that fell we would lose the war. But it never fell. So that we won the war. Or did we ?

Well, from there, ah landed in Manchester this time, Nell Lane Military Hospital. When ah got back tae Blighty here, oh, there wis thousands o' recruits bein' pumped in. They were even bringin' up the miners by that time. They even took up ma brother James who was 40 years old. And he wis killed.

Anyway there wis all these folks waitin' tae be instructed and nae instructors there. So ah wis sent back up tae Nigg and that's where ah stayed until the last. That wis the end o' ma war.[13]

Bill Hanlan

At Christmas 1914 ah wis in the trenches in France wi' the 8th Battalion o' the Royal Scots. And there wis an officer come out wi' me and the man that wis on duty. And there were three or fower Germans come ower and shook hands. We spoke tae each other, wished each other a Merry Christmas. And they said that the war was gaun tae finish. They always maintained that the war wis gaun tae finish. We said we didn't know, we'd never heard. We hoped it did. That wis a'.

Ah think they said it wis diplomatic, ye ken, through diplomats talkin'. It must ha' been in their press or somethin' like that. It never wis in oors that ah'm aware o'. And we used tae get a daily paper every day for nothing.

But there were oor officers and NCOs, sergeants and privates went oot an' a'. In fact, they were desperate some o' them for tae get oot for tae talk tae the Germans. They were volunteerin', ee ken: 'Let me on guard the night!' There wis officers goin' oot and talkin' tae each other. It wisnae jist us, it wis up and doon the line. No more fraternisation took place efter that, efter Christmas 1914.

Well, ah went tae France in October 1914. Afore the war I worked on the pithead at Newbattle, near Dalkeith. And there were two fellows—Alan Halliday and Jock Scott—and it was through them talkin' about bein' in the Territorials, they asked me if ah wid care tae come doon and join. So ah said, 'Aye, ah wouldnae mind.' Ah think ah wis aboot nineteen year old. Ah wis born in 1893, the 15th o' December, so it must ha' been aboot 1912 or 1913. There were no drill hall in Dalkeith at that time. Ah wis tae come tae the Auld Meal pub and see them there and they wid tell iz what tae dae, ye ken. So oo went intae a room in the Auld Meal and there was an officer and a sergeant. He was a Regular, this sergeant. He wis stationed at Edinburgh Castle. He used tae come oot and train the Territorials.

Ah found it tae be quite nice. It wis interestin'. There were two nights a week that oo trained, ah think it wis a Tuesday and a Thursday. The sergeant from Edinburgh Castle used tae come and train us wi' oor foot drill—form fours and a' the likes o' that. He wis quite nice, he wis quite civil. There would be about two dozen o' us, ah think, used tae go there. They were jist aboot the same as maself. They were mostly miners. And there wis a lot of Dalkeith men—shopkeepers and things like that.

As ah say, they had no drill hall in Dalkeith at that time. We used tae go intae a room at the Auld Meal and oo done oor drill there. And we marched from there down to the King's Park wi' our civilian clothes on, and a bandolier and a rifle, and done drill in the King's Park.

So ah had twenty-eight drills tae pit in tae become a Territorial, twenty-eight nights tae go there, thae two days a week. And ye had tae be there for two hours. Oo used tae have a dance, tae. There wis a fellow played the melodeon. There were some girls that used tae come that the fellaes knew.

Then they started tellin' us about the camps, about goin' tae the camp. Well, we joined the Territorials because we never had a holiday, we never could afford a holiday very well, accordin' to the wages at that time. Aye, men joined the Territorials for that purpose. That wis the idea. And when we went tae the camp we got a shillin' a day and our food and we got a uniform and we got sleepin' in tents, because it wis summer weather. It wis always in July, when the pit holidays wis on, that we went. We went for two weeks. And if ye had tae stay over and above the two weeks ye got your pay that ye had at your work. Ye always got paid full up, ye never lost anything.

Ee didn't get provided with any clothin'. It wis yer own clothes until ee went tae camp and then they issued ee out with a uniform: a pair o' britches, puttees, a tunic and a glengarry, and a bandolier of course wi' blank cartridges in it in fives. Ee'd always tae buy yer own boots. And underclothin' ye bought yerself. Ee never got any allowances for it, not at that time. Ee just done it on your own. Ye got yer hat, of course, yer bandolier, yer rifle, and things like that.

At the camps we done drill and we done trench warfare up tae aboot four o'clock at night, tae tea-time. Then after tea-time ee wis finished until the next mornin', till reveille. And then ee paraded at reveille and ee got sort o' physical exercise, marchin' up and down and runnin' and that, for about an hour or two hours.

The camps ah wis at, prior tae the war, wis Stobs at Hawick, Crieff and Irvine.

Well, jist before the war ah happened tae leave Newtongrange and ah went away through tae Caldercruix, tae get out the pits. Ah wanted tae leave the pits and ah went there and started in a paper mill until ah wis cried up on the 7th o' August 1914.

Ah went from there at Caldercruix tae the Waverley Market in Edinburgh. We stayed there at the Waverley Market for aboot three weeks. We got provided wi' no bedclothes. We had tae sleep in our own gear. We got our food certainly, they provided food. And we done rifle drill and marchin' up and down and round about Edinburgh, out to Leith, Bonnyrigg, Portybelly and back again. And that wis for about a fortnight or three weeks. Then they decided that we's goin' tae Haddington. And we marched from the Waverley Market tae a school in Haddington.

The school wis on the main street as ee gaun intae Haddington. Ah wis there frae the August tae the October. At Haddington we done soldierin'. We done rifle drill, route marches, had oor dinner out on the march and wis always back for tea time. We wis never any later than that. We done twenty to twenty-five miles a day.

We had a uniform by that time. We got issued with uniforms after we left Edinbury and went tae Haddington. Ye maybe got a pair o' trousers or a tunic. Ye got them at odd times, ye see. At that time ye'd always tae wear yer own footwear and

13

underclothes. They didn't supply them.

We had rifles and bayonets and dummy ammunition. We had a bandolier and it had pouches in it, and there were ten rounds in each pouch. There would be about sixty rounds all told, but they were dummies.

The people in Haddington were quite friendly tae us, especially the shopkeepers, of course. We wis makin' business for them. There were no restrictions against us. Ah mean, we could go anywhere we liked. We could go tae a dance or could go to the pictures. The pictures were only comin' intae vogue at that time. And that wis our amusement.

Oor main object wis girls. There wis a lot o' the fellaes did get married there, of course—married Haddington girls, oh, yes, a lot o' them.

Ye got instructed that ye wis tae go tae France. We wis a' desperate tae get tae France, every one o' us, at that time, we wis desperate. If ee thought ee wis goin' tae France ee wis ready tae go. There were no conscientious objectors. There were a lot o' people didnae want tae go but not because they were COs. Ye could either volunteer or not volunteer. At the latter end they left the men that wisn't goin' tae France in Haddington and the men that had volunteered for France they sent us down tae Prestongrange school.

I volunteered. Ah wanted tae kill Germans, tae tell the truth. That wis ma ambition. Ah wanted tae be there and have a shot at the Germans. Well, they were fightin' against us and, ah mean, the papers and everybody was in the same frame o' mind that ee didn't like the Germans because ee wis fightin' them. And there were wounded comin' hame by that time, people that ee knew personal, and, well, ee wanted tae have a shot at the Germans tae. There wis some men that came home—probably had been wounded and got home—that wis sent tae oor battalion before they were sent out again in a draft.

Well, ah went tae France in October 1914. We left Prestongrange and we went down tae the Waverley station in Edinburgh. We went from the Waverley down tae London and we got the boat from Folkestone across tae Le Havre in France. It wisnae the whole battalion o' the 8th Royal Scots—jist the volunteers. But there was so much of the Highland Light Infantry and so much o' the 6th Royal Scots wis sent tae make up the battalion for tae go tae France. They made up for the rest that hadnae volunteered.

It didnae take ee long tae cross the Channel, of course. There wis a lot o' them seasick but no' me. We had ta'en oor transport and all. And there wis horses seasick. And there were a lot o' us on duty, ee took turn about for doin' guard, ye see, and we had tae attend to these sick horses. We laughed at the time when we first heard about the horses bein' seasick but they were really seasick. It wis a pretty smooth crossin' but the horses did get seasick and were inclined tae lie down. But we wis made tae keep them up. Ye'd tae force them tae keep on their feet, because if ye let them lie down apparently it went for them.

It wis the first time I'd been abroad. We stayed there at Le Havre for a week. Of course we were stayin' away up a big hill but it was a camp, it wis under canvas. And we wis ta'en up there and puttin' intae marquees and tents. It wis a' canvas. And we stayed there for about a week at the very least. Then we wis transferred from there tae Fleurbaix. When we arrived in Fleurbaix the Germans wis about thirty mile out and we had tae go and meet them. We wis ta'en out tae meet them. But the whole British army wis retreatin' at that time and we fell in wi' the retreat. And the Germans made trenches and we made trenches. And that wis the first trenches that wis ever made at that time.

There were no trenches and no dug-outs or anythin' like that, no parapets that we could stand up on or anything. It wis jist like a drain and ee stood there. The weather wis terrible, terrible wet, terrible wet. And we had nowhere tae go. Wir beddin' and everything—ye could wring it: it wis saturated. We had no dug-outs, there werenae such a thing as a dug-out. We didn't know anythin' aboot dug-outs, of course. Dug-outs were places for gaun intae tae sleep in, for stayin' in. Ye lived in the trench, and ye wis there and that wis it. Our trench wis like a drain. It wis jist like diggin' a drain and standin' in a drain and lookin' ower the top o' it wi' yer heid. Ee hadnae tae dig it too deep or else ee couldnae see. But they learnt for tae make parapets and stand on them and be able tae look ower them. And when ye wis on duty ye got clay or sandbags, filled sandbags and made them so that ye could see ower the top.

We learned aboot trench warfare from the Germans. After we took the first line o' trenches from the Germans we knew what trenches wis. Oors wis only a hole in the ground. The Germans they had a parapet that they could stand on and go down. They could walk about the trench without their head bein' shown. If they wanted tae see ower they stood on this wee parapet that they made. And the back o' their trench wisnae as high as the front o' it. The back o' theirs they could always jist take a step and walk away back. Oor trench wis the same height back and front.The Germans learned us trench warfare. We didn't know it but they knew it.

The cold wis terrible, oh, aye, it wis cold. It wis rainin' and oo wis standin' in it and couldn't do nothin', couldn't go anywhere. The officers wis jist the same, they were in the same boat. They were walkin' up and down this trench, and sergeants, NCOs. The troops they did two hours on and four hours off.

The food was a' cold, everything, nothing hot, nothing hot: bully beef and Maconochie rations. That wis the meat part of it. The bread it wis sodded wi' water—ye couldn't know if it wis a bit o clay that ee wis pickin' up or a half loaf. They made wee half loaves wi' a sort o' crust on the top. Och, they'd be aboot the size o' a big orange. And ee used tae throw them at each other.[14]

It wis a' horse transport that we had. And we had to go out the trench and go back about two or three kilometres tae get the food and carry it from there up to the trench. They had containers made that ee carried it in.

Cooking wisn't allowed in the trenches, that wis prohibited. Ye couldn't do that. Well, the Germans would have putten over bombs right away, wi' the smoke. They were in the same boat as what we wis. They were livin' the same way.

We had no heating, none whatever. Yer clothes, if it was rainin', they got soakin' wet. Ee had an overcoat and eer uniform. If your overcoat and uniform got soakin' wet ye'd jist tae wait until it dried. Ee'd no change o' clothin'. Ee'd no change o' underclothing. Ee'd nothin' like that.

The Germans they had a lot o' buckshee clothes. When ee went intae their trench ee knew that it wis extra clothin' that wis belongin' the troops that wis left, and there were plenty. Of course we couldnae use them because they were blue or green.

Aye, the autumn o' 1914 and that winter wis bad, oh, aye, wi' the weather especially. This state o' affairs lasted, ah reckon, for aboot three or four month before there were any improvement. The improvement wis they were sendin' up new underclothin' which was wet when ee got it, because everything wis open. It wis jist horses and horse transport. Latterly they come tae have motor transport and it became a wee bit better, especially the food.

It wis a long time afore we got any mail and we wisnae cheerful. But the British sojers took it very well. Ah don't know how we took thon and never done nothing about it. They reckon the Germans wis prepared for this trench warfare, which we wisnae. We wis prepared for extension and fightin' in the open.

I wis really very healthy. There were no gas at that time. The first glasses we got—it wis tae save the eyes, not to save the mouth. Ye had tae put thir glasses on for tae save yer eyes. There were a lot o' bad eye infection at the very start. The ammunition that they were sendin' ower affected yer eyes. It made them like they were gaun tae run oot. Oh, ah had that for a long, long time, a lot o' times. Ah dunno how ah wasnae affected permanently wi' it. But there wis a lot o' them went absolutely blind.

The worst part o' that first autumn and winter o' the war wis the weather, the bombin' and the shells, because we had no retaliation for them. And I don't think that we had the same guns as what the Germans had. They had far bigger guns than us at first. They had guns that wis, oh, bigger than two hooses thegither. They used tae make a hole! Ee wis sorry for the casualties. That's all ee could say, ee wis sorry for them. But they were ta'en away and we didn't know where they were gaun tae. They were gaun doon tae a camp, some camp where there were a dressin' station. There were no dressin' stations up in the trenches. The only dressin' station wis yerself—eer own men. It wis usually them that wis in the band that done the Royal Army Medical Corps work. They done a' the bandagin' and things like that, that's the only dressin' we had. But there were nae hospitals. Ye'd tae go away back twenty kilometres before ee came tae Étaples and a' these places.

Well, casualties got quite common and ee didn't really bother about it. I've seen men lyin' moanin', they would be big holes in them and we couldn't do nothing aboot it. And we wis told not to touch them: 'Anybody that is wounded, that's lyin', leave them. There's somebody'll come and eventually attend to them.' But the most o' them at that time died. Ah wis there frae the beginning tae the end and never got wounded.

We wis at Ypres and then we shifted doon the line again tae Loos. And we wis back and forrit and back and forrit. We wis mostly on the Ypres side. Ah wis in Ypres. It wis a lovely wee village, a nice wee village. And the people were there. The cattle wis goin' up and down the street, the horses, the cows and sheep: they were roamin' up and down the street. But at the latter end there were no Ypres left: atween us retreating and fightin' the Germans there, and them retreatin' and them batterin' us, Ypres wis nappoo—finished.

Ah wis a machine gunner, of course—a Vickers Maxim. The artillery used tae be quite close tae us, at the back o' us. And they used tae blaw up the parapet that the Germans had on their trenches. They made big gaps in it and when the Germans went past there they either run—ye had tae run, of course—or gaun doon on their hands and knees. Some o' them took a chance—the same as what we din oorsels—and jist run. And wi' the machine gun we used tae jist watch the movement and press the button. Oo killed a lot o' Germans that way.

Well, at Christmas 1914 ah believe carols were sung in some places in the trenches, but no' where we wis. Ah never heard any carols.

Tae let ye understand, the Germans had a listenin' post come out every night, and so had the British. That wis from our front trench. Ye went out about, say, thirty yards and you lay down there. Now this was every night and every company in the British army that wis in the trenches done the same. They sent out two or three different bodies at a time, for listenin'. This was what they called the listenin' post. And ye had a' tae take a shot at it. Ye a' took a turn: NCOs, everybody, officers and a'.

Of course the officers only done visitin'. They didn't stay there all the time. There wis probably a lance corporal or a corporal in charge o' the men that wis there. But the sergeant used tae come out and talk tae ye, ask ye questions and that, and retire back tae the trenches again. The same wi' the officers: they only came out to enquire and then go back again.

Now the Germans carried on jist the same. They were doin' the same as what we were doin'. Of course we knew where their listenin' posts wis and they knew where oors wis. But we never attacked each other at the listenin' posts. Ye never got one listenin' post throwin' a bomb at another. Ye never got that—no' wi' oor regiment anyway. Ah don't know aboot other regiments, it may have happened, but no' wi' us.

Ye went oot in the dark, ye didnae go oot in daylight. Ye had a special road that ye went tae a listenin' post. Ee'd crawl along under a tunnel like, and it wisnae where ee come oot frae, ye see. At first, we used tae go straight oot and jist lie doon. Some of them used tae take oot their waterproof sheets wi' them and lie on them to keep the dampness off them because it wis aye bloody rainin' yonder. Wi' a' the gunfire it couldna ha' been onythin' else. The Germans kent oo wis lyin' on water- proof sheets and they done the same.

The first Germans we wis facin' was the Saxons. But you wisn't always in the same trench. Ye got shifted but ye'd tae do the same work as what ye'd left— listenin' posts and things like that. Well, ye went out there and the Germans knew. They said, 'You're new, you're different.' And we said, 'How d'ye know?' They said, 'It wis Englishmen that wis there before.' We got tooken the place of English- men. And they said, 'Ye talked Scotch.' It wiz amazin' the amount of Germans that could talk English. We couldn't talk German. We couldn't say, 'Jah!', never mind anythin' else. They could talk aboot as much Scotch as what we could, to tell ye the truth.

Ah met two German fellaes that had worked in Edinbury and they could speak jist as good as you and I. They were in shops. One of them told us what he done—it wis mair of a factory than a shop. It wis footwear that he told me he wis in. He laughed when ah said, 'Ah, well, ah'll ken where tae get ma boots cobbled now.' Of course he could talk jist as good as you or me in Scots. And they weren't in love with it—they weren't in love with the war. He says a' the Germans wanted tae be in front o' Scotsmen because they got it easy. They didnae want tae be in front o' Englishmen! They didnae like the English but they loved the Scots, ah don't know why. But they werenae blate in tellin' ee that.

It wisnae every time that ye got the Germans tae talk tae ye, tae fraternise wi' ye. Ee used tae say, 'Is that you?', ye ken, and ee never got any answer. And ee knew then that they didnae want tae talk wi' ye, though ye asked them two or three times. So ee jist stopped. And ee went back and forrit at nights until they wid talk and speak tae ye in English and say, 'Is that you, Jock?' And ee'd say, 'Aye.' And ee'd maybe say to them, 'Well, how is it that you're talkin' now?' And he would say, 'Well, it wis the other guys. We've relieved them. They're away.' The Germans sung regular. They sung more than we did. They knew that we were Scotch and they sung Scotch songs. And they could sing! They were good singers. And that's how it started. They used tae shout: 'What aboot singin' so-and-so? Let us hear it.' And that was it.

The German officers knew that ee wis talkin' tae each other. In fact, some o' the German officers used tae come oot and talk. Ah spoke tae a German officer often. And he telt me that he worked in Edinburgh—that wiz a' that he telt iz, that he worked in Edinburgh. And he telt iz they were bein' strict. 'They're bein' strict here on us talkin' tae each other. So,' he says, 'don't depend on it too much.'

Well, at Christmas 1914 ah wis in the trenches. The whole regiment wis in the trenches, the whole British line wis a' in the trenches—ye had tae be there at Christmas. These trenches wis never empty. There were no agreement until the two men that wis oot in the listenin' post, the German and the Scotsman that wis wi' us, well, the German had shouted tae the Scotsman: 'Happy Christmas!' And the other yin repeated it: 'Merry Christmas!' The German must ha' been talkin' good English and he says, 'And where dae you come frae in Scotland?' And the Scotsman says, 'How d'ye ken ah'm Scottish?' 'Oh,' he says, 'ah know. Ah've been in Scotland. Ah worked in …'

Well, the Germans knew about the fraternisation and they allowed it. There were two officers went out and met each other and spoke tae each other. There was an exchange o' gifts. Oh, we used tae get a lot o' stuff any day, every night. They were very, very scarce on cigarettes and we wis anything but. We used tae get a guarantee o' an issue o' twenty aboot every third day. The Germans used tae give us food, meat, bully beef. Anything that ye asked for they would get it for ee. They would tell ee they would bring it.

But on Christmas Day 1914 there were two officers went oot and shook hands wi' a German. We a' did.

The fraternisation lasted only for aboot half an hour where we wis. Ah don't know aboot the rest o' the line. But ah know that we wis allowed half an hour. And there wis an officer come out wi' me and there wis the man that wis on duty. Ah wis the NCO.

And there were three or fower Germans come ower and shook hands. We spoke tae each other, wished each other a Merry Christmas. And they said that the war was gaun tae finish. They always maintained that the war wis gaun tae finish. We said we didn't know, we'd never heard. We hoped it did. That wis a'.

Ah have no recollection o' any disciplinary thingmies through that fraternisation, because they all knew it. The officers knew it. There wis officers goin' oot and talkin' tae each other.

No more fraternisation took place efter that, efter the Christmas. It might have happened but no' tae ma knowledge, no' wi' oor regiment anyway.

Ah don't know why it wis only at Christmas 1914 that this took place. It wis goin' on before the officers actually knew that the thing wis goin' on. It wis bein' done until it got bigger and bigger. We all knew that they were talkin' tae each other.

In 1915, efter the Christmas fraternisation, the Germans took the Saxons away and put the Prussians in their place. We wis that stupid, of course, we didn't know. But we knew when, instead o' them comin and shoutin' tae ye and talkin' tae ye, ye got bullets instead. We lost two or three men through that. We discovered that the Saxons had been ta'en away from these trenches and the Prussians putten in front o' us. And there were nane o' this 'Hullo, Jock! How are ee gettin' on the nicht?', or anythin' like that. It wis mair shootin' or anything else. Of course, the Germans wis the same, 'cause we started shootin' them tae.

The singin' got put a stop to because that wis the Saxons again. Then they put the Prussians doon aside us. That wis a different story a'thegither. And they used tae tell ye: 'Aye, you can sing as much as you like. You keep your heid doon or we'll let ye know what we're doin!' We'll no' sing tae ye!' And that wis enough. Oo kent then no' tae.

Ah wis at every battle frae '14 right up tae the finish. Well, tae me, a' the battles was the same, except Ypres. They were aye battlin' at Ypres, ye wis aye fightin' wi' them. The battles were a' much the same. Ye wis only oot there for tae fecht and kill Germans and take their trenches. And if ee got the first trench ee tried tae take the second trench, the reserve trench. And if ee wis lucky ee took that but sometimes ee couldnae haud it. Ye got battered that much wi' artillery and machine gun fire that ee had tae retreat back tae the front yin again. That wis a' ye done a' the war—back and forrit, back and forrit. But ah wis at the battle o' Loos, Neuve Chapelle, Cambrai, Arras, and the Somme. Ah wis in Albert on the Somme. Ah remember the Virgin on the church at Albert lyin' doon. She wis lyin' towards the German trenches. And the French people reckoned that she wis keepin' the Germans back. They didnae think it wis the British that wis haudin' them back, it wis this Virgin that wis haudin' them back.

Well, durin' the battle o' the Somme ah got a leave and ah come home and ah says tae John—that wis ma brother—ah says, 'Ah'm no' gaun back there again.' He says, 'Ye have tae go back.' Ah says, 'Ah'm not goin' back.' Well, what ah went through—that wis the reason. 'Cause the Germans were somethin' tae fight, ye know.

So ah went oot tae Newtongrange tae ma sister's. Now there were policemen at ma brother John's hoose every day, every other hoor, wantin' tae ken where ah wis. John said, 'Ah don't know. He left here. He went away back tae the army, as far as ah know.' They said, 'He's not in the army. Where is he? Have you any friends?' 'Yes, ah've a sister in Newtongrange and a sister in Bonnyrigg.' 'Right, give us their address.' And they were oot at Newtongrange. They were at the door. Ah wis in the hoose. And Margaret, ma sister, wis tellin' them: 'No, Wull's no' here. No, he's in the army. He's oot in France. Oo've no' heard frae him for a while.' They took that for an answer and they went away. And ah wis sittin' in the bloody room! They didnae come in and search the hoose or anythin' like that. They only made enquiries at the door.

Now ma brother had a fruit shop in Edinbury and he had a hawkin' van and ah used tae go oot and hawk. Ah went oot and got away wi' it—a' up Newtongrange, Dalkeith, Bonnyrigg, Gorebrig, Leith. Ah used tae go doon tae the Hibs' gate and stand wi' ma van and sell fruit there. Ah went tae a' the fitba' matches—either Tynecastle or Easter Road. And ah used tae put maybes twae aipples, a pear, a bunch o' grapes, some nuts, row the bag up—ninepence a time. Ah made as much money doin' that—more than hawkin' fruit or sellin' it in the shop.

Ah wis oot o' the army aboot five month. Then ah went down tae the recruitin' office in Cockburn Street and ah joined up in the artillery. That wis how ah got intae the artillery—under a different name, under ma *ain* name. Ah wis brought up as Wullie Kerr frae ah wis weeks old till ah wis twenty-odds. But ah knew by then that ma name wis Hanlan. Ah went tae the thingmy office in Edinbury and got ma birthlines. Ah got tae ken that ma mother and faither was married, that ah wisnae illegitimate—which ah thought ah wis.

So ah volunteered tae go intae the artillery, cause they were beginnin' tae look for iz. And ah knew that ah had either tae do that or ah'd get caught. And if ah wis caught ah wis feared for what the result wid be. Ah got the wind up. 'Now,' ah says, 'ah must gaun intae the army or else. If they catch me ah'll be ...'

Ah knew one or two fellows that—in the regiment like—had been court martialled and got shot. Ah wis at the shootin' o' them. Ye see, when there wis anybody shot in eer regiment there wis so many NCOs and so many—the youngest—recruits in eer regiment tooken tae see the shootin'. They actually watched them shootin' until it stopped. Ah did see two or three shot.

Ah wis never in a firin' party maself. Ee wis there for the occasion. Well, ee went up there. They had tae take a machine gun up, ee see. They didnae depend on rifles too much, because when anybody was bein' shot there might ha' been other sojers no' pleased at that, no' wantin' it and goin' tae cause a bit o' trouble. And the machine gun was there in case o' that, to keep order if it wis required.[15]

Billy Cordrey, as far as ah know, he did desert in France. And it so happened when he came back, which wis six weeks efter he had been knockin' aboot France and couldnae get anythin', he couldnae get across the Channel on the boat—he had tried apparently—and he decided tae come back tae the regiment again. Now on his comin' back there wis an officer that had gotten wounded in the leg. Billy happened tae see him and he wis lyin' wounded. And Billy picks him up and brings him in. And Billy gets the Distinguished Conduct Medal for this, for savin' the bloody man's life apparently. Now Billy was gettin' intae trouble if he hadnae brought in this officer. That made a' the excuses possible for Billy. His desertion was never mentioned. It sort o' pleased them.

But there were not a lot o' desertions, no' that ah ken o'. Ah cannot remember many in ma regiment. It wis a very rare occurrence. When ah deserted, says I: 'Now ah dinnae want tae gaun away back tae the trenches. The best thing ah can do is jine the artillery', says I, because the artillery at that time wisnae near the trenches. They were aboot two mile back frae the trenches. But ah jined the artillery and they had their guns in the trenches. Ah made a blunder there of course. Ah'd been as weel in the infantry as in the artillery because ah wis in the trenches.

Ah don't remember any conscientious objectors in France, no' that ah'm aware o'. There were plenty in the regiment of course, wantin' tae be conscientious objectors, talkin' aboot it and a' the rest o' it. They werenae a' a hunder per cent for the army. But ah knew two fellaes that belonged the Highland Light Infantry. Now we had a company o' the HLI attached tae us tae make up oor battalion tae get us oot tae France in 1914. And thir HLI fellaes wis a different kettle o' fish frae us a'thegither. Well, they were discontented. They werenae a hunder per cent sojers. And ah knew them tae be the same way as a regiment. Everybody knew them tae be like that, the HLI. It wis definitely a bad rotten regiment. Ah'm no' sayin' that there werenae a lot o' good sojers in it. There were good sojers. But there were a helluva lot o' bad yins in the HLI, there wis. And if there were any mutinies it wis in the HLI. I seen one at Étaples and that wis the HLI. That was after ah'd went back tae France, efter ah'd joined up again. Ah wis at Étaples tae bring horses up, because oo'd gotten horses killed in oor transport.

Well, ah wis at every battle frae '14 right up tae the finish. Ah started the war, ah finished the war and ah actually went tae Germany after the war, when we took the occupation o' Germany in Cologne.[16]

21

James Marchbank

I was born on the 14th o' June 1900. We landed at Le Havre on the afternoon of the 5th o' November 1914. So here ah was in France. I was then fourteen, four months and three weeks old. And consequently I became the youngest soldier on active service in France durin' the whole war.

How did it come about? Well, I think there was a combination of circumstances. I've been told by near relatives that from a very early age I had always expressed the desire to become a soldier or a sailor. That wis number one.

Number two: at our home in Dalkeith, Mum and Dad, four sisters and another two brothers. My father was a miner and I'm sure economic circumstances wis another influence on me, tending to move me to become a soldier. You've got to keep in mind that miners in those days weren't paid very much—possibly £2 on an average per week—and to bring up a family of seven on that, well, it was pretty hard going.

Then we had an old granny. She lived with us. You might call her a patriotic woman. Her room was plastered with pictures of the Royal Family. I was always conscious when I moved about in her room that Queen Victoria or some other Royal Person was busy watchin' everythin' I was doin'.

Then the Scout movement set up somewhere about 1908 or '10. At age eleven I joined the Boy Scout movement in Dalkeith, whose headquarters were in Eskbank Road, opposite the Catholic chapel. The scoutmaster was a retired Indian army cavalry officer. Now he was a splendid gentleman. Ah might say he was also a philanthropist. Comin' from a workin' class home we didn't have the means of course to get fully equipped. But out of his own pocket he helped us along. Consequently you had a troop second to none, where every boy was rigged out with full uniform, caps, the staff, and what have you. We also had a bugle band.

We were taught lots of things in that place there, apart from the drilling and military discipline that was shown. We were taught scouting, trekking, first aid, and on the sports side we got boxin', fencin', swimming, rock climbin'—you mention it and we got it, with instruction from the assistant scout masters.

In 1913 I learned there was a vacancy in the local company of the lst/8th Royal Scots Territorial Battalion in Dalkeith. Their headquarters were in Buccleuch Street, close by where the Arts Centre is now. There was a drill hall there. And ah went along—ah think it was in about the lst o' November, or thereabout—and enquired if they considered me suitable, because ah had already become a bugler in the Scout movement.

So they jumped at the chance. They says, 'Fair enough.' I, of course, accepted the king's shillin'. Now once you accept the king's shillin' you become a soldier. That's you. So I was in.

Durin' the months that followed of course I got the same trainin' as the other lads in the company, in the form o' musketry trainin'. And I can tell you that at thirteen and a half or thereabout I was considered as bein' a very good shot and ah was continually bein' told that ah could shoot tae kill any time ah liked at that age.

I was still at school but on the 14th o' June 1914 I decided to leave school because that was the school leavin' age in that day. So for a few weeks I did a roll round, newspapers in the evening, and so forth.

About mid-July the Territorial Company was due to go to camp at Stobs. I went with them there. While we were there, of course, there was talk of war and rumours of war, etc. But we came home.

On the evening of the 4th of August, when war was declared, my calling up paper came through the post. It read as follows: 'Embodiment Notice to Join. 4585 Boy J M Marchbank, 8th Royal Scots. The Army Council, in pursuance of His Majesty's Proclamation, has directed you to attend for enlistment immediately. Bring rations and fuel light to last 24 hours.' That was signed by the lieutenant in command at that time, on the 4th day of August 1914.

Well, in reportin' I first went into billets in a drill hall at Tranent. Then we were all collected down to Haddington in East Lothian. And we put in three months very, very hard trainin'—all foot sloggin' more or less. In these days there was no mechanised transport. Officers were allowed a charger but if you were an infantryman you had to slog it, no matter where you went. And we practised very hard and marched sometimes ten, fifteen and twenty miles twice or thrice a week. So that fairly toughened us up. That went on for about three month.

On the 2nd of November, though, we got a quick order that we were due to go abroad. We entrained at Haddington. Now the Battalion at this time was just over 900 strong, but we were supplemented by a company from the 5th Highland Light Infantry from about the central Scotland belt. They made us up to a thousand in total.

So we entrained, set off, and landed down at Southampton. We had a short break in camp there. Then, the following afternoon, the 4th, we marched down to the docks. And ah can tell you we got a marvellous send off from there. Ah've never forgot it. All the people turned out and we were laden with gifts of all descriptions: foodstuffs, fruit, whatever. One dear old lady I remember gave me half-a-crown. Well, she never would know how pleased ah was about that, because ah had no money at all. The only money ah had was this half-crown. So ah cherished this half-crown.

We got aboard this ship—it was an old cattle boat—and off we went, across the Channel, escorted by a couple of destroyers. On the next afternoon, the 5th, there was a submarine scare, and these two destroyers went harin' about and tossin' these depth charges. I don't know whether they succeeded in gettin' rid of the submarine but it certainly didn't sink us.

So we landed at Le Havre, as ah say, on the afternoon of the 5th. Early the following morning we were marched down to the docks railway station at Le Havre and we were shipped into cattle trucks which held eight horses or forty men. And while the transport was bein' loaded up of course we just wandered about the yard. Outside the gates of this place the local youngsters were millin' around, offerin' to do all sorts of things for us: buy chocolate and what have you, anything you wanted, even offerin' the services of their sisters and a' that sort of thing. However, ah thought, well, ah wanted some bread. Ah said to this wee boy could he get chocolate and bread? Oh, yes, he would do that. So ah gave him ma half-crown. And this wee character set off across the road and disappeared round the building. Ah said to maself, 'Ah wonder if he'll come back?' And just at that he looked back and thumbed his nose at me. And that was the end of ma half-crown. It was gone for ever.

Well, we entrained and we eventually landed at Saint Omer, where we joined up wi' the 22nd Brigade of the 7th Division of the First Expeditionary Force. Then we moved into the line in a section of what was really no line at all at that time, on the way to Armentières—a place named Bois Greniers.

Within a few hours the first casualty happened: a sergeant was killed by a sniper. These snipers were very, very skilful. It wis learned later on of course they were usin' telescopic sights. The nature of the so-called trenches in these days was they was just simply holes where people had dug in and some were water-filled and what have you.

The weather became so bad that both Jerry and ourselves decided, well, 'Ye better try and make yerselves comfortable for the winter because ye cannot fight over these conditions.' The weather was extremely cold, heavy rain and snow, places filled up with water and men were standin' yonder. And we were doin' a four-day stint, night and day in the trench.

Consequently, the men became ill. Number one, of course, was the trench feet due to continually standing in water, you couldn't get dry clothes, you only stood up in what you had. There was no shelter, just a rubber sort of mackintosh thing that you wore, and that was all there was to preserve you. So you can understand there was a heavy illness list. But ah can tell you that unless you wis bent double, or the medical officer thought you were likely to take pneumonia, you just had to soldier on and lie in the billets. If they thought you were goin' to have pneumonia you were shifted away down to the 'ospital.

Well, this went on. Then there was another bugbear started. It was lice. Now this is a fearful thing. Lice affected everyone without exception. Every person was verminous. And in addition to being disease-carrying, these body lice, setting up a trench fever, were very discomforting. So it meant of course ye had to try and contend wi' this sort of thing as well. We more or less overcome it a wee bit by burning the bits off the inside of the seams of your trousers or whatever uniform there was wi' a match or a candle, or kill them in other ways. You'd hear them going pop, pop, pop, pop. Och, a horrible din. Chats, we used to call them.

Whilst all this was going on there were other discomforts: rats. At this period possibly they weren't as numerous as they became later on in the war. But I can tell you that even at first the rat menace was serious. They were livin' on bodies—lads who had been killed. They were even attacking people who had been wounded and unable to defend themselves. When you were lying around on a firestep they run around there and they run over your face. Some lads complained of bein' nipped in the extremities, and so forth. So that was another hazard.

Apart from that, there was always the other side of the business—the shelling and machine gun fire which had to be contended with, and the menace of these snipers. And of course raids were organised on a small scale. Raidin' parties went out and you'd try to take a machine gun post or attempt to find where a sniper was. Various things was tried. Ah can tell you these lads were very, very good, because ah've seen when we'd just put anything up and the next thing—crack! They werenae always firin' from fixed sights but they were very good. However, as ah say, they became very menacin' and raids had to be made.

Then, as ah told you earlier, the weather was getting very, very bad and on the cold frosty nights the place was still. You could hear in the distance Jerry coughin' or somebody whistlin', or transport and things goin' up in the distance.

One evening I remember. At school I had been taught a German song named 'The Lorelei'. I don't know what prompted me to do it but ah wis standin' this night and ah started to whistle the first bar of 'The Lorelei'. The next thing is ah hears the second bar comin' up in the distance! So ah repeated it again. Ah whistled through the tune, and lo and behold this Jerry ...

This story got around and ah can tell you ah wis severely reprimanded for it and wis told ah wisnae tae repeat it again. That was what I got out of that lot.

Later on in '14—I wasn't there when it happened—I believe there was a sort of undeclared armistice by some of the boys, who went over and exchanged cigarettes and so forth with the German lads. But that was stopped as well. It was forbidden. Nobody was allowed to continue that sort of thing. But on lookin' back, ah think that possibly if that spirit could have prevailed and got through the whole lot it would have been much better. It would have saved millions and millions of lives.

Well, after the fightin' started in '14 they become more ambitious. Ammunition was very short in the early stages but when more ammunition become available they started. The British made an attack on Aubers Ridge. Well, it was really a mudflat they were makin' on to but they succeeded to a certain extent. Then of course the attack fell flat because communications broke down. That was a very important thing. They lost touch and of course the reinforcements didnae come up and Jerry counter-attacked—and there you are.[17]

Later on, I believe, about that period Jerry used gas: phosgene. That was a tragic thing. Fellows were in a very bad state. From there of course our lot started—they introduced mustard gas. And then Jerry was usin' mustard gas as well later on. So there the atrocities all got started and continued.[18]

In '15 and '16, well, there was Festubert and Loos. They were all really jist tragic events. There is no question about that. Ah was in the vicinity. Ah was doin' different

25

jobs at various times. Ah was at that time a runner actually.[19]

And then of course in '16 the Somme came along. Everybody was involved in that. It was jist a hellish thing altogether that. The casualties on the first day alone, if ah remember rightly, about 19,000 or 20,000 died. Casualties was really very, very heavy. On the lst of July—that's when the battle really began—the losses were 57,000 men. Just imagine that, the slaughter that went on there: 57,000 losses, of whom 19,000 were killed. By the end of September 200,000 men were lost. Many were unburied. Some were in shallow graves. Some were buried—and blown out again. Buried and blown out, buried and blown out. Ah mean, it wis fantastic what was really happenin'.[20]

Well, there were battles all on similar lines, where men lost their lives and were blown to smithereens. Then in the later stage of the war Jerry was havin' a turn. Of course, you went on the defensive. In 1918 he made his great effort to break through. And this was a terrible thing. There was a terrible bombardment and of course he eventually succeeded in breaching the line. Jerry had built up a line o' defences which extended miles behind his trenches: wire, trenches, gun emplacements and what have you. And we had started doing this similar. From our front line to the support lines and reserves—barbed wire, miles of barbed wire, and trenches dug in readiness for this big stink comin' off. And it did come off. Jerry eventually succeeded in breakin' through. Ah can assure you it was a fearful time that. But it was the first time in the war when we really got going at one another into the open, into new ground out of the trenches. But ah can tell you there was some very sad stories to be told about that.

You can imagine some o' the artillery barrages went on for days—six days. You can imagine men tryin' to live under conditions such as that. It was fearful. And you had no choice: you just had to stick it out. Because if the army caught you showin' cowardice in front of the enemy in the front line, well, it wis jist a case you had tae be disposed of. You wis shot. You would have upset the rest. And there were no doubt truth in it. Ah have seen a young soldier run amok—he certainly gave the whole position away. And, well, possibly it's no correct tae say they should hae been destroyed. But that wis the only hope for the salvation of the rest of you. Ah witnessed a case like that: he wis destroyed.

Well, there was five days of that, when Jerry made his breakthrough in March 1918. There was an awful lot of sacrifice took place—needlessly. But that's another story. Men suffered intolerably. It went on for five days. Then we were taken out on rest. We were reinforced. But Jerry was still pressing on.

We went out for a so-called rest up into the Artois area, round about Lillers. Then Jerry made another attack in that same area. And ah'll tell you this story because ah've never forgotten. It was outside a little village where we were immediately put on the alert and marched off—of all places, a little village named Paradis. Heaven knows, it never resembled that, ah can assure ye. Haig, the commander-in-chief, issued his famous message of 'Backs to the Wall'. It meant that if we lost this one things were goin' to be really bad. And ah think the message got home and everyone stuck in.

Well, we marched off to in front of Paradis, this little village. Ah had been in this place about three year previous under different circumstances. Ah wis familiar with the lay-out. That night ah wis detailed, along wi' another lad, to try and make contact. We didn't know what the situation was, it had become so fluid. Portuguese troops were comin' back and some of our lads were comin' back. So it would appear that our forward lines had got the worst o' the argument.

So we took up position and ah wis detailed wi' this other lad to go out wi' this patrol and try and make a contact. Ah'll never forget this all the time ah live. After we had passed our forward post we wandered up this little farm road and came to this wee farm. Ah listened and inside ah could hear movement—very little, but it was there just the same. And ah thought, 'There's somebody here.' So we knocked. But eventually we just banged the door and went in. And here was an old man sitting, an old Frenchman. He must have been eighty years old. He was sitting there with a cavalry sword in his hand. Ah said to him, 'What are you goin' to do?' He said his intention was to have it out wi' any Jerry that come in the door. Ah tried to persuade him to leave but he wouldn't leave.

Well, we left him there. Shortly afterwards we ran into a Jerry patrol. After an exchange of shots eventually we had to pull out and alert the others behind us. We didn't pass by where the old farm was but I've often wondered what would happen to that auld man. He was so convinced that he had been successful in the Franco-Prussian War of 1870 that he would destroy any German that come into his house. He had no chance whatever.

Well, nobody likes war, let's face it. But at the same time the propaganda machine gets busy and people sometimes become persuaded to think in another direction. Possibly that is the answer to why so many people carried on. Plus the fact, there was a strict military discipline. I think had there just been a voting paper and you issued it to a soldier and said: 'Are you in favour of continuing the war or not?', you would have invariably found that there would have been an overwhelming vote for stopping it immediately. But that didn't apply. So you just had to soldier on. A lot o' grousin' and groanin' went on, make no mistake about that. And a lot of injustices were done. And all were glad at the finish to see the end of it. But they themselves couldn't end it. As I said, if the key had just been taken from what happened in the first Christmas period and New Year period of 1914, millions of lives would have been saved. The war cost over fifteen million lives throughout the continent. The British alone had three-and-a-half million casualties. No one has any conception of what really did happen unless you were involved in it. My God, you know, it's fearful to come across men in a' sort of situations, standin' up, lyin' down, bent up, sittin' as if nothing had happened—but dead. There were others scared out their wits. Some lost their reason. Other lost their sight. There were some awful things happened. And there were atrocities committed, too—make no mistake about that—on both sides. What are you going to do if a man gets tuned up? He'll stop at nothing. That's the situation, I can tell you.

Robert Irvine

When Lord Kitchener's pointing finger was on every hoarding throughout the country—'Your King and Country Needs You'—I was one of the innocents who was enmeshed in this web of patriotism at the First World War.

I was only a shop assistant at the time, and on reflection I think it was more that I wanted to escape from the humdrum life behind a grocer's counter and see a bit of the country. I've since been sorry that I took that decision, but not having a social conscience I was just swept up in the wave of patriotism that swept the country.

However, some time after I was in France news of the activities of the Shop Stewards' Movement were filtering through to the soldiers in the trenches. The married men in particular were a wee bit resentful, because they were getting letters from their womenfolk that the landlords were putting up the rents and so forth. Gradually this resentment spread to the young unmarried members of the Forces. And we also heard that the French army had practically gone into revolt for similar reasons. I believe it was verified later that Earl Haig had written to Lloyd George: 'For Heaven's sake, resolve your war there in Glasgow and Scotland or you'll lose the battle here.' The resentment was growing to such a pitch.

There is no doubt whatever about it that the Clyde Workers' Committee and the shop stewards' activities did have some impact on the troops fighting there, because the more we experienced the incredible folly of war out there the more we appreciated the work that our comrades at home were doing. We realised that we were fighting for the capitalists while the shop stewards at home were fighting for the workers.[21]

We knew through letters from home what was going on at home. The only press we saw was *John Bull,* and even that was at a premium. I think most of the soldiers bought it for the sake of some competition that was in it.[22]

Anyhow I was wounded at the battle of Cambrai and I landed up in Trouville, the holiday resort of the millionaires on the Channel coast of France. And this incident, I think, done more than anything else to sort of give birth to a sort of social conscience in me. There wis nobody in that millionaires' paradise except soldiers, wounded and convalescent, and a few key workers. But what attracted me was the fact that a stable boy was exercising race horses along the sands. And in conversation with one of the stable lads I asked him where the owners were. 'Oh,' he says, 'they're away from it all.' So there you are: the people who owned the race horses and the property and everything else, they were away in Canada and America and away out the place altogether, away from it all—while the lads, married and unmarried, were out in France dying before they knew what it was to live.

Anyhow on my return home to Glasgow I knew there was something wrong and I tried to form an ex-servicemen's group. I got about half-a-dozen members. We had rooms in Eaglesham Street. This was shortly after the war. And I suggested we have a march up to the City Chambers and kick up a row. So here I was marching my small platoon along Paisley Road, and Harry McSharie and John Maclean were going down in the opposite direction. I learned afterwards they had been at the City Chambers to see the Lord Provost. Anyhow John and Harry gave me a wave and I told my troops to fall in behind John's big platoon and we marched down, I think it was to Shieldhall housing scheme.

Well, I attended one or two classes of John Maclean's and latterly I joined the Independent Labour Party and I remained with the Independent Labour Party till they disaffiliated from the Labour Party in 1932.[23]

Allan Young

For my sins, I was the grandson of a shepherd and the grandson of a farmer. My grandfather bore the same name as myself, Allan Young. He shepherded on Loch Eil side on a famous farm called Fassiefearn, noted during the Jacobite Rebellion as one of the places that Prince Charlie slept in.

My grandfather, herding 900 sheep twelve miles from the slope of Ben Nevis, received the princely reward of something like £15 a half year and a boll of meal and a boll of flour. After he retired at the age of seventy and had turned blind through cataract—not getting skilled operations and with no Medical Health Acts in those days—he wasn't even allowed, after having given his lifetime to that, to graze a cow on the hill opposite, on the other side of the road. I think when I learned that, the iron entered my soul.

Then again I happened to be in the misty isle Eilan Sgiathanach (Skye) on the outbreak of war in 1914. And I saw the men being called from the shielings and the glens and the bens there, going away to fight in a foreign land. I reflected then as to what it was all about and I saw in the *Glasgow Herald* questions being raised in the House of Lords as to certain events that were taking place in Glasgow. Now brought up as I was in a Free Church atmosphere and with, if you like, feudalistic parents and grandparents, I had never heard of such outrageous bodies as Labour Parties and trade unions and so on. And I thought I would learn for myself.

Again for my sins I was a schoolteacher. Reluctantly I joined what was called the Derby Scheme, and you weren't called up until they thought it was a time fit for you to go. So I was in the army from 1916 until the end of the war. I saw just exactly what war meant.[24]

Now the *Forward* and the *Labour Leader,* as it was known then—not the *New Leader,* but the *Labour Leader,* which was the organ of the old Independent Labour Party—were forbidden to be sent out to France. But my wife used to cut them up in columns and send them out as if it was a letter. And I got that letter there. It used to be passed round the battery in which I served.[25]

Now I used to have very great debates with several people. One of them stands out in my mind and that was Professor Holland Rose of Cambridge University.[26] It was the beginning of 1917, when peace pourparlers were in the air. He was sent out to deliver propaganda to the troops. The title of his address was 'An Unjust and an Unlasting Peace'. By then Russia had caved in and Germany could concentrate on one front instead of on two. And they were showing us this thing that we were not to lose our morale, although we were now going to have to fight the whole weight of the German army.

Well, that was the tenor of Professor Holland Rose's speech and after it, when questions were asked, I asked him if he had remembrance of the Three-Power Treaty between Nicky, Geordie and Ben—Russia, Britain and France. He said, 'Yes.' I said, 'You'll admit then that that meant an association of birds of a feather flocking together?' He said, 'Yes.' 'Now,' I said, 'you mentioned at the outbreak of your address that it might have been a good thing to have a Russian Revolution. Now,' I said, 'if it's the case that we are all birds of a feather, might it not be a good thing to have a British Revolution after the war?' He said, 'Young man,' he said, 'the British Tommy will see that he gets the government that he wants after he returns home.'

I wasn't just quite content with his answer and at the end, as Scotsmen always do, I pursued him. And he began to ask me various questions as to the sources of my information. I referred him to the *Cambridge Magazine,* as he was a professor of history there. He said: 'What—that, written by the miserable pacifist remnant at Cambridge?' My retort to that was this: 'You as a professor, especially of History, should sift all evidence, no matter by whom it is written, and come to a logical conclusion.' He turned to the Reverend Mr Yellowlees, who was in charge of that Woodbine hut at Harfleur, and said: 'Give Jock a pair of socks and clear him out of this.'[27]

That was my wee bit of trying to do a bit of propaganda there. The following day I was down drying my shirt in the drying shed—we washed them in petrol cans when we could get water out of the Somme or any other where—and the fellow who was in charge of the place said to me: 'Jock, were you the speaker last night?' I said, 'No.' He said, 'Come on now,' he said, 'we can't mistake the Scots voice.' He says, 'If you don't want to tell me I'll tell you about myself.' He said, 'I was a non-combatant. I was one of these conscientious objectors and I sailed away from Britain. I was going to have no more to do with it. I got as far as San Francisco then I thought better and I came back. I was sentenced. The standard sentence in those days for conscientious objectors was 112 days, commuted to 34. 'And,' he said, 'I got 112 commuted to 34 and I was sent out here. And this is the job they have given me as a non-combatant. Now, Jock, I've told you about myself. Where did you get your information?' 'Well,' I said, I got it from a wee book, Bertrand Russell's *Justice in Wartime*. And the most illuminating thing of all in it, on its first page, is that the first casualty in war is truth.'[28]

He asked me if he could get a copy of that book. I told him I had spoken to Bertrand Russell at Charing Cross when he even went and lectured on the street just after he was fined and imprisoned and his Columba gold medal—the university award that he got in America—was taken from him. I said, 'I don't know if we'd be able to get that book, seeing it was written by a sedition monger.' But I got my wife to send it out.

I used to write a little to the front pages of *Forward*—and I regret its passing, because that's what we lack today: a live political journal that would keep us *au fait* and sometimes reassure us when we become depressed. I used to write a little to the front pages of that, under the heading 'Socialist War Points'. One I sent was this: that the papers here at home used to tell you about 'destroyed by Hun shellfire', and all that sort of thing. I was with the artillery, first of all the 136 Heavy Battery, then the 138. And we calibrated our guns on Lens church—that is to say, we fired on them to test the accuracy of the firing. So I sent that information along and it appeared in *Forward*.

On another occasion I sent *Forward* a little official government manual. It dealt with co-operation between aircraft and artillery and said that we were permitted to fire on steeples and churches, the excuse being that there might be snipers in these.

The third point that I sent to 'Socialist War Points' was this: Major Lloyd George, as he then was, the son of Lloyd George, and who wrote the biography of his father, commanded the neighbouring battery to the one that I was attached to—the 222 Siege Battery.[29] That was at a little place Lanouville, so many kilometres west of Abbeville. He had the dug-outs of his battery underneath the civilian graveyard there. The privet hedges round its boundary he used as the camouflage for his guns. Of course, he fired from there. Of course, Jerry spotted where the fire came from. Of course, Jerry retaliated. Then the papers at home said: 'Civilian cemetery destroyed by Hun shellfire.' But they didn't tell you we were firing from there.

Harry McShane

Just about the beginning of July 1914 I became a shop steward. I wasn't long a shop steward. The first thing that I did when I became a shop steward was to take the men out on strike for the reinstatement of the man who had been shop steward before me. And we were actually a fortnight on strike before the First World War broke out.

Well, actually, for about five years prior to the war I was already quite active in the socialist movement, having joined the Independent Labour Party in 1909 and left it to join the provisionally formed British Socialist Party in 1910.[30]

Around that period there were a whole lot of industrial struggles on Clydeside, the most prominent figures being, I would say, John Wheatley, John Maclean, Tom Johnston, Emanuel Shinwell and Pat Dollan. John Maclean was a sort of heretic, not being a member of the Labour Party, but he was very, very active. He wanted his Party—the Social Democratic Party, later the British Socialist Party—to join the Labour Party. But that did not happen until 1916.[31]

So during that period there was a host of industrial struggles: a number of national strikes in 1911, and a number of rank and file strikes—of girls in a particular mill in Neilston, engineers in Singer's, led by an unofficial organisation, and a number of other similar disputes in various parts of Glasgow. And the idea was mooted then of a rank and file movement among the workers in the factories. It didn't catch on then to any great extent, although it was being preached everywhere. But to my surprise, when I entered Weir's engineering works at the beginning of 1914 I found a works committee—I think the only one in the country—in actual operation, led by Jim Messer, a member of the Independent Labour Party. This works committee met once a week, had a properly appointed chairman and secretary, and it kept minutes and did everything possible to carry out the decisions made by the committee in the intervening days between the meetings.[32]

So about the beginning of July I became a shop steward. A man named Mulloy had been shop steward before me, and we were actually a fortnight on strike before the war broke out.

The negotiations with the employers took place on the very day the war broke out. A lot of men were being called up to the naval reserve, and immediately after the war broke out there was a considerable amount of confusion. A large number of the men were already prior to the war leaving Weir's, because there was a feeling that unemployment was coming and they wanted to get to places like Brown's, where they were building a big battleship, and to other places where they thought there would be some sort of permanency of employment.

I left Weir's shortly after the war broke out and wandered about from place to place and took part in the ordinary agitation to arouse feeling in connection with the war itself, being opposed to the war.

I will say there was a sort of hesitancy on the part of the socialists in connection with the war. All the parties in Glasgow without exception—including the Independent Labour Party, the British Socialist Party, and the Socialist Labour Party—were split on the war. A large number of the British Socialist Party leading figures left to follow H M Hyndman, who was supporting the war. The Independent Labour Party finally came round to an anti-war position, as did the Socialist Labour Party. The British Socialist Party was anti-war in Glasgow because the pro-war elements left it, and left the anti-war elements—who were in the majority—in charge, the leading figure in connection with that being of course John Maclean.

The first meeting held in Glasgow that was advertised as anti-war was not held until September 1915. But there was prior to that a good deal of anti-war propaganda mixed up with the general propaganda. But 1915 saw the height—but that was also connected with the industrial movement and the rise of the shop steward movement.

I said that Weir's was the best organised factory on the Clyde when the war broke out. The Amalgamated Society of Engineers put in a demand before the outbreak of war for the biggest rise they had ever asked for. They used to ask for a ha'penny, expecting a farthing. But this time they asked for tuppence. And no one really believed that they meant it. But the war broke out and some engineers were brought from America to work in Weir's, with wages that were fabulous in comparison to what were being paid in Weir's. And that was the cue for the Weir's men to walk out. And then all the other engineering and shipbuilding establishments followed suit and you had something like 17,000 Glasgow engineers out on strike. This was known as the 'Tuppence or Nothing' strike: they said, 'Tuppence—or nothing.'

They were offered a ha'penny, they were offered three farthings, they were offered all kinds of sums. Finally, it finished up with three ha'pence of a rise—the biggest rise that the engineers had ever had. But they formed out of that what was known as the Labour Withholding Committee. The officials of the Amalgamated Society of Engineers had come out against the strike and were howled down in the Palace Theatre in the Gorbals. The employers showed a great bitterness towards the workers who were on strike. And the press—all the newspapers without exception—called them Clyde shirkers and Clyde slackers. There was a big campaign. The *Daily Record* was very vicious. A boycott was instituted against the *Daily Record,* and the Fairfield workers in particular boycotted the *Daily Record,* and the newsagents had piles of newspapers that they couldn't sell.

Later on, of course, the fight developed. The Labour Withholding Committee became the Clyde Workers' Committee, with Gallacher in the chair, and with Jim Messer as secretary.[33] A large number of struggles took place, one of which Charlie McPherson can tell you about better than I can. He was one of the victims of that particular struggle.

Charlie McPherson

Well, earlier on in this struggle there was the vicious lock-out of the boilermakers in 1910. You folks who are younger could hardly believe the employers would have been so vicious as what they were then. Some small local strike took place in the north-east of England and nobody on the Clyde knew anything about it. And the posters went up that from twenty-four hours afterwards every boilermaker in the country was locked out—just like that.

Gradually then the other tradesmen were paid off as the days and the weeks went past. Govan in particular was very badly hurt. And out of that strike there grew up the famous Govan Boilermakers' Whistle Band. Well, this band was organised to go round begging just, seeking for money—boxes on poles, up the windows. The Glasgow magistrates wouldn't allow them to collect in Glasgow. But Partick was a separate burgh then and so was Govan and other places, and they had to keep to the boundaries and go round with the Whistle Band collecting money to try and keep folk alive. That was in the year 1910.

Well, I wasn't a boilermaker, I was a shipwright. After about six weeks I was paid off. And I always remember that notice that I got: 'Paid off.' It was a lesson to me, mind you, because it said on it I was paid off because 'Work was too far advanced.' I had done too much work and I was paid off and there we were—into the heap.[34]

The unions were never very aggressive then, they weren't aggressive at all. They were fairly helpless. It was just local folk that were campaigning. That 1910 lock-out gave an impetus to the socialist movement. The worker could see the class struggle in its bare nakedness then. And then the Irish strikes came on—the Dublin strike, with Larkin and Jim Connolly. We were helping here in Glasgow to send food over to Dublin, to the Dublin strikers. A curious thing about that was I came on some papers in a shipbuilding firm. As I say, we were collecting—concerts and everything—to send a food ship over to Dublin with food. And here in these papers I found that the Clyde shipbuilders were levying themselves to pay the Dublin employers, so that they weren't losing anything at all. So all our efforts were going for nothing. I had these papers but I was frightened for them and I gave them to John Maclean. I don't know what he did with them. Anyway it proved all that, you see.[35]

Well, all these troubles were growing up. The war was looming then. The Independent Labour Party's campaign was anti-conscription before the war, because the militarists were yelling for conscription to prepare for this war. But the war started.

We shipyard workers got a nice little notice telling us we wouldn't be called up. We were needed where we were and we didn't need to worry about being called up. Then the employers, later on in 1915, passed what was called the Munitions Act. Under this Act the worker became just like a chattel slave. He was tied down to his job. He couldn't leave. He couldn't lift his head hardly and he had to get a certificate from his employer before he could leave his job at all. And employers weren't giving any certificates at all.[36]

Well, I got mixed up with trouble like that. I was a young fellow and I was a shop steward. But the shop steward I was wasn't a fighting type of shop steward. My business was to see that the men were paying their dues and see that they had a card. And I was probably fighting my own tradesmen and trying to get them into the union. That was the job of the first of the shop stewards. We weren't called shop stewards in our trade. We were called the Vigilant Man. The man in the yard came to us with his complaint: it might be demarcation, it might be something wrong with the timekeeper, something wrong with his wages—these kinds of things. And we went humbly to see the management about it. We had no status at all. If the manager cared to see us he would see us; if he didn't care to—well, he didn't see us. And then the war came and, as I say, we were tied down to our jobs.

Trouble started in Fairfield. Men were dismissed because, as I found out afterwards, there was a quarrel between a young manager and a foreman. To get down on this foreman this young manager dismissed two of his men on the plea that they were loafing at work—they weren't being properly supervised. They came to us and somebody said to me: 'Charlie, you're a better speaker than I am. You take the chair here'. And that started the trouble, which rolled on.

We agreed to go out on strike. Then we sent a deputation to management. I remember that we picked some nice, elderly, quiet men to go and see the manager. The manager said: 'Why don't you send some o' your young spitfires here? I'm surprised at sensible men like you taking part in this.' And when they came back and reported that to us, somebody says: 'All out the gate!' So we were all out the gate and Fairfield was on strike.

We got a hall and organised that strike a bit. Then the Ministry of Munitions—we were summoned to the Sheriff Court under this Munitions Act and tried by Sheriff Fyfe.[37] The day of the trial we managed to get a lawyer. He was an old club lawyer: he dealt in clubs—drinking clubs and so on, licences for clubs and that kind of thing. That was the kind of work he was doing. He had never seen a shipyard. I marvelled at that, because the information he got and the way he put it across in the court you'd have thought he'd served his time in the shipyard. You should try telling a man about barbettes, twelve inch guns, ammunition passages—tell a man that had never seen anything of that![38]

Anyway the day before the trial we got this lawyer. But when he came into court he tied up this Fairfield management completely. First of all, they had to discharge a whole lot of men who weren't at work that day at all. They were so lax about it. They thought all they had to do was just say, 'Bring them into the court. They'll be condemned.' No—the lawyer saw to that. A number of them had been discharged, they hadn't been at their work—and yet they were summoned for going on strike!

I was put in the dock as a kind of leader and it depended on me. The lawyer for the Ministry of Munitions was a man called Turner McFarlane, a little man. I was told he was known then in legal circles as Little Tich. But this lawyer of ours put the Fairfield management, from the timekeeper to their manager, right through it and showed their confusion. They didn't know where they were.

The sheriff said he admired us for our stand for our fellow men. 'But unfortunately,' he says, 'the law is your officer. It says Thou Shalt Not Strike.' Our lawyer had argued that we weren't on strike. We had left our work but we weren't on strike for a change of conditions or an increase in wages or anything like that. He had tried to argue that we had left our work as a protest but not as a strike. But the sheriff washed that out. And then Sheriff Fyfe—he was a famous sheriff in those days—said, 'Well, I admire you, I admire your stand. But unfortunately the law says Thou Shalt Not Strike, and you've gone on strike.' So he fined us £10 or thirty days' imprisonment.

So we decided that after the court we were going to have a meeting but a lot of the men got drunk. We couldn't get a proper meeting. And most of them rushed back to their work. I went back to my work and asked for my books. And the manager said, 'We're not giving you your books.' Well, I went on a stay-in strike. I walked about Fairfield doing nothing at all. But, you see, they were frightened to speak to me. And after a fortnight of that, the Fairfield management changed their attitude completely and gave us our books. It was a mistake on our part. Every rebel in the yard then left. We were scattered all over.

And then we were summoned to the court and, as I say, we were tried in the court. Then the union sent for us and said: 'This is terrible. We'll try and save you from going to prison.' And they said, 'All you've got to do is sign these papers and it will be all right.' Well, most of the fellows signed the papers—and that left just three of us. Three of us were left. We didn't sign it. And about twelve o'clock one night I was arrested and hauled down to the police office. The prison van was waiting for us, the old horse van. And we were put into Duke Street after twelve o'clock at night, in through a wee gate. I can remember that yet. A man came with a lantern, a lantern with a lid. It was like a scene from some old Irish play that I had seen in the theatre. And of course we were put into our cells. They put me into a cell that must have been meant for some dangerous criminal, because the pot was made o' *papier mâché* and the stool was fixed to the ground. There was nothing I could kill anybody with! In the morning we were taken out and got our clothes and so on, and settled down to prison life. There was no distinction between prisoners—there were no political prisoners in those days. Porridge in the morning, soup at dinnertime, and porridge at night again.

I didn't know anything about the trouble that was going on on the outside. But there were great meetings outside everywhere. The whole Clyde was coming out on strike. And this night, after we were in a fortnight, the warder says to me: 'When ye gang intae yer cell at night dinnae take aff yer claes. Ye're gaun tae a meetin' or something.' But what we were going to was another trial—by Sir Lynden Macassey and Lord Balfour of Burleigh. The government appointed these men to look into this. And we went through another trial—inside the prison. Oh, it was just the same as the trial in the court. Lord Balfour of Burleigh was like the judge and Sir Lynden Macassey asked all the questions—about conditions in the yard, all the conditions of work, and so on. And then a week or so afterwards we were slipped out by a back door and released.[39]

Grace Kennedy

I married during the war, in 1917. I married a man who was gassed and come back from the war. I went into a single apartment in Govan.

During the war years there was people getting put out of their homes because they couldn't pay their rent. A lot of their men were in the Forces and at that time the soldiers' allowance was a shilling a day and they got half pay. The rent courts were full of people. And then there was what they called enrolments, re-enrolments and other re-enrolments. Sometimes the sheriff said you had to pay seven shillings. If you couldn't pay five shillings a week rent how on earth could you pay seven shillings a week ?

Well, the women got together and we decided that not one soldier's wife would be put out of her home. And guided by Baillie Mary Barbour, who was a plodder and who did tremendous work—we picketed these homes. They barricaded themselves up and we picketed the homes.[40]

They couldn't put anybody out between sunset and sunrise. The picket had to be between sunrise and sunset. Then after that you could go home. Then you put the food up to the people who were barricaded in their houses.

Then later on there was the Rent Strike. The landlords decided to put the rent up and they did get a 47½ per cent increase, which was supposed to be for repairs. Then we had nine months of a Rent Strike. Well, quite a lot got into difficulties through the Rent Strike—financial difficulties. A lot who hadn't stopped at the proper time they were told to stop it, generally got into difficulties—maybe didn't save the rent. Some of us saved our rent and had then to pay a certain amount and pay the arrears. But then the Rent Restriction Act was brought in and I think it was due to the work of Baillie Mary Barbour particularly and the women that the Rent Restriction Act was brought into being.[41]

John Heenan was a great man in the Rent Strike and I think he was on the Clyde Workers' Committee at that time. But he attended the rent courts. He was a councillor for a period and he was chairman of the Trades Council and of the City Labour Party.

I mind being on duty one day and I threw a pail of water over a gentleman that I thought was a sheriff officer. He came round the corner and it was in Drive Road, Govan, and we were picketing this day. We were determined that this woman wouldn't be put out of her home. But the gentleman turned out to be John Heenan.

He had been at a funeral and he had on a bowler hat.

John Heenan and I think there was a man McBride, they attended the rent courts.[42] And I used to go up to the rent courts, just more or less as a spectator. Sometimes I was allowed to speak on behalf of tenants. In fact, you didn't get speaking. They just said, 'Do you owe this rent?' The tenants said, 'Yes.' 'We'll say seven shillings a week.' If it was five shillings a week then it was seven shillings. How on earth could you pay two shillings more? It became so bad that Lloyd George came to the city and I have a memory of going up to some meeting and I think we bawled him out.

As well as Andrew McBride there was Harry McShane, Davie Kirkwood and John Heenan went up to the rent court to represent the tenants.[43] We couldn't send anybody up as a political party. So we had to set up this Housing Association. That was the position. Baillie Mary Barbour was president and there were others on the committee. It was individual membership. The membership was only a shilling a year at that time. And the Housing Association sent Andrew McBride and Harry McShane and other people up to defend the tenants. I took an active part in it, which brought me into the Independent Labour Party.

I hadn't any background at all of a socialist nature. I was brought up more or less in a religious atmosphere. But I remember the Boilermakers' Tin Whistle Band going round Govan during the boilermakers' lock-out or strike in 1910. My father was one of the victims of that strike. I remember the Parish Council at that period giving my mother I think it was either 1/6d. or two shillings a week of a line. You weren't allowed to get the money. You went round to Roddie McDonald's in Hamilton Street and I mind my father saying, 'Go round and get tea, sugar, and butter, etc.' for the two shillings. My father said maybe I could get half an ounce of tobacco, which was a penny ha'penny. And Roddie McDonald says, 'No, you can't get tobacco. It's not allowed.' So we had to take food, you see, so the men got no tobacco. Now that was my experience as a girl, just a school girl, going round with that line because my father was one of the victims of the boilermakers' lock-out, with the Tin Whistle Band going out. We did get maybe 1/6d. or two shillings a week from the boilermakers through these collections but there were so many of them it was terribly hard to distribute out. My father at that time used to go out and do cobbling. A friend gave him a job and he done a wee bit cobbling on the side.

It was injustice, it was fighting for what was right, and it was injustice that made me a socialist.

William Carey

I was in a family business. The family business started because my father, who was a member of the union of cabinetmakers and upholsterers, was sent down in 1888 to Beith to organise the chairmakers, who were below the Glasgow level of wages. He had to pick up a house here in Glasgow and go down and take up house in Beith, get a job in Mathew Pollock's the chairmakers, and stay there for three years until he had organised the chairmakers.

Then he come back to Glasgow and for a whole year he travelled all over, looking for a job. There was no job for him for a whole year. Because of that experience, over the years my mother had to start a business. And that was how I wasn't a trade unionist until about twenty or thirty years afterwards. But the impression left on my young mind as a boy implanted that working class bias that I never forgot, not even to this day.

Prior to the 1914 war an older comrade took me under his wing and he took me to the Socialist Labour Party Economic and Industrial History classes in Renfrew Street in Glasgow. Tom Bell took Economics, and Paddy Fitzpatrick took the Industrial History. And I got my early training there.[44]

The two classes were in the same buildin' in Renfrew Street but at separate times. There would be up to about thirty or forty students, all working men. I think there would maybe be two or three women. I can't remember. In these days politics wasn't the interest of women.

The books I read for the classes, oh, I started to read Karl Marx's *Das Kapital* but I gave it up. It was a hopeless task! I realised I had begun at the wrong end. There was a general textbook set by Tom Bell and Paddy Fitzpatrick—Daniel De Leon was the author. It was a book of definitions.[45]

Up there in Renfrew Street they printed *The Socialist* paper in the same building. The members ran off that paper.

Well, after the war came I was called up and I was taken away to Hamilton Barracks and I was told that I was now a soldier. I said, 'No, I'm not a soldier.' So they took me up to a room and an old soldier met me, a very kindly old fellow, and he says, 'Now what's your name ?' Ah says, 'Wullie.' 'Oh, well,' he says, 'Wullie, I've got a grand new suit for ye. That one that you're wearin's not very good.' 'Oh, but,' I says, 'ah didnae come here wi' ma best suit on.' 'Well,' he says, 'this is a better one.' Ah says, 'Ah don't want it.' He says, 'Aw, well, it's like this: if you don't put it on ah'll make ye put it on.' And ah looked at him and ah says, 'D'ye think ye're good enough tae do that, Jock?' 'Oh,' he says, 'we'll no' argue about it. You do it.' So to please him ah put on the uniform. 'And,' he says, 'there are yer puttees.' 'Oh,' ah says, 'ah'm no' wantin' them.' 'Oh, ye'll need tae put them on. Ye cannae go out on parade like that.' So two soldiers come and put me in a sheet, put ma legs up and wound the puttees round. And that was me. They stuck a bag in ma oxter and then the band started up and they shouted: 'Quick march!' Well, ah didnae quick march and ah dropped the bag. And a soldier at the back very near fell over it. But he kindly lifted it up and he carried it down the station for me. So that was ma first battle.

Then ah wis taken to Hawick and they had quite a scene there in Hawick. And after a fortnight there the regiment removed to Wormit, away up facing Dundee. And I was court martialled there. And I had a very pleasant experience: after the court martial the prosecuting officer come forward and shook hands with me. I don't know why he did it and I understood that he was a VC. So there must have been some sympathy—a young man standing up to the might of the British army.

Well, the attitude of others to my conscientious objection—I seemed to have a charmed life. I don't understand it. Unless they said things behind my back, what they said in my hearing was quite complimentary to me. They believed I was sincere. And I never shirked an argument. If they were willing to discuss my attitude I was always willing to have a go, and they apparently thought I had great justification for what I was doing. I could always answer all their questions. And it was the same all through.

In the army I found that the ordinary soldier was quite sympathetic. When we were detailed to go to London to Wormwood Scrubs there was a young fellow in the guard who took me to the court martial and he was quite upset about it. He didn't like this idea of a man being forced to do what he didnae want tae do. Ah says, 'Well, we'll see. We're going to London tonight on the train. Ah hope you're one o' the guards.' 'No, no,' he says, 'no, ah'm no' takin' a man tae prison that disnae want tae soldier.' He says, 'Ah didnae want tae soldier. Ah wis told tae go intae the army but ah hadnae the courage tae do what you're doin'. Therefore ah'm no' takin' you tae prison.' And he didn't.

Major Dan Bonnar

I joined the army as a boy piper in June 1914 and I was posted to the 2nd Battalion of the Highland Light Infantry, stationed in Aldershot.

I was a very happy boy. I liked my piping, I was a good dancer, and I was well and truly appreciated. I was no sooner in the battalion and, being such a good player, I was doing duty as a piper, getting up at half-past five, playing reveille and all the calls throughout the day, right till lights-out at night. I was terribly keen. My ambition was to be pipe-major and of course I practised like blazes. I was never without my pipes or my chanter.

In those days the soldier got no privileges of any kind. He got his three meals a day and his weekly pay. He got one furlough a year, which entailed paying his fare all the way to Scotland.

Now in the pipe band in Aldershot the majority of the pipers in those days were Highlanders, Gaelic speaking. And there were two lance corporals in the pipe band. One was from Plockton and the other was from Lochboisdale. John Smith was from Lochboisdale and Lachlan MacKinnon was from Plockton. MacKinnon got hold of me one day and he says, 'Poy, you know when you go on furlough you've got to pay your fare. And what are you doing about saving for it ?' I said, 'Nothing.' 'Oh', he said, 'you better start. And any money you can get I'll look after it for you.'

Well, in those days the food was good: a good breakfast, a good lunch, but at tea time there was nothing for tea. There were no dining rooms: you ate where you slept. When it came tea time, the night before you got your pound of bread issued and you put it in your locker. And when breakfast came up you cut off what you wanted, and when lunch came up you did the same thing. Well, when it came to tea there was nothing to put on the bread. One could purchase pennyworths of butter, pennyworths of jam and pennyworths of cheese in the canteen. We boys used to run the cutter for those things. On the majority of occasions we got a penny to ourselves. I gave all my pennies to MacKinnon. The result was when the war broke out MacKinnon got hold of me. He said, 'Poy, I've got some money belonging to you', he said, 'we better count it out.' So he took it out of his box and put it on the lid of his box, counted it out. The Post Office was within sight—in Stanhope Lines—and he took me down to the Post Office and he opened me a bank account. And I've still got that bankbook. Every time I got promotion throughout my service I put two-thirds in the bank and one-third to spend.

My pay as a boy was a shilling a week. But when war broke out in August 1914 it went up to four shillings. I don't know why that was, but I never asked any questions! Another three shillings a week was a terrific boost.

The boys—the band boys and the piper boys, of which I was one—were sent off to what was then our depot at Hamilton Barracks. I was only fifteen. Of course, it took a long time for things to settle. After we got there there were no pipes for us to play. But we soon got cracking and got a little pipe band going amongst ourselves. Altogether it was a very happy existence.

In Hamilton Barracks we had a combination of the Cameronians and the Highland Light Infantry. I was doing my duty as piper. Altogether it was a nice existence. I was happy. It was just a matter of waiting until we became eighteen to be eligible by age to go and do our war training for the front.

I was in the barracks at Hamilton three years. How I came to have contact with the conscientious objectors there was the bugler boys mounted guard and stayed in the guardroom for the twenty-four hours' duty. There was one chap in particular, he was a London boy, Hudson, became very friendly with the conscientious objectors. They were in the guardroom and were treated as prisoners.

I think there would be five or six at a time. They were a good class of men. They had money. The food was not all that good when it was carried from the kitchen to the guardroom. And they used to send this chap Hudson for delicacies for themselves—pies, and rolls, and butter and what-not. And altogether Hudson got to know them very well and told us lots of stories about them. I do remember quite clearly one objector. He was in the guardroom. He was a prisoner in the Hamilton guardroom. Hudson became very friendly with him because he ran all his messages for him. He was an independent chap and could afford to buy what he fancied. Hudson told us lots of stories about this objector, who was a very kind man, understanding and friendly and treated the boys as something.[46]

But when I played my pipes in the morning the conscientious objectors had to get up as well. When reveille sounded everyone had to be on two feet. The conscientious objectors could hardly refuse to get up and fold their blankets.

There wasn't much comfort for them. They were in prison cells—just the four bare walls and a board with a piece of wood for a pillow. In the wintertime they had four blankets. It was very cold. I don't think there was any heating in the Hamilton Barracks guardroom. Oh, no, it was a miserable, miserable place. There weren't many home comforts, I can assure you! The conscientious objectors were allowed visitors and they brought goodies for their friends. That was all allowed, there was no objection to that. It eased the situation when they got visits and little tit-bits to eat and what not.

With the little contact I had with the civilians at Hamilton they were pretty hostile to the conscientious objectors. Well, we were fighting for our liberty and people thought that nobody should do otherwise. It was as simple as that.

On hindsight, of course, I thought very little at the same time about a conscientious objector. I was hostile to them. Well, we were soldiers and we couldn't think that anyone had a right to think other than to fight for his country. But as we grow older we get more sense. I remember feeling definitely resentful of these men. Oh, yes, we looked down on them, we looked down on them as unequal.

I left Hamilton Barracks in the autumn of 1917. I didn't go out then to France. In those days every division had its own reinforcement school and every reinforcement for all the regiments in the division went to that school before they went to their battalions. They got hardened up—as if they hadn't been hardened up! The first big experience of my life in the front line was as a result of the 21st of March German offensive in 1918. The British army was being knocked about and there were great gaps in the line. As a result of the fighting I did think that the conscientious objectors weren't very far wrong.

Dorothy Wiltshire

My father was called up when conscription came in and he was called to appear before a tribunal. An army captain presided who was really vicious in his hatred. All the details were in the papers. I was sent actually to relatives, in order to spare me this experience.

My father's conscientious objection was on religious grounds. Well, he didn't want to take life. He believed that it was wrong to kill and take life and he refused to do so, because in the Bible it is said that you must not kill. And Jesus said that if his Father had wanted him to do anything like that … Anyway my father wanted to obey God rather than men. And he stood firm on that.

At that time my father was employed with a big firm and his boss was furious because he was a very patriotic man. All the staff who joined the Forces were given a certain amount of their salary to be retained for them. But not so my father.

He was told by the tribunal that he had to find work of national importance, because he wasn't to be sent to prison. So he contacted a firm where he had worked as a young man as an engineer. He had had to give this up because he had had a very serious illness at one time and was quite ill for a long time. However, the firm were very pleased to hear from him again and they said they would be delighted to have him work with them. He went to Kirkcaldy from Perth, where we lived, to work. So he worked there for quite a long time and his salary at that was £5 a week, which had to cover his board and lodging and keep us at home. So you can imagine we had quite a hard time.

I was at the secondary school, Perth Academy, at the time. When I went back to school after this happened it was just like being sent to Coventry. The pupils just ignored me, except for one or two of my own special friends. The teachers didn't ignore me. The teachers didn't even mention it. It was just the pupils, which rather surprised me but I realised then that their parents must have read the newspapers.

I can't remember my mother being taunted as a result of my father being a conscientious objector, I can't remember that at all. I think the neighbours were all very pleasant to her. I can't remember my mother being taunted in any way by anyone.

I do remember shortages of food, I do remember that very well, because my mother wasn't too strong at the time and my brother and my grandmother, who stayed with us, were quite ill on occasions. And mother wasn't able to go out to the shops. We weren't rationed in those days and you had to be out at a certain time, quite early. When you got to the top of the queue very often the door was shut and that was all for the day. So it meant that many a time I came home and mother was really distressed that there was very little for a meal. But she was very, very good at getting things from the butcher. She would get a sheep's head from the butcher, get all the meat cut off it and make soup with the bone and a lovely pie with vegetables with the meat. In fact, she really did a wonderful job.

Then I had to leave school eventually, when money was running out and we couldn't pay fees. I also had to give up music. This was a heartbreak to me and my teacher as well. So the firm my father worked for before offered me a post, which I got 7/6d. a week for.

During my lunch hour I used to go to try and get some shopping for mother but at that time nearly all the food was finished—butter and marge and whatever there was. It was a very, very difficult time as far as food was concerned, and we really had no money for extra clothes. Mother was a great mender and I learned to mend, too. We just had to do with what we had.

Then my father used to cycle all the way from Kirkcaldy home to Perth every week-end to see how we were getting on. I don't know really how many miles that was. But there's one thing: there were very few cars in those days, and he often told us when it had been snowing his cycle tyre was the only mark on the road.

I must say my father's post was kept open for him and when he came back after the end of the war everything was just as it was before. No one else was unkind or nasty to him. I do remember that his wartime experiences had the result of giving him an ulcer, because after the war, he was always having those severe stomach pains. And it turned out it must have been the result of all the anxiety he had had, because he had an operation to remove an ulcer.

William H Marwick

When the First World War broke out in August 1914 it came to me, as to most of my contemporaries, as a complete shock. But it evoked a great deal of enthusiasm at the time. Many people who had no experience of military life or any particular taste for it rallied and joined up. They were anxious to get into the war before it stopped. One of them, a friend of mine, used to say bitterly: 'But it didn't stop.' As the war went on they became more and more disillusioned. By the end of 1915 or the beginning of 1916 it was realised that the war might go on for a considerable period longer than had been expected. The government found that if they were going to have a sufficient number of people in the military forces they would have to intro-duce compulsion. They already had the Regular army, they had the volunteers who came in the earlier part of the war, and an Act was passed early in 1916 laying down that men between 18 and 41 were liable to military service if they were medically fit. An opportunity was given for those who would take advantage of it to enrol them-selves, to enlist, or be attested, as the phrase was. And if they didn't do that within a fixed time then they would be called up and imprisoned. Well, that happened in my case.[47]

I was born on 16th October 1894 at Creektown, Old Calabar, in Nigeria. I was the first child of the Reverend William Marwick and Elizabeth Jane *née* Hutton, both United Presbyterian missionaries. My father was the only son of William Marwick, who, with his elder brother James—afterwards a well known Town Clerk of Glasgow—had taken up practice as a solicitor in Edinburgh. These two brothers came from Orkney and were descended from a family of crofters in the island of Rousay.[48]

My father took an Arts course at Edinburgh University, but did not graduate, and a theological course at the United Presbyterian College in Edinburgh. In 1892 he volunteered for the United Presbyterian mission in Nigeria. My mother was the only daughter of John Hutton, a draper. She became a mission worker in Old Calabar, under the famous Mary Slessor.[49]

Both my parents suffered in health in the then 'White Man's Grave', and shortly after my birth they returned to Scotland. After some time the now United Free Church appointed my father to the Jamaica mission. My parents decided to take all the family with them. I went to school in Falmouth, Jamaica, and then when my father moved further inland we older children were taught by a visiting governess,

Arabella Barrett, daughter of a brother of the poetess Elizabeth. Arabella shared the literary talent of her family.[50]

Granny Marwick came to Jamaica in 1905 and took me and my sister home for our education. I was enrolled at George Watson's College in October that year and my sister in the corresponding girls' school.

My interest in politics was aroused by the general election in December 1905, when I enthused over the Liberal triumph. A more serious interest was aroused by the events of 1909-10, when I became an ardent supporter of the People's Budget, Irish Home Rule and Women's Suffrage, and an opponent of the House of Lords, taking Lloyd George as my hero. I had become an active member of the school Literary Club or debating society, which apprenticed me to public life; and in my last session at school, in April 1912, I stood as Liberal candidate in the annual mock election, losing by a small majority to William Morrison, later a Tory cabinet minister and Speaker of the House of Commons.[51]

My father had been converted to socialism in his student days and subscribed for the short-lived radical *Daily Tribune*, for the *New Age*—then under A R Orage—a forum for all heretical standpoints, particularly for Guild Socialism, and for the *Christian Commonwealth*, which advocated Christian socialism and the new theology preached by R J Campbell and W E Orchard. Both considerably influenced my thought. I became a Sunday School teacher, a communicant member of Mayfield Church and secretary of the Youth Fellowship.[52]

In my later school and early student days at Edinburgh University, while still supporting the Liberal Party, I became critical of the government's policy, especially of the foreign policy of Sir Edward Grey, and supported the criticisms of men such as Morel and Ponsonby.[53]

At the university I entered for honours in Classics. A F Giles, lecturer in Ancient History, was a Watsonian who had been held up as a model to us at school. He was a first rate lecturer. I won the medal in his class and decided to transfer to an honours History course. In my second session I attended the First Ordinary class in History, conducted by Professor Richard Lodge. My turning to History led me to abandon the University Classical Society for the Historical, with which some of my deepest memories are associated. It was very popular, attracting not only students in the History School, but others. Among those with whom I became most friendly were Laurance Saunders, who later became Professor of Constitutional History, and Francis Hood, later Professor of Politics at Durham University. I also joined the Philomathic Society, one of the Associated Societies to which my father had belonged, and the Christian Union.[54]

When the war broke out in August 1914 a fellow student wrote to me: 'I am sitting in the ruins of my own particular cosmos.' While not yet completely pacifist, I was shocked by the bellicose sermon delivered by the minister of the church which I attended the following Sunday. While fully accepting the criticisms of British foreign policy and of the declaration of the war, I was at first disposed to accept the need for home defence, and I joined a voluntary Home Guard that was formed at Watson's. But after some months I became convinced that this was an impracticable compromise and resigned my membership.

I felt much in sympathy with the Union of Democratic Control and joined the Edinburgh branch and thus became close to its secretary, Raymond Holt, minister of St Mark's Unitarian Church. Among visitors who addressed the UDC was Arthur Ponsonby, who became my political hero. His meeting, like others of the UDC, was disrupted by Australian soldiers.[55]

Opposition to the war at first seemed negligible. But there were those who expressed their doubts about it from the start. There was a group of Radical MPs who had been critical of the foreign policy of Sir Edward Grey—particularly the military alliance with Tsarist Russia. And they and others like-minded had formed the Union of Democratic Control. It was not specifically anti-war. It included not only pacifists but some who actually served in the war. One such was Maitland Hardyman, a fellow student of mine, who was killed shortly before the Armistice in 1918 and who was described as the youngest lieutenant colonel in the British army. The leading figures in the UDC were two of those Radical MPs, Ponsonby and Trevelyan. They subsequently held high office in post-war Labour governments.[56]

Then there were those who were definitely opposed to the war—not to all wars—but opposed on what would be called ideological grounds. They held it was a capitalist war in which they as proletarians had no share and no business to take part. Prominent among them, in Edinburgh at any rate, was Arthur Woodburn, long afterwards Secretary of State for Scotland in a Labour government. He used to jest when he was Secretary of State that the offices which he then dominated on Calton Hill had formerly been the site of the old Calton Jail, where he had spent some years as a conscientious objector during the 1914–18 War.[57]

Then there were those who objected on religious grounds. The Society of Friends, or Quakers, had since their origin in the seventeenth century opposed all war as contrary to Christianity. And there were members of various other churches who took the same position. One of the best known in Scotland was John MacCallum, who had been captain of the Scottish rugby international team. Afterwards he became my family doctor.[58]

There were others who opposed the war on religious grounds, not because they were pacifist but because they objected as religious people to sharing in what they considered one of the activities. There were a considerable number of those Christian Brethren or Plymouth Brethren, as they were more generally known, and also those who are now known as Jehovah's Witnesses, who would fight in the final battle of Armageddon but wouldn't fight for any earthly cause.

Then there were those who objected on various other grounds. So it was a very mixed lot. And I remember, when a number of us were in prison later on, rather an illiterate warder, addressing a group, said: 'You con- con- ... What is it you call yourselves? You contentious objectors.' And he was really wiser than he knew, there were so many varieties of opinion.

As the war went on there came to be greater disillusionment, both on the part of those who were serving at the front and of those who at the beginning had given their support to the war. Notable among these were such war poets as Siegfried

Sassoon, who expressed their bitterness, and two notable clergymen who had been, I think, army chaplains: Dick Sheppard, who afterwards founded the Peace Pledge Union, and Charles Raven, a leader in the Fellowship of Reconciliation. There was also, as well as a change of opinion, an actual change in the conduct of the war from the idealism with which it had started.[59]

Well, in 1916, for the first time in Britain—at least in modern Britain—conscription was introduced. For all men between the ages of 18 and 41, unless they were exempt on one ground or another, service in the army was imposed. And to combat that there was formed the No-Conscription Fellowship, of which Clifford Allen—a leading figure in a later Labour government—and Fenner Brockway were leaders. The NCF received the support of quite a number of people who were themselves supporters of the war but disbelieved in trying to enforce conscription on people who didn't support military service and persecution of conscience. These people included Dr Clifford, a leading figure in English non-conformity, and even Lord Hugh Cecil, a prominent Tory aristocrat.[60]

There were set up by the government tribunals to hear objections by those called up to military service. These included objections on the grounds that, for instance, it would be more useful remaining in civil life, on the grounds of ill-health and physical unfitness, and so on. So a very miscellaneous lot of people, not only conscientious objectors, came before the tribunals which were set up for the purpose in each locality and which consisted mainly of local worthies—town councillors, and so on—who were not at all familiar with the ideas of principle. And so a great many applicants were turned down, especially of those who pleaded grounds of conscience. An Appellate Tribunal was set up to hear cases. To this were submitted those who had been turned down by the local tribunal, and the military authorities' objection to men who had been reprieved, who had been granted exemption. The tribunal in Edinburgh was presided over by a certain Sheriff Maconochie, who was a judge of the brand of Jeffreys and Braxfield. He turned down practically every case, usually with personal abuse of the applicants. I remember a friend of mine saying with regard to the treatment of her husband, who was a quiet scholarly man, nearly over military age: 'The Sheriff just gave William a lot of impudence.' Well, those who were turned down were liable to imprisonment. And so, like myself, after a little lapse of time they were deemed to have been enlisted.[61]

Well, as I say, that happened in my case. At the beginning of the war I wasn't quite assured of taking no part in it and I did undergo, as I've said, a little voluntary military training in the Home Guard. But as the war went on I, like many other people, became more and more sceptical about it being any good and finally came to the conclusion that it was my duty to refuse to have any part in it. I had been influenced too by my father, who was very Left in his political opinions, though he was not an absolute pacifist to begin with.

In 1916 I was a student aged twenty-one. When I became liable for military service under the Conscription Act I was at first granted temporary exemption to enable me to sit my final degree exams in June 1916. The general practice was that those who were due to graduate were allowed a short time of exemption to enable them to do so. So I had been allowed to graduate that summer and finished my studies at Edinburgh University with first class honours in History

Before the introduction of conscription I had volunteered to serve with the Society of Friends—the Quakers—with which I had had no previous connection, either in their ambulance work or in work for the relief of refugees and others whose homes had been destroyed in France. It appeared to me as a particularly good, practical, constructive alternative to war. I can't remember now how I first heard of the work of the Society of Friends, but there was some representative of it who gave a talk in Edinburgh about their work in France and that attracted me and I thought that was the kind of thing I'd like to do. And so I wrote to their headquarters and they had me visited and interviewed by Edward Walton, who was a leading Quaker in Edinburgh and also a very well known artist of the day. He had two sons who were both engaged in Friends' work in France. So he recommended me for it and I was accepted by the Society, either for their Relief Corps in France or their ambulance service.[62] And in other cases—there were quite a number of other cases, like Walton's two sons—that was accepted by the tribunal as an alternative to military service. So I thought I was all right in that respect. I asked the tribunal for exemption from military service in order to undertake this work. But the tribunal refused to accept it in my case. They didn't give any reasons. That was very general in Edinburgh. There were very few exemptions granted in Edinburgh in comparison with some other places. I think the reason was largely the personality of Sheriff Maconochie, who was a dominating figure in the tribunal. He was a strong militarist and a High Tory. And it was before him that I appeared in the tribunal. He was generally rude to applicants. Oh, I remember him quite clearly! I don't remember him saying anything particularly to me but certainly he was very offensive in his remarks to some people. Maconochie was a notorious character.

My appeal against the decision of the local tribunal was rejected by the Appellate Tribunal. Again no reasons were given for the rejection of my appeal. They just said 'No', and that was it.

I was deemed to have been enlisted in the Argyll and Sutherland Highlanders. Then a summons came, which I ignored. So I became liable to arrest as a deserter.

On Monday evening, 4 September, 1916, about 4 pm two plainclothes constables called at my home on the south side of Edinburgh and asked me why I had not appeared at the recruiting office as summoned. I stated I had nothing to say beyond what I had written to the military authorities. The constables were quite polite. They said they had come to arrest me. They recognised that it was a matter of principle on my part. But they had no alternative but to take me to a police cell. I protested that I had not avoided the military authorities and had stated in writing my willingness to appear in the civil court. They took me to Causewayside police station, the nearest one, where I was searched and the contents of my pockets confiscated. I spent the night in a cell alone.

Next day, about six o'clock in the morning, I was taken in a black maria to High Street police station and there confined in a large cell.[63] After about two hours I was taken to a cell by myself and given some breakfast sent in for me by my family. At ten o'clock I was handcuffed and taken to the Sheriff Court. I at once got 48 hours' adjournment to prepare my defence and was bailed out for £2.

The day after that I called with my father on the Town Clerk of Edinburgh, Sir Thomas Hunter. I think this was on my father's initiative really, because he knew some of these legal people. My father had some hope that a legal authority like that could somehow secure my exemption. Sir Thomas bade me stick to my principles. Professor Hume Brown of Edinburgh University was also approached by my father and he wrote in my favour.[64] I also saw the clerk to the tribunal and the military representative there, who was a lawyer. Both were very pleasant. The military representative said to me: 'Now you've made your protest don't you think you'd be just as well to bow to the inevitable and join the Forces?' And I said: 'Wouldn't it be just as bad for me if I professed to have a conscientious objection to military service as long as I was left in peace, and succumbed as soon as I was liable to get into trouble?' He replied, 'Oh, no! Second thoughts are always best. And you'll change your opinion when you see that there is a perfect chorus of approbation.'

Next day I surrendered to my bail and was taken again to the Sheriff Court. Sheriff Guy, who was more polite in his manner than Sheriff Maconochie, heard the case and gave me great latitude in pleading my defence. Formal evidence against me was given by the military and the police representatives. I was fined £2 and handed over to the military, Sheriff Guy saying he had no alternative and could not overrule the tribunal.[65]

A sergeant—Sergeant Baker—was there ready and I went to the recruiting office with him. He was very agreeable and tried to persuade me to join. He filled up medical papers which I signed. He got me an hour and a half's leave to go home for dinner. On my return I got a medical examination and was passed for Class 'A', general service. Finally, as I think I had heard that conscientious objectors were treated very reasonably at Dreghorn Camp on the outskirts of Edinburgh, I expressed a preference for going to the 3rd Argyll and Sutherland Highlanders there. I realise that seems a bit odd. The whole experience had been very strenuous. I was certainly nervous beforehand and I think I was rather relieved to find it wasn't such a harrowing experience as I had expected. It was all over pretty quickly.

Well, Sergeant Baker asked if I would give a promise to serve, offering me a night's leave. But I declined to give any undertaking. He bade me then await an escort for the depot at Stirling. Another sergeant just waved to me—'Come along'— without bothering whether I was coming or not. He took me down to Waverley Station and we went off to Stirling, where of course the barracks of the Argyll and Sutherland Highlanders were.

On being taken to Stirling Castle I was handed over with papers to the orderly sergeant as an absentee. He took me to the guard room. I found there two conscientious objectors—Syme of Arran and Neilson of Beith—besides other prisoners, and was given some soup and three blankets. I had to sleep on the floor, the beds being 'booked', and was much disturbed by a drunk soldier put in late at night. He kept up a monotonous wailing about the man who had put him in the guardroom: 'You want me to tell you what you are?! I'll tell you what you are! You are a dirty lousy f... b... c...!' I'll leave you to fill in the blanks. So there was quite a miscellaneous group put into the guard room—conscientious objectors were mixed up with serving soldiers who were returning drunk from leave or from jaunts down to Stirling.

Next morning I had a wash and a good breakfast and spent most of the forenoon in the guard room. I was allowed out for over half an hour for fresh air. I was taken for medical examination and later taken before an officer who received me kindly, spoke of acquaintanceship with my family, and seemed familiar with my case. He ordered me to go to the quarter-master sergeant for equipment. But I refused to obey the military order formally to try on army boots and was sent back under escort to the guard room.

During that week-end I was sent under escort to the commanding officer before whom formal evidence of my offence was given and I was remanded for a district court martial. On the Sunday I had a short airing in the forenoon and received letters from home. The secretary—Jack Crockhart, who was a very prominent member also of the Independent Labour Party—and another local Stirling member of the No-Conscription Fellowship visited us. It seems strange that the army authorities allowed this, but they seemed to be very casual in allowing people in. Relatives came to see me as well.

My father was present when next day I was taken before the commanding officer. I'm sure that it would be my father's idea to be present. I was offered but refused service in the Royal Army Medical Corps. My reason for refusing was that the RAMC was under the military authorities and you were liable to transfer to a combatant regiment.

Throughout these days in the guard room at Stirling Castle I received letters from various members of my family and friends. There was apparently no restriction on receiving letters. I was also allowed to write as many letters as I wished. I also did some reading. I had some books with me and again there seemed to be no restrictions on them. One I read then was by Peter Kropotkin, the Russian anarchist.[66] I also did some German grammar.

I had never learned any German at school and then I just thought—well, there were some German works useful from an historical point of view. It was partly for that reason I tried to learn some on my own. I don't remember any suspicion on the part of the military authorities that I should be learning German while I was in detention.

On Monday, 25th September I received the summary of evidence and notice of my trial by court martial next day. But it was postponed till the Wednesday, when it took place in the recreation room of the Castle. On the following Saturday my sentence was read out to me: 112 days' hard labour. I think I knew pretty well beforehand that that was the kind of stock sentence. Another conscientious objector named Clinton was given the same sentence as me. That same day three brothers named Morrison—all three conscientious objectors—arrived at the Castle and one was an invalid with sciatica.

My sentence was to be served in Wormwood Scrubs prison in London. On the Monday after being sentenced I was taken to the quartermaster's stores at Stirling

Castle and got equipment. I put on the uniform voluntarily—the military authorities did not force me. Some conscientious objectors refused to put it on under any circumstances. But, you see, you had gained the point. There was no reason to worry about it.

That same day my mother came in to visit me in detention at Stirling. She was rather upset.

That Monday night, about 11 pm, I left Stirling under escort—a sergeant and two privates, who travelled with me down to London. We detrained next day at Willesden and got a lift in an army waggon to Wormwood Scrubs in North London. So real imprisonment began then.

On arrival I was deprived of kit, boots and money and put in a cell. Then I was stripped, given a bath and the grey prison garb to put on and taken before a doctor. I was put in cell B483.

The prison authorities had become familiar in the previous few years with another type of political offence—the militant women suffragettes. One of them I came to know very well later on claimed that experience with the suffragettes in these prisons had familiarised the prison officials with a type of offender who was not the ordinary criminal, and they also obtained certain ameliorations in the treatment of such persons, although there was not officially any difference in the treatment of political and other offenders.

So at Wormwood Scrubs it was a case of solitary confinement in a cell, and in a way that was, at first, something of a relief after the very mixed society of the barracks guard room, where you didn't get a moment free from the most varied company. But then of course it got rather boring to be shut up alone for some time at Wormwood Scrubs. I wasn't there long enough to receive any of the privileges, such as visits and letters. Those were given after one had served the first month or two of the sentence.

We were allowed out in company to march round the prison yard to get a little fresh air and exercise every day but without opportunity—unless in a very clandestine way—of communicating with any others, as speech was forbidden. Then almost every day we were taken to a short service in the chapel. We were supposed to have a chaplain to visit us. The prison chaplain came along and looked into my cell and asked what denomination I belonged to. I said Presbyterian, as I then was by my upbringing, and he said, 'Oh, well, you'll have to get a chaplain of your own denomination.' And I was to have had one—there was one appointed specially for that purpose—but I didn't stay long enough to have his ministrations. These were the only breaks in the day's routine.

It was the solitary confinement, as compared with the relative freedom of the guard room, that was the most striking feature at Wormwood Scrubs. Two people there I got to know well. One was William Kitchen, a brother of George Kitchen who was a lecturer in Edinburgh University for a long time whom I knew previously. William had some business of his own in Edinburgh. The other man was also a conscientious objector—a Roman Catholic postman. He was already in Wormwood Scrubs when I went there. He was given some job going round with a warder.

55

It was rather unusual to find a Roman Catholic who was a conscientious objector. Most objectors were non-Catholics—Dissenters, in more senses than one. But the postman was very pleasant and cheerful and kept up my morale.

The only other two things I can recall of any account were that there was an air raid warning one night. Whether it was a genuine one or not I don't know but there was a great row, various prisoners ringing their bells and shouting out and wanting to get out. The other thing I recall was that I spent my twenty-second birthday in Wormwood Scrubs. I remember that because it was on that date, the 16th of October, 1916, I got notice that in a few days' time I was to appear before the Central Tribunal.

I wasn't quite sure why I had been sent to Wormwood Scrubs, because a good many of the Scots conscientious objectors were sent to local prisons in Scotland. But the main reason, I think, was because the government had now decided, as a result of so many people being imprisoned, having been turned down by the Local and Appeal Tribunals, to give a final Central Tribunal. And those who had given some proof of their sincerity by submitting to imprisonment were brought before this Central Tribunal. It was to give a further investigation of objectors who were actually in prison.

There had been agitation against the treatment of conscientious objectors on the part of some sections of opinion in the country who themselves approved of the war but disapproved of conscription, which they thought was one of the evils of German militarism against which they regarded themselves as fighting. Among these were people like Professor Gilbert Murray, the famous scholar, and Dr Clifford, the leader of English Non-conformity.[67] The result of their protests against the treatment that conscientious objectors had had in a great many cases was that this Central Tribunal was set up, which was to visit people in prison and hear their case over again.

The chairman of the tribunal was Sir George Younger, a well known brewer and Tory MP.[68] There I got quite a fair hearing. The result was I was offered an alternative service—not the service with the Quakers which I had sought and been accepted for—but what was called rather ironically 'Work of National Importance'. It was a Home Office scheme. For that purpose at least two former jails, one of them being Wakefield, were set apart for conscientious objectors. There we were put to ordinary prison tasks—for instance, making ropes—but were given a considerable measure of freedom: still dressed in prison garb we were allowed to go out for the evening. The conscientious objectors usually got on quite good terms with the local inhabitants. The Society of Friends had a centre at Wakefield which acted as a kind of social centre for many of us. And we were allowed a visit home about New Year.

At any rate I was very glad to get away from Wormwood Scrubs. I had spent more or less exactly three weeks there. I had the feeling that I didn't know how long I could have stood it—well, the loneliness and the boredom.

Well, the Wakefield scheme continued over the winter of 1916 for some months. But by the spring of 1917 it was felt that while these former prisons were being crowded the work which was being done in them was not of very great national importance after all. So there was an innovation in the scheme by which certain approved work, that was more in the nature of national importance, was brought into being. Parties of conscientious objectors were sent out to various other places such as Dyce in Aberdeenshire and Talgarth in Wales to perform what was really more useful work. The place to which I was sent was a work camp near Brecon in Wales, which was concerned with digging the foundations of a national hospital of Wales. As I was found to be not very suitable for navvying—ten hours of digging every day—I was made the camp orderly. I continued there until the spring of 1918. And then it was decided to extend further alternative service for those conscientious objectors who were prepared to accept it. They were allowed to go as individuals to various other forms of work.

Now at long last, more than two years after I had first applied and been accepted to serve with the Society of Friends either in their ambulance work or relief of refugees and others whose homes were destroyed in France, I was allowed to join the Friends' relief work there.

Whilst this work was organised by the Society of Friends, quite a number of those who like myself worked with them were not themselves members of the Society, at least at that time. Among those with whom I was particularly associated were, for example, two very typical Cockney working men of very advanced social opinions. Among the Quakers themselves there were of course very great varieties. There were some British Quakers and also American Quakers after America had joined the war in 1917. Among the American Quakers there were two very distinct types. There were those of the eastern States, particularly Pennsylvania, which was originally a Quaker colony, who were generally speaking very similar in type to the ordinary British Quaker. They had broad religious views and were generally very well educated. On the other hand, there were those from the Middle West who were mostly farmers, not very educated, rather unsophisticated, whom one of the more sophisticated Quakers used to refer to as '*les cultivateurs de Kansas*'. However, they managed to carry on together.

At the time I went out there there were two work places, both in the south of France in the Département of Jura. There they were engaged in constructing wooden huts of which the various planks and so on were constructed in the workshop. So I was employed at that time as a very unskilled machine shop worker.

Then as soon as the Armistice came in November 1918 a number of us were drafted off to the old front line in the Verdun area. We weren't in Verdun itself but in villages in the locality. That was my first view of the front line. One of the things that impressed me most there was the sight of the German burial grounds, where you had little crosses inscribed *Hier ruht in Gott* or *Hier ruht in Friede,* where the German soldiers had been buried. And there we were engaged either in putting up these wooden houses or in seeking to mend the houses which had been damaged by bombardment. And then again we were very well received by the local population.

Incidentally, while conscientious objectors were the subject of a great deal of abuse by non-combatants in this country—politicians and parsons and journalists like Horatio Bottomley and Lord Northcliffe—the relations between conscientious objectors and fighting soldiers were in my experience always very good. They looked upon each other with mutual respect and goodwill.[69]

So we remained there in the Verdun area until the Conscription Act released us to go home. Conscientious objectors were supposed to be disenfranchised for five years after the war.[70] In contrast was the attitude of the French government, which awarded us all certificates, thanking us for the service which we had rendered to France.

I came home to Edinburgh some months after the Armistice, in the spring of 1919. I was looking out for a job. I had intended to go in for teaching so I tried for various teaching posts. But I think I was turned down on account of my war record. But then what happened was that I took a course for teachers' training at Moray House College in Edinburgh and at the same time I took a course in Economic History, which was then conducted by J F Rees, who was afterwards principal of a Welsh college. I had known him before. Rees had been active in the Union of Democratic Control—democratic control of foreign policy. When I was taking his class he was also a prominent figure in the Workers' Educational Association. They were just about to appoint for the first time a tutor organiser in Scotland. Rees asked if I would be willing and able to take up such a post instead of an ordinary post. I was very glad of the opportunity.[71]

You were usually supposed when applying for jobs to present testimonials from those who had taught you. So I had applied for testimonials to my principal teachers at Edinburgh University. Professor Lodge, who was then Professor of History, and who was a Liberal professedly but of a rather imperialistic type, demanded to know what I had been doing during the war. When I told him he said, 'Well, I wouldn't give you a job and I can't recommend anyone else to do so.' Another professor—of Constitutional History—who was a rank Tory, refused to have anything more to do with me. On the other hand, Rees said to a colleague: 'If that's the way they treat Marwick we must do our best for him.' So he was responsible on that account for getting me this job with the Workers' Educational Association, which I held for twelve years.

My friends among my school fellows and fellow students, many of whom went to the war themselves, always remained on very good terms with me. There was one apparent exception, a very strong Tory, very militarist in his opinions. When I came back after the war he wouldn't have anything to do with me and made rude remarks about conscientious objectors in my hearing. Later on, however, he was quite cordial to me and said, 'Oh, I don't care what a man's opinions are so long as he is honest with regard to them.'

So far as I can judge myself now at my time of life I would retain the same position towards war whatever the issues were. I have not changed my opinions at all. I was more convinced than ever by the Second World War that war was futile and vicious and wouldn't have any good results. I think a good many people came to that conclusion when they saw what the results of the war were. In the 1914-18 war there were those who were somewhat disillusioned by their actual experiences at the front, and there were quite a number of others whom I knew who had supported the war in the first instance and as a result of their experiences were converted to pacifism—for instance, the well known Scottish clergyman George MacLeod, and Dick Sheppard, who was similarly a chaplain in the war.[72] So I must say that I feel as strongly as ever the views I had then. I certainly hold that the making of compulsory military service or conscription was beyond the legitimate use of the power of the state.

J P M Millar

When the First World War broke out I was in the general manager's department of the Scottish Union National & National Insurance Company's office in St Andrew Square, Edinburgh, where my prospects were very good indeed.

At that time I had become a young socialist. Originally, like my father, I had been a Conservative. Then my young brother, during a holiday at Pomathorn near Penicuik in Midlothian, fell from some logs in a farmyard. When we went back home to Musselburgh he developed asthma and it was quite pathetic seeing him trying to breathe. My father learned that some people who had asthma living at the seaside lost it when they went up to live in the hills.

So one Saturday he took my young brother on the back step of his bicycle to Pomathorn. By the time the boy got there his asthma had vanished. So my father said, 'I'll have to board you out here.' He therefore arranged for a railway signalman, who was a member of the National Union of Railwaymen, to accommodate him in his cottage, where the signalman's wife looked after the crossing gates. James Robertson, the signalman, was one of the early socialists and when I visited my brother he used to take me into his signal box, which was on a very quiet line between Edinburgh and Peebles, and argue against Conservatism. I, of course, argued against him but after many a battle I had to admit I was wrong. He was a great reader and introduced me to the socialist paper *Clarion*, edited by Robert Blatchford, and to Blatchford's many books and pamphlets, including *Merrie England*, of which a paper-covered edition sold a million or two million copies after being hawked about the streets by members of the socialist movement.[73]

I then joined the Edinburgh Central Branch of the Independent Labour Party. Its room was furnished very sparsely with some twenty forms and the same number of spittoons, because in these days many workers were very badly fed and suffered from catarrh. I also joined the Clarion Cycling Club who when out cycling in the country on Sundays endeavoured to sell *Clarion* pamphlets to workers hanging about their doorways.[74]

As a socialist I became greatly interested in the economics of capitalism about which Karl Marx had written his book *Das Kapital*. I was especially interested in imperialism as Britain had built up the greatest empire in history.

When the war broke out in 1914 I had to make up my mind whether I thought socialists had any business getting involved in the struggle. Like James Robertson,

the railway signalman at Pomathorn, I became convinced that socialists had no business getting involved in this struggle. I therefore became one of the miscellaneous
band called conscientious objectors, of which the Quakers were the best known.
The Second World War, when it came, was a different kind of war altogether
because by then the Nazis had destroyed the German socialist and trade union movements and set out to destroy the Jews simply because they were Jews.

When I made up my mind that I shouldn't take part in the war I wrote to
Thomas Johnston, editor of *Forward*, which was published in Glasgow, and suggested that those of us who weren't prepared to take part in the war should make
preparations for the fact that the government would no doubt in time introduce
conscription. He replied that he didn't think conscription would ever be introduced
in Britain.

But conscription did come and one result of that was the formation of the No-
Conscription Fellowship. I founded the Edinburgh branch of the Fellowship and
became its secretary. Its membership consisted not only of men of military age but of
women and of men too old for military service. The men included an elderly man
who was a Writer to the Signet and whose name I think was Shand. Another was
William Geddie, editor of *Chambers' Dictionary* and *Chambers' Encyclopedia*. Another
member was an elderly lady, Miss Jeffreys of Jeffreys' Brewery.

The first Military Service Act which introduced conscription made provision for
the exemption of clergymen, and also made provision for conscientious objectors.
Objectors could appeal to one special tribunal and if they failed there to get exemption they could appeal to a final tribunal. These tribunals were usually made up of
elderly gents who were anxious to get the young men to do all the fighting for them.
They normally gave conscientious objectors short shrift. None of my members got
absolute exemption. As secretary of the No-Conscription Fellowship I managed to
get non-combatant service, which meant I became liable to go to France and do
such jobs as bury the dead or paint barracks. The War Office invented a special
regiment for non-combatant conscientious objectors—the Non-Combatant Corps.[75]

Although the government decided that it was a Holy War it also decided that the
country's holy men shouldn't be conscripted. One of our members was the Unitarian minister for Edinburgh. He was a conscientious objector and was appointed to
understudy me against the time when I was arrested for not obeying my calling up
notice. I took him to court with me when any of our members were coming up for
sentence. Nationally one of the most active members of the No-Conscription
Fellowship was Fenner Brockway, editor of the *Labour Leader,* the Independent
Labour Party journal. Brockway was one of those who served a long time in prison
as a conscientious objector.

In due course a national conference of the No-Conscription Fellowship was
called to London and the delegates were warned not to ask anyone except a policeman for directions to the hall, which was a Quaker building. This did not prevent a
number of soldiers trying to invade the building when the conference was being
held. We were, naturally, very unpopular with the population generally and were
sometimes spat at or assaulted in the streets. Two naval officers in mufti were

mistaken for conscientious objectors and were handed white feathers by Edinburgh ladies who assumed that they had failed to join up.

The Edinburgh branch of the No-Conscription Fellowship was a very big branch and many of those who joined after the war helped me to build up the Edinburgh branch of the Scottish Labour College.[76] I also helped found during the war an organisation representing working class bodies who were opposed to the war. We held open air meetings at the Mound in Princes Street on a few occasions. At one of these the speaker was John S Clarke. At the end of the meeting, as we had no collection box, we borrowed his bowler hat and passed it round the small crowd. When Clarke got his hat back he looked into it and saw only a few coppers and said, for the crowd's benefit, 'I'm glad I got my hat back.' It was clear that the views of the anti-war people were not popular.[77]

The insurance office where I worked in St Andrew Square in Edinburgh was a very conservative office. I was the only socialist and the only trade unionist there. I had joined the National Union of Clerks, although my conditions of employment were better than the union ever dreamed of. My views must have been very un-popular in the office although I had said nothing about them. But I must say that the official bosses never showed any antagonism to me personally, perhaps because I did my work well.

Some weeks before my call-up was due I resigned from my job so that I could build up the Edinburgh branch of the No-Conscription Fellowship and, as long as I was free, represent the rest of the members when they were brought up before the courts. Most of the members when arrested were brought before the Sheriff Court but some were brought before the Police Courts—which was a mistake on the part of the authorities. When the first member had to appear at a Sheriff Court I hired a lawyer as I was led to believe a lawyer was necessary. He made a poor show and I afterwards sacked him. I had another lawyer for the second case but sacked him at the end, too. I then found an old radical lawyer who had been a member of the Young Scots.[78] He probably didn't agree with our views but he had brains and he was prepared to take suggestions from me. I had made a study not only of the Military Service Acts but also of the Military Manual used by the army. In most cases all I could do was to ask the court to give the arrested member time to prepare his defence and get him off on bail. I was successful in every case. This caused a scandal in Edinburgh, for the evening papers came out with bills reading 'More COs re-leased'. That didn't please the legal department of the army, which I understood was in Edinburgh, nor did it please the very patriotic citizens.

When I became subject to arrest for having not responded to my call-up notice I didn't go home to Musselburgh some nights but used a small flat that belonged to my Aunt Mary at the entrance to Greyfriars Church. This was the church to which people had gone to sign the Covenant, to express their opposition to the government forcing the Anglican church service on Presbyterians in Scotland. Aunt Mary had a sweet shop at the end of Chambers Street, where she stayed late on Fridays to re-arrange her window.

One night when I did return home I was awakened by my mother in the middle of the night. She told me that two gentlemen in blue wanted to see me. They took me down to the Town Hall where I was locked in a cell. The following day I was brought before the police court. The magistrate was a local master baker. The charge was that I had failed to present myself at Glencorse Barracks. I asked to be released on bail to prepare my case. I couldn't be denied that apparently and I left to phone the lawyer to acquaint him with my new position. A day or two later he heard from the procurator fiscal who had dealt with me at the court that my trial had been fixed for a certain date. He assured me that his request would be granted as 'we lawyers oblige each other in such cases.' He was mistaken. The Musselburgh lawyer had read in the papers about my activities in defending conscientious objectors and he assumed mistakenly that all the successes had been due to my lawyer and therefore told him that he wasn't prepared to alter the date. He was delighted apparently at the prospect of an easy ride when I came before his court. I had therefore to defend myself.

When conscientious objectors were brought before the courts a number of members of the No-Conscription Fellowship always turned up to provide moral support for the victims of the Military Service Act. When I got there to face the charge a small crowd of my members were waiting for me and when the police hustled me through them into the court the lawyer, who knew I was going to ask for a stated case to go to the High Court, told me that after I had made the request and it had been dealt with I was to move that 'proceedings be sisted pending the appeal.' I knew a good many legal phrases because of my experience in the general manger's department but I had never heard that one before.

Once in the dock the magistrate asked me if I pleaded guilty or not guilty to the charge of failing to turn up at the barracks as ordered. Instead of answering his question I said, 'I challenge the jurisdiction of this court.' This beat the baillie so he had to retire with the clerk of court to ask his advice. When he returned to the court he asked on what grounds I challenged the power of the court to try me. I replied that this court had only power to fine a man up to a few pounds, whereas offences under the Military Service Act involved much larger fines. The baillie again had to retire behind the scenes to get more advice. When he came back he said he rejected my plea. I then said that the notice calling me up had been sent out by the army one day before the conscientious objectors' tribunal had heard my case. The sergeants who had come to take me back to the barracks as a prisoner were then put in the witness box and swore that the notice had been sent out *after* my appeal had failed. The baillie therefore took their word for it and fined me £5 and handed me over to the military authorities.

I never paid the £5 but the two sergeants took me off to Glencorse Barracks, some little distance from Edinburgh, where I was shoved into the 'clink'. It was a bitterly cold winter's day and there was no heat in the room. I had taken the precaution of wearing two overcoats but the soldiers in the 'clink' had no overcoats and therefore felt very cold.

The following morning a young officer accompanied by a sergeant came into the room and asked if there were any complaints. I surprised him by saying: 'It's a very cold winter's day. These soldiers have no overcoats and they are very cold because there is no heat in this room.' The officer and his companion wheeled about and disappeared. Two hours later they returned accompanied by the colonel who said to me, 'I believe you have a complaint. What is it?' I told him there was no heat in the cell. 'There is heat in the room next door where the guard are,' he replied. His party then wheeled about and also disappeared.

The following day I was brought before the colonel. By this time the army had had experience of many hundreds of conscientious objectors. He said to me: 'What I should do with you is to send you to join your unit, the Non-Combatant Corps, at the barracks of the Highland Light Infantry in Glasgow and I should send two sergeants with you to see that you get there. If, however, you will promise to go there yourself I won't send sergeants.' As I knew that there was to be a meeting of the No-Conscription Fellowship in Glasgow that night and I wanted to speak at it, I had no hesitation in assuring the colonel that he could count on me showing up among the Highland Light Infantry. The next day I duly arrived at the barracks there and was at once accommodated in the clink, where my companion was a soldier who had escaped from the army time after time.

He told me of one of his escapes. He had been picked up in London and two sergeants had been sent from Scotland to make absolutely certain that he showed up in Edinburgh. When they got him on the train they made him take off his boots and these were put under the pillow of one of the sergeants. One of the sergeants took off his own boots and pushed them under his seat. On the platform two ladies were serving free cups of tea to travelling soldiers. The two sergeants wanted to get a cup. They therefore opened the door of the train and stood on the platform waiting. When they got the cups and stepped back into the compartment their prisoner had gone. A train travelling in the opposite direction had been going very slowly. The prisoner had therefore grabbed the sergeant's boots and stepped from one train to the other.

Before I had been arrested Miss Jeffreys, a member of the No-Conscription Fellowship in Edinburgh, one day said to me: 'I would like you to go and meet my friend Mrs Phillips who has invited you to tea.' I went and we had a chat. Mrs Phillips then said: 'You don't look well as a result of the strain you are undergoing. Would you be willing to see my husband, who is a specialist?' I went to see him. He examined me, wrote on a piece of paper, handed it to me and said: 'When you are medically examined by the army show the doctor this note.' It said that I had a shadow on my left lung. I seemed to have consumption but I was more worried about my future with the military. Later, when I was medically examined by the army I showed the doctor the note—I think he knew it was written by a well known specialist. Years later, on thinking about this experience and that I had never been treated for consumption, I came to the conclusion that the certificate I had got from Dr Phillips was the result of a plot by Miss Jeffreys and his wife intended to prevent me from ever being sent to France, where conscientious objectors were in danger of being shot for failing to carry out a military command. I was therefore marked for home service only and found that the home service conscientious objectors were being collected in Glasgow to be transferred to Aldershot, the great military centre.[79]

The day came when the home service members of the Non-Combatant Corps—a new regiment invented for us by the army—were told to depart for Aldershot. I was ordered to join the parade that was to go to the station. A day or two before I had been ordered to put on my uniform but refused. Three of the biggest men in the battalion were ordered to strip me and put on the uniform. I knew how roughly conscientious objectors were handled if that happened, so I put on the uniform but I didn't have the letters NCC, which should have been affixed to my shoulders. I was then seized by the army and marched up to the 'troops' outside who were ready to go to the station. The colonel of the Highland Light Infantry felt that troops leaving the barracks for another destination should always be played to the station by the HLI band. It must have been much against his principles to order the band of such a fighting unit as the HLI to play a bunch of conscientious objectors to the station, but no doubt he was a creature of habit and had to swallow his feelings.

When I was pushed into the ranks I realised that one of the three big men who had been ordered to dress me had been a fellow pupil at my school. Once we set off for the station I felt I had to make clear that I had refused to join the War Office's new non-combatant regiment. The only way I could do that was to persist in marching out of step with the rest of the draft. This annoyed my fellow school pupil marching by my side, who accused me of being a disgrace to the regiment.

When the draft arrived at Aldershot we were accommodated in a batch of newly built army huts. Our first job was to paint a large number of army bedsteads. I refused. My companions went off to carry out their duties. The colonel of our new regiment had been very carefully chosen. I was the only member of my draft who refused to do the bedstead job and was naturally brought before him for not obeying a lawful military order. As I was ushered into his room by two soldiers one of them tugged my hat off my head. The colonel, instead of going for me as I had expected, spoke to me like a father. But I still refused to join the bed painters.

For several days I was brought before him for the same offence. He then said, 'Well, all I'll ask you to do is to weed the paths round the huts. Surely that's nothing to do with war?' I told him I couldn't carry out any military orders.

Then a number of old soldiers were put on to make my blood curdle by telling me what would happen if I was court martialled and sent to a military prison, as conscientious objectors were at that time. I knew all about that because some COs had been very badly treated and questions had been raised by a few MPs in the House of Commons. My blood froze all right, but I persisted in my refusal.[80]

One day a new batch of conscientious objectors arrived. One of them was Palme Dutt, a middle class Indian student from Oxford University. I found that he knew nothing about Marxism and I spent some days tutoring him on the subject which so greatly interested him that he later joined the Communist Party and became their chief intellectual. He wasn't long in the Non-Combatant Corps because India was struggling for its freedom and somebody in the British government realised that it would play into the Indian nationalists' hands if they got to learn that an Indian was being sent to prison because he wouldn't fight for the British government. He was therefore discharged.[81]

When the colonel and his young lieutenant had for some weeks done their best to persuade me to obey a military order but without success, they had no alternative but to put me down for court martial. The No-Conscription Fellowship office had, of course, kept track of me and I was one day visited by Joan Fry, one of a well-known group of Quaker sisters. She told me that as I was appealing to the High Court in Scotland, they were going to send an advocate to explain the situation to the court martial.[82]

When the day of the court martial arrived I was marched to the Queen Consort's barracks. On the way a black man in uniform, accompanied by two sergeants, appeared on the road in front of me. One of my sergeants told me: 'That chap's in the same boat as you are—he's refused to carry out a military order.' I naturally asked what the order was, and the sergeant replied: 'He refused to change his colour at the word of command.'

When the court martial began the barrister was there and he explained that my calling-up notice had been sent me one day before my final appeal to the conscientious objectors' tribunal had been considered and that I should therefore not have been arrested nor should I have been tried at the Musselburgh police court. He said, moreover, that the court had no right to try me at all because it had no power to deal with conscientious objectors under the Military Service Act: that was the prerogative of the sheriff court, which had power to inflict far heavier fines.

The court martial was now quite puzzled and retired to consider what it should do about me. When it came back it had decided it wasn't going to take any risks and was referring my case to the General Officer Commanding Aldershot area. The No-Conscription Fellowship office had good connections and I learned afterwards that the general decided he wasn't going to take any risks either. He therefore referred my case to the War Office. It evidently decided that I might win my case and that I was to remain with my battalion until my case in Scotland was heard. I was to be under 'open arrest', no doubt because the army might be found to have had no authority to have me.

The Colonel told me that being under open arrest I was free to go out for a walk whenever I liked but I would be accompanied all the time by a corporal—presumably to see that I didn't run away. The corporal I got was not an interesting companion. He was quite stupid and suffered badly from adenoids. He was a home service soldier from a fighting regiment.

I naturally went out every day accompanied by this companion. In time I became a well-known figure in Aldershot among the fighting regiments that surrounded our huts: I was known as 'the Bloody Mystery'. After enjoying my new situation for a few days I saw more conscientious objectors arrive. Some of them refused to obey military orders and were court martialled.

After some weeks the colonel called me before him and told me the War Office had decided that I should be sent home until my case was settled by the High Court. I was delighted, because the court's very long summer recess had just started and I would therefore have some months' freedom.

When I got into the train at King's Cross there were only two ladies in the compartment. I was of course in uniform but still with no regimental initials on my shoulders, and they proceeded to share their sandwiches with me. I discovered that they thought that I was one of the heroes who was going to defend them from the Hun. I didn't think it politic to explain my situation but I felt very awkward when they told me I was to have a whole seat to myself so that I could have a good sleep while they shared the other seat. I felt inclined to tell them the truth since I felt very awkward as I was young and they were middle-aged. But as I thought they might throw themselves out of the carriage if I told them the awful truth I said nothing and had a good sleep with a guilty conscience.

When I got to Edinburgh I went to see my lawyer. He called me back about a week later and said, 'I have some bad news for you. The High Court has decided to have a special session in order to deal with three cases but in reality to deal with your case so that you won't have a long holiday. The other two cases are simply "blinds" '. I asked him whether I should turn up at the High Court to hear my case but he suggested that if I won it, as I likely would, because in Scotland they were sticklers for the law, I might be arrested immediately the case was over. When the case did come up the court was furious over the incompetence of the Musselburgh lawyer who had been advising the baillie. It wasn't long before I was arrested once again and found myself sentenced to 110 days' imprisonment as a first offender in Wormwood Scrubs.

This was far from a pleasant experience. The number of warders had been greatly reduced. I got no association work with other prisoners. The food given to prisoners had been cut down to help win the war. I felt so hungry that when we were allowed out for a short period each day to walk round the exercise ring—six paces apart and no talking—I was tempted to pick up the dry bread that newly arrived prisoners hadn't at first the heart to eat and had thrown out through the ventilation panels of the high windows.

My first few days there turned out to be the best days because a doctor discovered that I was suffering from itch which I had picked up from the army blankets. I was immediately put in a special cell for cases like mine and along came a warder accompanied by a prisoner carrying a bucket of yellow liquid and a whitewash brush. I had to strip naked while the other prisoner used the brush to paint the yellow all over me. He came back several days to carry out the same task.

In this special cell was a large novel which was a story about the Firth of Forth, which I read with interest as I knew all the places mentioned. When I was put into a normal cell afterwards I found that all the prisoners had got to read for some weeks was a copy of the Bible. In view of the fact that the Christian churches were practically all backing the war and hadn't protested about ministers being exempted from sharing in the fighting, I had little interest in the book.

My hard labour consisted of sewing mail bags—a very unpleasant job because the canvas was very thick and hard and it was no joke trying to push a needle through it.

When the warders came round one day with the dinner we were given a tin full of boiled rice which had no salt and no sugar. It was quite tasteless. I was so hungry afterwards that when they came round to collect the tins I nipped out to a recess near my cell where a number of tins had been placed. One prisoner, a new one, hadn't touched his tasteless rice so I shoved my hand into it, took out a handful and shot back into my cell with it. A warder spotted me. I forget what punishment he threatened me with but he made me put the rice back in the pan—so I didn't even get a mouthful eaten.

The only time I was out of my cell was for Sunday service. The conscientious objectors wearing one prison uniform sat on one side and the other prisoners sat in another uniform on the other side. In the course of his sermon the parson first addressed the ordinary prisoners who he thought were much more respectable members of society than the conscientious objectors. Then he turned to us and began: 'You have chosen to spend Christmas in this institution ... and so on. None of us had any raw eggs to throw at him.

The War Office in its battle with the conscientious objectors had to change its policy several times, whether at the behest of the government or not I don't know. At first the COs were sent to military prisons but they caused so much trouble by often being brutally treated—which caused questions in Parliament—that it was decided that in future they should be sent to civil prisons. There they continued to disobey orders.

When I was in Wormwood Scrubs there was another change. Although we had all been before local tribunals seeking exemption, which was provided for under the Military Service Act, and then before an Appeal Tribunal, the prisons were filling up with conscientious objectors. It was therefore decided by the government that we should have a chance of going before another tribunal by which we were given—if they thought we were genuine—a chance of working under better conditions in one of three prisons that were taken over by the Home Office: Wakefield, Knutsford and Dartmoor. I was treated as genuine and allocated to Wakefield. My great friend Arthur Woodburn, who could have escaped war service, I believe, because he was employed in an engineering factory, was deemed non-genuine and spent most of the war in Calton Jail in Edinburgh, which Margery Fry told me was the worst jail in Britain.[83]

In Wormwood Scrubs I had had nightmares nearly every night. Most of them consisted of my scaling the prison wall, then just as I was getting over it, being pulled back by the legs. I think the fact that I was really in solitary confinement all the time was responsible. The effect on my mind showed one day when I looked at a knot on the wooden floor of my cell and it grew bigger and bigger and bigger. That recalled that some of the conscientious objectors went off their heads while in prison.

When I learned I was going to get out and be with fellow COs at Wakefield I thought that would be the most wonderful day in my life. However, when I left Wormwood Scrubs and found myself outside that grim place I had no feeling of pleasure whatever. I had completely exhausted the joy I had anticipated so often in my cell of being free.

When I arrived at Wakefield Jail, which had changed its name to Home Office Work Centre, my first job was to stoke the furnace that heated the prison. But I was soon transferred to the weaving shed, where I and some of my fellow conscientious objectors sat all the working day at handlooms. Each loom had a legend at the top that said *House of Correction*. This was apparently to remind prisoners where they were. Our job was to weave material for prisoners' vests. The material was terrible.

The warders at Wakefield were at first old veterans of the prison service. They showed no affection for their charges. But some genius at the War Office, perhaps, had a brainwave: warders were scarce—why shouldn't they be replaced with badly wounded soldiers who would no doubt give us a rough time? That genius made a profound mistake. The conscientious objectors included many socialists, who immediately started arguments with the new warders. In no time at all their views were about as unpatriotic as ours were: the war had taught them history lessons.

We were allowed to go out for an hour or two in the evening and our cells were never locked, so we could run classes on socialist theory. I myself got a bundle of *Plebs* each month, for which I had a ready sale despite the fact that our wages were 8d. a week, i.e., 1d. each working day and (as it was a Christian country) 2d. for Sunday. Soldiers were at first paid a shilling a day.[84]

Amongst us conscientious objectors were members of some unusual sects, including Plymouth Brethren, Seventh Day Adventists, and some whom we called 'Holy Rollers' who worshipped God by rolling about in their cells and groaning. There were also a number of Quakers. But the overwhelming majority of objectors were socialists of various types.

A number of conscientious objectors had fled to Ireland to avoid being invited to serve the army.[85] Others were caught on the run. One slight looking chap had gone about dressed as a girl until an observant policeman spotted him. Being on the run became very difficult because the authorities arranged to stop people in the streets and ask them for their identity cards.

My father had a distant relative living in Leeds, which is not far from Wakefield. He wrote him and said his son was a CO in Wakefield and he suggested that the relative might invite me to come to tea some time. He knew the spartan conditions in which I was living. When I got the invitation I set out. I was able to go into Wakefield by bus—one of the rules was that we were not to go anywhere by train. This was to prevent our going home to see our wives or parents at the week-ends.

When my relative came to his door in Leeds he couldn't believe his eyes. He had understood from the abbreviation CO that I was a Commanding Officer. The figure before him was wearing a very shabby Home Office suit. I had to break the news to him of my far from glamorous situation, but he gave me my tea all right and treated me civilly.

One of the best known weeklies then was *John Bull*, edited by Horatio Bottomley, a clever scoundrel who eventually went to jail. Bottomley's paper had a large circulation and pretended that it was the voice of the people. He knew that conscientious objectors were very unpopular with the public, so he ran a series of articles on us which resulted in mobs attacking the COs in Knutsford and at Wakefield Jail. That didn't happen in Dartmoor because there were no mobs to be had there: the sheep on the moor had no interest in politics.[86]

One evening when I was coming back to Wakefield prison by the back way three youths were hanging about, obviously waiting to give any returning conscientious objector a rough time. I was, however, six feet one in height, so they decided to let me pass. Soon a howling mob was at the front gate of the prison waiting for COs coming back. By this time I and a number of others were inside. One of the jobs some of us had had to do was to demolish a building in the prison grounds. There were a number of pieces of iron piping lying about and some of our group who had arrived back early slid these up their sleeves and waited behind the gate in order to give a warm reception to the crowd if they broke in. A group of warders was there to man the small door in the centre of the big gate through which only one man could pass at a time. The late birds had to make their way through the howling mob outside, which didn't handle them like Christian gentlemen; and as they got to the door the warders pulled them in and immediately shut it to prevent the crowd entering. When the door was opened on one occasion the warders pulled in a conscientious objector who was dripping with blood. There was a roar of anger from the COs inside and they tried to push the warders aside and get out at the crowd, removing for use the iron piping from their sleeves. The warders managed to keep the door shut with a great struggle, but I had then the experience of what a mob feels like, which I shall never forget. Reason completely left our chaps. All they wanted to do was to apply the iron piping to the mob.

Shortly before that the local paper had published an article which told its readers that there were apparently at least two types of conscientious objector. One, they said, presumably a Quaker, had been seized by a group of Wakefield citizens and thrown into the dirty canal that ran through the town. He had offered no resistance. When he got to his feet, with water up to his neck, the police arrived and ordered him to come out. But he took the view that, as the citizens had thrown him into the canal, they would have to get him out of it. A policeman eventually had to go most unwillingly into the water, carry him out and take him back safely to the prison.

On the other hand, said the local paper, a stocky conscientious objector was walking along a side street in Wakefield when he was attacked by three citizens. Before one could say 'Jack Robinson' two of them were lying on the ground and the third was making full speed for safety. This CO's hobby was boxing and he had treated the three to a lesson.

One of the conscientious objectors at Wakefield determined to go home by train and see his sweetheart. This meant he'd be away for a couple of days. He worked in the weaving shed, the warder in charge of which was a wounded soldier whom we'd turned into a socialist. The warder agreed that he wouldn't make any report that the weaver was absent. He went further when we said that if the fellow was caught on the train or at the station he would be likely to be sent to Wormwood Scrubs. The warder volunteered to go to the station to meet the conscientious objector on his way back, and to pin his Military Medal, which he wore regularly, on the CO's chest to ensure that he would not be molested. But the CO didn't know about this last arrangement, and when he spotted the warder at the station he got out by an unofficial route and managed to get back safely to the prison.

Another of the conscientious objectors at Wakefield was Jock Millar, who was a member of my branch of the No-Conscription Fellowship. Jock wasn't interested in girls, unlike most of us. By this time many of the COs had picked up girls among the local population. I was one of these enterprising gents. I can still remember that my girl had a damaged hand, the result of working in a factory. The reason for the conscientious objectors' success with the girls at Wakefield was because men were scarce and because we as a whole were physically superior to the average local male worker who was a product of generations of factory life, low wages and poor feeding. Jock, however, enjoyed a joke and when he heard some of our young bloods complaining they had to leave their girls early to be back in the prison by 9 pm, he said that if they wanted to stay out until 11 pm he would help them back over the prison's high wall. They welcomed his offer. He told them where to congregate on the other side of the wall at 11 o'clock sharp.

That day there was a hue and cry because a very long ladder padlocked to a wall had disappeared. The warders and the governor searched for it in vain. Jock and a pal had removed it from its fastenings. The prison grounds were covered with rows and rows of cabbages and the ladder was lying snugly out of sight between two of the many rows.

The prisoners were not locked in their cells nor were they locked in the prison, but of course the prison door itself was locked. Jock and his pal therefore had no difficulty just before 11 pm in going into the grounds, recovering the long ladder and directing it against the prison wall at the right spot. Jock climbed the ladder and looked over. The lovebirds were all waiting for his kindly assistance. He said to them: 'I and my pal will pull up the ladder and lower the end of it to you. You'll come up one by one. But there won't be time to get the ladder up and down for each of you. So you'll each have to jump down from the top of the wall. But you won't get hurt because we've provided you with a soft landing.' The soft landing was a great pile of dung used to encourage the growth of the cabbages. The lovebirds had no choice but to jump down on to it and to go scented to bed.

At some stage the army had decided that they would use some willing German prisoners-of-war to build a road from Ballachulish to Kinlochleven along the side of Loch Leven. This road was to go through part of the Grampians and was to be built on the spurs of the mountains near the edge of the water. The army built both a number of huts to accommodate the prisoners, and a pier, so that the steamer which sailed between Ballachulish and Kinlochleven could drop supplies and equipment to the camp site.

Someone at the War Office must have realised one day that these patriotic Germans were being sent to a place many miles from any habitation. 'Why should we send patriotic German soldiers to a god-forsaken place like that when we've got so many of these bloody conscientious objectors on our hands?' The result was that about 200 of the inhabitants of Wakefield Jail Work Centre were sent up to this benighted spot. I was one of them. Two Home Office officials were put in charge of the unwelcome arrivals. The chief official was Guy Newcomen. I wouldn't say, when we first gathered in a group in the dining hall, that he spoke to us as if he were Father Christmas. Among the things he did say was that we could go out of the camp in our spare time but that we had to be in by, I think, 9 pm. That meant that no one could go to the nearest village—Ballachulish—and be back in the time stated, except at week-ends. He also said that if we had any complaints (and he hoped we wouldn't have any) we ought to appoint one of ourselves to receive such complaints and if he—the conscientious objectors' representative—thought it wise he could submit them to him.

Because a number of the COs there were from my Edinburgh branch of the No-Conscription Fellowship and because I was well known as a 'press magnate' who had sold *Plebs* at Wakefield, I was appointed to the post. That was the first time I was a shop steward. I didn't realise the difficulties it would put me in. We were living in a very rainy part of Scotland and we weren't expected to work when it was really raining. But that was the rub. The Plymouth Brethren were very grateful to God for preserving them from killing their fellow men and they were therefore prepared to work when the rain was quite heavy. On the other hand, the rest of my very varied congregation included socialists of every variety and some of these, when a spot or two of rain fell, thought it was too wet to work and that it was my duty to let them go back to the camp. I knew quite well that if I played the fool and they left off the road-building under such circumstances, they were likely to be sent back to prison; and because of the solitary confinement that was common they would be in a very unhappy position and some of them would go off their heads as some had already done in Wormwood Scrubs. I therefore used my common sense and refused at such times to let them go back to the camp. This aroused so much criticism that a meeting was called in the dining room to sack me as shop steward.

Two or three of the leading rebels got on to the platform and described my behaviour in unflattering terms. It came to my turn to defend myself. I made the most passionate speech I had ever made in my life. I began by saying what would happen to them if they played the fool by leaving the road when there was no sound justification for doing so. I finished by saying with great passion: 'Now do you think if the government, the War Office, the Home Office, the army, the navy and the air force can't make me do something that a bunch of bloody conscientious objectors is going to be more successful?' The meeting then broke up and I remained shop steward for the rest of my stay at Ballachulish.

As I don't think any of us had ever been navvies building roads we had about half a dozen experienced roadmen whose job was to see that we knew how to put gunpowder into the holes we drilled into the rocks.

When the steamer which brought our supplies to the pier was some distance off the captain used to blow his siren to warn these foremen, who had a hut of their own, to be on the pier ready to receive the goods. One day there was no response from the hut when the ship's whistle blew. The reason was simple. Some of our young bloods had through the night put large screws through the doors and windows of the foremen's hut. They had quite a job eventually breaking their way out and showing themselves to the angry steamer captain, who had kept blowing his siren all the way to the pier.

When summer came and the sun was very strong one of us looked into the hut in which the meat was hung. The meat was crawling with maggots. I had therefore to tell Guy Newcomen that the six vegetarians had converted the whole of the 200 or so of us to their view, and that we wouldn't take the meat under any circumstances. He thought I was joking until I took him to see the meat for himself. I can't remember what we got instead: no doubt it was as unattractive as possible.

There was no entertainment available at the camp—not even a bagatelle table—and week-ends were boring. Ballachulish was a very small village. I therefore as the shop steward sometimes had to play the role of being the entertainment. One Sunday a group of my fellow conscientious objectors burst into my hut and made for my bed at the other end. I was lying in it at the time. I jumped out of it and over the camp wall, followed by the mob. I ran up the mountain, taking advantage of the cover it provided. I was a good runner and outdistanced the pack. I had nothing on my feet and only a Home Office shirt on my body. It was winter time. By making a semi-circle I got back into the camp. Meantime, having lost sight of me, the pack began to get worried. I had taken them so far that they thought I might be lost and they started to look for me, not knowing I was safely in bed. As they didn't look either in the camp or in my bed they eventually arrived back very tired and wondering whether they would have to contact the police, who were a long distance away, to tell them I was lost in the mountains.

On another occasion I was sitting up in my bed one Sunday afternoon reading, I think, the *New Leader*. I then became conscious of a far from melodious sound coming from another part of the camp. It came nearer and nearer. It was made by a procession of my fellow conscientious objectors who were singing and carrying trays, kettles and any other object they could beat with a stick to make a noise. They were marching round the huts to gather support for a procession and in they marched to my hut. They entered by the far end from where I was. I had no notion of what their ideas were. But when the first four reached my bed they lifted it bodily with me in it. I was marched round the camp then down to the pier. I was put on the very edge of the pier, where there was a whirlpool close by. It was wintertime and bitterly cold. All I had on was my Home Office shirt and a thin army blanket. The wind was practically a gale and I had difficulty in keeping the blanket on me.

The crowd gathered round me and a fisherman named Sandy brought a little book out of his pocket and solemnly read the burial service over me. He then put the book back in his pocket and the whole gang made for the warmth of the camp. I was left on the pier in the howling gale. I thought I would try to get the better of them by not getting up and not making my way back to the camp wrapped in my scant coverings—no doubt to be greeted by howls of laughter and jeers. I therefore clutched the blanket closer to me and waited. And waited ... I had almost given up when some of them, thinking I would get pneumonia if I wasn't brought back, came clattering down to the pier, lifted me—still on my bed—and transported me at some speed back to my hut.

Another member of my No-Conscription Fellowship branch who was with us at Ballachulish was Clem Jeffreys, who was part-Polish and part-Scottish. Before his arrest Clem had obtained an MA degree. The foreman on the road, however, never succeeded in making him into a navvy and he gave up in the end, so Clem spent most of his time leaning on his shovel. He was, however, easily taken in.

One winter day Jock Millar, who was a tailor by trade, said to Clem as he left camp for the road: 'Clem, would you like a warm bath when you come back?' Clem, hardly believing his luck, nearly smothered Jock with gratitude. Our bath hut was an army hut divided by hanging blankets. On one side of the division Jock had his tailor's shop; on the other side was a big iron bath, two pails of cold water and a stove on which one of the pails was placed when warm water was required.

When Clem came off the road and made for Jock's repair department he could hardly believe that Jock would have kept to his promise. He timidly asked Jock if he had remembered the bath. Jock assured him he had and when he had seen Clem coming he had, moreover, poured in the bucket of hot water and sufficient cold water to enable Clem to step right into it. Clem was full of thanks and went behind the blankets, undressed and sat down in the beautifully warm water. He was quite oblivious that Jock and two of his cronies were outside the window watching the proceedings with interest. Clem was quite unaware that fastened to the beam over his head was a bucket of ice cold water from the stream outside, and that attached to the bucket was a rope that led across the beam and out of the window where Jock and his pals were standing. Once Clem had got properly warmed the rope was pulled. The ice cold water drove every word out of his body. But the language that came out of it later would have won a prize in any swearing competition.

Later on, when I was back in Wakefield Jail, the government or its minions decided that they were having so many conscientious objectors to accommodate in work centres like that that they ought to make better use of our labours. A number of us were therefore sent out in ones and twos to work on farms or fell trees or do similar jobs. I was sent to work on the home farm at Failand, near Bristol, of Sir Edward Fry, who had been the Lord Chief Justice. I have no doubt that I had been asked for by one of his family.[87]

I was put up there on the farm in a little flat above the stable. For half the week I worked on the farm, where there was a bailiff and an agricultural worker. During the other half I worked with the estate carpenter. His only son was at the front and he therefore hated me. He made a point day after day of not addressing a word to me except when it was absolutely necessary if I was to do the job he wanted done. I sympathised with him to a certain extent. But it wasn't a pleasant relationship,

On the other hand, Margery Fry, a member of the family, who had a house in London and who for a time was head of Somerville College in Oxford, told me I could use her bicycle any time I wanted. I got my food from the head gardener's house and had access to the kitchen in the big house.

Eventually my work at Failand ran out but not before Sir Edward Fry himself died. I had to help two other members of the staff to carry him in his coffin down to the ground floor by way of a very narrow stair. He had rather a rough ride.

I was then sent to a farm near Guildford. Unfortunately it was a dairy farm. That meant we had to get up at 4 am so that the Londoners could get their milk. The farmer had about forty cows. He handed me a stool and a pail and pointed to a cow and told me to get on and milk her. I was a complete stranger to the cow and she may have heard that I was an unpatriotic rascal. With an effort I got a few drops of milk out and then I noticed that one of her teats was diseased. I drew the farmer's attention to this but he seemed unconcerned. But he was concerned that I was getting little or no milk into the pail and took me away to prepare the cow's break-fast, a small boy successfully taking my place at the pail. The breakfast was to consist of sliced turnips. I had the slicing machine pointed out to me. I had the impression that farmers in those days treated their machinery with little concern. That machine was not only rusty but the cutting blades were very blunt and it was only with very great effort that I managed to chop the turnips into pieces. Forty of the cows were let out into a field but I noticed that one was not released from its stall. As a prisoner myself I felt rather sorry for it but the farmer said, 'Give that one a bucket of water.' I filled a bucket and started to get up to the cow's head. It was a very big cow and I had a great job pushing my way between its flanks and the boards of its stall. When I got to the drinking end of the animal it suddenly turned its head and I saw a big brass ring in its nose. It was the bull! If it had moved sideways it would have smashed my ribs but fortunately it decided to shove its snout into the water.

I hadn't been long on that farm when I got a letter from Bob Rogers, who was one of my Edinburgh branch members of the No-Conscription Fellowship. His letter came from the Scottish Borders. Bob said he was in the same position as I was. He and a Borders conscientious objector had been sent out to a forest near Dumfries to fell trees for a contractor who, thanks to the war, had been left with only a small boy to assist him in his work. Bob's fellow conscientious objector had badly hurt himself with his axe and was in hospital. The contractor was willing to take me on as a substitute. As I knew Bob and was feeling very lonely I at once said I would come if his boss made application for my services. Bob said his landlady would put me up in her house, which was near the first forest we had to tackle.

I travelled by train to Dumfries and then got another train to Moniave. When the train stopped at Moniave it was snowing but Bob was on the platform to meet me. He was the kind of chap who, if he had bad news, blurted it out at once. As he shook hands with me he said: 'My landlady is not prepared to take you. I think she's not pleased with me as I've shown no signs of courting her daughter. And I think she's discovered from my letters that I have a girl in Leith.' That news was a blow to me because Bob said my digs would now be in Moniave and I had four and a half miles to walk to the wood each morning and four and a half miles back at night. A few days later, however, Bob's landlady decided to take more drastic action for his failure over her daughter: she told him he had to find other digs. He therefore joined me in my digs in the cottage of an elderly lady whom I called Mrs Watery Eye. When I told her a joke and she laughed the tears ran down her cheeks. This enabled Bob, who had a bigger appetite than I had, to seize another slice from the plate.

Every time a tree fell it was money in the contractor's pocket. Timber felling was a dangerous job both for men and for the horses that dragged the logs which had to be loaded on to special vehicles. Several horses badly broke their ankles in the woods and had to be shot. One point that had to be watched was that among the spruce trees there were a number of dead ones which usually leant on a live one. Before Bob and I started sawing down the trees after the contractor had cut the necessary mouths to make them fall the right way, we had to look up to see if a dead tree was leaning on the one we were to cut. In that case our one could come down, if we weren't watching, long before it was expected and might fall on us rather than away from us. I wrote my insurance office to ask what jobs involved the highest premium for employer's liability policy and was told the most expensive policy was for a steeplejack and the second highest was for a lumberjack. We were lumberjacks.

Felling the spruce trees was relatively easy—they weren't very big and the wood was soft wood. Our next job was to deal with enormous beech trees on the sides of a gully among the hills. I was told by the contractor that beech wood was much used on butcher's counters because it was very hard. The trees were from four to five feet in diameter. Our two-handed saws were, I think, only six feet in length. So it was tough work putting a mouth in the trees with an axe and then using the six foot saws to cut through the trunk. We used iron wedges to prevent the tree from settling down on the saw and so making it impossible to move. This time we had to sned some of the trees—that is, lop off or, if they were large, saw off the branches. As the trees were lying on the steep bank of the gully we had sometimes to stand on the big trunks while lopping. But we had to be very careful that in cutting off the branches we didn't disturb the balance of the tree—that could send us flying as it rolled over. That's what happened to me one day. I shot over a drystone dyke and landed on my back, while my axe went in one direction and my cap in another. I lay stunned for some minutes but recovered consciousness and went home a bit shaken.

The time came when the hauliers came with their horses to remove the trunks lying on the sides of the gully. They had to use the narrow road at the top of the gully which was separated from the trees by a drystone dyke. The chief haulier decided to tackle the biggest trunk first. He affixed chains to it and three horses were fastened to the other end. Their job was to pull the trunk up on to the little road where tow vehicles specially built for carrying them were to be loaded. The chief haulier then seized the reins at the head of the first horse and his mate the reins at the head of the second horse, and with bloodcurdling yells invited the horses to pull with all their might. The trunk didn't move. So they yoked a fourth horse in front of the first horse. The chief haulier seized the reins at the head of the new leader then, having backed the horses several yards to get them going full speed before the tree started to move, both men uttered even more blood-curdling yells. Unfortunately, the tree didn't move an inch. Instead the horses were stopped with a fierce jerk. Two of them were thrown through the drystone dyke. Their chains broke and the first horse rolled several yards down the gully. The man who was holding its head flew through the air and fortunately for him landed in a bush which broke his fall. That was the end of the hauliers' adventure. They had had enough and departed with their vehicles and horses for safer parts of the countryside. That was also the end of my tree-felling days and I was sent to a market garden near Edinburgh.

The garden had a large number of tomato plants. My job was to water them every day. I was only there a day or two when the other men discovered that I was a conscientious objector. They told the boss that if he didn't get rid of me they would leave. So the boss invited me to take myself off elsewhere.

By this time I was back living at home in Musselburgh. My father, who was chief accountant in Edinburgh Corporation's City Chamberlain department, then happened to meet the chief sanitary inspector. He complained that the wartime Coal Control office, which was accommodated in the Art Gallery, had been put under his supervision and he was fed up running the two departments. My father said that as I had been trained in a big insurance office I might be able to help him. 'For God's sake send him along to see me tomorrow,' said the inspector. I went, and after a couple of days with him he decided that I could run the department.

One incident I omitted to mention earlier took place when, I think, we were at Wakefield Jail. We learned that a number of conscientious objectors in a non-combatant corps had been sent to France. Some had been taken up to the front line and had been court martialled and sentenced to death. The little office in London of the No-Conscription Fellowship got word of this. The result was that one of the few MPs interested in our case put down a question in the House of Commons. The cabinet minister responsible for the War Office knew nothing about this but they knew about our office. They had to phone our office and get the information to enable them to answer the question in the House. Our office was run by two ladies, one of whom was Miss Joan Beauchamp, and they were able to provide the details the War Office wanted. The sentence was altered to imprisonment.[88]

Dr Eric F Dott

Well, I turned eighteen in December of 1916 and was duly called up to the army about the following February or March. I received a summons to attend at the army place and ignored it. We lived in Colinton at that time, a nice little residential village in Midlothian then it was, outside Edinburgh, with a little railway of our own. Our Colinton policeman came up to our house and very bashfully and regretfully said he had to arrest me. He did so and I went off quite obediently and spent the night in confinement in Edinburgh somewhere. I was ordered to report to Glencorse Barracks, across the Pentland hills from Colinton.

I was very uncertain then for I felt very young and very inexperienced. I was younger than eighteen though I was eighteen years of age, and I didn't know what to do. I wandered along to Glencorse Barracks and from there I was told I must report the next day to Kinghorn Barracks. Being released from Glencorse I walked away home over the Pentlands back to Colinton.

Now at that time my objection to joining the army was essentially Christian in outlook. I thought that war was completely incompatible with a Christian outlook. I was strongly influenced by all I had learned of Christianity. Indeed at that time I hoped to become a minister in the church. My mother, who had died just before I was arrested, was a very earnest and very fine Christian. From that I derived a very earnest Christian outlook myself when I would be between fourteen and seventeen years of age.

My father, on the other hand, was in religion what you might call a freethinker but he was a very earnest socialist. He was Peter McOmish Dott, the proprietor of Aitken Dott & Son, the picture dealers in Castle Street. He I think had been brought up in a Conservative family but of his own thinking and interest had swerved over towards Liberal, and then before the First World War he had become a confirmed socialist. And on the outbreak of the war he was the more strongly influenced by the wrongness of war, its origin in capitalist rivalries and so on. So the war made him go even further and further into his belief in the necessity for socialism. So that I had that background of a very able and interesting man to guide me in that idea, and I had a double view on this question of being an objector to war.

I had left school in the summer of 1916. Before that, so far as I can recall, I hadn't thought very much about the time that I would be called up and what I would do. But after that, during that second half of 1916, I did begin to think a lot about it.

And I began more strongly than ever to think that I couldn't possibly reconcile my conscience and join the army in any shape or form. This was entirely my own personal conviction. My mother, though a devout Christian, didn't object to war and didn't press me in any way what to do about it though she would have liked me, I think, to join the army. My father, though an earnest socialist by that time, also didn't influence me. He left it to me to decide what I would do. So this was entirely my own conviction that was growing in strength that it was not a Christian thing to join the army.

After I had left George Heriot's School I decided to work in my father's business, Aitken Dott & Son, the well known picture salesmen and artists' colourmen. I did so for several months, working in the shop, making lists of etchings and so on, just the work that came to hand. I suppose at that time I must vaguely have thought that I might go on and work in Aitken Dott & Son. I'm not really quite sure if I saw very far ahead then. Well, my work at the shop was interrupted finally by my call-up and arrest.

Well, the next day after I had been to Glencorse Barracks I did turn up at Kinghorn Barracks. And there I felt 'Now I must come to the crunch with this business', which I felt extraordinarily embarrassing, because I was most earnest in my belief that war was wrong—wrong on Christian principles. But how just to make the break I found very difficult.

Well, the young new recruits were called out and put on parade. And I stood aside and wouldn't go when all the other recruits fell into line. The sergeant turned just blue in the face with fury as I stood there. He asked me what I meant. I stuck it out and said, no, I didn't believe in war and wasn't going to join the parade. Well, then he marched two men out of the file to take me away to the guard-room and await court martial. That being over, having taken the plunge I felt completely restored to my confidence.

I had a very interesting time in the Kinghorn guard-room waiting for a court martial, discussing my stand with the other fellows there. These other fellows were the riff-raff of Glasgow and other cities—some of them quite sympathetic to what I was doing, others just sarcastic and furious. I had about a week to wait in that place, a few days of great interest, quite restoring my feeling that I was doing the right thing. You can imagine how new all this was to me, coming from a very comfortable home in Colinton. I met there in the guard-room rough Glasgow men who were in for desertion or for various crimes. And they were interested in what I said. Most of them couldn't agree with me. I think they nearly all thought I was there because I was afraid to go to the war. But we got very conversational and discussed all this kind of thing and I heard all their old army songs, which mocked at war and the part that the authorities played in it.

Well, in due time my court martial came. It was a very civil and considerate affair. The three army officers there, who were very courteous, tried to argue with me as to why I should be a conscientious objector when the country needed me. They asked me all sorts of foolish questions and I gave the best answers I could. I remember I was able to argue with them that this wasn't what they were there for. They were there to know whether I was a true conscientious objector or not.

However, they decided eventually that I was a conscientious objector and would have to undergo a sentence of imprisonment. I was then sentenced to serve three months of hard labour at Wormwood Scrubs—and what beyond that, I didn't know.

Now this sort of thing for me in 1917 was much easier than the earlier COs had had. By that time the government had come pretty much to a regular way of dealing with us. We knew almost in advance just what would be done. But the earlier men had had a far, far harder time. They weren't only court martialled. They were sent out to France with the very real possibility of being shot there because they disobeyed an order. I believe it's true that none of them were actually shot. But they went out there fully believing they might be—and some of them must have been very, very near it.

Well, for me it was comparatively easy going. I was sent from Kinghorn Barracks to Wormwood Scrubs. A couple of friendly soldiers took me down by train. I remember that journey very well indeed. I just sat beside these two soldiers like an ordinary passenger in the carriage. They allowed me to slip out of the train at Carlisle and get some chocolate without either of them coming with me. They were very civil to me. I don't think anybody knew I was a conscientious objector. There was nobody there to make a demonstration of any kind.

Well, we arrived at Wormwood Scrubs and there things, I found, began to get very hard. I was ushered into that huge place, feeling very, very lost and far away from home. That was the homesick time that was perhaps the most difficult of all.

We had to do first of all a month's solitary confinement there. That was rather a miserable time, really wearisome and trying. The only thing we had to read was the Bible, which was left in every cell. As I was an ardent reader of the Bible in those days I found that very helpful. Again I was young and healthy and could take things so much better. The experience there was perhaps easier for me than it must have been for many of my colleagues.

There were a good many conscientious objectors in Wormwood Scrubs at that time. And of course lots of other prisoners on different charges. One thing that's very vivid to me: I can remember that there must have been a number of conscientious objectors from Scotland within the neighbourhood of the block where I was. In the hours of the day, and even more in the hours of the evening and night I would hear these men whistling Scottish tunes to each other. One would take it up from another. One of them would whistle 'The Banks of Loch Lomond' or something like that. And away from the other end of the corridor you would hear it replied to by some other tune—'Annie Laurie', or something like that, coming from one cell or another. The warders didn't like it—they were furious! They felt this was communicating between prisoners. But they couldn't do a thing about it. So there was this camaraderie that somehow got going even in that place. I didn't whistle myself: for one thing I wasn't a very good whistler, and I was very shy in those days. I listened but didn't take any part at all.

My own warder, who was a flat-footed old chap who must have been a retired policeman, I think, and about to retire, used to say to me—because he got talking eventually: 'You know, I'd rather have a dozen of our old usual type prisoners than one of you COs. You're just a nuisance to the whole lot of us.' They couldn't make much of us at all.

After the first four weeks of solitary confinement we were given a choice of book to read. One of the prisoners, under escort with a warder, came round with a trayful of books from the library. I remember I picked a history of the Thirty Years' War of all strange things, because I had wanted something serious to read. I can remember that book yet. I was greatly impressed. Later on I got Charles Dickens' *Nicholas Nickleby*.

As the time passed after the first four weeks of solitary confinement I began to find things easier. I think that was really because I was young and fit and settling down and had some reading, which made a great difference. But I got to know from many of my colleagues afterwards, because we couldn't talk then but afterwards, what a hard time they had. They'd left wives and children and so on at home and some of them weren't so young and weren't so strong and were perhaps more sensitive to it all than I was. Because I had no reason to fear. I had a very happy family at home who backed up my attitude. Many of my fellow conscientious objectors, however, had left people at home who were hard up, in penury. They couldn't subscribe any money to their keep at all. They got the mere pittance of some kind of allowance, of shillings a week, to try and live on. These men were very unhappy there in Wormwood Scrubs.

Well, the time went by. It wasn't a very great experience. But you're resilient at that age and you don't mind really too much how you are getting along. There were a good many Scotsmen. I don't know if this is true, but I have the impression there were a bigger proportion of Scotsmen among the conscientious objectors at that time. But at any rate in the halls of Wormwood Scrubs there must have been quite a number of Scottish COs and we were more or less kept together from the prisoners who were there for other reasons.

We got a pretty low diet and we felt pretty hungry on it. It was very monotonous but just adequate. We always got our porridge, morning and evening, and a little milk with it but without any salt in it. There was salt in our cells and we could have put it in. But these Englishmen didn't know to put salt in their porridge! They must have had some of the most awful stuff to eat. I remember one time when one of the men was called away to the governor's house and left his cell in disorder. The warder told me, he says, 'Here, go in and tidy up that cell.' And I found the man's plate of porridge there. And, you know, we were hungry. It reminds me now how hungry we were when I saw that plate of porridge. I started to devour his porridge at once. I took my first spoonful of it—and it was awful. It was unsalted and nearly uneatable. And then I saw his salt and put in a good spoonful of the salt and stirred it up. It was fine. I never had a better meal of porridge in my life. The English didn't know what to do with it.

Talking of the diet, there's another point comes back to my mind. We were allowed a certain measured quantity of bread for the day. We got this cut out. It was a favourite ploy among lots of the prisoners to claim that the bread was under weight. So they had to have it weighed. This gave a chance for people sometimes to get talking with each other while this procedure was gone through. The warders knew very well that this was a ploy. But we used constantly to challenge that the bread was under weight—which indeed it proved sometimes to be. It gave people a chance to see each other and whisper a message to each other—all of which wasn't perhaps very serious, but it lightened the time and annoyed the warders. My very nice old flat-footed warder used to say to us, 'You know, they talk of the patience of Job. But Job, if he'd had this job to do, would have given up altogether.'

Well, then there was the exercise period. We had to trek round this large circle, one after another. It was pretty wearisome. I remember being surprised how tired I felt. Whether this was because we were on a low diet or whether it was a nervous thing, I hardly know. But I used to feel sometimes I would just drop on my knees while I was walking round there. And yet we kept going. We had to keep a certain distance from the man in front and behind. We couldn't speak and this monotonous walking round lasted about an hour—and then back to the cell again.

Well, after the term of my sentence at Wormwood Scrubs was finished we were offered the choice of doing what they called Work of National Importance if we would go to one of the Home Office settlements, one of which was at the old convict prison at Dartmoor, another at Wakefield. And if we would agree to do this Work of National Importance we were under restraint in that we weren't allowed to leave but had relative freedom compared to a prison. Well, most of us accepted this. I agreed to go to Dartmoor.

But there was a fine body of men with whom I couldn't agree then or now but whom I have a great admiration for, whom we came to know as the Absolutists. They wouldn't take the Home Office scheme because they said, 'This is coming to truck with a government whom we are utterly up against. They've no right to have the war. They've no right to send us in here. They've no right to bargain with us to send us anywhere else.' And they stuck it out to the end of the war, there in Wormwood Scrubs under very hard conditions, rather than go to the relatively easy life of these settlements. These were the Absolutists.[89]

Well, I didn't see anything to it if I got a chance to go to better conditions. I had no great minding what the government thought about it. And I went to Dartmoor— that must have been about July 1917—and found it a most interesting place. It was the old convict prison adapted for a Home Office settlement where we were under restraint in that we weren't allowed to leave but had relative freedom compared to a prison. The place was entirely cleared of its former prisoners. A great many of them went to the war and those who didn't must have been moved elsewhere, because the place was entirely given up to conscientious objectors. They used the term 'Settlement', they didn't use the term 'Prison'. It became the Dartmoor Settlement for conscientious objectors. There I met a large number of fellow COs who proved to be a most interesting body of people for me to meet, I being quite inexperienced and meeting people from different backgrounds that were a complete eye-opener to me.

I would say some 300 or 400 gathered there in the Dartmoor Settlement who were all conscientious objectors but who were conscientious objectors for all sorts of different reasons. We had there earnest Christians, we had Quakers, we had men from the rest of the smaller, extreme Christian elements, such as the Jehovah's Witnesses and the Christadelphians and the Seventh Day Adventists—bodies like that, of whom I had never heard before, earnest men, believing that what they did was right, objecting to the war on religious grounds.

They would be a slight minority of our numbers, because the greater number were committed socialists, many of whom—not all—were atheists, but who were all united by being utterly committed socialists of various brands, as we would say now perhaps Left and Right within the socialist movement, though we didn't talk perhaps much then of Left and Right. Of course, the Communist Party hadn't been formed at that time but I know that many of my friends would have certainly, and no doubt later did, become communists. On the other hand many of them were broad-based socialists who believed in socialism for its social justice but were not otherwise strong political people. But they all objected strongly to the war on socialist grounds. All these men got on well and were interested in each other's views. They were tolerant and good talkers, all men—or nearly all men—of ability. It was quite remarkable to be among this group.

Well, I got talking with all these men and made very good friends out of many of them. Naturally, the discussions we got into interested me greatly. I had the background of my father's teaching, who was an earnest socialist. And I met these men who could discuss it all with great knowledge. A great many of them came from Scotland, and I naturally got to know those better: they had so much in common. They were fine characters. Perhaps a majority of them came from Ayrshire and that region round about there. You know, it was a great place there for men of independent thought. It was the Burns country. Though this was such a good long time after Burns' own days, they had the tradition there of independent thought. They were strong independent men of socialist outlook. I can remember many of these men.

Perhaps the most outstanding of all was an Ayrshire man from Newmilns, Bill Deans, a tailor. He was a radical socialist of a very, very earnest and high idealistic type, a very fine man. He was himself a gifted man, a poet, a good speaker, a good organiser, and a tremendous enthusiast for the aims of socialism. He had many and many a story to tell us all. We would often meet in his cell, which of course was quite permissible there at Dartmoor, and have evening talks with him in which he gave us his recollections. He was an enthusiast and a poet and a real emotional and fine type of man. He loved art, he loved poetry, but above all he loved freedom. Bill was a great Burns scholar and about the finest reciter of Burns' poetry that I have ever heard, because he had the dialect of course natural to him. He lived there almost in the Burns country. He used to recite the Burns poetry to me. To hear him recite that poem 'To a Mouse', with the feeling that he put into it, especially that last verse, when Burns says:

> But och! I backward cast my e'e
> On prospects drear!
> An' forward, tho' I canna see,
> I guess an' fear!

The meaning Bill put into that, and his 'But och! I backward cast my e'e' was really an experience to me, although I knew my Burns and enjoyed it. Bill wrote poetry himself, I believe. I remember some odd bits of it that he liked.

He told me of some of the rugged times he'd been through. When he was arrested they came and took him from his home, and his old mother, who was as staunch as himself, saw him off. As he went down the stairs of his tenement under police escort his mother shouted down over the bannisters: 'Aye, on ye go, Bill! Dinnae gie the buggers an inch!' Well, they put him in Barlinnie prison in Glasgow. He would tell me how he was so fed up with all this he left his cell all untidy and wouldn't make up his bed, which was against the rules in Barlinnie. The warder looked in on Bill and said, 'Here, ma man, you'll be getting into trouble.' 'And what the hell d'ye think ah'm in now ?' says Bill. He was like that, just all this rugged but fine and idealistic nature. There was a warm heart full of affection in that man.[90]

Another man I recall so vividly was Walter Bissett of Kilmarnock. So many of them were from that district of Scotland. Walter Bissett was a fine, intelligent, well educated man and an earnest socialist as so many of them were then. He didn't go very much to the Left. He was also keen on literary things, a keen Shakespeare scholar. He loved his Shakespeare and he used to recite the Shakespeare sonnets very, very finely.

Walter didn't think much of the English. I always remember his story. They questioned him at his tribunal, which happened to be in England. He must have been taken to England. And they asked him what his trade was. He said he was a journeyman baker. 'Ah,' they said, 'well, we can't let you carry on with that because,' they said, 'if you're a journeyman baker you'll be going from door to door spreading your views to all the people.' They didn't know the meaning of the word journeyman. They thought it meant he went on journeys with his bread and bakery things.

One of my greatest friends at Dartmoor was a man called Dick Ashley from Norwich. He was a shoemaker operative by trade. He was an enthusiastic and rather left-wing socialist. He was a great idealist, a musician, a fine singer. He sang in the Norwich Choral Union or Operatic Society and they had travelled to Canada singing the Grand Opera stuff which he knew. He could sing screeds of it off by heart. He was also a great enthusiast for Shakespeare, which he could sing or recite by screeds too. I got to know Dick Ashley very well. He was a fine man, one of the most warm-hearted people I ever met. As a very left-wing socialist he couldn't stand Ramsay MacDonald and these people that he thought were just half-baked. I am sure Dick Ashley later became a communist. He used to call me The Youngster. He told me all about his fiancée Flo, and he would set her photograph there in his little cell in front of him and sing to her screeds from *Samson and Delilah* and all the operas.

I was one of the youngest conscientious objectors at Dartmoor. One of the others that moved me very much was a young lad, he wasn't so very much older than me. He was called Peter Brown, from somewhere in Ayrshire, I'm not sure of the exact place. He was a milkman. But he had tuberculosis. He knew it and we all knew it. He used to have temperatures and fever while he was there. We all knew that he was a very ill man. Well, the authorities couldn't have cared less. Peter Brown had left behind him at home a wife and small children in the utmost poverty and he worried over them no end. We got paid 4/8d. a day—I suppose for the work we did, which really wasn't worth 4/8d. a day I shouldn't have thought. But if you had dependants you could send back 3/- of that and retain 1/8d. for yourself. And Peter Brown used sometimes to be almost in tears about his conditions at home and that kind of thing. I used to get talking with him. He was a tender hearted soul, much grieved about his family. It was all about his family that worried him. He knew they were very hard up. I hadn't known how people lived until he told me many details of how they were trying to make do on just that tiny pittance. It used to bring tears to his eyes to think of them at home. Peter, with his lung tuberculosis, was very ill and he ought to have been in a sanatorium. I am quite sure the hardships of Dartmoor made his condition deteriorate greatly. He died soon after he got back home to Ayrshire.

There were one or two of my fellow conscientious objectors at Dartmoor who suffered from ill-health and I am quite sure that there were others who said little about it. We probably didn't know much of what was going on.

Another man that I remember well was a leader among us. His name was C H Norman. He was a lawyer of some standing. He made a great impression on all of us. He was a good organiser and a good speaker. He learned to study the tragedies and needs of many people who were undergoing hardship at Dartmoor. There was one man in particular who was a diabetic and who wasn't getting his proper treatment. C H Norman took this matter up and brought it before the authorities and struggled until he got the proper treatment for this man. But better treatment came too late to save this man, whose name I forget now. He died while we were there. He was a fine man, Norman, and we all looked up to him. He was very active in the socialist movement afterwards and outstanding in the movement against war and for peace.[91]

Another man I remember quite well was a quite different character. He was a young man, surname Francis, an artist and art teacher. I only knew later that he came from Edinburgh. He organised for us a little art class. We used to meet there and somebody would volunteer to act as a model. Francis would be the teacher. We had this little art class two or three times a week and I took this up and did my sketches and learned from this bright and lively young man Francis. He came back to Edinburgh again after the war and was a teacher, I believe, in the Art College there. But that class was a delightful little episode among the harder things at Dartmoor at that time.

Among the lighter things that I did then was to try sketching portraits of some of my friends, which I wasn't very good at but it served the purpose well enough. One man that I particularly remember was a religious objector who was older than most of us. I cannot remember his name but he was a member, I think, of the Plymouth Brethren. I sketched a portrait of him which he sent back to his wife. He told me afterwards with extraordinary feeling: 'You know, Dott, when my wife saw that portrait she burst into tears. And, you know, I cannot really tell you whether it was because it was like me or because it was not.' I remember his extreme eagerness, that touched me very much indeed, about the strict truth which was so typical of these religious men. He didn't want to praise the portrait more than it was worth.

During the summer of 1918 I went out a lot, because we were free to go out onto Dartmoor. I would go out walks in the country and do sketches round there. I remember in particular one sepia sketch of the Dartmoor Prison, seen from a little distance, which I found very interesting. I sent these things home. My father was interested in my efforts at art and painting pictures.

At Dartmoor living was quite harsh. We slept on boards with a very thin mattress. But we got quite accustomed to that—or I did anyway. I think some of the older men found some of that part of it very difficult. And of course we were in the old convict prison with stone floors and inconvenient ways. If we'd run away as we could easily have done they'd just have fetched us back. So there was no great point in that. We could wander over the moor when we weren't at work and lead a comparatively easy life. I say comparatively easy because physically it wasn't very easy. And we were given what they called Work of National Importance. Nothing could be further from the truth. It was just anything to get us there out of the way and keep us safe.

While we were at Dartmoor we were divided into different groups and sent on different work, supposed to be of national importance, such as digging drains for water courses and things like that, some of which were very hard labour for those of us who were older and not so fit, but which I as a young man really quite enjoyed, except in the severe winter weather. I had to pass the winter of 1917-18 at Dartmoor and as you can imagine it was sometimes very severe. I remember one time when I was walking back from Princetown to the prison against the bitter blizzard and wind when I really honestly wondered whether I would ever get through it or whether I would drop down dead. It was a severe place.

The work group that I was in was called the Mis Tor group, and we were there digging some sort of water course or drain of some several hundred yards. I can hardly remember what it was for. But when we broke off at lunchtime we were able to have meetings in a sort of shed that was for the purpose. We got up great lively discussions. We made great use of lunch-hour time. We discussed socialism and the pros and cons of what we would do under different circumstances and that kind of thing. It was a very lively lunch-hour that we had then.

It's very strange to me to think now—it shows how innocent I was and how little knowledge I had of what was going on—that just about that time the two great Russian Revolutions, first the Kerensky Revolution, which had happened just about the time I was arrested in Edinburgh, then the Bolshevik Revolution in October 1917, which had happened while I was there at Dartmoor, I was hardly aware of. It hadn't made the impact on me that of course it made on all of us later on. But these men at Dartmoor were vitally interested in all that and they managed to get the information somehow or other.[92]

So I became greatly influenced by men like Bill Deans and Dick Ashley, and I had to think about and discuss these views. Well, that led to my changing from being a religious objector to war to becoming really a socialist objector to war. By the time I was discharged after the end of the war I was really a convinced socialist and something of a freethinker as regards religion. I remember so well our fine Colinton minister Mr Marchbanks being really interested in my state of mind in that way. Well, I went to him in the earnestness of my conviction to do the right thing and told him that I felt bound to leave the church because I no longer really believed in church doctrine. I had meant—before all these events and my calling up to the war—to become a minister. But by the time I was discharged I realised I couldn't possibly be a minister because I didn't believe in the detailed creed of the Christian religion. I only believed in my intense admiration for the moral teaching of Christ but without believing in the orthdox religious teaching of the church. So I went and saw Mr Marchbanks and he reluctantly agreed that I should cease to be a member of the church.

Well, after some time on this Mis Tor work group at Dartmoor I was transferred to what they called the harness room. This was the place where the governor of the prison kept his coach and horses. I was under the regular attendant for these things to assist him and I had to clean and polish the harness. I learned to harness horses. I learned to help in grooming them. I also had to milk cows in that establishment. All of which were most interesting and new accomplishments for me. It was quite an eye-opener to a different type of life from what I used to have.

We were free to go down to Princetown, the nearest place to Dartmoor. The relatives of many conscientious objectors who lived in the south of England would come up and be able to visit them in Princetown. I sometimes went down with a friend, though I knew nobody there and was introduced to some of the relatives of some of my fellow COs in that place. We could get a meal down there but only for limited hours: we had to be back again at the Dartmoor Prison.

I can't remember that the local people either paid very much heed to us or showed any great opposition to us at all, perhaps partly because they had got pretty used by that time to the group being there. It was walking back from Princetown, which was about two miles from the prison, that I met this severe blizzard where I felt almost so exhausted that I really quite seriously wondered would I ever make it. The summer time of course was a very different story. I was able to roam the scenery of Dartmoor and enjoy the larks singing and the wonderful conditions that Dartmoor can offer in the summer.

I must have been about fifteen months or so in Dartmoor, because towards the end of my stay there and actually shortly before the end of the war we were offered to be allowed to go home if we would undertake to do Work of National Importance such as, say, gardening and horticulture and that kind of thing. I think this would be September or October 1918. I accepted this offer because a man in Colinton, where my home was, was a religious objector to war—though too old to be a conscientious objector like us—and offered to give me employment in his nursery garden there which would satisfy the criteria of Work of National Importance. So I got my liberty from Dartmoor then and was given a pass on the railway to get home. I remember that journey well. I had to find train times and everything myself and managed to make the train journey and arrive in Edinburgh and get out to my beloved Colinton, which then had a little railway service—no buses in those days. I got a great welcome home. It was really an extraordinary homecoming. I remember so well how soft my bed, which was a perfectly ordinary bed, felt after the hard boards of Dartmoor which I'd got quite used to.

I then had to undertake this work in the nursery garden of Mr Thomas Downs at Colinton. He was very kind in taking me on, because I don't think he really needed my services but he wanted to help a fellow objector to war. I had another ex-CO who joined me there—a man I got to know and like very much indeed. His name was Bertie but I can't for the life of me remember his second name. He was a chemistry student. We had many an interesting discussion on our views as regards objecting to warfare. We had a fellow employee who was a delightful man, an elderly signalman on the railway, who used to come out after working eight hours as a signalman and dig in the nursery garden and chat with us all and tell us of his experiences among which were how he regularly knitted bed socks in his signal box. He used to give them to his friends, myself included. I have many happy recollections of that man and his work in the nursery garden.

Well, the Armistice came in November 1918. It took a little time for me to be allowed to leave this work in the nursery garden at Colinton. But some months later—I just cannot remember exactly when—I was free. As I had given up the idea of being a minister altogether I searched for something—a work of kindness and compassion to my fellow men that would be the nearest thing possible to being a minister. And that—and partly because my brother had then become a surgeon— led me to choose the medical profession.[93] So my decision to become a doctor really arose out of my experiences as a conscientious objector during the First World War. I tried to join the University of Edinburgh to become a medical student but was told that because priority must be given to the returning soldiers I couldn't join then.

Well, I took out an Arts course at Edinburgh University, starting in October 1919. I did about a year of an Arts course, really to fill in time, and found it extremely interesting. Finally, in the following October of 1920 I was able to start my medical course.

Well, that lasted five years and I qualified in Medicine in 1925. After that I did much of the usual kind of thing. I did several appointments in the Edinburgh Royal Infirmary in different parts of the wards there, to really finish my medical education. After that—there was no National Health Service in those days and one had to make one's living—I put up my plate in the west of Edinburgh, first of all in a little street called Eltringham Gardens in Gorgie, just at a venture. I soon began to build up a little private practice just by getting known in the district. After about a year or two I moved over to Western Terrace in Murrayfield and further built up my private practice, which lasted me on till about 1938.

Now during that time I was doing my best to foster a specialty in the work for children, to become a child health doctor. I attended the Sick Children's Hospital in a voluntary capacity, helping in their outpatient clinics. In 1936 I got appointed— which was my great ambition—to become a member of the staff of the Sick Children's Hospital. All this of course at that time was entirely on a voluntary basis and without pay, so that I still required my practice to make a living.

Well, then came the Second World War and that made no immediate difference to me until the advent of the National Health Service in 1948. That immediately made a great difference to me because under the NHS I would be paid for my work in the Sick Children's Hospital. So I was enabled to give up my private practice altogether and become a full-time children's consultant in the Sick Children's. From that time onward I was entirely a specialist in sick children's care.

I don't think after I was freed from Dartmoor I personally suffered any sort of victimisation at all. I must have been perhaps rather unusual in that way. I was delayed in my entry, as I've mentioned, to the Medical Faculty. And by that time things began to be forgotten a little. I don't suppose most of my fellow students in the Faculty of Medicine knew that I had been a conscientious objector. It's not a thing that I talked about. I was far from inclined to boast of it or anything like that or to enter into discussions of it. I just didn't meet the circumstances that would lead to any victimisation. But that wasn't true of all. I believe that many conscientious objectors had rather a hard time afterwards. If it was known they hadn't been in the army they were discriminated against. It was the same for that matter for people who were of German origin. Very good friends of mine were terribly hard treated simply because they were of German origin. The prejudices were so strong and bitter.

Most certainly I've continued to feel entirely convinced that it was right to oppose war to the extent of refusing to join the army. I've never wavered on that— if possible I've become more and more convinced that that was so.

In the Second World War there were certain differences. I wouldn't then perhaps have taken the religious objection that I had in the First World War because my views, through the experience of all this and just through growing up and read-ing, had gradually changed on that. Although I remained an earnest Christian as regards Christian behaviour I'd quite dropped my belief in Christian doctrine in many ways, in the strict sense of the church teaching. So that I don't think that I would have been a conscientious objector on religious grounds in the Second World War. I think I probably would on socialist grounds, because even though it was a Hitler war and the whole set-up was very different from the First World War I still believed that war was wrong and led to a stultifying of results in the end. I would rather have seen, if it was possible, a pacifist non-combatant attitude, even towards the Hitler war. But it didn't arise, you see, because by that time I was a consultant physician in the Sick Children's Hospital and as many of the staff had been sent away I was ordered to remain at home and staff the Hospital. So that I was never called up to go abroad. I think probably I would have gone in a medical capacity. I certainly wouldn't have gone in a fighting capacity.

There is one point that I feel I would like very much to emphasise in connection with the conscientious objectors of the First World War. One sometimes hears it spoken of as though some of them had a fairly light time, or some of them perhaps rather light-heartedly undertook such a position. Now my impression of these men of whom I met a great many at Dartmoor, and men of all sorts of different types of conviction, is that that they were men of tremendous earnestness, of very fine idealism, men prepared to suffer a great deal for their views, as indeed many of them did suffer a great deal. They were men of the very finest calibre, of great ability, and of very great earnestness whether it was in the line of religious conviction or of socialist conviction, men of the highest quality and most devoted feeling.

William Murray

The night war was declared in August 1914 we played the final o' a football tournament in Denbeath and we won the tournament. And the whole team joined the army the next day, the whole team. 'Your King and Country Need You' and all this sort of stuff—patriotism, patriotism, it wisn't the sense o' excitement, it wis patriotism.

Ah wis in the Territorials—I joined the Fife Artillery before the war. Well, some o' ma pals were in the Territorials and ah gave a false age. I said I was eighteen and I was only sixteen. I didnae join tae get a holiday, no' really. A lot o' ma pals were members o' the battery, the Fife battery. It wis 15 pounders, field artillery. They had a drill hall down there in Leven, and the drill hall is still down there.

I was born in the Newton o' Falkland in February 1898 and ah came to Denbeath as a child, tae The Links, what they term The Links o' Buckhaven. That wis where the Wellesley pit was. And ah stayed in The Links o' Buckhaven durin' ma school days.

Ma father was a slater. In fact, he got killed. He fell off a roof in Buckhaven and got killed. I was jist at school then, I'd be under twelve years o' age. Ah had two sisters and a brother. I was the oldest o' the family. I was the breadwinner.

Ah liked the school but straight away when I left the school ah went down the pit. That was ma first job. It must have been 1912. Ah wis fourteen. Ah worked in a pit called the Isabella. It wis jist at Muiredge, Buckhaven. It wis owned by the Fife Coal Company. Ah jist filled the tubs and drew them out the road and pulled them down the hill—filling and drawing.

Ah wis only three weeks started wi' the man ah worked wi' when he got killed. At that time they had tae lie down and hole the coal, then they bored a hole, they bored the shot and blew the coal doon. The rances gave way and the coal come ower on top o' him. The rances were the props that held the coal up the time they were lyin' holin' the coal. Ah had come out wi' ma full tub, run it down the brae, got an empty, come in, and when ah come in the place was in darkness. That's what had happened.

Oh, shocked! It made me feel ah wouldnae go back tae the pit. But I had tae go back.

Ah worked jist about a couple o' year at fillin'and drawin'. Then ah got a job in the Rosie pit and it wis strippin' coal. Machines cut it and ye jist stripped it. I wis aboot sixteen or seventeen when ah wis doin' that.

When the war broke out I was called up at once. Ah went tae France in September. We were at the battle o' the Marne.[94] And we were at the battle of Loos in 1915. Loos wis pretty awful, in this sense that we were outnumbered and our guns were droppin' on our own trenches wi' the lack of range. Ah dunno why that was. It was 15-pounders in the original Fife battery before we got the 18-pounders. The Germans had everything up to date. And a lot o' our people were killed wi' our shells droppin' in our own trenches. And then we were heavily outnumbered. Oh, it was a costly battle that one! Some dead men there.

Ah wis invalided home from Loos, wounded in the legs. Well, it wis a funny thing. We yaised tae go down tae a wee village for groceries and things o' that description. Ah wis down there at this village gettin' these groceries and there werenae a sound tae be heard. And all of a sudden when ah wis crossin' a ploughed field *AWHIZZZZAAACHH!* And a shell must have burst just quite near me. Ah believe if it had been on the hard road I'd have been killed. Ah must have lain there for a while because the explosion had rendered me unconscious. The ambulance people, the RAMC, they got me lyin'. Ah wis sent home.

Ah wis in Beckett's Park Hospital in Leeds for a long time and then ah wis sent tae convalescent in Scarborough. Ah wisnae badly wounded. It wis jist shrapnel. In Scarborough there wis a house and big grounds, and the man who owned it wis a major-general. Ah wis there for a long time, in fact ah wis there when the Germans shelled Scarborough from the sea.[95]

Then I went out tae France again. I wis at the battle o' the Somme in 1916. There were more men killed every morning before breakfast time there than was in the whole o' the Falklands war. We were wi' the battery, further up frae Albert. They reckoned there was over 600,000 British soldiers killed on the Somme, 60,000 casualties on the first day.

After the Somme I transferred into the Argyll and Sutherland Highlanders. I wanted tae go into the infantry, well, they wanted us tae—this underground minin' business. Now ye were minin' below the German positions and ye could hear the Germans minin' towards us. And it got on your bloody nerves. You never knew when you were goin' to go up in the air. Well, there were engineers attached to us. But they asked for ex-miners, ye see, tae assist. So ah volunteered, as an ex-miner.

I was in the battles o' Cambrai and Arras[96] and I was at Ypres, aye, ah wis at bloody Ypres. That was a terrible place. Och, if you stepped off the duck board ye wis drowned. The Belgiums flooded the place.

And ye couldnae dig down. And they built pill boxes. Whenever ye dug about a couple or three fit down ye struck water. The result was ye couldnae dig trenches and ye had tae get intae these bloody concrete pill boxes. And the Germans used tae hammer them, ah could tell you.

We were inspected by the king. The king wis a wee man, a wee bandy legged man, and they put a kilt on him. And we stood about six hours in the rain waitin' on the salute.

Lieutenant Lauder, Harry Lauder's son, he was in the Argylls, too. Oh, he wis a bugger. He wis very unpopular. In fact, he wis shot in the back. Ah mean, he used tae wear a raincoat and ye didnae know if he was an officer or no. Ah think he did that deliberately. And ye maybe passed him and didnae salute and he would grab you. Ye would get a fortnight's detention for no' salutin' an officer. Oh, he was very unpopular. He wis shot in the back a'right.

He had no confidence in his men at all. Ah mean, he jist treated them as outcasts. Ah don't know whether he was class conscious or not. Ah didnae see why he should have been, because his faither wis only a comedian. But he was killed on Christmas Day on the Somme. We were going over the top and he was shot in the back. The boys must have known. It wis somebody in his own unit. I never had any dealings wi' him but the men all knew he had been shot in the back, oh, aye, they all knew. Well, if anybody is shot in the back it was deliberate.[97]

So I was at the battles of Arras and Cambrai. Arras was in April 1917, and Cambrai—that wis when the Yankees came out. We were attached tae the 6th Division, and the first thing we got from the Yankees was, 'Where is this goddamned shootin' gallery?' They wanted tae know where the shootin' gallery wis. They werenae bloody long in findin' oot where the bloody shootin' gallery wis. 'Cause there wis an attack and they were centre battalion and efter they went over they were supposed tae take their hand grenades and do thir dug-outs, 'cause the Germans they used to get behind us. And the Yankees didnae do that. And the Germans captured the bloody lot o' them. And oor boys on the left and right were left exposed. There were aboot 300 killed due to this action o' theirs.

Ah fought in France for the rest o' the war. Ah wis at the battle of Passchendaele, too—Third Battle o' Ypres. It wis a hell of a place. In fact, there wis nae nice places at that time![98]

1918 ah wis demobilised. I went back in the pit—the Wellesley, at Methil. Ah wis strippin' coal. Johnny Brown he was the manager. Ah can always mind ah wis at the bottom o' what they term the run, the bottom o' the coal run. Ye see, they had the pans and ye stripped the coal and put it in the pans and the pans jigged it down. Ah wis strippin' at the bottom o' thir pans and one of their well known men was attendin' the Wellesley, ye know, high men, and him and Johnny Brown the manager was talkin' at the bottom o' the run. He said tae Johnny Brown, 'By the way, Mr Brown, how many men work in the Wellesley?' And Johnny Brown the manager shouted: 'Half o' them!' Oh, he was a terrible man!

Ah worked at the Wellesley for about a year. Then ah went tae England tae play First Division football—Coventry. Before that ah had played Juvenile and Junior. Ah played for a team you called Wellesley Juniors. And they took about six or seven people to Celtic and one—Dominic Currie—he went tae Hearts. There wis the two O'Donnells, Hugh and Frank. Hugh wis eventually an international centre forward. Frank died, he died quick because he had a tumour on the brain and the doctor said it wis through heading the ball. At that time the ball wis heavy, ye know, heavier than it is now. And then ye had heavy boots. Joe Cowan and Gene McFarlane went tae Celtic tae and Jimmy O'Donnell went to Tottenham. That wis a' oot o' the Junior team. They were practically all miners.

The O'Donnells, their father wis a bookie in Denbeath.[99]

Ah signed for Coventry from that Junior team. Ah believe that Pat Currie, the secretary o' the Wellesley Juniors, said that if ah had hung on for another three weeks ah wid ha' went tae the Celtic, too. We had played for a Juvenile team called Denbeath Celtic.

Ah wis supposed tae be wi' Coventry for four year. But what happened was, ee werenae supposed tae go out on a Friday night, because of the match on the Saturday. And ah went away tae a dance in Coventry, and there was a girl there and ah had a dance or two wi' her. She was wi' a boyfriend. At that time, in the old fashioned style, at the finish o' the dance it was the Ladies' Choice. So she come across tae give me Ladies' Choice. Of course, ah wis only twenty or so at that time. Here her boyfriend come across and he called me a Scotch bastard. So ah let him have it. And they sent for the police. Ah wis hauled in front o' the Coventry club board and ah was suspended for six weeks without pay. Ah could still play but ah was tae get no pay. So ah said, 'Tae hell, ah'm comin' home.' So ah come home 'tae Leven, tae ma mother. Coventry wouldnae give me ma papers. They put me out o' football a'thegither. Ah had only played two years wi' them.

I was unemployed for a while then ah got a job in the Leven colliery. Ah wis there when the 1921 lock-out came on. They withdrew the fires. The pit was flooded, of course.[100]

Ah wis on the committee o' the miners' union. I was branch secretary and then on the soup kitchens ah wis on the committee—in fact, ah wis in charge. We had tae organise the soup kitchen in Leven. It wis in the washing-house, just where the sawmill used to be, where people used tae do their washin'. They jist cleaned out a boiler, cleaned it out perfectly and used it as a soup kitchen. They werenae allowed tae wash in it.

That was all the food that we had, the soup. But we wis well fed, mind. We went round and scrounged the food, stole it from farms. And then we went to the butchers and they gave us all the bones and things o' that description. We made pots o' soup wi' the bones. There wis a lot o' support from the shopkeepers and farmers.

Then ah wis on a concert party. We went out to the various places as a concert party.

After the '21 lock-out ah never got back to Leven colliery. Ah wis victimised for two years. Ah didnae get a job for two years.

It wis a difficult time. Ah got married in the November after the lock-out. But we were fortunate. The wife's mother was able tae support us. Her father always had a contract goin' in the pits and he had a bit extra money. And then we lived wi' heez mother, an old lady frae Dundee. We lived in her room. But she died so we got the house. The rent was only 3/6d. a week. We had 24 bob a week on the dole for the two o' us. Then the first o' our family was born a year after we were married. But ah got a job in the Wellesley in 1923 and ah wis there till the 1926 lock-out.

Well, my recollections of the 1926 General Strike is very clear. We knew that the position was that the miners were being treated in a very niggardly fashion as far as the government was concerned and we had no option but to strike.

We were a hundred per cent solid. It was practically no use authorising pickets at Leven No. 1 colliery because there were no man made any attempt for to return to work during the whole period of the miners' strike.

During the General Strike my job was to organise an office in the High Street in Leven and no lorry or truck of any description could come past the pickets without authorisation from that office. My committee controlled Leven. Nobody could pass through on any pretext unless they had a permit from that office.

Of course, when the General Strike was terminated the office was no longer used. But the next thing I had to do was to organise for the purpose of feeding the miners because there was no Social Security or any help at all given to the wives and the children of the miners at that time. Ma specific job at that time was to organise the soup kitchens and provide finance. This was done successfully for a period of over seven months. The traders of Leven were pretty good and also the outlying farmers who supplied us with potatoes, turnips and various other ingredients necessary for to make soup.

At lunchtime the people came to the soup kitchen with their pitchers and their jugs and they received a jugful o' soup and as much bread as would do them until the following day at lunchtime. At teatime we also tried to give them a mug of tea and margarine to put on the bread which they already had. And that was the staple diet of the people. Some of them had families who were working and they were able for to get a little luxury, but in the main the whole of the people in our area were dependent on this particular soup kitchen.

The farmers were good but at times we couldn't receive the stuff from the farmers, so being desperate of course we used to go to the outlying farms and take it. That perhaps wasn't etiquette. But necessity as far as I'm concerned knows no law. The people had to be fed and we were determined that they would be fed.

We had trouble. On one occasion we had massed pickets at Leven station for to try and stop an incoming train but we were met by a big contingent o' police under the auspices o' their Inspector, and they immediately drew their batons and set about the pickets without any provocation at all.

I was addressing a meeting at the Shorehead at Leven when I was ruthlessly hauled off the box, taken up to the local court and given thirty days' imprisonment in Saughton Jail for sedition.

In the hall I was in in Saughton Jail—'B' Hall—the whole of the Bowhill strike committee was incarcerated: the chairman, the secretary, the treasurer and the whole o' the committee were in Saughton at that particular time. And I may tell you they put us through the mill. They had us out in the fields, pulling sugar beet and we never got our back up. The food was deplorable. In the morning they gave us a stone jar full of porridge, or lumps of porridge, no milk. That was your breakfast. At dinner time we had some watery soup and at teatime one slice of bread and margarine and tea without sugar or milk. That was our diet on which we had to pull sugar beet.

Every week they had a concert for the inmates o' the Saughton Jail but we were not allowed to attend. We were not allowed any library books or any comforts of any description. They were making sure that once you were in there you would never come back.

Well, it was comical, too, because first thing in the morning the boy in the first cell he used tae start and sing 'The Red Flag'. This warder used tae say: 'Stop that bloody singin'!' And the boy would stop but the boy in the next cell would start. And it was up and down the place.

When we wis in jail ah remember the minister there an' a' these prisoners sittin' there. And he used tae come on a Sunday morning' and talk tae the inmates, ye know. And his subject that mornin' was Man's Trust in Man. And the first thing he did wis tae take a great big key and lock that vestry door. He was talkin' aboot man's trust in man and he didnae hae one inch o' trust in thae men or he widnae ha' locked that bloody door.

Ah, well, when ah wis goin' out the warder says tae me, 'Ye have tae come and see the chaplain.' Ah says, 'Ah'm no' wantin' tae see him.' 'Oh,' he says, 'but ye'll have to.' 'Oh,' ah says, 'ah'll no' have to.' Ah said, 'Ah don't want to see him.' And ah didnae see him. And that was the reason, because he had no trust in these men at a', or he wouldnae ha' locked that door. Whenever he locked that door that finished the trust business.

When the strike finished I wis victimised. It wis the buses at that time, and ah got on ma bus and went up and went in tae ask for ma check at the office at the Wellesley colliery. And the clerk there said: 'There's no check for you. There's no job for you.' Ah was the Leven branch secretary o' the Miners' Reform Union. And all the rest o' the men were behind me at the colliery office. And ah said tae the men: 'What are ye gaun tae do about this?' And they just all walked past me and went tae their work. And ah wis left standin'. Ah wis victimised for five years after that.[101]

It didnae maitter where ah went at that particular time, whenever ah mentioned ma name wis Murray that wis me finished. The Wellesley colliery was the Wemyss Coal Company. Ah tried the Fife Coal Company. Ah applied for jobs at builders and various other places. But whenever they knew who ah was ah wis out. Ah wis unemployed for five years.

To be frank I'll tell you what I did do. I'll be quite frank aboot it. I used tae lift bettin' slips and got a bob or two out o' that. I wis a bookie's runner for a number o' years. That wis ma only income. I had £1.20 a week off the dole for ma wife and two kids. I had £1.2.0d. for the wife and me and a shillin' each for the kids. That wis my income £1.4.0d. Oh, we had a hard time o' it.

There wisnae a lot o' unemployment, no' really, in Leven in the 1920s and '30s, because there were Durie Foundry workin' then. And they employed a tremendous amount o' men—a good bit over a thousand men. And there was the textile mill— flax. It wis still open at that time. Several hundred people worked there. There were the sawmills, too. And then they started these housin' schemes. And there were a lot o' men employed on the housin' schemes. We were the first tenants in this house in 1931. Oh, aye, there was a good lot o' work goin' on at that time. There werenae many unemployed in Leven.

Unemployment was very slight as far as this area was concerned. There wis jist the miners, which were very few and far between, living in Leven but working outside, because both o' the Leven collieries had closed.

A lot o' miners lived in Leven and travelled. They travelled tae the pits in the west o' Fife and places o' that description, travelled each day. At the Shorehead in Leven there wis two pits. There wis Leven No. 1 and Leven No. 2. What happened there wis, they started tae reconstruct them and they spent aboot £400,000 in drivin' new mines towards the supposed tae be new seams. And when they did eventually get tae the end o' the drive they discovered there wis no coal there. And the old miners told them they were drivin' the wrong way. The geologists said they were right. And when they arrived at the place where it should ha' been discovered there were no coal. That wis before the General Strike, in the middle '20s. They closed them down.

I was Leven branch secretary o' the Reform union and then later on ah wis branch secretary o' the UMS—United Mineworkers o' Scotland. When ah wis no longer in the pits ah remained in the Reform Union but ah wis no longer secretary. Ah wis never a member o' the National Unemployed Workers' Movement. There wis a branch in Methil but not in Leven.[102] The only thing ah can associate maself wi' them wis that if there were a case tae be fought at the Leven Labour Exchange they used tae come tae see me. Through the miners' union I used tae fight all their cases at the Labour Exchange in the 1920s and right on, when ah became secretary o' the Municipal Workers. Ah wis very successful that way, very successful. Any case that wis gaun tae the Labour Exchange they used tae come and ask me if ah wid represent them, irrespective who they were. So ah jist went. Ah wis their sort o' spokesman as far as cases were concerned. They were maybe disallowed at the Exchange when they signed on. They got no money. And then they appealed and they came tae me and ah used tae fight their case at the Labour Exchange.

Ah wis a member of the Communist Party, Davie Proudfoot and I. I joined it after the '21 lock-out, '21, '22, aboot then. But they stabbed us in the back. Ah'm sorry to say that, but we were stabbed in the back and we both resigned frae the Communist Party. Oh, ah didnae stay long in the Communist Party after what happened wi' Davie Proudfoot. What happened was we used to meet in Glasgow to formulate the agenda o' the business for the meeting for the United Mineworkers o' Scotland, and then take the decisions we had arrived at in the Communist Party and try to put them across to the UMS. And we were tricked all roads. And Davie Proudfoot wisnae gettin' no pay, ye see. He wis the General Secretary o' the UMS but he wis gettin' no pay, no pay at all, until he jist got to the stage when he said, 'Ach, ah'm sick o' it a' and ah'm havin' no more o' it. What about you?' Ah said, 'Ah, well, if you're sick o' it ah'm sick o' it, Davie.' And we both packed it in.[103]

Later on ah wis chairman o' the Board o Directors o' the Leven Co-op, and Davie wis chairman o' the Methil Co-op. Ah knew Davie well, oh, he was a genuine fellow, Davie, a very able man—oh, the most statistical brain I've ever known. He used tae go round the various co-ops and he would translate the whole o' the business o' the co-ops down to what ye could understand.

Ah never saw any Hunger Marchers passing through Fife in the 1920s and '30s.

Ah wis invited tae come on tae a Hunger March but ah wis always too busy. Tae let ye understand, ah wis treasurer of the ex-servicemen's club in Leven. Ah wis forty year treasurer o' the Earl Haig Club. We set up a club for the ex-servicemen in Leven.

Well, as ah said, I wis unemployed for five years after the General Strike and the miners' lock-out in 1926—victimised. How ah did get a job wis they were up in Letham Glen. The producer o' the musicals in Leven—Simonson, you called him—he wanted tae play *Rob Roy* in Letham Glen. And there wis a fellow had the leadin' part but six weeks before the show he packed in. And Mr Simonson came and asked me if ah would take it on. So ye'll understand ah'd done a bit o' elocution and things o' that description previous tae that. Ah had recited in the picture halls. I was a singer, I could sing. So Mr Simonson produced this *Rob Roy* in Letham Glen. The Secretary of State for Scotland at that time was at the first performance—Sir John Gilmour. And after the show Sir John come across and he congratulated me on the show, and he said: 'By the by, where do you work, Mr Murray?' 'Oh,' ah said, 'ah havenae worked for aboot five year.' He says, 'What's been wrong?' I explained the circumstances of course. 'Well,' he says, 'I'll see about that.' So the following fortnight there was a job advertised for a Town Council street sweeper. Sir John says, 'Put in for that.' So ah put in for the job and ah got it. And of course after ah got that job ah had tae leave the miners' union and join the Municipal Workers' Union. The fellow that wis secretary o' the branch died and they asked me if ah would take the job on. So ah took the job on. I wis the branch secretary from then, 1931 until 1982.[104]

I wis a pal o' Bud Flanagan. Ah wis a member o' a concert party on the Buckhaven beach and Bud was a member o' a concert party at East Wemyss. And they were doing nothing there. And Bud used tae come down pretty often tae oor concert party. We used to give him a couple o' pound a week and a pint and a fish supper. And then he left and got connected wi' Chesney Allen and they made a hit o' it in London. Ah can remember going down there tae a co-operative conference and they were playin' at the Palladium. Ah went doon tae the stage door and ah says, 'Can ah see Mr Flanagan, please?' 'Have you an appointment?' Ah said, 'No, I havenae got an appointment.' 'Oh, you can't see Mr Flanagan without an appointment.' So ah pleaded wi' him. So he says, 'Look,' he says 'I'll go and ask him.' So he says, 'What name?' Ah said, 'Jist say Mosie wants tae see him.' In two minutes he wis back: 'This way, sir, this way.' Flanagan and I went oot tae an hotel in London and we baith got fu'.[105]

Hugh McIntyre

I was a caulker to trade, a ship's caulker. I served my apprenticeship in Brown's in Clydebank. That was interrupted by the war in August 1914, when we who were Territorials were mobilised.

We had joined the Terriers simply in order to get a holiday down at Campbeltown. The year before we had had a wee cycle trip, four of us, three young friends of mine, who were the same age as myself, and with whom I had gone cycling and playing and generally running around. But in 1914 we hadnae a bean amongst the four o' us to go on a cycling holiday as we had done the year before. But we met some of our other pals who had joined the Terriers in 1913. So we decided that we would go up to the Terriers. We knew that the camp that year was to be down at Machrihanish.

In these days nearly every village had a drill hall. Here in the Vale of Leven there was one in Renton, one in Bonhill, one in Jamestown, one up here in Alexandria. And they all had a recruiting sergeant attached to them, and a house usually attached to them in which he lived. Some of them had a family, because the one at Jamestown, named Morrison, his son was in the school. We were in the same class. So we decided to go up and get the aid of Sid Morrison to ask his father to make it possible for us to get into the Territorials before the camp in July 1914. He let us in early in 1914, although I think he must have forged the papers to do it because he told us no' tae tell anybody that we were in. So I was in the Terries before I was seventeen, because I wouldnae be seventeen until later in 1914: I was born in 1897.

But you had to do so many drills, as it was officially called, before you were eligible to go to the camp. However he arranged it I don't know, but we got to the camp in 1914 at Machrihanish. I can remember going down the Clyde on a very old paddle steamer. It took us down to Campbeltown and we went over to Machrihanish and the Territorial camp was there. We had a very enjoyable camp. We got into Campbeltown every now and again.

But we only got back home from the camp and within two or three days war was declared on the 4th of August 1914. And the Terriers were mobilised. I was in the 9th Argyll and Sutherland Highlanders. They sent us away from the locality, first of all to Dunblane and then down to Bedford.

Between August 1914 and February 1915 we were just getting prepared for joining the Expeditionary Force in France. We went over from Dover to Calais in February 1915. Then the whole of the 9th Argylls as a unit were drafted into the

Highland Division, along with other units of regular soldiers and I think there was another Territorial unit.

We went into the 51st Highland Division in February 1915 and in the course of time moved up to outside Ypres. Two places that I remember very well indeed in Belgium are the village of Hooge and the city of Ypres. This village of Hooge was about three or four kilometres outside Ypres. The Germans had made an advance and then had retired quite a distance outside Ypres. We in the 9th Argylls went in to occupy a part of the line just beside this village of Hooge.

This thing I'll never forget. We went into a vacated German dug-out. The Germans had used it when they had been surrounding the whole of that area in opposition to the British forces. Its doorway faced into the German lines instead of the back of it. The British dug-outs always had their doorway facing the German lines, so that artillery fire coming over went over the doors.

Well, the four of us—the other three boys who were pals of mine in Vale of Leven—were sitting down in this German dug-out. Whatever happened, I think to this day it was a shell from the Jerries that came in and came right down the bloody stairway and exploded amongst us. I got a wound in my leg and a bit in my cheek, but the wound in my leg was the more serious.

I remember asking the stretcher-bearers who took me up to a first-aid post about my pals. And I can remember them to this day saying, 'There's nothing can be done for them.' They were killed with the explosion of this shell. You can still see the wound I got on my leg. It reminds me of the thing too much. They were my closest pals.

I got sent home to Newcastle with that wound. We went to Dumbarton Castle, which was the headquarters of the 9th Argylls. The 9th Argylls was a purely Dunbartonshire unit from Kirkintilloch out to Helensburgh and Balloch and up the loch sides.

The 9th Argylls had been so badly decimated as a unit outside Ypres at Hooge that they couldnae exist as a unit. So the 9th Argylls sent those of us who were left— and there wisnae a great deal of us left—to join the 8th Argylls, who were still a full battalion unit. We went back to Dumbarton Castle for a wee while and were then drafted out to the front again, oh, it must have been towards the end of 1915.

The 8th Argylls got a pummelling later on in the war and we were drafted into the 7th Argylls, which was a Stirlingshire battalion. The 6th Argylls came from over in Paisley.

We were at Ypres in 1915, we were in Doullens in 1916, we were in Cambrai early in 1918, in the Cambrai advance and withdrawal. I went through the 1916 Somme advance, in which I got back to 'ospital again with a piece of shrapnel in my back—a premature explosion from one of our own shells actually, outside Doullens. I was wounded there and sent home to a hospital in Gloucester. They gave me operations. But I'm told the bit o' shrapnel is still there. Recently, after my latest heart attack I was sent up to hospital to get an X-ray. It was there they discovered the bit of shrapnel in my back. It had apparently went in close to ma spine, about an inch or so away. It's not given me any trouble. But I thought they'd taken it away.[106]

Earlier than that the Germans started to use poison gas and I got just a wee whiff of that and I was sent down to a base hospital for some treatment that time. But that left me with a sort of asthmatic condition. Later on they gave me a pension for it of about one and tanner a week or somethin'.

These were the actual big scraps that I took an active part in. The rest of it you were serving in the trenches when there was little or nothing doing. I mean, odd people were being killed. Both sides were trying to shell the other's positions. But that became run of the mill as against the warfare you were engaged in early in 1915 outside Ypres and then in 1916 and later, in 1918, at Cambrai.

There wis advances and withdrawals on a larger or a smaller scale from time to time all along that Western Front. The memories of it arenae very bright because ye were wadin' about in the trenches in winter-time up to yer waist in muck and water. Ye want tae forget as much o' it as you can. As I say, that wound in my leg from Ypres constantly reminds me of one of the worst moments I had. These other three pals were killed and their names are up on the war memorial in Christie Park in Vale of Leven.

Well, I was demobilised early in 1919. We were brought up by train to a place somewhere near Paisley or Johnstone. I cannae remember the actual place where the final particulars were given or taken from us. And then we were officially de-mobilised.

And getting home here in 1919 I was attracted by a public meeting at the Fountain in Alexandria. It was addressed by Willie Gallacher. What he said made me go and buy pamphlets and books. And about the end o' 1919 or the beginning of 1920 I joined the Dumbarton branch of the Socialist Labour Party. And almost at the same time, about June or July 1920, the Communist Party was formed by the Socialist Labour Party, sections of the Independent Labour Party, dissident members of the Labour Party, and so on. And I've been a member of it ever since.

They promised you when you were in the army in the First World War that you were defending a land fit for heroes to live in, and it was going to be a great show after the war. But they were unemployed from early on, when they come back like myself.

There was a huge unemployed population here in the Vale of Leven. It was one of the unlucky places from the point of view of employment in the whole of Scotland. For maybe a year or so the highest rates of unemployment throughout the country were being registered down there at the Bank Street Labour Exchange—och, it wis away up![107] Well, I got in and was agitating among the unemployed from 1920 until 1922 when I was elected a parish councillor. We were a very early branch of the National Unemployed Workers' Committee Movement and we had a very strong branch here in Vale of Leven. We had a big membership. I was the chairman for two or three years. Over these two or three years I cannae ever remember bein' refused if I approached an unemployed man and knew that he wisnae a member and asked him to join.

We had street captains working. We had a person in every street in the area. And that's saying something because in them times there must have been about forty or fifty streets. We had about twenty or thirty members on our committee and all of them were street captains, either male or female. They collected the penny a week that the National Unemployed Workers' Committee Movement charged its members. And they kept us in touch with things that were happening, such as people being threatened with evictions.

We could get masses of unemployed people out on to the street to march to the place of eviction and then indeed on occasions—two or three occasions that I personally participated in—we stuffed the house of the person who was threatened with eviction with unemployed members from the march, to such an extent that when the bailiffs tried tae get in they couldnae open the ootside door o' the house. We would pack them in so that they were standing against one another. The bailiffs couldnae get in the door, even with police help, tryin' tae push the door in. They couldnae get it open. It was packed full o' human beings. The first one o' that kind that ah had anythin' to do wi' was up in an attic in Jamestown. There was one at the head of Govan Drive and another one—either North Street or Alexander Street. They are still there as streets but the houses are completely changed.

Some of the activists were former soldiers like myself. But they were unemployed from early on when they come back, when that depression struck after the war. So here in Alexandria we had one of the really active branches of the unemployed. And they carried out boycotts of the local cinema owner because she wouldnae give the use of her cinema as a public meeting place to the unemployed. The Strand Cinema in Bank Street was owned by a Mrs Wingate. The Unemployed Committee had the free use of the Co-operative Hall in Bank Street and of the public hall, which was also run by a group of local people. We held weekly meetings of the unemployed. The committee met every bloody day of the week. Then the committee would have a public meeting every week either in the Co-operative Hall or in the public hall. And there was another place that we used to get—the Empire Theatre. We staged concerts there. There were concerts being held in the Co-operative Hall regularly by professional artistes and the Unemployed Committee used to get some of these artistes to come down and give a concert in the Empire Theatre to the unemployed. They would give us a concert free of any charges for their services. That kind of thing went on for years. When we asked Mrs Wingate of the Strand Cinema to make it available and she wouldnae, we got the Unemployed Movement, with the assistance of the general public, to boycott it by marching up and down the street in front o' the cinema and publicly appealing to people during the times when they were going in. So effective was the boycott that she came to the Unemployed Committee after about four or five days of boycotting and said that she would give us the use of the Strand Cinema.

I can remember the first Hunger March by the unemployed was held just before the December 1922 General Election. We recruited a number of people to represent Vale of Leven branch of the Unemployed Movement in the Hunger March. We outfitted them with boots and clothing as far as we could. The March was to London. It was from various parts. The Dundee people and the Fife people and a group of people from the Vale of Leven, numbers of branches of the Unemployed in

Glasgow and the west o' Scotland were in the Scottish contingent that took the road about the end of November, beginnin' of December 1922. We were prevented from goin' on it by the Unemployed Committee—prevented in the sense that we were prevailed on not to go because we had an election coming up for the local Parish Council.[108]

A doctor saw the men, gave them a medical examination, and we saw them off on the March. We marched with them to the Fountain in Alexandria and saw them off to the train to join the Glasgow contingent, to be ready to start out on the March the following day from Glasgow.

The 1922 March, well, its chief achievement, I think, was the spreading of the realisation throughout the country that there was very, very severe unemployment existing, and that 'The Land Fit for Heroes' that many of the people who were affected had been promised wisnae materialising even three years after the war. Indeed, the reverse was materialising. Instead of having jobs and homes fit for heroes to live hundreds of thousands of them were on the unemployed lists. And there were various marches to Guardians and to Parish Councils all over the country, which stimulated the interest of the people who werenae themselves unemployed. It had a tremendous impact on the 1924 General Election, which returned for the first time a Labour government.

All the time in those years, even in local disputes in the local factory or anywhere in Dumbarton, in the likes of Denny's shipyard, the Unemployed Movement were always very, very quick to get in and inform the trade unions that they could look to the Unemployed Committees for whatever support or help they needed. They would be glad to give them it and to organise men to give them it if they needed practical help in doing anything. But one thing the unions must always be sure of was that we in the Unemployed Movement would do our best to stop the unemployed from scabbing against anyone who was in dispute. That had always been made perfectly clear, so far as I know, by every branch of the National Unemployed Workers' Committee Movement—and certainly by our Alexandria branch. That was one of the first things they did. When there was a dispute of any kind the workers involved in it always could depend on the unemployed not to strike-break.

The next thing of any importance that happened was the General Strike in 1926, in which the unemployed in Vale of Leven played the usual part of assuring the strike committee that they would do the best they could for them and help them in any way they could. The people who were participating in the General Strike would realise that the unemployed werenae goin' tae scab on them in any way and that they would take steps tae see that none o' their members applied for any o' the jobs that might be made available.

Well, in 1926, I started work as an insurance agent with the co-op. So that my contact with the Unemployed Movement wisnae severed by any means but it was severed from the daily work that they were carryin' on. I went back and helped them to organise the Hunger March to Edinburgh after that and then the second National Hunger March to London in 1929. I was still working hard then as an insurance agent trying to build up a book and I was only able to give them my spare time. I wasnae constantly on the move as I was when the Unemployed Committee was at its best for about four or five years here in Alexandria.[109]

Then later on, in the 1930s, complaints about one o' the 'Slave Camps' for the unemployed had been made direct to Harry McShane because o' the position that Harry occupied as the sort of chief organiser of the Unemployed Movement in Scotland. And he immediately contacted me because he knew that I had just got this wee second-hand car for work in the winter time and I didnae need tae go oot on a push bike. And I ran Harry down to this 'Slave Camp' at Glen Branter, which is at the bottom of a village called Strachur on the side of Loch Fyne, jist above Loch Eck. There they sent men who had been a long time unemployed and they were supposed to be getting experience in working conditions which would enable them to fit back speedily into their normal kind of work if and when their normal kind o' work came back. The Ministry of Labour ran the camp.

We were refused admission. But so far as I can gather the men slept on the floor. Simply they were taken down there and they were put up in the same kind o' conditions as travelling workers, tattie lifters and so on used tae be.

Barns and things of that kind had been hurriedly commandeered by the Ministry for these camps. People who had been scored off the register of unemployed altogether after aboot so many weeks' benefit were offered the chance of going to one of these camps. They had to do a certain number of weeks there and then if they proved satisfactory—willing to work and able to work—they were put back on the register. But that was the object of the camps. And they were called Slave Labour Camps—facetiously called that by the unemployed, because after an experience of them they discovered they didn't help them in any way to get a job. But that's the one that was used very extensively in the west of Scotland, Glen Branter.[110]

Harry McShane I've known all my days, all my political days since I joined the Communist Party in 1920. Harry and I mixed regularly either on platforms or on committees. And Harry did a powerful job. He was much closer to John Maclean for many, many years than anybody I knew. I differed with Maclean—and some of the rest of us differed with him—on certain political and electoral questions. But he was a devout socialist worker, John Maclean. And I don't think the movement treated him very well. They were inclined to pooh pooh his approach to a whole lot of questions. In his latter days some sections of the working class movement—and this included some sections of the Communist Party—were beginning to look on Maclean as a man who had kind of lost the place to some extent, that he was a wee bit gone up here. I never thought that about John Maclean. I certainly didnae see much of him in the last two years of his life. But I liked John Maclean and I think Harry McShane liked John Maclean and if you've read John Maclean's history you're reading Harry McShane's history. Harry was a devout and active socialist for the best part of his life. He had a wee bit difficulty in his speech, Harry, a wee bit thickness in his speech: even when he was in the best of his days his diction wisnae all that could be desired. But by heaven I've never had any reason tae doubt his conviction that there's a better system o' society possible in the world, and he would work for it like myself, work for it as long as we can.

Harry McShane took as much place in the Unemployed Movement in Scotland as Wal Hannington took first of all in London and ultimately throughout the country. Hannington was looked upon by the unemployed as the real leader of the movement. I first saw and heard his name at the Manchester Congress of the Communist Party in 1923 or '24. He was active in the Communist Party as I was myself and he appeared at that Congress. He had the facility of being able to express himself very, very fluently and to impress people by his general courage in approaching questions of working conditions and his insistence that the worker's point of view must always be heard. He was accepted really almost unanimously as the leader of the unemployed in this country. I had the pleasure of speaking with him on platforms. When he was up here speaking in the Co-operative Hall in Alexandria he stayed wi' me shortly after I was first married in 1928, when we were staying down in Burn Brae. The Co-operative Hall was one of our great places for holding meetings. Any party who had any following at all used the Co-operative Hall in Alexandria, because they had a big hall capable of holding 600 or 700 people and a balcony that would maybe hold a couple o' hundred, and a very big fine high platform. So that it was an excellent place from any speaker's point of view. Well, Wal Hannington spoke there one night for us. And I had other occasions to speak along with him when Walton Newbold, the first Communist MP, was elected to the House of Commons. Indeed, I think I was speaking along with them—Newbold was the main speaker in that campaign of his down in Motherwell—when Newbold was asked: 'Is it true, Mr Chairman, that the candidate, Mr Newbold, doesn't go to church?' The local Communists said afterwards, 'Oh, he's a well known Orangeman who asked that question.' And Newbold got up boldly at the front of the platform and said: 'I am and have been since I was capable of thinking, a confirmed atheist all my life.' And sat doon. And it's said to have lost him hundreds and hundreds of votes, because apparently there was a very, very strong Orange element in that part of Scotland. However, Newbold finished up, I'm told, by having his house plastered with Union Jacks and working actively for the Unionist Party in London after he broke his connection with the Communists.[111]

Locally, there was Allan Campbell who was known outside his locality as a man who was active in the Unemployed Movement. I believe that he was actually asked to go on a deputation to Bonar Law when he was prime minister and came up to visit Glasgow.[112] Allan was a great agitator but a wee bit of a crackpot in many other ways—at least, that was my personal opinion.

Allan belonged to Bonhill, the other side of the River Leven here from Alexandria. I knew him from 1920 or thereaboots, when I joined the Communist Party. But my chief association with him was in the Unemployed Movement. He was an extremely good organiser and worked many, many hours in the organisation of the unemployed in this town and other towns in the west of Scotland. He was rated highly in Scotland. He wis in the same sort o' category as blokes like Alex Moffat and Jock McArthur in Fife.[113]

I don't think Allan was actually able to go on Hunger Marches. He wisnae a very physically strong man. But he had a great ability on the platform, and a great organising ability to follow up his platform ability. I'll give you an illustration that's stuck in my mind over the years. Bob Stewart, who was a Communist organiser, was jailed for working amongst the unemployed in Dundee. A young woman, she was Jewish, lived in Glasgow, Sadie Span was her name, was active in the Communist Party. I was active, Allan Campbell was active, and Bob Stewart was in jail.[114] There was a by-election in Dundee—I think it wis a by-election, it may have been a general election, I cannae mind, it's so long ago—but Scrymgeour was standing as a Prohibition candidate. Now whether Churchill was involved in that particular fight or no' ah cannae remember but Churchill wis in one o' the fights there that we were up in. But there was some bugger present in that campaign who created a terrific interest in every kind of political thing. It didnae matter who held a meeting ye got crowds. And we three—Allan Campbell, Sadie and I—were asked if we were willin' tae go up. Nane o' us were workin': Sadie wisnae working and Campbell and I were unemployed. Bob Stewart got a helluva poor vote even in these days—well, Communists were gettin' better votes in these days. But he got a poor vote compared with what Scrymgeour got wi' his Prohibitionist label.[115] Well, we three went up tae Dundee. We were young, capable (that's maybe boastin' a wee bit) platform hands. And we held this meeting—I'm sure it was in the Foresters' Hall—and ah can always remember Campbell had a helluva hatred of local officials of the Parish Council or the County Council or anybody who had a government label of any kind on him. He used tae call them Tweedledum and Tweedledee. And he sometimes got up my bloody wick wi' it. However, I liked him so well that I could forgive him a' that. But this particular night he wis on aboot this Tweedledum the councillor in Dundee and Tweedledee the council official. And he Tweedledummed and Tweedledeed for a hell of a long while. He made a good enough speech. And when it came tae the question time a bloke—ah don't know whether he was a wag but I don't think he got the best of it, judging by the laughter—got up and he said: 'Mr Chairman, Mr Campbell there, who has been talking for about half an hour, has been mentioning very often Tweedledum and Tweedledee. Could Mr Campbell tell me the difference between Tweedledum and Tweedledee?' And Campbell got up like a bloody shot. He says, 'The same difference as there is between a spiug and a sparrow.' And the whole bloody crowd in the hall burst out with laughter. Now that was really Scottish wasn't it? He meant there was nae difference between the official Tweedledee and the Tory councillor Tweedledum. I thought Campbell had got the best of the exchanges against the heckler.

Allan Campbell was drowned in the North Atlantic during the war. I think his ship had been torpedoed. Harry McShane once told me on one of his journeys out to parts of America and Canada he went into Vancouver and he read in the papers something about some seamen who had been jailed and Allan Campbell was amongst them. Harry had gone up to the jail and had a word with Campbell.

But that was the word that we got here at home, that he had been torpedoed or he certainly had drowned. His father and mother, or the people he lived with up in Bonhill, were dead by this time. There was one other member of the family still alive—he would be younger than Allan and he worked in the local Cleansing

Department. He didnae seem tae be clear whether Allan wis really his brother, his foster brother, or his adopted brother. Allan Campbell was highly rated in Scotland. He was in the same sort o' category as blokes like Alex Moffat and Jock McArthur in Fife.

I was a Communist councillor for many years. In 1922 I was elected a Parish Councillor. We stood as Trades Council candidates actually. It was later on that Communists were banned from being associated with trades councils. The Trades and Labour Councils were done away with and became just Trades Councils.[116] In Vale of Leven part of the Trades Council's programme for the local elections affected the unemployed very, very greatly because we said that we were prepared to give them more than the official scale of relief that they were getting. By this time riots in Dundee had compelled the government to give the Parish Councils a power that they previously didnae have to pay able bodied relief. Prior to that—I think it must have been between August and December 1922—the local Parish Councils would only send people to the poorhouse if they said they had nae income. There were riots in Dundee which showed clearly that the people were starving because the rioters broke intae some o' the food shops and carted away food to take home to feed their families. Very few other shops were broken intae except food shops. So this compelled the government to give the local authorities—the local Parish Councils—power to pay able bodied relief. Able bodied relief meant that an able bodied man who had run out of unemployment benefit got relief from the Parish Councils. That's to say, the Parish Councils were given the legal power by the government to give them cash instead of giving them either a line for groceries or a line into the workhouse—their tramcar fare or whatever it was to the workhouse in Dumbarton. At one period the Unemployed Movement's activities was to organise people who were prepared to go to the workhouse when the scales of relief had been reduced to such a point that it was nearly as well for the men to take their families and go into the bloody workhouse as to try and exist on the scales that they were being paid.

Allan Campbell and I and Dan O'Hare, Erchie Peters, Thingmy MacFarlane, Jack Black—we were a' standing as candidates for the Parish Council at the December 1922 election.[117] Between the Trades Council candidates and the Unemployed candidates there was a majority elected over what was called the Moderates of the Parish Council at that time. There were fifteen members on the Council and there wis eight between the Communist Party members who were running as Trades Council candidates and other Labour Party candidates who had been on the Parish Council before that. A fellow the name o' McInnes, for instance, and Adam Shearer had been on the Council before 1922.

Well, we immediately started to implement our election promises. And we introduced as part of the relief to the able bodied unemployed an increase in the relief paid him by the Mond scale. Mond was a capitalist in the Tory government and had produced a scale of relief that got the name of the Mond scale. We paid them that and, I think, three bob a head or something more than that.[118] We also issued lines for women who were carrying babies to get maternity bundles, as they were called. All that kind of activity was going on not only in Vale of Leven but in various parts of the country. And you had marches from the Vale, for instance, up to Park Circus in Glasgow, where the Education Authority sat, in order to ensure the continuation of boots and clothing to children of people who were unemployed—'bootless bairns', as they called them.

Well, by 1924 the Bonhill Parish Council had got so far ahead with its election pledges of 1922 that it was now paying a scale of relief which was slightly in excess of the Mond scale. Because in 1924—I cannae remember the exact month—the Parish Council of Bonhill received a letter from the Scottish Department of Health in Edinburgh. They had an office in Princes Street in Edinburgh, and they sent word that they were proposing to introduce a surcharge against us for the period up until then when we had been paying this scale of relief in excess of the Mond scale and when we had been giving people extra bundles for children. The practice in these years was for the banks to give every Parish Council who asked for it an overdraft, which was secured by the local rates, to enable them to get on with the payment of this able bodied relief and other things which they had just been granted power by the government of the day to do. The Department of Health letter listed the names of the people they were going to surcharge and these were the names of the majority of the members of the Bonhill Parish Council. I think we had a majority of one, not counting the chairman's casting vote, over the Moderates as they then called themselves, who were a mixture of active members of either the Tory or Liberal Party locally. One of them, John Patch, was an active Liberal; Ferguson, the Balloch Post Office man, was an active Tory. These were known, everybody knew that. I mean, they didnae disguise it themselves. But they were in a minority for the first time on the Parish Council. They had carefully taken the right—and it was a right—to enter their dissent when we had moved any of the proposals which increased the scales of relief or in any way gave benefits to unemployed people which became the subjects of the surcharge. They had always carefully entered their dissent under a kind of leader that they had. He was a bloke the name of Barton, who had a grocer's shop at the head of North Street. He seemed to be the head of the Moderate minority in the Bonhill Parish Council, because he always took the initiative in opposing our proposals. All the rest of the Moderates consistently voted with him and followed his lead in this thing.

Well, the Tories in charge of the Department of Health in these days—because the permanent officials in most of these government offices were Tories to the bone—had an objective. We were looking around for assistance and realising that if they did surcharge us we would have to admit that we were bankrupt. We werenae able to pay them, so far as the majority of our eight were concerned. Peter Talbot, Adam Shearer and Tommy McInnes were married and had housefuls of furniture which could have been impounded if they hadnae the ready cash to pay. The rest of us were single persons who hadnae houses full o' furniture and so on. So they wid ha' declared us bankrupts and as bankrupts ye couldnae stand for election. So that was the aim.

We got public meetings. We got agreement from the bulk o' the people who came to the public meetings, to take a financial collection to recompense these fellows if they sold up their furniture, so that they could refurnish their houses. To that extent the public here were behind us, if it had come to a surcharge.

However, we approached Willie Gallacher and Davie Kirkwood and said, 'Can ye help us? Can ye get anybody tae help us?' And Kirkwood and Gallacher said: 'We'll get Maxton and Wheatley on to this thing.' Wheatley had just been appointed Minister of Health in the new Labour government.

Well, from that time onwards we never heard any mair about it. Neither Wheatley nor Maxton nor Kirkwood told us any more about it. Whether they knew I don't know. But we had tae come to our own conclusion and my conclusion was that Wheatley went in as Minister of Health and asked for a look at the Bonhill Parish file and never brought the damned thing back. That's the only conclusion I could come tae. What other conclusion wis there? I cannae think o' any other. He couldnae very well officially go tae parliament and get parliament to excuse us. At least, he never did. And the Labour government, so far as I know, never raised it. There wis nothing mair heard aboot it. Not a bloody cheep from anywhere. In fact, auld man Lindsay, who was the clerk to the Parish Council at that time, wis very, very angry when he wis asked by one o' the Moderates was there any further communication from the Department of Health about the surcharge? He said, 'No. No further communication.' He hadnae received anything.

Now I jist cannae understand how Wheatley did it other than jist forgettin' aboot it, losing it. Whether he was prepared to do that and risk his reputation and a' the rest, it certainly was important to us because it prevented us from bein' surcharged and it might have had some effect on other councils in the country. Wheatley may have had that on his mind. I don't know. But we certainly never heard another word about it.

In the interval we had gone to the co-operative to get help, because the banks had stopped, on the instruction of the government, giving us an overdraft. Our rates so far as the banks were concerned were to be considered not a sufficiently secure security for any advance that they made. There was the possibility that we widnae be there as councillors at all to levy a rate. So the banks closed down on us and we went to the local co-op and they for a wee while subsidised us. We went into the Parish Council chambers, two or three of us, along with Macleod, the assistant to old Lindsay the clerk, and him and Miss Tagg, who was the clerkess to the council, turned over thon old fashioned duplicators to print chits that we gave to people and they got them stamped with the co-operative stamp and that wis them in credit to the amount marked on that chit. But they were a small co-operative society. They werenae getting any money at all from the unemployed because they werenae gettin' any money from us. And the co-op had to call off after, I think, about five or six weeks of financing us. And by this time they had reached the stage where Wheatley handled it in some way and that was the end of it. We were restored to the position we were in before. The new rates were startin' tae come in and we were back on to put down the rates as security for the banks. And we were back where we were. To that extent we had spiked the guns of the Department of Health and we carried on with our work.

I was a member of Dumbarton County Council from 1928 until 1952, and chairman of their Housing Committee, Public Health Committee and General Purposes Committee. And I've got a watch that I got from the Workers' Union with an inscription on the back of it: 'Presented to County Councillor Hugh McIntyre, Transport and General Workers' Union, for services to trade unionism. The Alexandria Branch,1925-1950.'[119]

John Lochore

It was early November 1936 and I had volunteered to join the International Column in Spain.

News had come from Spain of the formation of the column by men who on hearing of the combined attack on the Spanish people's government had banded together and were actively fighting against the Fascists at the gates of Madrid. Democrats from all over the world flocked to join and within weeks this unique force grew in size, eventually to become the now legendary International Brigade.

Men and women from all walks of life made their ways to Spain, especially from the underground anti-fascist movements in Germany and Italy. They went by boat, by mountain tracks over the Pyrenees and by every conceivable and devious method of travel. They were men and women from almost every country in the world. In Spain they gathered and created a fighting machine that took part on every front.[120]

The first news I had read of this magnetic force was whilst I was on the Scotland to London hunger march in October-November 1936. Nat Cohen, a young London East-ender, had, with a friend, cycled through France and made his way over the Pyrenees to join a few others in Barcelona. Initially they formed the Tom Mann Centuria (named after the veteran British trade union leader) and, alongside the German anti-fascist Ernest Thaelmann Battalion, they presented themselves in the forefront of the defence of Madrid, which was then under siege by the Fascists.[121] Some Glasgow lads had also joined the column and assisted in this gallant stand that thwarted Franco from entering Madrid.[122] Phil Gillan from Polmadie, a colleague in the Glasgow Youth Movement, was one of those. He was seriously wounded and narrowly escaped death when a spray of machine gun bullets rained down on his spine. Phil survived and later became an organiser in the Transport and General Workers' Union.[123]

Other news dribbled out, of distinguished writers, poets and artists being among the fatalities in other parts. John Cornford, the young student and distinguished poet; Ralph Fox, writer and biographer of Ghengis Khan; Felicia Browne, woman artist; Hans Beimler, German parliamentarian; and many others were among the dead reported.[124] Franco was stopped from entering the capital on his white steed, as the drunken broadcaster Queipo De Llano, broadcasting from Burgos, had boasted he would. He had said that four columns would enter the city led by General Franco and a Fifth Column would rise and take its toll of vengeance on those who resisted.[125]

The epic heroism of the original volunteers was truly magnificent and will be imprinted in the annals of history's freedom fighters.

It was in a back street in the centre of Glasgow that I, along with some fifty others, gathered on a murky night in November 1936 to embark on our mission. Two rather old and worn looking buses lay in wait and a few confidants were there to say farewell. It was supposedly a secret departure, but just as the buses were geared ready to leave some dozens of well wishers emerged from the closes to say their farewell also. I can in my memory see and hear one of the girls who had come to say goodbye to her young sweetheart. She was Isa Alexander, a beautiful brown-eyed girl from Arcadia Street. He was John Connolly, a lad from the Gorbals who had previously been on the hunger march to London. With tears in her eyes she cried, 'Don't forget, John, to come back—I'll be waiting for you.'

No one came to wave to me. I had told no one of my departure, although I came back to Glasgow specially to have some last hours with my mother who never had stood in my way—she had great faith in me. That last night at home a visiting aunt, who was well known for her outspoken remarks, said, 'John, you've got awfa big tackity bits on your feet to be gaun trevellin'.' 'Aye,' I replied, 'I've got an awfa lot of walking to do.' (My story: I was joining a team of travelling canvassers working for the Beaverbrook *Sunday Express*!).[126]

On the bus travelling to London I was elected the leader and spokesman for my colleagues who included Lanarkshire and Fifeshire miners, unemployed friends of hunger march days, a school teacher, a newspaper reporter and three ex-soldiers. We travelled the identical route that we had traversed only a few weeks previously on the hunger march and by sheer coincidence the bus broke down when crossing the Shap Fells, almost exactly on the same spot our 'soup' lorry kitchen during the march had broken down, when we had had to walk the full distance of almost twenty miles without the midday bowl of soup. On the bus it was just as dreary a journey as it had been before on foot, because through the night the wind howled and blasted its way over the desolate moors and mountains. This breakdown meant we were running a day late. On arrival in London we were delighted to 'kip' in a lodging house, since contact with our London friends, who would willingly have put us up for the night, was inadvisable due to the secretive nature of our mission. If the British government, which was opposed to our going to fight for the Spanish government, had known we were leaving the British Isles they would have spiked our guns. Later we were to experience the ferocity of that opposition by the withholding of arms from us by virtue of the treacherous Non-Intervention Pact operated by the Baldwin government in Britain and the Blum government in France.[127]

The next morning it was under some famous railway (the same arches sung of by Flanagan and Allen) that a little bespectacled man with crippled feet doled out our fares and documents of authenticity and introductions to our French contacts. That little man was John Ross Campbell, a Scottish revolutionary of great repute. As he passed out our documents he smiled and said, 'Keep your heids doon!'[128]

We divided into groups of five. The plan was to travel over to France via the

Dover-Dieppe ferry on a week-end excursion ticket, and make contact with the underground organisation in Paris. With no hitches we duly arrived in the French capital and on leaving the station, by presenting our secret address to the driver, we were whizzed through a maze of streets to a wooden hut attached to a building site. The emphasis on our trip was secrecy but I am sure the entire fleet of taxi drivers in Paris knew the address—a fact which was revealed by their casual confidence in conveying us to our 'secret destination'.

In attendance in the wooden hut was a bereted man who wore a long Abercromby coat and chain smoked through a thin cigarette holder. He interviewed our lot, one by one, and plied us with questions as to our backgrounds and the reasons for desiring to join the International Force in Spain. Without taking notes, in what was a veritable third degree, he eventually established *bona fides*. That night was spent at a working men's cafe *cum* hotel. Early next morning we were collected by taxi and accompanied by a small Parisian, whose job it was to pilot the group through the busy station and safely aboard a south moving train. He pushed ahead of us in the melee, moving through the crowds of travellers who were gaily bedecked winter sports men and women with ruc-sacs and highly polished skis over their shoulders and who presented an almost impenetrable barrier on the platform. Choosing this time, I learned later, was a carefully timed feature of our departure—to get us out of Paris in a crowd without being noticed.

Safely aboard the train we settled together as a group. This part of the trip to the south of France stands out in my memory. As we volunteers sat in the carriage, another passenger excused his presence and politely asked if the remaining seat was occupied. We indicated it was vacant and he, with all the gentle mannerly gestures he could muster, showed his gratitude and settled in the corner seat. He was a round faced, jovial peasant. I guessed he came from Britanny because of his brown tanned skin and well worn beret with a bright kerchief tied round his neck in the traditional knot. His smile was permanent and his eyes—his brown eyes—gleamed with kindness and captivated one instantly. Continually he tried to attract our attention and at the least excuse made pleasing gestures. We politely ignored him. Halfway along the journey a most heart-rending decision had to be taken. He took down from the luggage rack a red spotted kerchief which contained his snack and a bottle of wine. He offered his snack round and held the bottle over to me. Politely I refused the offer and the others followed suit. I can still see the hurt on his face, and his smile almost faded.

We travelled via Narbonne to Perpignan and then terminated a most mentally uncomfortable journey. We volunteers had been prisoners: for fear of treachery, we could not afford to trust a living being with our secret. We had over-reacted. But we took no risks.

That evening we were taken to a farmhouse and lay around the barns and out-houses impatiently awaiting the go-ahead to cross the Pyrenees into Spain. It was two long days before we were alerted and ushered into a small bus with no seats and told to lie down, with no talking or smoking. The bus showed no lights and soon it was on its way jumbling and jostling uncomfortably in low gear over the rocky mountainous tracks. The journey lasted some hours. We rumbled on endlessly and I felt physically sick. Then the engine revved up to a terrific speed—obviously travelling downhill. There was a crash of wood. It felt as if we were in a collision. Then came the quick echoes of gunfire and the crack! crack! of bullets hitting the rear of the bus. Not long afterwards the bus halted and its lights flashed. The driver alighted from his cabin, jumping excitedly. '*España! España!*', he shouted. We had arrived. We had crashed the mountain frontier post and the guards in their surprise had fired recklessly and aimlessly. We were now in Catalonia and like mad schoolboys we alighted and jumped and danced wildly, hugging and jostling each other in our excitement. We sang lustily on that early dark morning amidst the snowcapped peaks of the Pyrenees. Aches and pains in our bottoms and backs were soon forgotten when we disembarked at Fort Figueras.

In the morning, as we assembled to our first roll call, who should we cast our eyes on but our travelling companion from the train—'the Breton peasant with the permanent smile'. He jumped with joy as he hugged me and the others in turn and I felt embarrassed and so humble to think how we had treated him on that train. Tears streamed down his cheeks from his lovely brown eyes—tears of joy, of relief, of satisfaction that he realised now, as we all did, that we were companions, soldiers in the same noble cause. After that I never saw our friend again. The French Battalion was cut up badly at Jarama and I often wonder if he died, and if he did would he still be smiling at the end of freedom's long, devious mile.[129]

Fort Figueras was a relic of the past and reflected a past feudalistic landlord- and priest-ridden system. The place was truly a fortress. I believe such places are quite common along the Pyrenees. Whether the fort was originally built to withstand the invasion of the French or the native Catalans I don't know, but it certainly stank of a past when soldiers, conscripts and mercenaries, were treated and barracked like animals in the frigid cells, with slits as windows and slabs as bunks, with the straw tethered frames and troughs for horses, which still in character furnished the place. The surrounding countryside was picturesque and reminded one of the rugged scenes of Scotland.

For some days we lay around talking and debating, mingling with Germans, Italians, Irish and Yugoslavs. It was here I met the members of the 'original' Irish Republican Army who were later to form the Jim Connolly Battalion, led by the legendary Frank Ryan and by Kit Conway, the latter a Dubliner, a brave and gallant man, whom I saw later shot down at the battle of Jarama. It was elation and inspiration to meet such great characters whom usually one only reads about in books.[130] We heard the stories of concentration camps in Germany and of the escapes to freedom. The Italians sang their *Avanti Opopolo Bandiera Rossa* battle hymn, and the strains of *The Soldier's Song* came from the Irish. When as a youth I had read Jack London and Upton Sinclair I had entered a new world in literature which sparkled with such legendary figures.[131] Now I had actually entered this new world of living figures. They were the men who were to lead on the battlefields in Spain and in the Second World War and later in the socialist emergence in the various countries— that is, those who survived Spain.

Christmas day 1936 was spent at Figueras and the entire British contingent was laid up with diarrhoea and sickness. We slept on straw mattresses in dungeons with only the traditional slits in the wall which allowed the sun to blink in and the stink to seep out. There was no plum pudding for us, nor even castor oil. We spent the two days of Christmas sitting on latrine seats.

Eventually we set off for Barcelona, which I had previously visited during my days as a seaman. What changes was I to see? Everyone who has visited Barcelona knows the Ramblas, just as everyone who has visited Glasgow knows Sauchiehall Street. On my first visit—in 1934, the year of the Oviedo uprising, when the Asturian miners revolted against the old regime, we had walked along the streets where people sat on the sidewalk drinking, smoking and eating. Chicken spits had tirelessly turned, emitting their choice smells, taunting and teasing the appetites of the passers-by, and bootblacks had offered to polish our shoes. The smell of strong scents and eau de cologne had pervaded the air and puffs of self-made black cigarettes gave an atmosphere of continental relaxation. Fashionable senoritas had chaperoned the young. Girls and boys always seemed to walk in threes but in opposite directions. I had memories of late nights when one went to the cinema to see Laurel and Hardy in *Bonnie Scotland* dubbed in Spanish, and Charlie Chaplin advertised as '*Charlot en Tiempos Modernos*' (*Modern Times*), and the big streaming adverts about American drinks and French perfumes.[132]

What differences now at the beginning of 1937? Everyone seemed to be dressed in overalls or quaint army uniforms mainly of corduroy, with berets or split little khaki hats. Buildings were bedecked with banners in black and red with the letters CNT, FAI, JSO, POUM.[133] Loudspeakers blared out messages calling for efforts to beat Fascism. Pictures of a woman and a dead child alongside the profiles of young militia men and militia women looked down from posters on walls and hoardings. All was confusion at first and to understand and appreciate the whole scene was very difficult. The overall message of 'Smash fascism!' penetrated the mind but what was to take its place? That was left to the befuddled imagination of the onlooker.

One could feel the unanimity of the population in their commitment to the cause of smashing fascism and all the reaction it stood for. Everyone, girls and boys alike, was a soldier. One could also detect the political confusion that existed, especially shown by the posters everywhere and by the various factions that flourished—Anarchist, Syndicalist, Socialist, Communist, Trotskyist. It was to be hoped that the military command was more united in its central aim than the varieties of political view displayed in Barcelona.

We were taken to the barracks and paraded through the streets in military formation. Spain was a country at war. Rationing and the blackout were in operation. Every car was commandeered by the military. We had food and went to sleep in barracks which reminded me of horses' stables—the smell of dung, human and animal, pervaded everywhere. Gradually pieces of military dress began to appear in our contingent, mainly hats and caps. I had a leather forage cap which could fold down over the ears as protection against wind and rain and it was very soldier-like. My raincoat was one from my *Sunday Express* days and was the type used for horse-riding with a flap and appeared to be officerish. I suppose, in my way, I was vain and needed some bucking up. The time of action was getting nearer and I now felt integrated in the struggle of the Spanish people, which I had come to accept was the struggle of the world's people against the creeping paralysis of fascism.

Our group—the original group which had joined the buses in Glasgow—was still intact except for one man who had been rejected in Paris and another who had been left on the London railway station platform as incapable and not worthy of the honour of being a member of the International Brigade. Despite our detestation of drink and its incompatibility with service in the Brigade, this latter mate of ours eventually arrived in Spain. He proved himself a remarkably able soldier and carried on through the war, showing examples of heroism in the face of the enemy. He died in the battle of Brunete in the summer of 1937.[134]

We left Barcelona and travelled on through Valencia and then to Albacete, a garrison town in the middle of Spain, which was the reception centre for the International Brigade. There we again went into barracks which I remember to be more like Paddy's Market in Glasgow. We drew our uniforms, which were khaki and comprised a small bum-tickler jacket and trousers that buttoned round the ankles. They were all misfits. Some of us received long, and some short. With a bit of swopping here and there we were eventually dressed as soldiers. Looking back now at some of the old photos we were like MacNamara's Band. All our civvy clothes were thrown on a gigantic heap and it was with the greatest reluctance I parted with my best and only suit, which I had bought for thirty-five bob.

Our stay in the bomb splattered garrison town of Albacete was short-lived. Soon we were rumbling on our way in an old bus to the training base at Madrigueras. It was on this bus, leaving the outskirts of Albacete, that a bullet cut a clean hole through the glass of the window, missing my head by the merest fraction and embedding itself in the wooden framework. The Fifth Column was no idle boast! On arrival at the base camp we were met by the remainder of our original companions of our departure from Glasgow. It was almost like being home again except for the uniforms and the quaint Spanish peasant atmosphere. There were also many comrades who had been in Spain for some time. They had received no publicity—that shocked but didn't surprise me, knowing these lads and their dedication. One was Tommy Flynn, who came from a staunch Roman Catholic family, and had fought right through from the first days with the German Thaelmann Battalion. He died only a few days after that meeting.[135]

The introduction to the Brigade was routine. A meal of stew was served in the local church, the first of many to follow—always stew. Our group was billeted in the local squire's house: where he was we never enquired. It was one of the best residences in the village; the floors were in picturesquely designed terrazzo and the walls were of the best decor. There were eight large rooms in addition to a very large and commodious kitchen, and in comparison to the small peasant houses it stood out like a palace. We certainly made ourselves at home. We slept in neat formation on straw mattresses. One large room was more or less used as a lecture and study room. It resembled, I should imagine, the traditional British army billet without the trimmings of rifles and other military equipment. No weapons were to be seen, apart from one machine gun, a relic from the First World War, and a revolver possessed by an officer who wore a Sam Browne belt.

A few days after our arrival George Nathan made his appearance. He was a British ex-army officer and was rumoured to be the black sheep son of a wealthy Jewish family. He arrived with another notable character, Jock Cunningham. They were rough, dishevelled, unshaven, from an earlier campaign in Aragon and had all the makings of seasoned, professional soldiers.

The following day Nathan was walking down the rough street of Madrigueras impeccably dressed in full officer's gear. He wore corded breeches, a short style British army officer's coat, with nice neat brown lace-up boots, a peaked cap and was smoking a French briar pipe. He swanked a well trimmed moustache. Where Nathan obtained his gear is anyone's guess. (Doc Bradsworth, a gentle soul from Birmingham, did possess such a coat as Nathan wore but never a word of complaint escaped the lips of Doc.) Jock Cunningham typified the sturdy well built Argyll Highlander. His profile could have been carved from the coal of his native Lanarkshire. Jock hailed from Motherwell. He was a dauntless fighter and a leader of men. Nathan eventually was promoted on to the International Brigade General Staff, and Cunningham identified himself as the warrior he was in leading the troops at Jarama.[136]

Other leading officers at the base included men like D F Springhall and a mysterious, boastful character who had all the swagger and swashbuckling antics of a typical mercenary soldier. He was Captain O. There was T H Wintringham, with cigarette holder, bald head, aristocratic trimmed moustache, and a diminutive Sergeant McDade from Dundee, who followed T H. Then there was Wilfred McCartney, who wrote *Walls Have Mouths*. Wilfred as a lad had fought and been trained by Compton MacKenzie in Greece during the First World War. He became the Battalion commandant but due to an accident, and I believe while he was still on parole, he had to return to Britain without having led his troops into battle, a task he would no doubt have carried out with distinction and honour. Most of the officers were working class. They included a London bus driver, a coal miner and a number of British ex-soldiers.[137]

Around this period the Largo Caballero Government was changing and an all out effort was made to mould the Republican army into a modern fighting machine that could cope with the entry into the war of the German and Italian Fascist troops.[138]

This was the period when the Anarchist Syndicalists and the rather primitive mode of warfare had to be changed if Spanish democracy was to survive. Although leaders like Durruti and his men made great sacrifices in keeping Franco from entering Madrid, nevertheless modern methods and strategy led by a united command was the urgent issue of the moment. In this period of the war the names of Modesto, Lister, Walter, and of course Chief Of Staff Miaja became known and prominent in the new co-ordinated command.[139]

Our task at Madrigueras was reflected in this general picture. Training and drill were the order of the day. In our billet I slept in the same room as McLeary, Douglas, Rae, Connolly and a small, burly, stout man who continually smoked stubs of cigars. He hailed from Oldham and he was the toughest guy I was privileged to meet. He was Clem Beckett. Clem was one of the most outstanding speedway riders to grace British tracks. His speed and daring on one occasion during his speciality stunt on the Wall of Death was so sensational that it caused a number of onlookers to faint, one being the Queen of Demark.[140]

Another of my room mates was a quiet, thoughtful and extremely good looking young man who would systematically dismantle, and lecture on the intricacies of, the only machine gun in our possession. He was Christopher St John Sprigg, a specialist in the technicalities of aviation and an outstanding writer, under the name Christopher Caudwell, of poetry and philosophy.[141]

There were also a porter from Covent Garden, a Welsh university student, and a bulky Londoner, Jack Sylvester, who used more swear words than anyone I ever knew. That was a snapshot of my mates.

The training was thorough and exhaustive. It was regular for the roll call to be at 6 am and to have a route march before breakfast. We starved, waiting for the midday meal of stew. Always stew! On one of those early morning marches I put my hand in my tunic pocket and found a crust of bread—quite small in size, coated with the usual dust that accumulates in one's pocket, and put it in my mouth and sucked it till every bit of goodness and nutriment was extracted. Today, if anyone asks me what was the most enjoyable meal or feast I've ever had, my mind goes back to that dear little crust.

The one great treat we all looked forward to at Madrigueras was to visit the homes of the peasants. Hospitality and kindness is in the nature of the Spanish peasant. It was quite common for a child to come to the billet bearing a slip of paper inviting a group to his or her home at the request of the parents. At a gathering of the whole family we would all sit round the table with a pan of wooden embers glowing at our feet under the table keeping us warm. The vino would be passed round in the goatskin bottle and the meat, always in garlic which I never relished. But how could one refuse such kindliness and hospitality? One dear old mother, whose sons had all gone off to the militia and were fighting at the front, invited us as a group to her home. Her dwelling resembled the Scots or Welsh cottage and an unusual feature was a 'well' in her porch from which she drew water by the bucket. Inside were the open beams and pieces of meat and ham hung from hooks. After the meal the old lady invited us to see Dolores in her bedroom. Our Spanish wasn't too good but we explained it was unusual for us to go to a girl's bedroom. She laughed and ushered us into the room. We also laughed then: Dolores was a donkey! She was bedded in a back room and accepted as one of the family, as were all the other animals.

Never a day was missed in improving our military efficiency. Visits by experts took place. One was Professor J B S Haldane, the eminent scientist, who turned out to be an expert on the throwing of hand grenades and he imparted his profound knowledge to us. He gave another lecture on poison gas and how to cope with such a contingency should it arise.[142]

There was still quite a lot of confusion in our ranks as to the role of the Brigade and the nature of the struggle taking place. Confusion arose from the failure to recognise the difference between a Socialist Red Army establishing workers' power and a Republican Army fighting against fascism, the force that aimed to destroy democracy and social progress. Therefore, whilst mainly we were socialists in the International Brigade, our task was to assist the Spanish people to resist fascism and protect democracy. The Spanish people themselves—and themselves alone—would determine the fate of their country and the eventual system devised, be it socialist or otherwise. So political discussion and lectures were part of our life and much was learnt in the process.

Our greatest weakness was lack of arms. The so-called Non-Intervention Pact thought up by the Baldwin government in Britain and the French government of Blum prevented the free supply of all the essentials. Gallant seamen ran the blockade with food and arms sent by the Soviet Union and Mexico. Food ships were sent by the democratic forces of Britain. Unsung heroes like Potato Jones sailed and burst the blockades to San Sebastian time and time again, to ferry food to the beleaguered people.[143] Armaments that had been bought and paid for by the Spanish Republican government were 'frozen' in France at the behest of the government there. The achievements at the front and the defence of Madrid could have been greater and more significant than they were but for the Non-Intervention Pact. The men who formed the governments that starved the Spanish people of arms and food in 1937 committed a grave crime against humanity and paved the way to the coming of the Second World War and the death of millions. Franco carried out some beastly and dastardly acts of inhuman vengeance against Spanish people with the open help of Hitler's Germany and Mussolini's Italy.

Our needs, therefore, were arms and a more sophisticated modern army and to those ends the Popular Front government were working feverishly. La Pasionaria (Dolores Ibarruri), the great woman legend of the time, reached the heights of patriotic fervour in urging and stimulating her people to struggle. And the people responded.[144]

The introduction of the International Brigades helped immensely in the introduction of new fighting skills and techniques and also in taking the brunt of the Fascist attacks while the new People's Armies were learning.

At the rear the task was hampered, especially in Catalonia, by the presence of the deadly Fifth Column and their activities and the paralysis being created by the POUM, who called for social revolution when the need was for the Popular Front's victory against fascism as a first priority. In the early months they fermented unrest to such an extent that large forces had to be deployed in that direction, thus taking vital energy away from the front lines.

The picture in Madrigueras was a reflection of the influences operating around us. Life was spartan and apart from training and reading the textbooks on modern methods of warfare our only recreation was our visits in the evening to peasant friends. Perhaps one of the most remarkable departures from our routine life was the organisation of a Burns Supper on the 25th of January 1937 in a local assembly hall where I gave the traditional toast to the haggis and we celebrated with tatties and sardines. That night Scottish, Irish and French songs were lustily sung and we even had two Dutch militiamen yodelling and playing concertinas.

All the time that I had taken part in the socialist movement I had never been asked to do anything which offended my morals or principles, but in Madrigueras I was asked to join the intelligence services. I have always had an objection to spying and 'telling tales' against my compatriots. George Aitken approached me and asked me to join the Intelligence and to make out reports to him. No question of compulsion, reward or revenge was mentioned in the interview and I said I would submit any reports of anything that was untoward, treacherous or otherwise, against the progressive cause. But I never had the occasion to report any incident during the whole of my stay in Spain. My career as an Intelligence officer bore no fruit and I could never expect to be rewarded for services rendered in that direction.[145]

New forms of army organisation were taking place and we were now classed as the British Battalion attached to the XVth Brigade, but it didn't make any difference to the shortage of arms. We were still practising with wooden poles and having our regular lecture on the working and manipulation of our one and only machine gun by that patient man, Christopher St John Sprigg.

Money and its benefits never seemed to bother me since I didn't smoke and my only requirement was to send an odd letter home or to go to the 'churo shop' in the morning. The shop was a little house in a side street where a man and a woman squeezed dough out of a bag through a nozzle into a pan of hot fat. The dough circled to the bottom in an endless trail like a long worm, and this was served in portions with a mug of milk coffee. It was delicious.

My pay was so insignificant that its irregularity caused me no hardship. At home, I learnt later, my mother received a mysterious pound note each week. I never found out who was the sender of the gift but my mother was very grateful.

Taking turns as guard was a monotonous, cold duty but one that was very necessary. At night on duty we were issued with one of the very few rifles available and a large blanket-like cape. Many nights I stood in a dark corner hoping that no one would come and attack because there was no ammunition for the gun. He must have heeded my prayer—no one ever came. It was on the occasion of those long, black, bleak watches I made the acquaintance of an Irish minister of religion. The Reverend R M Hilliard hailed from Killarney and embraced the Protestant faith. He was known as 'the boxing parson', and with his short cropped hair and broken nose he certainly fitted his nickname. Beneath that outward appearance he was a very kind, sincere person with a fine sense of humour and no task was too big or too small for him. He would come during my watches and chat for hours on end and relieve the boredom of the night. Later I helped to bury the Rev. R M in Murcia.

One morning the Battalion was assembled in the village square to hear an important announcement. A celebrity from headquarters would be present. The surprise announcement was that the British Battalion had been integrated into the XVth Brigade and rifles and other equipment would follow. The celebrity was a French general by the name of Vidal.[146] This surprise announcement was obviously the cover to tell us that we would soon be on the move. Sure enough the next morning we were told to get ready. Excitement reached a high pitch and the speculation was that action was imminent. That morning the first firearms were issued to us. Apart from the rifles that we had used at the training targets and which were of the older and varied types dating in some cases back to the Great War of 1914-18, this was our first individual issue. I received a brand new Russian rifle with the longest imaginable bayonet attached. A cold feeling went down my spine when I thought of its use. Oh, God!, I thought, let it never be that I shall be involved in hand to hand combat, especially with the cold bayonet of steel penetrating my body. I imagined the blood spewing and spurting from me. How the issue of these weapons affected the other recruits I'll never know.[147]

Busily preparations were made to move off to the front. I wrote a letter home saying that everything was fine, victory was just round the corner, and soon I would be home again. Soon, very soon, the whole Battalion was paraded again, this time for final. The children and the parents of the village assembled to wave and say farewell. The sad mothers looked on with their lined, brown faces and prematurely greying hair as their children clung to their aprons, staring in silence and wonder at the troops lined up. The few men gathered, mostly old, stood in a corner respectfully touching their hats as they recognised each of their new found friends among us. There was a feeling of foreboding as they looked on, tears glistening on their cheeks. Dust rose from the square when the soldiers stood to attention. It was a brief ceremony. The commander thanked the villagers for their hospitality and promised that every man leaving for the front that day would do his proud duty.

As we broke ranks and made for the lorries ready to transport us to the front, a young girl dressed in poor dark clothes and with a sweet, sad face which carried the glimmer of a smile, stepped out, ran towards me and handed me a note. As I took the paper from her she leaned over and reached for my face and gave it a fleeting kiss. Then she turned back and joined the crowd of onlookers. Little had I known that I had a secret admirer. Amidst my blushes and astonishment my mates let out a loud howl of delight and derision, chided me over the mysterious lover and demanded to see what was in the note. It simply contained a name and address which I interpreted as an invitation to correspond. I am afraid I have always been an unreliable correspondent. Anyhow the order was given later that all notebooks and addresses should be destroyed for obvious reasons. So I travelled as usual with my pockets empty and my mind full of wonder and expectation, still wondering who the girl was and how did she fit into my scene.

We piled on the open Russian lorries and soon were rumbling along the unmade roads towards Madrid. Fifteen men to a lorry, each with his kit-bag and holding a long polished rifle with the bayonet shining in the sun, did not provide for any travel comforts and it is surprising that someone wasn't stabbed before the front was reached. For the best part of the day we travelled mile after mile, and apart from stopping on two occasions to have mass relief by the wayside our bruised bodies swayed uncontrollably as the wheels of the lorry sank into ruts on the dusty road. No one in our group knew the destination. We passed through barren villages with not a face to be seen. Everywhere seemed to be deserted except for peasants working in the fields.

As the sun was losing its height we arrived in a village. Dismounting we were directed to a building resembling an old school room where staff members had already arrived and cooks busied themselves making their stew. The place smelt like a mixture of cabbage water and sweaty socks. Everyone ate, but the same robust appetites of previous times were not in evidence even though it was the only cooked meal that day. I felt edgy and didn't eat much and soon had settled in a corner with my pack and rifle. The rifle somehow felt human and commandeered a place in my life and received the respect it warranted. The other lads were also quiet and one or two settled down to write notes; in particular John Connolly (Isa Alexander's boy-friend) painstakingly wrote his *billet doux*, and Jimmy Rae, bespectacled and deadly serious, wrote his despatch as Battalion correspondent to his trade union branch. McLeary and Douglas, the seasoned Highland hikers, were slumped in a corner in an ideal setting for relaxation. Beckett I can see now, the natural leader of our group, still nursing his machine gun and looking the dare-devil he was, with a small stub of a cigar in his mouth. Around nine o'clock I decided to step out to buy some vino—a strange thing for me to do then. I was sick with fear and worry at the thought of impending action and the consequences. My idea in getting the wine was to give me Dutch courage at the vital moment. I managed to contact an elderly peasant who introduced me to someone who supplied the vino. Back in the billet with my boots placed together as a pillow and an old blanket for a cover I lay down to try and sleep, but couldn't doze off. The rumbling of shell fire could be heard, and the drone of planes overhead. We were close to the front. I lay stiff with cold and fear, wondering what the morning would bring. Terribly lonely now for the first time since leaving Glasgow my mind kept going back to my mother and young sister lying in their beds. I lay wondering, wondering, what would happen? I have, in circumstances of worry, been able to compare my lot with someone in a less favourable position and achieved a sense of relief by comparison, but on that night I could find nothing to equal my miserable soul.

With the rise of the sun the company was alerted and feeding and packing occupied our attention. The foreboding and fear experienced the previous dark hours soon melted and the lorries were on their way carrying us to the front. It was barely half an hour's run and we dismounted with instructions to move towards a ravine and to take heed of all cover and proceed in the direction of a hill at the end of the ravine. With discipline to keep pace and following the man in front I kept with a group of fifteen men as we wound our way forward. Our ammunition pockets were now filled. Beckett and Sprigg led the way, still hugging their machine gun and belts of ammunition.

On our way to the right was a large farmhouse which appeared to be the Brigade headquarters, which we steered well clear of and proceeded ravine-wise. At one period we walked along a deep gully and the first sign of enemy activity was heard. A large plane roared up the ravine—someone said it was an Italian Caproni. Beckett gave the order to cover and every man-jack threw himself to the ground as the distant spatter of machine gun bullets could be heard. I rolled over to a piece of scanty gorse-like bush and tried to make myself look as inconspicuous as possible. As the plane boomed out of sound Beckett called, 'She'll be back again—keep cover!'

As sure as anything she came back in the opposite direction but somewhat lower than before and Becket and Sprigg mounted the machine gun and fired a burst towards the plane's belly. The plane didn't come back and fortunately we suffered no casualties.

At the end of the ravine we saw to our right what appeared to be the Irish Battalion and later the American Lincoln Battalion, and to our left were the Spanish.[148] At the head of the ravine was an olive grove which stretched for quite a distance and presented a measure of cover from the stray bullets that could be heard whizzing, for we were virtually in the front line. We were now approaching the Jarama River and the Fascists were making an all-out effort to cut the main artery and surround Madrid. Again we heard a plane overhead but nothing happened. Shell fire could now be heard distinctly in the immediate vicinity. We plodded on and had a short rest at one period. It was then I decided to have a drink of my vino and I held the bottle up to my mouth and gulped quite a long drink. I found that instead of giving me infinite courage it simply came out of my body in beads of sweat. The Dutch courage had still to come!

A Spanish scout contacted us and explained the near vicinity of Moorish troops and directed us to a hill in the distance where a house had once stood. The old footings provided a natural barrier out of enemy sight. Beckett, looking through his binoculars, spotted an enemy grouping of Moors and peeping over the bank I saw a black-bearded face in the thick undergrowth. He looked fearsome, grizzly and inhuman. In that direction we concentrated our baptism fire and in the ensuing battle my fears and foreboding went unnoticed and the sound of fire from the enemy seemed to fit into the already imagined picture.[149]

Our first casualty was Noel, a young schoolteacher. A bullet had hit a rock and splintered his face, which was a mass of blood, and I was certain he was blinded. It was around this time, as the sun was dropping, that a plane came over our position and dropped what appeared to be a lighted torch near us. Within minutes hell was let loose as shell fire began, trees disappeared, and the whizzing screaming noise shook the ground around us. We recognised our position was vulnerable but there was little to be done in the bombardment apart from an occasional pot shot at the opposing infantry, whom we sensed would be crawling in the undergrowth and edging up whilst the bombardment continued.

Across the valley I could see a group advancing and firing almost in front of our position. It proved our intuition to be correct. The enemy was almost upon us. To our right I distinguished Kit Conway, the Irish leader, making the advances and going over the hill, followed by his men. At least three went down.

The bombardment seemed to increase and carried on for what must have been an hour. A London lad whom I knew back in Madrigueras took a bolt to a new position and almost instantaneously folded up like a pocket-knife as a bullet penetrated his body. He cried aloud in agony and I rushed over to drag him out of the line of fire behind a tree clump. As I bent over him I had such a bump on my right shoulder—it was just as if a sledge hammer had hit me and I must have rolled over in the position where I was trying to pull the wounded Londoner over. What happened then I'll never know. When I came around I couldn't move and felt as if my right arm was paralysed. I was saturated in blood. Gun fire could still be heard but it seemed to be in the distance. The hill was deserted and no sign of my group could be seen. Lying by another tree in the olive grove was a soldier, also wounded. The young lad I had gone to help lay dead by my side. With great effort, which all seems a daze now, I moved over to the other soldier who was in great pain and had been hit by shrapnel. It was almost dark. The fire was decreasing and seemed to consist of shots in the distance.

Later I learnt Beckett, St John Sprigg, Rae, Connolly and Douglas were killed. McLeary received terrible wounds that crippled him for life. Jack Sylvester, I suspect, also died but Len Cochrane, I believe, survived but died later as an airman in the Second World War.[150] The number of deaths at Jarama was very high. Often the tears of remembrance creep into my eyes when I recall those gallant, honest, dedicated mates who died on that hill.

Can I ever forget that trek back to the Field Hospital? We, my new found comrade and I, crawled from tree to tree from the scene of that hell's fire where our mates lay dead. It was when we seemed to reach the end of the grove that bullets could be heard whining over our heads again. They seemed to be coming from the direction of our own fire. Had we crossed back over the lines of the enemy? My arm was useless and gave me gyp. My mate dragged his leg. At one point we cuddled into a tree stump. He managed to light a nub of a cigarette.

I felt sick. We decided to stay put in a hollow till the sun rose and we could take our bearings. It was endless, cold and miserable. We managed to keep one another warm by placing our bodies together. At one stage just as the first chinks of sun peeped over the horizon he hitched on to his side, unbuttoned his flies and managed to relieve himself. I may have done that (without the contortion) in my pants. No firing commenced at dawn as was expected, which seemed to make the position more ominous. Were we behind enemy lines? If so, I thought death would have been a more relishable end than that.

It was later that voices were heard. They turned out to be of some Spanish militiamen who were in the same plight and were endeavouring to reach the dressing station. We tagged on to them and eventually came to a point where an officer approached, pointing a revolver at us in his duty of intercepting deserters. Our wounds were evident and he insisted we both sit down and he gave us a drink of water. He then directed us to the bottom of an incline where a field ambulance was busily attending to the wounded. As we were being attended to, a male orderly cut my tunic sleeve completely off and padded the wound with a swab and gave it a rough dressing. An ambulance donated by a Swiss friendship organisation drew up and the wounded were loaded into it. Along with my colleagues I settled in the ambulance but felt ashamed to think I was occupying a place that could have been occupied by someone in a worse condition than me. One unconscious casualty had a leg off. Another had his face so smashed up it was completely hidden. Another died on the way.

For some time we jostled along a wavy, bumpy path until a terrific concussion and explosion occurred and the next thing I remembered I was being dragged out of the window of the ambulance and forcibly pushed into some bushes. A bomb had hit the roadway and the ambulance had descended into the crater. Along with my wounded mates I lay there for some time—how long, I don't know.

A French first-aid worker along with some peasants arrived and helped us through the rough foliage and eventually to a building—a school?—which had been furnished sparsely as a casualty station. Without undressing or washing I lay on a bare mattress on the floor which was covered in blood and mud and fell fast asleep. I awakened in the darkness—I don't know how long I had slept—and I wanted to go to the lavatory. I remember groping my way past beds on the floor and to a door. The place smelt of lysol and death and as I entered the room I saw the bodies and the limbs of dead men. I had wandered into the makeshift mortuary.

The concussion of bombs and shell fire could still be heard. The next day or the day afterwards—time had no meaning—those that could walk went on an ambulance, the others who were stretcher cases went on open lorries. This journey went better than the first and soon we were at a railway siding which was pock-marked with bomb craters. A train with empty carriages stood there and we boarded. Soon the train filled up and once in a seat it was for the duration. The main bulk of mobile cases sat on the hard seats, the stretcher cases were laid down the passages. Fortunately, because the train was of old vintage, it moved slowly—very slowly—and by virtue of its country route it regularly stopped in orange groves and then there was the exodus of hobbling soldiers on 'make do' crutches and in blood-stained bandages who climbed from the windows to pay homage to nature. The stretcher cases—poor creatures—had to relieve themselves as best they could lying flat on their backs. On one occasion the train started quicker than usual due to enemy aerial activity and some of the soldiers with their trousers down had to scramble aboard in the most undignified fashion.

Where we travelled I'll never know. We thought the train was heading towards Valencia but that was only guess work. After almost two days aboard the train we arrived at Murcia where there was a big hospital manned by leading surgeons and personnel from all over the world. To the best of my knowledge three of the stretcher cases had died on the train. The hospital was certainly an improvement in facilities. The wards, although overflowing, were well organised and had a devoted staff second to none. I had never been in hospital before, but I have been since then. I would give Murcia hospital top marks even so long ago and in a country that clung so tightly to its feudal past.

After a week's attention and regular sleep and food I was out and about, although my arm, still heavily bandaged, gave me much pain and would be useless for some time. The doctors would give me no assurance about it. Evidently I had been hit by a spent bullet which when in the decline carries great force and the impact is felt much more than a bullet at its zenith. I was fortunate that it didn't hit me on the spinal chord for, if so, this story wouldn't have been told.

D F Springhall landed at the same hospital with a most unusual wound. He had opened his mouth to speak and a bullet went through one cheek and came out the other. According to an eye witness, it looked as if he had been hit on both cheeks with a lump of steak. When I saw him he couldn't speak and looked quite pathetic. However, he recovered and was soon back in action. Noel Carritt and Jimmy Campbell, a pal from the Hunger March days, with Tiny (a very tall man) and a dapper little Covent Garden porter, were my bosom friends in those Murcia days.

The war hadn't seemed to affect the populace there as much as it had in the Madrid area or even in Catalonia and it was not uncommon for us Brigaders to be forced off the pavement by other pedestrians which was strangely different from other places where we had been and where the peasants had showered kindness upon us. There was of course an historical reason for treating soldiers as second class citizens since the ranks of the old regime's army had been mainly recruits from among the peasantry and conscripts from Spain's colonial territories and their lot hadn't been a happy one.

The second week of our stay was saddened by the news of R M Hilliard, my Irish priest friend of Madrigueras days. We buried him in Murcia and Peter Kerrigan gave the oration at the graveside.[151]

In the third week we, as a group, left Murcia to go south to convalesce on the Mediterranean coast at Beni-Casim, a little village by the sea. Beni-Casim possessed villas and bungalows which were creations out of this world and had been built for some very wealthy owners who had left for more peaceful climes. The view was one of the sea and of lovely sandy beaches. We slept four in one room on mattresses spread on the floor and when the sun rose the great french windows were opened and we walked out to the sea. As I looked out to the beautiful blue Mediterranean and saw on the horizon the outline of a tramp steamer sailing freely with the smoke emitted from its funnel, my mind was taken back to my days as a cabin boy on the old tramps. Memories so fresh, yet so distant! I thought of how I used to gaze in wonder at what was behind those hills on the Spanish mainland and little did I think that one day I would climb those mountains and take part in a war for the survival of decency on earth.

We paddled in the sea with the waves dashing themselves against our bodies and basked in the glorious sun. Little was the wonder that in our discussions the subject of ethics arose, asking how millionaires who gave nothing to society could live a life of luxury like this when so much poverty existed not so many yards away.

However, our stay at Beni-Casim was helpful and provided the wounded with the necessary elements to recover. Noel and I found some champagne in our villa's cellar and each evening we would go to a little cafe tucked away in the village and enjoy omelettes and champagne. The seaside peasantry were as interesting as the country peasants and I saw them playing a game of hand-ball with exactly the same rules and style that I had seen as a child in the Ayrshire village where I was born.

Our general recoveries were quick and it was necessary to take only the minimum of convalescence since the amount of casualties coming from the front was increasing every day and beds were badly needed. Our group elected to go back to Albacete, although two of our number would never fight again and Noel wasn't quite fit enough and I wouldn't hold a weapon for some time.

When we arrived in Albacete it was like a blitzed town of the Second World War. The main buildings were almost demolished but the town buzzed vigorously with military activity.

Soldiers of all nationalities on leave from the front frequented the cafes and salons and quite a number of distinguished personalities were around. It was rumoured that Paul Robeson had passed through, as had Harry Pollitt and Ernest Hemingway.[152] I met a Glasgow friend, Alex Donaldson, who was attached to the editorial side of the Brigade paper and by him was asked to take on a job as courier. The job entailed being based at Albacete and when a group of volunteers arrived from Britain and they had gone through the procedures of uniform issue, my job was to convey them to Madrigueras. I carried this job for almost a month but the strain was quite strenuous since every time I arrived at the old training base with recruits everyone was inoculated and I was getting a jab every time I arrived there. Soon I was quite ill and my wound was playing me up and through another appointment I gratefully lost my courier position.

In Albacete at that time we had Peter Kerrigan, George Brown (later killed at Brunete), and Walter Tapsell, a cockney wit and *Daily Worker* man, who was also later killed.[153] The building Alex Donaldson and I slept in was a second rate type of hotel without any staff and we simply had a room to sleep in. We dined (?) at a local canteen. The room we slept in was on the third floor and one side of the building had been sliced off by a bomb and at the side was a terrific crater. It was said, and confirmed later, that Hitler had tried out there some of his bombs similar to those that were later to drop on Britain. Our room was barricaded and if we had gone through the thin plywood we should have dropped three stories down into the crater. Thank goodness we didn't sleepwalk. Complete blackout was in operation.

I was invited to attend a regional conference of the JSO (the Young Socialists) and it was quite an interesting experience. I had an intepreter provided and it was there that I met Santiago Carillo, later famous but then only of my own age.[154]

My strangest mission, one I wouldn't have liked to repeat, was to visit an International Brigader who had contracted venereal disease and was confined to hospital. Peter Kerrigan was the man who took the responsibility of visiting the wounded and performing many tasks relating to their welfare, including contacting their relatives at home. He was a busy person and delegated quite a lot of his tasks to me. This particular job I don't think he relished mainly because of his very puritanical attitude to drink and loose women. It was a job which I never thanked him for. I tried to get out of it but failed and so had the unenviable task of visiting hospital.

The victim was a middle aged man from a town in ———. He was a prominent co-op man and was a highly respected Labour official who held posts on his local trades council. He had a devoted family and some grandchildren, all of whom were proud of him and especially of his presence in the International Brigade. This man, however, had visited a brothel in Paris en route to Spain and it was after he had trained at the Madrigueras base that to his great dismay and shame he discovered he had venereal disease. He was sent to hospital, where he had lain for well over six weeks. Between remorse at his indiscretion, letting down his mates—many of whom were by now dead—and the prospect of having to go home and face his family and the Labour Movement, he had suffered what I thought was a complete nervous breakdown. I had never seen venereal disease and like all naive people wondered what happened to those who contracted it. In those days before pencillin was discovered it was classed much more seriously than it is now—although it is still a serious social problem.

The hospital lay just outside Albacete and I went by car on this dreaded mission. My ignorance made me afraid and I decided to open the doors only after wrapping a handkerchief round my hand and touching nothing. But just as I entered I bumped into a German Brigader I had met at Fort Figueras. He immediately shook my hand in a very warm, friendly fashion. He was in hospital for a hernia operation. So my resolution to touch nothing with my bare hands was broken right away. However, when I was shown into the cubicle to see the patient I was absolutely shocked and sick at heart. The poor man had wasted away almost to a shadow. He was staring and commenced shouting and gesticulating. He raved that the place was full of Fifth Columnists and that the Spanish doctors were deliberately not treating him properly and were making his disease worse. He stood up in his bed and lifted his night-shirt to expose his private parts. He showed me how his testicles were swollen and full of blue matter. He then accused me of being party to the conspiracy and told me to clear off and to tell Kerrigan he was the arch conspirator. The man was certainly deranged and presented a terribly sad picture—one that I have never forgotten over the years and would never like to see again. I left the hospital very depressed and feeling I had achieved nothing. I believe the man did eventually recover but as to his fitting back into his old setting I never enquired. I remembered only the lesson that that poor soul gave me of how a being can be so rich in pride, in achievement, in love, and yet can, by a mindless act of indiscretion, be reduced to a state of mental rags and tatters overnight. Fortunately, this was only a very rare case of social misfortune that occurred in the International Brigade to my knowledge. Of course, I recognised that the volunteers were not all angels and possessed their fair share of human faults. But the general conduct of the Brigade was second to none.

It was around this period in the war that international intrigue was doing great damage by the infiltration of spies and Fifth Column agents, and everyone had to be alerted to the dangers. Consequently posters, leaflets and broadcasts were made to pinpoint the mortal danger of this treacherous enemy in our midst.

In Catalonia mainly the POUM was a force that had been causing a lot of discontent. It was a vociferous propaganda machine which opposed the centralisation of government and campaigned against any steps of modernisation of the army through a General Command.

Also in the ranks of the International Brigade a group of young writers and poets had misinterpreted the discipline of an army which was fighting for its life, and through their indiscretions and outright disobedience landed themselves in trouble and behind bars.

It was then that Stephen Spender, the celebrated young English poet (who was not in the International Brigade), made his appearance in Spain and was known to be campaigning to have his friends released. He failed and made preparations to leave Spain and go to the south of France.[155]

During this period a fair number of about to be discharged volunteers were being sent back to Britain. I was put in charge to convey them safely back home and with the necessary documents and money I set about my task. It proved to be not so easy a job. In the group was a jute worker from ——— who had a family problem, his presence at home being necessary. Another man had developed tuberculosis. One young lad was under age. A fourth was a person who had mental illness and needed careful handling. My assignment was to see them over the borders of France and into Britain safely again, remembering we had left the country illegally and possessed no passports. We arrived in Valencia and spent the night at the Soccorro Roco Hostel (similar to the Red Cross). It was there that we met some recruits travelling to where we had come from. One was a middle aged widower who had left his one and only dependant with a friend. His dependant was a dog and it worried him so immensely that he asked me specially on arrival in Britain to send to his friend some money for food for the dog. This job I duly attended to.

The man with the mental breakdown was becoming a handful and it was touch and go if we could manage to hold him with the party all the way home. However, with patience and tact we succeeded. Our friend who had tuberculosis was progressively getting worse and it was necessary to get medical help in Valencia.

Eventually we arrived in Barcelona and put up at another hostel. The city buzzed with activity but presented a picture so confused that it was giving great concern to the central government. In Barcelona the British Foreign Office still operated and all five of us had to visit the consulate to obtain visas to re-enter Britain. It was here I really realised there were two kinds of Englishmen—or Scotsmen, for that matter. One was the old school tie type, and the other was like ourselves. The consular staff were as stiff as starched shirts. Our first interview was with an object who possessed the most revolting projecting teeth and hair parted down the middle of his head. He swanked an old Etonian tie and spoke as if he had swallowed an overgrown plum. He insulted us and said we had no right to take part in a war that was none of our business: we had broken the law and no help of any description could be given to us to re-enter the United Kingdom since we had taken part in a war that our government had banned! His only advice was 'to try and get into Britain and take the consequences.' It was significant that he took all our names and descriptions before he told us to be on our way. Our Dundee colleague had to be bodily restrained from attacking him. I am afraid we drew a blank at the British Embassy. So where could we go from there?

The next day we went to the Clothes Exchange to get our civvies and hand in our army misfits. We were all still in khaki uniforms caked with mud and creased, and altogether didn't present a very respectable looking picture. I dreaded the experience of wearing second-hand clothes. The reception was a bit different from the place where we left our original civvies in Albacete. We were met at a counter by a Spanish civilian who, as each showed his certificate of discharge from the army, stooped under the counter and presented each of us with a bundle of clothes already made up in a parcel tied with string. On undoing my lot I was disgusted. It had a black jacket with red specks running through the pattern—it resembled a circus crowns burlesque jacket—and also a pair of pin striped trousers with an Oxford type shirt and no collar. I refused to accept this rubbish, remembering I had handed in my best suit and coat. The attendant simply indicated if I didn't like what was offered I could clear off. I really felt let down, insulted and cheated. The others also grumbled and made some very disparaging remarks and comments on the general running of the war, of how men who were prepared to die for a country were treated like hoboes. It was then that the attendant who was the butt of our abuse walked from behind the counter and showed that he had an artificial leg attached to his right stump. I felt ashamed when the reality of the situation struck me. Here were we, five men who soon would be out of Spain and back to the peace and calm of home, making such a fuss about a few clothes when the news was still fresh of the massacre of Malaga, when the fleeing people—hundreds of them—had been mercilessly followed and strafed and bombed by the Germans and Italians. The bombs were still raining down on Madrid and the bodies of the slaughtered children of Guernica were hardly cold. How could we assess our life and existence by the mere value of a few rotten stinking clothes when our mates, our friends, our comrades, lay dead on the very battlefield we had not long left? When I thought of Beckett, Connolly, Sprigg, Rae, Douglas, Flynn, Hyndman, Cornford, Fox and all the other young men who were dead, never to return, and of dear Hilliard in his stony grave in Murcia, who was I? I felt ashamed.[156]

So we dressed in the clothes that were given to us. When we had originally donned uniform in Albacete we had looked like McNamara's Band. Now we looked like clowns in Billy Smart's Circus. My jacket was long, the trousers short, and I still wore my big tackety boots. But what did it matter? The attendant, who now saw that our co-operation was genuine, disappeared into the back shop and brought some raincoats. On donning them we didn't look quite such ridiculous and noticeable freaks. That night in the transit hostel, where we met some fresh volunteers on their way to Albacete, one of them gave me a brand new pair of flannels and a pair of brown brogue shoes and I felt quite good and smart again.

We remained in Barcelona nearly a week, due to travel difficulties, and it gave me a chance to explore the city that I had known so well in the past. Everywhere bore the pockmarks of battle: the buildings were studded with bullet holes. The political atmosphere was thick and rumours of impending internal trouble were rife. The POUM was churning out anti-government propaganda obviously for revolt. Loudspeakers dominated the plazas and posters of an anti-government nature were posted all over the place.

I learned that Bob Smillie, a boyhood friend of mine from Larkhall, who was chairman of the Independent Labour Party Guild of Youth during my days as organiser, had arrived in Spain and was attached to the POUM Regiment.[157] I set out to see if he was in the vicinity of Barcelona. On calling at the Hotel Falcon, POUM headquarters, I met McNair, who was acting head of the ILP contingent. I believe Bob had been his assistant, but McNair's new assistant, a girl by the name of Eileen, informed me that he was not around. Present also was an extremely tall, chain-smoking, sallow person dressed as an officer, with his Sam Browne belt and revolver, by the name of Blair. At first McNair was amicable but after a few minutes and knowing now that I had come from Albacete and was an International Brigader, his attitude changed. Blair made one or two snide remarks about the Brigade and all in all it was obvious I was not welcome. I left them to their cigarettes, polished revolvers and women.

I discovered afterwards that Blair was no other than George Orwell, the writer who later showed he had a pathological hatred for anyone or anything associated with the International Brigade and accused us of Communist intrigue against democracy. I'm afraid the numerical facts of dead and dying for the Republic rather refuted his contention. What has struck me all these years in his outpourings of hatred: where did his love lie? It certainly wasn't for the Spanish people and the country he was so eager to leave.[158]

In addition to being very angry at the attitude of the POUM and the ILP (represented by McNair) I was puzzled to know what the set-up was in that hotel. Why was McNair present, occupying comfortable quarters with a secretary and the ILP group who were serving in the POUM? It seemed ominous to me then that here was a bunch of men in the comparative safety of Barcelona churning out propaganda for social revolution and evidently with plenty of arms, whilst the Republic was fighting for its very life against fascism. The message was so clear: either win the war against fascism and then sort out the road the Spanish people were going to travel—either to remain a Republic pure and simple or establish a socialist system—or suffer the grim reality of being beaten by the forces of Franco, Hitler and Mussolini and live in chains for decades with all the accompanying torture and slaughter characteristic of fascism. In any case, surely the Spanish people themselves would decide the destiny of their country, and all foreign volunteers irrespective of their political, ethical or moral convictions would retire from the scene.

Outside in the streets lorries with soldiers in the old type militia uniforms—mainly corduroy—waving the anarchist colours, ferried to and fro. Noticeable was the great number of girls on the lorries. Loudspeakers continued to dominate the air with messages and calls to action from all shades of opinion. Many called for the spirit of July 1936. This was when the working class particularly had taken over the factories and telephone system, manned barricades and had put paid to the elements against the Republic. Of course, the slogan was linked with the call (mainly by the POUM) to establish workers' power—with no mention of defeating Franco first.

The anarchists evidently controlled the Telephone Exchange and there was talk of the government forces ratifying this anomaly which was leading to disunity and an intolerable situation, with the military command being subjected to 'ultra left' censorship and in some cases to open sabotage, with espionage being so easy and field intelligence so futile.

On the fifth day we left Barcelona. It was not before time. The man who had tuberculosis was not very well and looked a sad creature. Our friend who had the mental trouble was beginning to become more than a handful and it was only with skill and cunning that we, as a group, managed to contain him. On the station platform was Stephen Spender, the distinguished poet, whom I've already mentioned, and by design more than desire we chose his company. He was rather a friendly person, effeminate and generous. He bought all of us food on our way to Port Bou and the French border. To get across to France was simplicity itself. We simply dismounted from the train and followed Spender through a tunnel past some gendarmes and on to the platform of another railway station. Spender left us and was staying on in the south; we were going to Paris.

The journey, like our original passage in the opposite direction, was punctuated with uncomfortable moments. Spies, Fifth Columnists, agents provocateurs, were reported as being everywhere along all exits from Spain. Port Bou was bound to have its quota awaiting the opportunity of picking up a group like ours which no doubt possessed information which when sifted could be of great assistance to pro-Franco intelligence. And so, as the case happened, we picked up our fellow traveller in the guise of an International Red Cross courier. He claimed to be a Swiss, which we had no reason to disbelieve. He was blue eyed, fair haired, pale skinned, immaculately dressed in navy blue uniform and spoke charming English with just a slight continental ring. I was his choice of companion; and with the finesse of a cultured cavalier he offered his cigarettes, so neatly arrayed in a silver case. Being a non-smoker, and remembering 'sealed lips', I politely refused. He boldly opened the conversation by stating he had noticed us on the train from Barcelona in the company of Stephen Spender and he assumed we were discharged International Brigaders. He said he was himself on his way back from the Madrid front and was going back to Switzerland for more supplies. It was a very feasible story and connected in all details as far as I could see, but I became sceptical eventually because of his curiosity as to where we were going in Paris and what our connections were. Each time he approached the question I would guide the conversation away but he continually returned to the point, using different tactics. His strategy was evident to me and the red light was up. He could see I was an obstacle and his attention became directed on the man from Dundee but the one lesson I have learnt is that, despite the friendly, helpful nature of working class Scotsmen, once they feel they are being pumped, they fold up. And Dundee was certainly no exception. He, like myself, smelt our friend as a subtle spy.

As previously in dealing with our mentally disturbed colleague, Dundee and I had a prearranged signal to go to the toilet and have a 'pee' conference. On this occasion we decided there was only one way to deal with the Swiss Red Cross man, which was to ditch him, and the plan was laid.

On arrival in Paris we all adjourned to the lavatory and, true to life, the Red Cross man followed. As we all assembled to pay our respects to nature, Dundee went into a cubicle and beckoned the Red Cross man to follow and share the pan. The door then closed. A few seconds later a terrific howl was heard. Dundee hurriedly left the cubicle, slamming the door, and followed the group up the stairs into the crowded station and away. I never asked Dundee what he had done but I have a suspicion it was some deed not in the rule book of the Marquis of Queensberry. Whatever it was, our Swiss friend bothered us no more.

That night we slept in the same working class cafe I had slept in on my way to Spain. It was there that I discovered I had company which I had suspected for some days. It was in the privacy of the bedroom when I took my vest off that the evidence was there. I was lousy with body lice. I had had the experience of bugs on the *North Anglia* and of occasional fleas at the cinema but never, never had I had before the dreaded experience of lice on my body. I could remember some horrible nights in the company of rats at sea and the fear of death before battle but the lousy beastly feeling of lice on one's body was the most lowering form of human existence. It was among my worst experiences.[159]

Walter Tapsell (Tappy) of the *Daily Worker* once told me that in the trenches a method of cleaning one's underclothing of lice was to put the garments over an anthill. The ants just waded through them like an army and cleaned them out in no time. But, alas, we were not in the trenches and anthills didn't exist in Paris lodging houses. I didn't go to bed that night.

The next morning we were up early and on our way to Dieppe. On the train was a party of nuns and priests. Now instead of being afraid of our fellow travellers it was quite the reverse. It struck Dundee and myself instantly that mingling with nuns and priests was the ideal cloak in boarding the cross-channel boat and disembarking in England: our identity would not be so conspicuous.

I have always found it easy to get into conversation with clergy but never having had the occasion to converse with nuns that was an unknown quantity. To our united dismay on trying to get into conversation we were made abruptly aware that the party spoke only French and none of our party spoke anything but English. However, in a way this may have been better because it didn't raise the question of who we were and what our business was. Dundee was the star on this occasion. He commenced the discussion in our company, which comprised three priests and three of us—Dundee, the mentally disturbed colleague and myself—in the carriage. The other two of our group—the sick colleague and the boy—were with the party of nuns and by all accounts made friends with them. Dundee, in very hesitating short sentences, repeated slowly and deliberately: 'We are going to England and then to Scotland. Where are you going?' The words 'England' and 'Scotland', must have registered because the priests laughed knowingly and repeated to one another the words mingled with their fluent flow of French. Dundee began punctuating his short sentences with sign language, which led to confusion and laughter from our friends, and in a short space of time we were a jovial company mixed up in the ridiculous mess that we had experienced in Spain and France in trying to communicate. By the time we arrived in Dieppe each of us was deeply in discussion in our rough sign language technique. Boarding the ferry to Dover I can still picture the scene. Immediately in front of our group, comprising priests, Dundee and myself, was the party of nuns two of whom held the arm of our sick TB colleague as he walked up the gangway. Dundee had his hand on the shoulder of a young smiling priest as he chatted away and I carried the bag of another. All in all it looked like a genuinely acceptable party of dedicated shepherds of God looking after five lost sheep.

The customs and other personnel turned a blind eye to our party and the short trip across the Channel was embellished with the same conviviality that had marked our initial train journey. All good things come to an end and this brief ecclesiastically sponsored party was broken up as abruptly as it began. One by one as we walked down the gang plank at Dover 'the men from the Ministry' stood there and systematically plucked our party like apples off a tree. The nuns and priests looked on in utter astonishment at this dismal end to their good deed for the day; and I am sure as I was marched away I could see the nuns with tear-filled eyes crossing their hearts, and the pink-faced priests looking to the skies as if they were asking forgiveness from the Almighty.

Dundee was the first to be quizzed and although he was taken into a separate room, I could distinctly hear him say, 'I have been hiking in France.' And I can proudly say that not one of our group would divulge any accurate information on their movements. When I was interviewed my name and description was on the table and the gentleman from MI– knew damned well we had come from Spain— the International Brigade—and I am equally sure their informant was our Eton friend at the British Embassy in Barcelona. Despite our detention and interrogation there wasn't much the police could do and we were eventually allowed to leave— but not before the boat train had left for London. We had to wait a long time before getting a connection and we certainly cursed MI–.

That evening I was in the office of my friend John Gollan in London, and was discussing my campaign for food and volunteers for Spain, which was eventually to take me from Land's End to John o' Groats. John arranged for me to be deloused at the local public baths and provided fresh clothes. The remainder of my stay in London was in the flat of a young budding writer, Ted Willis, who was then the chairman of the Labour League of Youth.[160]

Mark Hurny

In August 1939 I returned home to Lubliniec in Upper Silesia, Poland, from my summer holiday on the Baltic Sea. I received then a mobilisation order to report to my regiment, the 74th Infantry, which was stationed in my home town.

I was born in 1915 in Western Poland, one of a family of six—three boys and three girls. My father was a civil servant. I went to high school at Lubliniec, which is near Katowice. Then I began studying at the University of Cracow. But I was unable to continue there because of financial difficulties. I worked for a time then as a civil servant in the regional government, while hoping of course to be able to resume my studies at university.

At that time there was general conscription to military service for young men in Poland so when I was conscripted I became an ensign or officer cadet in the 74th Infantry Regiment.

Eight days before the outbreak of war I was posted near the Polish-German border in charge of a platoon consisting of sixty-six soldiers and non-commissioned officers. I posted my men in a line covering about a mile, and about four miles from the border. On August 31st—it was a Thursday—I spent the night sleeping in a ditch near my men. At 4.50 am next morning I jumped from the ditch on hearing artillery fire coming from the Germans. I soon noticed small German tanks moving in our direction. The motorised German armies and their heavy guns crossed the Polish frontier at several points, supported by tanks, while fighter planes roared overhead.

I was slightly wounded in our first counter-attack but I was able to remain in command of my men after a dressing was placed on my wound. My regiment was retreating for two days, being in constant fight with the Germans, till we were relieved by another regiment. On the 3rd of September, being encircled by German infantry and tanks, we made a desperate attempt to break through their lines. In our successful counter-attack our regiment lost many men. From my platoon, consisting originally of sixty-six men, I had now only eighteen fit for further fighting.

The Polish forces put up resistance to the Germans as best they could. Bayonet charges took place. Our cavalry, brandishing their lances, attacked tanks and dragged the crews out. But this was futile and carnage was inevitable. This gallant resistance had no hope of stopping the Germans from blasting their way into the heart of Poland.

Worse was to come. The Russians crossed the Polish frontier from the east on the 17th of September 1939. They say they came as brothers to protect us, to restore peace and order. Some brothers they turned out to be! Many of our troops now fought not only against the Germans but against the Russians as well. The Russians in a few days took 180,000 Polish prisoners. And all this happened in spite of a non-aggression pact signed by Poland and the Soviet Union in 1932. The fight against the Russians soon came to an end. But the fight went on against the Germans.[161]

I was taken prisoner-of-war by the Russians. Along with two other young Polish officers and two senior officers, I was loaded onto a Russian open truck driven by an armed driver with an armed soldier beside him in the cabin.

Because of the masses of Polish soldiers who were being allowed to go home and the masses of Russian troops, tanks and guns, our drive on the truck soon came to a halt. In the small town where it was halted one of our guards left the truck for cigarettes and other goods. This was a most opportune moment for us three young officers to leave the truck unnoticed, mix with the masses of passing soldiers, and find a place for the coming night. After three weeks of fighting I slept for the first time under a roof and had a cooked meal prepared by the owner of the house, a doctor's wife. Her husband had not yet returned home from the army, where he was a medical officer.

The following day I made my way to the city of Lvov, which was then in south eastern Poland but is now part of the Ukraine. Lvov is sometimes called Lemberg, its German name. I went to Lvov because it was the biggest place in the area where I had escaped from the Russians and I thought it would be easier to hide there. It was over 300 kilometres east from my home town of Lubliniec.

Well, I spent the next eight months in Lvov. For a while I worked as a stoker in a Polish hospital there that was still managed by Polish staff but with Russian wounded and sick soldiers as patients. As a stoker I could spend my whole time in the boilerhouse, there being fed by the Polish nurses. But this soon came to an end and I found lodgings in the flat of a woman whose husband, a joiner, had been taken prisoner by the Russians and sent to a camp in the Soviet Union.

During my stay in Lvov I managed to procure in various names of various nationalities documents which I hoped would prove useful one day. The room I occupied was so small that it had only a bed and a small chair. One night, at about two o'clock in the morning, I heard loud voices on the staircase. A few seconds later banging on the door of my room convinced me this was the NKVD. The Russian secret police had come for me.[162]

There were five men in Russian uniforms who tried to get into my room. But the tiny size of the room allowed only one to enter. 'Get up! Get ready!' shouted the Russian who entered the room. The other four waited outside. I was seized by fear. What to do with all the various documents which I had in a little linen bag hanging round my neck? I was ready in a matter of a few minutes. I had hardly any luggage. But I asked the Russian officer to let me go to the toilet. While I was in the toilet the door was kept open but I succeeded in taking the documents from the little bag, tearing them into small pieces and dropped them in the pan.

136

I was soon in the street outside, where there were many other people—men, women and children—surrounded by Russian soldiers. Children and women were crying, saying goodbye to their relatives who were trying to comfort them and who brought some food parcels, loaves of bread, and so on.

The Russians took us under the cover of darkness through side roads to a train waiting in a disused place away from the town. We were surrounded by guards with rifles at the ready who warned: 'One step to the right or left and you will be shot!' In front of us in the full glare of lights was a goods train so long that its end was not in sight. The waggons were of the type usually used for carrying cattle.

Once we were inside the waggons their doors were bolted outside by iron bars. A very little light was coming through small barred windows high up on each side of the waggon. There was a hole in the floor which we had to use in full view of each other for our urgent needs. Several times during our trip we were awakened at night by stamping on the roof—a routine check to prevent escape.

We were without food for days and in despair we banged on the waggon door, shouting 'Bread! Water!' The guards responded by hammering the door with their rifle-butts and yelling: 'Shut up, you Polish swine!'

Soon we were in the Soviet Union. We went to Penza and then back again to Moscow, Vologda, and finally on the fourteenth day of our journey from Lvov we reached the deportation point of Tarza, about 120 miles from Archangel. Then from Tarza we walked about seven miles to our camp. There we saw ten barracks in which we were to live. About fifty people were herded into each barrack.

The following day we all, except the children, had a medical examination: a complete farce. An old man—he was not a doctor—sat at a table with a wooden stick with a hole drilled through it. It was supposed to be a stethoscope. He would place this so-called stethoscope near our chest and pronounce immediately almost in every case, 'Fit for work as a lumber jack.' Our camp was in the vicinity of Tiga forest. We were marched into it for tree-felling. At half-past five every morning the barrack doors opened with a clatter and the silence, disturbed only by the last sighs of sleep, was broken by a loud shout: 'Let's go!' A moment later a prisoner responsible for the march out to work walked briskly along the rows of bunks, tugging the sleepers by their legs. The prisoners moved heavily on their bunks, threw aside the coats covering their heads, and slowly—as if their bodies were held down by invisible bonds—sat up, only to fall back on to the bunks with moans of pain a moment later.

Those few minutes while the inhabitants of each barrack lay on their bunks without moving were devoted to a peculiar form of prayer. It began invariably with swearing and curses and ended with the formula, 'Oh, what a bloody life!' That expression, which I heard repeated every day on all sides, was a complaint which contained everything that a prisoner knew and could say about his living death. In other lands, in normal prisons, the place of this short cry of despair is taken by a real prayer. For a man robbed of everything but hope should begin his day by turning his thoughts to hope. Soviet prisoners had been deprived even of hope. For not one of them could ever know when his sentence would come to an end.

We had to work hard until the evening—a good eleven hours—under the eyes of the overseers to earn our meagre rations at night. These consisted of a piece of black wet bread, for 24 hours, a plate of liquid mess in which you could detect sometimes a piece of rotten potato or a piece of cabbage leaf. Our drink consisted invariably of boiled water. For our so-called lunch in the forest we would be provided again with boiled water and soup. After a frugal meal we laid our weary bodies back together on the hard planks of the barrack bunks.

The common complaint of both sexes in camp was blindness, which affected people from dusk till dawn owing to lack of fats and vegetables. No wonder Peter, a former schoolteacher, was keen to be a kitchen cleaner and a latrine attendant—a job which gave him a ration of a quarter of a litre of milk a day. When his fellow men and women were escorted to work some way outside the camp each morning he was able to remain behind. Therefore it was not surprising that many men and women tried to snatch his job.

Peter was also the keeper of the delousing station and the attendant of the steam bath. The delousing station was the pride of the Russians, who said: 'It is the pride of our culture.' They also used to say: 'We are the only country in the world which puts people into prison for swearing in public.' Every Russian in the camp was constantly using about ten swearing words in all sorts of permutations.

The steam bath, similar to the Turkish bath, is an old Russian institution. It's called *banya*. I took one one cold dark evening and had a feeling of entering heaven. A small hut, built entirely of logs, with a wooden floor, had a large oven made of stone, the top of which had holes covered with smaller stones. The oven with its stones was brought to intense heat by burning wood. I stripped naked in the ante-room, entered the so-called bathroom, dark except for a flickering glow from the oven, lay down on a bench along the wall, resting and sweating profusely. After a while I lazily left the bench, picked up a wooden bucket full of water and dragged myself towards the oven, not too close and slightly to one side. I threw the water on the stones and enjoyed the dense clouds of rising steam. At last I lifted another bucket of water, sluiced myself, dried with a towel, dressed quickly and left the place feeling reborn. That was one of the happy memories.

The short spring and summer had many sunny days and for several weeks the nights were as bright as the day. We had to cover the small windows of our barracks to enable us to sleep. These were the white nights of the Arctic. The warmest months were July and August, with frequent showers. During this time nature was coming to life. I enjoyed hearing the hum of various insects—but not the whine of angry mosquitoes. Swarms of them attacked us fiercely, making our life hell. A few people developed malaria.

In the winter, on the way to work, there was a white desert, a small plateau covered with snow and the forest in the distance. There was nothing in the way, apart from breath vaporising as each of us exhaled. The air was pure. The sky was clear, with a weak sun. Perfect visibility, not the slightest breeze. The dead silence was broken only by the crunching sound of the horses' hooves, and of our boots treading in the thick snow. The constant reflection from it tired our eyes, causing moisture which rapidly turned into icicles.

On the 22nd of June 1941 Hitler's armies poured across the frontier into Russia. Barely four months after they were just 64 kilometres from Moscow, forcing the Soviet ministries to be evacuated to Soviet Asia. Then on the 30th of July an agreement was signed by Stalin and the Polish General Sikorski which proclaimed a general amnesty for Polish people in Soviet prisons and labour camps like our one. And on the 14th of August it was decided to form a Polish army on Russian soil. Both these developments were in consequence of the Russian treaty with Great Britain that had been concluded a little earlier.[163]

In September 1941 I left the camp with many others. We had decided to leave the cold north and go to the warm south of the Soviet Union where the Polish army was then being organised. We wanted to go to this Polish army and fight against the Germans again.

We were able to board a goods train full to overflowing with Polish people—men, women and children—some in rags and rotting clothes. During this journey I witnessed a horrifying epidemic of measles which brought unbelievable mortality, especially among the very young. At every few stops the small bodies had to be removed from the train and left behind. It was a nightmare. Grieving hysterical mothers often refused to part with their dead children. Other travellers tried to calm them, telling them it was the only way. When persuasion failed, the dead body was taken by force. But then some railway authorities refused point blank to take the bodies. 'We have too many already and can't take any more. Try at the next stop.' Looking out of the train, I could see masses of Russian refugees from the west, fleeing from the Germans. Railway lines were blocked by trains with evacuated equipment and by trains full of wounded Russian soldiers, casualties from the front. I felt compassion for them. It struck me that I had no hatred against the Russian people.

If you take the ordinary Russian people they are like you or me, with plenty of compassion for other human beings. One would have to distinguish between the attitude of the ordinary man and the attitude of the government, which channels its will through various bodies, administrative and so on. But even amongst those who were in charge of us prisoners you could find traces of great compassion, willingness to help, and so on. I remember distinctly one of the commandants of a labour camp who tried to help an old lady who happened to be in that camp, who had three very young sons. The boys were unable to work and she was unable herself to work because of some illness. Well, the commandant tried to help her by sending his wife with a piece of bread to the barrack where the old lady lived with her young boys. Of course you could find people who showed some sympathy and who could show some other human feelings towards the prisoners.

So I had no hatred against the Russian people. They were given law, order and injustice. They never knew freedom. Their individual liberties had been taken from them a long time ago. They lived in perpetual fear—harassment, arrests, executions. Their rulers, the Soviet government, were killers, slave-drivers, brain-washers. Blunted by the lack of liberty, deprived of self-respect, the Russian people became resigned to their lot.

Well, after a long journey I arrived in Gizak, near the Afghanistan border, a small town in Uzbekistan. From there I went to Kermineh, where I joined the Polish army. Then from the Soviet Union I went to Iran, Iraq, Palestine, South Africa, and finally came to Britain about the end of 1943. Scotland became my country and now I have spent the best part of my life in this beautiful land. And English is my tongue, though I have never mastered the accent.

Irena Hurny

I was fifteen on the 24th of May 1939 and, well, we happened to be in Warsaw because school started always on the 1st of September or the nearest day to it. The 1st was a Friday. But the school never started that year because Warsaw was already bombed. And father insisted that my mother, my brother and I should go back to the country near Oszmiana in eastern Poland. Oszmiana was near Vilno, which is Vilnius now, the capital of Lithuania, but of course that belonged to Poland at that time.

I remember the bombs on Warsaw. Warsaw was very badly hit in the first few days, but luckily not our district. We lived in the suburb of Praga on the right or east side of the Vistula, which flows through Warsaw. There was bombardment and we see could fires from the distance, and smoke and all the rest of it, and this terrible noise. Everything was in a rather grim way.

We lived in a block of flats in Praga, on the second floor, and the whole house shook with the bombing. It must have been very early morning, I couldn't tell you the exact time. But it was terrifying, terrifying. The second bombing wasn't as bad as the first. But I remember my stupid pride that I wouldn't go down to the air raid shelter. Well, our block of flats survived and I certainly didn't want to leave Warsaw. But father insisted and that's what happened, against my wishes but of course they didn't count. I still have this little sort of complex of guilt about it. On the 8th of September we left Warsaw.

Father had written a letter to us in August when we were on holiday in the country at Oszmiana, that he would love us to come to Warsaw, where he was a civil service engineer in the Department of Communications. I remember that letter very clearly. He said, 'Well, maybe this will be the last time we shall see each other.' And we had come to Warsaw, I think probably on the 20th or 22nd of August, just before the war broke out. And father felt when the war broke out he had dragged us away from the safety of the country. So he sent us away again back to Oszmiana.

During our journey by train from Warsaw to Vilno we were attacked several times from the air by German planes. Machine guns were going all over the fields The planes were coming pretty low and they were shooting civilians. So when the train stopped—all out and under the train or wherever, just on the field, as flat as possible. I remember lying amongst the cabbages beside the railway track. I wasn't alone, there were even younger children. It was all the country in the same boat. It was not a pretty war—but which war is pretty? Eventually we got to Oszmiana. Somehow no one thought that Russia would step in. However, on the 17th of September the Russian army marched into eastern Poland. So at Oszmiana we were cut off completely from Warsaw, not knowing what happened to my father. And actually we never learned until after the war. I believe he was killed in the bombing of Warsaw in the middle of September or so. We don't know place or date exactly.

My own name is Irena Sawicz-Zablocka. I had been born in Vilno in Lithuania in 1924. It belonged to Poland at that time, so many people of Polish nationality are still living in those parts. When I was three my father had been transferred to Warsaw to the Ministry of Communications. He was an engineer. He was chief of the department of mechanical or technical experiments and research. And of course we moved to Warsaw. But I always had very sentimental links with Vilno and its surroundings, including Oszmiana.

My father was Polish and his family had been settled there near Vilno for a very long time. When there was the union between Lithuania and Poland many Lithuanian people, particularly—it sounds frightfully snobbish—of the so-called gentry, became entirely Polonised. Among them were many great writers and patriots— even Pilsudski. When he was cross with Warsaw people he said, 'I am Lithuanian.' So my father came from that part of the country. We used to spend our holidays there near Oszmiana and it was really wonderful. Nowadays that little town of Oszmiana is beyond the Lithuanian eastern border in White Russia or Byelorussia.[164]

As a civil service engineer my father travelled quite a lot. He knew languages. Very often he was in London, and quite often in Paris and Berlin. He had to do with industrial machinery, absolutely not war machinery.

Old Poland of course had been partitioned near the end of the 18th century and until the First World War that part where my father's family belonged was inside the Russian Tsar's empire.[165] So of course all the young men had to go into the Tsar's forces. My father was conscripted and because of his education he was a lieutenant in the Tsar's navy during the 1914-18 war. He was very lucky that he wasn't killed during the Russian November Revolution. It was a very bloody revolution and it actually started when my father was on his ship at the naval base in Kronstadt, near Petersburg. I don't remember the name of his ship. Father never talked about it but my mother was telling me that father was always very popular with the sailors. I loved my father very much, probably I idealised him. But I remember his attitude to people was not only extremely liberal but I would say it was more than that. There was not a bit of any silly snobbery or class consciousness, nothing like that—and I was brought up that way and I am very grateful that I was. Well, mother said that father was saved by his sailors because some others wanted to kill him during the November Revolution. And he was Polish, too, which wasn't very popular either, particularly in 1919-20, when there was already this offensive in Poland.[166] Anyhow he ended up in the Lubianka prison in Moscow as a political prisoner for about three or four years until 1920-21. I'm not very sure if he was in Lubianka all the time. I can't give you all the details. But my father must have been out of prison for a while because my parents got married in 1918 in Moscow. And then he was arrested again just after they were married. But after the 1920 war between Poland and the Soviet Union he was taken to Poland when there was an exchange of political prisoners.

In earlier times my father's family had owned an estate with a large house near Oszmiana. But the size of the estate had shrunk greatly with the passage of time. And it and the large house had been ravaged—in fact, the house was more or less destroyed—during the fighting in the 1914-18 war. My father had had a small house built there on the remaining part of the estate in 1937. That's where we spent our summer holidays and where my mother, my brother and I were sent back to by father after the war came in September 1939.

My mother—it's a long, long history. My mother's father was the son of a Pole—again, from that part which we now call Lithuania, well, it was Lithuania historically. In 1863 there was an insurrection in Poland and this grandfather of my mother took part. For that he was sent to Siberia. There he met a Russian girl and married her and their son—my grandfather—was born in Irkutsk, half-Polish, half-Russian. Later on my grandfather married a Swedish girl, from Helsingfors—as Helsinki was called then. He actually met her in Tokyo, of all places: he was a geographer, but whatever he was doing in Tokyo I don't know. Anyway their daughter was my mother. My mother's father—half-Polish, half-Russian—died when she was only six years old so the languages my mother knew from her childhood were Swedish and Russian. She had very few words in Polish, because of course her mother was Swedish. And my mother was brought up by the Swedish part of the family in Helsingfors. So mine was very much an international family. Well, I feel absolutely Polish but probably there is some Lithuanian blood, and of course my mother was half-Swedish, and a quarter Russian and a quarter Polish.

And then my mother had a step-father. He was born in Irkutsk too, strangely enough, like her own father. This step-father was the son of a Polish Evangelical pastor from Warsaw—although his name was very German: Wittenberg—who had also taken part in the 1863 insurrection and had been sent to Siberia. I remember that Wittenberg family from Warsaw. They visited us before the 1939 war.

Anyway my mother's step-father Wittenberg was a surgeon in Helsingfors. And just before the 1917 Revolution in Russia he was taking some sort of medical equipment to St Petersburg or Petrograd and my mother went with him. There were some friends in St Petersburg, which of course was very near Helsingfors. My mother liked St Petersburg very much as it was a very beautiful city and she had quite often travelled there. Well, the 1917 Revolution came and they stayed in St Petersburg. My mother's step-father, whom my mother adored by the way, managed to get back to Helsingfors but neither my mother nor my grandmother did. They were left under this revolutionary state in Russia—it wasn't the Soviet Union yet. My mother applied and was admitted to medical school in Moscow. My grandmother died in Moscow, and my mother met and married my father there. I don't quite remember all the details and I couldn't tell you exact years. But my poor mother went twice to prison during the Russian Revolution. And mother came, as wife of a political prisoner, with father to Poland in 1920-21.

So ten days after we left Warsaw in September 1939 for Oszmiana the Russian army marched into eastern Poland. Somehow father and so many other people who knew Russia quite well—it never occurred to them that the Ribbentrop-Molotov Pact would have this sort of result for us.[167] Father actually felt when the war with Germany broke out that he had dragged us from the safety of the country in eastern Poland. Somehow he felt that we would be safe there.

I remember the Red Army coming into eastern Poland in September 1939. First of all everything disappeared within a couple of days from the shops. There was looting to some extent. This part of Poland was, well, rural—not much industry. But comparing it with Soviet Russia it was a very rich country. The Russian soldiers who came were poor soldiers who had never seen a watch in their life. They were very, very primitive people, generally speaking.

The soldiers were to some extent quite orderly themselves. They were told that they had been asked by the Polish people to protect them from Hitler, and they believed it because they were told that. They didn't behave very aggressively towards the local population. Later on they were arresting people but you didn't see much brutality. Under the German occupation of Poland the Germans were shooting everybody. Well, nothing like that happened.

But I remember another lovely little Soviet idea. When the Russian army came to this part of Poland the Polish money was the zloty. Suddenly the zloty just wasn't worth anything. It wasn't exchanged for roubles, nothing of that sort. It was Christmas Eve, 1939 when we were all left penniless. Could you imagine a situation when suddenly you are told that the zloty is not worth the paper it's printed on? So apart from all these terrible other tragedies you find yourself in the situation where you don't know where tomorrow's bread can be got. But then again my mother, my brother and I weren't alone—there were millions of people who went through the same times.

Well, after we had been a while at Oszmiana mother decided, quite rightly, that my brother Olgierd, who was about two years older than me, and I should go to school there and try and finish our education. But since mother wasn't very well— she had a heart condition—we were given the choice: one of us would have to stay with her and one would go to school. Naturally we decided—it seemed perfectly natural—that the boy should go and the girl stay with her.

So my brother went to Oszmiana school and he was doing quite well. He was quite a bright young boy. But the pressure began that he should really join the Communist Party Youth and things like that, which of course was very much against the way we felt about it. He managed about Christmas time 1939 to escape through the Lithuanian and Soviet border, which was west of Oszmiana and east of Vilno. And he got to Vilno. We had friends and family there—he had some homes to go to. And actually my mother and I never heard from him any more because on the 5th of April we were arrested. Years later I learned that my brother had been killed very, very early in 1940. He had joined the Polish Underground Army, as most young people of that age did in Vilno. He was fighting against the Germans. He was in the underground organisation and he was travelling illegally between Warsaw and Vilno. I don't know the details exactly but he was killed on the Russian occupied side because he was buried later on in Vilno. But we didn't know anything about it until years later.

Well, on the 5th of April 1940 my mother and I were arrested by the Russians. They just arrived, I mean, they came dressed like soldiers. Who they were—NKVD or Red Army—I wouldn't know. I think it was a Thursday evening but frankly in a way that very moment is not very clear in my memory. I suppose I must have been in a state of shock. They knocked at the door. They said, 'Well, you can ask questions but you won't get any answer.' They didn't attempt to explain why we were being arrested: they were not obliged to explain anything to you. You were just taken. We were not given time to pack a bag. We just had to go with actually what we had on.

Fortunately we had reasonably warm clothing on and we were allowed to take coats and things like that. In Poland spring starts at the end of April. By May we have orchards in blossom. Somehow the spring explodes quicker after a cold winter. But at the beginning of April, which was when we were arrested, you can still see patches of snow. So we were allowed to take those things but not anything else. That was the horrible thing. Later on in the camp I got one parcel, some clothing from the girl who worked for us. She was for years working with our family. She sent me that parcel and I was very, very grateful. I remember it was a woollen shawl and one of my mother's warm suits,which was rather big for me but still it was something to put on, something to change.

My cousin Ludwika, who lives now in Poznan, was only eleven at that time. And what had been happening, when the Soviet army came into Poland in 1939, some of the mansion houses of the landowners were robbed by local people. Well, we always had such friends around us—my parents were really extremely liberal people and they always treated everybody as friends. Strangely enough, we even had a guard of our workers around our house so that nobody would harm us. But my poor aunt Victoria—she was a wonderful storyteller and I loved her very much—she very often spent the night with us, too. Practically everything had been taken away from her. Her husband—her second husband—was in hiding. And her little girl Ludwika was very often with us because my aunt felt she was safer with us. So poor Ludwika, at eleven,was arrested with mother and me as well. It was terrifying, but after a day or two they let her go to her mother.

Well, we were arrested—it was just some weeks before my sixteenth birthday— and first we were put in a tiny little cellar: that was a prison in Oszmiana. Then we were moved to Molodeczno. That was east of Vilno, quite near the pre-war border between the Soviet Union and Poland, and still on the Polish side. At Molodeczno it was a prison that was very newly built. On principle the Soviet authorities always tried to separate families when they arrested them. That was one of their principles. However, luckily enough, in Molodeczno there was only one women's cell. So I was together there with my mother. And then there had been a garrison of some Polish army unit there and we had quite a few ladies sharing our cell who were wives of the officers. Well, that was their crime, that was why they went to prison. And the ladies said that the bricks which had been used to build that prison—which looked frightfully new and unfinished, just rough—were part of the building material stored to build the garrison church.

I remember one funny thing happening while we were in Molodeczno prison. We had one extremely nice woman. We called her Sophie. I don't remember her second name. Sophie was the only criminal prisoner with us. She was extremely nice and a very, very kind person. We didn't know the details—maybe she had helped herself to something from the canteen. So she was with us. She was working out her sentence in that prison, cooking in the prison kitchen. And I will never forget there was one guard at Molodeczno prison who was very human, who was even trying to smile to us and treated us well. I wouldn't say we were ill-treated, brutally treated: it was just that the conditions were brutal. Usually it was the same sort of soup—water with barley and a sort of horrible frozen bit of potato. But still that was a potato and I enjoyed it enormously. And very occasionally we got a few bones of fish—I suppose cod, or something like that—and some sort of taste of smoked fish in it, which we considered wonderful. Well, one day that guard I mentioned opened the door of our cell and Sophie came in with one onion in her hand. And in that cell there were about thirty of us. And I remember how we divided that one onion into so many little portions. That was the most wonderful piece of onion I ever ate in my life. It had got such a pungent smell—and the vitamins! We were lucky, very lucky! It was a great luxury.

Probably about June 1940 we were moved further east to Polock. That's in present day Byelorussia. I think it's quite a big town. And the prison there was a very old monastery which was changed into a prison. And again there was only one women's cell.

I must say I was never ill-treated, physically ill-treated. But it was always this interrogation there at night. That was very nerve-wracking. The guard would come and say, 'Well, somebody whose name starts with the letter A'—or B, or whatever. And so many women would have to stand up in the cell and then he would say which name and that person had to go for interrogation.

At the interrogation there were a lot of silly questions: what your father's doing, and you were bourgeois and a blood-sucker, and all this sort of jargon. The interrogations were conducted by one of the NKVD, a man wearing uniform, a sort of khaki. Orally, the interrogation was very harsh and brutal. They were shouting and, well, they always asked about the organisation and 'What do you know about this people and that people?' Well, it's paranoia: paranoia was ruling that country, no question about it. They were suspicious of everybody. Quite honestly, I did not belong to any organisation. I was just sixteen by then. But sometimes even younger people went, too.

To begin with, I mean, we were all in a state of shock. Of course, they asked if you knew about the store of arms here and there and all this sort of ridiculous nonsense. I mean, I knew nothing about any arms. It didn't make any sense whatsoever, to be frank. But, oh, they suspected everybody, they suspected everybody. And you were an enemy of the people.

It tended always to be the same sort of question. 'Where is your father ?' Probably they suspected that my father was in hiding somewhere. I didn't know myself where he was but I said, 'Well, the last time I saw father was in Warsaw on the 8th of September'—which was perfectly true. Probably my answers agreed during the several interrogations, because I was speaking the truth. I had nothing to hide.

Strangely enough, they never asked me about my brother. Maybe they didn't know—nobody told them—that there was a young boy who had disappeared from Oszmiana. I was very glad that they didn't know. But they never mentioned my brother. So obviously they didn't have very much information about us.

It was always in the middle of the night that we were taken away to the interrogations. But what time it was I couldn't tell you, because nobody possessed a watch there. You were just asleep and you were called. There was always tension in the cell. It was a very, very funny thing, you know, because we all noticed after a while that they would call probably two or three people the same night, not every night. And all of us always kept a little bit of our ration of bread for the morning. And we always started eating bread when someone else was called for interrogation. It was some kind of moral or physical support, because we were tense. It was very funny. To begin with, we never noticed. Later on one of the ladies mentioned it: 'You know, we are all reaching for our slice of bread.' If we had had cigarettes we could have lit up a cigarette. That's what people do in a time of stress.

When you were interrogated you were always alone in front of the interrogator. Even though two or three people might have been taken away for interrogation from the cell each was interrogated in a different cell or room. The interrogator was not always the same—it varied. It was never a woman who interrogated us but always a man. Searching us there were women—we were searched whenever we changed prisons. But we weren't searched immediately before the interrogations, just when we entered the prison. You had to strip completely. There was a woman searching us, a warder or whoever it was. She was in uniform too, but what was her rank I have no idea. But when you appeared in front of the interrogator you were usually alone with him. Sometimes some other soldier or an official was there. But mostly it was tête-à-tête! It was a small room, with a small table, and that was it.

Conditions in the Polock prison were the most primitive you can imagine. There were about fifty of us women in that cell. We had no toilets. There was a wooden tub standing in the cell and that was your toilet. Once a month they took us to the so-called *banya*: it's like the sauna—it sounds frightfully luxurious. Anyway we were given a little basin of hot water and a cubic centimetre of soap. And that was incredible luxury. So the result was of course there was lice, filth and insanitary conditions. Such things as medication or any sanitary conditions were simply non-existent. It is very difficult nowadays to believe that one could survive this sort of condition. But, well, millions of people did—and do still: I hope not in Russia any more, but probably in other parts of the world.

Well, eventually the day came—that would be in the middle of September 1940—when they called us one by one and they said, 'Well, you have five years of labour camp' or 'You have eight years of labour camp.' I was sentenced to five years, my mother eight years. There was no trial, we were just told. I don't know if a trial existed or the prison authorities decided about it. I have no idea. Of course, we were told in the very official language, 'By the Court of the Soviet Union, such and such ...'

I didn't know where I was going when I was sentenced. I only knew that my mother was going to a different place. And of course she didn't know where I was going either. So I was taken away.

Well, those trains we were transported in were just cattle trucks. I was taken from that train in Orsza. That's quite a large town. I think it's now in Russian territory but that's how I write it in Polish. And in Orsza I was put into the most terrible prison. I mean, parting from my mother was naturally very difficult—particularly not knowing how we could get in touch or even if we would be able to get in touch again. And at Orsza for the first time I was put into a cell where there were very few Polish women. Most of the prisoners were Russian criminals. Well, I suppose nowadays I could be tolerant. I could say that life made them like that. But that was the very first time in my life that I was among this sort of element. And of course being strangers—that's human nature—I and other newcomers were resented. They were after all Russians and we were such-and-such foreigners.

Well, that was a very bad time for me. First of all I was taken away from my mother and I didn't know if I would ever see her again. Secondly, I felt absolutely lost and absolutely alone. And I heard people screaming in Orsza, in that terrible prison. I think men there were treated very badly. Probably it was my imagination but I heard screams from somewhere and I imagined that I could hear my brother's voice. And it wasn't true because he was never there. But it was a sort of nightmare.

Orsza was certainly a nightmarish experience. That first night, when I was pushed into that horrible steamy cell, full of terrible faces—well, these criminal women were terrible, their language and their behaviour and everything. I know it was probably a small detail compared with the tragedy which was happening outside. That was my worst time, in Orsza, the most difficult one.

I always had some sort of childish pride. When they were taking me away from my mother at Polock I wouldn't let them see me crying. And then at Orsza I broke down and I was crying like never in my life. Then I felt somebody come and put her hand on my arm in that cell. It was a Polish lady. She said, 'Don't cry, child. What happened?' I said, 'Well, they took me away and I don't know what's happening to my mother.' And she said, 'Well, they took my daughter away a few days ago. Maybe you will meet her.' And indeed I met her daughter later. And that Polish lady met my mother in Pothma camp. So it was a strange coincidence.

But I didn't stay long there in the prison in Orsza—just probably three or four days. I was then taken to a small police station in Orsza and another four Polish girls about my age were there. We were transported to what they called a colony for young offenders in Starodub, near Orlov. One soldier with one little gun took the five of us to the train. I felt, 'Oh, goodness, if there is ever a chance to escape it's now. But where to?' And the soldier was afraid of us. He was very young and he said, 'Now don't you try to escape because I will have to shoot.' You could see that the responsibility for him was really terrifying, too. And I thought that we went like silly sheep to the slaughter. But then I felt, 'Well, I don't know Russian. I will be spotted instantly and then I will be put back to Orsza or somewhere worse than that.' And probably apart from this five years which I had I would get another five of prison. So maybe reason prevailed. But there was a certain feeling of shame, to be led so meekly.

Starodub—it meant in Russian Old Oak—was in the district of Orlov, in the south of Russia, not very far from the Ukrainian border. The place we were sent to at Starodub used to be—according to what I heard—a seminary for young Russian Orthodox priests. It was quite a nice building in almost park grounds. And we were allowed to go and see some of the greenery. But it was an old building and of course there was no plumbing, nothing like that. And another very difficult thing for us was, well, there were twenty-one of the Polish girls, so-called political prisoners, and—later on—a couple of Russian political prisoners. One of these was a girl of about our age, about sixteen, with absolutely grey hair. She was a nervous wreck.

Well, she started talking to us and then later on she was avoiding us. She was obviously told not to mix with strangers. But the rest of the prisoners were young criminals, about 200 to 300 of them. And most of them were, well, to put it mildly, difficult.

At Starodub we worked in a factory which was making things out of cotton thread on machines. The other girls had to sew with this stuff and make underwear, vests and such like out of it. Then there was the place where they dyed it the most bright colours: deep blue and green and such like. So that was the work ten hours a day, which was quite a long time, especially when you were there after a good few months of prison and undernourished. But it wasn't such tortuous work as I had to do later on in another camp.

Another thing: we had the duty to attend some sort of lessons. We had to learn Russian, naturally, which was difficult for us Polish girls. And there was another thing there which I appreciated very much—a library. Of course they were Russian books. But that was the way I started learning Russian, by taking these books to read. The first book I remember I took was by the Russian poet Mayakovsky.[168] I hadn't learned any Russian at school in Poland. But my mother, who was brought up in Helsinki—Helsingfors it was called then—when Finland was still under Russian domination, had had to learn Russian. So she knew Russian quite well. And I remember during our time in prison together at Polock she was trying to teach me the Russian alphabet. Of course there was nothing for us to write on. We were sitting on the concrete floor, I mean there was no furniture there of any description. At night we put our shoes under our head and that was the way we slept. It was just the floor, that enormous wooden tub for essential purposes in the middle of the floor, and that was it. And I remember when my mother, licking her finger, had tried to write on the floor the letters of the Cyrillic alphabet for me. Then there was an incredible row because the guards saw that we were writing something on the floor. I don't know what they imagined we were trying to do but with their paranoia … We tried to explain to a guard but he wouldn't understand what we were doing.

At Starodub conditions were very primitive. We weren't starved but we never had enough to eat and naturally the quality of the food was very poor. It wasn't really starvation yet, although we already showed certain signs of troubles—teeth and skin trouble, and the curse of Soviet Russia: lice and scabies. It was horrible because it was so contagious. They used to give us a sort of ointment and for two days it was all right but then it came back. And when it's neglected it becomes sort of infected. I remember I had my elbows covered with scabs—very unpleasant, horrible in fact.

I remember too that on the 1st of May 1941 I foolishly enough let myself be provoked by one of the officials. Of course the 1st of May was a very great day of celebration in the Soviet Union. We had the day free of work and it was even special food that day. We were allowed to go outside the building.

May already was pretty warm. I remember the 1st was a beautiful sunny day. And of course we Polish girls were always sitting together. Well, it was not that we wanted to be stand-offish but it was very difficult really for us to find much in common with the other prisoners. Probably ours was the solidarity of any people who are persecuted: they cling together. We were always talking in Polish to each other and we became very great friends. Anyway on that 1st of May 1941 I let myself be provoked. How childish it was when I look back on it now. Some of the senior guards said the most insulting things about Poland and Polish people. I was very young and very foolish, and I just wouldn't let them insult my country. That wasn't a very clever thing for me to do at Starodub. So I was separated from the others and put into a cell on my own. It was a rather ugly situation for me. I was still only sixteen then, not quite seventeen. But the camp authorities were talking about counter-revolution and this sort of thing. Some of the Russian girls were talking the most terrible rubbish about my expression of opinion. Later on I learned that I was supposed to be saying that the Polish king would return to his throne. However, I was let out but I was always guarded.[169]

At Starodub we had one Jewish girl who was absolutely wonderful, Barbara Tropp. I remember her well. She was from Grodno in Poland and she was a very ordinary Jewish girl but extremely loyal and a very great Polish patriot. Barbara was just one of us completely. We really all liked her very much, we got very, very friendly. But there was another Jewish girl who said she didn't want to speak Polish, she didn't want to understand Polish, that she was a great Communist, and all the rest of it. So we just ignored her.

One wonderful thing that happened there: I got a letter from my mother. Later on I learned that when I was taken away from her and put on that train from Polock to Orsza one of the guards had told my mother where they were taking me. Mother was in camp at Pothma and was allowed to write one letter a month. So that's how it was.

There were prisoners treated in the most brutal fashion in Russia—Russian prisoners as well as any other nationality. But the ordinary person, well, he was just a human being. In a way, being a prisoner myself, I felt very sorry for Russian people. I remember the woman who was teaching us Russian in Starodub. She was an extremely nice person, very kind. I was allowed to write only one letter a month, the same as my mother was. And this Russian teacher said, 'If you want to write to your mother I will just take and post your letter.' Normally, I had to write in Russian: my first few letters were written in Polish but in the Russian alphabet, because you were not allowed to close a letter from prison—you left it open and they sent it away unsealed. But she wasn't a prisoner and she was very generous and a very, very nice woman. She was really kindly and, well, sort of motherly toward us, which we appreciated very much. If she had been caught by the authorities posting those letters for me it would have been very bad for her. She would have lost her job. Probably she trusted me, she knew I wouldn't say anything to anybody.

And then at Starodub there was a man I remember, too. He was some sort of worker who didn't stay in the camp. He was coming to it from the town. And I remember he had a very Polish name—Kwiatkowski. And right enough, when you look back at history, to what we Poles call our First Republic, before the Partitions in the later 18th century, Starodub belonged to Poland-Lithuania together. And I remember that I once somehow met that man Kwiatkowski and he whispered to me, 'Remember, Poland was here, too.' So obviously he must have been of Polish origin.

Then on the 22nd of June that year the German-Russian war started. And in the Starodub camp we Polish girls were attacked as Germans by our fellow Russian prisoners. Well, we were strangers. That's how pogroms probably begin—just because somebody is different. It was so ridiculous to accuse us of being Germans. If somebody is German they can't help it! But, I mean, none of us had anything to do with Germany. We were Polish. But for them we were strangers and that was enough. That was rather a frightening experience. We were physically attacked: they pulled our hair and punched us and all the rest of it. The camp officials intervened. And five of us, including me, were put in isolation. I was already the black sheep after the 1st of May—a troublemaker.

And we didn't know what was happening. Everybody said, 'Well, this is wartime. We are not going to put up with counter-revolutionary people', and things like that. I was called for interrogation by somebody who came from maybe Orlov, somewhere outside, a rather high official. And there were other officials from the camp sitting there too. It was then I learned what I was reported to have been saying about the king who was going to return to Poland and the other accusations which were quite ridiculous. Well, again they put us into that cell. It was really a very strange cell, because it had iron beds screwed down into the floor and without any mattresses. Lying on the floor was much more comfortable than lying on those wires!

However, we learned that all the Starodub camp was going to be transferred to Siberia. So all of us were taken to the station, put into these cattle trucks again as usual, and the journey started. The five of us Polish girls who had been in isolation at Starodub were put in a separate corner in the train. The others were not allowed to talk to us. We were in a rather dodgy situation. Of course, in our truck there was just a tiny window with bars and it was almost impossible to look through the window because the stronger girls were sitting there and wouldn't let any other body near it. At least there was some fresh air coming through it.

I think we were just passing the river Volga when suddenly it was some sort of stop and they delivered hot water and bread for us. Then officials came. They said they were so happy that they had such patriotic young Polish girls there, because an agreement had been made with the Polish government in exile in Moscow. So here we were being shown as an example of patriotism and bravery and all the rest of it! The change in the atmosphere! For us—particularly for the five of us sitting in isolation—it was a very great relief.[170]

As the train went on we could see through the little tiny window some rather strange countryside. Obviously, we were already on the other side of the Ural Mountains, in Asia. I remember the great steppes—just flat, nothing there. And I remember the stations where the children used to come to beg for bread from us prisoners on the train. I heard the same story from other people on their way to Siberia. So, I mean, it must have been a pretty bad situation in the country altogether.

Eventually, however, they got us to Barnaul, in Siberia. Barnaul was quite a big town, near the Altai Mountains and just south of Novosibirsk. We were put into the ordinary labour camp. Comparing Barnaul camp with Starodub camp, Starodub seemed like luxury. Barnaul was absolutely terrible.

We were in wooden barracks. The most awful thing was bugs which were living in the sort of moss between the big trunks of trees of which the barracks were built. It was tree trunks, not planks, because in Siberia they were needed to give some sort of protection, otherwise the prisoners would freeze to death. But at night the bugs in the moss between these tree trunk walls were practically eating people alive. There were huge bugs and small brown flat ones. When you killed them—a horrible smell. Well, we couldn't sleep because we were being eaten alive. Whenever you put your hand down then lifted it there were hundreds of bugs. It was terrible. Lice seem to be frightfully subtle creatures compared with those bugs.

Our work at Barnaul consisted of going out in the morning to a little pond, full of water and mud and straw. For fourteen hours a day we had to go round this pond, stamping with our feet, so that later on they could make some kind of straw bricks. They built houses in Siberia out of these bricks. It was terrible work. It was September by then and there were already frosty mornings—pretty cold. And starvation really started then. We got some sort of watery soup once a day and a tiny bit of bread, which was almost always running with water. Somebody later on explained to us that according to the law they had to give us so much bread in weight. So of course they put water on it to make it heavier.

The camp officials kept telling us, 'You are going soon to be free, according to the amnesty for Polish citizens you are going to be free.' Well, on the 22nd of September 1941 we were set free. I was left for a few hours longer. I suppose they just wanted to frighten me, to tell me to keep quiet or whatever!

Then we were sent to a sewing factory in the town of Barnaul which was making uniforms for the Red Army. Our Polish group was given a tiny little cottage on the river Ob to live in. We had no fuel, we had no bedding, we had no pots and pans, not even a cup or a spoon to our names. We just huddled together and slept like that there on the floor.

In the mornings we went to the factory. We usually had some sort of dinner, well, soup and our ration of bread in the factory. And then the winter set in. It was a terrible winter, that winter of 1941-42. It was absolutely awful. All winters in that part of the world are very, very severe. I remember we had over minus 50 degrees centigrade at Barnaul. Luckily, Barnaul was very much inland and very dry. Otherwise I don't know who would have survived the winters.

We had no clothing, we were in rags. I remember I went with my friend, another outspoken girl, to the man who was the main executive of that factory. He was the only man I ever saw in that factory. All men otherwise were in the army. We said to this executive: 'We are going to freeze to death. We have no fuel in that little cottage where we are living. And we must have some clothing.' So eventually they provided us with some clothing. Actually, it was a wonderful thing—a quilted anorak, and we were also given quilted shoes with sort of rubber soles. That made us relatively warm. But of course whenever you went outside it was so cold that your eyelashes froze. Your breath froze around your mouth—it was like Scott of the Antarctic. It really was frightfully cold.

And there was not a single drop of milk. There was no milk. I remember once going out of the camp in Barnaul and there was some sort of market going on. And I thought, 'My goodness! Not that we had any money to buy things. And I saw slabs of a frozen sort of bluish white thing. It was milk. It was frozen stiff. You just chopped it. But of course we couldn't afford that at all.

Lala, one of the girls from our group, suffered from pelagra. Well, I didn't know then it was pelagra. I learned about it later on in Teheran, when I was working in a hospital, because we had so many cases of it there. It's an illness connected with starvation, and I think the climate has something to do with it as well. At Barnaul we were all terribly thin, like skeletons. But the skin of this girl Lala became frightfully hard and very brown, and she had certain mental disturbances too. I will never forget poor Lala. I remember her coming to us with tears running down her face and she said, 'If only I could have a drink of milk.' There was nothing we could do for her, we couldn't possibly get any milk for her. We were starving ourselves. But somehow she was the only one who was affected in that way: it was obviously some sort of natural inclination or whatever. But later on I learned that Lala had survived. She got somewhere down south after I had left Barnaul. She got herself into the army and into hospital and they cured her. I was very glad. Lala was a very nice girl.

We were near to breaking down, I suppose, each of us. I remember in Barnaul once I was out of prison and we were freezing in that little hut, I thought, 'Well, we are going to perish from cold'—and of course from insufficient diet too, because you feel the cold much worse when you are hungry. And we were working very hard in that factory. But I wouldn't say that Barnaul was the worst time for us. There was a certain freedom of movement which was very important to us. After all, we were allowed to walk to the factory and we could go into Barnaul.

Among us at Barnaul there was one Polish girl I always remember: Wladka. In

Oszmiana, Molodeczno and Polock I was the youngest of the prisoners. In Orsza, well, I wasn't really quite sane there so I don't remember ages. Maybe there were young Russian girls there. But in Starodub there were younger girls among us Poles and one of them was Wladka, that's short for Wladislava. I can't remember her second name. She would be about fourteen, maybe fifteen. She was very slim. She was the smallest of us and really she looked as if she was suffering from tuberculosis— and probably she was. She was a very nice child.

Wladka was a very tragic story. Actually she was from Katowice in western Poland. She was the daughter of a Polish communist. When her father learned in September 1939 that Russia had occupied eastern Poland he decided he was going to the workers' paradise. He took Wladka—she was the eldest of his family—with him. And of course they were arrested by the Russians crossing the border between the Russian and German occupied area. It was frightfully tragic because often Wladka said, 'I wonder what my father is thinking now?' She was a very, very charming and nice girl. We all liked her very much. She went with us from Starodub to Barnaul.

While we were at Barnaul there was this great parade during the anniversary of the Russian Revolution in November 1941. And of course it was bitterly cold, bitterly cold. Wladka must have been brainwashed from her childhood. She said: 'Well, I came to this country. So I can take part in that parade. I am going.' And it was so cold. We said to her, 'You will freeze to death with your very poor little coat.' I remember we had enough heart to dress her warmly with whatever we had. And she went—she was of course the only one to go to the parade. She said, 'You should all be going.' We said, 'No, no, it's far too cold. We are not going.' Of course we didn't go because of what we thought about Russian rule but we said it was because it was far too cold. It had been a great surprise to us that she wanted to take part in that parade. I remember Wladka came back blue with cold, poor soul. We felt so sorry for her but we asked, 'Did you enjoy it?' She said, 'Oh, no, oh, no, it was horrible. Silly speeches and shouting "Hurrah! Hurrah!"—you know, somebody gave a sign and all the crowd shouted.' Poor Wladka, I don't know what happened to her. She was still in Barnaul when I left.

Well, I stayed at Barnaul until January 1942. I was pretty ill there. I think it was just the climate. I didn't know what was wrong with me but all my joints were swollen. It may have been arthritis or rheumatic fever. I could hardly walk. But I was sent from Poland the address of my cousin. She was fourteen or fifteen years older than me but we were always very close. Actually she had stayed with us for several years in Warsaw when she was studying. She had been deported from Poland by the Russians. It wasn't really imprisonment. They took so many people, families from Poland, and deported them to Kazakhstan or Siberia. They just unloaded them somewhere in a *kolkhoz*—collective farm—and they just had to manage as best they could. Anyway I was sent her address in Kazakhstan and I got in touch with her. And since she was much older than me she was always very protective towards me. And she wrote to me: 'Irena, please come to me if you can.' So I went to the director of that factory in Barnaul and said how I would like to go to my cousin. So I got the permission and I got the railway tickets.

That was the most fascinating journey I ever made in my life. I boarded the train in Barnaul and went to Novosibirsk. Novosibirsk station was very, very beautiful. It was marble and bronze and all the rest of it. But all the floors of that station were covered by people in rags and starving. The contrast was terrible. I think it was a showpiece of the Soviet government. I don't know when they built it but it was a good few years before the war.

From Novosibirsk station I had to go westwards to Petropavlovsk and then change to Karabanda, down south again, and then to a station called Kokchetav. But nobody knew at Novosibirsk when the train to the west was going to come. So I just sat there at Novosibirsk station. I had managed to save a little slice each day of my bread ration and had dried them and I had these rusks with me. Knowing that I was going on that journey I managed. And that's the way I survived. I was sitting waiting six days in that station at Novosibirsk, afraid to fall asleep. Well, I'm sure I was dozing óff—but always I was listening. People would say, 'The train to Petropavlovsk is coming.' Eventually, after six days, the train came.

Again it was not really a passenger train—it was just the usual cattle or goods trucks. But I got in there, into one of the trucks. I remember there was a little fire in the middle of it. That was January, the end of January, so it was frightfully cold. I just dropped off and slept, I don't know for how long.

Eventually somebody dragged me to the fire in the middle of the truck. I had been sitting against the metal wall of the truck and my legs were practically frozen. However, an elderly man helped me. Later on I learned that he and his family were Germans, Soviet Germans. There used to be a German Republic in the Soviet Union, somewhere near the Volga. Of course, when the war with Germany started in the summer of 1941 they were thrown out—deported. Nobody wanted them anywhere. I believe they were just sort of travelling all the time through Siberia and Kazakhstan and elsewhere, trying to find a place that the Soviet authorities would let them stay. I don't really know what happened to these people. But I was very grateful to that old German in the truck. He had obviously noticed that I was freezing and in danger and he helped me.

Then suddenly, in the middle of the great white nowhere the train to Petropavlovsk stopped. The railway officials said, 'This train doesn't go any further. But there is a train along the line and hopefully you will find a place in it.' So everybody rushed along the line toward the other train. The snow was chin high. Nobody on that other train wanted to open the door to us. And the train was full anyway. So that was a very grim situation. I don't know how many people were left stranded there and died of cold.

But we all ran along that train and knocked at one carriage, then another carriage. Suddenly in one carriage when I knocked I heard somebody saying in broken Russian, 'Sorry, you can't come in here. Here are only Polish men going to join the army in Kuibyshev.' 'My goodness!', I said. So I started shouting in Polish: 'Surely you will let me in? I'm Polish!' Of course, they opened the door then and dragged me in.

They were Polish prisoners released from this terrible place Kolyma—coal mines and gold mines. They were young Polish men, well, most of them were young. Some seemed to me—then seventeen—frightfully old: about forty, probably! So I stayed with them and, oh, I felt so safe. For the first time I felt safe. They were so wonderful. They all wanted to talk about their experiences in Kolyma. It was very tragic. I just tried to listen. But they really looked after me. I was the first, well, not Polish woman as I was just a young girl, but the first person that they were able to talk to in Polish since they were let out of those terrible camps.[171]

Their stories were absolutely shocking. There was a very, very small percentage of people who survived even for a year in those conditions. And so many committed suicide. It was really quite an unbearable life. Well, those men on that train were really terribly kind to me and they kept bringing me bread because, as they were going to the army, they had better conditions. They were allowed to buy bigger rations of bread and they shared all that with me. It was wonderful. And they said to me, 'Why don't you join the Polish army with us?' There was that temptation to go with them to Kuibyshev, on the Volga, where the Polish army was forming. But I knew that my cousin was expecting me. So I said, 'Well, no, I will see my cousin and probably I will join later on.'

I arrived at Petropavlovsk on that train. It was the only passenger train I experienced in Russia. It was packed like anything but still it was more like the trains in other parts of the world. Then I reached Kokchetav and from there I had forty kilometres to go to this farm where my cousin was. She had written to me: 'Irena, when you get to Kokchetav go to such and such an address. There is one Polish lady there who will direct you and help you.' And, right enough, that Polish lady was extremely nice. She had two daughters, one about my age, another younger, and she gave me wonderful soup. And her little cottage was quite warm. Oh, it was wonderful luxury! She said that the transport, as they called it, was going towards my cousin's place next day. The local people, those Kazakh people, who were generally very kind, said they would take me there. Well, not exactly there but a few miles or kilometres from my cousin's place. But they said they would see that I got there all right. They put me on the sledge and gave me the reins of the poor little horse. But I had no idea how to drive it. There were probably ten or twelve sledges going altogether. They never travelled in winter alone because of the wolves. It wasn't funny. It wasn't safe. It was too dangerous.

I don't know if my horse didn't want to listen to me but I was always left behind. The Kazakhs, however, waited for me. In broken Russian they would say, 'If you stay behind the wolves will eat you up'—which was very encouraging! But they got me there, and again they said, 'There is a Polish woman staying in that cottage. Knock at her door. She will help you.'

Again it was night when I arrived. And I remember I slept under the table in that Polish woman's little cottage because there were no beds. But still I was under the roof and the cottage was relatively warm. In the morning the woman told me, 'Take the track all through the snow and you will get there.' And somehow, by instinct, I got there. Everywhere it was all white and there was just a little track that was always covered in snow. But that's how I got at last to my cousin, a very special cousin. Her two children and her sister were there as well.

I remember just after the war had begun, when the Russians were transporting those Polish families, thousands and thousands of people, my cousin had come to visit us at Oszmiana. She was staying in the same part of the country, about twenty miles from us. Her husband was arrested. Poor man, he had to go for an appendicitis operation, and the second day after the operation they came to the hospital and arrested him and she never saw him again. She was left with the two children and she was sure that she was going to be transported somewhere so she was getting ready for it with her sister. They were making for the children warm boots, fur-lined. Later on she said to me, 'Those things helped us enormously.' They had had time to get the most important things ready, especially for the children. Even half an hour of notice, or forethought, could make a lot of difference when you were arrested or were to be transported.

Well, one day a Polish sergeant in uniform, more or less Polish uniform, arrived at my cousin's place in Kazakhstan and said he had an order to take everyone south to Kermineh. Well, they included me as well. And that's how I joined the Polish army in Uzbekistan. I got to Uzbekistan in June or maybe the end of May 1942 and I joined the Polish army then and was sent to work in an office. The office work was rather boring but of course one had to do something.

Then in August 1942 we were taken to Krasnovodsk on the Caspian Sea. After a couple of days of waiting we got a legal exit from Soviet Russia to Pahliveh on the Persian or Iranian side of the Caspian Sea. Later on people in Poland were told that we had all escaped and it was illegal and all the rest of it and that it was treason against Soviet allies. But that was not true. Stalin wanted Polish people out there and we went out with the blessing and polite treatment of the Soviet secret police and everybody else.

When our boat was still in Krasnovodsk I did the most awful thing. It was August and incredibly hot. So I decided I would go to the sea and have a bath. I went in—and the sea was full of oil: Krasnovodsk and Baku were oil country, and the Caspian was full of oil. I scratched myself like mad because there was not enough water nor soap to wash it off. Such luxuries hardly existed! But that was a minor thing.

But I remember when I was standing on the upper deck of the boat as we were preparing to leave Krasnovodsk for Pahliveh—and we all hoped and prayed that it really would leave the Russian shores!—I saw a poor woman, who was really a skeleton of a person, boarding the ship. She had no strength to walk. So she just sat down by the entrance and the Russian police came and dragged her off the boat. Maybe she thought it would be the way out, the chance, for her. I was pretty far away from her so I didn't hear the conversation. But the dragging of that poor screaming skeleton off the boat—well, I shall always have that picture in front of my eyes when I think of it. It was terrible. It was really very frightening that they could still do that if they wished. One felt extremely insecure in those last few minutes in Russia.

That journey through the Caspian Sea was absolutely wonderful. And Pahlevi was like paradise. There was a lot of poverty in Iran. But you didn't see people in rags everywhere and dying of starvation, as you did in Soviet Russia.

I was sent to work in an orphanage in Pahlevi. Then by chance I learned that my mother was in Teheran, nursing in the hospital. After a couple of weeks they transferred me to Teheran and I met my mother again, which was absolutely wonderful. From the northern part of Russia where her labour camp was she got to Kuibyshev and into the Polish army much sooner than me. But she had lost track of me and I of her. We couldn't communicate. There were two waves of Poles out of Russia. The first one was in April 1942. My mother got out then. The second one—in which I got out—was in August. My mother was very ill. And it was then, too, that I learned that my brother Olgierd had been killed very early in 1940.

That made me feel that I couldn't leave my mother on her own. So I asked to be exempt from the army and I worked as a nurse in the civilian hospital in Teheran for two years. Then they moved most of the staff of that hospital, plus some patients, to Kenya. That was a long journey, first to Achwaz on the Persian Gulf. It was June and that's about the hottest place on earth. We experienced absolutely terrific sandstorms. We had a few patients who died from heatstroke. The heat was incredible and we were just in tents, which didn't give very much protection. However, from then on we were at least not hungry, we were clean, and we were treated as human beings.

We had to wait for transport but eventually they took us to Basra. From Basra we went on a very, very old boat to Karachi. It was a creaky and horrible boat, full of great big brown beetles—cockroaches—running all over the place. On the boat I met Indian people for the first time and I remember them giving us curry, frightfully hot curry. It was the first time I'd eaten curry. They decided, however, that it was not really suitable for ill people. At Karachi there was a very modern and beautiful Dutch vessel waiting for us and that took us to Mombassa on the east coast of Africa, and then we were taken to a transit camp at Makindo, half way between Mombassa and Nairobi.

When the Second Front started with D-Day in June 1944 they said they would need more nurses in Europe. My mother and I and some of our friends volunteered. Well, we were sitting in that transit camp for seven months waiting for transport to Europe. I was working in the meantime in a small hospital there at Makindo but I'm not made for hot countries. It was very hot and I got malaria. About that time too we were getting news through the radio about the Warsaw Rising. That was in August, 1944 and I remember every evening we would go and listen to the BBC Polish service. The news was worse and worse. It was really terrible.[172]

Eventually, in January 1945, we were transported back to Mombassa and then to Suez. From Port Suez we were taken to somewhere in Egypt where there was a Polish army camp. We waited a couple of weeks there for transport to Europe. I decided Egypt was the coldest place on earth: there was even a little mixture of snow with rain. As we just had tropical things on they gave us jumpers and sweaters to keep us warm. We had blankets but we were shivering because it was such a terrible contrast of climate from where we'd come near the Equator. Eventually, we went to

Port Said, through the Mediterranean, Gibraltar, over to the Azores, then Ireland, and we landed in Liverpool. I think I'm an extremely lucky person that I landed in this country—but Liverpool docks on a grey raining February morning are not the most beautiful sight! But that was lovely because when we were coming on shore there were volunteer ladies with a hot cup of tea and biscuits. It was lovely.

And then they decided to send a group of us, including my mother and me, to Scotland. We had no choice in the matter. We boarded the train and arrived in Carlisle. It sounded very strange. Our Polish people pronounced it Carlissla! And then a sort of jeep came from a small hospital we were sent to Eliock House, near Sanquhar in Dumfriesshire. It was really a hospital for the war wounded. I shall always remember that jeep and the beauty of Scotland. It was so much like home in Poland, compared with Africa and with my years in Teheran. The birch trees, which I always loved from my childhood, well, the Polish ones are frightfully white and very, very tall and straight, but those in Dumfriesshire were still the birch trees. Well, that's how I landed in Scotland and I've remained here ever since.

They never sent us to France or Germany. The war ended three months later in May. And of course there was Yalta and all the rest of it.[173] There was this terrible decision for us Poles: what are we going to do? I think for many people who had gone through Russia, as I had, there was the element of personal fear, apart from the matter of principle that we could not agree with the new rulers of our country. We had had pretty nasty experiences under Soviet rule and wouldn't voluntarily go there again. I don't suppose my mother and I would have been in any particular danger. It's difficult to say. But that's the way we felt. We had some sort of choice. And to choose Communist rule would have felt like some sort of betrayal of our principles. It was a frightfully difficult decision and a decision which I still don't know and won't know to the end of my days if it was the right one or not.

It was just after the war, in 1945 or so, that I met Mark Hurny. He was sent to that little hospital at Eliock House in Dumfriesshire and I met him there. But then I went for over a year to Perthshire because, well, I was fifteen when the war had started and I, or my parents, always had certain plans. Anyway I always wanted to learn. Of course, I had no English whatsoever. But I learned there was a sort of grammar school of Polish girls in Dunalister House in Kinlochrannoch in Perthshire. I wrote there and they had a place for me. I had to get permission from the authorities to go there but I managed to get all that and I went to Kinlochrannoch and got my Polish matriculation in 1946. I worked like mad and not learning any English because I was concentrating on at least having that Polish matriculation—not that it was very much use to me. But it gave me some sort of satisfaction.

Later on I met Mark again and in 1949 we were married. For some time afterward I was nursing again in the little Polish units, first in Edinburgh then Gullane, and then at the Polish maternity unit in Bangour Hospital in West Lothian. That was my last nursing job with the Polish units. Our daughter Anna was born in 1951.

The name Hurny is a Czech name really. But Mark's family lived in Poland near Poznan for generations. I feel absolutely Polish myself—but, as I said, my own family were a mixture of Lithuanian, Swedish, Russian, Polish, and even—in my mother's family—French. So when I'm thinking about my grandson Christopher, whose father's grandfather was Greek—how many different nationalities in him! So we are just Europeans.

Well, in September 1939, our world collapsed over our heads in Poland. But there were millions like us.

Paul Dunand

One of the most beautiful things I have ever seen was while I was working at the Hispano-Suiza factory in the Bois Colombes in Paris. It was on the day in November 1942 that the French fleet was scuttled at Toulon. London had asked for a minute's silence, and in the factory at the hour indicated all the workers stopped the machines and stood to attention behind them singing *The Marseillaise*. The Germans took two of them from each workshop. They were sent away. They were never seen again: *Nuit et Brouillard, Nacht und Nebel*, Night and Fog. I do not know what became of them.[174]

I was born on the 20th of October 1924 in Paris. I am an only son. And I am an only son in a double sense, because my father's brother and my mother's sister married each other. Two brothers married two sisters. But my uncle and aunt couldn't have any children. So I had two fathers and two mothers! My parents were married after the 1914-18 war. They met in Catholic youth clubs in Paris. For I am the son of a very Catholic family. My parents were both religious.

My parents lived in the rue des Belles-Feuilles, in the XVIth arrondissement. My father was a bank clerk. He worked at the Banque de Paris et des Pays Bas.

My father was of Savoyard origin. My paternal grandfather was born under the law of Sardinia. He wasn't born French. But he could remember the referendum in Savoy in 1860 as a result of which it became French. He recalled that all the Savoyards had come over the mountains to vote. Everyone was overjoyed, and he told me: 'Ha, there was only one of them in my district'—that was St Julien-en-Genevois—'there was only one person in my district who had not voted for France. And he was a rotten Italian!' So there![175]

Grandfather, who had been only seven years old when the return of Savoy to France took place, also lived in the XVIth arrondissement in Paris, where he had a grocer's shop in the rue Spontini beside the Avenue Foch, which at that time was called the Avenue du Bois.

I remember my grandparents but not all four. I did not know my paternal grandmother, who was originally from the Beauce, and my maternal grandmother died when I was five or six years old.[176] I remember her—just. My mother's parents were from the region of Tournon Saint Martin in the Department of the Indre, near the centre of France. My mother was born there.

My father began work in the bank when he left school. Always he was employed

161

in the bank, that was his occupation. During the 1914-18 war he was in the artillery. He was a conscript, he had been called up. My father was in the Class of 1914. He was twenty years old then. He fought throughout the war. He was at Salonika, he was in the Greek campaign, the Middle East campaign, and before and after that he fought in France, too. When he came back on leave from the East he was put into the part of his regiment that remained in France. He remained there till the end of the war. He was in the heavy artillery. He was a sergeant—well, in the artillery it's not called a sergeant but *maréchal des logis*.

My father was at the taking of St Mihiel near Verdun by the Americans in 1918. It was at St Mihiel that he won the Croix de Guerre medal. The Americans attacked the St Mihiel salient. My father told me it was terrible because they were young soldiers who had arrived and they had not had the training of French soldiers. It seems when they attacked the salient they went into the attack marching upright. They were massacred. They took St Mihiel but they had enormous losses.

In the war my uncle, my father's brother, was killed. He was in the 39th Infantry regiment from Rouen. He is buried at Toul. On my mother's side I didn't have anyone who was killed. My father himself was not wounded in the war, not at all. In the East he was gassed a little. It wasn't very serious. It didn't affect his life after the war. What affected his life after the war was malaria. That was common at Salonika. He had malaria all his life.

My father often spoke to me about the war. His opinion was that it was necessary to defend France. The war was a hideous butchery but it was necessary to stop it ever happening again. I often heard him say that the war had been won but the peace had been lost.

In 1919, after he was demobilised, my father resumed his work at the Banque de Paris. It was quite a safe and secure job. He worked in the investments department. He never suffered unemployment between the two world wars.

Like many ex-servicemen of 1914-18 my father admired Marshal Pétain.[177] My father wasn't at Verdun and hadn't fought under Pétain. It was a general admiration for Pétain's role during the war. Oh, he saw Pétain but he never met him.

My father was not a political activist. He had political opinions. After the war he joined the Croix de Feu when Colonel de La Roque created it in 1924. The Croix de Feu at the beginning was an association created for all the ex-servicemen who had been awarded the Croix de Guerre. Then after that it became a political party, the Parti Social Français (PSF), still under the direction of Colonel de La Roque. It was a party of people on the Right.

I remember when I was quite a young boy taking part in the meetings of the Croix de Feu and of the Parti Social Français. My father was a militant. I went with him to the meetings. As with every political party the objective was electoral—to have elections, be the majority in order to take power. Otherwise as activities I recall fêtes which raised money for social works. I recall also a meeting at the Parc des Princes with the Loie Fuller ballet. All that was marvellous. There were fireworks, etc. There were many activities which included families because the party did a lot of good works. They gave parcels to needy people. Like all political parties they needed to collect money. And in those days there was no embezzlement by party officials!

The Croix de Feu took part in the events of February 1934 in Paris. I was nine years old then. Well, that really is a memory. I remember that. The ex-servicemen, with Pétain at their head, had come down the Champs Elysées and were marching on the Chamber of Deputies to take possession of it. Violence broke out. That was a fight! There were many people killed. The government fell, that's to say, was changed.

I didn't go myself on that demonstration nor my father either. My father wanted to go on the march by the ex-servicemen but my mother made such a song and dance about it he was forbidden by her to go.

On the other hand, I have a memory about school then. There were two gangs in school at playtime. There was one that represented the demonstrators and the others were the forces of order. We really laid into each other. When I came back from school my mother saw me with my overall torn and my face scratched, etc. She said, 'What a state you are in! What happened to you?' I said, 'It was a great fight but we took the Chamber of Deputies!' Those are old memories.

My father remained a member of the Croix de Feu until 1939—but by then it was not the Croix de Feu: the Parti Social Français had replaced the Croix de Feu, but still under the direction of Colonel de La Rocque . Membership of the Croix de Feu was limited to decorated ex-servicemen. There were many members of the PSF, and there were Deputies besides. And as often happens, the majority at that time in the Chamber of Deputies had changed the electoral system in such a way that the PSF had the smallest possible number of elected members there. My father spoke well of Colonel de La Roque. I saw him. My father talked with him but I was too young to do so.

After 1934 there was the government of the Popular Front. My father wasn't at all in favour of the Popular Front. I have memories of it—of strikes by workers, of workers in processions and demonstrations. There were many of them. Here at Tournon, I was on my school holidays. We generally came to Tournon. But occasionally we went elsewhere. We went to the Ile d'Oléron and to Veules-les-Roses, near Dieppe. But here at Tournon there was a demonstration, with *The Internationale* played by loud-speaker, processions, red flags. At Tournon there was everything but it was above all socialist, or rather radical-socialist, rather than communist. There were communists, of course, but not many.[178]

I began school at the age of six. It was a Catholic school. I attended primary school at the parish school, and then I was at Sainte Croix secondary school. I went as far as the sixth form—the year of the Baccalauréat—and then the war came and I stopped studying.[179] I confess, to be frank, I didn't much like my school! It was strict, perhaps there was too much discipline. There was not corporal punishment, not at all—apart from some smacks with a ruler on the fingers, but that wasn't serious. But I preferred more freedom, I just didn't like it much. The subject that I liked best was history. I was always very fond of history, whether it's the history of Egypt or Greek or Roman history I've always liked it.

At school there was no co-education for boys and girls, it was boys only where I was. At that time there was no co-education. I passed from the primary to the secondary school at eleven years of age. What upset me was the change between the two sorts of education. I was a brilliant pupil in primary; in secondary everything changed: it's all so different. I quite liked mathematics, but the practical subjects—I have never been very good with my hands. I learned English but it hasn't stuck with me! Oh, you lose it. I've been to England and to Canada. I could make myself understood, I could talk with people because it came back, then after that it got lost. It's difficult to pick it up again. Sometimes if you hear it, it comes back.

I read a great deal, oh, I read the books of Fenimore Cooper, Walter Scott. I read Balzac. My father was an enthusiastic Balzacien, oh, la la! And I still have the complete works of Balzac in my house. I very much enjoyed reading and I read widely. I read a great many things. Everything interested me, especially history, historical novels. I liked novels very much, histories of the Middle Ages.[180]

Anyway I remained at secondary school till the age of seventeen, in 1941. For my father had been mobilised; I had to start work. When I was sixteen or seventeen I hadn't any ideas about employment. We who were young at that time thought about one thing—the liberation of France. That was really something. I was a member of a church youth club. I played basketball and all our team, all our friends, were prepared to fight to liberate France.

As a boy I had religious views—naturally, since I was in a Catholic school. But politics—no, I was not at all a political activist, not like my father. The activities of the Croix de Feu interested me but not enough to become an activist, nor was I inclined to turn to the Left or the Centre. That was not my problem. I was always on friendly terms with my father. I loved my father very much. We weren't always in agreement politically. But I always had a great affection for my father. My father, as I told you, followed Marshal Pétain. I did the opposite. Father never held meetings in our house, no, never. He was not a militant. All the same, my father could not stand the Germans, believe me. No, he was in favour of Pétain but did not support the Germans.

At the time of Munich in 1938, I remember that people were happy because it seemed there was not going to be a war. In reality it was a surrender. Chamberlain and Daladier made an enormous mistake. At the time of the remilitarisation of the Rhineland in 1936 I was much younger. But I heard my father say it was completely mad. Hitler himself said that if we had moved in to stop him then he would not have been able to continue, that he would have even abandoned power. It was bluff on a grand scale, what he did there.

And I remember the Anschluss with Austria. All that we lived through.[181] As for the war in Spain, my father was for Franco. Personally, I didn't have views, as you will understand. I was too young. My father didn't have the idea of going to Spain in order to fight: he was too old, and in any case he had his work and everything. I didn't personally know people—neighbours or anybody—who went to Spain to fight for the Republicans or on the side of Franco.

I remember the beginning of the Second World War, the declaration. When I learned of the mobilisation I was here on holiday at Tournon. And of course that was a shock for everyone. People spoke a lot about the war, but no one thought they would have one. You had two camps: one camp said we had to fight. And one camp said, 'Oh, well, better to live under the Boche than die French.' I think that's a matter it's necessary to emphasise. In general, the people who didn't want to go and fight were the people of the Left, the same people who afterwards went into the Resistance! You could say that's very much what one would expect from the French character but that's how it was. Events changed a great deal between 1939 and 1941. That's to say, the Communists really went into the Resistance when the Soviet Union was invaded in 1941. Before then I even found pushed under our door in Paris a clandestinely published copy of *L'Humanité* which said it was necessary to serve the Germans. I regret not having kept it.[182] And there was the Nazi-Soviet Pact in August 1939. That was a big about-turn. In that business, my personal point of view is that Hitler conned Stalin. Because he certainly intended to march into Moscow. Just as he conned us at Munich.

I remember the Phoney War in 1939-40. The Maginot Line was impregnable, and we just sat and waited for a German attack. Our military leaders made a very big mistake, because once Poland had been invaded we had either to attack or not go to war at all. It was one or the other.[183]

My father was mobilised in April or May 1940 with the blue call-up papers: those who had fought in the 1914-18 War had blue call-up papers. They were called up after the rest. Well, he was called up to the Army Service Corps who were at Fort Ivry at Paris, and afterwards he was posted back to his own unit, the Colonial Artillery. He was in the heavy artillery in the 1914 war and this time he was in a regiment with 75mm guns. He was at their departure from Rueil Malmaison, near Paris. It was he who closed the gates of the barracks in June and who left with his Blacks on the arrival of the Germans. And I have a memory that when I went with my mother to say goodbye to him a British man gave us a lift back into Paris. And I remember this man informed us that Italy had just entered the war. And he said to us with his British imperturbability, 'Oh, you know, the Italians like ruins very much. Well, we'll make a few more for them!'

I didn't witness the arrival of the Germans in Paris. I was still at school. But I took part in the exodus with everyone else, with my mother, my aunt and some friends. We just set off down the road at the beginning of June. The Germans arrived in Paris in the middle of June and we were on the roads while bombs were dropping.

We went on foot. We went as far as Orléans. I had a bicycle of course but since my aunt and my mother and my friends didn't have bicycles I walked along with my bike, with luggage piled on top of it.

We spent two and a half days on the road between Paris and Orléans—120 kilometres. And when the bombing took place I saw people killed. I saw heaps of bodies. I saw appalling things. I was 15 years old.

Always the bombing was taking place from aeroplanes, and there was machine gunning. The road was crowded with people. It was an appalling experience. I have very, very clear memories of it. It was a matter of chance that I was not hurt or wounded, because I saw people killed beside me by the machine-gunning from the German planes. They were machine-gunned ruthlessly. All were civilians. Those who got it really got it!

There were some military people who passed along. I remember some Air Force men on board a lorry with a bren gun on top of it. When the plane fired they didn't have cold feet but fired on the plane—without success. But the plane hesitated to come back over us as a result of that.

We passed the nights in barns during our exodus from Paris. The weather was fine—just as well. We didn't have rations to eat en route, not at all. We lived off whatever there was available in the countryside. We asked if there was anywhere open where we could get food. Or if there were peasants we asked if we could have eggs, or whatever there was. We asked if they could give us something. That's how we managed. We got something to eat on the way to Orléans . We were not totally hungry. We always found something to eat. And drinks of water. Well, I saw one place where people were making a profit. They sold us a litre of water for a shocking sum so that they could make money out of it. That was disgusting.

When we left Paris we hoped to reach Tournon here. My grandfather at Tournon didn't expect us in any case. There was only my grandfather. He knew nothing of it at all, it seems. It wasn't possible to telephone him. At that time my grandfather didn't have a telephone. We wanted to cross the Loire at Orléans so that we could go and see my grandfather. You couldn't cross the Loire.

Orléans wasn't on the frontier of the Occupied Zone. The frontier of the Occupied Zone was near here at Tournon, south of the Loire. Tournon was in the Unoccupied Zone and the line of demarcation was at Petit Pressigny or Grand Pressigny, I no longer remember which. Saint Aignan sur Cher was likewise on the frontier. On the other side of Tournon the frontier ran above Chauvigny. But Tournon was very close to the frontier.[184]

We stopped at Orléans, I don't know, about ten days before returning to Paris. As I say, you couldn't cross the Loire. I saw the Germans for the first time at Orléans, apart from those in the planes. They didn't frighten me particularly.

I saw them kill a French soldier near me at Orléans. He had his Lebel rifle on a bicycle. When he saw the Germans arrive he tried to grab his Lebel. The Germans machine gunned him. It was over at once. That was an experience for a boy like me to undergo, but I was one among thousands of others.

We had arrived at Orléans during an air raid and there we found the Germans. They began to put me up against an embankment. They threatened me with their weapons, and then they left. I saw the columns passing.

So then we returned to Paris. We went back on foot. It took a bit longer than two days. When we returned toward Paris there were still bodies, heaps of bodies, in a state of decomposition, on the route. It was something really frightful. What a smell! Women, men, children, soldiers—Belgian soldiers, I remember. I didn't see any British soldiers. I have the impression the British had gone to Dunkirk.

Reactions on the subject of Dunkirk were very mixed because many people said the British had embarked the French soldiers only when they could not do otherwise. Is that true or not true? I do not know. Many people did not understand the way the British went about things—that is to say, to go back home with their Air Force and all. But the English had above all to ensure the defence of the British Isles. The French understood that.[185]

On the road back to Paris from Orléans we were in a state like gypsies—appalling. My mother was extremely tired and full of worries, of course, about my father. She did not know where he was.

As I told you, it was my father who had shut the barracks of the Colonial Artillery at Rueil Malmaison when the Germans arrived and he set off down the road on foot with his Blacks. He arrived at Rivesalts in the Eastern Pyrenees, quite near Perpignan. I don't know how many kilometres from Rueil that was. It was when he was at Rivesalts that the end arrived for France. There was the Occupied Zone and the Unoccupied Zone. The soldiers who were from the Occupied Zone—as was the case with my father—were not demobilised. So he demobilised himself at Tournon in August and came back home to Paris in August or September. He was able to cross the demarcation line secretly.

In June 1940, after the Fall of France, Marshal Pétain signed an armistice with the Germans. We learned of it while we were on the exodus from Paris. Then, at the outset, we were relieved but afterward one did all one could—above all, young people—against the policy of collaboration. In the Unoccupied Zone above all, many people thought that Pétain was playing a double game. But that was not the case.[186]

Pétain was one of my father's heroes and that remained the case after the armistice in 1940. I can tell you something amusing: when we went to the cinema and saw Pétain on the newsreels, I hissed and my father applauded. This made for family dramas, so much so that my mother, for the sake of a quiet life, eventually persuaded my father not to applaud and me not to hiss! An armistice! But my affection for my father was not affected by this.

Later on, too, I remember, after I had left school and begun work, we disagreed over Pétain's portrait. In the dining room of my parents' home was the portrait of Marshal Pétain. When I came home from work I used to be in before my father. The first thing I did was to turn the portrait face to the wall. And of course when my father arrived: 'Who did that?!' 'It was me!' Every evening there were frightful scenes in the house! But outside of that business my relations with my father were excellent. However, I used to get angry because he read newspapers issued by collaborators.

The paths my father and I followed politically diverged from the moment of the armistice. That was often the case in France. Families were divided on the issue. But there was something else—the view of things in the Unoccupied Zone and in the Occupied Zone was different. Here at Tournon it was very marked. The people who called themselves Pétainists, the Légion des Combattants, etc.—I don't mean the Milice, who were traitors—could also be Gaullists, whereas in the Occupied Zone that was not the case. It was very distinct.[187]

I had not heard of General de Gaulle before 1940. The first time he came into prominence was through his appeal of the 18th of June 1940. I heard afterwards what he said when it became possible to listen to the English radio, which was very difficult to hear—pah-pah-pah-pah-pah—even so, one began to hear plenty of things.

Before 1940 de Gaulle was not a general. He was a colonel. And he alone won a victory in 1940, at Montcornet, with his tanks. He had written books, *Towards the Professional Army*, *The Sword's Edge*, etc., which advocated armoured divisions, which was ironic since Guderian, in Germany, did as de Gaulle advised. And this is what beat us.[188]

I left school in 1941 when I was sixteen or seventeen. I had an ambition to make a career in the army because I have always had a love of my country. And then things turned out otherwise. France was liberated in 1944. And then after that I wanted to get married. Then that changed my way of looking at things.

Well, I left school not necessarily with pleasure but I wanted to work. I didn't shed any tears. I began work as a writer at the Mutual Assistance Society of the Town of Paris. It was an insurance company. I was in the fire damages section, that's to say the payment of damages after a fire. The work was O.K. I had good colleagues at work. I quite liked it. It was quite lively sort of work. I was busy with files of losses and damages, small losses and damages. There were many extremely interesting things.

At that time, during the German occupation, food was difficult because one had nothing, above all at the beginning, because the French had not yet got themselves organised. There was nothing at all to eat of anything whatever. One thing I still have a memory of was sausage or black pudding—*boudin*. But it wasn't pork sausage, it was sausage made of beef blood or some such stuff. It was enormous. It was absolutely uneatable. There was also fish paste. It was made with crushed fish bones, etc. You see the sort of stuff it was. There wasn't much for eating, nothing much at all.

One day in 1941 or 1942 I saw a German soldier kill a Frenchman in the Paris Metro. I was leaving for work. Two Frenchmen were chatting alongside the door of the Metro and a unit of Germans arrived, equipped with rifles, helmets, etc., who barged into us and settled themselves down. Those two Frenchmen who were there continued to talk about things and then something must have passed through the head of one of these soldiers. He began to swear at one of the Frenchmen, and to call him all sorts of names. One couldn't understand it very well but what he was saying wasn't very nice. The other man said nothing. He pretended not to hear. And on arriving at the Concorde station—that's right, since I myself was getting off at the Tuileries—this Frenchman got off and the Germans got off behind. And this German, as he got off, carried on insulting the Frenchman. What did the Frenchman do to his friend who was with him? He put his finger on his forehead to show that the German was mad. The German saw the gesture and he took his rifle by the barrel and brought it down on the Frenchman's head, breaking his skull. The Metro was moving off, but the force with which the German struck him made it evident that he could not survive. I was badly shocked.

In Paris I saw Goering in the Champs Elysées. He was enormous by then. He had decorations, etc., etc. In the Champs Elysées he was going into a perfume shop with all his guard—a gangster.[189]

I was requisitioned by the Germans in 1942. 1 was the youngest in our office to be requisitioned. That business of requisitioning was again a piece of treason by the Vichy government. In theory the Germans had no right to requisition Frenchmen under 20 years of age. But they took them from age 18. And then in order to deceive the enemy (that's to say, the French), they had to sign a job application. I was on the requisition list and I was called up on to the German labour service, in the rue de la Chaussée d'Antin. It was German women serving with the army who received us. This girl, who spoke French, said to me: 'Look here, you're lucky because you are requisitioned to Hispano-Suiza for a period of apprenticeship. So you won't be leaving immediately for Germany.' I said to her, 'Is it as rotten as that in Germany?' Ha, ha, ha! She was a very pretty girl.

I then turned up at Hispano-Suiza, which was in the Bois Colombes. I arrived at the personnel office there. I was told, 'You must sign your job application.' 'I don't want to. I want to go home. I work at the Mutual Assurance of Paris. I was getting on very well there. So I don't see why I've got to sign this job application.' 'You must sign!' Then I saw some Germans coming, etc. It was extremely difficult. 'Either you'll sign or you'll be taken immediately to Germany.' Well, I signed! I was put into maintenance. I had decided not to work. So I was sitting in the middle of a workshop when the foreman arrived. He said, 'What are you doing there?' 'Send me back.' 'Ah, you've been requisitioned?' 'Yes.' 'These requisitioned Frenchmen, there's nothing to be done with them!'

So this went on until the day when there took place one of the most beautiful things I have ever seen. It was on the day in November 1942 that the fleet was scuttled at Toulon. London had asked for a minute's silence and in the factory at the hour indicated, all the workers stopped the machines and stood to attention behind them singing *The Marseillaise*. The Germans took two of them from each workshop. I was young, perhaps I had shouted louder than the others. Anyway I found myself pushed into the office. With the foreman in his overalls, German military police at the door, some Gestapo were there and the man before me who went into the office began to be beaten with fists and booted feet. I went in afterwards.

When you are 18 you feel a bit funny when you see that. 'Communist! Gaullist! Liar!' I let him say it, and then afterward I said to him: 'Monsieur, no. I have just been requisitioned and I am not a Communist.' He asked the workshop foreman for my dossier. Then I shall always remember him saying, 'They're sending me kids now! Get out!' And he sent me back out the door by which I had come in. The others left by the other door. They were sent away. They were never seen again: *Nuit et Brouillard*, *Nacht und Nebel*, Night and Fog. I do not know what became of them. I was sent back through the door I had come in and received some thumps from the Germans. It wasn't too bad.

Then some people whom I did not know very well but whom I knew were in the Resistance, asked me to make them a little sketch that showed where the petrol depots were. The RAF were then able to bomb the petrol tanks and destroy them.

It was that experience that made me decide to join the Resistance at the age of 18. I began at Paris with some friends. We went into the woods near Paris, the Bois de Chaville, and picked up leaflets sent by the RAF. These leaflets were copied and then distributed. They were put into letter-boxes. It was one line of Resistance, you see. That was in 1942.

There were no more Zones in 1942. That was when the Germans took over the southern or Unoccupied Zone. I left Hispano-Suiza at the beginning of 1943. I was unwilling to join the STO—the Service du Travail Obligatoire, forced labour—in Germany. An accident was faked that involved the lifting of metal parts. I fell on top of them. I was taken to the doctor, who told me to leave. I went to Cour-Cheverny where my cousin who was in the Resistance lived.[190] Doctor Grateau faked my X-rays to try to have me declared unfit. But that didn't last long. I was chased up and the factory had been bombed by the RAF. Some people came to tell my parents, 'Do not return to Hispano-Suiza. Everything has been destroyed. You haven't seen your son. Do not return to the factory.'

When I was at my cousin's place at Cour-Cheverny I got to know the Resistance men of the freelance corps called 'Vengeance'. They were shot by the Germans. I was at Cour-Cheverny when the Allies invaded Sicily in July 1943. And then I went back to Tournon and I found myself in the Resistance. At first I was involved in little things and then bigger ones, until the struggle for Liberation.

I had already met my future wife here at Tournon. I had known her for ten years, as my grandfather was a neighbour of my future parents-in-law. It was destiny! Her father was Parti Social Français. He had a builder's business. He was part of the Tournon Maquis group. It was a territorial group. He helped, rendered services to it. My fiancée helped too when she could. She was a young girl—in 1944 she was seventeen, I was twenty.[191]

After I went to Tournon in 1943 I made the acquaintance at the nearby.town of Le Blanc of a teacher at the college there, Monsieur Peche, who in the Resistance used the pseudonym 'Papillon'. This teacher realised my views, and entrusted me with some minor errands—giving messages on paper to people, that kind of thing. Most of the time I was here at Tournon, until the D-Day landings took place in June 1944, and on D-Day and immediately afterwards we took to the woods.

Round here at Tournon there were not people—Maquis—who were always in the woods. There were those who were dodging the STO (Service du Travail Obligatoire) who worked on the farms. We regrouped and got going immediately after D-Day came.

At the Normandy landings in 1944 I distributed mobilisation orders to officers and NCOs of the Armistice army to rejoin their units at such and such a place. I did all that on my bicycle. I began that work because the message of the landings was passed across in two parts, as the first gave the alert and the second said the landings would take place immediately.

D-Day was a very, very remarkable event in history. I carried messages telling officers, etc., to join the Maquis, and where to go, etc. I remember all the planes that

170

passed overhead. In this region before D-Day there was an enormous number. There were a lot of planes coming and going. And we were very glad, you know. Fortunately, there was an inrush of people into the Maquis.

I had a chance to be in on some parachute drops by the English at that time and also to help to hide arms, above all sten guns and bren guns. The sten gun was very dangerous as a gun. I was a specialist at firing the bren. The only awkward bit about the bren was that sometimes the ejector took off the base of the round and left the casing inside, so that the second round couldn't be fired. To get it going again we used to put in a smaller blank round. That's what happened to us at Ville Jésus, a small locality where we tangled with the Germans. That's where I was hit by a bullet. You can still see the scar. The Germans advanced. Our bren jammed. But I recalled the trick I had learned and I was able to get it going again—fortunately, because things were going very badly! We also received Canadian rifles from the RAF. There were eleven bullets in the magazine. And revolvers—a small barrel with a plastic grip—and defensive grenades. With the British rifles there were bayonets. And then we received American arms. We also received carbines that fired fifteen rounds. That was a very, very accurate weapon. And also Colts. And then we received a great deal of plastic explosive. Anti-tank bazookas too. With the bazooka you had to be careful and wear a mask: the rocket blew back flame and some of the lads had their hair burnt with it! At the end we had Canadian mortars. But we didn't really know how to use them!

We had a sort of uniform. We picked up jackets from the youth camps, green jackets and green shorts. The British never or very seldom parachuted clothes to us. We also had French army uniforms. There was the First Regiment of France, a regiment that the Germans had authorised Pétain to have. And we had part of that regiment stationed at Le Blanc which joined us with arms and equipment. And that brings back a certain memory. It was before the Normandy landings. There was an arms depot on the road between Le Blanc and Bélâbre, I think it was in an old chapel. The arms had been placed inside there. Had someone given us away? Well, the First Regiment of France came to take these arms. So our Peche-Papillon requisitioned an old bus from a commercial company. We were in the bus, about forty of us, that's all, and we stopped. In front of us there was a whole company of the First Regiment of France with machine-guns, etc. And Peche-Papillon got out. And he said, 'You're going to give us your arms or we're going to give you what for.' I'll never forget the look on the face of the officer, Commandant Noel. 'Let's take into account the number of men you have and your weaponry. We don't want any bloodshed. We leave the arms to you and off we go.'

Immediately D-Day came arms were distributed. The town of Bélâbre was occupied. Arms were given out to the people who joined us, etc. We saw the local curé arrive. The lads who were with me were afraid he was going to remonstrate with us but he took a weapon for himself and said, 'I fought in the war of '14-18. Give me a weapon. I know how to use it.'

When on 10 July, 1944 the Germans of the SS Das Reich Division attacked us, they had begun to gather women and children in the churches, to do as they did at

Oradour. So this brave curé along with the local mayor went to find the German officer and said to him: 'If you are looking for hostages, I am the curé, he is the mayor. We're first. Yes, there have been battles. Germans have been killed. But we gave them proper burials.' They went to the cemetery, where they saw the graves with the German helmets on them, and the papers were at the town hall. That calmed them down a bit.

At that time we hadn't heard of the fate of the people at Oradour-sur-Glane, near Limoges, and about 85 kilometres from Bélâbre. But these Germans belonged to the same Division. We had been warned that the Germans were coming to attack us. We had forced back some elements from St Hilaire des Bois who were awaiting us. And a Maquis company arrived from the region of Chauvigny in Vienne. We told them that the Germans were coming and it was necessary for them to join up with our group: 'We'll see tomorrow. Tonight we rest.' Probably they were informed on, as usual. The next day the Germans were there and they were all shot. That was done by the SS Das Reich Division. It passed close to Tournon.[192]

After that there was the business with the 17th Panzer Division (General Elster). The 17th Panzer Division was not SS. It was an armoured division which was coming back up from the south of France to rejoin the troops on the Normandy front and which was completely pinned down by the Resistance. They were completely prevented from coming back.

In the region around Tournon there were people who were killed in the struggle against the Germans. There were quite a lot. You see the evidence everywhere. There are little crosses. There is one beside the road from Tournon to Le Blanc. I know what happened in that business. It was a member of the FTP Maquis.[193] The road to Le Blanc passes through some rocky country. All the German convoys that passed along there were attacked. All the signposts were changed throughout the countryside so as to send them that way. So this convoy was attacked and then he, a young fellow without experience, jumped out from the ambush in order to fire on the last lorry in the convoy. Well, the German who was at the rear of it fired, and that was how he was killed.

In this region there were killed and wounded. There were 120 shot, 537 killed in the fighting against the Germans, and more than 800 who were interned, imprisoned or deported for acts of resistance. Not far from Tournon there's a farm that has been rebuilt at Boussay. That's where the headquarters of my group was based. Being in the freelance unit and also a medical orderly I was attached to headquarters. All night, trees had been blown up to impede the movements of the 17th Panzer Division. We arrived in our big Citroën car, put the plastic explosive in position, ran out the detonating cable, and set the igniter. There was a sort of plate one rubbed that lit the cable. And after that night we lay down to sleep quite worn out. It was about two or three o'clock in the morning. And I was in the hay in the hayloft on that farm, and then in the morning I was awakened by a mate who called me and said: 'Look here, I have blisters on my feet. Have you any stuff for that?' I said, 'Yes, of course.' We had some products that had been parachuted in by the English, some sulphamide ointment for skin troubles. It was very good. I said, 'O.K., I'm coming.'

I went down the ladder. Bang! Bang! The farm was surrounded by the Germans. 'The Boche are here!' So, right. I didn't bother going down the remaining rungs of the ladder. I jumped. The Germans weren't too numerous and there was a unit protecting our group, and a section of the First Regiment of France commanded by Lieutenant Pannier protecting the commander and the headquarters. They attacked the Germans with their bayonets. And we accompanied them with sweeps on the submachine-gun, with the result that the Germans pulled back, taking some wounded with them, to cut a long story short. So then we evacuated the farm. And there was a young man on that farm. The commander said to his parents: 'Let him come away with us. He won't fight when it's all over. He will come back. If the Germans come now they will kill him.' But they wouldn't agree. At the edge of the road now there is a monument where the Germans shot him. And he had done nothing.

Some friends of mine, young people, were killed of course among those that fought before or after D-Day.

I mentioned that in this region 800 people were interned, imprisoned or deported. There was a camp near Tournon at Douadic where the Germans, using French guards, had gathered Jews who were afterwards deported. There weren't many Jews living in the region, they were rather in the big towns. But there were some at Tournon. I recall one who was hidden at my cousin's place. He went under the name Le Blanc and was the director of a big store in Paris, Les Galéries Lafayette. A lot of Jews came to this region to go to ground. But those people didn't say they were Jews. And then they were nice people.

Gypsies, too, were victims of the Nazis but we didn't have any here. But there were some gypsies who gave people away. The headquarters of the battalion to which I belonged—the 27th demi-brigade Charles Martel—was at Chateau du Verger at Liglet. Well, the headquarters and all the groups had left the Chateau du Verger at Liglet in order to join up with the rest of the 27th demi-brigade and to liberate Loches. It was there that we came across elements of the Elster 17th Panzer Division. I had gone by way of Tournon, along with a lieutenant and two other comrades. We stopped at the restaurant at my cousin's place. My parents were on holiday at Tournon and came to eat with us. We discussed things, etc. The next day a German convoy passed through. My father was sitting at his door reading. Then, when he looked up there were three Germans threatening him with their rifles. They said, 'The gypsies in the caravans across the road told us, "Maquis here yesterday"'. Then one of the Germans took my mother away to the foot of the garden, with his rifle pointing at her back. I had left a parachute behind me that was in full view. There was a German grenade—and what else besides? Yes, there was still some tincture of iodine that had been parachuted down in various containers. All that was in full view. This German passed right in front of it. He saw nothing—or said nothing. Afterwards they came to my cousin who had the restaurant. Her daughter had a bottle in her hand ready to pour. One of the Germans broke the bottle with the butt of his revolver. Same thing again: 'Maquis yesterday. Lunch here.'

I reported this to Commandant Marceau, who was furious and said: 'Go with a section and take incendiary grenades and set fire to all those gypsy caravans.' I said to him, 'Commandant, there are three families of them.' Which one had denounced us? There were women and children among them. The mystery has always remained. Which of them had denounced us?

There were not many Germans in this region before D-Day. At Le Blanc there were Germans to ensure the trains ran and to guard the station. And then also when the electricity lines were sabotaged the Germans came to repair them. But there were not all that many Germans there. They passed through. There was not a garrison. There was a garrison at Poitiers or Châtellerault but not at Le Blanc. At Le Blanc was the First Regiment of France. There was no garrison but there was one at Châteauroux, of course, at Poitiers and in the big towns. And then there were convoys that passed through. You had to be careful.

There were Gestapo at Poitiers, at Châtellerault and at Châteauroux—in the big towns. At Le Blanc I don't know. But they moved about to make their enquiries, arrest people who had been denounced and take them to their office at Poitiers or at Châteauroux to interrogate them. I had the opportunity to see a member of the Resistance who had been arrested with a group. After being tortured they were taken into the forest of Châteauroux and shot. That man had been lucky. The bullets hadn't seriously wounded him and when the German warrant officer came to deliver the coup de grâce he turned his head away. So the coup de grâce had simply broken his jaw. He was lucky. He was taken care of by peasants who afterwards led him to the Maquis where I was. The Germans had stuck knitting needles into the calves of his legs. He was taken in charge by his network and I think he left in a Lysander for London.[194]

There were some of the Abwehr in this region too but it was very difficult to know who they were since it was the Intelligence service of the German army. And these people spoke French very well, were just like Frenchmen, and there were denunciations of Resisters, one didn't know how. I even think that we had in the group some Abwehr types who were there posing as Resisters.[195]

It was more difficult for the Abwehr to function in a region like this than, for example, in Paris. One knew everyone in Tournon, and it was very difficult for a German. They were outsiders. I knew one character who belonged to the Abwehr and who was at Bélâbre. He repaired shoes. He was a White Russian. And as there were denunciations of Resisters and different things, he was arrested and brought to the Maquis. And so he repaired our shoes until one day his mistress came to the Maquis because she had learned that he had played some mean tricks on her, and she brought the stubs of his pay cheques from the Germans. We executed him.

For us the enemies were not so much the Abwehr but rather the Milice and the collaborators—those who denounced others. There were all kinds of them. One day when I arrived at my grandfather's at Tournon he said, 'Don't go to my nephew and niece's place. Are you still in the Maquis?' I said, 'Of course, you know that.' 'Because they've told me that they will throw you out.' I wanted to see that happening and I went to their place at once. The nephew said to me, 'It appears that you are in the Maquis?' 'Of course,' I said. 'I don't want any bandits at my place.' I said, 'We'll see about that', and I left. And this character, who was married to the niece of my grandfather and who had fought all through the war of 1914-18, hanged himself when Liberation came. He had his own views of things but there was no proof that he had actually denounced anyone.

There weren't all that many cases of denunciations to the German authorities. Otherwise there would have been a lot of fear among ordinary people, because people did not know who their enemies were. I don't think there were very many denunciations to the Germans. To my knowledge in the region there weren't any denunciations except for the woman who took in the mail at Be, who had denounced some of those dodging the call-up.

I should say that those opposed to the Resistance and opposed—how shall I say?—to the liberation of the country, were very few in number. Here at Tournon was the Unoccupied Zone. The veterans of 1914-18 were in Pétain's Légion—the Légion des Combattants. It was a movement of veterans of 1914-18. Pétain was its chief. He created it when he became Head of the French State in 1940. Well, there were leaders of it all over the region. And those people who were in the Légion believed that Pétain, as I told you, was playing a double game. So they worked for the Resistance, apart from the police service of the Légion which afterwards became the Milice or Militia. The Milice was commanded by a certain Monsieur Darnand, he was the chief.

We didn't have Milice here at Tournon. There were some at Le Blanc. I met two Milice chiefs who were making enquiries at Tournon on the subject of a parachute drop. I was there for the same reason, for the containers which had not been picked up by the Resistance had been collected by the Vichy police. We found ourselves by chance at the same restaurant and these two men from the Milice began to praise the Germans to me. Everything was fine, marvellous, etc. They even went so far as to say it was the French who had in 1915 first used poison gas. But I said to one of them, 'Monsieur, you say that and you say you are a French officer. You ought to be ashamed!' That passed off well all the same.

On Liberation B. and C., the Milice chiefs of the region, were arrested. B. was put on trial. He was sentenced to penal servitude for life and pardoned. C. was shot by the Resistance.

While I was in the Resistance I was arrested myself. Once it was actually the Milice people who saved me. I was coming back from Trimouille, where I had made a contact. I had a 7.65mm revolver in my pocket and some documents. I came to a level crossing above Le Blanc. Two members of the Milice were there and made me get off my bike. I was wearing a youth camp jacket. 'Come on. Our chiefs are going to sort you out. You are in the Maquis.' And they did not search me, thank God. They took me to the gatekeeper's house and there I met the characters I told you about that I had seen at Tournon. 'Ah', they said, 'we know you.' 'I saw you at the Hotel Grateau.' 'Ah, yes, we met you. Oh, he's not really bad. He's a bit of a nut but not really bad.' And they let me go. I had a rendezvous at the Hotel Central in Le Blanc. I checked the rendezvous. I was like that. I said, 'Listen, give me something to drink. It doesn't matter what.'

Another time approaching Preuilly when I was coming from a contact with General Chome the gear went on my bike. A German convoy passed. One vehicle passed, then a second. A light vehicle stopped. A German officer got out of it. 'What are you doing?' I said, 'My bike's broken.' He spoke French. I said, 'I'm an insurance agent. I'm visiting clients.' 'Ah. Get up on the lorry at the back.' I got up on the lorry with my bike. There were tyres in the lorry. I didn't know what they were doing with all those tyres. There were also two German soldiers. With his boot one of them touched the back pocket of my trousers where I had my 7.65mm. revolver. I moved over. What else could I do? As I was approaching Preuilly one of my pals hiding at the side of the road had seen me. 'That's it, they've got Dunand. They're going to shoot him.' And then the Germans kindly let me off at Preuilly. And of course I thanked them!

The organisation of the Maquis was a little complicated for the groups were progressively being transformed. The group where I was at Bélâbre belonged to the 27th demi-brigade Charles Martel, which was part of the ORA (Organisation de la Résistance Armée). The headquarters of the battalion to which I belonged was at Château du Verger at Liglet. The commandant—Commandant Moreau, alias Marceau—had been an officer-instructor at St Cyr. He was a Regular officer.[196] The demi-brigade Charles Martel consisted of the 17th Light Infantry (Maquis Carol) and the 27th Infantry Regiment with two battalions, ours and a second one in Indre-et-Loire. In the Maquis Carol (Carol de Beauregard) were Prince Murat, who was killed, and also Prince Napoleon, alias Bonaparte.[197]

And afterwards there was the AS (Armée Sécrète). The Armée Sécrète were little local Maquis formed by people of goodwill but there were all sorts of incidents. I'll tell you about a case that involved me. I came back here to Tournon often to see my fiancée, of course, and—I didn't say what I did—I was a Parisian. I had come there to see my grandfather. I could have been a member of the Milice, the militia, or something. So one fine day a mate who knew what I was up to said to me, 'Watch out. They want to kill you.' I said, 'That's the last straw!' I warned my commander and told him I no longer wanted to go on missions to Tournon. His wife and daughter lived in a farm near here. The core of the battalion was stationed at this farm and had already been bothered by this local Maquis. He called to an officer cadet: 'Go with Dunand to the Marne' (the name of the farm where the Maquis was). We found one of the people in charge and the lieutenant told him, 'You want to execute our liaison agent? You are completely mad.' 'Ah, well, we didn't know, we didn't know.' That's all very well. But when you want to kill people it's as well to know who they are. This shows you what could happen. There were also personal scores to be settled, for political or family reasons. There were some unfortunate things that happened, that's certain.

And then you had the FTP (Francs-Tireurs Partisans). These were Communist groups. We had an important Communist group in the region of Le Blanc. It was often I who went to make contact with them and Guy Lebon was their commander. He was a brave man but without military training. He was a mechanic in a garage. Commanding a group was a little tricky. They fought well. They were at Bélâbre near us. We were at St Oprien then at St Jacques, they were at Château Guillaume, a fine chateau. Among the FTP there were not only Communists and there were some problems with the Party.

The Maquis wasn't organised on a party-political basis, not at all. There was a whole spectrum of ideas. In this region the people of the Maquis were patriots rather than political activists. You know the boys of the Maquis were young men—I was going to say mere lads, as I was if you like. So we weren't centred on politics. Of course we were against Pétain. But apart from that, as to whether one was a socialist or a Gaullist ... All of us, even the FTP, were following General de Gaulle. That was very clear. For the rest, ideas, you know ...

We did have here in the Maquis people who before the war had like my father been in the Croix de Feu—just a few, since the majority of us were only young people. We hadn't been active in political parties, and the officers didn't mention such matters. It was indeed very complex. And it must be said that the majority of the priests—up to ninety per cent—were for the Resistance.

As I've said, the Maquis was mostly young people apart from some officers. In the ORA (Organisation de la Résistance Armée) it was mainly officers who came. But the mistake the Reserve officers made was not to have commanded the Maquis. The Maquisards were often attacked in these words, 'They had no proper commanders in charge, they covered themselves in gold braid', etc., etc., because there were no officers who wanted to come. And yet we sent for them. Everything was done to encourage them to come. Then, finally, when they saw things beginning to hot up they came.

In this region a majority of the Maquisards were, in my opinion, farming people. But there were also many draft dodgers—*réfractaires* refusing to go as forced labour to Germany—people who were sought by the Germans, and escaped prisoners-of-war: men who had been taken prisoner in 1940, who had escaped from Germany and who rejoined. There were many.

There were a lot of women in the Maquis. These women weren't in the Maquis in order to fight. The wives of the small farmers did our cooking, etc. But I knew women then, in the Resistance, who did Intelligence work. There were a few who actually fought with weapons. But personally I didn't know any. It was rather a question of taking part in some other way.

We didn't have children in the Maquis whose job was to pass messages. There was no rule on the question. It was a question of whether the person concerned appeared able to cope. But normally those who came were from 17 upwards. There were not many old people.

There were some Spanish members of the Maquis. I didn't know any. They didn't remain there. They went away and regrouped in the south because it was said that the Spanish would form Spanish regiments to get rid of Franco. We were even told that if necessary our group would leave with them. And then our group went off to the Atlantic Wall.[198]

We had a few Poles. Where they came from I don't know. But at one time we had a Polish section.

Some of our prisoners told us that they were anti-Nazis. When you take prisoners and then they tell you that they are anti-Nazis, well … There weren't any Germans in this region who had escaped from Germany after the rise of Hitler in 1933, nor Italians opposed to Mussolini either. What there were on the other hand were many Alsace-Lorrainers who did not wish to fight for the Germans. After all, they were Frenchmen. One of the most bitter men whom I found among the German prisoners we took was I suppose an SS man.[199] He was an Alsatian and we had not treated him as a prisoner but put him to work in the kitchen for that reason. But he was a Nazi, ah, yes, he was a Nazi. It was there I learned something about the problem of Alsace. When in 1870 the Germans occupied Alsace-Lorraine the Alsatians had the choice of either becoming German or leaving for France. Some left for France. But they were replaced by Prussians. And this lad was one of the latter. His family had come to Alsace in 1870. He was a small farmer. He had been to a French school. He spoke French very well. But do you think he was French at heart?

In our group we didn't have prisoners who had been collaborators, except the one man I have mentioned. As for German prisoners, they were taken to a camp at Grand Pressigny, in the caves there. And there were also those who came perhaps from Loches or elsewhere: Milice, and women with shaven heads who had slept with the Germans.[200] They were guarded by veterans of the 1914-18 war who volunteered to do so. They were armed with hunting rifles. Believe me, there was no point in those prisoners trying to escape.

A German prisoner had given me his address and told me, 'Whatever you do, if you come to Germany after the war and if I'm still alive, come and see me.' I carried that piece of paper about with me for a long time and then—lost it. I was sorry about that.

But those prisoners weren't harmed. There were some prisoners who were executed. They were Indians who had been taken prisoner with the English army in Cyrenaica and whom the Germans had enlisted into the German army. When they had arrived at Yzeures, a little place near Tournon, the German officers in charge of them had let them do as they wished. They raped women and young girls. I was one of those who first went into Yzeures after they left it. After their rear-guard had been fought we went into that area. It wasn't a pretty sight. We saw four people who had been bayoneted because the father had defended his wife and daughters. We took prisoners but there were some whom we were sure had taken part in these things and they were executed. They wore a khaki German uniform, but I don't remember seeing them with turbans. Perhaps one or two wore them but in general they had German helmets. Anyway they were brown.

Well, after D-Day the Maquis in this region began operations that were a lot more overt—attacks on German convoys, railways, sabotage, etc. The first time I blew up a pylon was on the road from Le Blanc to Bélâbre. And I'd never done that before. Nobody showed us how to do it. We were told, 'Look, plastic explosive—this is how it works. You attach a detonator, etc., and then you put the cable round the pylon.'. But we forgot only one thing: to lay the charges asymmetrically. When the pylon blew up it went up and then came straight down! Ha, ha, ha!

We attacked convoys and blew up the railway, too. Once things nearly went badly wrong. We went to blow up the Paris-Bordeaux line near Port de Piles. It was an operation that had been mounted with Résistance-Fer, railwaymen in their Resistance organisation. Trains with troops and materiel were going up to the Atlantic front. The railway guards were for us, they were firmly attached to us. They laughed and then our charges were laid. I don't know if you have seen a sabotage system. It was like a telephone earphone with two points. You placed it alongside the rail and between the two points was a sort of ring and you laid the fuse cable through it. You made a hollow in the ballast that stabilises the rails or sleepers, and you put the plastic inside. When the train passed along, the wheel of the locomotive broke the circuit and everything went up in the air.

Well, that particular day everything was ready when we saw an SNCF (the railway authority) official arrive on a bicycle. He said, 'Oh, stop, lads. This is terrible. The Germans are sending the Paris-Bordeaux train just in front of them.' It was the Paris-Bordeaux that was about to go up in the air. Oh, I can tell you that everything was cleared away immediately!

There were some British agents in this region parachuted in before and after the D-Day landings. I knew them personally. I knew Captain Crawley very well. He was a very nice lad, an Intelligence Service man who taught us sabotage. He had been parachuted in with two other Englishmen at the beginning of 1944. There was also a flying boat which landed on the lake called La Mer Rouge in Brenne and which brought some agents and flew back others. The son of a friend of mine was cornered by the Germans the last time the flying boat came. Afterwards that game was not played again. It was very, very dangerous. I knew one woman agent who dropped in but I don't think she was British. I think she was French. And of course there were Frenchmen and French women among the agents who came down by parachute, too.

There are things I remember that I haven't told you and that now come back to me. Some people one remembers very well, others ... well, it's fifty or so years ago. But I was very young and impressionable and I was very affected by all that.

Outside of the business of Pétain's portrait, relations with my father were excellent. He knew I was in the Maquis. However, I used to get angry because he read newspapers issued by collaborators. As I told you, he used to come to Tournon on holiday. One day I came to see him with my fiancée. I said to him, 'Papa, may I offer you an aperitif?' This was at my cousin's place. He said, 'I don't want to take anything from *your* paymasters.' That had profoundly upset me. But he apologised later on, when he realised, when he saw how things turned out. He said to me one day, 'If you need someone, I fought in the war of '14!'

After the war I continued in insurance. I married my fiancée in Tournon in 1946. And then my wife's health broke down in Paris. So we came back here to Tournon to work. I worked for a time with my father-in-law and then that didn't work out for all sorts of reasons. And I went back to Paris again. I worked as an industrial accountant, a kind of back-room job, at Radio Air. Then Radio Air didn't work out so well. It was all right for me but not so much for the company because it was before the war in Indo-China and there were no orders coming in. They made cameras for planes. And I went to work in an English company, Hoover. I stayed there something like twelve or thirteen years. After that I got into a household electrical applicances shop.

After the Liberation with Guy Lebon and Peche-Papillon, my network chief in the resistance, we formed the RPF (Rassemblement du Peuple Francais). After the war I met General de Gaulle. I was elected a town councillor for Orléans on the Gaullist ticket. I have always remained loyal to General de Gaulle.[201]

I have no contact with the British I met during the war. I have regretted that but it hasn't happened. For a long time I was in the Franco-British Association when I was at Orléans and then I used to meet British people. I remain active in Les Combattants Volontaires de la Résistance. I am president of Souvenir Français, an organisation dedicated to the upkeep of the graves of soldiers who gave their lives for France.

For my Resistance activities I received the Médaille du Combattant, the Commémorative de la Liberation, and the Médaille Franco-Britannique.

In retrospect I certainly do not have any regrets at all about my activities in the Resistance. If it had to be done again I would do it.

James K Annand

Having been a Conshie, or a potential Conshie, I was quite glad when I was called up in July 1941 because I felt that I really ought to be involved in what was happening in Europe. And I went quite cheerfully. In the 1920s and '30s I would possibly have been a Conscientious Objector as I was anti-war. That was the fashion in those days. But I was influenced by the Spanish Civil War in the late '30s. That made me think that maybe pacifism wasn't enough.

I remember vividly the outbreak of the 1914 war—and the end of it, too. I was only six in 1914. I was born at Mackenzie Place, Edinburgh, on the 2nd of February 1908. The house is still standing, it's next to St Bernard's Well at the Water of Leith.

My father was born down at the Water of Leith and brought up there. He lived in the sound of the Water of Leith all his life. My mother came of a mining family in Lesmahagow in Lanarkshire. My father was a plumber and I think they met when he was on a job as a plumber in the Lesmahagow area. I had three brothers. I was the second of them and I'm the sole survivor.

As I say I remember vividly the outbreak of the 1914 war. There were no Sunday newspapers in those days. And my granny lived in the upper flat of the house that we were in, and I used to often spend time up there. Well, my brother and I were up there with granny this day and there was the *Dispatch* and *News* man calling across the Water of Leith from us. And I remember my granny saying, 'Either the king's deid or there's a war broken oot.' And she gave my elder brother some money to go and buy the paper—the *News,* I think. In those days it was either a halfpenny or a penny. And the news-vendor was charging sixpence for it! War profiteering!

I remember that very clearly. And also there were two things in the war itself I remember. By then I had begun school at St Bernard's primary. We were half-time, of course. Flora Stevenson's school and St Bernard's used the St Bernard's building because Flora Stevenson's was a war-time army hospital. Flora's, I think, attended in the forenoon and we attended in the afternoon. And one afternoon in the gloaming the janitor came round with a taper to light the gas and he remarked to the teacher that Lord Kitchener had been lost in the sinking of the *Hampshire.* And I remember thinking, as so many of our friends did, that that was us beaten, as he was the head man of the army.[202]

I was eight years old then—too young to take a close interest in the war or follow the campaigns through the newspapers. But I remember seeing men at Waverley station coming off the train, their kilts caked with mud. I had an uncle in the Gordons and I remember seeing him when he came on leave.

Then again in November 1918 I remember being off school in the forenoon and I was down at the Co-op in Hamilton Place getting messages, when somebody came in and told us the war was finished. That evening or afternoon, after the school was over, I remember going up to Princes Street to see the crowds there. The place was hoaching with folk. There was an open horse-cab going along with some soldiers, I think, and some girls in it, and a sailor jumped from an open-deck tramcar into the cab—without injuring himself! Well, I went home after that and began feeling a bit guilty, because my granny had fallen and been dragged along by a tramcar a few days earlier and was very ill in bed. So there was poor old granny—and me out enjoying myself at the Armistice celebrations! So I went home—and granny died that night.

My father hadn't gone off to fight in the war. He was too important a tradesman for that, although he did get a shilling for registering in what they called the Derby Scheme. That was at my mother's insistence—just thinking if you're registered you'd maybe no' be called up! But my father did a lot of war work. He was employed a lot at Rosyth, for example.

Looking back on it I don't think the First World War had any effect on my thinking about war and peace.

From St Bernard's I went on to Broughton Senior secondary. It was selective in those days. As far as I remember there were only two of us from St Bernard's went along there. Mark you, there were a few more—not many, maybe a handful—who possibly could have gone but their parents said no. You were supposed to sign on for three years and leave at fifteen instead of fourteen. We paid ten shillings a year for books. Otherwise it was free. My parents felt able to afford that, and all four of us—my three brothers and I—went to Broughton. From Broughton I entered Edinburgh University.

When I was in the Senior Secondary I began to take an interest in literature and history. My parents were very encouraging but it was more the influence of teachers at Broughton and at St Bernard's as well. There was Tommy Walker, who had been wounded in the First World War in the Royal Scots. He was a greater encourager of me. And then Albert Mackie was in the same class at Broughton as my older brother and I met him a lot. He was writing and produced a manuscript magazine.[203] I thought I'd do the same when I was still at St Bernard's, with mock advertisements—'Buy Gibb's Soor Plooms', or such things. And there were stories made up. Tommy Walker, my teacher, had noticed this being passed round. I thought, 'Oh, I'm going to get the belt now!' But he said, 'I'll let you have this back. But your punishment is you'll have to produce another one next month.' So that was my literary inception. I'd be eleven.

I went to Broughton in 1920 and I was there until 1926. The teachers there who influenced me most were the principal teacher of English, George Ogilvie, who had influenced Hugh MacDiarmid, and there was John Sinclair, who became principal teacher of History later on. And there was a lad called George Young who taught me

English. He was actually a Classical scholar. At least he had taken a degree in Classics but I think he got a Third and that didn't allow him to teach in those days. But he did the general History and English. These were the teachers that influenced me most, they were all very encouraging. The influence was in their teaching rather than in direct personal encouragement, except in the case of Ogilvie. He gave me personal encouragement, as he did in other cases. That was in my fourth, fifth and sixth years at Broughton, when I was in his class.

I was very fortunate with somebody like Ogilvie as my teacher but there were quite a number of Broughton pupils who had benefited from his teaching: Albert Mackie, C M Grieve, and another poet—Roderick Watson Kerr, author of *War Daubs*, poems published in 1919, and one of the three founders of the Porpoise Press. He got a job on the *Scotsman*, like quite a number of other pupils through Ogilvie's interest, and he became, I think, editor of the *Liverpool Post*.

George Ogilvie was the author of *Secondary English*, which was a textbook in those days, along with Edward Albert, who was another pupil of his. But in the school magazine, which was very much a literary magazine, he had many interesting reminiscences and articles. Ogilvie never published any poems or novels. His strength lay in his teaching and his encouragement of young people. Later on, when I was at the University, he went off to become headmaster of a primary school, which was what they did with principal teachers in those days. It seemed a bit of a waste of his talents.[204]

When I went to Edinburgh University in 1926 I had been thinking that I might do Honours English. So in my first year I took the English class and the History class. Grierson was the English prof. and of course was easy to listen to. Basil Williams was the History one: he was a lousy, most uninspiring teacher. I got a merit certificate all right in History but only a Duly Performed in English. So that meant I had to go on to the History side. I would rather have followed the English, which was my greater interest.[205]

At Edinburgh University I was active in the Labour Club. I was on the committee and took part in two rectorials—one the year I went up, when they elected Sir John Gilmour, and then, three years later, we put up the first woman for the rectorship: Beatrice Webb. In fact, I had to go and interview the secretary of the University to make sure that a woman could stand.[206] But Churchill was elected.[207]

I edited two issues of the *Rebel Student*.[208] And in my final year I organised a meeting in the Usher Hall for Ramsay MacDonald. He was the prime minister at that time. I was also a delegate from the University Labour Club to Edinburgh Trades Council. The Labour Club wasn't a huge organisation—it had about a dozen or so attenders.

I had gone to the University just after the General Strike. I was still at school when the strike was on. I actually went down to Hillside Crescent, where the strike committee was based, and did some work on their paper, the Edinburgh Strike Bulletin, helping with the publication of it. I had just turned 18 then. I had become interested in political issues at school.

My father influenced me a lot in those. He was a socialist—not a very intelligent one. He used to take me along to Pringle's Palace, quite a big cinema in Leith Walk, where the Gateway is now, when the Communist Party used to have a Sunday meeting there. I remember hearing them all—Willie Gallacher and J S Clarke ... My father was never a member of the Communist Party. It was just a sort of general socialist interest that he had.

I graduated from university in 1930. I thought of going into journalism but it was too difficult to get in, and also I felt it was a bit too precarious. I sat the Civil Service exam for inspector of taxes and revenue, and just failed to make the mark. In normal years I would have been all right but they were recruiting so few in 1930. So I went to Moray House teachers' training college. It was a sort of second or third choice: I wasn't keen to become a teacher.

But even after qualifying there—I finished in June 1931—my first bit of work wasn't until January 1932, when I had a week filling in at Watson's.[209] So I was really unemployed for fifteen months until September 1932. And there were dozens like me. You just couldn't get a job. Teachers were ten a penny.

I started in James Clark's secondary school. It was only temporary to begin with. It was maybe three or four years before I got made permanent in the job I'd been doing there. I was actually appointed as a teacher of shorthand and book-keeping, knowing nothing about either. They evidently had a lassie in the place who couldn't keep discipline. And she also had to do a little History. Somebody in the Education office had noticed that I had History and sent me along. I remember my interview with Mike Oldham, the headmaster. He says, 'Come away in, laddie. Come ower tae the window and let's have a look at you.' He says, 'Let's see what sort o' a cratur they've sent me this time.' He asked me my qualifications and he says, D'ye ken any shorthand?' I said, 'No.' He says, 'Will you learn it?' I said, 'If it means a job.' He says, 'You'll dae.' So I was in.

I learned some shorthand and got a certificate in fact. I probably taught that for about a couple of years, along with some History and so on, and then I finally went on to more English, as it was in those days. There were no separate History departments. The History was taught with the English.

I was lucky because Chapter III teachers—Ordinary graduates—started at £200 and went up by £10 a year to £250, or whatever it was. But Chapter V teachers—Honours graduates, as I was, started at £250 and went up to £400. Well, they kept most of the Chapter V people in a primary school for five years until they had reached the £250, then they put them in a secondary school. It was penny pinching, oh, terrible, terrible. It was very discouraging. So I got the permanent job before I got married in 1936. My wife was a nurse.

During those years as a teacher I wasn't really politically active. I was a member of the Labour Party when I graduated. In fact, I was the election sub-agent or whatever they called it for North Edinburgh. Gibson, later Lord Gibson, was the candidate then.[210] But once I became a teacher I dropped away from any active political work. I was all too concerned with my job.

Moreover, I was becoming disillusioned, because being in the Labour Party and knowing what went on—the disputes with Ramsay MacDonald, and the Trades

Council as well, I knew the jiggery-pokery that was going on within the Labour Party, Left and Right disputes, and so on. I remember one time—I must have been at the University at the time, so it would be about 1927—there must have been a move in the Trades Council to prevent trade unions appointing Communists as delegates.[211] In the University Labour Party we opposed this and I must have spoken against it at one of the meetings, because I remember getting a letter from Ramsay MacDonald's secretary—I've forgotten her name now—saying that this meeting we had had in the Usher Hall had brought us in quite a bit of money (which we needed because the Party's rectorial election funds had been snaffled by a divinity student who was the treasurer), and the letter from this woman said MacDonald was very annoyed or perturbed about the University Labour Party supporting the Communists. So I just sort of drifted out of the Labour Party eventually.

But I remained interested in events in Europe. I used to subscribe to *Le Monde*, edited by Henri Barbusse. It kept my French up. But that was about my only interest in international affairs.[212]

When the war broke out in 1939 I was in the Local Defence Volunteers—the LDV. Then I was called up in July 1941. There wasn't any tradition in my family of being in the navy, but like most boys I had had a notion to go to sea in my early teens. This was the chance to fulfil it. So I joined the navy. Well, you had a general medical examination and then they passed you on to the Services people. The chief petty officer who interviewed me, I remember him saying: 'Of course, you're a volunteer now. You're all volunteers in the navy. There are no conscripts. You're conscripted in the Forces, but you've got to volunteer for the navy.'

I went to Skegness—Butlin's Camp! The recruiting chappie saw I could read and write and said, 'Oh, signalman for you.' And all the signal people were at Skegness. When I got down there I was told within days the headmaster-commander wanted to see me. He was sitting there with his three gold stripes and a warrant officer schoolie beside him, a half-striper. And he said, 'I've been looking at your qualifications and so on and I'd like you to consider joining the Educational Service.' He said, 'Of course, you'll be given this rig here'—the half-stripe. I listened to his story. Then he waited for me to answer. I said, 'I'm not interested.' He said, 'Why?' I said, 'Well, first of all if I was of value as a teacher I should have been left where I was. Secondly, my training and standard of qualifications takes the same length of time— five years—as it does for a doctor or a dentist. If you can give them two stripes you're not getting me for half a stripe.' It shook him a bit. 'Thirdly, I said, 'I joined the navy to be a sailor.' Well, within another week I had another interview. Would I consider a commission? And this time I felt, well, this barrack room life made me a bit—although varying at times—well, my wife could do with the money, you see. So I agreed to that. Then I was sent down—there were a dozen of us, I think—to Devonport and into the barracks there, and from there went through the usual interview and so on, and was sent off to sea.

When war broke out they were giving public schoolboys, yachtsmen, and so on, commissions right away. I don't know at what point they made the change. But by the time I was in everybody had to serve first in the lower deck—prove yourself at sea. Of those who were with me a number, including public schoolboys, were turned down. There was this Lord Dirty Neck, we called him: the Honourable Stoker Michael Moore-Brabazon, son of a lord. And he had been a stoker and somebody had said, 'Oh, he should be commissioned.' Well, he couldnae get a commission as an engineer. Consequently, he was a CW candidate—Commission on Warrant—but, och, he couldnae make it. As far as I know he remained a stoker. So it was all very much on merit.

My first ship was HMS *Tartar*, a Tribal class destroyer. Devonport was its base. So after a few weeks' initial training I went to sea at the end of October 1941 on *Tartar*. I was an ordinary seaman. I started writing a journal—keeping notes—from November 1941.

So from October 1941 until April 1942 we were based at Scapa Flow on *Tartar*. We were with the fleet. On the lower deck you never knew what you were doing, of course. We were never told what the ship was doing. But we would go out into the Atlantic and up to Iceland, up off the Norwegian coast. We were never on convoy duty, except as accompanying the fleet which was looking after the convoy. Eventually there was this convoy to Russia. But even on the trip to Russia we weren't in the close escort. We were certainly with the convoy lots of the time, but we were being sent off with cruisers and all that because there was a possible incident or emergency somewhere else. But as I say, we never knew what we were doing. It was only after the war we discovered what we had been up to. We were kept in the dark pretty well all the time. Principally, I would say, it was to prevent word getting about.

It was very dull and unexciting in a way. We left Scapa to go up to Iceland and we were in Seydisfjord on the east coast. I remember we were looking forward to our Christmas dinner—it was my first Christmas in the navy—and in the mess they got all the dainties in. And then we sailed just before Christmas Day. And the weather was so bloody rough that we couldn't eat our Christmas dinner. The mess deck was in a hell of a shambles—all the gear here, there, and water on the decks. It wasn't particularly cold, not going up to Iceland. But the galley couldn't operate, conditions were so bad. We used to get a drink and mixed in it were odd bits of cold tea and cocoa. There was no hot food at all at that time. When we got to Iceland we had our Christmas dinner then. We were still there at New Year. I remember being ashore at Seydisfjord.

Our worst enemy was the weather. We were never sunk—I never had that misfortune. While I was on her there wasn't a single casualty on the *Tartar* though the ship had been in the war from the beginning. She had been out after the *Bismarck*, for example, before I joined her.[213] I joined her just after she came out from her dock in the Thames. And there was a leading seaman killed there in dry dock: he came aboard drunk and fell in the dock. He was the first casualty. After I left the *Tartar*, after the Normandy invasion in 1944, she had it pretty bad. The captain was killed and there were a great number of casualties. In my time aboard her we suffered damage of various kinds, mainly from the weather or heavy seas.

While I was on the *Tartar* we were under attack—presumably from submarines—

I'm not sure—but certainly from aircraft. But my action station was in a magazine, two decks down below. You were locked in, hatch down, and you were sending the stuff up in the lift. And the only thing you heard was our guns and and sometimes you got a real old shake. This was a bomb landing somewhere in the sea. But we were never actually hit. But you didn't know what was going on, there was no communication at all. We could have got out, I should imagine, if we had been hit. I can't remember now what the procedure was. But certainly they kept every compartment watertight, for flotation purposes. It was a pretty claustrophobic experience.

I was in action on anti-submarine work, attacking subs. I'm not certain that we ever got one. We were on patrol once at the mouth of Seydisfjord where they had an anti-submarine loop, just in case anything got through it. And whiles planes came in and there would be only an essential couple of look-outs and an officer on deck. Once when a plane came over I went to the nearest Oerlikon, I think it was, and got behind it.[214] What a difference from being down below! This was a German plane. And you could actually see. I didn't shoot it down—but there was fighting! It was quite an experience to be active, rather than just suffering in silence down below.

Then some time in April 1942 I went back to Devonport and then eventually to *King Alfred*, which was the officers' training place at Hove, near Brighton. I was there a few months and on 17 July 1942 I got the commission: Temporary Acting Sub-Lieutenant, the bottom rung of the commissioned ranks.

I went back to sea again on the *Bute*, an anti-submarine mine-sweeping trawler, which I joined at North Shields. Then we came up to the Forth and were working up for mine-sweeping from Port Edgar.

Then we went to Tobermory. We were working up under the command of Commodore Stephenson or Stevenson. He was very good. He was very active. He must have been certainly in his 60s. And any time you saw his barge leaving the depot ship you were on your look-out. He'd come over and on the ladder and he was up and tell you to do this, that and the other thing. He kept us on our toes, oh, by God, aye. He made the ships very, very efficient.[215]

Tobermory was just the working up and then we went off. The base ship was one of the Shetland boats or Orkney boats. I remember we were up in Loch Ewe on Christmas Day, 1942. We sailed for Iceland shortly after Christmas with a convoy. The ships gathered there to cross to other staging points across the Atlantic. And later on all the Murmansk convoys sailed from Iceland.

I was a watch-keeping officer and it was some months before I got a watch-keeping certificate. We did a lot of minesweeping and accompanying in local ships, sometimes sailing right round Iceland with a single vessel, sometimes with a convoy—general sort of work. And we were several times back to the UK or Scapa Flow in Orkney. I went to Loch Ewe with a convoy and I think that was the farthest south on the *Bute*.

I was on the *Bute* for a couple o' years I should think. Then she went in for a refit and paid off. I was on leave then got an appointment to stand by for the building of a Loch class frigate—the *Loch Fyne*—at Burntisland, which was right up my street!

So for a month or so I was living at home. By this time my wife and I had two girls, one born before the war and one just after the war started. It was a worrying time for my wife when I was away from home for months at a time. She never knew, she had no idea where I was.

Once the frigate was ready we were based in Greenock, again doing escort work, sometimes escorting the fleet, mostly escorting convoys. By this time I was a lieutenant, in fact I was a lieutenant before I left the *Bute*. And I got the watch-keeper's certificate.

I was away on a lot of escorting in the Atlantic. For a while we were escorting mostly troop ships and other merchant vessels down to Gibraltar. By that time— 1944—the Mediterranean was fairly free and the convoys went through without us. We stayed at Gibraltar for a day or two's respite, waiting for a west-bound convoy. And meantime we took our turn of patrolling the Straits, to prevent submarines getting through.

Eventually, when the Germans packed in in 1945 we were to go out east. Japan was still in the war. But I remember going through the Straits of Gibraltar into·Gib. I must have had the first watch because I was due off at midnight and on the way I went down and looked into the WT where they had various wireless sets and the boys were listening to the BBC. And there was Attlee announcing that the Japs had packed in! So that was a cause for jubilation. We spliced the mainbrace next day.[216]

Then we carried on through the Med. and the Suez Canal. We picked up some motor fishing vessels at Aden and took them out to India. We had to go into a place on the east coast of India, Cochin, I think it was. I never got ashore in India but we left the vessels there and went down to Ceylon, to Colombo. Och, we had a great time there. The ship was leaking steam. The thing needed reground and a couple of days would have done normally to get away. But it took them six weeks to do it out in Colombo! Which suited us fine—ashore every day and swimming from the nice beaches with palm trees. We even had a trip up to Kandy that was very interesting. But I never got across the Equator. I crossed the Arctic Circle but never the Equator. Then I got a draft to another ship that was coming home anyway. And that was that.

We were actually in the Gulf of Suez waiting to go through the Canal when—it must have been an afternoon watch and I was having my head down—one of the WT ratings came down with this signal for me: 'Twin girls born.' I knew my wife was pregnant before I left the UK and my brother had sent me a cable, which didn't reach me. By the time this second cable from him reached me the twins were six weeks old! I was wondering why I was never hearing. I wasn't expecting twins though! Anyway we came through into Gibraltar and then up to Sheerness. I left the ship then. That was the end of my naval career.

I had no interest in remaining on in the navy after the war. But it was an experience I wouldn't have missed. Oh, it was great. The war had no influence on my political views but, oh, it gave me a wider experience of different classes of men and of how people reacted to unusual circumstances and so on. It was a good experience.

I think the experience influenced my writing later on. Some years later—in the 1950s—I began writing remembered experiences. I never was politically active after the war. I've become a bit of a cynic about politics.

I went back into teaching, I went back into James Clark's. I had three spells in James Clark's altogether. I had first gone there, as I said, until I was called up in 1941. And then I was back from 1946 until 1947 and then I went to teach Civic Studies at Regent Road College of Further Education. And then after five or six years they were having to appoint principal teachers of History in schools. And James Clark needed one, so I went back there. I was there until 1959, when I applied for a job in Wigtownshire in Whithorn—partly *Candida Casa* and all that, history.[217] It was a junior secondary and a primary school combined. But we only stayed there four years. I thoroughly enjoyed it but it was a bit restrictive for the family. If you wanted to do shopping you'd to go either to Dumfries or Ayr—a long way away. By that time two of my girls had left school and one of them was at Moray House College of Education in Edinburgh. The other was working. And the twins, born just after the war, they were needing trained and so on, and my wife was getting a bit fed up. So we came back to Edinburgh.

I started at Darroch Secondary, which I was glad to get out of pretty quickly. It was a terrible place. I soon became principal teacher of History at Firrhill, where I remained until I retired.

All through those years I was doing a lot of writing. Down at Whithorn it was children's and adult's stuff too. When I was down there the *Weekly Scotsman* was publishing one a week for me. And on a Sunday night I used to retire into a wee study I had, and I would think it was time I was getting one off. I'd maybe do two or three and I'd send them off to Denis Carabine who did illustrations. And he would send them on to the *Weekly Scotsman*.[218]

That kept me going. It is essential to have an interest like that if you're a teacher, otherwise you can get in a terribly narrow rut. And I had contact with other poets as well. Robert Garioch I knew very well. He was the poet I was closest to. He taught in various primary schools but he was not really a teacher—he was very uneasy and uncomfortable. And he was down in England for a bit. We corresponded quite a bit: all the letters are in the National Library of Scotland now.[219]

I was never very close to Norman MacCaig. We've read our poetry together and so on. But he's a different type from myself and his work is quite different, too. But I reviewed MacDiarmid when I was 17 years old, when *Sangschaw* came out. I reviewed it in the Broughton School magazine. And I corresponded with him on and off from then on. I had a lot of contact with him. Alan Bold got a lot of help from me doing his biography of MacDiarmid. It's a magnificent biography.[220] I had quite a contact with MacDiarmid and right up to the end I used to go and visit him down at Brownsbank. And I knew Sidney Goodsir Smith. Sidney and I were good friends. We used to have a drink together at Milne's. Oh, I liked Sidney. Some of his Scots was pretty, oh, unusual. He was not a native speaker. But, oh, great stuff.

Bill King

I was actually in church when war was declared in September 1939. Mr Galbraith, the minister, announced it from the pulpit. He just asked for a bit of attention. He said he was sorry to declare that Britain had declared war on Germany. We were now at war. The effect on the congregation—it was St John's Church in Dalkeith—was just absolute quietness. Most of them that was there maybe didn't know or didn't realise just exactly what war was.

I was seventeen. I wasn't a really serious or committed Christian but I was quite interested in the church then. Well, I used to go, I was a regular attender, and I was in the St John's Church boys' club. And I can remember that Sunday in church when war was declared I was wondering if I would have to go. I wasn't worried at the prospect.

I was born in September 1922 at Westfield, Eskbank, Dalkeith. My father was a miner all his life. He didn't always stick in the one pit. In fact, he worked in all the pits round about. When he got peyed off in one he had tae go to another. In the First War he was in the Royal Navy. I think he would be a volunteer because he was a miner. He was at Jutland, though he never said much about it.

Nobody ever talked much about these things. I think HMS *Marne* was the name o' his ship.[221]

I don't know much about my father's father: my father never spoke much about him. My mother's father he stayed in Musselburgh; I don't know much about him either. I was sixteen when he died but I just wasnae interested, though I was at his funeral. I never seen him; my granny and him had split up long, long before I was born. But I remember that granny when she stayed in Westfield. And it was 1929, I think, when they started that slum clearance—1928 the Slum Clearance Act came in—and she got a house down in Gibraltar in Dalkeith. In 1935 we came up here to Dalkeith as well. All Westfield was cleared out because it was a slum clearance area.

I've got seven brothers and two sisters. I'm the second oldest. Our housing conditions at Westfield werenae conditions at all. We had just two rooms. There were ten o' us in the family but there werenae ten o' us up there in Westfield. There were two of them born later on after we moved to Dalkeith. But with my parents it meant there were ten o' us altogether living in two rooms. Most o' us slept in the one room. It was only a kitchen and a bedroom. The boys were in two different beds. The girls were only wee and they were in the big room as well actually: they had a bed tae theirsels. Och, that was the norm in those days. Everybody had the same conditions. A lot o' the Westfield houses belonged to Widnell & Stewart's carpet factory. Mostly Westfield was set up for a' these people, but not the houses we stayed in. The houses we stayed in belonged to Dunbar, who was a property owner in Dalkeith at that time. He come and collected the rent. I was thirteen when we left Westfield and came to Spalding Crescent in Dalkeith in 1935. We had five rooms then—a huge difference.

I went to the primary part of Dalkeith High School and when ye passed your Qualifyin' ye went on to the secondary there. I can't say I disliked the school but no way was I an enthusiastic scholar. There was no subject I particularly liked or enjoyed. I was more interested in football. But I had an excellent memory—even now I have it—so I didn't have to pay too much attention in the class. If I heard somethin' it went into the head then and when it was necessary I could remember it. Well, I stayed in the secondary at Dalkeith High and left as soon as I could, when I was fourteen. Oh, I wanted tae leave the school. I don't think I would have stayed on even if I'd had the chance. I was quite happy tae get away fae the school.

I knew I could get a job easy enough. I was in St Cuthbert's Co-op for a month, a message lad delivering groceries. Then I got an apprenticeship as a saddler with Thomas Wilson & Son in Dalkeith. That was in 1936. It was a five-year apprenticeship but I didnae quite do my five years because I went away to the Air Force in 1940.

I enjoyed that work, learning the saddlery trade, oh, first class. It was very skilled work then. You learned a great deal. But when ye're young like that ye don't realise how important it is ye're learnin'. Wilson had two shops in South Street in Dalkeith and another one up in Pathhead. I was in Dalkeith then I was sent up to Pathhead to work there.

There were three o' us—old Willie Thomson, who was the journeyman really, myself, and Bobby Miller, who was an apprentice under me and who just come about six months afore I went away to the Air Force—and a girl Nessie Hall, who was the clerkess, and Tom Wilson hissel. Then there was Old Bob Kirk, another journeyman, up at the Pathhead shop. Willie Thomson and I and Bobby Miller were in the one shop in Dalkeith, and Tom Wilson and Nessie Hall in the other.

We had a lot of farm work. That was mainly these big high top collars for the likes of Clydesdales. And then they brought in these Polish horses. They were a killer, oh, their necks were a terrible shape actually. Ye had to make a completely different body for the collar.

Ye had tae make collars individually for the horses, ye had tae for the neck. We didnae actually make the collar. The body o' the collar was made by a collar maker. That was a separate trade. They used to be in Johnston Terrace in Edinburgh. Then you had to shape them intae the horse's neck and cover them wi' leather.

If a horse got a skint neck—sometimes it could happen—well, the carter would actually bring the horse in and let ye see what it wis so you could, what we'd say, chamber it. Ye had tae see exactly where the sore was—well , ye could see if ye took the collar off. But ye maybe couldnae get the collar off until the horse was in its stable. So they brought the horse tae let ye see. And what ye din wis try and mark it wi' a bit chalk. Then when ye got the collar in ye knew just exactly. And the thing to do then was to cut the straw and a' that away and then get a hollow, much bigger than the sore wis, so as ye covered that wi' chamois leather, soaked it and then moulded it in. So when it went on the horse again there was no pressure at all on the sore bit. The sore could begin out in a field, wi' a wind blowin' and dust, and it got under the collar when the horse was pullin'. Then it widnae take long tae fray through the skin.

We made the harness as well. I mean, people use the expression 'Put the hames on ye', but most people don't understand what it means. The hames is the metal bit that goes round the collar and then you're chained into the cart from that. That's what it means if you've got the hames on you: they've got control over ye.

Oh, ye got a lot o' satisfaction out o' the job. You learned all about leather, ye learned about the bits o' leather that you need. Ordering the leather was never ma province, Mr Wilson did that himself.

Then we used tae make the dog muzzles for racin' dogs that were kennelled doon in the stables in the Buccleuch estate in Dalkeith. They used tae bring their big vehicles tae take the dogs intae Powderhall for the Saturday racin'. Well, ye did that and covers for greyhounds. But then ye made canvas tarpaulins as well. Ye worked wi' canvas as well as leather—ye had tae because ye had the horse-drawn binders, and ye had tae make the canvasses for them.[222] And then later on when they done away wi' the horses and they brought in the tractors that wis mair work for us. When a horse wis cuttin' a field wi' a binder and got a grip—the likes o' catchin' a stone—it would stop. But a tractor widnae stop. It wid jist carry on and before ye know where ye are it had stripped a whole side o' canvas. So it had to be taken off and a new one put on. And that came intae us tae get either a new side on it or new slats.

So our work wis very closely connected wi' agriculture—that's what it was actually. Then ye had your coal merchants. They had tae get harness for their horses. Then there were van horses as well. There was a difference atween a cart horse and a van horse. The Store used tae have van horses. That was a different type o' harness althegither, a lighter harness.

We repaired a lot o' ridin' harness as well. But a thing we never did was repair stirrup leathers. If a stirrup leather broke ye put on a new stirrup leather: if it broke once it could break again. But ye would get a lot o' ridin' schools would say, 'Oh, repair it.' No way, because your head would be on the chopper. Ye could splice it so ye couldnae see it. But if it broke again ye'd be in trouble for repairin' it.

In Dalkeith Hall's the butcher used tae have horses, and McCluskey, the dairy, they had them, and the Dumfries Dairy, the Store, and Grieve's the grocer. I remember round about 1935-36 ye used tae see a' these vans wi' bills up: 'Buy British. Don't deal with the Axis!' And that was on every van in Dalkeith.[223]

We started at eight o'clock in the morning—but ye had tae be there at eight ready to start. And ye worked right up till one o'clock. No tea breaks—they'd never heard o' them actually. Ye worked right up tae one o'clock and then ye went away for your dinner. The other lad went at twelve. I had tae be back there ready tae start

at two. And ye had to work right till six o'clock before ye cleared up your bench and
swept up. It was generally half-past six afore ye got oot the shop. Ye hadnae far tae
walk home but finishin' time was six. So every night we had a half hour extra but ye
didnae get peyed for that. So as a laddie ye were really goin' tae yer work at half-past
seven in the mornin' and not home till half-past six at night. Ye worked a half day
every Saturday—tae one o'clock. Ye never worked on a Saturday afternoon or a
Sunday. Well, ye couldnae do that. We were indentured apprentices.

But ye were supposed tae do overtime at night at certain times, when the harvest
was bein' cut or they were doin' the fields and needed pole straps. Nowadays if they
heard this they'd say, 'You're kiddin'!' But I used tae get tuppence for every pole
strap I stitched up. You've got to stitch on a buckle wi' two loops on it, fold it
thegither and leave a splice at the other bit so it fits round tight. But when you do
that with it there's actually a space through the thing. It was just so if there was too
much pressure it would burst. But that's what ye had tae do. And ye got tuppence
for that.

The wages began at seven shillins a week. And then it went up 2/6d. a year:
9/6d. the second year, 12/- the third year. So by the time I went into the RAF. I
was doin' quite well, actually. I was gettin' quite a bit more than any other apprentice. I think they got aboot 22/6d. It wis good for me. I don't think *now* it was good
when I think of the work I used to do—the quality o' the work ye were doin' for
that amount o' money: nothin' like it. But that was the way wi' everybody actually.

And Wilson's had never heard of a union! Oh, God it wouldnae ha' made any
difference even if there had been one: as an apprentice a union cannae dae anythin'
for ye. So I was not in a union before I went off to the war. And I wasn't really
interested in politics either. I was always interested in sport and before I went away
tae the Air Force I was actually runnin' St John's Boys' Club, because a' the older
ones were away.

I was seventeen the week after the war broke out in September 1939. Just after
that I went into the pit. It wis part o' the war in as much as everybody was getting
more money than ah was gettin' at that time for workin'. So ah thought, 'Right,
ah'll go to the pit as well.' I went to Easthouses pit. It was in the winter of '39. My
old man used tae say I wisnae in the pit long enough to get black—which was true!
So I gave up my job at Wilson's and went to try and make more money. Och, ye
could get intae the pits easy enough then. I never worked on the surface: straight
underground, drivin' a haulage engine down the pit for the coal, haulin' the hutches
out and puttin' them in. It was a bit of a change from the saddler's. I was in the pit
maybe about three months.

It wasn't a job I enjoyed. But the pit's interestin', the pit is amazin' actually.
There's an awful lot goes on in the pit, an awfy lot tae learn in the pit to do the job
right. Well, you're workin' wi' people. It's like the army: ye're workin' wi' a squad
o' people. In a saddler's shop ye're workin' yerself. When ye're in the pit ye've got
a lot o' good friends, and a lot o' good laughs. Hard work, yes, but it didnae seem tae
be hard work. It's the only place other than the Forces I've seen that sort o' atmosphere. But I came out there very quickly and went to the RAF.

I wasn't in the RAF volunteers. There wasn't very much of flying, I mean, you're talkin' about 1939: nobody knew very much about flyin' then. I hadn't been up in an aeroplane and I never thought of joinin' the RAF before the war broke out. It wasn't my ambition to become an airman. I was only there eventually because I thought I was missing something.

I volunteered for the RAF. A couple o' ma mates were goin': George Louden and Alex Todd. The three o' us decided tae go actually. We were mates. We went to the dancin', we went out together. I think the three o' us thought we were missin' something. I don't know what it was. The war was only tae last six months. I've always been lookin' for the person that said that but I could never mind who it was. But quite truthfully ah don't regret goin' tae the Air Force. Ah thoroughly enjoyed it.

I don't think there wis any specific reason I went to the Air Force rather than the army or the navy, except the Air Force was needin' people and we thought we'd mair chance o' getting away. I think that wis mair the reason we volunteered: we didnae want tae go in the army. God Almighty! Just imagine yourself rushin' across a battlefield wi' a bayonet and a big six foot man comin' rushin' at ye! Ah'd ha' died o' fright! Up in the air everybody's the same size.

But we knew nothin' about the Air Force, and I don't think we volunteered for it because o' there maybe bein' some glamour about it. I don't think that applied actually. It wis mainly because we were hopin' tae get away quickly. The three of us all went through thegither. Ye jist went tae Edinbury—the Music Hall in George Street—and ye got an interview and a medical and everything there. Ye'd tae say ye wanted tae be aircrew right from the beginnin'. You went through the examinations. It was either aircrew or ground. I had no doubt I wanted to be aircrew: if you were in the Air Force you've got to fly.

Well, ah got accepted for the Air Force that day. And ma two pals were accepted but they had to wait. That was the Saturday we went intae Edinbury. On the Monday there wis a letter at my door tae report. I reported in there and that wis it. I was off, down tae Padgate. But George and Alex didnae get their letters till later on. The whole idea was we were a' goin' tae be thegither but ah only saw them when we come home on leave. Well, I seen Alex down in Lincoln later on, when he was a flight mechanic and I was down wi' the squadron there.

It was late in the spring of 1940 when I went intae the Air Force, nearer May, I think. I did three months' basic training at Padgate. And oo never got outside the camp. We were stuffed up tae the gunwales wi' bromide—like Zombies! Ye never got outside. Mind you, it was a big place.[224]

Square bashin', rifle drill, hygiene, and a' that sort o' thing—the basics—that's the training we did at Padgate. It was a big change from my normal way o' life. I remember once standin' on the parade ground and it was a beautiful day. My mind wisnae there at a'. It wis jist such a good day. But ah heard a shout. It wis the sergeant. He shouted ower—ah never forgot actually—'Hey, you! Little man! You wi' your hand on your … and your mind in China!' And ah looked at him. 'Yes, you!' So ah went oot there when ah wis ca'ed oot and it suddenly dawned on me what he'd said. Ah started laughin'. And ah wis walkin' up tae him and ah wis still laughin'. And them that wis in the ranks started guffawin'. And he took one look at me and he started laughin', tae. He took me by the shooder, took me richt off the parade ground. He says, 'Where's your billet?' Ah said, 'Across there.' He says, 'Well, get intae it—quick!' And that wis it. But ah distinctly remember that, thinking tae masel', 'What the damn am ah doin' here?' It wis jist such a good day and at that moment ah must have regretted ma decision tae volunteer. I certainly wisn't fed up. It wis jist a case o' it wis such a beautiful day and tae be beltin' aboot square bashin' on a day like that wis sacrilege. Ye should have been lyin' on yer back, lappin' up the sun.

The strange thing aboot square bashin' for the first two or three days ye think it's wicked. But after ye start gettin' intae the way o' it ye find out ye enjoy the precision. Ye enjoy the precision: when you get a command everybody does it at the same time. Once you've got into the thing ye thoroughly enjoy it. So we did that for three months and we learned weapons, the basics o' a rifle, everything.

From Padgate first of all we went doon to West Drayton in London tae get settled up and then we went tae White Waltham, no' far from London. We went there and trained as observers, plane spotters. I think the Battle o' Britain wis jist startin'. Ye were trained tae recognise any aeroplanes silhouetted, in one hundredth of a second. They did that by flashing it on a screen. But ye could cheat, because if ye shut your eyes immediately before they switched it off ye could still see it for two or three seconds. We spent practically a' day aircraft spottin', lookin' at silhouettes. And cards—playing cards: ye used tae play each other at cards, like snap. That sort of thing. The RAF provided us wi' these special cards.

Then we went from White Waltham by train tae Stranraer and across to Larne in Northern Ireland. We moved all over the Six Counties from then on. My first place was outside Ballymoney, a wee place called Dunloy. We jist had a Nissen hut aboot five miles intae the middle o' moors. There were only seven o' us. It was a wireless intelligence screen.

We had no beds in our Nissen hut. We slept on a palliasse. It wis stuffed up wi' gress and heather and the like o' that. And by the time we got beds we'd actually wore a hollow in the cement where we were lyin'. It never seemed to bother us. Eventually we got somebody's house to go to and get a bath. Before that we dug a hole in the peat and whenever the rains came we were off wi' the clothes and into that hole. If it was too cold ye wouldnae go in. When the water is comin' off the peat it's that soft when ye put your soap intae it and ye started latherin' ye couldnae see the place for lather!

I got hame on leave in May 1941, that was the first since I'd joined up a year earlier. And then I got home again early 1942, because we used to have a wireless for sending out messages in the Nissen hut. I had picked up an accumulator and the damn thing burst. It sort o' sliced ma hands, and wi' the acid in it and the cuts and what, and ah had tae get stitches in the thumbs, so both hands were bandaged up. They took one look at me and they said, 'Oh, send him on leave. He's nae use tae us.' The leave wis only supposed tae be a week. But the hands turned septic and ah used tae have tae go down to Newbattle Abbey and get the Medical Officer there. And then eventually they sent me intae Edinbury Castle tae get a look at ma hands. Ah couldnae do very much wi' ma hands. So ma leave became about a fortnight.

I went back tae Ireland after that but of course a' this time ah wis still waitin' tae be called on for air crew. But at that time they didn't have the demand and so ye had tae take what wis goin'. But if ah had been here ah'd probably have been pushin' more than what ah did when ah wis in Ireland, because ah knew it wis a waste o' time. You were doin' a job out there and you'd been trained for that job and there was no way you were goin' tae be taken off it. But then about the middle o' 1942 ah come back here and it wis Grangemouth ah went to. Ah wis on the RAF police force there—guard duties, that sort of thing. And ah could write, so ah wis getting the guardroom writin' up duties, the keys and a' that sort o' thing.

And that's really how the air crew question got pushed, because there were one day Flight Sergeant Panchard says tae me: 'Jock, there's a purge on. Jist watch who comes in. If ye're not sure o' him, ask for identity card.' 'Fair enough.' And ah'm standin' at the gate, pistol ready, no' the size o' tuppence ha'penny, and a big black car draws up. Ah says tae the bloke who's drivin' it: 'Identity card. Anybody in the back?' 'Aye,' he says, 'there's somebody in the back.' So ah opened the door—and a' the gold braid's shinin'. 'Can I see your 1250, sir?' The 1250 wis your identity card. He said, 'What?' I said, 'Your 1250, sir.' He says, 'Ye're jokin', are ye not?' 'No, sir.' 'Do you know who ah am?' Ah said, 'No, sir. That's why I'm asking for your 1250'. 'Ah've not got ma 1250 with me.' Ah says, 'That's all right, sir. If ye jist go across to the guardroom and tell the Flight Sergeant in there.' 'Are you serious?' Ah said, 'Yes, sir.' So intae the guardroom he went. And ah seen him comin' oot and he come right across tae me and he says, 'Now, I'm the Commanding Officer. You'll recognise me the next time.' 'Yes, sir.' So off he went and the corporal came out from the guardroom and he says, 'Bill ye've got tae go in there.' Ah said, 'Oh, oh, here we go again.' So old Panchard was sittin' there, a smile reachin' tae his ears. He says, 'By, you've done it now, Bill.' Ah says, 'What d'you mean?' He says, 'The CO's fair chuffed. There's been a push on here about the lack o' security on the place. And he come in and said he was quite cock-a-hoop: "There's nothing wrong wi' your man, Flight." He says, "He stopped me and there wis no way ah wis gettin' past him."' So Panchard says, 'he wis askin' who you were. Ah said, "That's the lad who's waitin' for aircrew." He said, "Tell him tae see me on Monday."' So the Flight says, 'Ye've tae go and see him on Monday.'

When ah went tae see the CO on Monday—MacWalters wis his name—he says, 'Waitin' for aircrew?' 'Yes, sir.' He says, 'Right, there's a helmet there. Let's go.' And that's when he took me up in a Tiger Moth. That wis the first time I'd been up. Ah wis air-tested there. I passed a'right. But that's what they did—ye'd go up wi' a pilot and they'd jist kick an old Tiger Moth about and see what happens tae ye, actually—vertigo or anythin' like that. But ah wis a'right. And ah got ma Selection Board there.

And then ah wis sent down to London to St John's Wood and Lord's cricket pitch. That's where air crew used tae get sent to. And we stayed in Stockleigh Hall, one o' these big mansions where Regent's Park Zoo used to be. We were bein' trained there as air gunners. Ye did the night vision tests and that there. No use sendin' ye any further if ye were blind. But these were palatial surroundins—a wee bit different from oor two-roomed house in Westfield, Dalkeith: the bathroom at Stockleigh was bigger than that, actually!

You were designated as an air gunner, which means you go any damn place on the plane—rear or upper turret. Ye had tae learn about hydraulics and aboot guns, because your guns are a' worked by hydraulics. If you have no hydraulics you have no guns. It was a Fraser Nash system on the Lancasters, and a Bolton and Paul system on the Halifaxes. So you had to learn both systems. It doesnae seem much now but there wis a terrible lot to learn. It comes like drivin' a car: ye don't think about it— ye do it withoot thinkin'.

The guns were Brownings. 303s. Later on they got .5s, which we should have had from the beginnin' actually. Ye had four Brownings, but the bullets were too light. Tracers, ball, incendiary, armour piercin': a' these bullets were in your belt. They had a set pattern. Ah cannae remember now what it was. Every five or six was a tracer, or somethin' like that, to guide your aim. The tracer wis tae let ye see where your shots were goin' and ye could correct your aim by the tracer. Mind you, you only had a snap of the fingers to do it in.

For firin' practice we moved up to a place near Morpeth—Ambleside. We used tae fly in a Botha and there was a wee Magister or Master used to tow a drogue—a target like a windsock—over Ambleside and ye had tae fire at that. There were maybe about four or five o' ye as pupils up at the same time and ye a' had different colours o' paint on your bullets. Ye couldnae cheat. So they could count how many hits ye had. But ye could be quite clever about that. If we thought we werenae doin' too well then one o' the best ones o' us used tae shoot the drogue away, so they couldnae check. Ye werenae supposed tae fire tae the front o' it but if ye fired tae the front o' it wi' the bullet pattern ye got tae see it. At 150 yards the wey your guns are synchronised you've got an eight feet six inches pattern o' solid lead. I mean, that's compact bullets. The further away ye go of course the wider ye get the spread. 150 yards was point blank.

So Ambleside was where you did your trainin'. Ye went tae a range. Ye sat in a turret on the range and ye could fire. Well, firin' on the ground is not a great deal o' use tae ye, because if ye're firin' on the ground all ye've got to worry about is yer distance for a trajectory o' your bullet and your range—that's all ye've got tae worry aboot. But when you're flying ye've got bullet drop or lag, and ye've got wind resistance and ye've got air speed—the relative speeds. So a' these things have got tae be taken intae consideration. But it's no, as difficult as you think because ye've got a ring sight and ye could look at your target and ye could say, 'Right, it's a 50 mph ring sight—if it's right ah'm goin' 150 mph quicker than the fighter. O.K. Lay off three rads.' And that was it. It's like drivin' a car—it becomes automatic.

From Morpeth ah wis made a sergeant, once ah had passed through trainin' and got ma wings. That was the beginnin' o' '43. Ah went up tae Kinloss then. It was an OTU—Operational Training Unit—there. So ye trained up there on flyin', night flyin', and all that sort o' thing. Ye did that trainin' and a terrible amount o' gun turret practice. Ye went tae a big Nissen hut and ye jist sat there in yer turret and there wis a light flashin' in front o' you. And ye had tae follow that wi' your guns. That went down and round about. Jist turret manipulation till again it wis jist second nature—when ye seen somethin' ye could … Ah mean, ye're workin' on hydraulic control. Ye're bringin' guns up, ye're bringin, guns down, and at the same time you've got tae whirl them. But once you've done a' that manipulation, ye could take it—wheech!—and yer guns were right on the target.

As an air gunner ye're in a revolving turret. But you're makin' it revolve—wi' your hands. Ye had tae have good control because that wis bringin' your guns up or down, that wis guidin' your turret. They're easy enough to move. It's the pressure o' your hydraulic oil that's doin' the movin'. But you've got tae open up the right valves for that tae happen. Well, then ye can swing your guns roond and get on tae a thing and open fire straight away.

I wis at Kinloss for gettin, on for four or five months. You've got tae wait tae get crewed up—that's where ye got crewed up. Well, maybe no' quite that long: because once we were finished there and we were crewed up we shifted tae Findhorn and we did night flyin' from there. That was more or less Whitleys—two engines— we were on. And once we'd done all that we went down to Riccall in Yorkshire. It's near a place ca'ed Osgodsby. And that wis for conversion on to the four-engined Halifaxes.

The Halifaxes and the Lancasters wis heavy bombers. Well, at the time ah wis trainin' that wis the bombers. That wis it. I've actually flown in Wellingtons as well. It wisnae a heavy bomber but it wis the only bomber ye had at one time. The Wellington wis two engines but no' only that, it wis a canvas body. It wis jist a doped up body: geodetic construction and jist covered like how ye used tae cover the old aeroplanes long ago and then dope them up. The other bombers were a' two engines. The Stirlin', it wis a heavy bomber. But it couldnae get up the height. It wis suicide. And another one was the Whitley. Its nose wis fa'in off in appearance. Then there wis a Manchester—again, it couldnae take the height. Ah mean, ye've got tae get above 10,000 feet before you're safe from normal sort o' anti-aircraft guns. If ye get above 12,000 feet then it's only heavy flak that can hit ye. The Stirling and these other ones they were lucky if they could get up to 10,000 feet wi' a bomb load. That's why there werenae sae very many big raids earlier on in the war actually: they didnae have the planes that could get that height.

So when we got to Riccall that wis the first time we had been in the Halifax. As far as air gunners were concerned there was more room in the plane but there werenae very much difference in the gun turret. I mean, the gun turret was much the same in them a', except in a Botha—that's an awkward shaped one, and a Blenheim was another. Blenheims and Hampdens—bombers—they were a' there earlier on in the war. That Glasgow laddie Hannah that got the VC, he was in a Hampden actually. The Hampdens were still about, well, ah widnae say so much in '43.[225] But the Halifax when it come out had a heart-shaped tail fin and it wis long enough afore it ·was realised that that wisnae clever, because we were losin' Halifaxes on raids.

When they shoved them down intae a steep dive they couldnáe pull out. That cost a lot o' lives. So that's why they changed them tae a square fin. So it was Halifaxes that we went on to first when we went tae the squadron at Pocklington at the end o' July or August 1943.

Ah think ma first op was the 4th o' October '43. It wis Cassel. I might have done one before, I'm no' jist quite sure. But I remember one wis Cassel. That's the one I remember obviously I first done. I didn't have any sense of fear, none at all. We were all like that, our crew, actually. There's only the two gunners and the pilot that see what's goin' on. The rest o' them are enclosed. They don't see anythin'. So they're dependin' on hearin' you.

In the Halifax there was a crew o' seven: the pilot, two gunners, the wireless op., engineer, navigator, and a bomb aimer. They had went through Kinloss. Frae Kinloss we were all together. And the same crew stuck together up till we were finished— that wis the case wi' our crew. Well, the first lot were nearly finished before the bomb aimer dropped out. He wis Canadian. But then ah went on tae Lancasters after that—a different crew. So in the Halifax we were there, the same seven o' us since Kinloss right through till the middle o' August after D-Day in 1944.

We were mair than fifteen months, and fully a year on the squadron—102 Squadron—which was a long time, because they had got a system that after a while ye were termed as Mains crew. Ye had Freshers, Mediums and Mains crews. Mains were the most experienced. We done so many operations, well, they jist decided the number themselves. This is nothin' tae do wi' the set up. This was only the Squadron.

The Freshers were on trips tae France. They were the ones wi' not so much experience. The Medium runs would maybe go on a mine-layin', or Holland or somethin'. The Mains crews were kept for the big targets. If we went on a French raid that only counted as a third of an op. Ye had tae do three o' them tae get one op., us as Mains crews. And ye could jist as easily get killed on a French yin as ye could on anythin' else.

We were lucky 'cause the bad time wis between November '43–December and intae January and February 1944. That wis a bad time for Bomber Command. We were doin' main targets. It wisnae so much a switch on to main targets as a case of now we could do it, 'cause we had better planes. Ah mean, ah wis at Berlin maself, I think it wis three nights within a week. That wis more than the usual.

Now, ah mean, it gets a wee bittie dicey, because we were on Berlin, Mannheim, Stuttgart, Leipzig, Stettin—a' these sort o' main targets. Essen was a different kind o' target. That wis done earlier on wi' the 1,000 bomber thing. But Hamburg, the Ruhr Valley, that wis jist a past thing that actually. But the big ones that ye could be oot for seven or eight hours on—that's seven or eight hours o' concentration—it can be a bit hairy.

But my first raid I think it wis early October '43 on Cassel. Ah can remember it pretty clearly only because ah know Jackie Pretsell, a Dalkeith lad, who was on 10 Squadron, was killed in that raid.

Och, there were nothin' special aboot that raid. The only things that ye can remember—when took ye off ye either had tae go tae Portland Bill or Selsey Bill and circle to get your height. Ye were climbin' all the time before ye set course. And if it wis ten tenths cloud or somethin' like that—it really wouldnae be ten-tenths or ye wouldnae be goin' if ye couldnae see! But when ye got tae these places and it wis aboot eight to ten-tenths cloud and you're circlin' around it could gie ye a wee bit o' a start when another Halifax went ower the top o' ye about twenty feet above yet It could frighten the life out o' ye! Oh, that could happen often. That used tae be the hairy bit. But once ye were away from that it wis O.K.

Ye see, a lot o' people think we jist took off and headed straight out willy nilly. We didn't. We had tae get a certain height by a certain time and set a certain course at a certain time and fly that course for a certain amount o' miles and a certain amount o' time. And then alter your course. All that was all worked out by the navigators. It wisnae a case o' sayin', 'Right, we're here, there's Berlin. Let's go straight to it.' Ye didnae do that at a' because ye'd ha' got annihilated by the Germans. Bomber Command would put on a raid some place else at the same time and hope that the Germans would think, 'Right, they're goin' there.' Then when they went there we could get through to where we were really goin'.

And then again because o' the heavy weight o' bombs in a Halifax or Lancaster you couldn't just climb straight up. Ye had tae do it gradually. We tried tae get up tae aboot 10,000 or 12,000 feet. Ye had tae get up to ten here. Ten's alright here. But if ye got mixed up wi' a German raid comin' in here and you were goin' out, ye were jist as likely tae be shot down wi' yer ain guns as anythin' else. That happened sometimes. We got shot up yin night over Ipswich. We didnae get hit but we were mixed up—the Germans were comin' in tae bomb here as we were goin' out.

Ah never experienced great fear, ah wis never panic stricken. Ye maybe got a fright at Selsey Bill when a plane would appear suddenly above ye. But ye get the same fright if ye're flyin' along in beautiful sunshine on the top o' solid cloud, white cloud, and then suddenly come tae a break: ye're grippin' on—ye think ye're gaun tae fa' off the end! Ye get that. But ah never experienced great fear. It's a job that ye're trained for. And if ye're quite confident in your own capabilities and your crew's capabilities ... Well, ye knew that they werenae goin' tae let ye down. Ye'd been together so long. And ye used tae live thegither in the same hut. The same crew were all thegither.

The pilot was the skipper but, och, ah mean, if you speak to him he says, 'No, ah'm no' the superior. I'm jist the message laddie, the taxi driver.' Ah used tae tell him that. But the key figure really wis the navigator, because he had tae get you there and get ye back and a' he had wis a wee place tae sit in and a wee table and a map tae work it oot on.

The bomb aimer should in a lot o' instances have been workin' as the co-pilot. But, ah mean, when it got tae that time in the war they were jist purely and simply bomb aimers. The bomb aimer wis there tae drop the bombs. He could be down in the front with the navigator and checkin' off the things on the Y-sets and the G-sets, because it wis a lot o' work, too. But durin' the time when ye were approachin' the target the bomb aimer wis lyin' down on the front and he wid take over then.

So if the pilot had been badly injured there wis naebody else could fly the plane. Jist the pilot. Ah never thought aboot that.

Sometimes I wis in the middle turret and sometimes in the back—rear gunner. If I'd been badly wounded somebody—maybe another gunner or somebody—might have been able tae double up for me. But the trouble would be gettin' ye out. On maist o' the aircraft it wis very tight at the back end. In the middle turret, no: ye could get straight up intae it. At the beginnin' we also had a front turret. But the front turret was no use because nobody attacks frae the front—the closin' speeds are too quick. Ah mean, if you're doin' 200 miles an hour and the other man's doin' 200 miles an hour, that's 400 miles an hour. Ye've no' got time tae shoot at one another. So front turrets were done away wi' in the later part o' the war.

They did lots o' things actually. They actually brought oot a turret that ye didnae have tae look out o', that ye could work the pedals wi' yer feet and ye could see an aircraft comin' and ye could work in, 'Right, that's him at 350 yards. Open fire.' But there were only one thing wrong wi' that. If it wis a plane that was goin' at the same speed as you all we got was peep-peep-peep-peep-peep—if it wis one o' yours. Well, if it wis only goin' the same speed as you it wis one o' your own. But if it went pip-pip-pip-pip-pip then it wis an enemy. Well, if ye thought ye could spot an enemy by that—could you damn! If he wis flyin' across ye that way ye got pip-pip-pip-pip-pip—but it could be yer ain planes! So, ah mean, it wis ridiculous. Ye really had tae depend on your eyesight rather than on sound.

We got another thing that we called Monica. And that wis another one that gave ye the sound peep-peep-peep-peep-peep: that wis one o' yer ain planes. The other sound went pip-pip-pip-pip-pip when it wis somebody that wis comin' at ye faster. So it gave ye a warnin' tae pick it up. But most o' us didnae keep the Monica machine on, because if a plane wis flyin' sideways at ye then it wis goin' faster than you, so ye got the pip-pip-pip-pip-pip. It nearly blasted yer ear off! And it wis one of your own!

When we were on operations if ye could tell the skipper, 'Tip the kite on its side port.' Then 'Tip the kite on its side starboard.' So we had a view below. Of course, if the enemy got within 150 yards o' us we were dead, quite truthfully. The furthest away ye could see them really to be effective was 600 yards. But a fighter pilot has got a hard job, 'cause he's got to fly the plane, he's got to see you, and he's got to look at his instruments. Now at night, whenever you start lookin' at instruments that's your night vision goin' for a Burton straight away. But when the fighter pilot sees you he'll generally see you flyin' level, and then when he sees you he's got to come up bankin' to lay off his deflection, because there's nae use shootin' straight at you: if you're goin' at 250 miles an hour, by the time his bullets get there you're no' goin' to be there. So he's got to lay off deflection—he's got to fire ahead of where he thinks you're goin'. But in a bomber we're only lookin' for him and we're no' watchin' any instruments. We're only watchin' oor gunsight on him. And if we can see him we can lay off oor deflection right away. And immediately we see him he's bankin' tae lay off his deflection. Once he's done that he's got to bank the other way tae come intae ye. And immediately he does that tae start his attack we've already telt the skipper: 'Prepare to corkscrew!' And we didnae say any more. 'Prepare to corkscrew!'—whichever way, port or starboard. Then say: 'Starboard—go!' And down he'd go. Now that's the fighter's deflection a' tae pot. If he follows we've already laid the deflection off. He's got to go through that. And we actually dive down like that for about 800 feet and then, if he's still comin' the skipper'll actually roll and start climbin' up. Immediately he does that we jist fire straight at this damn plane, because if he's followin' he's got tae come through again. And if he's still comin' after that—jump oot! He'll blow us up!

People used to say, 'Oh, the gunner has no chance.' Ah used tae say, 'If you've seen the fighter first there's no way he should get you'. You had always tae be vigilant. Oh, God! Ah mean, ye've got tae see him. If ye cannae see him there's nothing ye can do about it. That's how they got most o' us, actually. They'll never admit it but that's how they got most o' us. If you're flyin' along, you're up about 16,000 feet and you're flyin' along and somethin' comes underneath ye they'll see your red exhausts. Now if they can synchronise their speed tae come up underneath all the time—well, it's a very gradual climb—and then once they are within shootin' range they can open up, fire on your belly and just drop off ...

You've very little chance o' seein' them unless you say to your skipper, 'Tip up. Tip up one wing and let's see what's underneath'—which you should do all the time. We never had a gun in the belly o' the plane. So if a fighter approaches you from below you're supposed to tip up on a wing one way. Now immediately you tip up on the wing the mid upper gunner—him that's on top—he can look down all the way he's goin'. And at the same time as he's doin' that you're flyin' it on your wing edge, he's lookin' doon. But your rear gunner swings his turret round on the beam and he's watchin' up the other way. So you're covered. And then when ye change over to look the other way you reverse the position.

So the danger is there all the time. But a fighter's got to be very clever tae synchronise his speed tae come up. And when the bomber turns on its wing and the gunner spots the fighter comin' the fighter has tae get oot the road quick 'cause he has no defence. The bomber disnae spend a lot o' time flyin' on its wing. Ye just flip up, have a look down, flip ower and have another look. That's jist occasionally. Well, we would actually say, 'Let's have a look underneath.' The belly o' the bomber isnae really very vulnerable: there's very little in it. They could shoot the belly off the thing and it's no' goin tae do any harm—unless you're in the road o' a bullet. It's up in the wings and there—if they get at that ...!

Ye got bombers firin' on each other from time to time. At D-Day actually ye seen it happenin' because we werenae used tae flyin' in daylight. But we had tae dae it then. Well, we were jist goin' out, comin' back, goin' out, comin' back, goin' out, and comin' back. We were tryin' tae bomb the submarine pens and the defences along the coast o' France. By then ah didnae have very many raids because ah wis aboot finished.

Thirty operations wis the maximum then—well, not the maximum, but thirty was the set-up, the tour o' duty. Ye did thirty separate missions. But ye see wi' us bein' Mains crews, as ah'm sayin' a France only counted as a third o' an op. Ye had tae do three o' them tae get one full one. It wis very seldom it would happen that anybody did ninety operations, because the ops were a mixture. But we actually come off for the simple reason that we got a swing on take-off—swerved off the runway—and ye're no' supposed tae correct a swing, straighten it up. Ye're supposed tae let it go. The skipper must have tried tae correct it and of course the under-carriage jist folded up. So that wis oor kite—the end o' our plane.

And we were that near the end o' the thing anyway ye'd a' tae go tae the Medical Officer and get checked—a thorough medical examination. And once he checked us he said, 'Aye, ye've had enough.' I didnae myself feel strained or fatigued—I never suffered frae that. But some o' the other members o' our crew did. There were some o' them actually used tae say, 'There's flak off your port quarter.' 'Is it much ?' 'Aye, quite heavy. Move away roond aboot.' Before then oo would have jist flew straight ahead. The crew tended tae be more cautious as ye get on. The operational hours you actually do wis about twenty-seven, ah think. That's what ye'd be allowed: twenty-seven hours—then you was dead! Well, that was aboot the average then, taking all the casualties in Bomber Command. So if you survived for more than twenty-hours operational you were on borrowed time.

Three to four raids was about the average expectation o' life then for bomber crews. But there were any amount o' fellows who went up and were killed on their first raid. I knew quite a few.

When you came back in the early mornin' from a raid and ye found that fellows ye'd known didnae return ye coped, ye coped. Ah wrote quite a few poems just after it. Ah started writin' them soon after ma first raid. Well, a lot o' folk think ye didnae think at all, ye see. When ye come back intae the mess: '*A glance at the empty chairs: Where's Jack, Freddie, Dixie and Pete?*' Well, we used tae get bacon and eggs when we come back. It wis the sheer fact o' what we were thinkin' aboot at that time that made me do that. The thought jist used tae run through your head and until ye wrote it down it wis still in your nut. Ye see, this is a thing that ye learn after a very short period of time. Ye learn tae cut yerself off—from feelin' too much, from too close friendships.

Strange enough ah didnae have close friendships wi' the other fellows in ma own crew. Ma mate Johnny Lyons, frae Dundee—was in another crew altogether in ma squadron. He was a gunner. We had been through everythin' together. Johnny didnae survive the war. Oo were supposed tae fly together but at Kinloss the gunner leader said, 'Well, you're the best two we've got and there's a couple o' crews goin' out and they're needin' the gunners.' And ah telt him, 'Well, we want tae go thegither.' He says, 'Oh, you two are the most advanced and ah'm goin' tae have tae take you.' Ah says, 'We don't want tae.' And ah argued wi' him, all the way ah argued wi' him. But we were taken, and Johnny Lyons had tae go wi' one crew and ah had tae go wi' the other crew, though it wis tae the same squadron. He was killed on the 18th of January 1944. That shattered me a bit. But ye jist had tae carry on.

If ye didn't go out on a raid yerself your documents were marked LMF—Lack of Moral Fibre. You were taken right off the squadron. And you were sent any place, out the road. I objected to that system actually. I objected aboot it to the Commanding

Officer quite strongly. Mind you, we could do that. There wis a certain freedom o' speech. We could do that. But ah said nobody knows your breakin' point. What's the breakin' point for one person is not necessarily the breaking point for another one. And if a man's done six or seven raids, or even if he's only done two, and then he finds he cannae do any more then there's no lack o' moral fibre. That man has went his limit. And that LMF should never have happened. But it did.

In ma squadron ah remember one lad, Pete. It wis just after D–Day. And he had been goin' back and forward and the next time he come in he says, 'Ah'm tired. Ah don't want tae go. Ah'm tired.' And they said, 'Aw, you're yellow.' He said, 'Ah'm tired.' But they took an Australian lad. Now Pete wis the rear gunner but the mid-upper gunner went intae the rear turret and the Australian lad went into the mid-upper. Well, they took a direct hit and his head was blown off him. So if Pete had been in the plane, obviously, all other things being equal, well, it wouldnae have been him, but the other gunner would have been in the mid-upper turret. But Pete was accused of Lack of Moral Fibre. And ah remember goin' intae the mess that day and Pete was sittin' at the table. We a' had our own tables actually. But ah knew ma crew wouldnae be comin' so ah just sat down beside him. And Pete said, 'You'll be gettin' intae trouble for sittin' here, Bill.' Ah said, 'What for?' He said, 'Ah've been sent tae Coventry.' Ah said, 'What for?' So he telt me. And right enough up come a lad and said tae me, 'Excuse me, you're not supposed tae be speakin' tae him.' Ah says, 'And whae are you?' He says, 'Oh, ah've been sent across tae tell you.' Ah says, 'Who are you and who sent you across?' 'Ah, well,' he says, 'Pete didnae go and somebody else wis killed in heez place.' Ah says, 'So what are you wantin' Pete tae do? Commit suicide?' Ah says, 'Away and go and rap off.' Ah says, 'When you've done as many operations as Pete's done you come and tell me. And', ah says, 'when you've done as many operations as ah've done you'll be dead.' I'd done twenty-seven by then.

There was no lack of sympathy among the crews for somebody who just felt tired and couldn't carry on. It's the old thing that ye see if they show ye an old war film aboot a man gettin' shot for cowardice. It wis only tae boost up some officer's ego. It wis only the common ordinary man that wid be a coward, not an officer. So they shot the private that wis runnin' in the wrong direction. Now the same thing applied in the bombers. When somebody gets tae the stage that they cannae go intae an aeroplane it's not because they're a coward but because they've given their all. They cannae do any more. And, oh, that happened a lot more than what has been made public.

In my squadron at that time there would be twenty-four crews. But that's only twenty-four crews if they all went through. In actual fact, most of the crews that were with me never got through. So there would be crews comin' all the time. Now twenty-four crews and seven in a crew—you're talkin' roughly about 150 men. Well, ye'd very seldom get twenty-four planes up at the one time. There were always planes that somethin' was wrong wi' them. But out of that 150 men you'd get five or six who were Lacking in Moral Fibre. Well, there wis any amount o' squadrons. But it would never be made public. LMF men were posted away, straight away. Ye never heard any more what happened to them. They were taken off flyin'.

I said that Pete should never have been criticised at all, because he was actually actin' in their interests. If he wis tired—and he was bound to be tired because they were goin' out, back and forwards—and he says, 'Ah'm tired.' Well, if you're up there and your life is dependent on that man you'd listen to him. But in our squadron we didnae have very much of it and nine times out o' ten ye wouldn't know. Ah knew about Pete.

One o' ma poems is about a pilot named McPherson in ma squadron. He went tae Berlin, I think it was, and he come back and he wis goin' round the Drem system. It's posts round about an airfield, and on top o' these posts there are lights. So you go round about them and it will lead you into a funnel tae come intae land at nights, ye see. That gives you the light there. And he wis jist comin' in tae land when his damned engine fell off—complete engine fell off! But he brought it in and landed. But the strange thing aboot it was after debriefin' he wis comin' back on his push bike and he fell off and split his lip. He had tae get stitches and twa teeth oot! Fell off his bike!

There was another pilot. His name was Dusty Miller, an Aussie. But ah wis watchin' him. They were doin' circuitin' landin' actually. And the Halifax is funny, because you've got two levers and one's the undercarriage and one's the flap. Now when ye're comin' in tae land and instead o' landin' you're goin' tae overshoot, what ye do is lift up your undercarriage. Ye've got so much degrees of flap on ye when ye come in to land. Well, they come in tae land and—ah don't know but ah think—instead o' pullin' up the undercarriage they pulled up the flaps. The plane struck the deck. They got burnt tae a frazzle.

When wee Freddy King wis killed at Morpeth ah went back tae the billet and when ah looked here ma bed was stripped. But Freddy King's bed was still made and heez kit bag was there. So next mornin' on parade: 'Sergeant King!—Oh, sorry, lads.' Ah said, 'Here.' 'Uh?' Ah said, 'Here.' He said, 'Come here.' So ah seen, 'W King, Deceased.' Ah says, 'No, it's the one below that—Freddy King.' 'Oh, ah'm sorry about that. Ah'll get that changed.' And ah says tae him, 'Ma kit wis away yesterday as well.' He says, 'They better no' be sendin' the coffin tae your hoose, Wullie.' And it suddenly struck me then and ah went round tae the officer responsible for the arrangements—Flying Officer Tooth was his name—and ah says, 'Excuse me, sir.' He says, 'Well, what is it that you want, lad?' Ah said, 'Ah want tae know where ye're sendin' King's coffin.' 'We'll send it home.' Ah said, 'But to what home?' 'What do you mean ?' Ah says,, 'Ah'm King.' And he looked at the photie— you get a squadron photie taken and as ye get knocked off they ring your face off. And it was ma face that wis ringed off. Ah says, 'That's me. That one's Freddie.' So he says, 'Oh, just a minute', and he went away then came back: 'Oh, no, the coffin's goin' to Sunderland.' Ah said, 'That's fine, sir.'

When Freddy King got killed when ah got in it jist so happened ah had No.1 parachute. And when ah come back ah jist whipped the parachute on to the counter.

And the WAAF lassie says, 'What number are ye sergeant?' Ah says, 'No.1.' And she looked and she says, 'Oh, see: Deceased.' Ah says, 'Dinnae worry, ah'm no' deceased. Ah jist dinnae want ma mother tae get chairged for this.' And ah walked oot. And it wis Jackie Pretsell frae Dalkeith, he come in then and says tae me: 'What a damn shame. That lassie wis greetin' her hert oot.' Ah says, 'What for?' He says, 'Well, you had said ye didnae want your mother tae get chairged for the parachute. She didnae ken there were two o' ye Kings.'

Every year oor squadron has a reunion. There are a hundred o' them, veterans o' the squadron. But, mind, the ones that wis on the squadron wi' me in '43 to '45, there's only aboot three crews actually survived. The rest were a' killed.

As far as we were concerned it wis a job. Ye were telt tae go and bomb. Ye went and bombed. How could it be indiscriminate? We had tae get tae a certain height by a certain time and fly a certain course and drop your bombs on a certain target. It wisnae a case ye jist went out there and dropped them any place at all. It had to be precision done, well, as near the target as we could get it. If they werenae dropped on the target it wisnae for the lack o' tryin'! As far as ah'm concerned there should never have been any bombing at all of French marshalling yards or French coast line or anything like that at all. When we were able to bomb Germany we should have been bombin' it. I don't suffer from any sense o' guilt about that. You'll see in one o' ma poems where ah say, *'Ah glanced down at the holocaust explodin' below. A moment of pity for the people slain. Yet knowin' full well when ye build it up, ah'll be back again.'* Ah mean, there were never any motive. As far as ah'm concerned it wis a job, ah wis trained for it. All the Germans were in the war. There were no Fifth Column in Germany. For a' these people now that apologise and that I would say to them: 'Bollocks!' That's what I would say, quite truthfully. The bombing should have been more intense. If the governments as they were had been governments at all we wouldnae have been in the state in 1939 we were in. There's no way that 30,000 o' young blokes in the Air Force should have been killed or missin' before the end o' 1943.[226]

Quite truthfully ah didn't regret goin' tae the Air Force. Ah thoroughly enjoyed masel.

But now if anybody came tae me and said, 'There's a war comin'. Should ah go or ...? Dependin' on who they were ah wid say, 'No, don't go. Let them that the country is giving a livin' to, let them go.' The people who were fightin' the 1939-45 war were the right people tae fight it. But they didn't get the treatment they should ha' got for doin' it. Ah don't mean me personally, ah mean them that did sacrifice— ma generation. In one o' ma poems it says: *'A treacherous thought enters my brain: was it worth it? Was their sacrifice in vain?'* At the time it wisnae in vain. People got a wee bit o' hope for they had no hope at all on what wis happenin'. But what has happened since has been a waste o' time. We'd jist been as well handin' things ower to the Nazis. We've done it now. The Nazis are still there and trainin' the younger ones.

Well, in the war I would say I did aboot forty-seven operations. But when ye count the bits as thirds, ye see ... As a matter o' fact, if ah could have wangled it ah wid have went longer, ah wid have carried on. I wis reluctant tae be taken off ops. But I wis taken off aboot July 1944 and then I went to Kinloss as an instructor. Then ah wis remustered into Transport Command and ah finished the war oot in Ceylon as a motor transport officer. Ah wis demobbed in May 1946.

Eddie Mathieson

Since I came back from Burma nearly fifty years ago I've had these terrible night-mares. The war is the source of them because it's all this violent stuff. I'm always fightin' for my life. I'm always retaliatin' or wardin' off or sometimes bein' chased. They're shapes, they're no' people in Japanese uniform. They're jist shapes. They've a' got weapons.

I never had nightmares like this when I was in Burma, never, never, never. Because I think most o' the time when you went to sleep there you were exhausted. You just dropped off to sleep. I've stood on sentry duty, I've stood on watch. I've found that if I've had a rifle I always fixed the bayonet and put it under my chin and stood that way. And if I nodded off I would get it—it's the only way you could keep awake. I'd get a wee cut and it would hit the bone—it would only have a nick like. But that was to keep awake. It was a trick everybody knew. Aye, a lot o' them did that because you'd maybe gone three or four nights wi' a couple o' hours' sleep. And sometimes you'd maybe no' slept properly for days on end, you know, just had an odd forty winks here and there. So if you were standin' to, all these guys were tryin' to steal an hour or two's sleep, it kept you awake just! If you didnae have that you'd be in your foxhole and you'd get your fightin' dagger out and you'd put that under your chin' and you would sit like that, watchin'. And when you nodded off … It kept you awake.

So I'm still havin' nightmares about my experiences. I wake up shouting or kicking the bedboard sometimes. There was one dreadful occasion four or five years ago when I had my wife Nan by the throat. I've got the thumb round there where I've been trained to put it. That's bad. It's dangerous. That wakened Nan. So I mean she got a terrible fright. And I've never forgotten it. I'm terrified I ever do it again. I'm still pretty strong, you know. On another occasion when I was havin' night-mares I kicked out and I hit the wall with my foot and near broke ma toe. The nightmares are pretty horrible. I wake up wi' the sweat runnin' off me, you know, shakin' like a leaf. Nan's always aware because I'm movin' violently in the bed or I'm sittin' up starin' wi' my eyes, you know. 'Come on, you're O.K.,' she'll say. And I just go to sleep again.

I go once a month now up to the hospital for the psychology. It's less than a year ago I started goin'. A mate says to me, 'Eddie, are you gettin' nightmares?' He says to me, 'My ears have become affected: I've got a perforated eardrum.' He heard a lot o' gunfire in the war. He was on board the *Coventry*. I think it was a cruiser. That went down, that was sunk in the Med. Anyway he did a lot o' action in the *Coventry* and he says that gunfire ruined his ears.[227] Just about two years ago—he's a couple o' years older than me, he's 73 or 74 now—somebody told him, 'You can claim a pension for that.' He claimed. He never got a pension but he got three thousand quid in a lump sum! So he says, 'Eddie, you're havin' nightmares. Get intae it.' Ah says, 'Ah, but you've got physical proof that your ear's damaged.' I says, 'I've no' got anythin' physical,' I says, 'it's all in here.' He says, 'Nevertheless,' he says, 'it's worth a letter or two.' So I've written a letter or two. The wheels are in motion now! Ach, I'm no' worried really but I thought, 'Well, if it's there I'm goin' tae have it, to make up for that shillin' a day Japanese campaign money!'

I was born on the 31st of July 1924 and I've lived in Edinburgh all my life, apart from the war years. My father was a paintmaker with a pretty well known firm, Craig & Rose. These people make the paint for the Forth Bridge and have done for a hundred years or more. My dad was a Leith man. He wasn't highly paid at Craig & Rose. He finished up in charge of a department after many, many years and after ruining his health, needless to say, in that horrible place. I visited him a couple of times when I was on leave during the war and I was horrified at the conditions my father worked under. I didn't realise till then. He used to come home with blue paint all over his mouth and breathing it in—disgusting. He would be in his seventies when he died—he was born just about 1900 or 1901—but, I mean, he was ruined, his chest was completely ruined, similar diseases to what miners get but probably more virulent: red lead powder floating about, just breathing that in every day in your working life for years and years. His health was completely ruined by his occupation—and no compensation for it either.

Unfortunately, my father wasn't in a trade union. With me bein' in the buildin' trade, I was. But my father and I politically were totally opposite. I would say he was Conservative, which was ridiculous, a Tory working man, the worst thing you can have, I think. The firm Craig & Rose was run by a Sir Hugh Rose, who was a commander in chief of the Royal Scots, I think. Everybody thought this guy was wonderful, this Sir Hugh Rose. He was a rank Tory, paying them pitiful wages, and yet they thought he was a wonderful man. I could never swallow it or understand it. Of course my dad thought I was a bit of a rebel and a bit of a Communist probably. But my dad's wage was quite low, oh, it was terrible.[228]

Until the tender age of five I lived in the High Street, one block down from John Knox's house. I remember our house there. It had one room, and it wasn't a room. It was what you called a single end with a bed closet off it. I had one sister, so there was four of us living there. I remember it was on the top flat. It was on the corner of Jeffrey Street. You could look down on to Jeffrey Street out of one window, and into the High Street or St Mary's Street from another window. And that was it.

We had indoor water but I can't remember havin' a bath. I'm sure it was a tin tub in front of the fire. And I believe that the toilet was outside. I think it was a shared, communal toilet. We didn't have electricity, we had gas lighting and a coal fire. Aye, ye had a bunker inside where ye kept the coal in. The coalman brought the coal into the house. And you can imagine the dust. A terrible life for a woman, oh, awful, awful. The fireplace had to be all polished with black lead. Everything spotless clean. My mother scrubbed floors and polished. I can always smell Mansion polish. I can smell it yet. The furniture was polished.

My mother was originally from Bathgate but came into Edinburgh at an early age and spent all her adult life in Edinburgh. She came as a girl with the whole family—my granny and so on—from Bathgate. My mother came from a big family: I think it was three brothers and four sisters. My mother became a laundress—very humble beginnings in my family. She worked after she was married.

As I say, my father wasn't highly paid. My mother was working throughout my childhood in a laundry; if she wasn't doin' that she was cleanin' houses, she was cleanin' offices, very menial work, hard work for a few coppers.

But lookin' back, you know, my dad was a wee hard man. He knocked me about occasionally but I suppose I deserved it. He was pretty strict with me actually. He was always soft with my sister but with me he was a wee bit hard. My sister was a year and a half older than me.

As I say, until the tender age of five I lived in the High Street. I got started in school when I was four years old. My mother was lucky, she got me in some way or another into Cranston Street School. Shortly after that we moved from the High Street to Lochend, which was just built at the time. This was the move that was on, a' these council houses were gettin' thrown up. We would be among the forerunners of these people gettin' moved out o' slums. It was slum clearances actually. The High Street was a slum.

My mother thought she was going into a mansion at Lochend, I think. It was a brand new house, we were the first tenant. At Lochend we had two bedrooms. We thought we were in a mansion. Lochend Gardens was the address. It was four in a block, with a garden. My dad got stuck into plantin' potatoes. He wasn't a gardener as such but he dug it religiously every year and planted spuds and I had to give him a hand. So Lochend was a big transformation for us. Oh, we thought it was the greatest place in the world. My mother was so house-proud and delighted. This was a huge big house compared with what we had lived in in the High Street: a bathroom, a bathroom, you know!

When we moved to Lochend I went to a school called Hermitage Park, which was a good bit away from Lochend. It was at the bottom of Lochend Road. There was actually three schools there: Hermitage Park, Saint Anthony's—a Catholic school we played at football—and Leith Academy.

I hated school. I hated every minute of it. I hated every school I ever went to, every school. It worries me now to think it might have been my intelligence—incapable of learning, you know. But on the other hand I could write in these days a fair wee composition. I used to get quite good marks for composition. My spelling was pretty atrocious and it remains so to this day. I don't want to knock the education system then. I think they were dedicated people in the schools, even in these days. But they did believe in usin' the strap in the schools I was in. And I got my fair share of that. I got belted all over the place, because I was incorrigible really. I was in all sorts of mischief. I used to play truant as well quite a lot. In the summertime particularly I roamed up Arthur's Seat. I knew every nook and cranny on Arthur's Seat. And I used to play cowboys and Indians up there. It wasn't just myself, oh, no. I had a good mate that did the same. Him and I got thrashed stupider, but we used to do it just the same. It was this being cooped up in the classroom: I just couldn't bear it. I was an energetic laddie and I liked to be out in the fresh air.

And I'm afraid most o' ma playtimes I had tae take on somebody out in the playground, to fight them. It was a big ring and I was in there. I was always fighting—not viciously. I boxed in the Forces later on a wee bit, but not at school, I wasn't a school boxer. My uncles—I had a few uncles—I did a wee bit with them, though it was more gymnastics than boxing. My uncles tried to get me interested in gymnastics. one in particular, a younger brother of my father's, was a good gymnast and won a few cups. But occasionally while I was at school I got the gloves on wi' them and some young boys.

I played football but I never got a game for the school. I was never good enough! I used to run quite a bit. I was quite a good runner at the school sports, I could do a good 100 yards. But I was never outstanding at sports, though I liked sports and that was my chief interest really as a laddie. But I had a lot of private fights! I did quite a bit of that. I had quite a reputation for it.

I was an assiduous reader. I read and read and read as a laddie. I went to McDonald Road library, at Leith Walk, which was a long walk away. I would go home with three or four books. I've read all my life and still do. I gobbled up just about everything: boys' stories, adventures, some o' that, but I read the theory of evolution when I was about sixteen. I very early on formed an opinion that religion was a load of rubbish. I couldn't swallow the stories out of the Bible.

My father wasn't a churchgoer. He never talked to me about church or anything. My mother went regular and my sister. I always remember my mother speaking, 'I'll need to go this Sunday. It's communion.' Stuff like that. I was never at a communion in my life, even as an adult. I was sent to Sunday School as a kid: I hated it. I didn't play truant but I spent the penny for the collection to buy sweets with, which was a crime. But my mother never made me go to church and I never went. Once I got to the age where I could do what I wanted I just didn't go to church. In fact, later on when I joined the Forces I used to try and dodge church parade on a Sunday until I found out that if you dodged church parade you got stuck into cleanin' boilers, or loadin' coal, or workin' in the cookhouse peelin' spuds. So I then became Church of England or something like that! Anyway I picked out the one that had the shortest service and then I got out and had the rest of Sunday to myself. I had to get out of this fatigue business, peelin' spuds and what not.

After I left Hermitage Park primary school I went to Norton Park secondary school—it was called Albion Road School then—and that's when the horror began for me. The teachers there were tougher, harder, and more prone still to use the belt! I have no happy memories at all about that school. Again it was the discipline, and my work was going wrong. I was a keen reader—but mathematics, oh, terrible. My spelling wasn't too good. Though, mind you, my spelling could have been better then than it is now. I had two good subjects. One was technical drawing and the other one was art. I developed a bit of a flair for the technical drawing. Everybody hated it and I thoroughly enjoyed it—strange. But it wasn't that that led me to think of becoming a joiner. I actually got woodwork at school and I never finished a model yet! I was hopeless The woodwork teacher hated me, of course, and I hated him. He used to throw lumps of wood at me for talkin' when I should have been workin', or puttin' a chisel down the wrong way or whatever. He always had a lot of wee bits of wood on his desk and he was a dead shot! He would get you on the skull wi' this wee lump o' wood. I hated joinery work. I used to make all these daft wee tooth brush racks and pipe stands—everybody smoked pipes in these days. But I never finished one of them. I certainly hadnae any intentions at the school o' becomin' a joiner. I just didn't have any ambitions at the school. All I ever thought about was gettin' away from school! That was about all that was in my mind.

I left school I think it was a month or two before I was fourteen. I couldn't get out the door quick enough. Of course, a few years later I looked back with regret and thought, 'Why did I ...?', you know. I must have left in the summer of 1938, just a year before the war broke out.

I got a job in a shoe shop in Earl Grey Street. The shop was called Truform. My mother, she was very keen to have me workin'! She liked to get the money comin' into the house. I got stuck in this shop and I hated it from the minute I walked through that door. There was a couple o' prissy old women and a couple of guys. I had to polish floors and clean windows. I stacked shelves with shoe boxes. I wasn't actually selling the shoes, oh, no, I was there to clean up. If they dropped things I picked them up. And then we had certain clients came in and ordered shoes and wanted them delivered—didn't want to carry them home. Then I had to deliver shoes all over Morningside. Oh, I wasn't allowed to take the tram. I could if I had used my own money but I didnae have any money. I wasn't given fares, I just had to walk. I enjoyed gettin' out the shop. But then I always got a row because I was away too long. I'm talkin' about walkin' two or three miles, away up into Morningside and back. It was maybe a two or three miles round trip with a couple o' boxes o' shoes. I dawdled a bit because I hated the thought o' goin' back into the shop. I knew I was goin' back in tae get the big tin o' polish out and polish the counters or whatever.

I can't remember what the wage was when I began. It was a pittance, a few shillings, and my mum got most o' it. I got pocket money out o' ma wages. But I was only in that job a few weeks at Truform when I got this brilliant job as an apprentice joiner. Oh, this was the greatest. You would think I had been knighted. You know, my mother was saying: 'Now there's nobody round here in Craigentinny got a job like this. You're going to be a tradesman!' That was the accolade—a tradesman. A tradesman! Oh! That was it: my dad, you know. My mother had heard of the job through somebody and she dragged me along. I hated her goin' with me for jobs, of course. I'd sooner have gone myself. But she dragged me along. The joiners' workshop was away in Blackhall and by this time we lived in Craigentinny, near Lochend, the other side of the city. I had a bike, of course, so when I did get started there I was bikin' for an hour goin' to work in the mornin' and an hour comin' back at night. And when I got there, once I was old enough to go oot and do window ropes and things, the boss used to say, 'Just put your tools roond your bike and go!' So I was away out to Barnton or Davidson's Mains from Blackhall on my bike, my own transport.

It must have been the late summer or autumn of 1938 when I started as an apprentice joiner. I hated joinery at school but I really took tae it right away. I really began to take an avid interest in joinery and carpentry. My tools I had tae buy one by one every two or three weeks—save my coppers, buy it. I would get a tool for my birthday, a chisel or something like that. I gradually built up my kit o' tools. I loved these tools and I looked after them, I really did: linseed oil doon them.

I worked there wi' a cantankerous old tradesman Peter Davidson, who was a terrible old man. He was really a martinet. Put your plane blade down on the bench— a lump o' dowellin' across your fingers! 'You know about that?' It was like bein' back at school. So you turned the plane on its edge so it wasn't lyin' on the blade. Things like that. He taught me, he taught me. I've got a lot to thank that man for. That man gave me the best groundin' in joinery anybody could ask for. Peter Davidson was the finest tradesman I've ever seen in my life.

He was what they call the bench hand. There were two or three young joiners and a couple o' apprentices who went out and did bits o' building. They built the odd bungalow and put the roof on here and there. They did the occasional shop front. But Peter Davidson did anything like cabinet work. He actually made coffins. The first year I was there I went out a couple o' times wi' Peter and measured bodies. In these days you had to go out and measure the corpse and make the coffin accordingly. Well, you can imagine a young boy o' fifteen year old goin' wi' the auld guy. He was quite callous about it. You cannae measure a corpse properly in bed, because in these days all the mattresses, you know… So you had to get them flat on a table and you had to put a straight edge across the highest part of the body. That gives you the depth. And then of course you took the length and you measured shoulders. And that's a' the sizes you'd take for a coffin. I was shaking to begin with, but I got quite used to it. It was just a job after a while. But at that time, particularly in the country—and this shop I worked in, although it was Blackhall, was more or less a country shop—most country joiners were coffin makers, too. We didnae do that many. And then they stopped doin' it because coffins started comin' in in bulk into big warehouses. Now they've got stock sizes.

You started work at eight in the morning so I would leave home about seven, maybe just before that. It was a good hour's cycle and that was in all weathers. I'd get into my work soakin' wet and have to work all day with wet clothes on. When ye got to the workshop ye maybe had two or three hanks o' sash cord and got sent out to Barnton, to go round a dozen houses puttin' window ropes in. I think I had a big yellow cycling cape but when you put it on you sweated under that and you'd get wet anyway. My main concern was keepin' my tools dry. I hated the thought o' ma tools gettin' wet. I really was daft about ma tools. I wouldnae let anybody touch them. I kept them in the workshop but when you went to do these jobs you had to take your tools.

Another job I remember gettin' to do when I got older—by the time I was two or two-and-a-half years in—I was actually makin' garden gates to design. I used to have to take these garden gates, get gate posts, cement, sand, and go and instal new gate posts. We did a lot o' it in the Blackhall area. There was a tremendous amount o' wooden gates in the Blackhall area at that time, bungalows wi' wooden gates. And sometimes there were double gates for the garage or a drive and there was the smaller gates. But you had to dig out these old gate posts. They were set in cement. You had to dig them out, break them up with big pinch bars and—16 or 17 year old nearly, I'm doin' this—set the posts in, rack them up and concrete them, hang the gates on them, then trim the tops into fancy acorns and shapes on the top. And that was after having made the gates. Oh, I did all that. It was hard work and skilful work—and very little machinery. We had one huge big saw, a big dangerous brute it was, too! The mortice machine was a thing wi' a counterweight on it and a steel blade and a big lever handle. You just punched your mortices out with this manually. I had muscles like Tarzan! But I enjoyed the life. Oh, it was great, it was great! I liked it outside the shop, gettin' away frae the old guy now and again, workin' wi' the other younger blokes on roofs and that. I loved workin' on roofs, climbin' about on roofs. I had a head for heights. I could go up tenements, I worked on the tenements in Blackhall and in the town. I worked on a lot of factories, like the tannery at Beaverhall. I did a lot of roof work and absolutely loved it. Och, God, there was a tremendous range and variety o' work. Well, it was a wee shop, a wee firm, and ye got cabinetmakin', ye got garden gates to make, huts, coalboxes. People had coalboxes in these days that they kept outside. We made hundreds of these. We were fed up makin' them. I had tae creosote them all, of course, once they were made. And huts—many different sizes and shapes o' huts—and I built sectional garages, greenhouses.

It wasn't unusual to start as an apprentice in those days at the age of fourteen, it was normal. In the first year my wages were five shillings a week. Of that I gave four shillins to my mother. I had a shillin' to myself. The second year it would go up—I cannae really remember how much. Your first year was very, very low. It went up considerably more every year after that. Then it sort of levelled out. When I went away to the Forces I think my wages were round about £3 a week. I don't remember what I got when I became a journeyman because I never finished my time. I was away in the Forces. My apprenticeship was interrupted. I had only had something like three years at my trade.

I remember the hours all right. You started at eight o'clock. You finished at half past four. But you had half an hour dead for your lunch break. You got no morning tea break in these days. You worked a 44-hour week. So you worked five days at eight hours, and you worked Saturday morning—that wasn't time and a half or anything: you started on Saturday at eight o'clock, finished at twelve. No breaks in the morning.

Overtime in these days was virtually unheard of, unless it was something really, really special. I wasn't in a union as an apprentice. I could have joined but nobody approached me or told me. There were a lot o' non-union members goin' about. It wasn't a union shop at Blackhall. It was a wee small shop. Had I been in a bigger shop I would have had to have probably been in the union. I wasn't politically inclined or anything, and neither were the guys that I worked beside.

That was a great life when I think back on it. I always remember workin' on some villas out at Barnton, lovely big houses. It was summertime. The men took their tea out of billy cans in these days, just syrup tins wi' a wire handle. I used to have to build a fire outside, just two or three bricks wi' a perforated metal sheet, a bit o' corrugated iron wi' holes banged in it wi' a pick, laid on the fire, and dozens o' these drums on it. And I had tae remember how much tea I had tae put in this one and how much sugar—or this one didn't take sugar. I had tae remember a' that. Ye had tae memorise every drum and whose drum it was. If ye got it wrong—oh, dear! So somebody sent me for cigarettes or something and the shop was a good bit away. I should have been puttin' the drums on. I says, 'I've got to put the drums on.' 'Never mind the drums, I want my fags. Go and get me ten Woodbine.' Away I went. Of course by the time I got back and got the drums on the foreman came out, and blew the whistle. Ye got half an hour dead. The tea had to be ready for the guys. Of course, it wasnae ready and they started cuffin' me about and a' the rest o' it. I went over and I got my boot under the corrugated iron. I kicked the whole lot up in the air! 'Your tea!' I said. Oh, I just about got my books for that. 'That's you, you're finished,' one o' them says, 'as soon as the boss comes in.' The boss came in in the afternoon and I was tremblin'. I says, 'Oh, God, I've blew it. I've lost my job.' He took me aside. He says, 'What's this I'm hearin' about you?' I explained to him. 'Bob there,' I says', wanted me to go and get cigarettes,' I says, 'and I was just about to put the drums on. But he hit me and he made me go!' 'I'll let you off this time,' he says, 'but anything like this again and you're finished.' So I had to be on my best behaviour after that. I was a wee bit impetuous, you know. They got no tea! Oh I wasnae very popular after that! Funny, after that I got treated wi' a wee bit respect.

The year or so I was working in the joiners' shop before the war came I really don't think I was beginning to get interested in world events. I was pretty naive. It was only after the war I became politically aware.

One of my mates in Craigentinny—which was unusual for these days—was a coloured laddie. His father was Jamaican, his mum was white. His father wasn't there. I never ever saw his father. He was dead before they came to live in Craigentinny. There was two boys born of that union. One of them was younger than me and one of them was older. I became very friendly with the older one. I don't know why. He was a pretty ugly looking guy. He wasn't a handsome coloured laddie. He was downright ugly. David McCrae was his name. He would be about three or four years older than me. But I think he had difficulty making friends. He was a nice, a lovely guy, he really was. But I think people would be a bit frightened of him. He was an ugly looking boy. But he was a great person. And I was really friendly with him. They were living in a top flat in a three-storey in Craigentinny. I got friendly with both of them. They played football. And we—David McCrae and me—we went to school on the same bike. We had a bike between us and he went to David Kilpatrick's School when I was going to Norton Park. I sat on the handle bars and sometimes he would. He was bigger than me and he would usually pedal. I would jump off at my school and he would carry on to David Kilpatrick's and then pick me up on the way back. This is what we did. It was a long way to school.

Well, David McCrae tried to join the navy. He tried to join Boys' Service at fourteen. I believe that was the Boys' Service age at that time. They refused to have him on account of his colour. They just wouldn't have him. And he finished up instead in the mercantile marine. I don't know how he managed this but he went to a nautical college in Leith and went to another one in England. But anyway he finished up on merchantmen, plying out of different docks in this country. And at the time of the Spanish Civil War he would be about fifteen. As a deck boy or a deck hand, whatever he was, he actually sailed into Barcelona on a ship with munitions and came under bombardment. It was probably German Stukas they were usin' at that time. The Germans were practising in Spain for the big war, I believe. I have vague memories. All he told me was that there was bombs flyin' about all over the place and, he said, 'I was terrified.' He actually lost his life during the Second World War, going down below to get somebody. He was in docks somewhere down south. There had been an explosion and there was gasses escapin'. And he went down to help people up and he died down below by the time they put the rope back down for him. He got the George Medal for it, posthumously of course. I was at his funeral.

I remember the outbreak of the Second World War, the declaration, and Chamberlain's speech. Aye, I remember all that. I also remember the first sortie the German Air Force made up the Forth. I was actually working on a bowling green roof with my boss, because by this time all the young joiners were away. Two or three of them had been in the Terries. They were whipped away. In fact, one of them was an apprentice. Jackie Quinn his name was. He was cryin' when he went. He was only seventeen. And he was whipped away! He didn't want to go. He was Artillery and he used to like strutting around with his spurs and bandoliers. He used to love goin' about in that. And then all of a sudden he realised it was for real. It was no' a dressin'-up affair. The real thing was on him. He survived the war but he took a bayonet in the stomach in the Ardennes. He finished up in the paratroopers in the Ardennes debacle near the end of the war. He was comin' down and there was a guy waitin' for him. He virtually landed on the German's bayonet.

Anyway I was on the bowling green roof with my boss, Willie Johnston. He was a mad hat. He was a crazy man. We heard a lot o' bangin' and cracklin' goin' on down in Granton. We could see one of the spans of the Forth Bridge. But there was a lot of flashes there. I says, 'What's goin' on up there, Willie?' 'Oh,' he says, 'That's them practisin', he says. 'They're jist practisin'.' Oh, tae hell, it wis German bombers and it was the Spitfires up after them! And then this bomber came flyin' from the Bridge area right down, as though they were goin' down the east coast. And they were gettin' lower and lower and lower. Apparently at the time all the crew aboard were dead. I believe it eventually crashed somewhere in East Lothian. And when it passed us on the bowling green roof—just two or three hundred feet above us—we could see the big black Maltese cross on its side. And ah says tae Willie, 'That's a

German plane!' 'Don't be daft.' he says, 'it's a hospital plane that.' And it was a black cross tae on it. Oh, he was the boss so ah says, 'Oh, aye, O.K.' But it was a German plane! So that was my first experience of seein' anything at all o' the war.

As the war went on ye heard that people round about—and it didn't daunt you either—you heard o' guys goin' down wi' their ships. 'Oh, so-and-so had a telegram. She's lost her man. She's lost her son.' You know. That didn't put you off. You still wanted to go. There was a glamour about it. You know, it was ridiculous. Everybody thought it was great to go and fight. There was a terrific atmosphere of comradeship, if you like, of gettin' together. People seemed to get together, closer to one another. There was what they called a war effort—and it was an effort. People really made the effort.

My father tried to volunteer. He had been too young for the First World War. He would just be 18 after the First War. But he was of age and he actually volunteered—I give it to him—for the Second War. And he was the most disappointed man on earth when he failed his medical. He was really cut up about it. He wanted to go.

My dad didn't volunteer in the First World War. He was just too young for that. But his elder brother did at sixteen and got taken. And when he went over to France he was terrified. He actually deserted and made his way into Spain. He was a character. His name was Arthur and he was a bit of a wandering man. He went on trawlers, drove lorries. But the story goes in the 1914 war he faked his age and volunteered. Arthur got sent to France, of course, and he didn't fancy that one little bit so he deserted. Oh, it was infantry he was in because I think it was trench warfare that he got frightened off. The fact that he skipped, you know, deserted was a bit of a disgrace in the family. It was never discussed. I only got it out o' him in later years, when I was old enough to have a drink wi' him. He was in Spain for quite a wee while, months, months. He had a terrible job trying to get back here. I don't even know if he had to wait until after the war. I don't think so. But some way or another he got back. I don't know how.

Uncle Arthur had so many adventures. He married somebody and had a child by another woman, and things like that, you know. That wis horrific things tae happen tae people in these days, that was a real disgrace. A lot o' it was hushed up, a lot o' it you were never told. Just before the Second War he had a lorry he used to drive around, delivering pigs' meat or collecting pigs' meat, or something like that. It was a stinkin', smelly lorry. And I remember him takin' this lorry intae a field and sayin' tae me, 'Right, you're drivin' it.' And I was drivin' this huge lorry round the field at fifteen-year old! That's the kind o' man he was. He was full o' fun. People would term him a careless man but he had a life about him. He was an excitin' guy tae be with, you know, in spite o' all the daft things he did—sometimes dishonest things. He was a rogue but he was a likeable rogue. He really was. He was older than my dad. It was only after the Second War that I heard about Uncle Arthur's adventures in the First World War.

I had other uncles. I had an uncle who was in the Artillery in the Second War. He was called up, conscripted. He was a young uncle but obviously he was a good bit older than me. He didn't want to go but he had tae go! He'd be in his early thirties, or late twenties. I don't know what he saw by way of action. I didn't see much of him after the war.

Once the war began I joined the Home Guard. I was 15. Ye had tae volunteer. You could join at fifteen year old. It was young boys and old men, that was what the Home Guard was comprised of. The Home Guard was formed I think it was durin' the first year of the war—the very last line of defence. It was the Edinburgh battalion. It was a Royal Scots badge on your cap. Ye had nothing really to do with the Royal Scots but that was your cap badge. All the Edinburgh Home Guard wore the Royal Scots cap badge. My dad was in the Home Guard as well.[229]

The Home Guard trainin' really was invaluable to me. We saw no action, of course. We spent our time plowtering about on golf courses. We could throw hand grenades, dismantle a hand grenade, take a Lewis gun to bits with a blindfold on, things like that. I learnt about the Lewis gun, learnt about the old Lee Enfield rifle, which was a 1914-18 weapon. All these old soldiers in the Home Guard knew everything about them.

I wanted to join the Air Force. I wanted to join as an air gunner. To be quite honest with you, I don't know why. My mate Bill Reid—who is now my brother-in-law: my wife's sister married him—he was an engineer. He worked wi' Bruce Peebles. He served his time at Bruce Peebles. He lived near me in Craigentinny. He was a year or six month older than me. But we discussed various things and, oh, he fancied the Air Force. And he got me thinkin' the same way. He was on about bein' a tail gunner—that was a suicidal job! But we were dead keen to get into this—mad!

Certainly we both went up quite jauntily to George Street, where they used to sign you up, and we put our name down for this Air Force lot, air gunners. But we failed lamentably. Our education jist wasnae good enough! We had to have good mathematics even as a tail gunner. I think we did not too bad in the intelligence test—well, Bill did better than me. He's a pretty intelligent guy. But our education just wasn't up to it. We were offered instead Air Force ground duties, guardin' aerodromes or drivin' trucks, or doing sentry duty. Bill jumped for it but I says, 'No, I'm no' havin' that.' Ah says, 'If I can't get into the Air Force I'll go into the navy.' One of my grandfathers fought on the North West Frontier in India, but none of my family had been in the navy. I thought I'd maybe get better fed in the navy. I was a hungry wee bugger at that time. I could eat a lot. I ate big meals every chance I got. I had a fair appetite. So that was my belief: if I joined the navy I'd get better food than I would in the army! 'Cause I had stories from the '14 War of guys livin' on bully beef and all that. I finished up eatin' quite a lot o' bully beef myself!

So I put my name down for the navy. I passed the physical O.K. I was pretty good because I was pretty fit, climbin' about on buildin' sites, and a wee bit o' boxin' occasionally and football now and then. So I passed grade one. And when I got my papers—it was for the damned Marines!

I had put in for the navy. But, mind you, had I waited till I was conscripted—which I would have been in another four or five months' time—I'd have been duffed into the Black Watch or the Cameronians or something like that. I didnae fancy that.

I cannae remember exactly when I volunteered for the Air Force and then for the navy. I would be seventeen-and-a-half. So it would be late 1941, early 1942. I went as early as I could. Within a week or two Bill Reid, my mate, he was away. Bill survived the war. He was in the Air Force through the war. He didnae see a lot o' action, because he mostly drove a lorry. A wee bit o' strafin' here and there but he didnae see combat as such. But he actually finished up at Belsen. He finished up helpin' to clean up Belsen at the end o' the war. 'Horrible,' he says, 'terrible'.[230]

They hadnae asked me anything about the Marines at the interview I got for the navy. I hadnae much idea what the Marines were all about actually. I never even thought about them. Well, I went from Edinburgh down to Deal, which was Marine Holding Battalion. All recruits at that time passed through Deal, and I believe there was other centres. All Marines are affiliated to some naval port. My regimental number I can remember now after all these years: Plymouth X107253. It was PLY then an oblique and then an X and then the number. That was Plymouth. PO with an oblique—that was Portsmouth. There wis four naval divisions: Plymouth, Portsmouth, Exeter, Chatham. Chatham was CHA oblique X and number. I don't know what the X was for, nobody ever queried what the X was. But every Marine had an X.

I was about six weeks at Deal—basic training. It was very hard going. We were never allowed out the barracks because we couldn't walk properly, according to the drill sergeants. We shambled about like orang-outangs, according to them! Because I'd been in the Home Guard before I joined up I was well into arms drill and stuff like that. I was well into the use of weapons. I did a bit of target practice. I was used to marching, because a' the old sweats really put us through it. So I had already done about two or two-and-a-half years in the Home Guard before I went into the Marines.

The barracks at Deal had German air attacks on them. They used to hop across the Channel. You were only about twenty mile from France. They would strafe the barracks when we would be goin' through drill manoeuvres. There was a dive for the shelters, of course. That was maybe not daily but every two or three days. The whole of the south coast of England was virtually evacuated of women and children. It was just all men in that area, most of them servicemen of some type or another.

Then we were sent up north to Whitley Bay for weapons training principally, route marches, aircraft recognition—all sorts of things. I was there a couple of months, I think. Then I went on a non-commissioned officers' course to Filey Camp in Yorkshire. Actually, it was a Butlin's holiday camp, the first one that had been built before the war. And I don't think it had ever even been used because the war came along. It was an ideal training place for troops. At Filey there was Marines and RAF Regiment. And it was training to make you a non-commissioned officer, starting wi' one tape and hopefully you were goin' tae move on from there. I was at Filey, oh, about six weeks, I think. So when I left Filey I was a first-class Marine. I had one tape up. There is no such rank in the Marines as lance corporal, you were a first-class Marine, although they would call you corporal.

After Filey I went back to the Whitley Bay area, I think. I am bit hazy now about my movements, because I moved around a lot. I don't really remember. But I did go to Portsmouth, to a place called Whale Island. That was a gunnery course. It was anti-aircraft—ack-ack, Oerlikons, the pom-poms, Bofors, and I think it was a heavy machine gun of some sort, a Vickers—I'm no' sure. But we were trained on anti-aircraft defence. We fired at rogues and things—that's aircraft pulling a sock behind them and you fired at that. I was only a few weeks there, and then I went to Leigh in Lancashire. That was a good place.

What I remember about Leigh is a lot of route-marchin' and general infantry training—hand grenade throwing, firing machine guns, rifles, general stuff like that, and a lot of sentry duties on the camp. It was a mixed camp of naval personnel, WRNS, and Marines.[231] The Marines were in a minority there. I think it was a training camp, because we werenae guarding anything specifically. We seemed to be just guarding the camp itself.

I got into a wee bit trouble at Leigh. The Marines, and I think the army, have a funny notion about time. You got a leave pass to go out every night if you weren't on duty. We were outside of Leigh a few miles and you had to get a bus into Leigh. On any leave pass in the Forces your time for coming back is 11.59—one minute to twelve midnight. You must check in and hand this leave pass in then. So from Leigh there was a bus left that got you back to camp for about ten minutes to midnight. So we got the bus as usual. It was full of Marines, very rowdy and noisy, everybody had a good drink of course. Here the damned bus got a puncture. I can't remember if another bus came or the guy managed to fix it. Some decided to walk. But eventually we got back one way or another. The result was we were all straggling in after twelve. And the duty sergeant of the guard that night was a real idiot. He must have realised that there was no way all these guys can be comin' in late and that there must be something wrong. But he's just bookin' them all and puttin' them on a charge as they come in. Just an idiot. There was always one or two guys came in late and they went on a charge. They got extra drill the next day—something like that. On this occasion it was nobody's fault. We'd got the bus and we should have been there on time. But this sergeant's no' listenin'. So I've had a drink, quite honestly. But anyway ah says tae him: 'You're not bloody well listenin' tae anybody, sergeant, are ye?' I says, 'Do you think we're all deliberately being late? Isn't it obvious to you that there must be something wrong?' 'Who do you think you're talkin' to?' he says. 'Ach', ah says, 'shut up.' 'Corporal, did you hear that?' he says to one o' the guard, 'insultin' talk to a sergeant, a superior officer.' And ah says, 'And, corporal, did you see this?' Bang! That was it. I thumped him. I lost my head, didn't I? And I was wheeled away right away down to the cells and tossed into them. A couple of days later I'm marched out in front of my company commander and I'm given a month or six weeks or something in jail. This was naval detention—Marines are under naval discipline.

Preston jail was at that time taken over as a naval detention centre. It was a medieval jail. I think the ceilings in the cells were six feet high and I think the length was about six feet six, and the width was something like four or five feet. It was stone—thick stone—and freezin'. No heatin'. A wooden bench wi' a wooden block thing, like an executioner's block, for a pillow—a wooden pillow.

I think you got one blanket, I'm not sure. It was cold. I don't think this was the winter, or it would have been much colder. They would need to have given you some sort o' heatin'. I mean, it couldnae have been that bad wi' us. But it was cold and dank and damp in there. It was solitary, you were in the cell yourself. But you weren't locked up 24 hours a day. No. You were out and worked. Work would have been O.K. if it had been constructive work. But it was the most stupid work. We were pullin' a big roller up and down a yard, things like that. And, oh, filling sandbags with sand, carrying them 100 yards or so to the other end of the compound, emptying them out, filling them again and carrying them back—all day. Soul destroying, stupid work like that. They were trying to crack you, of course, tryin' to break you, to make you go back and do everything on the word of command without question.

The roller was heavy and when you got it moving you couldnae stop it, once it got momentum. Ye had tae put everything into it to stop it—and you were going for a wall about fifteen foot high. So there were injuries—broken fingers, broken toes, gettin' your feet caught under the roller, and broken arms. It happened several times while I was there and apparently it had been goin' on for they still weren't stoppin' this stupid, horrendous business, trundling this thing up and down. I wasn't injured myself but some people there were maybe a wee bit slower on the uptake o' realisin' what was on.

The guards were naval men—and they hated Marines. There were naval prisoners in there, too. But these naval guards picked on the Marines harder than they picked on the other blokes. But everybody had a hard time.

I think we were up about six in the morning. It was an early start anyway. You had to shave first, cold water shave. Then the razors had been taken away from you and were handed to you as you went in. You were allowed a minute or something to shave and you scraped away and you handed the razor—a safety razor—in at the other end. They were obviously afraid of suicides. We were issued with open razors when I joined the Forces. Open razors were part of our kit. But when you went into detention all your kit was taken away and you were given denims to wear all the time you were in there. You got your kit back when you left. You took all your kit with you when you went to naval detention and it was stored and you got it when you came out. There weren't any suicides when I was in Preston jail but there was stories of it.

I couldnae really say how many prisoners there would be, because ah wis confined to a certain area o' the prison and there might have been a compound somewhere else in the vicinity. I don't know. There was about up to twenty other lads I worked with. It varied as they came and went in the group I was in.

You worked after you got your breakfast. It was usually a thin gruelly porridge. When you were in there at that time you didn't get full rations—part of the punishment again. You didn't get smokes either—not allowed to smoke. I was a pipe smoker and most of the others were cigarette smokers. They were goin' mad for the smokes.

So you started work round about seven and worked right through till the dinner break at twelve. You got a gruel sort o' thing, a very watery soup, and a couple o' boiled potatoes and that was it. You got an hour. You had to regulate your bowel movements to suit that hour, of course. Because when you were out there there was no way that they would let you go to the toilet. It meant an escort taking you—no way. So you had to more or less get your physical needs sorted out very early on or you could be in dire straits. And then you went back to work after your dinner. I think it was five o'clock you finished. You got your tea such as it was—bread and dripping or something like that. And you got a cup of cocoa later on: that was handed in to your cell.

You were locked up after your day's work and after your tea. It was a pretty grim experience. From six o'clock you were locked up till six the following morning. You weren't allowed any reading—no books, just the Bible. I tried reading the Bible but I couldn't make much of it. And ye werenae supposed to talk even when you were outside. Ye did, but ye werenae supposed to. I was never caught doing it but you had the odd shout: 'Who's that talking?' You tried to speak out the corner of your mouth.

Some of the lads in Preston jail were very distressed. I think mentally a lot of them were affected by it. You had to be pretty tough. And then I lost weight. I was in there about six weeks or two month, I cannae remember, but I lost more than half a stone as far as I remember. I was really thin when I came out.

Some of the fellows must have been in longer than me. It varied, well— there was one guy in for rape. He had climbed in through a WRNS's window or something. He was in for a long time—it was years he had. I don't know if he would survive that treatment or not. Oh, ye got stories about people dying in detention, aye, ye got all that, ye got all that. Kickings, well, kickings were quite common. I witnessed a few of them. These guards were a wee bit vindictive. If you had to speak to them it was 'Staff'. That was the title. And they carried wee swagger cane things. They used to walk about and if they were displeased with what you were doin' or how fast you were doin' anything they could jab you and they would get you right on the funny bone. They were adept at that. They would catch that nerve on the elbow that makes you tingle. Or they would prod you right in the kidneys. Oh, you know! And they were just dyin' for you to take a swing at them. And before you knew where you were there would be six of them round about you puttin' the boot intae ye. I saw that. But the bad one was when six of them really pounded this boy. He had retaliated. I don't know how it started. It flared up. Of course, things could flare up. I imagine prisoners in general are like that, that there could be a flare-up at any time. The guards certainly didn't get any disciplinary action for this guy that was badly beaten. They were there the next day doin' their job, the same as though nothin' had happened. He was in hospital.

The guards wore a sort of naval uniform. They had navy blue battledress. They never wore hats. They were naval personnel, not Marines. You very seldom saw any officers. You saw what you would call the head warder. His rank in the navy would be master-at-arms or something, a warrant officer, like a sergeant-major in the Marines or in the army. We never saw a commissioned officer.

I just tried to stick to the rules. I just wanted to get the days in. I didn't want any hassle. I didn't want any kickings. I didn't want to be rebellious. You were just heading for trouble. You couldn't buck the system. It wisnae a very nice experience.

You weren't allowed to write letters or receive them, no' in there. You got to write a letter before you went in. I didn't tell my parents what had happened. I told them I was going on a special course! And the unfortunate thing was my sister was getting married when this happened. She was just getting married. And I had already asked for special leave. And I was still waitin' to hear from my commanding officer at Leigh whether I was being allowed a leave pass to go to my sister's wedding. So my last letter was, 'I'm sorry I won't make the wedding. I'm going on a special course.' It was after the war before I told them actually what had happened.

In Preston jail I think your mind went into a certain slot, an acceptance slot. You say, 'This is it. I've just got to put up with this until …', you know. And at times you actually forgot how long you had to go. At other times you were countin' the minutes and the days.

I didn't make any friends or keep in touch with any of the other fellows there. They all came from different units anyway. They come from all over. It was difficult to strike up any acquaintanceship at all. You'd get the odd smile frae one or a body movement sayin'—you know. No communication at night, of course. The walls must have been three feet thick o' stone! They were jist wee dungeons really.

When you were discharged the sort of warrant officer guy, he says, 'Well, we don't want to see your face in here again. You'll now be a good Marine.' You got the pep talk on your way out! Och, I was glad to get out of that. I was a very good soldier for a long time after that, I'll tell you.

From Preston jail I went back to the unit at Leigh. Within it would be a couple of weeks, I think, I learned I had been selected for the commandos. I never volunteered for the commandos. What you've got to do in all training establishments like Leigh, you always have to look at your company notice board, always. It's just a daily habit, because there's always something at some time or another goin' up that appertains to you or that you're goin' to be involved in. Everybody's waitin' for moves out to different units. And that was mine came up. And of course that was me separated finally from my mates, a couple of guys I had left Edinburgh with when I joined the Marines.

The notice just said: 'Report at so many hundred hours for travellin' visas and so on and with full kit.' You had been posted to commando unit. Contrary to what everybody thinks, not all commandos at that time were volunteers. There was a unit that was formed for volunteers to start with but when they began to realise the usefulness of commando raids and commando units as such, I think this was their way of filling up the necessary numbers. There was people like me that had done a wee bit inside. I found as time went on there was some like me found when they came out o' detention that they had been 'appointed' to serve with the commandos. As I say, I never volunteered for the commandos.

I was aware of the existence o' the commandos at that time. There wis talk about them then. There had been the Lofoten Raids and so on, and the commandos were comin' into their own then. I cannae really remember when I was sent to the commandos. It would be the end of 1942, I think.[232]

I got sent to Achnacarry in Inverness-shire. We left by train. On the way north from Leigh I went somewhere where there was two or three people gathered, blue beret Marines, ordinary Marines like myself. We went intae a sidin' somewhere. The train we got on there was all sorts of people on it goin' different places. But the train we finally got on was goin' one place, I think they were just gathering people from different units, from all over the place. We got off at Spean Bridge station.

There were about twenty or thirty of us marched from Spean Bridge to the camp at Achnacarry. There was a big house there but we were in nissen huts in the grounds or round about it. There was French Canadians, Poles, army guys—it was army commandos at that time. Nowadays there is only one commando unit, and that's Marines. But at the formation of commandos, there was army—in fact, everybody wore different cap badges. I can't remember any Air Force men there. I think they were mostly army guys. Difficult to know how many men there were at Achnacarry. I would think it could have been hundreds. There were some pretty full-scale operations carried on out in the hills. But it's difficult to be sure of numbers because everybody was scattered about. The nissen huts were even all separated from one another. I was in a hut with thirty guys. There was thirty bunks in my nissen hut. There was a central cookhouse or kitchen area. I would say there were maybe a dozen nissen huts scattered round about. Whether they were all inhabited by men or whether they were storeplaces, I don't know. Probably there would be 200 or 300 men at any given time.

And then there was a nucleus, a small group, of instructors. I think they all lived in just as Spartan conditions as we did. They were hard men and they had to keep fit. The only thing they didnae carry were the big weights we carried! They were more or less in gym kit when they took us out on speed marches and things like that.

Now a speed march is a fiendish thing until you get really hardened and used to it. It can crack your spirit as easy as anything. It can exhaust you. It can drop you to your knees. You can feel like givin' up. A speed march sounds an easy thing to do but bearing in mind you're carrying 60 lbs in weight … So you set off in a group and you trot for ten minutes—don't run full out, just trot—then you break into a walk for ten minutes. Then you trot for ten minutes. By the end of fifty minutes you have a ten minute break. And that goes on all day. Hours and hours and hours. You start off with a five-miler. You maybe do a couple of them, then you do a ten-miler, maybe do three o' them. Then you'll jump from ten mile up tae twenty! Ha! And you'll finish up doin' a thirty-miler after a week or two of this, gradually working your way up—30 miler. By the time you are headin' for the thirty mile you will be lookin' forward to it. A strange thing, You've gone through agony. You've had blisters. You've reached a point of exhaustion. You've reached where the sweat has blinded ye. You've reached the stage 'I can't go on any longer.' And something makes you go on or somebody says, 'Come on', you know. When you got to doing thirty miles that took all day—from early morning to maybe seven or eight o'clock at night.

I was at Achnacarry about a month, I think, six weeks, maybe longer. We were in a pretty isolated area. It was just in the middle of fir forests. We really didn't have any contact at all with the civilian population. It was very intensive training. Well, it was pretty hard goin'. It was very strict physical training. I hated every minute of it to start with. It was so vigorous, it was so hard physically and mentally, all you had to cope with, you know. You were doing things that you thought you couldn't do—physical tasks carrying heavy backpacks up steep inclines, and things like that.

The backpacks were about sixty pound gear in total—that would be backpack, plus weapons, plus ammunition, plus water. Sixty pound would be about the regular weight that you carried.

Then you had milling, which was a pretty barbaric form of barefist fighting! You formed a ring and the instructor blew a whistle and you were all numbered. So No. 1 and No. 2 would jump in. When he blew again No. 3 would jump in and No. 1 was supposed to jump out. But if you were No. 2 you could be fightin' No. 1—bare fist, mind—and No. 3 could come in at your back and he would clabber you one round the ear. You know—no rules: kidney punching, everything. The only thing that wasn't allowed was kicking—just the fists. You were stripped to the waist. Oh, the bloody noses! Milling was a toughening up exercise to make you physically tough. But I think it did more damage! Because there was broken noses and everything occurred. I was quite happy with milling, because having a wee bit o' experience in boxin' I managed to keep out all the wild swings I could dodge. It was the sucker punch—the one that you didn't see comin', a wild one from nowhere—that would get you now and again. That was the only thing you had to watch for. A boxer should be able to beat a guy that doesn't box but just goes in like a windmill. So as I say I came out o' millin' not too bad, with little damage, a couple of bruises. But some of them came out in a real old mess.

Milling wasn't a daily exercise. They would have had more guys in hospital than on the trainin' if they did. I mean, there were men gettin' knocked down and everything. Sometimes a broken jaw. So, I mean, it wouldnae be very good if half the recruits were finishin' up in hospital. If there were injuries from that or anything else there was a sick bay for immediate things. But if it was serious they would need to have been taken by ambulance to Fort William or something like that.

We did abseiling and cliff-scaling. Abseiling's coming down the face of a cliff in leaps and bounds controlled by a double rope, with a bit o' gear that you use for checking. We did, oh, swimming in rivers, freezin' cold water, death slides across water—always water: if you're goin' to fall you're goin' to land in freezin' water. You never landed on a nice bit o' soft bracken or anything. Oh, no, that was too easy. These death slides were always constructed in a place where you were goin' tae land in mud or water. Death slides was a bit dramatic name for them. But you had to have a wee bit nerve for to go down. You were shootin' down there at a fair lick.

We went out on night exercises. Exercises could last a couple of days, livin' out in the country. On some exercises—if it was an exercise against another troop—you had food. You were divided into teams. You'd maybe be against the French Canadians or a regiment or whatever. They'd be holdin' a position. You would need to attack it—general military sort of tactics.

But there was an occasion when two of you—men in pairs—were sent out to the mountains to live off the land for a couple of days. You had a couple of fish hooks, about three matches—and a block of emergency ration chocolate which you were supposed to bring back: you lost points for your team if you didn't. And you were supposed to live off the land. It was O.K. for guys like the Lovat Scouts and people that were stalkers and that kind of thing. They could snare a rabbit. They could guddle trout.[233] Us town boys—we had no chance! I don't remember catching any food. But it happened more than once somebody cut up a sheep. In desperation they killed a sheep and obviously they didn't get rid of the remains! And the local land-owners and farmers and what not were a bit put out, of course. I wasn't involved in any sheep-stealing. I cannae remember what I lived off o', I was completely ignorant of how tae set a snare.

I think I went hungry actually. Oh, God, and that was always my problem when I was in the Forces: I was always hungry! My mate was the same as myself. He wisnae up tae it either. It was hard goin'. But I'm sure we went into a cottage or some place and got something to eat. We couldn't have gone two days without eating—well, we could have if we had to. But I think we chapped at somebody's door. I don't suppose that was allowed either. The course was quite a hard, demanding one, it was, it really was.

We got special weapons trainin'. Fightin' wi' knives, unarmed combat, fightin' a man with a knife and you've got no weapon, disarming a boy with a knife, and coming up behind a sentry wi' a garotte and garotting. The garotte was wire. You could actually sever the head. It was just a cheese wire with two wooden handles. And there was a way you looped it—and then did that. The other way of doin' a sentry if he's got a chinstrap—the Japanese used to wear chinstraps, and as far as I hear the Germans did, too—come up behind and make sure it's not on his chin, flick the strap down, grap the front o' it and pull: and his own chinstrap should strangle him, you know. You became very enthusiastic about this kind of weapon because it was practice. But always at the back of your mind there was: 'I'm goin' to have to do this for real one day.' But I was fairly enthusiastic on all this stuff. It seems blood-thirsty now. But it didn't worry me at the time.

And then there was this element that you were something special. They instilled this into you right away, that you are going to be an elite force of men. You were going to be something different from the ordinary soldier. Half way through the course I could have quit, I could have failed. I felt it was too hard. And I felt the instructors were brutal. I felt they were goading you on all the time. They were driving you too hard. 'What am I puttin' up wi' this for? I'm goin' back to my unit. I'm no' havin' this.' But then something started to come up inside you: 'I'm going to do this.' Your attitude seemed to change, it was probably gradually. You started to say 'our' instead of 'me'. You started to say to your group, 'Our group's goin' to beat these bastards.' It became competitive then. And this was engendered. And after a hard day's trainin'—it got so ridiculous near the end—you would go out and challenge the next hut—'First round the battle courses!' That was crawlin' under the wire and runnin' across slippery logs and all that sort of thing—for a pint! Six against six, you know. And this was voluntary! I think the instructors pretended to turn a blind eye to this. But it was goin' on and this must have been satisfactory to them. They knew they were succeeding then and they'd got something inside of you that wanted to do this.

A large proportion of men at Achnacarry were returned to unit. They were gettin' failed all the way through on certain things. Some just couldn't do it physically, couldn't do it mentally, couldn't cope with what they were asked to do—and RTUd: Returned to Unit. The guys couldn't get away quick enough when they realised they werenae goin' to make it. And there were no comebacks, there were no second chances. You either failed or you didn't. A great day of course was when you take your blue Marine beret off and threw it away and you proudly put the green beret on.

We didn't at that time have a special cap badge. Later on there was a special commando badge. It was a dagger actually. But at that time there was army guys, there was Marines, there was all sorts. You wore your own regimental cap badge. The Marine badge is the western hemisphere—half the world, surmounted by a laurel wreath, and there's a crown on top of the world.

So the Marines were formed into a commando. A commando is a unit, a company, about 120 or 150 men. A commando is divided into troops: A, B, C, D Troop and Y Troop, which is, I think, signals or heavy weapons. Anyway I was in A Troop, which is a fightin' troop. We all wore the same cap badge bein' Marines. But it was strange to see in these days an army commando troop. You'd have them all with green berets on, but all with different cap badges. You'd see a Black Watch with the Red Hackle; and you'd see a Seaforth Highlander with the stag's head. You'd see all the different cap badges. And it looked strange. But they all had green berets.

The commando uniform was just khaki battledress. On commando weapons the one that springs immediately to mind is the commando fightin' dagger, which was a double edged type stabbing instrument, with a blade about eight inches, a black ebonite handle and a normal hilt. Nothing fancy about it, quite a plain but a deadly weapon. It wasn't an issue to the ordinary army or navy. Special services were issued with it and we were issued. Then guns: we were trained on every weapon—rifles, bren and sten guns. At different times it was interchangeable but mostly I used a tommy gun—a Thompson sub-machine gun—which was the old gangster weapon of the 1920s or '30s, I think. A tommy gun fired a .45 slug bullet. It's heavy. It's heavy to carry—that's the point I'm thinking about! A .303 was the standard rifle bullet. So you carried this .45. It was shorter than a rifle bullet. It was a stubby sort of thing. That was the ammunition for the Thompson gun. You also carried a pistol which fired the same ammunition. The one I had was a Colt Browning automatic pistol. It held six bullets at a time. Your tommy gun: sometimes you had a drum under it, and sometimes it was a stalk like a bren gun's. I think they held twenty or twenty-four bullets. Sometimes it had the old gangster's type of drum thing round about it. Generally speaking towards the end of the war it was always these stalk ones, because they were easier stacked in your ammunition pouches. It went underneath the tommy gun, in front of your trigger. It had a very short range. It was a spraying weapon.

The accurate weapons were Garrand rifles. The snipers had them. It was an American rifle. The good thing about a Garrand was you could dismantle it in seconds, shove it into a waterproof bag and go across water with it. It had a long range of course and also you could fix an 18-inch bayonet to it. It was a semi-automatic weapon in that there was no bolt action. With the Lee Enfield rifle every shot you fired you had to eject the cartridges physically and put a round up the spout again with the bolt. Every round you fired you were doin' this. But with the Garrand you just pressed the trigger. Then the Lee Enfield held five rounds. You could put five in your clip and you could stick one up the spout first, so you could actually put six in. But that would mean taking the sixth out a clip because they came in clips. But the Garrand had eight it fired. And the beauty of it when it fired was it was a dispensable clip that jumped out. So you were aware when your weapon was empty. With the Lee Enfield you had to count. It could be dodgy obviously. With the Garrand your clip jumped out—in with another one right away and you were in action again. And you had no bolt action. So a troop of guys with Garrands could put up a fair volume of fire, as against a troop with Lee Enfields. We carried Lee Enfields for a while.

The snipers with Garrands had a telescopic sight. I wasn't a sniper. We had snipers with us, trained. The best shots were generally picked out as snipers. Not a pleasant job being a sniper, I must admit.

Then everybody carried a rope. It was only about a yard long. But that was for climbin' or puttin' together. It was a short rope—obviously, you cannae carry big coils o' rope wi' all your other gear. But every rope had a loop on one end and a wooden handle toggle at the other. And by lacing all them together—very quickly, puttin' the wood through the loop and just a turn—you could form a rope for pullin' stuff. You could then specialise in weapons. Some guys after a while they were carryin' the garotte. Some guys picked up weapons in different situations and preferred to use them. The only problem there was it would need to suit the ammunition that they were issued wi'.

You had a specific job and a specific weapon that you had to use. Anything else would be an extra. You were allowed to carry extra weapons if you wanted to. But it wasnae a practical thing. There was not a lot o' guys did it because your biggest problem operatin' in jungle country or any hot country—or any country, in fact—is weight. Once you come off a landing craft and hit a coast line you obviously have no transport. Wherever you are going you are going to have to walk. So the crucial thing is to take bare essentials. And if the choice is food or ammunition you throw away the food! Your weight has got to be distributed in order of importance: ammunition first, water, food.

From Achnacarry we went to Wales, a place called Towyn in Wales. Now this was a place where they were goin' to form a commando brigade, as far I can make

228

out. They werenae getting whole brigades comin' through the trainin' process at one time. They were comin' through in small numbers, relatively small numbers. We were in Towyn quite a while, waitin' for the strength to be made up.

They just kept us fit. They gave us quite a lot of sports—football and what not. The trainin' was nowhere like Achnacarry, of course. We got a wee bit time off, actually we got a wee bit leave. We got runs into places—Aberystwyth, I think. I'm not sure. Anyway we did that and we had the usual route marches but no speed marchin' or anything like that. We organised a couple of boxing events.

Once you got into the commandos all the sort of barrack room and parade ground bull disappeared. Salutin' officers was at a minimum, too. You only did that very seldom. You got parades and inspections but to nothing like the same extent. There was no spit and polish. You had to look after your boots—I don't mean to polish them: dubbin. You never could get a polish on them anyway. Your boots were dubbined. Your webbing was black so there was no blanco used. The cap badge was to be green verdigris! Your brasses on your equipment were painted black or green. So you had no polishin' to do. And you didn't have to spend hours pressing your trousers and that sort of thing.

The emphasis was on fitness, ability to use your weapons, ability to obey the word of command immediately—that was one of the things they did. They were strict about it, however stupid it might sound. In fact, you did a lot of stupid things. But eventually you understood it was for a reason.

I think when you come through your training period you'd got a wee bit o' pride installed in you. And you really didn't want to do anything to hurt your corps. It's strange, it sounds just a wee bit daft. It was esprit de corps and I never thought I would be capable of havin' that feelin' but you did, you know. So nobody deliberately or wantonly spoiled the image o' their particular troop within what was then a specialist corps. Your own troop that you were in was the most important thing. It was your family really.

When we were at Towyn waiting for a brigade to be formed, that was No. 3 Commando Brigade. Within that Brigade there was four Commandos. There was No. 1 and No. 5 Army Commando. And it was No. 42 and No. 44 Marine Commando. I was in 44 Marine Commando. I was in A Troop of that Commando. And I was a tommy-gunner. I think it was at Towyn that I was promoted corporal. I was carryin' two tapes the first time I went into action anyway.

I was sent to Ringway in Manchester after Towyn. I often wish I had kept a diary. You werenae allowed tae. But there must have been some people kept diaries. And any letters that I saw that were ever sent were so badly censored you couldn't make sense out of them. They were ridiculous. Well, I didnae do a lot of writin' in this country anyway. I didn't write home as much as I should have. I was a pretty bad letter writer. It was a new life you were leadin' and your mind was full of a' sorts of things. I suppose it was neglect in a way.

Anyway at Ringway I just did a normal parachute course—twelve jumps, two from balloons and the rest out o' Dakotas. Havin' done a commando course we sort of took it in our stride really. I'd never been up in the air before, though.

The balloon was the most frightening thing you could ever imagine. You've got to really experience parachute jumpin' tae realise the feelins ye get. You come out of a wee trap in the bottom of the floor of the balloon. You're in a basket, three or four of you, round about this hatch—just an open space—in the bottom of the floor. So you sit on the edge and you just push off and drop drown. You drop like a stone. I don't know what height you're up but it must have been about a thousand feet. Anyway you drop. Everything comes up in your stomach! It's terrifyin', it is. There's a sort of hook thing from the basket in the balloon attached to your parachute. The 'chute opens automatically. And when the 'chute opens you get this terrific jerk in your armpits. The relief when it opens! And then you're floatin' down and then that's great.

It's the same when ye come out o' a plane. There's a line goes right down the fuselage of the plane. You're all hooked on and you slide your hook along as you're going along and as it's your turn to go out—and that's goin' out a side door. You can come out o' the floor o' a plane, too. But comin' out a plane is a dawdle compared tae comin' out a balloon, because you've got this terrific slip stream that catches you. You've no sensation of droppin' at all when you come out a plane. You've got a sensation actually o' swimmin' in air. Ye sometimes tumble head over heels. But you don't go down like that as you do in a basket. And again you don't pull the parachute open yourself. It's hooked on. You have got an emergency that you do yourself but I never used it.

I made two balloon jumps and then I went to planes. The balloon was terrifying. And even instructors hated balloon jumpin'. I never witnessed any accidents. All the lads got down safely. But there was what they called a Roman Candle. That's when the chute doesnae open and it all furls up like an umbrella. The guy comes down like a stone and is smashed to bits. I didn't happen in my experience but I heard about it, I heard about it.

The last jump from planes was a water jump. We jumped into Windermere! I had no problem, I could swim. But there was a guy with me actually couldnae swim. He was terrified. And he was a great guy and he'd passed everything. He wanted, you know, 'Should I tell them, should I not? I can't swim.' We didnae have any swimmin' exercise. We forded rivers but we got pulled across on ropes. It wasn't compulsory to be a swimmer. It seems strange. But he jumped out the plane at Windermere. There wis boats, pick-up boats and he was fortunate. If he had landed a good bit away from them … I don't think anybody ever knew that he couldnae swim except his mates like myself and two or three in his group.

The parachute course at Ringway was only a couple of weeks. It was a crash course! I rather enjoyed it actually. Once you'd done that you were a trained parachutist—on your shoulder you got wings with a parachute. I never jumped again though. We were supposed to have this elite group within our group that if it was called for we could be dropped. Ah wis one o' those. But it was never ever used.

I think it was around this time—either from Towyn or Ringway—that I got my first leave since I'd joined the Marines. I think it was just over a year I'd been away. Generally after a course you got a leave, because courses were pretty demanding.

Goin' home was emotional, it was strange. I'd known by this time my mother was actually operatin' an overhead crane in Redpath Brown's Engineering Company down at Easter Road. My mother! I couldnae believe it. So I had to go and see this, of course. So ah walks in uniform into Redpath Brown through the workshop and: 'There she's up there, son'. And there was my mother up in the roof. I would never have believed it, I would never have believed it. She was copin'. She was quite happy. Och, she must have been then well intae her forties. She'd been married quite young. Well, she waved down to me then she climbed down and had a wee crack wi' me. She was wearing a boiler suit, and a turban round her hair, operatin' this crane. Handlin' tons and tons o' metal, swinging it over these guys' heads. I said, 'I wouldnae work under there!'

My father wis churning out the paint and stuff at Craig & Rose. My sister wasn't a military nurse. She wasn't at nursing for very long anyway. She was never in the armed services. And of course she was married by this time anyway.

On leave I didn't take up wi' my old mates because they were all away. I was home for a fortnight. I jist wandered about. I was out o' ma depth. I didnae know where to go, what to do. I did take a pint even in these early days. But ye couldnae spend a' your time standin' in a pub. So by the time ye went and had your pint at midday and maybe at five o'clock at night again' all ye saw in there were old guys. Your own mates were away. There were maybe one or two guys on leave, the same as yourself. But ye maybe didnae know about them bein' there. I was restless to return before my leave was finished, which seems strange. I think by then my unit had become my home in a sense. I felt closer to the fellows in the unit. Because there's nothin' so intimate as livin' in a barracks, a tent or a hut, or bein' wi' the same guys day and daily, month in, month out, bad times, good times.

After that leave I went to Plymouth Barracks. That was the first time I had been in Plymouth. I had never been in ma home Division. This can happen, of course. Ye can get posted immediately from your trainin' area. Ye sometimes can go years without ever seein' your home barracks. The barracks at Plymouth was huge. It was a big Marine barracks—no naval, completely Marine. The fellows there were Marines, they were a holdin' battalion o' Marines, I believe. But there were a lot o' them wi' white caps, blue uniforms, you know—very smart! They were by no means all commandos. It was just a convenient place to keep us. Plymouth was a port, it was for that reason—that's where we embarked from. There would be about half a brigade o' us: two commandos, that would be 200 or 300 men maybe. A commando brigade was a lot less than an infantry brigade. Commando brigades are specialised units, they don't need the back-up, the amount of men of infantry brigades. Every man is self-sufficient, so it's a much smaller unit—about two or three hundred.

We were on what they call stand-to, waiting for shipping orders really, I think. But the rumours were rife. We were going everywhere bar the Far East. We were going to Europe, we were going to Norway, we were going to North Africa—everywhere. I can't remember exactly when this was; all my army records were lost long after the war. It wasn't the practice then to tell you where you were going because apparently all the naval establishments or naval towns—as far as I've read since—were hotbeds of spies. I didn't know then.

One thing maybe gave us a clue where we were going. On the very last day before we actually embarked we got issued with stupid pith helmets with a silver knob on top of them! I don't think they were white helmets, they were a sort of khaki colour. But they still had the silver knob on the top. And they were relics o' the Boer War, these damn things! But half-way across, maybe after we put into Ceylon—these things were thrown away and we were issued with bush hats. We never got any tropical kit until we reached, I think it was Ceylon. And then when we reached Ceylon we got shorts and stuff like that, khaki drill.

Anyway from Plymouth Barracks we marched down to the docks and went on board the *Empress o' Australia* or the *Winchester Castle*, I cannae remember which it was. It was a P & 0 Line ship, I believe. It was overcrowded. God knows how many troops were on it, but it wisnae jist our unit that was aboard. Och, there were thousands, thousands. We were crammed together, some were sleepin' on decks even. I had a hammock down on the mess deck.

The food wasn't too bad. And we got up for exercise and fresh air. And we did anti-aircraft duties. The ones that had done gunnery courses had to do watches. Everybody got somethin' to do. There was warnings. Goin' through the Mediterranean there wis bits o' panic stations, stand-tos and what nots, and there was attacks by air, though not by submarine.

We went through the Suez Canal but we didn't go through on the ship. We came off at Alexandria or Port Said and we went up the bank. There's a railway runs up the length of the Suez Canal and that's how they transported us to the other end. For some reason that ship turned where it was and went back the way instead o' goin' through the Canal. At Aden we got on another ship, the *Cap Touraine*. It was a French ship. Apparently it had been used for years up and down the Algerian coast wi' Foreign Legionnaires gettin' shipped from one place to another. It was a really ancient ship. It was rustin' tae bits, it was a rust-bucket. It was a coal-burner: everything was layers of coal dust everywhere. You were filthy, a' your gear was manky. It was salt-water showers. Ye had salt water to shave with—ye couldnae shave. Oh, what a life!

We were on the *Cap Touraine* three or four days and that took us to Ceylon. The crew were Lascars. And you could smell the curry all over the place. They were cookin' in their quarters and the place was 'stinkin' o' curry smells. The ship was overcrowded—even more so than the *Empress o' Australia*, even more so. There was almost a mutiny aboard there. The food was filthy. The food was off. It was bad. It was sour. It just about came to a mutiny. I mean, that's the first thing that gets servicemen goin' is no' gettin' their food. That's the one thing that does get them. All servicemen are like that. Oh, there was complaints. It was the first time I've ever seen people shoutin' at officers. It's no' done. Aye, they were shoutin'. Officers would come down with pistols on their belts! It was predominantly commandos on that ship because it was a smaller ship. It must have been mostly commandos. I don't think there was other troops on that ship. It was a much smaller ship than the big *Empress*. The *Empresses* were huge ships.

Well, the *Cap Touraine* sunk at its moorins a couple of days after we got off the damn thing in Ceylon. The bottom fell out o' it or somethin'. It should ha' been in dry dock and scraped and painted years before that. We'd had a lucky escape because it was shark-infested water we were crossin' to Ceylon. It's amazin'! Lookin' back on it, it was rather silly that the authorities had taken all this time and trouble to train us as an elite force and then they put us on this unseaworthy ship, when the whole lot of us might have been killed.

We were put up to a naval airfield in mid-Ceylon somewhere, right up in the jungle. It was just a strip that had been cleared out of virgin territory. There was a few naval aircraft there and we more or less guarded them, just to stop the natives stealing or pilfering. There were some anti-aircraft guns which we did duty on. We manned the guns through the day and at night time, too. I never did any at night but we did patrols at night, just to keep wandering natives away from the aircraft. The aircraft were pegged out in the open so they were vulnerable to anybody. It was a fairly isolated spot. There were small villages in the vicinity. But it was virgin jungle all round about this strip. There was wild elephants and hyenas and all sorts of wild life goin' about. There was an abundance o' snakes all over the place. There was a lot of monkeys and baboons.

I had a funny wee experience. In an off-duty moment I wandered into the jungle just to have a look around at things. And I came across a big family of baboons. I never realised monkeys could be dangerous. But they started to close in on me above in the trees. And they were angry. They were snarlin' and screamin'. I thought, 'I better get out o' this.' I had picked up a stick on the way, an old stick I had found lying, a fairly heavy thing. I thought, 'Well, if they come near me!' But then when I saw the numbers of them I was actually frightened of them. Och, it was a tribe of them. There were maybe twenty or thirty of these baboons. And there was one big fellow, obviously the leader of the clan, and he was gettin' closer and closer. He actually got on to the ground and was jumpin' up and down. He had huge big fangs on him. He was a big grey, furry thing with a black face. He was really a fierce devil this. I'm afraid I beat a hasty retreat. I didn't want to run in case—you know, but I walked pretty smartly away from it. I didn't go any further into this jungle. Well, I was obviously invadin' their territory. And I thought, 'Well, if I do go for another walk through here I'll have a pistol or something, it won't just be a stick.' I wouldn't have stood a chance if those baboons had gone for me.

My impression of the jungle was it was exotic. It was all I had read about as a boy—creepers and these baboons swinging through the trees. I really was in a foreign country and I was quite excited about that. I wasn't fearful of the jungle but totally inexperienced, of course, and I did get a fright with the baboons. My first impression was the jungle was intimidatin'. The trees were huge. You couldn't see. There was only glimmers o' sunlight comin' through. There was a lot of dark sort o' areas and shaded places.

I was two or three months at this airfield in Ceylon. I think the powers that be were waitin' for some operations for us to take part in probably. They've got their own way of movin' bodies o' men about. Sometimes you think you're forgotten about! You get stuck in a place and then all of a sudden you've got marchin' orders and off you go. I actually had a few leaves to Colombo and places like that, weekends and maybe an odd week. I didn't think very much of Colombo. We went to a place called Kandy which was more interestin'. The Temple of the Tooth was up there. The tooth was some Buddhist tooth or something, but it's in a casket there. And the country up there is hill country so the climate was better.

Then there was a holdin' camp of commandos up in a place called Trincomalee which eventually we joined. These people up there sort o' licked the brigade into shape. I don't know if we were reinforcements as such but some of these lads had seen action before anyway. Some o' them told us about their experiences in a general way. They were Marine and army commandos. It was a full brigade, this encampment up at Trincomalee, No. 3 Brigade. We were up there three weeks to a month, as far as I can remember. It's a bit hazy. We had the usual training, some jungle stuff.

They had taken us into the jungle when we were down in mid-Ceylon. The training there was just patrols, how you operate in jungle. You've got your lead man, you've got your tail-end Charlie as you call him—that's the guy at the back— and your patrol and centre. The number of men in a patrol could vary. If it was a reconnaissance patrol it would only be a few men, half a dozen at the most. If it was a fightin' patrol it would be a troop strength, which would be 40 or 50 men. I'm not too sure of the number really, but it was a bigger outfit for obvious reasons. At that time you didn't get taught much about how to live off the jungle, eating things found in the jungle. That became a science later on, as jungle war progressed. The commandos in these days were not so sophisticated in their training methods as later on and they hadn't got into all that. I think it was the war that really engendered all this later training for commandos as we know them now. Probably commando training now is away ahead of what we were. The emphasis on commandos then was to make them fit, strong and ready to accept orders—to do anything they were asked to do. But the emphasis was on fitness. We were the first commandos. A lot of the experience came durin' the war, in various theatres of war. Later training methods would derive from experiences that the initial commandos had. We had a wee bit training in Ceylon in how to use the jungle to our advantage, but not much— not enough, I would think. The training came actually under campaign conditions, under fire.

Well, up at Trincomalee we did a few route marches and things, played a bit o' football and did a wee bit o' boxing, whatever you fancied.

Then from Trincomalee we set off to India. We landed in the very south of India and entrained there and we went right up through the plains of southern India. It was a horrific journey. We were three or four days, I think, in the train—though I wonder if it was ten days? It probably felt like ten days! It was a terrible journey because it was wooden seats. It was purely a troop train but natives have a habit o' jumpin' on any trains and getting' a free lift. They hang on the outside of the thing and get on the roof. They do the same wi' their buses actually. We were all heartily sick of the hard seats and the cramped compartments by the time we got to Calcutta.

We then had intensive lectures on weapon cleaning. We were each issued with about 100 rounds of ammunition, also some special items were added to our equipment. I remember that. A small compass, the size of a florin. Now sometimes they were in the form of a button on your tunic. It was just an emergency thing. They were trying all sorts of wee things out on us, you know, and adding wee bits of equipment here and there, altering your battle order rig that you wore. We had normal army battle rig, which wasnae suitable for jungle warfare. For instance, tin helmets were ridiculous wi' camouflage nettin'. You were in jungle that used tae catch on it. So we generally finished up just wearin' our green berets or a cap comforter, these woollen cap things. And that was it. At one period I had a bush hat. But again in the jungle they're no good if you're crawlin' about. We found berets just about as good as anything, apart from the fact that you're not protected. Most army guys wore tin helmets. We didn't. They tended to rattle a bit. We were a sort o' creepy crawly outfit. We liked to move around silently if possible. Same wi' your weapons—any buckles on your straps were all blackened. I used to wrap rags round— well, most guys wrapped rags round their straps on their weapons, too, or anything that would clink or make a noise. As long as it didn't affect the handling of the weapon you could wrap them up. Silence was really important. And we had wee phials of morphine, of course. I think that was general in the army, too, though I'm no' sure about it. We certainly had them for dealing with your own wounds or somebody else's wounds. If you got any you could have self-administered this. And we had purifying tablets for water. Mepachrine pills to combat malaria. And this cream that was supposed to keep mosquitoes away but which didn't. I used to think it attracted them! Then we got mosquito boots, long-legged boots that laced up to the knees, with your trousers tucked in. At first we had standard army boots but they just fell to bits. The mosquito boots were a help, although the leeches could still get in. It's amazing where a leech can get to. They used to creep in. It depended on where you were. There werenae leeches everywhere you went in Burma. But when you did hit country where there was leeches these damned things always got in at places where you couldn't reach them: under your webbing equipment or in your boots. You used to pour the blood out your boots. Oh, horrible things, aye, terrible.

I would be in Calcutta about a month, I think. I cannae really remember. My impression of India was that it was a smelly, dirty, filthy country, that every second person seemed to be a cripple of some sort. The amount of cripples and beggars was just astounding to us. We'd never seen anything like it. Men, women and kids. A lot of them had elephantiasis and things like that. Disease was rife actually. It really was terrible. I found that quite shocking. I couldnae come to terms with it at all. It used to disgust me that these people should be allowed to get into that state. And don't forget they were under British government. It was part of the British Empire and this was the state of affairs. The living conditions were atrocious. Sanitation was just non-existent in some of the native areas.

We weren't popular. British soldiers just were not popular in India at all. And I think it was due to the fact that the peacetime army in India treated the native population rather badly. Cantonment areas for officers and their wives were notorious in the way they treated their Indian servants and what not. I had personal experience up at Poona one time. We were up there after a landing in Burma. We were put up there to Poona to reinforce, I think. We had lost a lot of casualties. We were up there at Poona and under canvas. Poona's up north, it's in the foothills. And it is Gandhi country and they did not like us one bit. I actually got stoned one night when I went into the nearest village to have a drink with one of my mates. He got under the weather a bit and I was having to assist him back to camp. And we were actually getting stoned on our way out of the village. It was a bit dodgy.[234]

I think my own political awareness, awareness of problems in society, was being aroused by what I saw and experienced in India. We come across old soldiers in different regiments who had been peacetime in India and they were equally as bad as officers. I'm not just blamin' officers. These soldiers treated the natives like rubbish, they really did. For instance, there was one place—I can't remember where it was— but you lay in your bed and the Indian lad came round and shaved you while you were lying in your bed. A soldier doesnae need tae be shaved. He shaves himself. But these soldiers were throwin' them a couple o 'annas, which would be about 2d. or 3d. And these old men, you know, shavin' lads. To me it was all wrong. I couldnae accept it. Other guys took it for granted and that was it. That was the way o' things and that was it. I can understand why they had so much trouble in India. They had risings, didn't they? They had all sorts of rebellions in India. Then again they had Indian troops who were loyal to the crown, as it were. But they were treated so much better for obvious political reasons. The British authorities were usin' Indian troops for policin' the place. But there was a lot of nasty terrible things done to the Indian people.

Then there was the Bengal Famine. I was there at that time. I remember goin' round and pickin' up old people and babies—dead bodies, you know—and takin' them to burial places, goin' round wi' lorries collecting corpses. We should have been goin' round wi' food for them and medical supplies. But there was a war on, I suppose—this was the old story. They cut our rations at that time. This was our contribution. But I mean that was no use because their diet was entirely different from ours. So cuttin' out a couple o' cans o' bully beef from our ration wasnae goin' tae help them. Because a lot o' the sects in India don't eat beef anyway. Other ones don't eat pork. I don't know which ones is which. The cow's holy to the Hindus, I think it is.

Well, the Bengal Famine was a pretty distressing experience for us. Well, we were all young guys. We had never seen anything like it in our lives. We were really shocked. Apparently there was thousands died. I saw dozens and dozens anyway. I had to handle the bodies and carcases—the old and the young. They were the most susceptible, of course.[235]

We didn't really do any special jungle training while we were at Calcutta. We seemed to get an awfy lot o' leave there, local leave. We could wander out into the town and what not. Apparently the area we were in was called Chowringhee and it was notorious. It is well known to most troops that have gone to India. There's a lot o' brothels in the area. And it's a pretty seedy run-down part o' Calcutta. The troops were prohibited from going to the brothels; they were out of bounds. But they went! The Military Police roved around there and if you were caught in there you were for the high jump—well, put on a charge.

Well, we were about a month to six weeks in Calcutta and then we went to Chittagong from there. Chittagong was a place where most troops went to, heading into Burma. It was held by us. But it was a sort of staging post into Burma. Chittagong was heavin' wi' people, all sorts o' people, Regular army guys, you know. It was fairly near the front line with the Japanese. It was a big port, well, big for a Far Eastern port. I think we would be there about a month. We just did the usual route marches and patrol work again. Then from Chittagong we went on our first landing.

I do remember we were lyin' on board the assault ship ready to pull out for the Arakan coast on a landing, and we seemed to be lying in harbour for a few days. Again, I don't know why that was. Maybe final orders or something. There was a lot of things that went on you didn't know about. Very often, very often nobody told you anything until it was actually happening. You wondered what you were doin' or where you were goin' until the very last minute. Then you knew all about it, of course. You can realise the feelings there, loafing about on board a ship tied up in harbour. We knew we were on our way now. This was it.

The ship was just an assault ship. It would probably just have a number on it or an initial. Assault ships were ordinary ships, as far as I could make out. But in place of lifeboats on the davitts there was landing craft. So when you did your landing the ship would drop anchor maybe a mile off-shore, you would get into your landing craft and lower with it, or you would go down scrambling nets into them after they were already in the water. You left the mother ship on the landing craft and headed for the shore.

The landing craft—well, there were some of those kind they called ducks (DUKW), like a barge but wheeled under it, that got you right up on to the beach. But the ones I was in had a ramp in front of them that went down: like the ones that landed on D-Day in Normandy. The ramp came down and you just poured off it. You were usually up to your knees in water. I mean, they could only get in that close. They couldnae get right on to the sands. You usually got wet from landing. The landing craft would hold about thirty men, I would think. Again I'm not sure. And then there was tank landing vehicles. We didn't very often have the tanks. In fact, I only did one landing with tanks.

Now eventually, after lying in harbour a few days we set off for somewhere on the Arakan. Now I can't remember the sequence of landings I was in. It could have been Myebon or Kangaw or Alethangyaw or some of these places. All these names are just a jumble in my head now. But these are places on the Arakan. Kangaw, I was there. I was at Akyab, Buthidaung. Anyway we went from Chittagong on our first landing. I can't remember which beach we hit first. It could have been Akyab or Myebon, round about there. It would be 1944, I think. I couldnae say if it would be the spring or the summer. I never thought about seasons out there, except monsoon seasons and the hot weather. There was just two extremes o' weather, and that was it. I actually passed my 21st birthday in Burma later on, in July 1945, and didn't realise it until days later that I was now 21!

Well, that first landing was assault ships and into landing craft as usual from there, and then ashore. I think that first one was unopposed actually. When we went in we penetrated inland and had a wee bit skirmish here and there—nothing too serious. Oh, ye saw Japanese soldiers, ye saw them and we exchanged fire with them, too. It was a bit hair-raising. That was the first time I had been in action. I remember feeling nervous, aye, very nervous actually. And then some bright spark said: 'Watch out for land mines,' you know, booby traps and all this stuff. You were prancing about like fairies, frightened to put your feet on the ground! It was a terrifying experience. But none of my mates were wounded or killed, not on the initial landing anyway. There was casualties later.

You were in there for quite some time. You seemed to do an awful lot of marching and digging and no contact with the enemy. It's a funny sort of thing, jungle warfare. You go for weeks and weeks and make no contact. Thick country. Burma was hills and jungle and chaungs—rivers. The jungle there was similar to the jungle in Ceylon, except that I would say the hill country in Ceylon is virtually jungle free. It's on the low lying ground that you get jungle. In Burma you get jungle right up to the shoulders of the hills. So you can be climbing up through jungle as well. It's hard goin', it's really hard terrain, by no means flat country. And it was pitted by these rivers, hundreds of rivers all over the place. Everywhere you went you had to cross rivers. There was a heavy rainfall.

I had I think it was a total of two or three landings that were unopposed. We were lucky sometimes. But most of them were opposed. We had one pretty early on and I'm no' sure if it was the first one, but I remember we were told that if our landing was successful we were to force our way inland, attacking and harassing the Japanese at every opportunity.

My experiences of Burma seemed to be digging holes all the time. Every time you stopped you dug a hole. You just didn't stop and lie down. You had to dig a hole. Maybe you were only there for an hour and away again. You had to have some form of protection. I don't know if it was a good idea or not, because there were plenty of trees but trees arenae always good when they start tossin' mortars. The Americans nicknamed these holes foxholes. I don't know where they got that. It was a personal trench. You dug it so that you could get your head down if there was a lot of stuff flying around. Again diggin' holes in Burma was a hit or miss affair because you could hit a big rock and that was you. You couldnae get any further. You only had a small entrenching tool. Roots of trees was another thing. Sometimes ye couldnae get a hole dug, so you just lay as close to the ground as you could. It wisnae a simple matter.

The entrenching tool was army issue. That's part of normal British army equipment. It was a wee shovel thing in a canvas pouch and it's got a wee wooden handle on it. The handle can be used as a club actually! In fact, when you went on regimental police duties you carried an entrenching tool as a truncheon. It was a wee spade wi' a spike on one end and a flat shovel on the other end. It was less than a foot long.

So you can imagine tryin' tae dig a hole wi' a thing like that. And it was back-breakin' work, too. But again it was an essential piece of equipment if your life was to be saved.

The action on this first landing lasted maybe two or three weeks. I think the longest I was ever actually in action without coming back out would be about two month. It was generally only a few weeks. You landed wi' 48-hour ration packs on you. They were called K-rations. They were just cardboard cartons with concentrated meat cubes and a big thing like a porridge oat cube that you ground—smashed up wi' a stone or something—and made a gruel of. A couple o' sweets. And three cigarettes and three matches! I smoked a pipe so I always—even from my trainin' days—I carried maybe about half a pound o' tobacco in an oil silk bag to keep it dry, because we were always gettin' wet. And I carried a really strong heavy pipe and I used that all the time I was out there. Bein' in the Marines I got issued with tobacco. We used to get an issue of either tinned tobacco or you could buy the leaf and roll it into what they called pricks o' tobacco when you had time. You used it when you had time to do that. But eventually I was smokin' Indian tobacco and stuff like that. There was a good Indian tobacco called Coolie Plug. It was a very strong tobacco. And I smoked that. There was a few smoked pipes but most o' them smoked cigarettes there. And then there was an Indian cigarette called Vs—Vs for Victory—and they were pure rubbish. You used to get issued wi' them free and hardly anybody could smoke them, they were that bad. They were terrible.

After that first landing we went back to Chittagong. That was our base really for operations. But sometimes we'd get a leave and we usually got the choice of two or three places in India. We never went on leave anywhere in Burma. There was nowhere really to go. Rangoon was taken by the Japs and other places, too. I went to Madras on one occasion, which was a mistake: it's about the hottest place in India. Oh, it was terribly hot. Bangalore was a great place. That was up in the foothills. It was really civilised up there and you could go horse-ridin' or you could hire a bike and cycle about. And there was dance halls of a sort—ticket dances, where you handed in tickets for a dance. You got a roll of tickets and it was Eurasian women, beautiful women, you danced with. Indian women were very submissive to their husbands. There was no romances or anythin' like that between Indian women and our lads—well, not to my knowledge! The situation didn't—I mean, you weren't liked anyway. Oh, you were lookin' for trouble if you started sniffin' around Indian women.

I don't remember if we were ever actually told by the authorities that friendships or relations with Indian women were prohibited. But we were always warned of course of the usual evil croppin' its head up—the VD situation. It was pretty rife actually among the troops. Oh, quite a lot, particularly in the leave centres. This is because there was prostitutes and they were gettin' used. And it was an offence if you got VD. In the early days there was fellows in my unit that went down with VD, but afterwards, no. Early days there were—the probably naive people, you know. I think the message got home after a few bad cases of gonorrhoea and what not and the horrific tales that these guys came back wi' after they had their treatment! Because in these

239

days it was the old lumbar puncture up the back and apparently that was a horrific experience. It was enough to put you off havin' any ideas in that direction.

But as I say, there was Eurasian women and there was quite a few romances amongst them. It was easier for our fellows to make contact with them. Because usually they spoke perfect English for a start. Most of the Indian people didn't speak English unless they were traders and that, so there was a language barrier there with them. And then Indian people had been treated very badly for generations by the British.

You generally got your leave after an operation. And then if there was nothin' in the offin' for you that obviously the higher-ups had you earmarked for you generally had a fairly good time when you were pulled out o' Burma and into India. Well, there were one occasion we were sent up to Poona, as I said, under canvas and we had a long spell up there. They were enjoyable occasions except for the unfriendliness of the natives. And it was particularly bad up at Poona because they were all Gandhi supporters up there where we were. And Poona had been a cantonment area in peacetime for officers and their families, which didn't enhance our reputations very much either. I mean, the British army was just unpopular in that area and that was it. I didnae personally manage to make any friends with Indian people. Ye were always on the move and ye filled your time wi' other things, such as football and swimming and eating! You tended to be with your mates. And to make your leave half decent there was like Salvation Army hostels. There were snooker tables and there would be a place where white people swam, or like in Bangalore you could hire ponies and go trekkin'. There was a colour bar, whether you were aware of it or not it was there. The swimming pools and other sports facilities were just for the military. The only swimming pools I can remember were attached to hospitals, because most of them were in places where people were recovering from illnesses or wounds or what not. Outside Calcutta there was a place called Beach Candy, and that was a big open air swimming pool. I'm sure there was Indians there. It was so big, it was a huge thing. It was a sort of natural swimming pool but they installed diving boards and steps and things, and that was a great place. There was restaurants at either side of the pool. All you thought about when you come out o' Burma was filling yourself up wi' beer and buyin' a steak or a chicken or something! Food was a priority. Food was the greatest pleasure ye had, I thought, when ye went on leave. Ye could go in and buy a meal—because you had plenty o' money, ye see.

Oh, the pay was ridiculous but there was an accumulation o' your wages that you didn't use when you were in action. Well, you got your tobacco for nothing. You got your tot o' rum every day, if possible, when you were in action. And, as I say, you got your food and everything. You had nothing to pay for, nothing to buy. In action you got your soap and stuff like that. Back in barracks you buy all that but in action you got all that. When you came back you just went into the nearest naval pay office and they would just give you what you asked for. The cost o' livin' was very low, it didn't take a lot o' money.

We were the poorest paid troops in the war, I think, the British troops. I think I had thirty bob a week when I first joined up. And then every year ye got a wee rise.

You got promotion but that was only a few shillins, it was nothing. But I do know this: all the time I fought in Burma I got a shilling a day Japanese campaign money. That's seven bob a week extra for fightin' against Japanese. You got seven bob a week more than guys stationed in India that never saw any action. For every man in the field there's a dozen behind him keepin' him supplied. So you got a shillin' a day more than them! That's all you got, a shillin'. That's what was marked in your book: Japanese campaign money, shillin' a day.

Money wasnae really important, because you always had a sufficiency when you went on leave. It was only when you came back after the war and thought about it: 'My God, all that for a shillin' a day!' But nobody seemed at the time to bother about money. If you didnae have any money your mate would have it or somebody else would have it and they would just give you it. And you would give one another it. Money wasnae really important. You never carried money in the jungle.

I sent my parents an allowance. It was five bob a week or something like that. That was quite a big part of my wages. Well, you see, as a lad all my wages went into the house anyway. But I never saved anything in my life. I spent everything I got my hands on. We never discussed whether any of the other lads had saved anything, we never discussed it. I think they would just spend it as they got it. Of course, you never knew if you were going to be alive from one day to the next. You never thought o' the future. All you thought about was, 'When is this war goin' to finish?' Survivin' for the time bein'. That was it.

As I say, I sent my parents an allowance but I wrote them very desultorily. I wasnae a great letter writer. They wrote me pretty regularly. But you got letters from home in big packs, because it took weeks and weeks. And generally even the letters from home were censored. Sometimes it was just a waste o' time. Accordin' to ma folks, they told me some o' the letters I wrote there was just hardly anything left o' them by the time they got them, censored, pencil through them, you know.

It's so long ago and I never took notes or anything but one landing I clearly remember was when I got behind the turret of a tank. I think that was at Akyab. Well, the story went out later on—after the ones that did get ashore we got grouped together—that the Intelligence people had got it all wrong. It was a colossal error o' judgement. They took the landing craft in when the tide was out. Normally you would land at high tide for obvious reasons: it cuts down the distance o' open beach you've got to cover before you get into the treeline and intae cover o' some sort or get to grips wi' the enemy. So if you've got a big wide open space—the tide's out— you're goin' to have a hell of a big open space to cover. And you're a sittin' duck, you're a target. It's suicidal really. And this is what happened. We landed and the tide was full out. The landing craft got in as far as they could. But lookin' at it—the sand was wet—you'd have thought it was water. But it wasn't. It was just pure mud. We come down the ramps and immediately you were up to your chest in mud. In fact, some guys went right under the mud—the unfortunate buggers in the heavy weapons troop who were carryin' machine guns and mortars, mortar bombs and all the rest of it. And even the rest of us were loaded wi' 60 lbs of weight on us. You can imagine landin' there in mud and strugglin' tae. So this is what happened. They landed at the wrong time. The landin' should have been scheduled for high tide. Their Intelligence wasn't good enough.

It was in daylight. That was another thing. I remember fellows for a time sinking into the mud and disappearing. My sole concern then was to try and get as close in and on to firmer ground. The closer in you got to the beach the firmer it was becoming. And that was the one and only landin' we had tanks. The tanks came in and we were supposed tae come in at the back o' them, using them as cover—go up the beach under the cover of the tanks.

Not a tank got ashore. They all bogged down. There was about a hundred yards I crawled through mud when I came off the landing craft. And I got on to this tank and I lay behind the turret. And there was guys inside it. I could hear them! They lifted the hatch and I was speakin' tae them! But I couldnae get in. It was a smallish tank. There wisnae enough room. So ah says, 'I'll be O.K. lyin' here.' Well, I was— except that the sun was up and I was gettin' roasted alive lyin' on the metal tank. I just had to keep slippin' off and gettin' mud on myself tae sort o' keep the sun off me.

I lost my weapon, my tommy-gun. I was left wi' a pistol. That was in the holster on my leg. But I lost my tommy-gun. I lost my hand grenades, because they were bogging me under. I actually had to throw them away when I was half swimmin' and half crawlin' through the mud until I got on to this tank.

And there was bullets panging off the top o' the turret o' the tank. I was under fire into the bargain! I was quite safe lyin' behind the turret, mind you, but I could have got a ricochet, I suppose. That would have been really bad luck.

The tank had sunk so far then it stopped. It must have hit bedrock or somethin'. I don't know. The top part o' the tank, which I was lyin' on, and the turret were above the water. The tracks and everything were under. They were out o' action, they were out o' action completely.

I would be on that tank a couple of hours. Well, the sun was actually goin' down. It was waning but it was still very hot. The tide was then coming in. I gave the lads in the tank a shout and banged on the tank. I said, 'I'm off.' The lads in the tank were Sikhs actually. They were Sikhs drivin' the tank. Well, they would be Indian Army guys. They had turbans, they had green turbans. I don't know if they got out of the tank. It was every man for himself. So you just sort o' did your own thing. They would.

So I sort of used the water, half swam, half crawled. And the further I got the firmer under foot it became. And eventually I got ashore. I was pretty tired, pretty exhausted. The mud was filthy, stinkin', smelly stuff. It was mangrove swamp,' ye see. Mangrove's hellish stinkin' stuff. It's a' rotten vegetation under a mangrove swamp. It's smelly, terrible.

It was actually dusk when I finally got ashore. I'd lost my main weapon, my tommy-gun, and lost my grenades. And I didn't know where to go. There was a bit of confusion. I had lost my particular unit, my particular troop. Some o' them had got ashore. See, landing craft usually come in in two waves. The second wave got the worst of it because all the mud was churned up by this time. A lot o' them did get ashore and somebody very quickly whistled up Navy MTB boats and they blasted the shore line and the Japs actually pulled out. So in the initial landin' we were under heavy fire and then, when the MTBs opened up, they were firin' over our heads into the treeline.[236] The Japanese pulled back and the guys that could get ashore got ashore unscathed like. There had been casualties before that. Terrible, terrible the initial landing. It was just a shambles. Och, it was awful.

And that was due to bad Intelligence. It was obvious there was no way you could get ashore at low tide and it should have been at high tide. We didn't do the reconnaissance that was carried out before the landing. It was a separate Intelligence unit probably. The Special Boat Service probably would do that. Someties you did land without some sort of reconnaissance beforehand. But I mean that's elementary stuff. The landing conditions should have been well noted. There was no way they should have landed half a brigade o' commandos in conditions like that. I mean, it was just throwin' men away. Possibly it could be an error of judgement, a navigational error, or a map reading error, or something. Well, I can't explain. Nobody explained it to us at the time. They just put it down to bad Intelligence. And that was it.

Anyway, when I did get ashore there was a stockpile of weapons and I took a weapon. I think it was a rifle I got, and some ammunition for it. And I was told that my particular unit was up a track. And before I set off they says, 'It's about a mile up that track. And you'll make contact with your troop leader and what there is of your troop up there. Watch how you go: there might be booby traps.' So I'm on my own! So I tripped the light fantastic up this track, watchin' every step I'm takin'. And fortunately I got there and it was O.K. I reported myself to the officer and it was the usual, 'Right. Dig in.' No sooner had I got the damn hole dug than we were on the move again: 'Right. We're movin' out.' We didn't know where we were goin' but we moved out. That was my experience all the time—diggin' holes. I had blisters on my hands!

Casualty rates were very high in these landings sometimes, they were, generally speaking. Twenty-five per cent was allowed for, accordin' to what we heard. That might be an exaggeration or barrack room talk. But this is what was said. I don't know where the figures come from. It might have been in the imagination o' the troops. But sometimes it would be more than 25 per cent. I think it was the landing with the tanks the casualty rate was about 40 per cent. That was pretty heavy casualties there. The initial landing was a bad one, as I say, wi' the conditions o' landing.

In jungle warfare sometimes you didn't see the enemy you were firin' at. Sometimes it was a movement in the bushes you fired at. Sometimes you did see them. Generally speaking, you were firing at shapes. And in night attacks it was just black shapes and dark shapes you were shootin' at. And you didn't know who you had killed or who you hadn't killed. On some occasions you did.

I remember a bizarre experience I had. It wis patrols, it wis two patrols. We just came head on to one another. You see, in the jungle you have clearings, wee clearings. We broke cover about the same time as these Japs. They actually had their arms shouldered. We were at the trail—I had a tommy-gun about here at my waist. And that was it. It was totally unexpected. The Japanese officer at the head o' their patrol was marchin' as though he was on parade with his sword at the present, I think. He had it drawn and was holding it upright. He was probably usin' it for leading his men on or directin' them where he wanted them tae go. But the Japs round about him had their arms actually slung. They broke cover at the same time we did. I blasted away right away. I got the officer through the middle. I near halved him in two. And I probably got the two guys at the side o' him. By this time our bren gunners and riflemen are takin' action as usual—down, and it was all over in seconds. We caught the lot of them. We got the lot of them. By the time they got their rifles off we were in action and firing at them.

The Japs thought they were invincible. But it maybe seems odd that officer was carrying his sword in the jungle. The reason was they could chop their way. A sword wouldn't be a useless thing altogether, though not much good for hand to hand fighting unless the officer could creep up quietly and use it! They used their swords as machetes, to hack their way through the jungle. We had machetes. Some of the country was pretty thick stuff. Sometimes it was a hackin' job gettin' through it.

But sometimes the Japanese officers would use their swords for fightin'. The Japanese philosophy of fighting is to get close enough to look your opponent in his face while you're killing him. This is apparently something the Japanese prefer to do. An officer if he was from a Samurai family—which they all weren't—but if he was from a Samurai family and that sword was handed down it would be a great honour for him to kill his country's enemies with that sword.

Well, I got that sword of that Jap officer I killed. I got it as a trophy. He wasn't the first man I was aware of killing. I had shot at people before and I was sure I had killed them. As I say, whether you were on the move or dug in' the next morning it was a case of clearin' bodies. We used to clear the Japanese bodies and if they were in a pretty bad way we used to roll them into the nearest river—chaung—and let the chaung carry them away. We buried our own men if we could. If there were some support troops coming up we left them to bury the bodies. We laid them as nicely as we could and covered them with their ground sheets. But the Japanese dead we treated like meat, I'm afraid. I've had the job of puttin' ma toggle rope round their ankles and draggin' them to the nearest river and then kickin' them in. That was because you darenae leave dead bodies lyin' about in that climate. Within hours the flies would be swarmin' all over the place and this would carry dysentery and disease. For hygenic purposes the problem was to get rid of bodies as quickly as possible. It wasn't to cover traces of fightin': the traces would be there anyway.

Malaria was rife. In all units operatin' in Burma malaria took its toll as much I would say as even weapons. I would think so. Malaria is a dreadful thing. So you got malaria and you got a thing called dingy or dinghi fever. It was similar to malaria, it was obviously a fever. Ye got lightheaded, dizzy, weak, sweating. But malaria was the worst, I would think. I had a touch o' dingy, not too bad. But I had malaria which didn't come out on me later on till we got to China after the war was finished, funnily enough. And ah went down in China with it. I jist dropped one night on guard duty. I just collapsed.

There was malaria and dingy and then there was smaller things. There were certain types o' scrub bushes, thorny bushes, if it pricked through your trousers or got you on the legs or anywhere within hours you had a big scab or a big ringworm. It was a sort o' ringworm, sort o' ulcerated legs you got with this. That was called scrub typhus. Everybody had that. That was a common thing. Ye jist wrapped field dressins round it. It didn't prevent you from marchin' but it was damned irritatin' and sometimes a bit painful. It would get raw, you know.

Crossin' any water at all you were almost certain to get leeches about your body somewhere. And if it was wet, sort o' marshy ground you were on for any length o' time the leeches could actually get in the eyeholes o' your boots. They were very small leeches. But then once they got in they started sucking and they jist expanded, they jist enlarged. They got filled up with your blood and then they burst. And then again if the head's left in your flesh that would go septic in a matter o' hours. And you would have a big nasty ulcerated sore on your leg where the leech's head was buried. The best way to get rid o' leeches—ye cannae pull them off, ye just pull the body away frae the head and the head's left embedded in your flesh—so the best thing was to get a cigarette and touch the leech with the cigarette and the whole thing curled up and dropped off clean. It's startin' tae swell up by that time anyway. I mean, the body would be stickin' out your flesh. If ye touched it wi' the fag end, the lit cigarette, it would drop off. But the damned things used tae get down your back where ye couldnae reach—down behind your collar and in the back o' your pack that ye were carryin', or in your belt, at your waist.

Leeches were terrible, they were horrible things. Ye got big ones and small ones, but they were black in colour as I remember, a dirty grey colour, a dirty muddy colour. You wouldnae sleep in a wet place if you could avoid it. I've actually slept up trees tae get away frae leeches! We spent a night in a mangrove swamp and we all slept in trees like bats! You put away your webbin' equipment or hooked yourself on' tae the tree wi' your webbin' some way so you wouldnae fall out. It is amazin' where you can sleep when you're really tired. If you've gone a couple of nights without much sleep you'll virtually sleep anywhere and in any conditions.

Oh, I've often felt despair at the horrors of the jungle! Oh, aye, I've lain in situations where I says, 'I'm never going tae see home again. Ah'm never goin' tae get out o' this God-forsaken place. Ah'm goin' tae die here.' I remember one time we were cut off on a hill one night and the Japanese were comin' up in droves, just literally droves. They reckon there was a whole division against us, all round about us, and we were cut off. And we were fightin' at half brigade strength because the other half o' the brigade was in another area. And actually they came in at dawn and gave us a hand out and the Japanese pulled out, because they were attacking a hill on which we were dug in. And it's suicidal. Even the Japanese had to withdraw on that occasion. Sometimes they appeared to be foolhardy. But, I mean, they did have a certain amount o' military dexterity. They weren't fools altogether. They were good jungle fighters. But some o' the moves they made did seem to be crazy, suicidal, you know. They didn't seem to know how to spread out. We were taught: 'Coming off landing craft, spread out right away. Don't bunch.' If a guy's got a machine-gun he's goin' tae get six o' yeez, ye know. If ye're spread out, he's goin' tae get one o' yeez.

I mean, it's common sense actually. But the Japanese ... They used always to attack in strength, the Japanese. You know, there was always hundreds of them against dozens o' us. We always seemed to be outnumbered! The Japanese had snipers. We had snipers, too. Our snipers went out after the Japanese snipers. We had specialist guys wi' telescopic sights. Ye heard a shot maybe up in front or behind you, and that was it. The story was that the leadin' scout wasnae the most dangerous job, as you would think it was. The sniper used to let him go past, because then he was lookin' for an officer in the main body o' the patrol that was advancin' through the jungle. He would let the scout go. The sniper's up his tree there. He'd maybe been up there for days. He's lookin' for the officer. But officers didn't carry insignia as such. We wore what you call jungle green. It's a blouse and trousers, mosquito boots up to your knees, and your equipment. The rank wasn't metal or cloth pips, it was done with a blue indelible pencil. You had to be a yard off the man to see he was an officer. And that was so he couldnae be picked out at a distance and shot. You knew who your officer was anyway, you knew him. So it didnae matter even if he had no insignia. But bein' military people they had to have some sign o' rank up. And he would jist have his pips drawn on his jungle green shirt. The same wi' your stripes. If you had any you just had them on until the next time you went on leave, and then you changed from jungle green to khaki drill wi' your medal ribbons and badges, commando flashes and everything. You went all dressed up. But in the jungle all your brasses and whatnot was all painted black or green, dark green, olive green. Your webbin' actually was black.

The Japanese were fanatical soldiers. They were good soldiers. I make the record clear here. They were excellent jungle fighters. They were really good soldiers. I thought they were all madmen at that time. I didnae understand the philosophy of the Japanese. But I've read quite a bit about Japanese since then. It was a total disgrace for a Japanese to be taken prisoner. When he takes his oath that as a fightin' man for the Japanese Imperial Army he's devotin' his life to that cause it's an honour for the Japanese to die for his country. Wi' us it wis lookin' after Number One, I'm afraid! But the whole Japanese philosophy is entirely different from Western think-ing. Well, the Kamikaze pilot is a particular thing—I mean, these were suicidal guys that just crashed their planes into battleships. And by and large that—as far as I could make out—that went throughout the Japanese army as a whole. They all had this Die for the Country thing on their minds. They were taken prisoner but only at the end of the war, as far as we were concerned. We couldn't come to terms wi' their attitude. You knew when you were goin' in against Japanese you were goin' up against a fanatical race of people who thought nothin' of dyin'. It was a bit frightenin'. When ye come up against people like that it's a bit of a frightenin' prospect to think, 'This guy'll go tae any lengths tae kill ye.'

The commandos didn't have a rule as such that they didn't take prisoners among the Japanese. But we couldn't look after prisoners. We were a fast movin' outfit and we were small compared to army units. We hadnae the facilities for cartin' prisoners along wi' us. I mean, we didn't dig intae a position. We were mobile. Army guys used to go and stick in one place all the time. Any ground that had been taken the army would settle in there, build their.defences and hold on to that. So they could handle prisoners. We couldn't. We were on the move all the time. You cannae lift prisoners along with you. You've got the job of feedin' them and guardin' them. You just can't do that. So we never took any prisoners. There was no instruction about what to do with prisoners. We never took any. A quick bullet was the story there. It happened. I was aware of it. I didn't do it myself. But I heard some of the other lads in the close vicinity. On the other hand, you were doin' them a kindness, because you would be movin' on and leavin' them lyin' there severely wounded, you know.

The philsophy in the jungle was kill or be killed. That was about it. Well, we were told on no account to surrender to the Japanese, because commandos by this time had a reputation ... Actually, Japanese wouldn't take aviators prisoners and they wouldn't take commandos prisoners. It was a beheadin' job right away. You were beheaded on the spot. I knew that and we were told that. Therefore you didn't surrender to Japanese. I don't know any instance in that theatre o' war o' commandos bein' taken prisoner, which meant they must have fought to the last wherever they were or whatever situation they were in. As a matter of fact, there's not many records of commandos havin' been taken prisoner anywhere, even in Europe, as far as I know. When I got back to barracks after the war and spoke to commandos from the European theatre o' war comin' in for demob, there was never ever mention of anybody we knew—I mean, guys that joined up wi' me that went to Europe when I went to the Far East—havin' been taken prisoner. And in our case in Burma the reasons were obvious: we were goin' tae be beheaded. We weren't given any specific instructions by our officers. We were just told, 'Don't be taken prisoner'. We didn't carry a poison tablet, no, no, no. Nothing like that. We made damn sure you werenae goin' tae be taken prisoner! And if you were goin' tae go down you were goin' tae take as many with you as you could.

I remember a position bein' overrun and a young guy about my own age, 19 or 20 or whatever he was, actually lying under dead bodies. The Japanese had pushed us back a bit and this lad actually had Japanese virtually kneeling on top of him firin' at the rest o' our company. And he lay under there frightened tae move. And then eventually we counter-attacked, pushed them back. And that guy was just away, away wi' the fairies. He was ravin'. The experience was too much for him. He was a lad in my unit. We didnae see him after that for about a year. He must have been hospitalised in India or Ceylon. And he was actually grey-haired. He was a dark-haired kid when it happened and he was grey-haired when we saw him again. The funny thing was his parents were British origin but they had worked all their life in the Argentine. His people were wealthy. They had a ranch in the Argentine, rearin' beef. His father took his family back to England and joined up. And then when the lad became military age he joined up in England. He survived the war as far as I know.

Bein' in the Burma campaign was a bit of a nightmare really when I think about it. It was a nightmare situation all the time. It's hard to describe what bein' in action is like. You don't feel brave anyway, that's one thing I do know about. I don't know anybody who felt brave. Some people looked as though they were brave wi' some o' the things they were doing. I think a lot o' these things were more desperation than bravery. The instinct to survive—I think that's all it was. There's nobody could convince me that they went in there and had no qualms, no fears, and relished what they were doin'. You would need to be wantin' in ... there would need to be something wrong—although there was one young officer in my unit who appeared to be fearless. He was my particular troop officer. He was only a lieutenant o' Marines, a young guy. He wasnae long out o' university apparently, and had gone through OCTU training as a Marine officer.[237] That guy would appear to me to be fearless. And yet, thinkin' about it, he must have had some feelings. He was an intelligent man and he couldnae jist have been disregardless of his own safety.

He was a big tall lad, he was over six feet, slimly built. He looked like a boy, a big overgrown schoolboy. And he stood wi' a tommy-gun and all that wis covered was his knees. The hole that he had dug for himself was totally inadequate for the size o' him. And we were under attack and he stood up and blasted away most o' the night wi' his tommy-gun. It was foolhardy. Everybody was keepin' their heads down as low as possible. And he was actually standing up and lookin' round about him, lookin' for targets and blastin' away when he thought he saw something. It wasnae in panic. He was doin' it quite deliberately and coolly. And the next morning he was cheery. Maybe he got the feelin' that he was untouchable. It can happen, I suppose, in certain circumstances. He survived the war. He never got a scratch.

The horrors of warfare—well, I remember the usual serious wounding cases: legs off, and so on; and the dead: heads blown off, bullet in the heart even, just lying there dead with no visible wounds on them. Bodies lying about, both ours and the Japs'. With the badly wounded fellows, well, where possible if you had back-up—you see, when we went in what ground we took another unit came in and held. And then Ghurkas brought up supplies and stuff. And we had medical officers with us, of course. But if they were so badly wounded they needed real hospital treatment—amputations, things like that—well, they were got out some way or another. They were evacuated wherever possible.

There was one thing we were on. We were going in as a second wave attacking a hill and there had been, I think it was an army commando went in in front of us, and this was a really bad experience. We were lyin' at the side of a track under cover and stretchers were comin' down this track with badly wounded men. I'm talkin' about bad, I'm talkin' about blood dripping out the bottom o' the stretchers, you know, and guys lyin' moanin' and guys wi' arms off and getting carried down past where we were waitin' tae go in where these lads had come from. And that was one of the worst experiences I had, lookin' at the wounded passin' a few yards away from us. It wis awful. It wis terrible. They were gettin' carried back to probably a base hospital or something. I don't know where they were takin' them but they were gettin' them out. They were badly wounded people, badly wounded.

I was lucky myself. I only got a slight fall-out from a mortar. I only got one or two bits o' shrapnel in ma back and they were picked out—surface wounds, more or less. I've no' even got a scar, no' even got a scar. I never got out of action with it even. I just got some field dressins slapped on it! I had to lie on my belly for a couple o' nights and that was it. I was lucky: that same mortar killed a couple o' guys and pretty badly wounded somebody else. There were quite a few others like me but lookin' back it was a lot o' luck, a lot o' luck.

We came across a few villages here and there in Burma. I think the Burmese people came and went with whoever was in their territory or whoever held that part of the country. They didn't want to fight with anyone. I just don't think they were pro-Allied or pro-Japanese. They were peaceful people.They were just villagers. They had a few cattle, chickens, and if they were lucky a wee rice paddy or somethin' tae exist on. They jist lived a bare existence and reaped their living out o' the jungle. I think they would spy for the Japanese. But equally they would spy for us. It was a case of who was in the area at the time, I think that's what it was. They were just people that were terrified because here their whole existence was being turned topsy-turvy wi' two big armies fightin' one another. And it must have been a terrible time for them. Generally ye tried—the Japanese and us—tae trade with them. Ye'd give them tobacco for a few eggs or a chicken or whatever. They didn't have an awful lot anyway. Or you'd maybe get some rice off them or somethin' like that. But you generally tried to give them somethin' in return—cigarettes or that kind o' stuff. Chocolate was our emergency ration so you wouldn't give them that. But you would give them maybe some o' your rations if you had enough. We didn't have an awful lot ourselves unless you were on manoeuvre. Tobacco was the thing that ye could barter with.

You couldn't trust the villagers, you couldn't trust them. Well, it made sense not to trust them, let's say that. Probably some of them were trustworthy enough. But you just couldn't take the risk. There was no way you could control what they were goin' to do when you moved on. They could send somebody away to the Japanese—maybe they'd been dealin' wi' Japanese before you came in contact with them. There was what they called Jiffs—anybody that you did think were Japanese col-laborators. I'm no' sure how you spell Jiffs, I just heard it spoken, I've never seen it written anywhere. These were Burmese who were reputed to have dealins with the Japanese. And we—my unit—actually shot some o' them in the field. I shot over their head. I wouldnae have any o' that. But they were shot anyway. And that was on the orders o' our commander in the field. We had interpreters talkin' to them and the interpreters were convinced that they had had dealins wi' the Japanese. That was enough for our boss: 'A Troop, firin' squad. Shoot them.' There were six Jiffs. That happened only once in my experience but it did go on elsewhere. I've heard stories about it.

There were people up in the Chin Hills. They were bigger than the normal Burmese. They were fine lookin' guys, the men, and they were lovely lookin' women. They were pro-British. It was the Chin Hills anyway we were operatin' in, and I'm no' sure exactly where the Chin Hills were. I don't know which tribe was which. You see, there were only fleetin' moments or a couple of days maybe when you ran across them, and you didn't get to know them. And there was the language barrier. It was all sign language and it was exchangin', you know.

I didn't come across any cases o' maltreatment of Burmese civilians by the Japanese. But it must have gone on, it must have. The Japanese were ruthless people. But as I say, we didnae see an awful lot o' the Burmese people anyway. We were on the move most o' the time and sometimes you would be a few days dug in in a place, or restin' near a river, wi' sentries out, and ye'd maybe use that as a wee spot to have a breather or maybe waitin' for orders comin' through.

We did come across atrocities by the Japanese, a couple o' times actually. One time it was people hangin' from trees. I think they were stretcher bearers. But the other ones were definitely stretcher bearers. They were pegged out first in this paddy field and then the Japanese had gone to work on them wi' the bayonet. They had been bayoneted and clubbed to death. They would be Indian Army stretcher bearers, in uniform but non-combatants with Red Crosses on their arms—quite obviously medical people. They had been bayoneted and their faces smashed in wi' rifle butts obviously. They were Indians. The Japanese wouldnae want them to be givin' treatment to wounded that could still possibly fight. I mean the Japanese were completely warlike people. And there was no way they were goin' to let these people run around giving aid to wounded that could come back into combat. I would imagine that's why they did it.

The war came to an end with the dropping of the atomic bombs on Japan. We didn't know at the time it had happened. We'd been on leave. We were recalled to do another job. We were to do a landing on Penang, off from the Malaysian coast. It's all built up now, it's all skyscrapers now, but at that time it was pure mangrove swamp and it was goin' to be a bad one. We were goin' to land there. And we had memories of landin' in mangrove. They were bad beaches. Anyway it was goin' to be one o' the worst landins ever we done, I would think. But the bombs had been dropped on Hiroshima and Nagasaki.[238] We were lyin' on board ship. We were actually aboard the assault ships, the mother ships, wi' all the usual landing craft on board, and we were all armed to the teeth. The balloon went up. The Japanese surrendered. But we still pulled out to sea. And apparently we were sailin' in circles. It was jist the brigadier in charge of the whole outfit—I think it was two assault ships—he was waitin' on orders. Nobody knew what was happenin'. When a country surrenders to another country the war jist doesnae stop like that. For instance, there's commanders away maybe in the country, or troops in areas where they've not got the news that it's finished: they're still fightin' on. The war's finished and they don't know: this happened actually.

So we had the news that the war was over, the Japanese had surrendered. And we actually thought, 'Oh, we'll be goin' home, that's the war finished.' So we sailed in circles on the assault ships but the brigadier was awaitin' on his orders. And then it came over the tannoy system: 'Sorry, lads, we're not for Blighty,' he says—he was an old time soldier, this brigadier. 'We're not for Blighty. We're not goin' home yet. Another wee job to do. A wee bit police work in Hong Kong, China.' Oh, the moans and the groans! You know, we'd all been out there quite a while.

So off we went to Hong Kong, took up police duties and looked after the place. We took over. The Japanese had an awful lot of prisoners in Hong Kong—Royal

Scots, who had garrisoned Hong Kong, they were taken right early on in the war. They'd been in the cages for two or three years. Then government officials, Hong Kong police—people like that who had all been in prison for years wi' the Japanese. And they were in a mess. The government people—civilians—funnily enough, weren't too bad health wise. But the servicemen and the Hong Kong police guys were livin' skeletons, somethin' like what the Belsen people must have been like. I saw them. We went in and took over, organised the Japanese into working parties and cleared up whatever had to be cleared up.

The Japanese liberated those prisoners themselves. Actually, the Japanese stacked their arms and let their prisoners out. The Japanese sat down where they were and that was it. They actually imprisoned themselves. They just gave in and the spirit went right out of them. They sat down and accepted whatever was goin' to happen to them. If you had gone up and chopped their heads off the ones sittin' beside them would have just sat and waited their turn. They were the most docile prisoners you could imagine. For such a warlike people, for such an efficient fightin' machine, to see them like that was strange. We had seen Japanese in action and to see them like that close up, sittin' in rows, just acceptin' everythin' that was happenin' to them … They had lost everything, they had lost everything. In fact, a few officers would probably commit hara-kiri, probably a few of them would do the suicide thing. Those Japanese were all ashamed. They looked ashamed to be prisoners. They just sat wi' their heads bowed. They were spiritless. They had no spirit left in them. They were totally ashamed o' the situation they found themselves in—prisoners, rather than fightin' men. And don't forget, they were almost an invincible army. They had swept right through south-east Asia totally unopposed. Nothing could stop them then. They rode down through Malaya on bicycles! They were great soldiers, they really were, in spite o' what everybody says about them. They were fiendish and they were cruel. That was the reason they treated prisoners so badly. They thought that the British army, or whoever else was fightin' against them, should never have surrendered. They thought that that was a disgrace. So it's well known how they treated prisoners. They were really brutal to them. And they would expect the same treatment themselves—but they never got it. Well, at the end o' the war it was the whole army. It was an order from the Emperor. And some of the generals wouldn't accept that even. I mean, we were out in the hills at Hong Kong roundin' up bands o' Japanese in the New Territories round about Kowloon, on the China coast and up in the mountains inland a bit. The Japanese just wouldn't give up, they wouldn't surrender. The same thing happened on some of the Pacific islands. They wouldn't give up. They carried on the war in their own minds months and months after the surrender. They just wouldn't accept the fact that the great Japanese Empire had been defeated in war. Some o' them went on livin' in the jungle for years after the end o' the war. The Japanese are a strange people. They've got a strange code o' ethics that we don't understand. And ye need tae really study the Japanese a long, long time to understand their mentality.

Well, in Hong Kong at the end the war there werenae any cases of murders of Japanese by the former British prisoners, not to my knowledge. But I imagine it must have gone on because our men were savagely treated. So there must have been retaliation when they got the opportunity. There certainly were beatins' o' Japanese and I'll be ashamed to admit we participated in that a bit, kickin' them around. We thought back on stretcher bearers that had been bayoneted. So we treated those Japanese at Hong Kong a bit rough. We didn't treat them wi' kid gloves, I can tell you. I put the boot into them myself. I'm ashamed to admit it now but I did.

It was evidence in front o' your eyes what the Japanese had done to the prisoners in Hong Kong. And we were lookin' after these guys that had done all this. Those Japanese were garrison troops, don't forget. They werenae even men that had fought. They had been garrisonin' Hong Kong since they captured the place. So tae us they werenae fightin' men even. They were Japanese soldiers but they had brutalised these prisoners. So they got a bit o' rough treatment—so much so that eventually it became an offence to strike a prisoner. Before that if they didnae do exactly what you said when you said it—it's the old entrenchin' tool I'm talkin' about. We were wandering about wi' them. You gave them that over the head. War brutalises you. I realise that now. Looking back now I feel ashamed, I feel ashamed, because I did do it as well. No' as bad as some did. Some people I pulled off. One guy I patrolled wi' in particular was so incited he jist couldnae keep his hands off them. It just needed the bat of an eyelid and he was crashin' ... He could have killed them. I said, 'Come on, Jock, you'll need tae stop it. You'll need tae get a grip. You're goin' off your head.' Nasty, it was a bad, bad thing. Man's inhumanity to man. It engenders more hatred, more viciousness. Terrible.

We didn't really get to know any of the former British prisoners of war. Most of them needed urgent hospitalisation. We had a few months in Hong Kong because we couldn't get a passage home, because the priority was given to all the ex-prisoners. There was thousands of them, thousands of them. Well, a whole battalion of the Royal Scots for a start—the survivors, like.[239]

The civilian population in Hong Kong were dyin' too, 'cause the Japanese army had been livin' off them. Their rice was gettin' consumed by the big Japanese occupation force in Hong Kong, in Kowloon and the New Territories, and China proper. And they were gobblin' up all the rice. So there was starvation. There was a dreadful shortage of food. Of course, the prisoners of the Japanese had got nothing. They were human skeletons, jist bags o' bones. It wasnae very nice there, because there were people dyin' o' malnutrition for a start. There was a lot of disease. It was reminiscent of the famine in Bengal.

We were doin' police duties. They were really tryin' tae get the Hong Kong police organised again. The RAF Regiment came in shortly after us to help us, and various other units of the British army. We were policin' the place, patrollin'. There was a curfew on. We were havin' tae control black market situations, opium smuggling, and pirates were operatin' up and down the coast. The Chinese are great pirates. They're great lads for the kidnappin' game, too. They were kidnappin' people that had money and they would lop a finger off and send it through the post and say, 'The hand will follow next', sort of thing. It was a role that we were entirely untrained for. But we did it. We did police duties. We had to search the ferries that plies between Hong Kong and Kowloon, search them for opium which was goin' back and forward across the harbour. The islands were a hotbed of pirates. Ach, it was like something out o' a boy's adventure book, that! It was a bit of a skylark really. We couldnae take it seriously after the Burmese campaign. But there was a few bodies o' Japanese out in the hills who inflicted casualties and actually killed a few of our lads after the surrender. Some o' my mates got actually shot and killed. We used to go out on horseback after these Japanese. They were individual groups who either refused to surrender or wouldn't or couldnae believe that Japan had surrendered. And I must say that was the only time we took prisoners, when the war was finished. That's when we did. We used to go out on horseback wi' a few days' rations. We were like cowboys! On these wee mountain ponies! Half o' us couldnae ride the damn things. We just sat on them and they did all the rest. We just a' followed one another.

There were also Japanese civilians in Hong Kong wi' their families and what not, Japanese officers and Japanese troops. After a while they were gettin' shipped home to Japan. And before we put them on the ship in the mornin' for Japan, we had to search them. So anything you found—if you fancied a ring, you just took it! A watch—you just took it. I had about a dozen watches. And then we got the word that some of them were smugglin' gold back to Japan wi' them. They'd maybe be carryin' personal foodstuffs like a bowl or a bag o' rice or a big container o' rice or something. Run your fingers through that and you would find a couple o' nuggets o' gold. Ye got to know about all this. So you went through their food. You put your hand into their food and everything. You searched their pockets. And, as I say, anything you fancied—cameras—you took them. So I'm afraid I was intae all that.

By this time there was American freighters comin' in, American merchantmen, American sailors that had just come out from the States and had never been anywhere. They were regular servicemen and you could sell them anything. I sold a Japanese water bottle for about five dollars! I sold a Japanese sword for about thirty dollars. So I was doin' all right. I sold the sword, some Japanese medal ribbons and stuff and some bits o' Japanese equipment. The Japanese wore their ribbons in action actually.

Then there was another story. It was a bizarre situation but there were so many deaths. My mate and I were out patrolling this graveyard, him and I on duty like, with a gun and pistol and whatnot. Believe it or not, in Kowloon, where we were billeted—in fact, in the whole o' that part o' China, where it's mountainous country— wood is at a high premium, even for kindling, for making anything. There is just no forests in that area. So with all the deaths it was difficult and expensive to buy coffins. And there was funerals every day—even after a while, half a dozen people every day, there were so many deaths. They would bury them through the day and they would go back at night, dig the coffins up, tip the corpse out, take the coffin away and re- sell it again. It was a racket. These were the undertakers who were doin' this or people sellin' them back to the undertaker. I think there were a lot o' people in- volved in it. So we had the job o' patrolling this cemetery. And if you got any grave- diggers at it, well, you either arrested them or all I used to do was fire a shot over their heads, like: 'Get out o' there!', you know. They would scamper, they would run away.

The Chinese cemeteries are strange places. They are built on hills, built on slopes. The wealthier you are the higher up the slope you are buried. The way they found out about this coffin-robbin' was one of our officers had been walkin' through a cemetery. He'd seen a tuft o' human hair or what looked like human hair stickin' up: they'd taken the coffin and half-buried the corpse. Then he investigated further and further up; he found a hand stickin' out the ground. They'd been in and they'd been takin' the coffins away! So from then on that was another duty we had: grave-yard patrol. Nobody liked it. You wandered through this graveyard for a couple o' hours at night and then somebody relieved you and then you went back and did another couple. It was a graveyard shift, it really was.

Well, we were in Hong Kong for a few months. Then we were sent home on a troopship. I think it was the *Winchester Castle* we came back on. And we pulled into Ceylon, got Blighty gear, Blighty uniforms—greatcoats we'd never seen for years! And it was winter, January 1946, comin' up Plymouth Sound it was freezin'. We were all on deck. I'd been away from Britain two and a half years maybe. I remember the first thing we saw was Plymouth Hoe, which is a promontory. It's a sort o' high green. That's where Drake played his bowls. That was the first thing you saw. It was a clear day but bitterly cold. We were huddled up wi' these greatcoats up, feelin' the cold, really feelin' it. But we couldn't stay below decks. That was the first bit o' the UK we saw, Plymouth Hoe on the horizon. Ah, what a feeling, it was indescribable. Oh, there was a lot o' talk, excited talk. And, 'Oh, there's so and so.' You know, some of the people that lived in that area would say, 'I'll be able tae see my house now in a wee while.' The sound at Plymouth is a great area for ships. It's a huge estuary and there's battleships lyin' all over the place—destroyers, battleships, corvettes—hundreds!—and ye sail right away up the sound and then ye dock. Where ye dock is not far from the Marine barracks and the naval barracks.

We were right into the barracks—not too long. I was there a few weeks. It was a case of waitin': your number told them when your service started. You had to wait until your number went up on the board. All the guys that came back from overseas, from Germany or wherever they'd been, were put in these small units. The commandos all fell in at the back o' the parade. By this time they had a lot o' recruits in, a' learnin' to be soldiers sort of thing—bluesuits and all that sort o' thing. They didnae want anything to do wi' us. There were no way they could have got us out there doin' drill. We would just have put our rifles down and stood and looked at them, you know. There was no way that some puffed up stupid colour-sergeant was goin' to order us about. I think they knew this. So they were fairly diplomatic about it. What they did do was—we had to fall in on parade and answer our names, to make sure that everybody was there. And then the colour-sergeant would be quite pleased to dismiss you: 'Right, parade dismiss! Keep away from the main barracks and from the main parade ground. Keep yourselves out of trouble! Keep your eye on the notice board for your number.' And that was it till the next mornin'. He was dyin' tae get rid o' ye. He wasnae wantin' ye out. He was wantin' ye back to peacetime livin'. He didn't want anything to do wi' us. So it was good. We were always first in the queue at the NAAFI and there was nobody was goin' to push us out of the road either![240] There was a lot o' guys—veterans, we were called—standin' there. So the young sprogs would come and talk to you and ask you about things. They always made way for you. Same when you went out for your grub! They would stand aside until—you know! So I mean we took advantage o' that situation, quite honestly. We always got our pint or our cup o' tea and our buns before anybody else. There was a bit o' jostlin' and shovin' amongst ourselves but nobody else would dare come in and push us, nobody wi' a blue suit on. We'd seen it all and there was nobody was goin' tae tell us anything. And we were civilians at heart. We were goin' back to civilian life. The guys that were in barracks were professional Marines who had joined up and were goin' tae make a career out o' it. They were marchin' about like wee tin soldiers. They had got their hats away down over their ears, and their polished buttons and blue suits and red stripes and a' that. And we were in khaki, just a commando flash up and a green beret. So we just ambled about.

So we got demobbed. There was centres that you got taken to and in that centre you got your money and you got a book o' clothin' coupons, and you got a civilian ration book for food, if I remember right. The clothin' coupons I later discovered were like gold! Ye could have got anything for these clothin' coupons! I never even thought about it. I had a suit and that. Everybody had a suit. You had two choices: dark blue or brown, both pin stripe, single breasted or double breasted, wide lapels. I got a blue double breasted like a gangster's! Black shoes or brown. I got the black shoes obviously. I think the shirts were all white. And the ties were a nondescript brown or blue. And a soft hat or a cap. I took the soft hat. I had a hat like Jimmy Cagney![241] And a raincoat. And it was like another uniform! Everybody walked around with the same! Thousands of men dressed the same, just the same, just like another uniform. It was funny! It was a joke for years afterwards: 'You're still wearing your demob suit?' The thing is—you were! Mine lasted, oh, years. I finished up wi' it in my work, wearing it under my overalls. But at first I used it as a suit because I had no clothes that fitted me at home.

I remember gettin' accosted when I came out o' the demob centre in Plymouth. A guy wanted to buy my parcel o' clothes. Ye come out wi' your parcel and touts all waitin' outside tryin' to buy the stuff off ye. Clothes were scarce. You could have got money for that then. Oh, I told the guy to f— off! I wanted tae get intae this civvy suit as quick as I could! I just gave him a shove out the road. They had a good wee racket goin' there. A lot of the guys would sell it.

I must have gone home up the west coast. And I always remember Carstairs, they changed trains at Carstairs. I arrived at the Waverley station in Edinburgh. My family werenae there waitin' for me. I wasnae sure when I was comin', ye see. Your name went up on the notice board at Plymouth Barracks and you were away the next day. You hadnae really time—and no phones in these days. So what you did then was you got on the train and you got home as quick as you could. I remember I arrived at night time and I remember comin' up all the way from England and lookin' out and all the lights were on. When I'd left everything was black—the blackout. I changed on the train into this civilian suit. It was the first time I'd had it on. Well, I'd got measured for it. The guy says, 'That'll fit ye.' Ye didnae get a chance to put it on in the demob centre. The guy ran the tape over ye and says, 'That's yours.' There was no trying it on, 'Aw, it's a bit slack here. Can you take a bit …?' No, there was nothing o' that! No, the suit hung on you or it fitted you. Acutally, mine was a bit tight. But I thought I was really smart lookin' in it. I thought I was the bee's knees wi' this suit on!

So I got off at the Waverley wi' my demob suit on, and I had a big kit bag as well. I brought back a kukri knife, which I gave away to a nephew of mine and he cut the top off his finger with the damned thing and his mother threw it in the bucket. I had sold my Japanese officer's sword to a Yank. But I brought a Browning Colt automatic pistol back with me and I had about twenty rounds, I think. Well, after the war there was amnesties for people that held weapons as souvenirs. Every two or three years you'd have this amnesty period when you had a chance to hand them the weapons in. A lot o' lads held on to weapons as souvenirs. I suppose I should have handed the kukri knife in, too, but nothin' was asked for. I could ha' taken a machine gun ashore at Plymouth. We went through a form o' Customs. They just said, 'What you got?' 'Oh, nothing.'

Well, I took the tramcar from Waverley station down to Craigentinny. I'd lived there since I was about 14 or 15. The house there was a wee bit better because it was of a later design than the one at Lochend where we'd gone from the High Street. My mother was an awful woman for change. She always wanted another better house, a better house, a better house. We lived in Loganlea Road, No. 5. It was the six-in-a-block type.

So my parents were delighted to see me back from Burma. Unfortunately, it was a few weeks after New Year and all the New Year celebrations were over! But they had a party o' sorts. The family turned out to greet me, but no' the street. Aye, there there were too many guys comin' home then. In a housin' scheme there was too many blokes, whether they were coming home or not coming home—you know what I mean. Well, guys like I had knocked about wi', played football with, boxed with and all that—dead, you know. Some o' the ones I was in the Home Guard wi', the young guys I was in the Local Defence thing wi', one o' them became a sergeant in the Tanks. He wis blown up wi' his tank. The guy that lived immediately below me lost his leg from below the knee. He was a young guy, the same age as me. Another one went down wi' his ship. He lived down the street from me. Then there was ma two mates: the coloured lads, the McCraes. One got the George Medal posthumously. He went below in his ship to take a guy up from some boiler explosion. Then there was his brother who run intae the back o' a lorry on a despatch rider's bike in England before he even got into action. He was killed. And there was other acquaintances tae. They were friends o' mine I'm talkin' about, immediate friends that I played football with. And there was other lads that I knew, went to school with. In the whole area—because a lot o' the people moved in mass from Lochend, a lot o' people all came at the one time to Craigentinny. It seems a sort o' migration from one housing scheme to another, you know. So I knew a lot o' them for years since they were kids. And a lot o' them were dead. A lot o' them never came back. Some came back that had been prisoners and they were a mess. They were psychological cases. Well, where does the country get its fightin' forces from? From the proletariat, don't they? The ones that are actually goin' to do the fightin'.

So I just had a family celebration when I came back. Ah wis intae the drink at that time! I think I astonished them wi' the amount o' beer I could put away! They hadnae had much experience o' me doin' that before I went but when I came back I could drink wi' the best o' them.

But you were disturbed. You were very, very disturbed. Because you wonder how you're goin' to settle down. I had worries about goin' back to my trade because I hadnae got my apprenticeship completed. I knew there was guys that had worked at their trade all the way through the war. But that was a needless, stupid worry, because when I did finally get back into building there wis hundreds o' guys the same as me. So it was O.K. And the guys that hadnae had war service helped you. They seemed to think, 'Well, this guy's been away tae the war. If he's no' as good as me he cannae help it. He's been away, you know.' I had had a good initial trainin' anyway and I probably didnae find it too hard tae become an efficient professional joiner. And I was keen and enjoyed the work, which goes a long way to make you good.

But I had difficulties fitting into the routine existence of civvy street, I definitely did. Because I had kindred spirits there I was workin' alongside. I had guys who would get the jacket off and have a go wi' ye if they felt they didnae like ye, and I was the same. I was quite honestly a wee bit too ready to lift the fists. Oh, I think I had always been a wee bit pugnacious. I'm entirely different now. But I realise, lookin' back to then, I couldnae ha' been too easy tae get on wi'. I had a flashpoint, and when that flashpoint went it was dangerous for anybody that I was goin' to tangle wi'. I would have a go wi' anybody, no matter how big. And then again I had certain specialist commando trainin' that made it dangerous for anybody to mess wi' me, and I knew that. I didnae take advantage o' the fact but I wasnae goin' to be messed about by anybody—I mean, by anybody. And that in a sense is a bad way to be. You're no' lookin' for trouble but you're ready for it. You're over-ready for it. Once I lost a job because I hit a guy who was out o' order and everybody knew he was out o' order. And I packed in before they fired me!

I lost jobs verbally after that because I then became very militant in the union, the Amalgamated Society of Woodworkers. I was a wee bit vociferous, I think, in my union. I wisnae very careful what I said tae bosses. I used tae go down and shout at them a bit. It cost me a job a couple o' times indirectly. They never said, 'You're gettin' paid off for this or that.' But I knew why I was goin' like. I mean, a shortlist: 'We're goin' to thin out the workforce.' Ah knew I'd be on that list, I knew it. I was pretty militant in union affairs. I got a lot o' disillusionment when I did participate in union affairs. I felt that the members let me down on several occasions, didn't support me at all. I was puttin' ma job on the line day and daily for them. And when I asked for a bit support it wasnae forthcoming on many an occasion. And I'm afraid the last maybe ten, fifteen years o' ma workin' life I went on to the management side. I was better off financially and I had less hassle. The only thing was that when I became management in the Edinburgh area all my union conveners and the president o' my union in Edinburgh, they had known me as a union man. But when there was a dispute and I'm representing management I had all the answers. I could read the book backwards. And I think they found me a tough cookie tae deal wi', because they knew if I was doin' anything there was no way I was bendin' the rules in the book. I was goin' strictly by the book and they knew that if there was a case brought up and I had anything tae do wi' it I usually came out on the right side.

My last full-time job was the skills centre at Granton. Before that I had three or four years wi' the YTS, teachin' youngsters. In fact, I was senior supervisor. That was a good job actually. I went from there to Telford Further Education College. I was only there a year and they paid me off before my year was up because I would then have been permanent. I was of course last in and first out. So I went from there to the skills centre at Granton and I had a couple o' years there. Then I was retired. In fact, at Granton they asked me to work on past my retirin' age. So I actually done another six months past 65 and it helped ma pension. I was amazed. I mean, I've got probably another tenner a week more than the normal pensions. That plus all my workin' life I've paid that graduated pension thing. Now that doesnae give you much but again it helps a wee bit.

Now lookin' back to the war, well, I don't like the Japanese. I can't possibly like them. But I've not got a strong hatred. I've not got a strong hatred for anybody now. Immediately after the war, oh, I did. I mean those memories were too close to the war then. But over the years I've read a lot more about the Japanese and I think I'm beginning now to understand a wee bit o' their philosophy o' life. I don't study them but if I read a book about Japanese, I think, 'Oh, well, that'll explain a wee bit what made them what they were durin' the war,' like. I can't fully understand the atrocities they carried out, the needless atrocities. I can understand torture in a certain sense—for information, or for the good o' the majority. I can understand it even if I can't condone it. But mindless killing or mindless inflicting o' pain on people I can't understand and I can't accept. I haven't any hatred for the Japanese. But I did have a terrible hatred. As I said, lookin' after them as prisoners in Hong Kong I was a bit brutal, along wi' everybody else. I sunk the boot in here and there and I used my fists and I thought nothin' o' cloutin' them.

But lookin' back on the war, I was a minute speck, I was just a number. If a war were to happen tomorrow I think there would be a lot of young men would act the same way as I acted then, like millions of us did. And I think we were kidded to death. I think we were manipulated. I think the war was glorified—you know, the spirit of Britain, and all that stuff. Self-preservation, that's all that was.

So I think war is abhorrent. And if ever a war happened again and I had any o' my family—grandchildren, for instance—I would try and persuade them at all costs to steer clear of it if they could, in spite o' what might be said about them. And certainly, if another war had broken out and I was still of military age I wouldn't have gone, I wouldn't have gone. I would have been a conscientious objector. I would have refused tae go.

In general I think war is needless, it's useless. War shouldn't happen. I know wars have gone on all through history. And I don't think wars'll ever stop. But the most powerful countries in the world now seem to be gettin' the idea that war is useless and serves no purpose. Unfortunately, smaller countries don't seem to have got the message. I don't know why. Nobody wins a war. To my way o' thinkin', nobody wins. I just think war's abhorrent.

Andrew Gilhooley

I remember the old man, when he come home frae the World War One, me and my twin brother were seven. And he said tae my mother, he says, 'Annie, if any o' thae boys join the army I'll shoot them.' That's what he said.

Father, he was sort o' strict upbringin'—he was a bit religious, that was all. He wasn't through the full war, I don't think. I think he maybe went in the last two-and-a-half years o' the war. Oh, he wasn't a volunteer, oh, no, no, the old man never volunteered, never volunteered. He was in the Highland Light Infantry. But he went to India and he'd be gettin' on then: he'd be over his thirties then. He was born in 1882.

I was born in Edinburgh on the 8th of November 1912 and brought up there. I had three brothers, one o' them my twin. I lived in Tron Square practically all my life till I came to live here in Restalrig.

When I left school it was mass unemployment: 1926. It was the General Strike, and there was no jobs, ach, no prospects for jobs anyway. It was only a job for two or three month, on the dole, then you had the Means Test. I thought that was the most horrifying thing of the lot. That was worse than the Poll Tax, because you were forced to leave the house. And through that four or five of us went on the tramp away up to the Highlands. My God, terrifying poverty, misery![242] Ah says, 'Well, that's it.' I'd be about 20 when I went up there: Hibs were in the Second Division, that's how I remember.[243] So I didn't have any regular sort of job before the 1939 war. I was on and off just. Oh, there was a mass of unemployment. Where we lived in Tron Square in Edinburgh it was terrifying.

If you were employed for a month or two at a time you didn't get much, it was only coppers. About 1939 I got a job in Weston's biscuit factory. Tenpence an hour it was—10d. That wis the wages. And you worked from 6 am to 2 pm or from 2 pm to 10 pm. Well, that's when I got sort o' militant and I just pulled the machinery off, you know, and I went in and I seen them and I said: 'We need more money than this.'

One o' the best temporary jobs I got before the war was deliverin' Corn Flakes round the door. And that was fantastic. You were getting something like ten shillings a day. Oh, my God, you were rich! Beer was only sixpence a pint.

When the war came in 1939 I didn't have a pacifist or anti-war background. It only happened through just pure luck. I went to the Mound a lot. So I used to hear the speakers. The man that impressed me was a man named Frank Maitland. He was a revolutionary socialist. Oh, he was a Trot, he told you, he was a Trotskyist. He was the man that sort of sent me going. And ye sort of asked him for the book of the life of James Connolly. From then on I got, you know, involved in it. But I've never been a member of any political party, never been a member o' nothing.

Another man that interested me and I knew him personally because I lived near him was a man named George Robertson. He fought in the International Brigade in Spain as a young man. He was a younger man than me, not much, but younger. And I read two or three of the books and I thought there was something in it. And I thought, 'Well, here's something too, if a man like Robertson can leave two young children, there must be somethin' to fight for.' Later on, Robertson committed a murder. When he came back fae Spain he had been wounded, and then he went to drink. His life was finished then. He was a handsome man, too, quite a handsome man.[244]

So my views came as a result of attending the Mound and I was influenced by this man Robertson. In a way you met people, well, they were left-wingers, put it that way. You got involved wi' people talkin' about politics. And one of our neighbours in Tron Square was a member of the Communist Party: Owen Mochan. He was a bit of a wild man. He come from Ireland, too, like we came away in the 1850s from Ireland—that's how we settled in Edinburgh in the 1850s, the Gilhooleys.

So that was more or less the start, about 1939, comin' up then, I'd be 27, and up to then I'd had just casual jobs, aye, jist casual. After the war broke out I was up in the Orkneys. I got the job frae the dole in October 1939. It was work to do with putting tanks, metal tanks, into the ground for oil at the naval base. We were on the mainland on Orkney, looking towards Scapa Flow.

I only worked there about eight or nine weeks. They were givin' us tuppence below the rate. It was a big contractor, one of the big ones. And we were sub-contracted. And I said, 'By the way, we're entitled to the same money, the same conditions, as the other men are workin' for.' The same job it wis. 'Well, get off the island,' they says. I got the sack, oh, it wis the sack a'right.

I came back to Edinburgh when I left Orkney. And I got my call-up papers, oh, as quick as that. But within days I was on my way to the Tribunal at Aberdeen, and tried as a Conshie. I told them I didn't want to fight, I didn't want to join the army, that I was a conscientious objector. Then they sent me down to Chesterfield.

Well, you got a medical. You got the medical and the only thing was I had to wait till the army gave us the papers. They gave you a five-shilling postal order. So I got the postal order and I went down to the town of Chesterfield. And that's where it started. I refused point blank to put on the army uniform. Ah says, 'I'm not puttin' that uniform on.' And they stripped iz naked and they put it on me and they said, 'Now you're a soldier.' So they forced me to wear the uniform but I would say they were very gentle. They were good about it, I would say that. But once I got the uniform on I still refused to do anything. They came, I was lying in the barracks—it was a school—and lying there you heard them shoutin' '244669 Driver Gilhooley!' That was my number. I was conscripted to the Royal Army Service Corps.

And they were shoutin' out the names, ye know, shoutin'. And this corporal came up—I'll never forget him. He's swearin', shoutin'. That's a thing I never do, never swear. But anyway, 'You're goin' to do this and do that!' And they put me on to the parade ground. And I wouldn't do nothin'. So they marched iz off. And they put me in detention right away. And I was there till I was court martialled. There was another lad in the barracks in the same position; I'm sure he was a Jehovah's Witness. I think he was a religious person. He was treated similar to me.

I was detained in a cell. The army were never rough with me, never. The food was good, everything was good. The Jehovah's Witness was in another room but you met when you were gettin' food and ye had a talk. That was all.

I was twice court martialled. To be honest, I've not got a clue where it was but it couldn't be far away from Chesterfield. It wasn't far away but I didn't know the place. I was ta'en there from Chesterfield in the car. I'd say lucky if it was ten minutes or quarter of an hour away. It gave you the impression it was a barracks.

I'd say there were seven or eight officers on the court martial. I remember one well, Captain Brown. I always remember him. Well, he says, 'You're a damned fool. Can you not join up?' Ah says, 'Well,' ah says—I just said what I thought—ah says, 'I think we were silly.' Ah says, 'Were you at the last war?' He says, 'What do you think this is?', you know, showing me his medals from the '14-18 war. He just says, 'Well, you've caused us a lot of trouble, a lot o' trouble.' But I just stuck to my principles, oh, I never altered, didn't alter.

To be honest, the court martial was jist a rumble-jumble. It was nothin' at a'. It didn't even convey nothin' to me. I wasn't interested. To me it was jist a formality. I stuck to my principles, no danger. Well, they sent me to prison. Right away, out to Chesterfield then on to Lincoln Prison. The sentence was three month in Lincoln Prison.

Well, I went to Lincoln Prison and then you go before the Governor. And the Governor reads out, 'Driver Gilhooley 244669'. He says, 'A fine number.' Ah says, 'Yes, sir, for a motor car.' 'Any more o' that,' he says, 'and you'll do what they call punishment—bread and water.' Ah says, 'Oh, well.' That was that.

After that, everything was brilliant. The prison was good: good porridge, every-thing was really good. I was in a cell by myself. They let you out just for exercise. You went out wi' the rest o' the prisoners. I was treated very well in prison, genuine. They were all right.

They put you in the fields, you had to do a bit on the fields, weeding, ploughing, aye. And what they call the mail bags, sewing the mail bags, that's a'. Yes, we were kept busy—mail bags. I never met another conshie in Lincoln Prison; the only one was the one in Chesterfield—I think he was a Jehovah's.

The only people I met in prison wis the IRA. They were in what you called the Concert Hall. It was a concert, you see, and it was very funny. You'll laugh at this one. The IRA at the time, you know, they were mad people. And you'd tae stand up, you know, when they played the National Anthem, the King and Queen. And the IRA men wouldn't do nothin' at all. They just sat down. But durin' the concert the song was 'There's no Place like Home'. I thought it was fantastic: 'There's no

Place like Home'. And these IRA men were doin' about seven or eight year and more. And they seemed intelligent people. I met two o' them and they were quite well educated.

Ah never smoked in my life, never smoked. I like readin' and in Lincoln Prison that's where I read quite a lot o' good books. I read what I thought was a brilliant book. It was *The Iron Heel*. And I read the Dean o' Canterbury's *The Socialist Sixth of the World*. Oh, I thought it was great.[245]

I got nothin' in prison, nothin' at all—no money, I got nothin'. I had got married in 1939 and I had a son. I was married in July 1939, just before the war broke out. My wife hadn't a clue about my position as a conscientious objector. She didn't understand. It was sad, because I knew that she wasnae goin' to live. Aye, it was just a matter o' time. She died just after the war, in 1947.

But every one o' the other members o' my family, I'm not jokin', they admired me for some reason. My father was in the First War and my three brothers were in the Second War and they didn't oppose me in any way. I don't say the old man was proud of me but my brothers never even thought nothin' about it. My twin brother was a Regular in the Cameron Highlanders. He joined in 1932. He was comin' home when the war started. He became a prisoner o' war. The youngest brother he was in the Navy Reserves down at Leith. He automatically went in right away when the war broke out. Then the brother just behind us, he joined the Navy too.

Well, when we come oot o' Lincoln Prison two of them, a corporal and another soldier, took me back to the army at Chesterfield. And the one says to me, 'Are you a communist?' Ah says, 'No. Never been a member o' nothing.' 'Have you got a sympathy with the Soviet Union?' Ah says, 'Well, I'll say "yes" tae ye if ye want.' He says, 'Well, I'm tellin' ye now Russia will be in the war in days.' And they were in the war. And it was the 23rd or 24th o' June 1941 I joined the army. Ah joined myself.

I went before a Colonel Penn Gilley. I'll never forget that man. Ah says, 'Well, sir.' He says, 'What are you doin' up here, Gilhooley?' Ah says, 'Well, sir, I think I've been bangin' my head against a stone wall.' He says, 'What do you mean, a stone …?' 'Well,' ah says, 'ah think I'll be a soldier.' He says, 'Gilhooley, you're a good man.' I think when the Soviet Union came into the war it changed ma views. It was a big factor, it was a big factor. Ah would say maybe I had a leniency towards the Soviet Union. I admired what they were doin'. So it was that week ah joined the army. I volunteered. I wasn't a member of no political party. I had a leniency towards the Russian system, put it that way.

I joined the Royal Army Service Corps. I went to the town Mumbles, that's in Wales, and Gloucester. The British Glory Match Company was the big house we were in. I was a driver, I drove a lorry. I did that for a couple of years then I went right over to Egypt in 1943. They put me in charge of a big massive hut with all the food in it. And that was me settled there. I was in Egypt eighteen month, till the end o' the war. I didn't get hardly any money. It was only five shillins a week I got till about 1943 and I got nineteen shillins. When I was in Egypt the holiday I went was the best holiday I had in my life: Beirut, Beirut.

I was demobbed at Kirknewton late May or June 1946. I got a job in the brewery when I came back—Willie Younger's, it became Scottish and Newcastle after that. Oh, they were a smashin' brewery tae work wi'. I thought it was a wonderful place.

I never suffered in any way after the war for having been a conscientious objector. The only time, maybe somebody in the pub talkin' and somebody got nasty wi' ye. You accept that. But I've never altered my views, no, I've never altered. I'll never alter that way. I still think, really, honest, war is silly. To me it's stupid.

Fred Pitkeathly

And when it came to the Tribunal I think it was the Earl of Eglinton in the chair, but I wouldn't swear to that. But on the Tribunal was Lord Provost Buist of Dundee.[246] The Tribunal seemed to be very short. Before we went in somebody said, 'It's forestry today.' So when I went in they had my statement before them and they asked if I had anything to add. And the chairman may have said one or two words. The only other one that said anything was Lord Provost Buist, who asked me if I did not think that Abraham Lincoln had been justified in going to war on behalf of the slaves? I said that I couldn't claim to any deep knowledge about American affairs but my impression always was that there was a lot more to the political side of their civil war than to the moral side. And that was that. They said: 'Forestry.' And I sat on and listened to one or two of the other cases—and the same thing. The only ones that wouldn't lay any claim to religious grounds for conscientious objection to service with the armed forces—they were the ones that were turned down. One fellow said his objection was on moral and political grounds, and he was turned down—just like that. This seemed to me like putting us all on the assembly line! That was my impression of the Tribunal.

It was really from my father, I would think, that I got my pacifist ideas in the first place. He had six good reasons for not wanting a war: there were six boys in our family. I was second from the bottom.

I was born in 1915 in Newtyle, a little village in Angus. But the family moved to Dundee when I was about six years old, after my mother had died. Some time later my father remarried—my aunt.

Father was in the office of Jute Industries in Dundee. He came under the influence of Dick Sheppard and he read all of his writings. Dick Sheppard was at St Martin's in the Field in London and he broadcast. I first heard him in a broadcast. And he started this movement, the Peace Pledge Union. It was after the Peace Ballot, I think.[247] But he asked all who agreed with him to sign a little declaration: 'I renounce war and I will never take part in another'—something on those lines. And as a result of that there then sprang up all over the country the Peace Pledge Union branches. I was a member of the Dundee one, which had meetings with speakers at them. But there was quite a lot of social activities, too. And when these public meetings took place we acted as stewards. I don't think Dick Sheppard ever came to Dundee. But I remember there was one large meeting in Dundee and George Lansbury was one of the speakers. And there was a brigadier: I can't remember his name, but he really looked like a brigadier, and he went into action that night on the peace movement as if he was going into battle.[248]

One thing I remember was a mock tribunal for conscientious objectors, run by the Peace Pledge Union branch. And they turned me down! They were really hard on me—which may have helped a little. This was a practice run, because they knew we were coming up before the Tribunal and they knew it would be a bit of an ordeal. Three members—older members—of the group grilled you in the way that you would expect to be. And then they gave their decision, which was a little daunting. One of the leaders there was Rev. Edwin Towill, a Church of Scotland minister, and he was a moving light. He helped me in many ways. I got his help in making up my statement to the Tribunal. But he didn't want himself to come to the Tribunal. He urged me to ask my own minister, a Congregational minister, Rev. Bowen. He was quite agreeable to come. Unfortunately, when he spoke he more or less said that, although my father was very much in agreement with me my mother was less happy about my views. And that was the part that the local newspaper, the *Evening Telegraph,* picked up which was a bit unfortunate! It was for personal reasons only that mother had expressed this opinion to the parson. I didn't know anything about it, of course. Anyway I was granted exemption from military service to do forestry work.

I had gone to school in Harris Academy, Dundee, and then I went into an insurance office. I did my home study and so on and qualified to be an Associate of the Chartered Insurance Institute. I might have been a Fellow if the war hadn't come! But that helped me in later days.

So when I went back to the office after the Tribunal my boss asked me about it. Then he had gone to Lord Provost Buist, whom he knew in a business way, and said, 'Look here, if you're not taking Pitkeathly to the army he'd be a lot more use in my office than he would in forestry.' That was the last thing I wanted—to remain in the office! But my boss hadn't made anything of it with Lord Provost Buist. But I must say the office, in their way, were quite co-operative because they were prepared to treat me in the same way as those who were in the armed forces, by making up our money while we were away. The forestry wages went up certainly, but within a couple of years—it showed the level of insurance wages—they weren't owing me anything. But they continued in that right until my Appeal Tribunal about four years later, in 1944.

All the people in the office seemed to accept me as being a little strange maybe but personal terms were good. There was only one exception really and I saw very little of him. He was an Old Contemptible. But I met his wife afterwards and little girl and they were quite friendly and charming.[249]

At the time of the Tribunal in 1940 I was also in the Scout movement. One of the things I wondered about was that the authorities wanted Scouts to act as runners for the Air Raid Precautions depots. They also got involved because they ran a series of lectures on dealing with chemical warfare, which I attended, but I wasn't too happy about that. I thought this was all concerned with the results of warfare, though

I suppose it was taking part in the war effort in a way. But it was very difficult to keep away from it.

I was on very friendly terms with one of the Scout Commissioners and I met him on the street after the Tribunal. In his usual bumbling way he finally said, 'Oh, well, you take vows to do your duty to God and the King—and how do you square that?' I said, 'Well, I think the duty to God came before that to the King.' And he accepted that. There was no animosity. But this was the general feeling amongst my friends and so on: although they didn't agree with me they were prepared to accept that I was sincere.

I'm not sure if my father ever persuaded any of my brothers to sign the Peace Pledge—I think one of them anyway would sign. But they didn't take an active part in the work of the Peace Pledge Union. And when it came to the bit one was in the army, one was in the air force, one was in the navy, and my two oldest brothers— one was a teacher and one was with Glasgow Corporation—were in reserved occupations, though I think both took part in the Home Guard. But there was no friction amongst us. One of my brothers suggested that I had made my point by going to the Tribunal and that I should now reconsider. But that was all. There was never any pressure of any sort put on me.

So after the Tribunal I was put in touch with the Christian Pacifist Forestry and Land Units. The Reverend Lewis McLachlan in Glasgow was their Scottish representative. I can't remember the procedure, but finally I was told that there was another Dundee chap, Alex Adamson, going with me. We met at the Dundee station and went through to Glasgow, where we met Rev. McLachlan—I think we recognised him through a red rose in his buttonhole. He was the co-ordinator, as it were, for the Unit and he gave us our instructions, where to go and so on. Another conscientious objector Tom Cunningham went with Alex Adamson and me.

So we got the train from Glasgow to Lockerbie. The forester had arranged for us to be picked up in Lockerbie by taxi. And we went from Lockerbie up to this hut in the hills at Eskdalemuir, miles from anywhere. You looked everywhere but apparently the only living object was a sheep! I remember there was afterwards some discussion about the taxi—who should pay for it, because the forester Charlie Parley had ordered it and I don't think we had the money to pay for it! Anyway there we were. Then there arrived other conscientious objectors: Dick Soye on his bicycle, and Gordon Clingan and Guy Cree from Glasgow.

Well, there were six of us there for, oh, a week or two and then others started to arrive, until we were up to finally fifteen. All of us were conscientious objectors, from different backgrounds, for different reasons, but all of us were conscientious objectors. And the grounds of our objection were religious rather than political.

The work was all planting of trees that we were engaged on. There was no felling. In that part of the country, there weren't established forests as such. So there would be very little felling done.

The wages, as far as I remember, it was 38 shillings a week and then it shot up to 42 shillings a week and then 45 shillings a week. But that was the sort of level. Agricultural workers were always at the bottom of the heap, of course. And forestry workers, I think, were always about two shillings ahead of them. I think that's the way it worked, though they came under the same Wages Board.

We started our day's work at half past seven. We had one break, and an hour at lunchtime, and a break in the afternoon, and finished at five o'clock. We would be up, oh, half-past six in the morning, because by the time we got up and had breakfast ... And there was always some way to walk, considerable walking to do—or bicycle—to be on the job at half past seven. And on Saturday we worked until about twelve o'clock.

We'd all been union members, I would say, of one sort of union or another. So we applied to become a branch of the Scottish Farm Servants' Union. And we were accepted. And when there was a meeting down in Lockerbie, when the union organiser Joe Duncan came down, I with one of the others—I can't remember who it was—went down as a delegate. It was quite interesting, though I found out that it was very much Joe Duncan's union. There had been a movement by the trade unions to help their fellow trade unionists in Holland, who because of the war and deprivation were very short of food. And the unions were trying to urge on the government a relaxation on the blockade, so that food and other humanitarian supplies could be brought in. So I put this to the Farm Servants' Union at that meeting in Lockerbie but it was, I am afraid, shot down by Joe Duncan. That was really the only experience I had of him.[250]

We also thought that we could make a contribution from our experience to welfare and improving conditions for forestry workers. So we did make a report and sent it to the appropriate authorities, suggesting improvements in working conditions, hours, and generally what appeared to us from our experience could be done. Whether it ever made any impact I couldn't claim, but at least we felt we had made the effort. So that our sojourn there wasn't without some fruit.

I don't remember many union meetings at Lockerbie, I admit, but we would be discussing those sort of things all the time—about wet time, and protective clothing, working conditions, and having some place where, instead of sitting out with the rain coming down and having to take your midday piece without any protection ... all these things. We felt that we might improve things in the future.

There were no limitiations at all on our movements away from our forestry hut at Eskdalemuir or from the forest where we were working. We had week-ends when if we had any holidays we could go up to Dundee, Glasgow, or elsewhere. On one occasion when we had a holiday Dick Soye and I went on a cycling holiday round about Perthshire. There was recognised agricultural holidays that we got. And if we took a long week-end we lost the pay. I think on the whole Charlie Parley, the forester, was quite all right about that, if you wanted an extra day or if there was some family crisis, for instance, as happened once or twice. But as regards paid holidays it was the agricultural holidays we got.

In our hut at Eskdalemuir, which was very basic, there were plain tables, wooden forms, a coal-fired stove, which was a brute to deal with till we got used to it, and cups and mugs of some sort, cutlery, and so on: all the essentials for cooking. I think Dick Soye and Gordon Clingan and me had had experience with camps and hostelling, which gave us at least some sort of background. I think it did help that some of us had had experience of cooking on a stove, because we had to do all the cooking.

There were, as I say, these six people for a week or two. At first we arranged that one would be released from work at four o'clock, to go back and make an evening meal. But when we were up to finally fifteen in the hut we thought that it was time we had a cook. So we got the Forestry Commission—or Charlie Parley, the forester—to agree that we take it in turn, a month at a time, to do the cooking and keep the place clean and tidy more or less. So that seemed to work out all right.

We seemed to gell into a unit, and our different backgrounds and our different attitudes and so on ensured that there was always scope for lively discussions. We tried to vary our discussions by inviting each man to give a talk on a subject of his choosing, because on the whole we were quite a literate, intelligent lot, I would say, and could discuss things on this level. I think there would be a feeling that we wanted to keep our minds active.

Different people arranged different ways of occupying their leisure time. Some thought several of us a bit daft because at week-ends, after a week of heavy work on the forest, we would walk over the hill to a youth hostel! The youth hostel was Shortwoodend, which is on the Moffat Water. It's now a private house again. But it was very friendly and we enjoyed meeting other people—mainly Glasgow people—that were coming down there. I think that was the real reason we went: to get a break.

In the hut there was a lot of reading done. I don't know where we got our reading matter. I suppose we bought it. Alex Adamson used to be able to get us books because he was a librarian. There would be a library in Lockerbie but I don't know that any of us were ever members of it. But I think we probably borrowed books from Charlie Parley, the forester, for instance. And we all contributed because we did have books, we did have reading matter.

And of course we got newspapers of one sort or another from home. In my case it was the *Manchester Guardian Weekly* and the *Perthshire Advertiser*. One man got the *Bulletin*. And I think we got the local Lockerbie paper. Quite a range of publications like that.[251]

We had a radio and we followed 'ITMA' every week and 'The Brains Trust'.[252] These were two of the programmes I can remember, and music, too. And then when you went visiting some of the local households we were quite welcome in, they were always avid for the BBC Radio News. In these households they used to talk about time, for instance. There were three times, according to them. The authorities introduced double summer time and we could see how it affected the rural community, because it really was ridiculous in there. And they talked about quick time and midtime and God's time. And if you spoke about the time it was always that or BBC time. But the News was the one thing you would hear on the radio. I can't recollect really ever hearing anything else in a farm or shepherd's cottage than the News. It would be switched on at nine o'clock. And then when the News was finished—off went the radio. And that was all I ever heard in a farm cottage.

I don't have any recollection of our playing chess, draughts, dominoes, these sort of things. It may have been with the hard work and the long hours and so on, by evening we were both physically and mentally exhausted. But it seemed that with letter-writing, reading and the radio we didn't have such long evenings really, because with early rising we had to get to bed. And after nine o'clock there wasn't very much doing. I can remember one summer we had a cricketer in our midst, Tom Cunningham, who'd played for Perthshire. We did have cricket but I don't think it lasted very long! There was Tom Cunningham and there was the rest of us. That was about the strength of it!

The hut itself at Eskdalemuir was divided into two rooms: there was the sleeping apartment and there was the living apartment, where the stove, and the table, and the forms were. In the dormitory part there was a coal-fired stove but otherwise it was just beds. There was a certain amount of privacy from having the beds separated from the living quarters. I think it was sort of recognised that within the dormitory there was no noisy work going on. We tended to have our arguments and so on round the table in the living room.

There were one or two members of our group who were members of rather fringe religious groups—Christadelphians or Christian Brethren—who did not take part in any communal activities. Though they were good singers they wouldn't join in the choir we had and wouldn't take part in any concerts, this kind of thing. They kept themselves to themselves. At week-ends they spent most of their time down in Lockerbie with others of the same persuasion. They were perfectly friendly. There was no division of any sort arising from that with the rest of us. We recognised that was their principles and let them get on with it.

There was churches, oh, about four miles in each direction—one at Eskdalemuir and one at Boreland. But I think David Sainty and I were the only ones from the hut who ever went, and that was only very occasionally. The minister did come up to the hut once or twice from the Eskdalemuir church. He was quite friendly, what we saw of him. I suppose we were really in his parish. His wife did come along once. She was a little strange. She claimed to be a poetess in her own right, from Aberdeenshire. And in the early days we used to have some sort of services within the hut, oh, non-denominational. Latterly, they were more of a discussion kind. But once again I suppose it was the week-end relaxation and so on, I mean, the distance...

We also devised other ways, apart from discussion meetings, to get on terms with the local people. We were very friendly with the people at the nearby shepherd's cottage. And we found out that Tom Cunningham, particularly, who was so friendly, used to get our meals if not made at least prepared there! They kept him right when he was on duty as cook. And the people at the road end, where the ganger lodged with the shepherd, we got on very well with them. Immediately we went in the house the kettle was on the fire and the egg was in the pan, this kind of thing! And one of our lads, Jock Ramsay, who went for the milk to the shepherd's cottage—we wondered why he was always prepared to go for the milk and then we found out that there was a lassie there, too. Later on Jock and Nancy got married.

We thought not only for all those people but for the other workers we would put on an entertainment. And we did so. And they seemed to enjoy it all right. There were songs and sketches, I think, some individual items. We had at least two of these concerts—three, I think, finally.

We would leave our bikes with the people at the road end when on the occasions—once a month on a Saturday—there was a bus which took us to Lockerbie: twelve miles. Although there were vans which came up to the hut and we got supplies off them, there was always something we were needing at the week-ends and we went down and paid the bills and got any supplementary things. But if we went on our bicycles that meant a twelve mile journey, which was mostly downhill going but was all uphill coming back! And the prevailing wind was south-west, which didn't make it any easier really.

The only antagonism, I would say, we encountered was on the bus. And it seemed to come from the younger people, the young farmhands, who were working on the farms or the forestry, and who were exempt from the Forces because of their jobs. They were discussing us, you know, in the back of the bus in loud voices: 'Yellow belly, conchie', 'You shouldnae be here', this sort of thing. And we met one or two when we were sent over to work on the farm: they weren't very friendly. But the older men, we got on very well with them. There was no animosity expressed.

Speaking about spare time, we all had our washing to do, our domestic chores, that kind of thing. There was a laundry and we would send away shirts, for instance, to that. But for our ordinary clothes and so on the facilities weren't very good. There was a sink. We washed them in the sink and we rinsed them in the river. On one occasion when the army came up—the army came up several times and had manoeuvres round about us: we were at the end of the road really, so they usually parked their vehicles and took off from there—and on one occasion when the army came up on a Sunday, I think it was, one or two of them started shouting at us. There was a rather nasty sergeant and corporal amongst them. We couldn't hear what they were shouting but obviously they weren't being complimentary. And I had been doing the washing of socks and so on, and the others thought I was being rather foolhardy by going out of the hut. But I had to get them rinsed in the river. So I went down and the sergeant comes along and he began asking what we were doing there, why we weren't in the army and so on. I tried to explain to him. I'm not sure that I got through! You can imagine the sort of passive resistance—and a mouthful.

But on another occasion we asked several of them in and gave them a cup of tea and so on and got chatting. I found out there was one Dundee lad among them. So we were able to compare notes about Dundee. He asked me, 'How long have you been here and what do you do?', and so on. 'Oh, I couldna be doin' with it here,' he says. 'I would do anything rather than be shut away up here on that kind of work.' So it was an interesting sidelight on the army.

In 1944 there was a break-up of the Unit and things did change. David Sainty and three others, I think it was, were moved to a cottage. And then the rest of us were moved over to the other part of the forest, which was on the Eskdalemuir side. It was a large mansionhouse: Castle O'er. It was pretty rudimentary in the provision.

But at least it had an indoor toilet, which was a big advantage! We hadn't had that at the hut. It had a bath, too. And it was in a very pleasant surrounding. But the thing was there were separate bedrooms. We had to split up into bedrooms. And that tended to give rise to cliques. You got into a bedroom with those with whom you were most friendly. And you only met the others at meal times. And I think this contributed to a change in the thing. So at times I felt it was no longer a Christian Pacifist Unit! But this was bound to happen. And several of the fellows of course found jobs elsewhere—still in forestry, but several of them went into the felling side because there was more money in that. And of course they had their other interests. When we had been at the bothy or hut we had had visitors but they were usually fiancées who came down. And the fiancée was invited to stay at the shepherd's house. So the lads at the hut were able to meet their lassies in that way. But it was more difficult at Castle O'er. It was more remote and there wasn't the same facility as there had been at the hut. So the lads tended to be looking for jobs nearer to Glasgow, where they could be closer to their fiancées or girlfriends. Tom Cunningham got married and he went back up to Perth to the felling business. And Jack got married and he went up, too. And Charlie. And they went up to be nearer their wives. Jimmy got married and his wife had already come down as a landgirl to one of the local farms, and they were set up in a cottage locally. And they lasted longer in the area than any of us but Jock Ramsay, who married the lassie in the shepherd's cottage. Jock lives now in Dumfries.

And then at Castle O'er there were Newfoundland lumberjacks brought over to do forestry work. And they were billeted there. They had to put in a water pipe across the road. And two of us were deputed to go over and dig the trench and then put in the water pipe and fill the trench up again, all in the same day. So we got our meals down amongst the lumberjacks. And that was quite an experience, believe me! They knew why we were there, as conscientious objectors. We certainly didn't advertise anything. They had arranged to give us our meals, and the atmosphere was thick, the food was thick, and the language was thick! They were a rough lot—you talk about roughnecks! It was quite an experience for us.

Well, in 1944 we saw this appeal for volunteers from the International Voluntary Service for Peace, which appealed to us. Being an international organisation it was affiliated to the Service Civil International based in Switzerland. But it went in for all sorts of relief work and for encouraging amity between the nations. So we felt that maybe the time was come when we should take a more active part in the problems arising from the ending of the war and afterwards work with refugees and so on. I don't think it was only a desire for pastures new that motivated us. But we found there were snags because the Forestry Commission weren't going to let us go. I don't know if we had impressed them as being such valuable workers but they certainly opposed our application for release—which meant us going to the Ministry of Labour to get a variation of the terms of our exemption from military service, which in turn was referred to a Tribunal. In my case, it was an Appeal Tribunal. I remember no details but at least I got my exemption. And that was the time that my old employer the insurance company said to me I would have to make up my mind, that they were quite willing to go along with the original terms of my exemption but not if I was to go rushing off to Europe or wherever. So I made the decision that I would no longer be—it was hardly their payroll at that time—in their employment. I knew in my heart of hearts I had no wish to go back to an insurance office—the commercial life—because of all that had transpired.

So then we went to London. I went to the East End, to a hostel, where they were all conscientious objectors of various persuasions again, and they were employed by the local council. There were three main jobs we did. We were assisting in building air raid shelters. We had some interesting experiences among the Cockneys there. We went round with meals for schools. And I had some very revealing insights into the state of some of the schools there. And the third job we did was if there were any incidents—it was the time of the buzz-bombs, and there could be incidents at night— we went out with manned canteens.[253]

Then I transferred to another unit nearby. They were engaged on demolition work, clearing the bombed sites. So I had some experience. My hands and my muscles were hardened. I didn't take too badly with that. Buzz-bombs were going off round about and we had the experience of one going off in the vicinity: wwwhhhsssshhhh. The next night I retired to the rather dirty air-raid shelter. But that was about the nearest we got to it.

During this time, I think, we were probably being assessed for our suitability to take part in foreign service. And I must have come through the test because I was accepted.

We had some training. One of the things was a series of lectures from the UNRRA people about what you could expect.[254] One of the things they said was, 'It's not glamorous. You are going into these countries to help with the refugees, with re-building, and your job is to make your job unnecessary.' Which I thought was quite a good thing to tell us. We weren't the glamour boys at all. We were to work with the local people and get them doing the job as soon as possible. I think we probably had some other training: I had certainly to get a driver's licence.

Then we embarked for Holland with our fleet of vehicles. I was a co-driver on one of the trucks. My job on the team was cook/caterer. I probably got more of that to do on the journey to Holland than I did when we actually arrived. We had several weeks in Tilburg. We were billeted with the Guides' and Scouts' teams. And there it was mainly ferrying relief supplies to hospitals.

Then we moved to Bildhoven and we had a variety of jobs. The hospitals were in desperate need of baby food and powdered milk, and that sort of thing. And I think their problem was the black market. So although they had large army lorries and their drivers we were sent with them, because I suppose we had the reputation of being above that sort of thing! I think that was justified. So with these people I saw quite a bit of Holland. The lorry drivers were always very friendly and they were very pleased because they always got a meal and they even spent the night with us in the billets.

Another job we got was when the people from the Displaced Persons camps were coming back we were assisting in taking them back to their home towns. That was quite a good experience. I remember on one occasion Queen Wilhelmina came to the station when we were there, to greet the returning Ostlingers. And there again I saw quite a lot of Holland.[255]

Then another job we had was with a clinic. With crowded housing conditions and so on there was a great deal of scabies. We treated them for that before they were rehabilitated.

We made contacts in Holland, and we contacted one or two people and they started an International Voluntary Service for Peace branch there. We also met one boy who had spent six weeks between the floor boards during the Occupation in Rotterdam, hiding from the Nazis. And they told us about the privations: there were no dogs or cats to be found in Antwerp, for instance, during the time of the food shortage; and in Holland they were eating bulbs.

What I didn't like very much was the women with the shaved heads. This is what they did to the women who had collaborated in any way with the Germans. But of course who were we to judge? We'd never encountered these sorts of conditions.

We were in Holland a matter of months then it was time for us to move on because once again the Dutch were ready to take over what we had been doing. And then we moved on to Germany. We finally arrived at a Displaced Persons camp in the Brunswick area.[256]

We there had various jobs. Mine was once again to oversee the cooking arrangements, to get the supply of food every day from the army depots; and, since they were German staff, just watch out for any friction between them and the Displaced Persons, who were of various nationalities. First of all there were the Poles and then there were the Italians. The Italians were the most vociferous. One day when I was on duty they came marching along and their leader, who spoke very good English but with an American accent, complained about bugs in the huts. I agreed with them and pulled my sleeve up and showed them the bites I had from these bugs—which quietened them down! But I promised them action and we did get action. They had to clear out the huts and fumigate them.

Then a bunch of Yugoslavian folk came into the camp—Tito's lot, his Partisans—great big men with bushy eyebrows and mustachios. So I was expecting trouble—confrontation with the Germans who were cooking and serving the meals—but no, the Yugoslavs were just like lambs and there was no trouble at all with them.[257]

Our other job there was going round the Displaced Persons camps and helping them if they were short of anything, trying to oil the pipelines between them and the authorities. We found all the camp leaders very good. The Polish folk—some I met had been in concentration camps—couldn't wait to get back to Poland and help by building things again. Well, when we left there we were on very friendly terms with the people in the various camps.

Then we moved again, this time into a terrace of houses. That's where we ourselves had a German cook, Willi the cook. I had to keep an eye on him because he was inclined to sort of do a bit on the side with our stores, perhaps just for his own relations. But he was a good cook. We were doing similar work there, going round the camps, but we weren't actually living amongst them, that was the difference. That was where I had a game of rugby. Another conscientious objector and I played for the local military unit. We always seemed to get on well with most of the military people we came across. There they didn't seem to mind having conshies in their scrum! Maybe they didn't know.

Then we moved up to Bremke, within a very short distance of the borderline between the British Zone of occupation and the Russian Zone. Every day the barriers between the two Zones were lifted and those who had been transferred from the Ruhr and the industrial districts to the east were now being repatriated. But we noticed they were all the old people and the kids. There was none in between those ages really. The only men that came through were in a sorry state. We saw some pathetic sights. One boy came through pushing a push chair and his aunt, who had taken charge of him to bring him over, was sitting dead in the push chair.

These refugees had to walk, oh, a mile or two from the station on the other side and then on our side down to Friedland, which was the camp. That would be two or three miles, I think. But we arranged transport only for the old people and the sick children.

The camp at Friedland was, oh, deplorable. It was just an old farm steading and it was knee deep in mud. On Christmas Eve we had a birth in the stable! But they did establish a new camp. And this is when we got the idea. German students had been already coming up and helping the people with their baggage on the road down. So we contacted them—our leader went in and spoke to them. And a group of them got a hut there—there was about a dozen of us all told and we added our army rations, which helped a bit—a change from the black bread (and it really was black) and the wurst.[258] And we formed a scheme there.

I remember I was working away with them on a hut and some German refugees passed and something they said caused my mates to start laughing. I said, 'What was all that about?' 'Oh, they said, 'they were pointing to your unform and saying, "This must be a punishment".' And there we did organise a concert. There was a three-piece band from the German Reformed Church. They used to go out at night. They didn't take any part in the camp discussions generally but they went out and played in the camp—mostly hymn tunes, I think! And once again there were sketches and so on. The Scottish compere with his very bad German appealed to them! With one German there I struck up a friendship and we've kept in touch ever since.

When there was no longer the same need at the border I went to a staging post in the Ruhr Valley, where the trains were still coming in with refugees from farther afield. And there we were just assisting them in their rehabilitation. But the work was becoming less necessary and I was due to be released anyway at that time. So having done my stint, as it were, I came home. It would be 1946.

I was with International Voluntary Service for Peace for a time and worked in a summer camp with them in Shropshire. And then I was accepted for one of the courses where they were giving a year's training and I chose to go on a farm to get experience and then go to the farm college. I finished up working on farms—in dairying mainly—up to 1961, and mainly in Angus and Perthshire. And then when they were advertising for mature students to enter the teaching profession I got into the Teachers' Special Recruitment Scheme, and thanks to my ACII qualification from my insurance days I did a one-year course of training instead of having to do the full thing.

Of course, housing then became a problem because I had to get out of the tied farm cottage I'd been in. Perthshire, Angus and Dundee weren't interested in my housing problems but Dumfries offered me a choice of three houses—which is why I landed back in Dumfriesshire. I spent six years in Thornhill as an assistant, was then a rural headmaster in the school at Bankend, south of Dumfries, and Torthorwald, till I retired in 1980, when I got a council house in Thornhill. So I'm back not so very far away from Eskdalemuir, where I was a conscientious objector.

There is no doubt, there is no doubt in my mind that I would take exactly the same position again. I mean, when you're confronted with some of the events that take place you just wonder. But I still feel the same. All wars were avoidable. In the early days the Peace Ballot was all in favour of sanctions—but effective sanctions. Then things might have been very different.

The fact that I had been a conscientious objector during the war never came up. In no case have I shouted it from the rooftops. I don't know in any of the interviews I had if they ever asked about war service. They would all know that I wasn't ex-army because I wasn't claiming, from the salary point of view, recognition of war service. But I haven't felt any discrimination at all. I never felt I was turned away from a job or lost promotion: it just never seems to have come up.

Bill Prentice

I was born in 1917 in Lanark. My father was a commercial traveller. He was a Tory. My mother, as far as she was political at all, was Liberal. And I didn't follow either of them in that respect—well, I suppose I did, when I was young. But eventually I was a socialist. And there was no pacifism or anti-war feeling particularly in the family. My father hadn't fought in the 1914-18 war, because he had asthma and was rejected. A number of my uncles were in the war, including one who joined up when he wasn't yet the age: he was keen. But I can't think of any family deaths because of the First World War. I think it was largely because of reading—reading writers like Aldous Huxley—and the Christian ethic that finally turned me into a pacifist.[259]

I did join the Church of Scotland but not very enthusiastically, and not for very long. I was a member of the Peace Pledge Union before the war and since, and more recently of course of the Campaign for Nuclear Disarmament.[260]

In 1937 or '38 I went to Glasgow University. I studied English, French and German, and while I was there I did have a vacation in Germany, a student exchange that was arranged, and went to a family in Hamburg, where the mother was bitterly anti-Nazi. But there was nothing they could do short of endangering themselves. So I suppose that underlined my feeling—because they were a very friendly family—that the whole thing was quite crazy. And other events in those years, like Mussolini's invasion of Abyssinia, just made me more convinced of the insanity and brutality of the whole thing.[261]

I wasn't active in student political associations at the University, well, I was a commuting student. I lived in Ayr—I had moved there on my ninth birthday—and travelled each day to Glasgow. I usually came back as soon as my classes were over. But there was a Pacifist Club which I occasionally attended while I was at the University. I haven't any clear memories of that really, just that it did exist. Oh, and Dick Sheppard of the Peace Pledge Union was elected Rector while I was at the University. It was probably those meetings that I attended, rather than being a regular attender at the Pacifist Club itself.

In Ayr itself there was already a group of the Peace Pledge Union. So I knew about half a dozen to a dozen other pacifists at that time there. We had regular meetings.

I graduated from Glasgow University in 1940 with an Ordinary degree. I went to Jordanhill Teachers' Training College from that. I was in the middle of my course there when I registered as a conscientious objector and had my tribunal. I've no clear memory of receiving the call-up papers. But I remember discussing matters with a school friend when I had decided to take the step of registering as an objector as it seemed a huge step to take and one that would be misunderstood and objected to. I must have had the use of my father's car at the time because my friend and I drove up to the Heads of Ayr and talked about it there and I revealed I was going to take this great step. The pacifist group in Ayr certainly gave me quite a bit of moral support, too. So I didn't feel entirely isolated. And although my parents weren't pacifist at all, they were immediately sympathetic as soon as they knew that I was going to register as a conshie. And the wider family were also sympathetic, although again there were no pacifists in the family.

The first tribunal, the ordinary tribunal, was in Glasgow, with Archibald Black, KC, as the head of the tribunal. I don't remember the other members of the tribunal at all but I remember Archibald Black as very aggressive. He was very determined to find out any chink he could in your objections. And he asked me about helping people in the event of an air raid. I said obviously I would be willing to do that. 'And you wouldn't rather do it in an organisation such as the ARP, rather than on your own?' I said I objected to the ARP as part of the war machine. And he said, 'So you would rather do it inefficiently than efficiently?'—and made some remark that my course in Logic at the University didn't seem to have done me much good![262] Anyhow, the result of the tribunal was that I got exemption, but only on condition that I did non-combatant duties. And because I regarded that as part of the war machine I objected to that as well. I appealed against the decision, and at the Appellate Tribunal in Edinburgh I did get unconditional exemption.

At the Appellate Tribunal I only remember this old boy who was the chairman and who I think was some relation of the present Queen Mum. He gave me the impression when I was listening to all the cases before my own that he really had no conception of ordinary people's lives but he was quite a humane sort of person. I think he was probably Lord Elphinstone.[263]

Quite soon after the Appellate Tribunal had given me unconditional exemption I heard about the Pacifist Service Units in London and the work they were doing during the Blitz in the East End. So with another Ayr friend who was a member of the Peace Pledge Union like myself, I went down to London for interview. We were both accepted. That was early in 1941.[264]

I was in one of the Pacifist Service Units in Stepney, which is now Tower Hamlets, for almost the rest of the war—from early 1941 until, I think, just after VE Day.[265] There were actually three Pacifist Service Units in Stepney. Ours was in a flat, in an old block of flats. Another was a flat in a new block. And the third was in a vicarage which had been evacuated by the vicar.

In our Unit there were about a dozen of us. There were two women, who were Quakers, who were more or less in charge of cooking and housekeeping. But we did in fact have a rota so that each of the men did have a week in the kitchen, when we did all the shopping and all the cooking—and quite a bit of entertaining, because we occasionally had social workers and other guests in the evening. I valued the cooking rota, in that it taught me to be able to cook. The two women Quakers in the Unit weren't conscientious objectors. They hadn't had to register for war service—was it a question of their age? They may have been beyond the age for registering. We also had part-timers in our Unit, people who were pacifists or conshies living in London who would perhaps do one night a week and join in the Medical Patrol or whatever might be appropriate.

We had a variety of work in the Unit. At night we did medical aid. We had Medical Aid Units, little kiosks, in several of the big air raid shelters like Free Trade Wharf. And we also did a Medical Aid Patrol round the small shelters in the railway arches that go through Stepney. During the day we rescued furniture from bombed houses and stored it in church halls or in whatever accommodation was available. We had a play centre for the young children and a club for the older ones. We did fire-watching for another club in Stepney, and in that connection later on I was called up for official fire-watching.

I objected to that on the same grounds, that I thought it was all part of the war machine, although I was doing it voluntarily. And I was sentenced to a fine or eight days' imprisonment. This is a part I am rather ashamed of. I refused to pay the fine and went into the cell in the local police station. I had wondered about taking any money with me in case I went to prison—someone had said, 'You might be turned out of Wormwood Scrubs at six in the morning and want a bus fare or some breakfast.' So I took with me a fiver, I think it probably was. Anyhow when the policeman at the local police station asked me to turn out my pockets he found the money. Of course, he couldn't understand why someone who had the money wouldn't pay the fine. And I suppose I was in a rather confused and traumatic state, as one would be. He said, 'Oh, if you have the money you've got to pay it.' I'm afraid I accepted that, so I never actually went to jail and I regretted it afterwards of course.

When I went to London early in 1941 it was really in the middle of the Blitz. In fact, when I arrived at the Unit in Stepney there was actually a large bomb crater in the ground immediately outside the flat. That was my introduction to the Blitz. And I think I spent the first night sleeping on the table in the kitchen because they hadn't yet got a bed for me. Destruction, deaths, injuries, were happening all the time. One of the most vivid memories: I had been on long leave home in Ayr during May the 10th 1941, which was one of the worst fire blitzes on London. I arrived back on May the 12th and as I walked down the street to the Unit Stepney was still burning, smoking and burning away. And someone—I suppose it was a gramophone record—someone was singing, 'I Don't Want to Set the World on Fire'!

I didn't like the V1s and V2s at all because of the uncertainty. You heard the threatening noise and waited for when it would cut out. We did have a V1 land on the vicarage. I happened to be there at the time and we piled down into the cellar and I got a chunk of the ceiling on my back, which was nothing at the time. But there were others, not in the Unit but round about, who were badly injured. But years later I did have back trouble as a result of that. The V2s were worse in the sense that you knew that it would all be over before you knew anything about it. With the V1 at least you did hear the engine cut out and waited for what would happen. But with the V2 you didn't know where you were at all.

We were fortunate in the Unit in that I'm sure there were no deaths. But some people were injured. One person, for example, had an incendiary bomb burst in his face and suffered a lot afterwards with headaches and depression as a result of that. But we really were lucky in that respect, considering we were in the middle of it all.

Well, being there in the Blitz was scary at times but it was also interesting. And obviously it was a sympathetic atmosphere because you were living with other pacifists, other conscientious objectors.

We had no uniform at all, there was no sort of uniform as such. We wore dungarees for purely practical purposes for all the dirty work we were sometimes doing. Otherwise we wore our own clothes. And some members did wear a PSU— Pacifist Service Units—armband but I certainly don't remember wearing one myself.

The East Enders themselves were certainly very friendly. They weren't—with a few exceptions perhaps—at all prejudiced against the conshies. They may not have agreed with us but they knew that we were there to help them as and when we could.

So they accepted us as part of the community. There were some incomers who were prejudiced, not the locals, not the East Enders themselves but people like social workers who came to function in Stepney and who didn't like the conshies doing their sort of work. But I remember East Enders inviting us to their homes, particularly when we were doing the social welfare work. They quite often invited us in and lavished very sweet tea on us, which wasn't exactly enjoyable always. But we did have that hospitality.

There was no supervision of us as conscientious objectors by the authorities in the East End. It was just taken for granted that we were carrying out our commitments.

In the Unit we had short leave, which was as far as I remember a couple of days every fortnight or so when we could if we wished—those of us who didn't live in London—go to a rest house in Chelsea, which was also run by members of the Pacifist Service Units, and where we could relax for a day or two. And then we had long leave, which was something like a fortnight each year, or it may have been twice a year, when we were able to go home, wherever home happened to be.

I kept in touch with my own home in Ayr. I wrote regularly to home and my mother fairly regularly sent food parcels—not that we were starving. It was more extras, because in fact the Londoners came off pretty well in the matter of food, in having less strict rations than many people had. And we had one member of another of the units in Stepney, Colin Somerford, who had been Compton Mackenzie's sort of gentleman's gentleman on Barra, who arranged bulk buying like big jars of marmalade and jams and so on, which were distributed among the three Units in Stepney.[266]

I think I probably attended some of the bigger meetings of the Peace Pledge Union while I was there. But on the whole there wasn't much time for that. We were too busy really, except for the leave, and then we were taking things easy. In our Unit at Stepney the grounds of objection varied quite a bit—Christian objectors and political objectors. There were no Jehovah's Witnesses or Christadelphians in our Unit but there were Quakers and I think one Church of Scotland. I can't remember if the political objectors were members of any particular political parties, such as the Independent Labour Party. We had discussions in the Unit and we certainly listened to the news of the war on the radio. But I think the discussions were more of our own views, since obviously there was a range of views from the Absolutists, as they were called, to those who were willing to compromise in certain ways. We had arguments about that.

There were two Welshmen in the Unit but I was the only Scot. Another Scot did go with me when I joined the Unit early in 1941 but he didn't stay very long. There were one or two Scots in the other units in London.

There was one member of our own Unit at Stepney who decided about half way through the war that he wasn't a pacifist after all. And I think he joined the Fleet Air Arm. But all the others, as far as I remember, went right through.

I didn't myself find any reason to change my objection to war. I think it probably became stronger as a result of my experiences at Stepney. They reinforced my objection. The Blitz reinforced the insanity and brutality of the whole thing.

Well, at the end of the war we were free just to go home. We chose to do so. When I left it must have been May or June 1945. I came back to Ayr.

I started teaching at Jordanhill College School and Hutcheson's Boys Grammar School in Glasgow. But I very soon decided that teaching was not for me and got out while the going was good. I just hadn't what it takes to be a teacher. I went back down south at the end of '45. I was for a time with a correspondence college at St Albans and then with NALGO in their education department, first in Marylebone then in Euston Road.[267]

I wasn't conscious after the war of any prejudice against me as a conscientious objector during the war. I didn't find any victimisation in my job or in promotion. I kept in touch with members of the Pacifist Service Units after the war and I still meet some of them whenever I'm in London. I have covenanted to the Unit and get their newsletter regularly, because they still carry on. They're not called Pacifist Service Units now but Family Service Units but doing similar work.

After the war I wouldn't say there was any change in my convictions to speak of at all. Well, I joined the Labour Party eventually and Campaign for Nuclear Disarmament of course. Let's say I would rather have been in the Independent Labour Party if it had still been in existence or still been active.

If history were to repeat itself I think I would act in more or less the same way as I did in the war, except that I don't imagine there would be conscientious objection and tribunals and so on in the event of nuclear war. It would be much too sudden and complete for that. But my feelings would certainly be the same. I haven't found any reason at all to change my views since the war.

Norman MacCaig

My mother came from the Outer Hebrides—the island of Scalpay. My father came from Dumfriesshire. They met in Edinburgh and several things happened—including me. I was born in Edinburgh in 1910. I had three sisters. I was the second youngest in the family.

I went to the Royal High School and then to Edinburgh University in 1928. I would be seventeen actually, just a few weeks off eighteen. After four years there—I took a degree in Classics, not English as most people suppose—I went to Moray House teachers' training college for a year. I was always sure that I was going to be a teacher. But at that date, 1932, when I left the University the teaching profession was overcrowded. Between then and the war I applied for four jobs teaching Classics—all in Scotland, I wouldn't leave Scotland—and got none of them. Meanwhile I was teaching primary school, as a temporary teacher, in a good number of schools, all in Edinburgh. And I got married the year before the war broke out.

I was influenced emotionally by international events in the 1930s because I hate war, of course. I detested war. The Spanish Civil War was a very big big thing in Scotland, in Britain—anywhere. All such things, of course, were sickening to read about and hear about. But I was never a very politically minded man. It just seemed to me horrible attacks by human beings on human beings for political reasons—which doesn't seem to me an excuse for murdering people. That really was all my response. It wasn't a knowledgeable one about politics. Oh, I dare say I knew a bit but not all that much.

Even I remember in the First World War my father got magazines and things, journals, all about the war, with photographs, rubbishy prose, you know, telling lies in every paragraph. Well, that was then—born in 1910, again I remind you—and I read these things with the interest that youngsters look at horror films now. Oh, but I was disgusted, I was very disgusted. And I suppose without me knowing about it, this was making my pacifism even more solid.

My family background in the First World War was that, well, relatives of course fought then. And I remember a friend of my parents and therefore of us, the children, who was in the army. But he was unscathed. He wasn't even mentally or psychologically damaged by his experiences. But I don't know what his experiences were. My father wasn't through the First War, because he was stone deaf in one ear. He volunteered but wasn't allowed. But I wasn't influenced by my family or their friends. I knew from about the age of twelve I wasn't going to kill anybody. Back to that simple statement. I wasn't influenced.

It was the violence in the world that really made me think about questions of peace and war and pacifism.

But that had nothing to do with me becoming a conscientious objector. I keep on repeating: I was just not going to kill people, whether it was in Abyssinia or anywhere else. I just refused to kill people: simple as that.

I wasn't a politically minded man. I didn't vote at all for a good many years. And I never joined any political party. In that sense, I was not a politically minded man. I just knew I was having nothing to do with killing and I still feel the same about it.

In the '30s an awful lot of people were certain there was a war coming— particularly, as usual, the writers. They've got a nose for such things—the poets and all that, you know, that are looked down on as being illogical, etc. They are not a bit. And we were all perfectly sure the war was coming. But there weren't writers who influenced me in that way. I wasn't influenced. My mind was made up— consciously made up when I was about twelve. And I wasn't influenced by anything whatever, except myself. I sound very aggressive and selfish but that's the way it was.

Well, I was actually called up in the winter of 1941, because I remember there was heavy snow on the ground that winter. I must have been 31. And I told my parents that I wasn't going to kill anybody, of course, And I think they thought, 'This is joking.' None of my relatives, nor even my friends, were pacifist. And my father, who was a wage slave in a chemist's shop and was an intelligent man with a lot of interests, thought I was just being a cheeky young man when the letter came. He was very disturbed indeed. He lost his temper. But that was only that morning. After six weeks or so it was totally accepted by both my parents. So that I had an easy journey compared with a lot of young men.

At the Tribunal I told them: 'You can't put a label on me. I'm not refusing to fight in the war for religious reasons or political reasons or anything like that. It's just that I refuse to murder people—to kill people.' And I said, 'I am very willing to join the Royal Army Medical Corps or the Red Cross or the Quakers. But I'm not going to kill anybody.' And since I'd said I was willing to join the RAMC they couldn't write me off as a hundred per cent conshie. And they put me in the Non-Combatant Corps, a collection of people that nobody seems to have heard about, a Corps made up of people like myself. The NCC were linked to the Pioneer Corps in order to have corporals, sergeants, captains, majors. All the officers and NCOs were Regular army people. But all the privates, as it were, were just like myself.

Well, when I was told to go to Ilfracombe in Devon to the Pioneer Corps, I wrote to the commanding officer and said, 'I'm no comin. You'll generally find me home after midnight if you want me.' Eventually two coppers appeared after mid-night and took me up in the black maria to the High Street police station. I think it was a Friday and there was no Police Court on the Saturday. So I stayed in the cell there over the week-end. I didn't get bail but the policemen were very nice to me. I said, 'I can't sleep. Is there anything I can read?' And a policeman went off and came back with half-a-dozen paperbacks. Then I was brought before the beak in the

Police Court on Monday. He said, 'This is a matter for the army. Just go back into your cell.'

Two soldiers came down from Edinburgh Castle and took me up to the Castle. I was put in jankers—to use the old fashioned word.[268] I was there for several days. Most interesting it was. I was put into a room—it was the guardhouse—with a great lot of soldiers under arrest. They were held there until they were brought before a military court. And most of them, I think, were up for absence without leave, that sort of thing. I was the only pacifist in the place. And they all knew I was a conshie. Because the first question they asked was, 'What regiment are you in ?'

Anyway a big shot—the Commanding Officer in the Castle—came round to inspect us in the guardhouse. Everybody had their beds tidy and their boots in the proper place. I'd just made up mine as if I were at home. In he came. We were all shouted at to 'Stand to attention!' They all sprang to attention. And I didn't. I was sitting on the edge of my bed and I just stayed sitting, I didn't get up. And the Commanding Officer flushed crimson and started shouting and bawling at me. I said, 'You don't realise I'm not in the army. I'm a pacifist. They've summoned me to the army but I'm not going because I'm a pacifist. I've resigned.' He nearly exploded. I thought he was going to burst. But I didn't get up on my feet. The rest of the soldiers hearing a major general or whatever he was being talked to like that, sitting on the end of my bed, 'Oh, no, I'm not standing up. I'm not in the army'— wonderful! So what they thought of me in that tough place suddenly rose. I was their lily-white boy after that.

Our lunch in the guardhouse was laid on a table and you just piled in—which I wouldn't or couldn't. They just swarmed like bees. And out of that dense mass an arm emerged from this tough guy—and he was a real toughie—handing me something to eat, and this fellow mutters, 'There ye are, chum.' To a conshie! Well, this tough guy was on his way to Barlinnie I think for the sixth or seventh time— probably for small offences or he'd have been there a lot longer, absent without leave, that sort of thing. And yet it's he whose arm came out of that mob and handed me my lunch: 'There you are, chum.' He was a soldier, not a conscientious objector. But again, you see, they had no resentment, no resentment at all. I was in good favour with them.

I was in the Castle guardhouse for several days and then a corporal and a private, who of course was a pacifist like myself, were sent up to Edinburgh to take me down to the Pioneer and Non-Combatant Corps at Ilfracombe. The whole thing was ridiculous, really. Any number of things made me laugh and laugh. We had some hours to wait for a train, so I took them down to my mother's house and she gave us a meal. And the corporal went off to the films—ludicrous!

We went down to Ilfracombe and I said I wasn't putting on the Non-Combatant Corps uniform. The Commanding Officer said, 'I believe you have offered to join the Royal Army Medical Corps?' And I said, 'That's what I told them.' He said, 'Well, put on your uniform. You won't be asked to do anything you wouldn't want to do. And apply for a transfer to the RAMC. You should get that in about a month.' So I did—until a notice went up that, 'The RAMC are no longer accepting conscientious objectors.' However, the Non-Combatant Corps proceeded to put us on jobs that I could see no connection with the army whatever—things like fire-watching, working on farms. They didn't know what to do with us, they actually didn't know what to do with us. They put us on some damn silly jobs, I can tell you, just to keep us occupied: trimming the hedges of country lanes, that sort of thing. They just couldn't think of things to do with us. A number of us worked on farms for a while. Well, I was very willing to do that.

In the Non-Combatant Corps at Ilfracombe I was in the Tenth Company and there were about 200 of us. I think there were twelve companies. I know there was an Eleventh, and I think there was a Twelfth. They all passed through Ilfracombe, one company at a time. They weren't all there at any one time. They were from all levels of life. And there were very many reasons for their conscientious objection. Far and away the biggest one was religious grounds. I don't remember one who stated his political grounds. They were nearly all religious objectors. I don't like putting a label on it but if one has to put a label I would say my objection was on moral grounds.

We didn't really have discussions and arguments about conscientious objection or pacifism at Ilfracombe among ourselves. We just all assumed that the other fellow was an honest conscientious objector. He was objecting on conscientious grounds. We just accepted that. I don't remember arguing with any of them. I think we were all very much individualists who had their views, whether they were religious or political or moral, and they were sticking by them—individualists.

As I've said, the Non-Combatant Corps was linked to the Pioneer Corps in order to have corporals, sergeants, captains, majors. They were all Regular army men. And if one came to join us they felt it was a fearful degradation, not being allowed to really go and fight but to look after a bunch of bloody conshies, you know. We never caused them any trouble pinching each other's this that and t'other, and all that.

For example, there was a sergeant, an Irish sergeant, who actually was known as Paddy because that was his name. And I remember on this occasion we were fire-watching in the docks at Newport in Wales. And of course the officers and all that—at least the NCOs, they went into town and got pissed on Saturday night. And several times Sergeant Paddy came back with plasters on his face. It turned out he'd got into fights in the pubs, sticking up for the conshies. That sort of thing kept happening. Paddy addressed us all the time, of course, as if we were rascals. He used to pretend to abuse us. 'Don't you say a word!' Odd mixtures of feelings. You met it all the time, all the time.

Let me say a little about the response to us conshies in the Non-Combatant Corps by the Regular army or air force people. Near Aldershot, when we were stationed there, we were continually meeting Grenadier Guards, Scots Guards, Irish Guards, meeting them at dances, and especially coming home on leave, the compartment filled with other soldiers. Not once did any of them abuse us, not once. I remember coming up home to Edinburgh once on leave on the train. Seven other Regular army chaps were in the compartment: four soldiers on that side, three on this, as well as me. Of course, I was wearing my uniform with NCC on the badge. One of the soldiers said, 'What does NCC stand for? Norwegian Camel Corps?' I said, 'No, no. We're conscientious objectors.' And there was quite a bit of talk about that. There were two ways of looking at it. One was, 'Oh, I'd have done that but I'm not clever enough.' I said, 'It's nothing to do with cleverness.' So—'Oh, no, no, they'd just twist me round their fingers.' And the other attitude was, 'Well, I'd have done it but I wasn't brave enough.' As if it was brave being a conshie. But never a word of abuse from the armed forces—just the civilians.

Oh, the civilians were different. When we were marching through the streets in Liverpool on our way to the docks, where we were fire-watching, quite often the general public would shout things at us. 'Yellowbelly!' was the favourite one. But never from the Armed Forces.

I never saw or heard of any brutality by our superiors—never. Not only at Ilfracombe but all the time I was in the NCC I never saw one sign of it. The only thing like that, there was a fellow there who was a Quaker. Now the Quakers more or less automatically were considered to be pacifists, and joined the NCC. And there was one fellow I met who had disobeyed orders and was sent to a military prison—which is terrible—back to his unit, then refused orders again, military prison: three times he was sent to the military prison. There was a name for that sort of thing at that time: cat and mouse treatment. But he was the only one I met who suffered that.[269]

Well, I stood the fire-watching, farming and other jobs we did in the Non-Combatant Corps for three years just about, till one day, away in some country place in the south of England, a notice went up that the following day we were going to work in a tank depot. And I thought, 'If I'm working in a tank depot I might as well drive a tank.' So I refused. I was duly court-martialled—in Aldershot, no less: nothing but the best for MacCaig. And you know the proceedings, don't you? If they think you're lying they send you to a military prison, which isn't fun, for six months and then back to your unit. If they think you're honest they send you to a civvy prison for 93 days.

I've met a lot of people—men—who were in the Second War and came out of it pacifists: 'Never again. What a fool I was.' You know, this is a very common attitude. It was beautifully shown when I was in the Non-Combatant Corps in 1944 after I had refused to obey orders. I was waiting to be court-martialled in Aldershot. And the captain in our company, who was an excellent man, said, 'I'd like to have a talk with you.' And we strolled up and down in the sunny field just outside South-ampton. And he told me that he had fought in the First World War—volunteered—and became a captain. And between the wars he did an immense amount of work for pacifism. I forget the names of the various organisations. But he spent a lot of his time working for pacifism. But of course when the war broke out in 1939—'What can one do?' I remember saying to him: 'That's like being a fireman until there's an actual fire. Anybody can be a pacifist in peacetime.' But he was an instance of so many men who after the First World War were pacifists—a lot of them. The captain was a nice man and a good man. But like so many, many others, once this government says 'Your Country Needs You!', off you go, sheep to the slaughter in many cases.

At my court martial in Aldershot I would say there were four officers on the court. And there was another lesser officer, I presume, telling them my crime. He wasn't really a prosecutor. He was just stating my case. He was neutral. He was explaining why I was there before them. Well, you can't expect a court martial to be sympathetic but they were certainly reasonable and objective. I didn't have any impression at all that they were trying to browbeat me. Well, they accepted my honesty and I was sentenced to 93 days' imprisonment in a civvy prison with remission. I was sent to Winchester Jail for a little while and then transferred to Wormwood Scrubs.

When we left the court martial I was walking along beside an army corporal and another conshie. I was their prisoner, you understand. And a group of immensely high ranking officers passed us. The other two, of course, nearly broke their arms saluting these officers. I didn't salute. I was just walking along. And the officers stopped a few yards away and sent their junior officer and he started shouting and bawling at me. 'Put him on a charge!' and that sort of thing. And I told him the same sort of story I'd told the commanding officer at Edinburgh Castle three years earlier: 'You're shouting at the wrong man. I'm not in the army. I've resigned.' Again, oh, boy, the veins bulged in his neck.

These two incidents—in Edinburgh Castle and Aldershot—with those two officers taught me that no organisation can make you do what you don't want to do—something serious that you don't want to do. They might punish you for it but they can't make you do it. In other countries they'd shoot you against a wall. I would have been shot against a wall, truly, rather than fight. I would. Naturally, that was a thing I thought of. I was prepared to be shot against a wall. But I wasn't going to kill anybody.

My recollection of Winchester prison is that it was full of bed bugs. Every night you went poking with a needle in the holes in the bed frame and the table frame. And the food was atrocious. People who applied to be allowed to work in the garden were allowed to work in the garden. So I did. And if you came across a potato that hadn't been picked last year we ate it raw: not a good idea, but we were very hungry. Most of the talk was about food—not, as you might think, sex. Some of the boys said, 'Oh, you should see the food they have in such and such a prison. My God, it is real good stuff there.' You know, some of them had been in prisons all over the place.

At Winchester they sent small bands of prisoners out with a sergeant, to work on farms, that sort of thing, which was marvellous—out in the fresh air, digging away or knocking in fences. There was none of that at Wormwood Scrubs—no wonder, it's in the middle of London.

There was only one other conscientious objector at Winchester. He came from the same company in the Non-Combatant Corps as me. And he was called a junior or under-age something or other, and they were kept separate. He was a young fellow of about twenty or twenty-one. They were all kept separate from the rest of the prisoners.

I was in Winchester prison I should think about three weeks. We went from there to Wormwood Scrubs. The food there was excellent. Wormwood Scrubs was an easier regime in a sense than Winchester. The amenities were better, in the sense of food.

We arrived in London to go to Wormwood Scrubs the very day the buzz bombs started operating. And really they were panic stricken. The driver of the van that took us from the station to the prison, oh, he was in a terrible state: 'The war's over! We can't stop them! They've not even got pilots in them! If you shoot them they just fall to the ground and burst anyway!' But they got used to them. It's marvellous what people can stomach.

I didn't meet any other conscientious objectors in Wormwood Scrubs, although they may well have been there. We didn't get much chance to chat with each other. We had a cell each both in Winchester and at Wormwood Scrubs.

As I've said, my wife and I were married the year before the war broke out. And our first child was born when I was in the Non-Combatant Corps. My wife never let on it was coming till it was all over, in case I worried.

My wife started as a teacher and she taught part of the time during the war and I think when the child was coming she gave it up. We couldn't then have managed financially had it not been that Edinburgh Education Authority, who'd been my employer in teaching, gave us while I was in the Non-Combatant Corps and in Winchester prison and Wormwood Scrubs I think it was two-thirds of what my salary would have been had I been teaching. It was paid all the way through, right through. They were extremely generous. Otherwise, oh, I don't know how we could have managed.

I missed my wife, of course. She used to come down and get lodgings nearby where we were, if we were to be in a place for any length of time. So I even saw her.

When I finished at Wormwood Scrubs I went before the Tribunal again. They accepted I was honest and I got my ticket, on condition I did land work or hospital work. I went back to prison and in no time at all—maybe the very next day—they dressed me in civvies and gave me my fare home.

I applied to several hospitals in Edinburgh and they wouldn't have me because I was a conshie. And yet I know conscientious objectors who did work in hospitals—in other places, not in Edinburgh. I don't know why that should be so in Edinburgh. I only know that I applied to two or three hospitals—three, I think—and they said they weren't taking C.O.s.

However, strolling in Colinton, a suburb of Edinburgh, I passed a nursery garden and went in and asked if the owner could give me a job. And he said, 'Delighted. Can you dig?' And I said, 'That's all I can do.' I said, 'I should tell you I'm a conscientious objector.' He said, 'I don't care what you are. I need a man.' So I worked for him for a couple of years, often in the nursery itself, but often in private gardens round about, you know, planting things and pruning things and all that. Colinton is a community of pretty douce Edinburgh bourgeoisy people, where you would have expected them to look down their noses at conshies, but they didn't. Oh, they knew, they knew I was a Conshie.

I didn't know a dandelion from a daisy when I started but I got books out of the library, of course, and swotted them up and became, I think, a pretty good jobbing gardener. On one occasion a professional jobbing gardener, who had been at it all his life, and myself dug over a lady's garden and when we finished he looked at it and said, 'That's the way I like to see it. None o' thae bloody flowers.' I was perfectly happy. Growing plants and flowers in the nursery I got 1/6d. an hour—the boss got 2/6d. an hour. Our second child was born while I was a jobbing gardener. As I've said, the Education Authority in Edinburgh gave me two-thirds of what my teaching salary would have been had I been teaching, all the way through. They were extremely generous. I don't know how we could have managed on 1/6d. an hour. Even in those days it was pitiful.

So I worked for the nurseryman for a couple of years, till the war was over, and then returned to civilian life. I applied for a job in a primary school and I got it and I've been teaching ever since.

The only thing I might add, as an aftermath of the war, when I was teaching I applied for promotion, to become a deputy headmaster. And I think I must have the British record. I applied ten times and was turned down every time. Now I was actually—it sounds boastful—a very good teacher. And the various headmasters I worked under during this spell couldn't understand why I wasn't getting promotion. Years and years later I was at a big 'do' in Parliament House or somewhere in Edinburgh, along with Hugh MacDiarmid—ladies stripped to the navel and gentlemen with bands round them, you know—and I was introduced to the Lord Provost. And he said, 'Ah, Mr MacCaig, the last time I met you you were asking for promotion. And,' he said, 'I was chairman of the Education Committee at the time.' And I said, 'Oh, were you? Is it true' (because several of my headmasters at the time suggested this), 'Is it true that the one who objected to me getting promotion was a minister?' And he said, 'I'm sorry to say it was.' That was ten, fifteen years after the war. So I was victimised in my own profession for years, in the sense of promotion being blocked. And it was the minister who did it.

Nothing, nothing at all was ever said by any of my teaching colleagues about my being a conscientious objector, and I don't suppose I actually told them, unless they said, 'What did you do in the war?', in which case I would, of course. And that must have happened. But I never got anything nasty from anybody once the war was over, except by the Education Committee who handed out promotions. And it was one man who was the stumbling block.

Well, the last seven years of my career as a teacher was in Stirling University English Department. I was an ordinary lecturer, except they started me—they were very good to me—away up in the salary scale, although I had taught nothing but Primary all my life and I had a degree in Classics. It was an extraordinary incident in my life. And then they invented a post, just to give me another £1,000 a year for doing what I was doing anyway. They called me a Reader in Poetry at Stirling. Very happy years they were.

Looking back on it now I didn't really have a difficult time at all in the war. Of course I have no regrets. If another war came—as if I could be called up now!—I would do exactly the same. My opinions, beliefs—they're beliefs, rather than opinions—are just the same as they always were. They haven't changed one bit. I just refused to kill people.

Dominic Crolla

Prisoners-of-war, in my opinion, are proud people. But internees are very sad ones. The military go to war with bands playing, people cheering, to defend their homes and country. Internees are picked up by the police from their homes and businesses and taken to camps with barbed wire and soldiers with machine guns. By the way, there is a Geneva Convention about the protection of prisoners-of-war; there is no law about how the treatment of civilian internees goes.

Well, that's what happened to us in the Italian community in Britain on the 10th of June 1940, when Mussolini declared war on Britain. It was a very sad day for us in the Italian community, because having spent nearly all our lives in this country as friends we suddenly became enemies. The feelings of the local population, to put it mildly, was deep anger against us. Where they could they smashed shops and looted the goods. Thousands of pounds' worth of damage was done. Businesses closed and families separated.

Of course at that time Britain was in grave danger. Hitler was nearing the French coast and getting ready to invade Britain. The British government had to protect themselves. And so all the foreigners—Jews, Italians, Germans—residing here were all arrested in great panic and put into camps.

Most were sent to the Isle of Man, and many others to Australia and Canada. One of these ships going to Canada with internees, the *Arandora Star,* was sunk off the Irish coast and about 700 or 800 people were drowned, including my dear father and many close friends.[270]

Personally I was put on a ship called the *Ettrick Star* and sent to Canada. We totalled 204 internees on board, all mixed, and we took ten days to cross the Atlantic. The conditions on board are indescribable. I landed in Canada on the 20th of July 1940.

Of course, the Canadians, far away from Europe, had a terrible opinion of the enemy and they had prepared a great reception for us. Barbers were there the night we arrived to cut our hair, starting from the front—you know, the cropped style. We had to strip off our clothing and we were given a blue uniform with a large red patch on the back. We were all given a number.

We found out that the Canadian government were expecting real prisoners-of-war to arrive and not internees, so that in case the Germans ill treated Canadian prisoners-of-war the Canadians could retaliate on the prisoners in Canada.

During the interviews with each man when we arrived in Canada we were asked what we did. And they wanted to know things about our family. About 180 of us answered firstly that we worked in chip shops and spaghetti shops and ice cream shops, or we were waiters, and that we had been taken from our homes and shops and shipped to Canada. This was a big shock for the Canadians: 'We were expecting dangerous prisoners-of-war and they've sent us a bunch of harmless shopkeepers.' Believe me, the phone between Toronto and London must have been very busy the next day.

We were lucky with regard to treatment—plenty of food, and apart from machine guns and barbed wire we were treated well. We had plenty of sport: ice skating in winter, football, swimming in the St Lawrence River in the summer. And so it was great fun. Although we were restricted we were well treated in this camp.

We all read a lot and some played cards all night. Some did sewing, joinery work, and they were paid 20 cents a day. It kept them going in cigarettes.

There was about a hundred Italians from Britain in our group and fifty Italian seamen who happened to be in British ports when Italy declared war. That was 150. And there was about 54 Jewish refugees—Italians who had run away from Italy in case of trouble. But these fifty or so Jews were released from our camp within about a couple of years, because they all discovered uncles and cousins in America who made an affidavit for them. They posted the affidavit to the camp commander in Canada and most of them got out. But they were very helpful when they were in the camp, you know. They were decent chaps. They had no money. They had come out with nothing. But these cousins in America helped them.[271]

We discovered in time that if you had toothache or a sore back they took you from the camp by ambulance with guards to hospital in Montreal. So naturally we were all trying to get out to see Montreal. We didn't see much. But everybody started to get ill so that they could get around to Montreal. But the authorities soon realised that the prisoners were just wanting out for a run, and so it was all stopped.

Well, my personal internment in Canada lasted about three years and then I was released, brought back to this country and made an interpreter in an Italian prisoner-of-war camp at Huntly. But that's another story.

Now I should add that Italians born in this country were considered more dangerous than people like me, because I was born in Italy, you see, and I had Italian papers. But an Italian born in this country had a British national passport and he could maybe go into places where I wouldnae have been allowed to go as an Italian. So they were considered more dangerous.

There were tribunals set up for them and some got out of internment and some stayed in it. But most of them, once they got in, they resented the fact that they were in. They resented it more than we did. We sort of expected it because we were born in Italy.

Some people did get compensation. There were claims made. But you had to claim within a certain time, say, a week or a month, to the City Chambers. And, of course, that wasn't done. You know, people were too upset with what had happened really.

A lot of my cousins were in the Pioneer Corps in the British army but that didn't save me from being interned. If you were over 16 and if you lived in Edinburgh— Glasgow was all right because it wasn't a protected area—but if you lived in Edinburgh you were kindly asked to move to Peebles or somewhere further away. Rosyth naval base was near Edinburgh, you see, and so Edinburgh was considered a protected area. Your shop was shut if you had a business, or you just lost your job. The family just moved out. My mother was in Peebles for, say, about a year or a year and a half. After that she came back to Edinburgh and she started up in a small business again and it was all right, I mean, after a wee while.

So what happened was that that—being away from Edinburgh—lasted about a couple of years and then you went to the Chief Constable and, you know, you laid your cards on the table. You told him where your man wis. And then very often sons started to grow up and got into the British army. And as soon as that happened of course the lady was immediately brought back to Edinburgh and she started up again. In most cases that's what happened.

Well, eventually, peace was declared and all was forgotten. Because I had lived so long in Scotland and I couldn't think that the Scots hated me, business was resumed better than ever. Most people here were sympathetic to our past circumstances.

Now we are all part and parcel of Scotland. Italian boys marry Scots girls and Italian girls marry Scots boys. Spaghetti, fish and chips and ice cream are selling better than ever. And every Scot knows Italian wine and the lovely beaches where they go in thousands on holiday. May it go on for ever. War is a terrible business and we all sincerely hope and pray that we have no more.

Joseph Pia

I am registered as Giuseppe Pia but on my will and everything it says: 'I, Giuseppe Pia, but known and always signing as Joseph Pia.' I was born in June 1910 at Raeburn Place, Stockbridge, in Edinburgh. My father had an ice cream shop there.

My parents came from the region of Lazio in Italy, the region of which Rome is the capital. My mother was married twice. She and her first husband were married in Italy and came to live in Glasgow in 1896. He had to go back to Italy to do his army conscript service. So he went back with my mother and by then they had a couple of kids. But he contracted tuberculosis and died. So my mother was widowed at the age of twenty with two kids.

In country places in Italy then marriages were always arranged. I heard that my Pia grandfather got a dowry of fifty sheep, plus other things, when my mother married my father in 1904. I think it's a good guess my father married my mother knowing she had three brothers in Edinburgh: if he married her there was a good chance his brothers-in-law would help him to come here—which did happen.

More than half of the Italians who came to Edinburgh came from two little villages near Picinisco in Lazio region. There was a Crolla village and a Pia village. My mother's maiden name was Crolla. Nearly always a Crolla man got a Pia wife, or the Pia boy got a Crolla wife.

My parents told me that in Italy they never, never saw hunger. They had enough for food—no money, it was always barter. They were on the hillside. They grew plenty of wheat, potatoes, and all that sort of thing but no wine. The men down in the valley had vineyards. So they used to swap: a couple of bags of chestnuts or wheat and that for a couple of barrels of wine or olive oil. Bartering: that's how they lived. So they were never ever hungry. But they had no money, no luxury. I was taken by my parents to Italy for a visit when I was four, in the spring or summer of 1914. I've got the vaguest, vaguest memory of it. But I remember it quite well when I went at the age of twelve, in 1922. It was just about the time that Mussolini was coming to power but I knew nothing about politics nor was it mentioned in front of me. But we stayed then in Picinisco, a communal town where the church was and two or three shops, with all these little villages round about.

Both my grandfathers had been in Scotland before my parents came here. But they didn't remain permanently. Picinisco was part of the Papal States when my grandfathers were young, before the unification of Italy in the 1860s. My grandfather Pia used to go down at Eastertime and Christmastime to Naples to play the bagpipes in the streets and earn money. He was a very good player. They used to think at home that he was great because he could bring back luxuries. Others used to do things like that, too. Most of them used to go to French places or Swiss and work there for six months or a year or so and then come back home. But towards the end of the 1800s they started to stay longer but intending to earn money and maybe in ten or fifteen years to go back to Italy and retire. But after staying here half a dozen or more years they got used to things here. They used to go to Italy on holiday and say life was beautiful here in Scotland compared with what they had there—except for weather: Italy beats us for weather. So that was the sort of background from which my parents came. Very, very few older Italians here—I don't know of any—before the Second World War ever became naturalised, because they were always intending to go back home. They were very, very Italian feeling. The next generation, the likes of me born and bred here, we feel more Scots than Italian.

When my mother and father came to Scotland after they were married in 1904 they came direct to Edinburgh. They lived in 23 Raeburn Place. They bought the shop there. It was an ice cream shop. But the big sale was chocolate, sweeties and cigarettes. They used to do a nice trade in the summer. Edinburgh Academy grounds are along in Raeburn Place and the tennis crowds used to come there. My father had seats in the cafe and they used to come. They could have a ball of ice cream with raspberry on top of it and a wafer. They used to call this a MacCallum.

My parents had long, long hours in the shop. They used to open the shop about eight or nine in the morning and stay open all day until eleven at night or midnight, seven days a week. Business was very, very poor during the day. When it came to about seven or eight o'clock at night then trade picked up. They'd maybe draw, well, in my day—their day would be worse—they used to draw £1 till about eight o'clock at night, and from eight till eleven another £2. So that was a good day's drawings—£3. On Saturdays and Sundays they doubled that, doubled.

Well, my father had that shop in Raeburn Place. Then when the 1914-18 war came a man with a shop in Rodney Street got called up to the army and sub-let his shop to my father. So my mother with the wee kids—I had two older half-sisters from my mother's first marriage, an older and a younger brother and younger sister of my own—looked after Raeburn Place and my father worked in Rodney Street.

I remember at Rodney Street we were told that some Zeppelins had come over and dropped a bomb and we went and looked and we saw the bomb hole. And we used to go up and collect cartridges at trenches that were built maybe to train the boys, where Drummond High School is now. But soldiers used to chase us. I had started school at St Mary's near the cathedral in Broughton Street the year after the war had begun but I was too young to remember the outbreak and I don't remember anything about the attitude of people in Edinburgh to Italy before it entered the war in 1915. But I remember that in the school playground somebody pushed me or something and I bumped my head and there was blood and I was bandaged. And the teacher said, 'Look at young Joseph. He's just like one of the wounded soldiers in the war.' I always remember that. I thought it was great. And I remember at the end of the war a man in Stockbridge, Joe Brattisani, who had a chip shop in Church Street, coming down the street in an Italian uniform when he was discharged from the army. The Italians were all called up to the Italian army. Two of my Edinburgh uncles went away to join the Italian army. Alfonso Crolla was one. Another one who was in the field ambulance was killed in the war.

My father was called up for the Italian army during the war. He had retained his Italian citizenship. But he was unfit. It was very unlikely that he could have swung the lead because they were desperate for men. But a lot of people said, 'Ah, he looks a smart chap. He must have bribed or something. Fancy him getting away with it.' But in 1919 when there was a 'flu epidemic throughout Europe he went down with it, with his heart. And then the talk was that he had had a bad heart. So my father died in 1919 when he was 35. I was only eight and a half. I remember him vaguely.

Both my parents were illiterate—no schooling at all. My father never found time to learn to read and write. He died too young, and then he had another shop. But if you went in the shop and asked for a quarter of chocolate caramels or candies, whatever, my mother would go to the jar right away. My mother could pick up and do almost anything, although she couldn't read or write. She learned to just sign her name. As a young boy, when my mother wanted to write to Italy to her brother or brothers-in-law, I did the writing. But the less education the parents have had the more they want their children to have. So my mother said, 'My children are going to read and write. They're not going to be like me.'

Speaking very frankly, I was a bright boy. I think I enjoyed every subject at school. I always did what the teacher told me. I was always an obedient boy and therefore got on well at school both scholastically and sportswise. When my father died people told my mother, 'Holy Cross Academy down in Leith is a better school.' So she got us transferred to there.

In every class at Holy Cross there were one or two Italian boys and girls like myself. We were all Catholics. Half the class were of Irish origin and the other half Scots, but always one or two Italians too. I was absolutely fully accepted by my classmates.

With all modesty, I was very good at sports. I was a footballer first but in the Interscholastic Sports I came second four years in succession in the 100 yards. You used to get a loud cheer. And I used to be the only person in Holy Cross to win a medal. The headmaster used to come round on a Monday: 'Come out, Pia. I must congratulate you.' I've got a very, very quick reaction. I think it's a natural thing, which makes an advantage in sprinting.

I was very good at football. I was an automatic choice for the first team as centre forward. And I was lucky, we always had a good team. Two or three Hibs football players used to come down and coach us. We used to walk away every year with the Colonel Clark School Cup, played for every year by schools' under-15s.

I am one of the very, very few schoolboys who have played at both Easter Road and Tynecastle.[272] I played for Leith Schools against Aberdeen Schools at Easter Road. We got beaten 2-0. When we played Edinburgh Schools at Tynecastle we won 1-0. I scored the only goal. The laugh of the thing was: a foul for us and our centre half was taking the foul. He kicked the ball forward to me. I had been facing

296

him so I turned round to face the Edinburgh goals. I said, 'Oh, I'll pass it to the outside left.' But the chap marking me and the man marking the outside left both ran to cover me. So I says, 'I'll kick it towards the centre.' So I kicked it and here it went away into the corner of the net. And of course all the Leith boys jumped on top of me—'Well done!' But at Tynecastle the crowd was nearly all Edinburgh boys: they all booed me like anything.

Then all the secondary schools in Edinburgh changed to rugby. It was either rugby or nothing once you were over 14. Well, in my first game at rugby I scored two tries, believe it or not. We used to have a special game twice a year against Trinity Academy. All the school used to get a half day to watch this match. We were playing in the first game and Trinity were sort of teaching us. One of us had kicked the ball too far forward so their full back had the ball and came trotting forward. So my captain said, 'Go towards him, Pia. Make him kick the ball as soon as possible. Don't let him gain too much ground.' So I went running up towards the full back and just when I was about half a dozen yards away from him he made as if to punt and I turned, of course, and put up my hands to protect my face. And the spectators—there were roars of laughter at me. And the Trinity full back, stupid ass, he had a laugh, too. So he stood there and I came forward another yard or two and he made to kick again—and I did the same again. And the spectators were laughing at him too. But with my very quick reaction I goes charging at him and here the both of us are lying on the ground, the ball there and not another person near us. So then I grabs the ball, goes running away to the line and of course I scored a try. And then in the second half one of us must have kicked the ball and does it not hit the goal posts and go curling up in the air. And of course here's us running forward and does it not come into my arms. So half-a-dozen yards and I'm over and scored a try again. So you can imagine, I was the hero of the school! I mean, we beat Trinity who were well established in rugby and we were still learning.

I stayed on at school until I was fifteen. I passed my Higher Leaving Certificate— not Highers. I was good because I was an obedient boy. So I had a month or two to go at school when, 'What are you going to go in for?' So I was fancying going in for Medicine or being a consul.

By this time—age 12, 13, 14—I was more conscious of my Italianity. By that I mean they had an Edinburgh Italians football team and they used to ask me to play for it. Although I was a young chap I was tall and they were only too glad to use me. The team was in the mid-week league, a sort of trades' mid-week league: playing against the fish trade, hairdressers, the Post Office. The Edinburgh Italians were a pretty rotten team but we played. We used to get beaten about seven or eight nothing every week. But that made us popular with the other side maybe! The Edinburgh Italians team was formed in the late 1920s and it was there right down to the outbreak of war with Italy in 1940.

My parents spoke Italian at home. 'Pass the butter', 'I'll give you a slap in the face', 'Do this or that' was always in Italian. Even at three or four when we were playing with the boys in the street mother said, 'Answer in Italian.' But we'd always answer in English and we'd get a slap in the face or on the backside—'Here, answer in Italian!' But, I mean, English was more natural to us than Italian was.

Well, when I came to about fifteen there was an Italian school—not that I went to it—that the Italian consul used to have. So I got it into my head that I would like to be an ambassador, a consul, or something like that. My other thought when I was leaving school was to become a doctor. My mother never had a doctor. They couldn't afford a doctor. They had a midwife. Maybe I'd met a doctor or two—I don't know. I know I was interested in it. At the same time I'd joined the Boy Scouts and maybe doing the first-aid there had influenced me. But I remember me thinking a bit later a big fault of being a doctor was mothers calling out at night to have a baby. I remember me thinking, 'As a consul I'll not have that trouble.' I didn't like the thought of being called out at night. But when I was wondering whether to go in for medicine or the Foreign Office there was an advertisement about bursary classes for Skerry's College, where you could sit exams for railway clerks, banking, insurance, and the civil service. 'Oh, I would like to go into the civil service.' So I sat that bursary exam and I was lucky and won a bursary. So I went to Skerry's College, in Hill Place in Edinburgh.

Well, after I had been there about a month or so the secretary called me to his office. He says, 'I hope you don't think I'm impertinent, Mr Pia. But, you know, your name sounds foreign.' I says, 'Oh, yes, definitely, it's foreign.' He opened a book. He says, 'Now can you read that paragraph there? It says you've got to be British born of British born.' He says, 'Does that apply to you?' And I says, 'Oh, no, I'm British born but my father was Italian born.' 'Well,' he says, 'in the civil service you'll never get anywhere.' He says, 'I advise you to change from the civil service. They might accept you but you'd only be a minor clerk. If you take my advice we'll put you in for the banking and insurance exams.' I said, 'Oh, yes,' disappointed, because I had really wanted to get into the civil service and into the Foreign Service maybe. I didn't want to be banking and insurance. So when it came towards the end of the course I got it into my head I would like to be a commercial traveller. My mother having a shop, travellers used to come to the shop and I used to see them all.

In the newspaper I saw that a firm down in Leith wanted somebody to sell wrapping paper. I says, 'Well, I don't want to sell paper but it's experience.' Anyhow I applied and here I got a letter from J & J Todd, which was one of the biggest wholesale grocers' provision merchants in the east of Scotland. When I went for interview the man said to me, 'We're starting a paper department and we thought we'd like you. Your name is Italian?' I said yes. He says, 'Oh, well, you know, the Italians do a very, very big trade. In Edinburgh they turn over about £4 million a year.' He says, 'There's a lot of chip shops that use a lot of paper and the confectioner shops use paper bags, too. So we'll give you a trial but you'll be on commission alone.' 'Oh', I says, 'I'm only too pleased to do this.' Well, to tell you the truth, half the Italians in Edinburgh were related to me. So when I went into their shops they couldn't chase me away. They had to give me an audition, you see. And I was lucky with my firm. J & J Todd was a grocery firm accustomed to grocery profits. A paper firm is accustomed to bigger percentages because of the smaller turn-over. A paper firm needs to get about 15 to 20 per cent profit. But a grocery firm would make a fortune at that. So Todd were maybe taking 10 per cent on their paper, thinking that was great, though it was small compared with Walker and Sinclair's and the other competition. So when I went into a chip shop: 'I've called from J & J Todd and my name is Pia.' 'Oh, are you Joe Pia?' Well, after half a dozen calls I knew I was on a good thing with my prices. 'Oh,' they would say, 'that's far better than the other ones'.' So you could almost say I never got a refusal anywhere. And of course down at Todd's, with all modesty I'm a wee bit of a sensation: 'What the hang's this? Making five or six new accounts every day! It's unknown for a traveller to do that sort of thing!' But of course they should have realised that it was Italians giving me the orders, and the prices were right.

Todd's had half a dozen managers. One was in charge of fruit and paper, one flour and sugar and cheese, another general groceries, one Greig and Douglas biscuits. 'Oh, what about giving Pia my price lists, too? Get him to sell my stuff?' I used to get two-and-a-half per cent commission on paper. So Gilbert Archer, the general manager, told me: 'We'd like you to have a full price list, Mr Pia. But of course on the other stuff you'll only get one-and-a-quarter per cent. We don't make the same pretensions there. And on sugar you'll only get 3d. a bag—it's a very small paying thing.' I says, 'All right. I'll do what you're saying.'

So I did very well there, too, I did very, very well. Well, when I say very—quite well. My big, big fault—and it is a big, big fault—was I was bad at collecting accounts. Of course all the other commercial travellers were bad at that, too. And the man whose job was to chase us—'Why's so-and-so not paid? You'll need to chase them up.' Well, what used to 'e a bad thing in the paper trade was, to get a good price a shopkeeper would maybe order a ton or half a ton, rather than just a hundredweight. That was enough for about three months. The shopkeepers had been accustomed before to giving their paper merchants a big order and they didn't pay for three months. So of course I told this to Todd's head cashier. He says, 'Yes, but we're making small profits. It's all right for the paper merchants. But our prices are based on monthly credit, not three-monthly credit. Demand the money now.' Well, I used to demand it but the shopkeepers'd say, 'Aw, tae hang wi' you. Not at all.' They used to refuse. The cashier says, 'Oh, but tell them we'll refuse to supply them.' But I didn't want to stop because it was two-and-a-half per cent, you know—nice commission for me.

Now on top of this my mother had two shops in Stockbridge—the original one in Raeburn Place, and one she'd bought in Kerr Street for my brother and me when we became older. The shop in Rodney Street had been given up when my father died. Well, the tenant she had in the Kerr Street shop wanted to leave, so my mother when I'd been with Todd's about one and a half years, she says to me, 'Instead of the cashier at Todd's giving you a telling off why not run your own shop?' So at the age of seventeen I went and took over the shop in Kerr Street.

I used to open the shop about nine in the morning and I was there till about eleven at night, seven days a week. Well, on a Wednesday, I used to get off from one o'clock for lunch but I had to be back again at nine o'clock at night to the shop. But I used to get these seven hours off every week. I did that for two or three years. On my afternoon off on Wednesdays I used to play for the Edinburgh Italians football team. Then I used to get Saturday afternoon off to play at rugby for Holy Cross F Ps. I was still very keen on sports. Then I joined the Portobello Rowing Club. I was picked into a crew. So I used to go there, well, one or two nights. We rowed on the Firth of Forth. So I was very keen: in the winter rugby, in the summer rowing. And then I had quite intense Scout activities. I was very active in the Scouts and used to be ambulance examiner for the Waverley District—boys wanting to pass first aid.

When I was about 20—that would be around 1930 or so—my young brother Gerard, three years younger than me, left school. So he came to help me in the shop. There was not enough work there to do. We were fed up doing nothing. And by this time, of course, I'm very, very price conscious: how to buy big to get better prices? I says, 'Oh, with Bassett's now you've to order fifty boxes. But we only go through about three or four a month. If I were to buy in the fifty, make sixpence profit and, you know, become a wholesaler ... ' So my young brother says, 'Oh, well, whatever you say, Joe, oh, yes, right.' So I remember on the 29th of February 1932, when I was twenty-one-and-a-half, I started off as a wholesaler.

I started off at Waterloo Place and went right down Leith Walk, selling. I had about half-a-dozen lines: Fox's Mints and Fox's Fruits, Bassett's Liquorice All Sorts, Highland Cream Toffee, and pandrops. These were my main lines. To tell the truth, all the wholesalers used to have an agreed price with each other. I used to cut the price and of course that's when I got the orders. I had the contacts—the same Italian community. They used to remember me before with Todd's. And they would put me on to a pal along the road.

As a traveller I used to travel on Monday and Tuesday, and my brother go out on Wednesday delivering. And then Thursday and Friday I'd go out travelling, and the Saturday he would go out delivering. When I came back at night both of us made up the orders for the next day and wrote out the invoices. And then I got other customers through the Scouts and the Wolf Cubs, too.

So I was working at that through the 1930s, right up to the war. I was quite well established as a wholesaler. So after two or three years I gave up the shop in Kerr Street. My older brother Philip went into it, and my younger sister went into the shop in Raeburn Place. So my younger brother and me got out of the shop and started our wholesale place along at Eyre Place. We rented a disused laundry there.

Now by this time, too, politics comes into it. The Italian consuls have always been keen to promote unity among the Italian community in Edinburgh. The Italian community in Edinburgh was 5,000 before the war. I'm sure I heard my uncle Alfonso Crolla saying, 'We've got over 5,000 Italians in Edinburgh.' But when he says Italians, that includes their children.[273] The clear majority of the community were drawn from the peasantry in Italy—children or grandchildren of peasants. I would say there were no members of the community in Edinburgh who had been industrial or factory workers in Italy. I would say not one was an artisan. There were one or two professional people—teachers or doctors or lawyers among the Italian community in Glasgow before the war but in Edinburgh only a couple of teachers. I think that's about all. I was considered most outstanding because I was a commercial traveller, not a shopkeeper working in either a chip shop or an ice cream shop. Yes, I was very, very rare. All the Italian boys and girls used to look up to me: 'Oh, you're lucky. You're not seven days a week from morning till night in an ice cream shop or a chip shop'.

There was one Italian in Edinburgh before the war had been a professional. During the First Great War I understand they had the Carabinieri Band touring all the capitals of Europe to rouse patriotism and the band came to the Usher Hall in Edinburgh. The assistant conductor was a man called Orazio Di Dimenico. He was tall, dark, and handsome—girls chasing after him. His father, I understand, was chief of police in a small town in Italy. Orazio married the Dagostino girl.

John Dagostino of Leith Street—the Alfresco side, on the right side going down Leith Street, not the Royal Cafe—was a well known Italian in Edinburgh. He owned half-a-dozen shops. He had two daughters and two sons. The two daughters married well socially. One of them married Di Dimenico, and the other one a chap called Garibaldi Arcari, who was one of the gentry of Picinisco in Italy.

John Dagostino made his money during or after the First War having gambling machines—penny in the slot. And his daughters have told me they used to go round the shops—my father's shop, for instance and they'd open up the machine and take all the pennies out. Depending on how big your trade was or how much John Dagostino liked you—my father was well in with them and he got halfers—some people only got a third, some only 25 per cent. So his daughters used to have the pennies in a big leather bag and then into a taxi. And they told me they used to go to the bank in Greenside Place and bring in about a dozen of these leather bags, loaded with pennies. And they have said to me, 'We're dashed sure the bank tellers helped themselves.' The girls didn't have a chance to count the pennies—there were so many. They had no grounds for saying that about the tellers. But they suspected it. They would have done it themselves so they thought other people would do it, you see.

The Dagostinos were rich but they were hated. Well, at the end of the First War they were fly lads with these machines. John Dagostino was well in with the police and he knew, either through the police or lawyers, that the machines were going to be made illegal. So here he goes round the whole lot, the Italian shopkeepers: 'By the way, too much work—I'll sell you my machine if you want to buy it.' They said, 'What?!' The likes of my father, his drawings from the machines from what I hear were about £10 a week, which was big time in those days. 'Well,' says John Dagostino, 'seeing you are my *compare* and I am godfather to your daughter Peggy, I'll give it to you cheap—£30.' My father said, 'What? Great! I'll get the money back in a fortnight!' But of course Dagostino wasn't so good to everybody. Some of them he charged £50 or £100. And of course everybody bought the machines from him. They couldn't believe their ears. How generous this was of Dagostino! And then, of course, after two or three weeks: 'You're not allowed to have them. The machine is confiscated.' 'Oh, the dirty dog that he is! Dagostino took advantage of us.' And naturally he was hated, oh, yes, he was hated.

John Dagostino was the president of the East of Scotland Ice Cream Federation. We were a branch of the British thing. But his two sons did not mix with us. They were rich. We were contemptuous of them. I suppose they were of us, too. We would ignore them and they would ignore us.

After the First War John Dagostino went to Italy. So he told his two sons-in-law, Di Dimenico and Arcari, 'You run the business.' So Di Dimenico says, 'Och, we must modernise these cafes.' So Di Dimenico, with Arcari, his brother-in-law, was the first man to have round table cafe style. He's the man that introduced cafes to Scotland, about 1920 or so. But an uncle of mine wrote to John Dagostino in Italy: 'Oh, you better come back. These two sons-in-law will ruin you. Fancy, you want to see the posh place they've built.' So John Dagostino came back and he was quite annoyed with his sons-in-law doing this without his permission. So then the sons-in-law started the Strand Cafe in Shandwick Place. Duncan's the chocolate firm owned the place but sold it them for £400. They went to Czechoslovakia and bought their chairs and tables for the cafe there—it was cheaper than buying it from Maul's in Edinburgh.

Among the other Italian families in Edinburgh there is no doubt the Crollas were the most appreciated. Then there were the Tartaglias. There were only two families of them but they were well known, well known. And the Di Marcos of Portobello: he had a big restaurant on the prom there, a big Maison Di Marco, they called it. And Luca, Musselburgh, was very well liked, he was such a nice man. So the leadership of families like the Dagostinos, the Crollas, Di Marcos and Tartaglias was based on a kind of mixture of personality, strength of character and also financial strength. All that would come into it. But they didn't look down on the poor.

My Uncle Alfonso Crolla was a very important man in the Italian community in Edinburgh. There used to be a wholesale grocer called Valvona, supplying Italian groceries, who was doing poorly in business. And he thought it would be a smart idea—which it was—to go to my Uncle Alfonso, knowing he was very well known and respected by all the Italians in the east of Scotland, and ask him to become his partner. Valvona had a little place off the Pleasance—in St John's Hill, I think. Valvona was in there. So my uncle became a partner of Valvona.

Now my Uncle Alfonso owned a shop at no. 19 Elm Row. It used to be what was called an ice cream shop. They did sell ice cream but they would have died if they had lived off their ice cream. Their trade was chocolate, confectionery and cigarettes. Ice cream was minor compared with these. They sold ice cream quite well in the summer but you had to diversify to keep afloat.

So Valvona and Crolla was founded just after the First World War. But Valvona played less and less an important part. He was pretty useless. And so Uncle Alfonso took the business over.[274] He had been born in Italy and had come over with his parents to Edinburgh long before the First War. He had been in the Italian army in the war. Uncle Alfonso had two sons, my cousins Dominic, who was born in Italy in 1912, and Victor, who was born here in 1916. Uncle Alfonso wasn't really a very good businessman.

Well, as I was saying before—this is where politics comes into it—Italian consuls have always been keen to promote unity among Italian communities here. Italian consuls throughout the world encouraged the community to be together. The

consul would have one or two dances every year to try and get the colony together—I presume to get the Italian boys and girls to mix and therefore to marry.
But to keep the Italian contact.

By the way, most of the Italian consul-generals here were rotten. I remember the
last one, before the Second World War started, when he came here he said: 'They've
called me in. I'm a consul of the first category. You've always been getting second or
third.' Remember, Scotland is almost unknown on the continent. In Italy they
speak about Inglesi. If you say to people you come from Scotland they look at you.
But if you say 'Edinburgh'—'Ah! Ah! Edinburgh!' They know the words Edinburgh
and Glasgow but they don't know Scotland.

In Edinburgh for about a dozen or more years before the war the Italian vice-
consul was an Edinburgh lawyer called Nicol Bruce. But there used to be one situ-
ated in Glasgow who was the Consul-General. He had vice-consuls in Edinburgh,
Dundee and Aberdeen. The vice-consul was a Scot rather than an Italian national.
Just immediately before the Second War or after the war had started in 1939 Nicol
Bruce gave up the vice-consul's job. So then they got a fellow Dr Trudu as vice-
consul. The Consul General was a man called Lupis. It was he who a year or two
before the war had come from Munich and said, 'I'm a Consul-General of the first
category.' The one immediately before him used to stay in the Caley Hotel in Edinburgh, though he was supposed to be resident in Glasgow. And he would go through
to Glasgow—not every day, but when it suited him. But he was staying in the Caley
Hotel all the time: a sinecure job.

Well it was the Consul-General from Glasgow earlier on, Tronchetti, who came
through to Edinburgh and I don't know why but he picked my Uncle Alfonso
Crolla to be the secretary of the Fascio—the Fascist Club.

So when Mussolini got the consuls to promote Italian unity here all the clubs
became Fascist Clubs. If Mussolini had been a Communist we would have been a
Communist Club. If he had been a Liberal we would have been a Liberal Club. We
were a Fascist Club—not that there was any Fascist activity—and we had the word
Fascist against our name, you see. They had a hall—they called it the Fascio Hall—
in Picardy Place in Edinburgh where they used to have a thing above the wall:
'Respect the country which has given you hospitality.' It had it in Italian: '*Respetta
il paese ci da ospita*'. So I don't think Mussolini encouraged them to interfere with the
politics of any country. I am saying what I think. There was certainly no political
activity in the Edinburgh area. I personally was never active politically. None of the
Italian boys were, absolutely nobody that I knew was. The leader of the Fascist
group in Edinburgh, my Uncle Alfonso Crolla, he used to run dances, I'll not say
every month, say four times a year, getting the lads and lassies to meet each other
maybe with the intention of getting them married. So the Fascist Club was a social
club. We really didn't have any political discussions, word of honour, word of honour. I have never voted in my life, not even at local elections. I was not interested in
politics. There wasn't any party that attracted me. Before the war there were never
any Italian Fascist candidates put up in Edinburgh in local or general elections.

When Uncle Alfonso was made secretary of the Edinburgh Italian Fascist Club he naturally had to have a committee. But with the Fascists you didn't vote for committees—you were selected. And to make his numbers big, naturally Uncle Alfonso put my mother down as a member of the Club and the whole of the family, although then we were just kids and didn't know. So he put all his relations on: 'Do you mind?' 'Oh, all right, go on, yes, yes, go on, swell up the numbers.' He did that—normal vanity, you know. So my two brothers Tommy and Gerry and I were all in the book of the Fascio Club.[275]

Later on they picked me because of my sporting activities and Boy Scout activities. I became second top man in Edinburgh, you could say politically. I was head of what was called the *Dopo Lavoro*. That's a Work Association, to promote all sporting activities. I restarted or rejuvenated the football team, the Edinburgh Italians. And then I got into the Table Tennis League. And then I started a golf club. But I used to get a chap—this is Fascist style, where I selected, it wasn't voted on— I'd get a fellow whom I knew was a very active golfer, Tony Capaldi, Antigua Street. 'By the way, Tony, what about us starting a golf club?' 'Oh, aye, yes, oh, aye, why not?' Anyhow this week or month we'd go to Dalmahoy, next month to Royal Musselburgh—a different golf club every month. Maybe twenty or thirty of us would go.

As a matter of fact, we were very much encouraged by the authorities. Italy had been an ally of Britain in the First War. So for Armistice Day we used to get a special invitation. We used to parade, come out with black shirts and fez and white gloves. And there was maybe about twenty of us who would go—youths. We used to meet at St Andrew Square and, you know, trailing round the Square there. We had a big procession and then away up to the Castle to the Unknown Warrior's grave, you see. And of course all the military went first, and then the civilians. But in the pride of place immediately after the military were the Italian Fascists. I remember some women's groups saying, 'Hey! What do these bloody Italians ...? The British should come first!' And my Uncle Alfonso says, 'Oh, it's quite all right.' He says to us, 'Fall out, boys. We'll go to the back.' And the women were coming in in front of us. And the man in charge of the whole lot was Colonel Robertson, VC. 'What's this that's happening? I beg your pardon! Have you no sense of manners? Don't you know that the guests always get pride of place? The Italians go to the very front because they are guests. The British give them preference!' And of course we were so picturesque. People would say, 'Oh, look at them!' It was something to look at, you see—quite different from the others. Leith used to invite us to go there, too. So I remember we used to go down there to Henderson Street and a big church there, where we had to sit during the service and then follow them to the Leith Unknown Warrior's grave.[276]

By the way, Mussolini did a lot of good in Italy. I found that out since then. He would tell the town and country planners, 'Now we want a railway station in Rome, Milan, Florence, Venice, Naples—all the big cities. Never mind what houses they're building there. Plan where the station's to be and the railway lines. We'll have first class communication.' And once the plan was drawn up—'Everybody clear out!' And of course the people who had to clear out were calling him all the names of the day. They had no say in the matter. Clear out they had to. But nowadays people say:

'What a marvellous …!' If you go to any Italian station they're magnificent! And trade unions: 'You must join the trade union. But you're not allowed to strike. If you're not pleased, a committee of nine—three of the union, three of the bosses, three neutral. The nine of you have got to decide what to do. Whatever the vote is, it must be done.' Does that not get things done?[277] And from what I hear he drained the Pontine Marshes. A lot of mosquitoes got into Rome. So he drained out the marshes. He built a first class causeway to Venice. He has done many good things. But—I'm saying what I think—many of the bad things or the good things, it's his henchmen that did it, not him. He gets the credit or discredit but it's his lieutenants. Well, Mussolini maybe had some good lieutenants but he certainly had some bad ones. I've heard that when Mussolini came to power in 1922 that was certainly accompanied by beatings-up and murders of political opponents. I've heard he used to make people drink castor oil. I'm sure that happened, although I'm also sure it's exaggerated. I mean, all journalists exaggerate.

Well, in Edinburgh before the war, whatever we got was Italian propaganda which was praising Mussolini. We just heard the good things, not the bad things. And to tell you the truth, the few good things I heard were very, very good—the railways, the Pontine Marshes. How did we hear? Oh, it was in the British papers. The Italian consul in Edinburgh didn't put round leaflets or hold meetings. I never felt that through the consul the Italian government was keeping a watchful eye on the Italian community in Edinburgh. I never felt that. The consul did use to come about the Fascist Club in Picardy Place a lot. He used to have a kids' party, a Christmas party, and also organised a 15th of August picnic—Feast of the Assumption. We would maybe go to Longniddry or maybe Stirling, where a few busloads from Glasgow, Edinburgh, Dundee, could all get together. And we used to have competitions—a tug-of-war and races and that. And to tell the truth I got the Edinburgh ones nicely organised, you see: we did very well because we were better organised. But the Italian community in Scotland kept in close touch with one another.

I would say 90 per cent of the Italian community of 5,000 in Edinburgh would be in membership of the Italian Fascist Club at Picardy Place. But nothing like that would actually attend Club. The Club was up half a dozen steps. There was a billiard saloon on the ground floor. And then we had the floor above that, just a single floor. We had a wee office and then a big hall. The hall would probably seat about 60 to 100 people.

I remember Wednesday afternoon, because I used to promote the thing, we used to have boxing. Yes, boxing or downstairs playing at billiards or snooker. And then on a different night—it might have been a Friday night—we used to have table tennis. We entered a team in the table tennis league, a weekly league. And we used to have a party at least once a month, not so much a dance as a sing-song or party, and we were taught Italian songs. But there was absolutely no pro- or anti- political talk at all. It was completely social. We'd maybe come in: 'Oh, good old Mussolini. Look at the good he's doing for Italy.' I don't consider that really political, though maybe it is. We never, never, never invited speakers who spoke about fascism or Mussolini or anything like that.

The Italian Fascist Club had no connection with the British Fascist movement, none whatsoever. We had no contacts or joint activities with them whatever. The only political event was Armistice Day, when we bought black shirts. We bought them just for that. We didn't wear them any other time, just Armistice Day. And in the Club we didn't mark Mussolini's birthday with a special gathering or anything like that. Not on the King of Italy's birthday either.

The majority view of the Italian community in Edinburgh was that Mussolini was a good thing for Italy. Most of them were really in favour of Mussolini and of fascism in Italy. Having said that, do not for a moment presume they were politically inclined, because they didn't know anything—just, 'Oh, is that right?' So they cheered for it. They were unsophisticated in the political sense. They weren't in the least in the habit of arguing about or studying politics closely. Not in the least. You can take it from me that is the case. As a matter of fact the younger ones knew the least wee bit about politics.

I was the Group Scoutmaster at St Mary's Cathedral. There was a Scoutmaster for St Pat's. We both had very, very good groups. So our Rovers—senior Scouts—had a debating society. And they for a great laugh chose to debate fascism. I was to be the mover of anti-fascism. I did my best but of the thirty boys there the vote went in favour of fascism. I lost the vote! Not that I was rotten in the debate, well, I might have been but I don't think I was.

There weren't any members of the Italian community in Edinburgh who came here as refugees from Mussolini's regime. From what I know nobody in Picinisco, our home town or village in Italy, suffered at all under Mussolini. He did nothing wrong there as far as I know.

There was one man in Musselburgh—Luca, brother of the famous Luca's ice cream there—who was opposed to Mussolini. He was strongly anti-fascist. Luca's name is really Scappaticci but Scappaticci being a big mouthful he uses his Christian name Luca, which means Luke. There were six brothers. The whole lot of them were Fascist except the one. I think this brother certainly had a chip shop in Musselburgh. He didn't mix with anyone. I don't know if he was a Liberal or a socialist. I just heard talk that he was against fascism: 'He doesn't want to join us to do work for charity.' We used to do work for charity, you see. We thought it was for that reason he was against it. It never occurred to us that it was for real political reasons. Although I think it really was political now that I think of it. But at the time we used to wonder because we saw no harm at all in fascism. But that Scappaticci brother was positively in a minority. I can't remember anybody else by name in the Italian community who was opposed to fascism. I would say—what I used to say, and I've said it often—nearly every decent fellow was a member of the Fascist Party. But they thought it was the thing to do.

I would say positively no member of the Edinburgh Italian community went off to fight in the Spanish Civil War for Franco or for Mussolini in the Abyssinian War. But I can say there were about half a dozen boys in Edinburgh who did service between the two World Wars in the Italian army. They went, they were conscripted. They thought it would be a good experience.

At the beginning of the Abyssinian War Mussolini made an appeal for gold. And all the ladies were told, 'What about making contributions? What about giving even your wedding rings?' So there was a collection made of the gold. Now to tell the truth my mother gave her gold ring. And we said, 'Would you send that, ma?' And she said, 'Well, to tell the truth, when I got married I had no gold ring. My parents couldn't afford a gold ring or anything. I bought a gold ring while I was here. So I've given it to them but not that's any value.' But I know gold was collected from us to go to them. I don't know if there was a lot.

During the Abyssinian War I would say there was not the least bit antagonism shown to any Italian in Edinburgh. If they made any mention about Mussolini and his soldiers doing things there—now I remember, I said: 'What are you talking about? He's done no fighting at all. He's bribed his way through.' I don't know how I got the information that he used to bribe this tribe and then bribe the other, and then his troops went marching through. I don't believe that Mussolini used poison gas in Abyssinia. What would he use poison gas for? You don't need to do that. He bribed his enemies in Abyssinia easily. It was cheaper bribing them. But there was positively no antagonism toward the Italian community in Edinburgh, not that I noticed, I never heard. I mean, I've heard people calling Mussolini names and I've heard people praising Mussolini, but just normal conversation.[278]

Just before the Second World War broke out in 1939 I went to Italy with the Scouts. I was the Group Scoutmaster at St Mary's Cathedral in Edinburgh. I had become very active in the Scouts when I was just a lad. I was twelve when I joined. And I was active right until the war. The Scouts I joined at St Mary's were exclusively Catholics but not exclusively Italian. There were about three or four Italians out of the thirty Scouts, and about three or four amongst the thirty Cubs.

Now Mussolini did quite a few good things, as I've found out since—I didn't know then. But what I did know then was he used to have a big seaside camp in Italy called Cattolica, where boys from all over the world—they were supposed to be poor boys—could go and have a holiday. You had to pay your own fare as far as the Italian frontier. But as soon as you were on the Italian railways you got at the Italian government's expense a fortnight's holiday in Italy for nothing. So they had Cubs and Scouts, Brownies and Guides amongst the Italians. Now, remember, I am Group Scoutmaster at St Mary's Cathedral. So here they asked me: 'By the way, we want one or two people to supervise them going across.' I says, 'Oh, aye, yes, I'm interested.' They says, 'Now you are absolutely free of charge. You get on the train in the Waverley station, you deliver them at Cattolica. Then for a fortnight you fend for yourself—go where you like for a fortnight. At the end of the fortnight you report back to bring all the boys back to Edinburgh again.' I says, 'Oh, well, that sounds fine.' That's what I did in 1937 just before the war broke out.

A train from Glasgow came to Edinburgh with kids, we in Edinburgh joined the train, and away we went down toLondon. By that time the British contingent was 384 boys and girls. There was one collective passport for the whole lot. I don't know why but they picked me to be the holder of the collective passport—all the passport was in my name. I presume it was because I had association with Boy Scout activity.

All the other ones were hairdressers or ice-cream men or chip shop men. Well, who would you pick to be in charge? One who has experience of looking after boys. My heart was in scouting so I was a very good Scout, with all modesty—not perfect, but very good. But anyhow they picked me in charge of these 384 boys and girls.

When the Second World War started in September 1939 Italy wasn't in the war and to tell the truth Italy was on a klondyke. Italy had ships coming into Leith Docks, two or three ships every week, coming in and loading stuff. I remember the Italian vice-consul Dr Mario Trudu—I knew him well, and he's still alive at this day in Genoa—I remember he used to get, I think it was a penny or tuppence on every ton. If it was a 10,000 ton Italian boat that came into Leith the master of the boat had to pay the Italian vice-consul 10,000 times tuppence. So Dr Trudu used to keep half and send the other half to the consul-general in Glasgow, who used to keep half and send the rest to London.

Now many chaps like me were of dual nationality. Quite a few renounced their British nationality, so as not to be called up. Remember, I am a commercial traveller who is going round all the east of Scotland. So I knew a lot of people. I used to say at that time, 'Oh, no, no, no, I'm not gasping to fight anybody but I'm quite willing to do my bit like anybody else.' Now that was my war-cry: 'Not gasping to fight but when I get called up I'll go like anybody else. I'm quite willing to fight.' I would say positively nobody in the Italian community in Edinburgh went off to join Mussolini's forces at that time. There was no anti-Italian feeling against us because they did not expect Mussolini to come into the war. Although I knew then that he was in the Rome-Berlin-Tokyo Axis, you see.

Then suddenly on June 10th 1940 Italy came into the war. I suppose like everybody else, I was flabbergasted. 'What the hell is Mussolini coming in for? He's on a klondyke making money'—you know, supplying both sides. 'Stupid ass, coming into the war!'[279]

A day or two later there was rioting against Italian shops, window-smashing, looting of goods, and so on. My mother had an ice-cream shop in Kerr Street and Raeburn Place. They did not touch us. My older brother Tommy used to run these shops. He was very, very well liked. Everybody called him Tam. He used to mix with them a lot in the billiards saloon. He was Hibs daft, you see. He was well known all over Stockbridge. Most of them were Hearts supporters. So they used to go in—'Aye, you and your Hibs!' And he used to call the Hearts supporters names. But he was very, very well liked, respected. So these fellows who smashed in the Italian shops after Italy entered the war, it wasn't patriotism, it was pinching. I would say half the Italian shops in Edinburgh got it. I don't know why it didn't happen in Stockbridge. But we sort of imagined it was because my brother Tam was so very well liked.[280]

Well, I went to bed that night, the 10th of June. The first thing I knew, about three or four o'clock in the morning here am I not wakened. The family is round about me and two detectives. 'What's this?' 'Are you Giuseppe Pia?' I says, 'Oh, yes, but I'm known as Joseph Pia.' They says, 'Oh, yes, you're the man we want. Do you mind coming to police headquarters?' I says, 'By the way, I'm not an Italian. I'm born and bred British. I'm a British subject.' 'Oh, well, but you must come,' he says. 'Now you may as well come clean. Have you any secret papers?' I says, 'What?! Search the place and find what you like.' Naturally, I had no secret papers but I had that collective passport for the British boys' and girls' holiday contingent to Italy in 1937. I mean, if that was incriminating I couldn't help it. But anyhow they picked me up and and they bring me to Gayfield Square Police Station. That was about two or three or four or something in the morning. So I'm laughing: 'No, it's all right. We'll get the mistake corrected there.'

But these fly lads knew what they were doing. They knew what I didn't know: there was a thing called DORA—the Defence of the Realm Act, section 18B. You see, we knew nothing about that.[281]

I was almost the last of the Italian community to be picked up in Edinburgh. Here at Gayfield Square Police Station they're looking for Mario Campanile, Vincent Macogni. I said, 'By the way, you'll not get them. They're in the Forces.' I says, 'I know Mario Campanile's in the Royal Air Force and Macogni's in the British army.' I mean, they were Britishers like me. They mentioned another couple of names. 'They're in the army, too,' I says. 'Is that where they are?' they says, 'because we were wondering why we couldn't find them.' I says, 'You have to go and find out where the troops are.' Me laughing, not for a moment thinking I was under arrest or anything. 'Right, come out into the car.' So I got into the police car. I thought they were driving me home. So here the next thing—a big door clanging. It didn't dawn on me even then I was going into Saughton Prison. So here I'm put into a little cubicle almost like a toilet in size—very small. 'I wonder what the hang is this here?' By this time I suspected where I was. 'Oh, this sounds like a prison. I wonder ... But it had no bars or anything. So then it was after a chap comes outside: 'Are you Giuseppe Pia?' 'Yes.' 'Age so and-so, address so-and-so?' 'Yes, yes.' 'And have you been in prison before?' A loud indignant 'No!' This happened to two or three before they came to me. I was surprised when they were going round that two or three Italian boys who had been in prison said 'Yes!'. But anyhow after a while— 'Right, come along here.' And here you had to get a bath. And there was a convict, washing you properly, disinfecting your hair. You've got to remember that a lot of chaps might bring bugs into prison. So everybody gets properly scrubbed, you see.

There were eighty of us had all been arrested that same night, once Italy declared war. But they grabbed a lot of Italians, too. But Italians were sent to Donaldson's Hospital, that's where the deaf and dumb were. Now they're Italians, but we're Brits, you see. All the people with Italian nationality only were sent to Donaldson's but all the Brits—like me —who had dual nationality were sent to Saughton.[282]

Now I found out afterwards we were all connected with the Italian Fascist Club. But of course, you know, they made dozens of mistakes. There was quite a few included that should not have been, and quite a few not included that should have been. The likes of my older brother Philip, he was not touched at all. As a matter of fact later on he got called up to the Pioneer Corps and then to another army thing, Ordnance Corps, I think it was. He was in the army for about three years. But I was in Saughton. My young brother Gerard was not touched on June 10th but about two months after that he got arrested and was brought into Saughton. My young sister Peggy, who used to be on the Ladies' Committee of the Fascio Club, was not touched at all the whole war. She married a British officer during the war. Whereas two girls—Celia Mancini and Elvina Scappatacci, Musselburgh—who were not on the Ladies' Committee were put inside Saughton. The lady in charge of the Ladies' Committee was Yolanda Coppola, and another member was Vera Luca of Musselburgh: that's all I can remember.

There were only four women put into Saughton Prison but there were about a hundred men to begin with. We had a hall to ourselves—C Hall was completely ours. I was Number C 98. But there were 99 altogether. The next man to me—a man called Brattisani from South Queensferry—he was Number C 99.

The warders, the first two or three weeks, were very, very strict. Of course, they all thought we were spies or traitors or things like that. Of course, when we came in the others said: 'Are you here?' 'Look here, have you done ...?' 'No, no.' 'Silence there!'—you know, you're not allowed to speak. But you're allowed half an hour in the morning and a half hour in the afternoon for exercise. You had to go down in pairs and you walked round outside in the fresh air. You're not allowed to speak but of course you learned to speak with the side of your mouth: 'Here, have you anything ...?' 'No, what the hang's this?' Now this was very, very strict for about a couple of weeks. But of course by this time the warders are weighing us up : 'What the hang? That chap there's useless.' And then they'd say, 'Oh, by the way, I go to his father's chip shop for supper.' 'Oh, I know this chap's father has an ice cream shop.' And here they're all discussing, weighing us up, you see, when we're walking round the exercise yard. They soon enough weighed up that we were from a military point of view useless. And they slackened up—allowed us to speak more with each other.

Now every morning we had to stand up in the hall and the Governor would come along and give a couple of minutes' speech. He was a very, very pleasant man, Captain Murray. I'm not too sure why this was done but it was nice. I think it was to check that we were being treated according to regulations. But anyhow I told him: 'By the way, sir, I understand there are eight boys here aged sixteen years—well, one fifteen and seven who are under seventeen.' I said, 'I understand you don't put anybody in prison under seventeen.' He says, 'Oh, that's true, but you're not in prison.' I says, 'I beg your pardon, sir. Where are we if this is not prison?' He says, 'Now, now, leave it to me. I'll look into the matter.' So about a week or two after, these eight got released. They were too young. One of them was Eduardo Paolozzi, Leith born and bred—Albert Street.[283]

Our treatment in Saughton was strict, not severe. But after two or three weeks it slackened off a bit. They then said, 'What do you want to do? Anybody know anything about ambulance and that?' And of course I was made in charge of the first-aid team. I was the only one that knew any first-aid. The others knew nothing. So I was allowed to pick three chaps. If there was an air raid everybody was locked up. But we four, our cells were opened so that we could rush out if we were needed. There were a few air raids while we were in Saughton, but not that we were needed.

I hear there were a lot of fire bombs dropped but nothing near Edinburgh, well, no serious damage.

You were allowed to write two letters a week but you could receive a hundred. You were given a special form to write on. It was a wee, wee tiny thing. I remember the head warder complaining to us. 'By the way,' he says, 'I mean I've got to censor that. I mean, give me a chance.' 'Well, well, they should give us more paper. We want to ... ' You see, we were writing tiny. We'd all the time in the world. I mean, I'm not a letter writer at any time—but there, take it from me! I wrote to my fiancée and to my mother.

All the 18B detainees like me were allowed to receive one visit a week, a half-an-hour visit. My fiancée's parents were very, very strict. We were not officially engaged, you know what I mean. So they thought it was scandalous her visiting a man—not the prison part, you know, but because it might seem she was hard up for a man. But my family—my sister and my niece—came to visit me regularly in Saughton. That cheered me up.

Well, after two or three weeks you get accustomed to anything. But to begin with it was very upsetting to be in prison: 'Well, what the hang's this?' I had done nothing wrong. You tried to wonder what you'd done, you see. And I was trying to remember. Maybe about a dozen and more years before that, I was a Scout—a boy maybe of twelve or fourteen—and they used to bring us to a place at Poole's for shooting wee pellets—air guns.[284] I'd been there half-a-dozen times with the Boy Scouts. I suppose they were training us for military things for the future. I don't know. But, I mean, it surely wasn't because of that I was put in Saughton Prison? I remember me thinking that. And then I remembered before Italy came into the war they wanted people to volunteer for first-aid in Edinburgh. I volunteered and of course considered I was a cert—ambulance examiner for Waverley District, holding St Andrew's Ambulance certificate. I mean, you could say I was a first-class chap to get for this. But no call came at all. I said, 'I wonder if ... They must have a mark against my name, suspecting me, I suppose.' Anyway, my nephew and eight of them got released because they were under seventeen. And then my young brother Gerard got arrested. I remember my nephew Ernie Crolla got released in the morning and then in the afternoon my brother came in and got his place in prison. Well, I mean, what family is not shattered and knocked out of gear with war? 'What's this?' And you wonder what the hang to do.

By this time the warders said, 'By the way, the Captain'—that's the Governor—'is very, very keen on boxing. Why don't you ask him to let you out your cells to box on a Thursday night?' We used to get out of the cells two nights a week to play at cards or dominoes in the hall. So every morning two warders—one would open the door, the other one standing watching. Three or four at a time you've got to go along and empty your slops. And one warder is watching you don't do something wrong when this other one's opening the door. And then come back again and you've got an hour or so to clean out your cell. You polish the floor and have everything neatly in front, blankets and all this sort of thing. It's examined—I suppose to make sure you're not smuggling in anything. We had an inspection every morning: very military like. But at the same time you had on your cell door a red card and a white card: white card if you want to see the doctor, the red one if you want to see the Governor. So the warder opens the door—'All right?' So you say, 'Doctor, please,' or 'Governor, please.' When you go into the Governor's office 'Number?' So you had to tell him your number—right military stuff. So, well, I said to the Governor, 'Excuse me, sir,' I said, 'I'm very keen on boxing. Quite a few of us are keen on boxing. I wonder if it would be permissible to have some boxing?' 'Ohhh,' he says, 'I'm very keen on boxing, too.' I says, 'Now I'm not a professional, just very amateur. I've been in the Edinburgh Amateur Boxing Club. That's Charlie Cotter's in Leith Street,' I says. 'And I used to do it in the Scouts.' 'Oh, yes,' he says, by all means, oh, yes, yes. You can pass round the word that everybody interested in boxing can go, but not any of the others.' Naturally, everybody wanted to go. I mean, very few had even put on a boxing glove before. 'Oh, yes, let me go'— anything to get out of the cell. Everybody but four went to the boxing. One was Professor Rankin. He'd been arrested because he used to teach Italian in the Royal High School. You see, the least suspicion—'Grab them and put them in.' Keep on the safe side and screen them and then if we're sure they're O.K. we'll let them out again. But any doubt and they must be kept in.' So this Professor Rankin's got no fingers at all. He's an old man in a wig. And then there was Dr Giulano from Glasgow, who was a cripple. He was a medical doctor. And then the other two were cripples as well. But anyhow everybody went to the boxing except these four.

So here I put my card into the Governor next day. I says, 'Oh, you know, Captain Murray,' I says, 'it's a shame.' I said, 'Not that we want to take advantage but, you know, everybody came to the boxing except four. And you should let the four come and see. I mean, it would do no harm.' 'Oh, thanks for bringing that to my attention. Oh, I'm sorry, I never thought of that. Oh, of course, by all means. Naturally, they must get out, too. Thank you very much for bringing that to my attention.' So they were allowed out as well to the boxing.

But also we were told: 'What about arranging football games?' So here we had about twelve teams, seven a side. We used to have football every Saturday and all the prisoners used to look out of their bars and watch us playing. They'd shout, 'Here, pass the ball!', and all this sort of thing.

Officially, we didn't have any contact with the ordinary prisoners. We had our own hall and were quite separate from them. But we had to bring down dustbins every morning, three or four dustbins, two chaps carrying them down to the boiler room. I remember I went down with them once, and here we were told one chap had been in a hold-up gang in Glasgow. And of course I said to him, 'By the way, is that right—you were in a hold-up gang?' 'Aye,' he says. 'Is that so?' Remember, we were greenhorns, we were honest greenhorns.

I remember also walking through a hall once there was a chap who was a prisoner. We got a telling off for calling them convicts. They called them prisoners. 'Oh, that man there, he's in for bairning his daughter.' 'Oh, don't kid on!' 'Go up and ask him.' 'But he won't tell me.' 'Go up and ask him.' So here I went up. 'Is that right, you bairned your daughter?' 'Oh, yes.' 'Did you?' 'Well, I mean,' he says, 'all the lads were having a go at her. I mean, I'm her father. If they could have a go at her why not me?' I'd never heard such a story in my life before. 'What the hang's this?' I don't want to say I knew nothing about sex—but almost that. Very, very green, you see. So my education was being rapidly developed in Saughton Prison.

By this time I had found out there were about twelve British Union of Fascists men in Saughton amongst us, and about half-a-dozen Anglo-Germans. By this time we were called Anglo-Italians and Anglo-Germans. One of the BUF men was a reporter from the *Edinburgh Evening News*, a chap called Finuchan or Finucane. And I remember one of the Anglo-Germans—I don't know why he was in—was with the *Dundee Courier*. When I say Anglo-German, I mean someone of German parent-age but born in Britain. One of them was named Von Stranz. His parents owned a laundry down by Peebles. They didn't use the name Stranz—it had been changed to Strange. Two Italians from Peebles—the Benignos—knew him: he was their laun-dry man. They with their ice-cream shop used to send their laundry to this German. But they used to call him Bill Strange, you see. The Anglo-Germans had been brought in to Saughton Prison just the same way that we had—they had the wrong parents, if you like.

Among the British Union of Fascist men—the British Union, BUs, that's what they used to call themselves—I remember one or two who were not BUs. I don't know why. I remember one chap called Richard Finlay, who was an author—posh and proper, hardly mixed with anybody although he was nice and polite and civil but he still didn't really mix with anybody. I don't know why he was in. But I suspect he must have had some Nazi connections. In fact, there were three or four who were not BUs but I presume they must have had other connections or were suspected of having them.

There was one boy among the Italians in Saughton who had been born in America: Tony Di Ciacca, Dalry Road. But he was kept separate from us because he was an American citizen. He was in D Hall. He was with prisoners but not allowed to mix with them. He used to request often could he come with us. He was allowed to come to us at boxing but not otherwise. See, you keep to a Hall. We—C Hall—got filled up. Then by this time they'd emptied B Hall. They started getting Italians in from Fife and Aberdeen and Glasgow. I'm not too sure about Germans, I mean, you kept to your own Hall, you see. But I suppose they were the same as us.

Some chaps named Maran from Pitt Street had been put in Saughton with us and they had written to the Home Office or wherever, saying, 'It's very unfair. We're not even accepted by Italians because my mother's English. And the Italians look down on us. If you want to verify this come and ask this fellow Pia.' So a warder said to me, 'Oh, by the way, Pia, somebody from MI5 wants to speak to you.' I said, 'What's MI5 mean?' The warder looked at me. 'You mean to say you don't know what MI5 means?' I says, 'No.' None of us had any idea what MI5 meant. And this was about late 1940. So here I went to this fellow—a nice chap—and he asked me my name and that and then he asked about George and Joe Maran. I says, 'Oh, that's true. They were not members of the Fascio.' Because my Uncle Alfonso Crolla had once made a speech. A nephew of his, Michael Crolla, Deep Sea chip shop, had married an Italian girl. And Uncle Alfonso says, 'It's good when Italians marry Italians. They shouldn't marry Scots at all. They should marry Italians.' And while he was making this speech about four or five Italians got up and walked out. It was because they had married Scots, you see. And of course the word passed round. I'm sure Uncle Alf repented saying that, because there were a few good lads. But the point is Maran was amongst them, you see.

In Saughton there were about half-a-dozen women detainees. Oh, there were plenty of other women, of course. When we used to go to mass on a Sunday the male prisoners went first and then the 18 B prisoners like me after them. Lady prisoners went next and the lady 18 B prisoners after them. Ninety-nine per cent of the ladies were prostitutes. I mean, I'm not running them down. And behind them at mass came our girls.

Now there was one girl in on an 18 B who should not have been there. I don't know why she was. Her name was Ercilia Mancini, from Raeburn Place. She was in, whereas, as I say, my sister Peggy who was on the Ladies Committee of the Fascio Club was not touched. I remember my sister was walking along Princes Street once long afterwards with Ercilia and a woman passing said, 'Oh, hallo, Ercilia.' And Ercilia says, 'Oh, the shame, the disgust! She was a prostitute in prison. Oh, to think of it!' Well, quite a few of the prostitutes knew Ercilia, having seen her in prison, you see. But Ercilia was mortified, to think of a prostitute recognising her in the street. Our girls were very strictly brought up in those days.

Later on all the three or four Italian single girls in Saughton were released. And the two married ones went with their husbands to a place called Port St Mary on the Isle of Man.

My mother died in 1940 when I was in prison. She was 58. My mother, by the way, was strongly pro-British. She used to say, 'Don't praise Italy. Here I'm a queen. I love here much better than Italy.' The war had started when she became ill. I was actually in prison when I got a letter from my sister saying, 'Mother has been brought to the Royal Infirmary—cancer. Now try and arrange a visit. But don't let mother know. She doesn't know.' So I put a card in to the Governor. And I went in and told him. 'Is it possible to get a visit?' 'Well, it's not usual. I have every sympathy', he says, 'my mother died of cancer recently, too.' So he knew I had bad eyesight: 'When do you generally ...?' I says, 'I go to Walls the optician in Forrest Road.' 'Good,' he says. 'Now without waiting for the Home Office to give you permission, I'll let you go supposedly to get your eyes tested in Walls. I'll get a warder to take you to Walls. You must let your friends in the prison know you're going to Walls. Don't tell them you're going to the Infirmary.' Oh, he was a gem of a man, this Captain Murray. He let me out to see my mother in the Infirmary, which of course is just round the corner from Walls' shop. And of course when I was with my mother the lady in the next bed said to her, 'Oh, when you get out you must come and visit me.' And my mother looked at me quizzically. I says to myself, 'Ha, ha, she does know.' But you know you both put on a show that you don't know. And then some time after that one morning a warder came up to me and he says, 'Oh, you better shave and that, Pia, you're going to the Royal Infirmary.' I says, 'Oh, it must be my mother.' So when I went to the Infirmary with a warder they asked me, 'Have you got enough money for a taxi?' I think they would have paid if I didn't have. When we went to the ward I went to the sister and I says, 'Can I get in to see Mrs Pia, please?' She says, 'What?' And she looked at me nonplussed. The warder guessed something was wrong. So he says to me, 'Take a seat.' Then he came back to me: 'I'm sorry. It's been a bad message put through. Your mother's already died. She died in the morning. But this is an exceptional case. If you would like I'll get permission to bring you down to the mortuary. It's not usual but they'll allow you down.' I says, 'Oh, please. I'd be very pleased.' So he brought us down and here I was quite hurt. The fellow there looks up, 'Oh, yes, that's no. 121. Oh, I'll get the corpse ready. You wait here.' And the fellow is stinking of whisky, you see. And then, 'It's ready now. Doesn't she look lovely?' You know, praising everything. And of course I was not interested in this kind of talk. But here was the fellow in my opinion playing up to get a tip. And I've got no money at all, and I says to myself, 'Oh, I hope the hang when I go away, if I don't give him a tip, he doesn't say, "The stingy dog", and slap my mother in the face or something.' You know how these thoughts pass through your mind. It was very sad. The Infirmary people said to me, 'We think your mother died of cancer. But if you're not satisfied we'll ....' I said, 'Oh, no, no, I'll take your word for it. I'm perfectly satisfied.'

My Uncle Alfonso Crolla also died—he was drowned at sea—when I was in Saughton Prison in 1940. He was a real Italian—born in Italy. Now, as I've said, all the Italians in Edinburgh were sent to Donaldson's Hospital whereas Anglo-Italians like me born in this country—were put in Saughton. Then from Donaldson's the Italians were sent to two different camps down in the Borders somewhere. And then, from what I understand, the British authorities were afraid of Hitler invading Britain and the Italians were sent off to Canada. What they did was they put all the young lads in one boat and all the older fellows like Uncle Alfonso in another boat. He was put on the *Arandora Star*. As they were sailing out to sea by a hundred to one chance a German submarine had come up to the surface in the dark. And here they saw the ship coming and of course they were able to line up. I heard they smacked the *Arandora Star* full on—beautiful target—and they sank it.

Now I heard when this happened there were many German seamen on the *Arandora Star*, prisoners of war, apart from the Italians. But the Germans knew what to do—went to stations or whatever you call them. The Italians—'Oh, what do you do?!'—were landlubbers, no idea what to do. But I know a few of them were on their knees. 'Oh, well, if you survive, give my love to my wife,' and all this sort of thing. Ci Alfonso—Ci is the Italian for uncle, I mean, I'm accustomed to saying Ci Alfonso—he went down with that lot. He was in his early fifties.

Now my brother-in-law Achille Crolla, who had been on the Fascio Club committee, was lucky. He was one of the survivors from the *Arandora Star*. The lifeboats were away and when the ship went down he was sucked down with it. But before that happened the captain on the bridge and one or two others shouted: 'Good luck, boys! Good luck, boys! Brave, these men were! Good luck!' You know, he wished them well. And here was the band playing away, going down with the ship sinking.

And a few wounded Canadian soldiers on stretchers further back—all went down with the ship.

So the ship went down and my brother-in-law Achi was sucked down as well. And here the next thing he remembered he bumped his head and come up again. He hung on to this floating piece of wood. He was covered with oil. He said he considered the oil saved his life—you know, cold. But there were two or three other men couldn't hold on any longer and sunk.

I think Achi was seven hours in the water when a rowing boat came up and pulled him on to a ship. He was lying in the bottom of this boat with two or three other chaps and they were brought on to a British warship. They went downstairs to get a shower, a hot shower, and here he'd been lying in that boat beside one of his best pals, Achille Coppola, a man from Waterloo Place, and Achi didn't know he'd been beside him. It wasn't till they got all the oil washed off them that they knew who they were. Of course he could hardly have said, 'Are you ...?' And of course they were nicely treated on the warship and then Achi came ashore to, I think it was Greenock. And then from there they were all sent to Edinburgh Castle and then to the Isle of Man.

By the way, Achi Crolla, my brother-in-law, was in his chip shop in Church Place in Stockbridge when he was arrested about seven or eight o'clock on the evening that Italy declared war. Of course he had to close the shop and he had to go up to his house and put on his other clothes or bring something, you know what I mean. And there were people calling him names—'Achi, hey, hey, hey.' But on the other hand two or three were saying, 'Here, what's wrong with Achi? He's a good friend of ours. Stop blaming him! It's not his fault. He's not created the war.' Two or three ladies were sticking up for him, telling the rest of the crowd: 'Shut your mouths!' Oh, it was a humiliating experience for people to be arrested and pulled out into the street. Nobody saw me, when I was arrested, because it happened in the middle of the night.

The *Arandora Star* was sunk not long after Italy had entered the war, because when we were in Saughton Prison we used to lunch in the open hall. One day they called out for a boy Di Ciacca from Cockenzie or Port Seton. They called him: 'A visit.' 'Fancy, a visit. It's not a visiting hour.' And of course anything out of the ordinary and everybody's interested, you see. So we were watching Di Ciacca go out. And then he came back again. He ignored everybody and went away up to his cell and locked himself in. 'What the hang's this?' And then my cousin Victor Crolla, Uncle Alfonso's son, was called out. And he did the same, too. There were about half a dozen boys did. The rest of us said, 'What the hang's this?' Of course, I went up to Victor's cell and banged at the door: 'What is it?' He ignored me completely. 'Victor! Victor!' Of course the warders were saying nothing because they knew what had happened. I was banging at Victor's door. So he opened the door and he told the other fellows to get out the road. He says, 'Dad's been drowned on a ship.' 'What?!' Of course, we knew nothing about this.

Now my mother was not dead then. She died in November 1940, and this was in mid-July. She was still at home, not in the Infirmary, and when they went to tell

316

her the *Arandora Star* had been sunk: 'Oh, Alfonso, Alfonso', crying out for him. 'Now, now, now, why Alfonso? You have two other brothers. Why must it be him ...?' 'Oh, no, no, no, Alfonso.' They considered that it was instinct that she knew. The three brothers were on the same ship. The other two were saved, it turned out, but Alfonso was drowned. Now why did she call out the name of the one that was drowned? And the laugh is that one of the brothers, Giovanni, who had a chip shop in Union Place, after he was saved he with a lot of them was shipped off to Australia. Off the shore of Australia did that ship not get sunk. So Uncle John got torpedoed twice. But he was saved again and landed up in Australia. He came back to Edinburgh after the war, oh, aye, grinned, 'Oh, well,' he says, 'that's war.' He shrugged his shoulders, 'That's war. What do you expect?' You see, you learn to be philosophical. Bad as you are, there is many a person worse.

I was in Saughton Prison about six months, from June to December 1940. After we had been in there for quite some time I got a communication from the authorities: 'You are accused of being a member of the Italian Fascist Party, of having had pro-Italian discussions with people. Tribunal on such-and-such a date, when you can defend yourself.' 'Of course, oh, well, that suits me.' So here I had to go before the tribunal.

There were about seven people had come to Saughton Prison and they were in a room seated at a table. There was about half-a-dozen of us done every day. But anyhow I had to go in alone. They says, 'Right, you're Joseph Pia? Right. What have you got to say for yourself?' I says, 'Well,' I says, 'you ask me any questions you like and you'll know from my answers I've done nothing wrong at all. I mean, I know nothing at all about military things. So ask me a question.' One of the tribunal says, 'Oh, we're not here to ask questions. We're here only to hear what you've got to say in defence of these things.' I says, 'Well, but I mean, I was a member of the Italian Fascist Party but there was nothing political in the thing.' I says, 'I've had arguments with people sticking up for Mussolini, I've had arguments with people against Mussolini.' I says, 'But nothing political about the thing, in the normal sense of the word.' 'Oh, well, is that all you've got to say for yourself?' I says, 'Oh, well, but I mean I've done nothing wrong.' So then I got out. It was quite a short tribunal. It lasted less than ten or fifteen minutes.

We should have been warned what you're supposed to do. I mean, I was not told before I went in. I thought they were going to ask me questions. That's what you expect. But—'What have you to say for yourself?' I'll admit I had the accusation on paper: 'You were a member of the Italian Fascist Party.' Well, my answer is honest: yes. But I was not political. What more can I say than that? I mean, what political activities were there in Edinburgh? They should have known there was none in Edinburgh. I'd never been in any military thing. Anyhow that's what happened.

Now after the tribunal, two or three weeks after, you were sent out of town. So when my crowd went out I was sent down to York racecourse. The government had commandeered it. My younger brother Gerard and my cousin Victor Crolla had been sent there before me. I don't want to say I was amongst the last to go there

317

but I certainly wasn't amongst the first. We left Edinburgh about four o'clock in the morning. We went by bus from Saughton to Waverley station, so as not to meet people on the way. We arrived at York racecourse about four or five in the afternoon. Now I found out afterwards that people interned in London and the south of England were sent to Ascot, and those in the north of England and Scotland went to York.

Anyhow when we arrived at York racecourse—it wasn't long before Christmas 1940—we were hungry, tired, cold—a drizzly day. There was barbed wire round a big encampment, where the tote and things were. We got into single file and here was an officer with a table and then you passed on from him to the camp. So when I came up to him, he says: 'What's your ...?' 'I'm C 98.' 'Giuseppe Pia?' 'Yes.' He says, 'Well, nationality English, of course.' I says, 'I beg your pardon?' He says, 'Your nationality is English.' I says, 'I'm not English,' I said, 'there's nothing English about me.' I says, 'I'm Scottish or British, if you like, or even Italian. I'm of dual nationality, British-Italian. Put down either Italian, British or Scottish but certainly not English.' He says, 'But I've got to write down English.' I says, 'Oh, yes? But I'm not an Englishman. So you can't mark English for me.' And all the others in the queue are saying, 'Oh, what's this?', you see. And of course naturally I've held up the queue: 'What is it?' And hundreds of people come to the gate, 'What is it? What is it?' 'I don't know.' 'Oh.' 'I wonder what that chap's doing?', you see. Here's a big crowd—two or three hundred people (there were only 400 in the camp)—so half of them were all excited, wondering what the hang's wrong. Anything for excitement, you see. But the chap behind me says, 'Oh, shut your mouth, Joe! Let him write down everything. What difference does it make? I'm tired, I'm cold, I'm hungry.' So I says, 'All right then, go and shove it down.' So here I go forward , but quite annoyed, you see. And of course in the camp: 'What is it?' I says, 'He wants to put me down as an Englishman! There's nothing English about me! I'm a Scot, I'm not an Englishman!' And I'm shouting, quite annoyed. 'Oh, are you?' And of course the word flashes right down. So here before I know it, a chap comes across to me, shakes hands and claps me on the back: 'Well done! Well done! Your name's Joe, isn't it?' I says, 'Yes.' 'Well done!' I says, 'By the way, who are you?' 'Oh, my name's Hamish Hamilton.' 'Hamish Hamilton?' I says. 'Why are you here?' 'Oh,' he says, 'I'm a Scots Nationalist.' I says, 'A Scots Nationalist?' 'Yes,' he says, 'oh, they consider we're anti-war as well. There are four of us in the camp are Scots Nationalists.' I says, 'Is that so?' He says, 'Oh, yes, and we've got Irish and Welsh Nationalists here as well.' 'Is that so?' And I says, 'And you are a Scots Nationalist?' He says, 'Yes.' I says, 'By the way, don't tell me that you let them write down that you're English?' 'Oh, well,' he says, 'what else could you do?' I says, 'Well, I mean, I've never bothered about nationality in my life before. But, I mean, you a Scots Nationalist letting them write down "English"? I who am not a nationalist make a fuss about being called English and you make no bother at all?' 'Oh, well, he says, 'you have to do it, you know what I mean.'

In the tote at York racecourse there were a lot of beds: without being exact, twenty beds on each side—forty of us. And then there was a big building, too, where there were a lot of camp beds all over the place. Maybe it was a sort of stables. When I came down the tote was full. I was in this other place. My brother Gerard and Victor Crolla were in the tote. And they applied so I got in beside them—F Hut, I think we called it. I was there at York racecourse about a couple of months.

By this time we were truly labelled Anglo-Italian to distinguish us from Anglo-Germans or Anglos. Now the Anglos: you could have been just Anglo or a BU—British Union of Fascists. They were the four categories. When we were there we were told: 'You can go to the Welfare Officer singly. Queue up, he wants to have a talk with you.' So I went in like all the others. The officer's name was Captain Cranstor. He asked your name and address and that, and verified who I was, you see. 'Are you willing to join the Pioneer Corps?' 'The Pioneer Corps?' He says, 'Yes.' I says, 'Oh, no, no, no. Why the Pioneer Corps? By the way,' I says, 'I've done no harm to anybody.' I says, 'If you release me from here with a clean sheet and treat me like any other boy,' I says, 'then let me volunteer for the Royal Scots, the HLI, the KOSBs[285]—any of these regiments—but certainly not the Pioneer Corps. If you want me to be like any other boy treat me like any other boy.' And while we were at this here does a major not come in who was inspecting various camps. So Captain Cranstor says to him, 'Oh, yes, Major. A very interesting case here. This gentleman here' (of course, they were nice and polite: remember, I wasn't a prisoner really), 'This gentleman here is protesting. He doesn't want to join the Pioneer Corps.' So the major says, 'Well, and what's wrong with the Pioneer Corps?' 'Well,' I says, 'to me they're the scrapings of the British army. All they're for is to dig roads and latrines and that. You don't get me for that.' 'How dare you despise the British army! They're as good as any other army!' 'Hold your horses,' I says, 'hold your horses. I'm not comparing the British army with the Germans or any other army. I know nothing about armies. I'm telling you, in the British army the Pioneer Corps are the scavengers. They build latrines, don't they?' I says, 'Well, you don't get me to build latrines. If you want me to go in the trenches I'll go in the trenches like any other fellow. But I'm not going into latrine-digging.' And of course the major just looked at me—not a word, about turned and marched out the place. Captain Cranstor laughed, which was right, by the way.

Now most people don't tell the truth. 'How did you get on?' 'Oh, ya-ya-ya-ya.' Now I suspect that the big majority of the Anglo-Italians at York racecourse said, 'Yes, I want to join the Pioneer Corps'—because they got out of internment if they joined it. About a quarter of us got kept in because we refused to join the Pioneer Corps. My brother Gerard, Victor Crolla and I, we refused to join the Pioneer Corps. We objected to being told 'Pioneer Corps or nothing'.

But we were very well treated in that camp, no complaints about the way we were treated there. We were up about seven o'clock in the morning and you had to be in at seven or eight at night—lights out or something. The food was very, very good.

Naturally we were curious to know about the British Union of Fascists men or Anglo-Germans who were there. 'What do you do? What is it?', you know. We tried to find out what they had done, why they were there. I was interested in the

BUs. I found out that four of the organisers for the BU used to be in the Communist Party. 'They were the opposite?' 'Oh, yes, but Mosley offered us bigger wages so naturally we came to the Fascists.' These were men that came from Manchester. But what do you think of that? They changed parties because of the bigger wages. When you're innocent you think politicians are true to a belief, you see. I'm a wee bit of a cynic now about politics. By the way, you couldn't meet nicer fellows than these four BUs., only politically they could be bought. Maybe we could be, too: you've got to wait until the thing happens to know what you're capable of.

By this time, too, we'd elected leaders. So I was on the Anglo-Italian committee. This suited the authorities to have us organised to do things, you see. Remember, in the First Great War they had found out that a person in detention is liable to lose his mind. It was so bad that they brought out the Geneva Convention: no person must be kept in confinement for more than three years. But of course Britain, Italy—any country you like to mention—keep their laws when it suits them and when it doesn't they break the laws. I was in for three-and-a-half years, although you're not supposed to be in for more than three.

We were at York racecourse from December 1940 until about February 1941. Then I was one of a dozen of our lot that was an advance party to go to Huyton, Liverpool. We were there for a few days before the main party arrived. The soldiers went round the streets at Huyton with us—a sergeant, a soldier and another man—and said, 'You can get twenty in there.' I had to find accommodation for about 200 of us. So that was done.[286]

The soldiers—you know how you become friendly—told us that before we arrived a lot of Jews had been in the Huyton camp. And after the Jews had been shifted out they went round the camp cleaning up, and according to the soldiers they had found four Jews who had hanged themselves. They were refugees from Europe. And you've got to remember the crowd of Jews coming into Britain. A few were sure to be traitors or spies, or whatever the word is. And there may have been spies amongst us Anglo-Italians, for all I know. I never really had any grounds for suspecting there were.[287]

Then of course all the boys, the main party, came to this camp at Huyton. The people at Ascot came in as well as York. Some mistake had been made at the Home Office about the rations needed. They were only given rations for, we'll say, 480: we were double that number. They were only given for York or it might have been Ascot, but we were double that number.

Now we had to cook our own food and I don't know how they picked the chef—we called him the cook. With about thirty boys cooking do you think they ate half rations? Do you not think they would fill their bellies and their brothers', and their pals'? And when you're allowed, we'll say, eight ounces of potatoes, so many eight ounces a hundredweight, you'll admit by the time you wash and peel them it's no longer a hundredweight. So you can imagine the rations we got. This went on for about four weeks.

Now we had four street leaders. I was one of the unlucky stupid buggers who was a street leader. I had to stand at the hut—we had three meals a day: breakfast, lunch and dinner—to make sure that nobody got into the queue twice. I was the last one to be served. I hope you believe me when I tell you that more than half the times I got no food at all. I was starving. I mean, can I remember that you were there three times a day? You've got to tell me you don't skip the queue. I mean, I was continually asking them: 'You been in already?' 'I haven't, Joe, I haven't.' 'Out you get!' 'No, no, I didn't, honestly, Joe! Oh, please, dinnae, please, Joe. I have not. I'm hungry.' 'Out you get! Don't kid me on. Clear out!' I hope to hell I haven't made a mistake. Well, what the hang can you do? And when it comes to the end of the queue—about six or ten or twelve of the men get no food at all. Who gets the blame but me: 'Hey, Pia, you're … '. One time I was battered and the policemen—I mean our policemen—had to protect me. There were half a dozen of the chaps were our policemen. They were there to protect me. I got battered to the ground by two or three chaps because they got no food. But I got no food either. The same would happen to the other street leaders, of course. I wasn't the only one. So we went protesting to the camp commandant: 'Oh, we'll need to do something.' So they quickly thought out having cards. But I mean, you are amongst a lot of smart boys: you know the word forgery. Oh, that was a pretty difficult time: hunger.

So Victor Crolla wrote to Miss Dennison, who was running his shop in Edinburgh—Valvona and Crolla, Elm Row. She had been their secretary or something and she was running his shop while he was away. So Victor wrote her a letter: 'Please don't let the family or anybody know but we're starving. Can you send us some bread? Nothing else but bread!' So here you could receive parcels in the camp. So one day: 'Parcels for such-and-such and such-and-such.' And you had to go to a certain building to collect a parcel. Here's a parcel announced for Victor Crolla. 'Oh, come on, we'll chum you.' We chummed Victor and here he got half-a-dozen I think you called them Yuma loaves. They were very nice to eat—I don't know if there were raisins in them but that was the impression you got. 'Oh, good!' Victor says, 'Back to the house!' We were eight in our house, we done 'Hey, la, la, ha, la, la! Right, a slice each!' Yum, yum, yum, yum, yum. And then another slice each. The six loaves didn't last long! Oh, that was a feast!

I'll tell you another thing. Every morning at Huyton you used to get two slices of bread and a cube size of cheese or jam and a cup of tea. That was your breakfast. So I got my breakfast one morning. When I went along to the house I says to myself, 'Oh, well, I've got to keep a slice of bread for later because I wouldn't be surprised if I get nothing again at midday meal.' So I put a slice of my bread in the cupboard and only ate the one for breakfast. So here at one o'clock or so, when I came back from the cooking hut: 'How did you get on today, Joe?' I said, 'No bloody food again! Why the hell must I be street leader? I'm the first one along there and I'm the last to get served! I mean, I'm going to resign this job. To hell with this!' That was the day when I got battered, you know, they knocked me to the ground and punched me. 'I mean, for all the thanks I get! Why the hell …?' So here I says, 'Thank goodness I've got my slice of bread from breakfast anyhow.' So here I goes to the cupboard—and has it not disappeared! One of the boys had taken it. 'Where, where's my slice of bread?!' My brother and Victor Crolla: 'Oh, I don't know.' So here we looked at this chap Bertie Dagostino. He was the nephew of John Dagostino I mentioned earlier—and John's son Freddie was in Huyton camp, too. But this is Bertie, who had the Royal Cafe, Leith Street, corner house behind Woolworth's. 'Eh?', says Bertie. 'Oh, I didn't know who it belonged to.' Of course, I goes for him. Luckily, they hold me back. I would have battered him to death, I think, for that slice of bread. I mean, food is the number one thing. In fact, we ate all the cats in the camp. I bit a leg of one that had been cooked but could not actually eat it. The commander spoke to us all about the cats disappearing and warned us that if we did not stop eating them a plague of mice and rats would follow.

The British army know how to handle people: you must keep them occupied. So at Huyton—'What classes do you want? Any of you want to teach?' We had one man amongst us, Dr Gordon, who used to teach English to the German police. He was quite willing to do a German class. He was a prisoner himself. To me he was an old man—he was a chap of about 40 or 50, a very, very nice man, a gentleman.

And then there were air raids on Liverpool. We used to come out and watch the aeroplanes. We says, 'Well, they'll never bomb us. They'll know that we're Fascists so they'll not bomb the Fascist camp'. So we used to go out whenever there was an air raid and it was a most beautiful sight. I mean, the British had tracer bullets—beautiful watching the tracer bullets. And the Germans had a flare, a wee parachute thing so that they could see to drop their bombs. And it was a most beautiful sight if you weren't afraid when you were watching it. As a matter of fact shrapnel used to fall on the camp. We used to go running to pick it up. We thought it was great collecting. I burnt my fingers once or twice till it cooled. But anyhow this happened for a few days until one morning when we got up: 'Keep away from the centre of the camp.' A German bomb had dropped right in the middle of the camp but it didn't go off. The soldiers had roped it off and none of us were allowed to go near it in case it did go off. It was there until the bomb disposal came to it. So after that, 'Oh, to hang with this!', we kept to our houses when there was an air raid on. We didn't have air raid shelters to go into.

There were two MPs amongst us at Huyton. I remember this one Beckett. There were two lines of barbed wire and a soldier marching in between them, and here's Beckett with a hand and a foot on the barbed wire, speaking with somebody. So the sentry says to him, 'Get your bloody hand in!' 'I beg your pardon? Who do you think you are speaking to?' 'Get your bloody hand in or I'll shoot you!' 'Oh, is that so? Right, shoot away, my lad! Come on, shoot away!' You're speaking with intelligent men, you see—I mean, this was the riff-raff coming out with this nonsense about shooting.[288]

Huyton was the one camp where we were badly treated. At the beginning, when the whole crowd came in we had to parade in a big field and go marching between soldiers with fixed bayonets. And of course, although the bayonet is a foot or two away, you think it's nearer, hoping they don't bump into you, you see. We were in three sides of a square. So this Major Veitch comes in to speak to us. 'Well,' he says, 'now you're here, if you behave yourselves, O.K. Any nonsense and we'll prick you.' You know, this sort of thing. Now you've got to remember that the likes of me and the big majority of the fellows were stupid, ignorant, non-military men. But most of the British Union of Fascists men there were true nationalists—not anti-British but pro-British, ultra—too much pro-British, you might say. And half of them had been in the Great War in 1914-18. And here's this Major Veitch telling them, 'None of your nonsense.' And of course a few of them stand forward—Captain So-and-so and Colonel So-and-so who had been in the First War. One of them says to Major Veitch: 'Obviously, in the last war you'd been away behind the lines. If you'd been in the front line like me you wouldn't be so anti-German as your talk. You're all talk. It's well seen you've been behind the lines.' So he says, 'Shoot me!', you know, baring his chest, 'Shoot me! I'm willing to die for my country! I'm an Englishman through and through!' About half a dozen of them were doing that, and of course we're looking with awe at this. We'd never seen such a thing before.

Of course, poor old Major Veitch, what could he do? I suspect his fellow officers were saying, 'You'd better leave, sir, you'd better leave.' Because it meant he had either to shoot or … So here he about turned. And there were loud boos. And of course after two or three started the boos, the whole lot of us started. Poor old Major Veitch got booed like anything off the field. And of course the other officers— 'Awwrrr, awwrrr, aahhhrrr'—got us back into the camp.

So every time Major Veitch's face was seen anywhere after that—'Boo! Boo!' They had to get rid of him, within a day or two they had to get rid of him. There would have been trouble if he'd been kept there.

We were only in Huyton about a couple of months, from February to about April 1941. Then we went to the Isle of Man. I was in an advance party again, this time going to the Isle of Man. When we were at Liverpool docks waiting for a boat there were half a dozen soldiers with us and they were speaking about an air raid the day before. They had shot a German plane down, and this soldier says that a German had landed in the water and as he was coming up he, 'Aaaaggghhh, I got the butt, you know, and I shoved him under. I made sure the bugger died.' So we were saying, 'Fancy being cruel like that.' But I mean, we were in war, we were in war. Are you going to say German soldiers didn't do that to our men? It happens on all sides. I mean, the majority don't do that but quite a few bad boys on both sides do these cruel things. And of course maybe these soldiers at Liverpool docks had seen the results of air raids—maybe their own families had been killed.

Anyhow we went to Peel. Oh, it was a beautiful camp—beautiful boarding houses. We had the whole front to ourselves: nine houses, from no. 1 to no. 9, with about 48 people in each house. The first three houses were all British Union of Fascists men, and then the next four houses Anglo-Italians like me, and the next two houses there were what we called the odds and sods. And then at the back, spread all over, were most of the Anglo-Germans and other odds and sods.

The odds and sods: no idea why they were in. There must have been quite a few intellectuals among them. Professor Darwin Fox, who was Professor of English at Lausanne University, was one. He was strongly pro-German and anti-British. Of course, maybe the war made him that, maybe the way he was treated, I don't know. But, oh, he was a gentleman. He had been in Huyton with us as well. He was a red hot Pape—a Knight of St Gregory, conferred by the Pope. There were quite a few other intellectuals. I remember a man Selwyn Wright. We used to call him Seldom Wright. And then I remember quite a few British soldiers who had been at Dunkirk were interned with us. I remember Lieutenant Sherston or Sheraton, a very, very nice man. He had been a street leader at Huyton. He was a lieutenant in the British army and he had been at Dunkirk. I says to him, 'At Dunkirk?' And he says, 'Oh, yes.' 'And you're in here?' He says, 'Oh, well,' and just smiled. A tall, handsome, very, very nice man. He had been, I suspect, in the British Union of Fascists. He didn't say very much. But he was certainly not Italian or German. He was English through and through. So that was the assumption, that he must have been associated with the British Union of Fascists. But he didn't take an active part with the BUF. I mean, there were a few fellows, the likes of authors and that, there. They must have had Fascist sympathies, I must guess. But they were not active BUF men. Richard Finlay was one. He was amongst the first to be in Saughton. He was in before us and he was there the whole time with us and then the whole time in the Isle of Man, too. He was an Englishman. But he was a funny chap. He was friendly but not very, very friendly. He didn't ask you anything nor did he tell you anything about anything private. We just knew he was an author from his card—it told you his occupation. So we were curious to know about him. Maybe a few tried to ask him what he did do, but I never asked him any personal questions. You know, you always volunteer it but you don't ask.

The top British Union of Fascists man in the camp was Captain Denovan, he'd been a captain in the British army in India. He used to give us talks on Indian religions. The BUs were pro-British—they were anti-Jewish, yes, but pro-British. I mean, I'm not far wrong when I say any of them would have fought for Britain in a minute. I had close contacts with the BUs in the camp at Peel—I mixed with every-body equally, it didn't matter who they were. Well, Captain Denovan was the BUs' top man and others I remember were the likes of Bill Eaton, who worked with me in the camp hospital and who was an MA of Lancaster University. He was quite big among them. He told me, 'If we'd got the whole of the BBC for a week we would have converted Britain to Fascism.'

At Peel the food was passable but not good, and there was not enough of it. The caterers or purveyors sent meat of the rottenest quality. We used to get kippers about two or three times a week. But the kippers were so rotten we refused to take them, and then we were served them again the next day. So we threw them to the seagulls. And of course the camp authorities: 'Hey, you mustn't throw them away! It's a waste of food!' We said, 'Well, look, if we give them back to you you'll give them back to us again so if we get rid of the stuff you'll have to give us something else.'

I can remember once the meat, oh, it was dreadful meat. And of course I was house leader. The meat was supposed to be for 48 boys, about two or three pounds of meat. This meat had maggots in it. So I went back with it: 'Over the wire, please. I want to go back to the catering.' And here is there not a big Cabinet minister visiting the camp? 'What is it? What is it?' I said, 'This here is for 48 boys. I've come back.' 'Oh, we'll need to get you something else.' I says, 'It's quite all right. Don't

324

think the sacrifice is a big one. That split among 48 boys would give us each a piece of meat about the size of an Oxo cube.' I says, 'Do you think we're going to complain about missing an Oxo cube?' You've to remember I'm not afraid of being imprisoned or punished. You could be cheeky to them. You had nothing to lose. So I said, 'Don't think I'm making a big sacrifice when I tell you: keep your meat.'

We had no idea of course how long we were going to remain there at Peel. Nobody said, 'You'll be released next week or next month or next year.' Well, you didn't worry. You took it as a way of life. And remember, they had a Welfare Officer there: 'Any activity you want you can have.' Now Bill Eaton, a great chap, a big-time in the British Union of Fascists, he came from Lancaster—he had a wholesale drapery business in Lancaster—and he was a harrier before the war. So here Bill went to the Welfare Officer: 'Can we have harriers?' 'Oh, yes, certainly.' So there used to be about a dozen fellows went as harriers.

By this time we've got policemen, not soldiers, looking after us. Soldiers didn't know how to handle us. They were causing more trouble than anything. So the authorities had to call in London Metropolitan police to look after us. They knew how to handle people. So this policeman used to go cycling behind the harriers. And at the first pub he would stop (I know this but the authorities didn't): 'Right, carry on, boys. Come back in about an hour's time.' He's sitting in the pub having a pint and the boys away running as harriers. Then when they come back, on to his bike again and back to the camp.

We were allowed out twice a week from the camp to play at football. I remember once when we went out to play here there is a lot of soldiers playing. So when we came up, 'Oh,' we says, 'we'll sit and watch.' 'Oh, no, no, you must play.' 'It's all right, we'll watch.' Here the authorities went and told the soldiers: 'Off the field!' I says, 'We don't mind watching.' But the officer says, 'No, you boys need exercise. You must—we don't want you all in the mental asylum. Our boys can wait till after.' So the poor old soldiers had to clear off the field to make room for us.

We also organised games. We had Olympic Games every year: Germany, Italy, and Britain, the three countries competing against each other.

And there was a nice tennis court, a red cinder tennis court. That was fully occupied in good weather. We had competitions there. I remember a chap Bertie Mills, who was a member of—was it Queen's Club, in London? He was quite annoyed that our Regno Benigno from Peebles, who was Scottish Boys' champion at tennis, beat him every time. Benigno's name is Dom Francesco really. I don't know why they use the name Benigno in Peebles: his father's name is Dom Francesco. But anyhow he walloped this Bertie Mills every time, and Bertie was quite annoyed, you know, being a member of the Queen's Club.

Time didn't hang heavy on our hands: we were well organised. For instance, I had a fellow who was of German origin. He used to teach German at some institute at Plymouth or Portsmouth. I got him to teach me German three nights a week. He'd come on a Monday night for an hour and he gave me homework, about three or four hours' homework. And then on the Wednesday night we'd do that in a quarter of an hour or so and then more stuff. But I got three hours a week with him and I used to give him 7/6d. a week. He used to earn money that way. After a year I'd gone through the German grammar completely and we could speak, him speaking in German and I answering in German. By this time he was interested in Italian. So one night I gave him Italian and the next night he gave me German. For a year I paid him, for the next year no: I was teaching him Italian and he was teaching me German.

But apart from that you could get classes in shorthand. So I learned shorthand as well. It's wonderful what you or anybody else is capable of. Oh, I was learning quite a bit. You could have taken Italian or French classes. But I had a smattering of French and Italian, I could get by. So I was better learning a new language. It came to the stage where I had a smattering of German. And I was very interested in history. So I had a chance there at Peel to read about history and to learn things I hadn't a chance to learn about before.

And I've always been quite interested in medical things. I wrote to my girlfriend—we were maybe engaged about the middle of my time in the camp at Peel—but I wrote to her: 'Can you get me a book on anatomy?' I wanted an elementary book. Here did she not send me a textbook—Cunningham's *Anatomy*. Well I didn't expect a big heavy thing like that. And of course when it came the police called me across the wire: 'Here, what the hang's this?' I says, 'Oh, I told my girlfriend to send me a book on first-aid. I wanted to learn a wee bit about anatomy. I didn't expect this.' They were watching me and looking at the book and of course they examined it to make sure that there was nothing concealed in it. But they believed me: it was obvious from my demeanour that I was an honest citizen. So I then learned quite a lot about anatomy from that book.

Of course, before going to Peel I was already a holder of the St Andrew's Ambulance certificate. But at Peel we were encouraged: 'What about going in for St John's Ambulance ...?' So four of us went in for it and the doctor who came to examine us in the work at the end says, 'My God! I've never heard such perfect answers! Better than I could have answered myself!' You see, the four of us had nothing else to do. The other three were all university graduates: Dr Alten, a German, from Sheffield, he was a Ph.D. And then Bill Eaton, the British Union of Fascists chap, he was an MA, Lancaster, and the other chap was Bertie Pacitti, MA, Glasgow. I was as keen as any of them. As soon as I was asked a question—how many kinds of fractures are there—rrrrrhhhh, I rattled off the whole lot. I remember the doctor saying, 'My God! I've never heard the likes of it before.' So time never hung heavy, I never got depressed at Peel. I was always too occupied, fully occupied the whole time.

There was a camp library. And we were allowed access to the British Museum or something. You got any book you wanted free of charge, oh, a good choice of reading. So I read quite a bit. I've always been quite a studious person.

One thing we weren't allowed in the camp was newspapers. We couldn't follow the ups and downs of the war when we were at Peel. I don't think we were allowed radios either. But we used to get told stories now and then, maybe from visitors. We knew when Hess dropped down in Scotland. So Adrian Coppola and I were the two massage fellows and we made up a story—it's wonderful how people believe it. So first thing in the morning: 'By the way, you know the latest?' 'What is it?' 'Oh, we've heard it from over the wire that Count Ciano and Italo Balbo have dropped down in a plane in Cornwall and have been brought to London, you know, offering terms of peace.' 'Is that so?' 'Oh, yes, yes. We've been told that over the wire.' And of course that story spread through the camp like wildfire. So when we went down at lunchtime: 'Oh, Joe, Joe, do you know that Ciano …?' I says, 'Oh, I don't believe it.' 'Oh, yes, yes.' I said, 'I don't believe it. Prove it to me.' 'Everybody's swearing it's true!' This is Adrian and me having a laugh. The stupid asses—we had made the story up. And when we told them, after about an hour or two, they wouldn't believe us!²⁸⁹

So we didn't follow the course of the war, we just had our activity there. If we heard anything: 'Oh, is that so?' By the way, there was a wee bit of hard feeling between the Italians and Germans or Anglo-Italians and Anglo-Germans in the camp when Italy dropped out of the war. The Germans were coming out with this story that the Italians were good runners—you know, running away. We resented that. And the Germans were annoyed: 'I wish these bloody Italians had not come into the war. They've let us down. They're a handicap instead of a help.'

Of course Mussolini maybe had some good lieutenants but he certainly had some bad ones, because during the middle of the war did he not find out that half of his cabinet—including his son-in-law Count Ciano—were in the pay of the British government? Imagine his own son-in-law in the pay of the British government! And Ciano got shot: the Italians shot him before they changed over.²⁹⁰ Well, as I said, we didn't have political discussion in the Fascio Club in Edinburgh before the war positively not. But inside the camp at Peel we did. Well, you had to talk about something. I would say that in the camp most of them had become pro-Mussolini because of the way they were being treated. Remember, most of them were bitter, annoyed at being dumped into prison, not trusted. You are treated like an enemy so you feel like an enemy. So really the British government's policy was counter-productive.

In our camp at Peel I would say there were about 800 to 900 of us. You were allowed visits—only your family couldn't come often to visit you of course on the Isle of Man. But there wasn't any restriction on the number of letters you could receive. But they had to be censored. You could receive a dozen but you were only allowed to send out two a week. They gave us special paper. It was highly glazed paper and we used to write tiny, to squeeze in as much as possible, to let our families at home know how we were doing.

At home my young sister Peggy was running my business for me. She got married to a British officer who had been in the Terries before the war, a chap called George Ford. He was adjutant on Inchkeith and then he was sent to Gibraltar and he was an adjutant there. By the way, he had been in the Scouts with me. My scoutmaster and assistant scoutmaster were in the army, too, and they used to contact my sister when they were on leave: 'Tell Joe I'm asking for him.' They had no anti-Italian feeling against me. When I was interned I wrote to half a dozen people to give me a reference, you know, as clean and above board. I got good replies from them and also from the District Scout fellow, who became a professor in Heriot-Watt University—Professor Joe Gloag.[291]

In the camp at Peel we had small wages. I think the government was paying it. I used to get 7/6d. a week. I worked in the camp hospital. I was in charge of doing the massage. We had a doctor, a German who was a naturalised Britisher, Dr Bode. In the First War he had been in the Uhlans—a vet for the horses in the Uhlan cavalry. But after the war they were shattered, so he became a farm labourer. Then he got a job in the local town, fitting shoes on to people. And from there got entrance to become a doctor. Instead of going into practice he became an assistant to a man who discovered homeopathy. So then, I don't know why, he landed up in London and became a naturalised Britisher. He used to write regularly in the *Lancet* and the *British Medical Journal*—articles on homeopathy. I'm maybe wrong, but I think he introduced homeopathy to Britain. I know that all the hospitals here used to write to him for information. He was very highly thought of.

When you went from one camp to the next you had to be medically examined. On the Isle of Man Colonel Flowerdew was the medical man. He used to come every day. He would sit at the desk with Dr Bode but Dr Bode was really the doctor. He would prescribe whatever it was. Flowerdew: 'Oh, yes, yes.' Flowerdew considered himself inferior to Bode, who had been the senior physician at the German hospital in London. He was official physician to the German Embassy, the Italian Embassy and the Spanish Embassy. So he had plenty of Fascist connections. But never once have I heard him say anything political—pro- or anti-Hitler or anybody else. And when you're in camp you become pally with each other. So me being a first-aid man Dr Bode says to me: 'By the way, Pia, I would like somebody to do massage—you know, people with lumbago and that.' So he showed me what to do. I says, 'Oh, well, then, right.' So I became the massage man or physiotherapist and then I got a fellow to be my assistant as well. So for three years I worked in the Peel camp hospital and I used to be paid 7/6d. a week.

When it was suspected a chap in the camp was slightly mentally affected he would get called up to the camp hospital for a check-up. Whenever it was a mental case there was a big sheet of paper came up from London with about fifty questions on it. So here they would ask the chap these questions and then they would send the paper to London and they would decide whether he was to stay on in the camp. The mental home on the Isle of Man was absolutely full up. We were sending them to the mainland. That was why we were given every activity so as not to be mentally unfit, you see. And of course when you're there just putting in time, everybody is getting every illness, you know what I mean? Lumbago was a common thing so I always had twenty lumbago cases every day, massaging their back.

My assistant and me were not properly trained in massage but Dr Bode used to tell me, 'Do this, do that.' I remember once a young Croat—he was pro-Nazi maybe—Dr Jerich came in to see me, so here I'm massaging his muscles. I says, 'What are you a doctor of, doctor?' He says, 'Medicine.' Quite a few were doctors there, but not medicine. I said, 'Oh, oh, oh, I'm sorry, I mean, I'm not a properly trained physiotherapist.' He says, 'Excuse me, you're doing the absolutely perfect thing. Get as much movement into the muscle as possible. You're doing perfectly well. Carry on.' Dr Jerich was a tall, imposing fellow—beard, magnificent physique. He could speak perfect German from what I could judge, and not perfect but very, very good Italian and French. His English was good but not as good as his other languages were. He had a loud booming voice and this most imposing figure. Quite a few years after the war I saw on television that he had been attacked by a gunman in Berlin but he survived. He was one of the characters in the camp at Peel.

As a matter of fact when Dr Bode was off ill or something Dr Jerich became the medical doctor there. I remember once he called me in: 'This fellow here's got a sprained ankle. He's had it a long time. So get him to go down to the sea front. Get permission to get a pail of water and get soap in it and,' he says, 'soak his foot in the soap and water. Tell him to do that for the next few days.' So here he was telling me this in, I think it was German. Anyhow I did what he told me. But the fellow was in my house so I says, 'That's funny, soap and water. I've never heard of that before.' So here the next day I said, 'By the way, Dr Jerich, that fellow there—soap and water. I mean, that's a funny thing, soap?' 'Well,' he says, 'in German saltz—saltz und wasser.' I says, 'Saltz? The English for saltz is salt, not soap.' 'Oh, oh, well, tell him', he says, 'I've made a mistake. I should have said salt and water, not soap and water.'

In my camp at Peel we were more or less British. I've said more or less because there was Dr Jerich: I fail to see why he was there as a young Croat. And then there was also Dr Brunmer: I think he was really Swedish. But he was a Harley Street specialist. I remember him telling me, 'Ach,' he says, 'you get these duchesses coming to you with their big fat backsides.' He says, 'I stick a needle in it and charge them five guineas. All they should have done was do the work their servants were doing for them. That's all they needed—to do a good day's work instead of sitting about doing nothing.'

By the way, in Peel next door to us was X-camp. We were called Peel Camp but in X-camp were all nationalities except for enemy aliens—so no Japanese, Italians or Germans. But Norwegians, Danes, Rumanians, Spaniards, Dutch, whatever you like, they were in there. And they used our camp hospital. So I was used for massage or dentistry. And I was interpreter to the Spaniards who could only speak Spanish. I couldn't speak Spanish but I could speak Italian, and there's quite a similarity between the languages. These Spaniards in X-camp were not refugees from the Spanish Civil War, they were seafaring men. I don't know why they were in there. It was the same with the Danes. One man I was treating was a Dutchman who had become a Mohammedan—I don't know why.

But also there was a Jew from X-camp who was being treated by me. He was a Rumanian Jew. I was told by other X-camp men that he was a well known international jewel thief. He was one of those international crooks that had to report every week or month to the police station, you know. But anyhow they were too much of a nuisance to the police when the war came: 'Dump them inside. Get them out of the way.' So when I'm called into the doctor's surgery, here is this Jew sitting in a chair and this Dutchman must have been anti-Jewish. In his house in X-camp he had picked up a big pot of boiling water and AAAARRRRGGGGHHHH!—right over the Jew's head. So here was the Jew sitting in the doctor's, obviously scalded all over, his shoulders and everything. He'd got stripped in there. He had a great big gash in his head. All you could see was this great big gash and all his skin swollen. Oh, it was a dreadful sight! So Bertie Pacitti and I, the two massage men, had been called in to help. Dr Bode was getting a dressing for the Jew. So after a wee while he tells Pacitti, 'You better leave the room.' So I had to hold this chap. There was not a murmur from him but his eyes—dark eyes—roving, searching, looking at me. The man must have been in agony. Fortitude is the word to describe it. He's looking at me without a whimper, studying my face to see my reaction. I suppose he was weighing me up to see if I was anti-Jewish. I mean, I don't know. I was doing what I was told. To tell the truth I was awed: the man scalded, a great big gash an iron pot had made on his head. The other fellow had done it because he was a Jew. I think there were six to a dozen Jews in my camp. I don't know why they were amongst us. Oh, yes, they used to say, 'They are Zionists.' We used to say, 'Oh, what's this?' I hear a Zionist is a sort of we'll say fascist. Well, if the Zionists were Jewish nationalists that's what a fascist is—a nationalist.[292]

There were many cases at Peel of quarrels and scuffles among us. In my house there—48 in a house—it was a beautiful place for a few weeks and then one morning at breakfast two chaps start fighting. And of course the poor old house-leader—me—had to go up and separate them. Then maybe another couple. So you used to have these scuffles for about four or five mornings in succession, and then nice peace for the next few weeks. And then suddenly a couple of chaps would start again, and that started us for the next few days. It went on like that all the time.

As house leader, I said to the 48 in my house: 'Now, boys, I've been elected house leader. We've got to do our own work here so I would like twelve volunteers. There are going to be four cooks, four servers and four cleaners. Can I get names of the first volunteers, please?' So here I got about sixteen names. I says, 'Right, we only want twelve but I'll keep the other four names for after. You'll be on for a fortnight at a time.' Then I says to all the chaps, 'I know most of your mothers are on the Parish. But those of you who can afford it, what about giving us a shilling or two a month to try and augment our rations?' So about sixteen or twenty volunteered certain sums of money.

When it came to the end of the first fortnight: 'Right, boys. That's the first twelve finished. Now I want another twelve names. I've already got four extra from the first lot.' No one volunteered. So that made me think. This is a cruel thing to say. I don't mean it, although I'm saying it. Most people who are poor deserve to be poor. They'll always be poor. They'll do nothing for nothing. All they know is to take things, not give. Whereas the ones who were making contributions at our camp were gasping to do work: 'Oh, no, no, I'll carry on, Joe. I'm glad to do work.'

At Peel there used to be an escape now and again. I don't think there was any kind of organised escape committee. They'd keep it secret, I suppose, so I was never told. In the three years I was there I think there were not more than three or four escapes. It was not publicised. But no Anglo-Italian was ever involved. None of them escaped or, I believe, tried to escape. You see, I was not interested and the crowd I was mixing with they weren't interested in escaping. Where were you going to go to? I was never in the least inclined to escape. You don't want to get your family into trouble. If you went home that would be the first place the authorities would look for you.

I know one fellow, a South African German, in the camp escaped. Burkhe was the fellow's name. He told me afterwards that when he was in London and staying with some woman, he was in a restaurant and he happened to say, 'Ach!'. And the people at the next table must have heard the German 'Ach!'. He had said, 'Oh, I hope they think I'm a Scot or something.' But he was reported and arrested and brought back to the camp. And here his girlfriend who had guarded him got into trouble and he was sent to Coventry by us for a quite a while. It's all right trying to escape but you mustn't get other people into trouble—you mustn't get a woman into trouble. There was quite a feeling against him because he got this girl into trouble.

Another chap who had escaped was caught on a boat and brought back to the camp. So he was being marched up the street. We had barbed wire keeping us in but across the road was a very big posh hotel. I've got an idea it was called the Balaquane Hotel. Well, while they were marching this chap who had been caught up the street between the soldiers to the guardhouse, here this officer—stupid ass that he was— made some remarks to us: 'We know how to treat you fellows that try to ... ' It was enough to rouse feeling. So the next minute—missiles. People were picking up stones and throwing them at the hotel and smashed up the windows. There was pandemonium for a day or two. Whenever any officer put in an appearance: 'Boo!' So the authorities must have decided: 'Let's get rid of the soldiers.' So that's when they sent London Metropolitan police to the camp instead of the army to handle us. And they knew how to handle us. I mean, they were used to dealing with people.

We never had got friendly much with the soldiers. They were only there a short time. They were being changed so often. But with the police we became quite friendly. As a matter of fact, they used to have a football team. And we played them for what was called the Peel Cup: the Anglo-Italians, the Anglo-Germans, England, and the police force. Once I got very, very loudly cheered. Sergeant Vickers was the police centre forward and I was Italy right back. We were both going after the ball and I gave him a dig—a fair dig—but he was only on one leg at the time. Of course, the poor lad went down with a crash. And I got the loudest cheer of the day. But he was a nice fair man. I wouldn't say one word against him. None of our guards were brutal or unpleasant. I would say not one person among us was ever punished. There was that mass rioting once when they caught that escaped prisoner. But they didn't pick out any individual for punishment. Nearly everybody in the camp behaved themselves—well, they might have been cheeky or something. But there was never serious trouble. I've got an idea they had a guardhouse. I don't know if anybody was ever put in it, apart from escaped prisoners.

The local civilian population at Peel ignored us completely. And we ignored them. We used to leave the camp to go to church every Sunday. There was a

Catholic church and we were Catholics. I don't know about the other chaps. But we used to march through the streets. The British people used to ignore us but we didn't bother with them. They were not unfriendly—in fact, maybe they were friendly because I remember once or twice they gave a concert to entertain us. There were a dozen turns and we did half of them maybe. But foul language was coming up from some of our boys on the stage. So much so that the priests and one or two other people got up and went walking out. I says, 'Oh, I don't blame them. I'd like to walk out, too.' But of course we couldn't.

So I went to church every Sunday on the Isle of Man. As a matter of fact, quite a few of our chaps became embittered with the Catholic Church or at any rate with the Pope. They considered that the Pope should have got them freed. You know how people expect ridiculous things. The Pope is not allowed to interfere in war or politics. We had to parade to go to mass so here I said, 'Right, boys, for the church parade.' And then all the other ones, you know, calling us names: 'Oh, oh, all the Papists!' But I used to grin. It didn't bother me at all. We just walked out and went to the mass.

We all wore civilian clothes in the camp, just our own clothes. While I was there I wrote to my sister Peggy in Edinburgh: 'Could you get me a raincoat?' I mean, three or four of my pals were now officers in the British army, and so was my sister's husband. Well, I don't think it was he, I think it was another chap called Alex Conlon went to Forsyth's or Jenner's in Princes Street and bought me a raincoat, a trench coat, which only an officer was able to buy. Anyhow my sister sent it to me at the camp: 'What the hang's this?' 'Oh, I didn't know it was anything special.' I was the hero of the camp. I never have been clothes conscious.

Some of the chaps in the camp were very poor and were poorly dressed. Oh, quite a few of their mothers or their wives were on Public Assistance. Their businesses had been all broken up when the war with Italy broke out. And all the Italian women had to leave Edinburgh. You had to be thirty miles away from the city. My two older half-sisters they had to clear out, but not my younger sister Peggy who was married to the British army officer. She was not touched in the least. She was in partnership with my older brother Tommy or Philip, who was in the army, and she used to run their shop. But she supervised my business, too, while I was interned.

As well as some very poor people there were some very rich people in the camp. One man who was very, very well off was Lorenzo Toma. He had a very, very good ice cream parlour in Gourock. He was arrested very late but he should have been arrested away at the beginning because he had been an officer in the Italian army. He was born here and was of dual nationality like me. But before the war he went and joined the Italian army. He was an officer so that makes me suspect he was a volunteer. And then after doing his time in the Italian army he came back to Scotland. As well as having the ice cream parlour at Gourock he worked, I think, for a firm of chartered accountants in Glasgow. But he played himself—he didn't really need to work. As a matter of fact he had a brother who used to go to university after university. He had—and I'm not exaggerating—at least half-a-dozen degrees. He had degrees from Glasgow and one or two Italian ones. While attending Edinburgh University he stayed at the Caley Hotel—so it gives you an idea that the Toma family were not too badly off!

Now another rich man I got to know in the camp at Peel was Tiny Rowland. His real name is Roland von Fuhrhop. But he told us, 'Everybody calls me Tiny Rowland'.[293] He was arrested in the middle of the war. He told me he was in the British army. He was a private but being very well off he used to get his uniforms tailored. And officers used to be quite annoyed with him because he was better dressed than they were. He was stationed at Peebles and being very rich he used to stay the week-end in the Green Tree Hotel in Peebles. And of course he used to sit in the lounge bar and him perfectly tailored and a measly private. And the officers used to look across and be quite annoyed with this upstart. They knew he was of German origin. He was born here and had dual nationality but his father was German. His father owned the Hamburg-London Shipping Line. Tiny Rowland was educated in Britain at a public school—perfect public school accent. His English was perfect and so was his German. And I've heard him speaking French and it was very, very good too. Well, suddenly he was arrested and brought to Saughton Prison.

In the prison hospital he met Lorenzo Toma. Toma said to him, 'Would you like to stay here in the ward? I get my food sent in to me here. It would be easy enough managed for you, too.' 'Ach, of course I would.' So Rowland before he knew where he was was in the hospital with Lorenzo Toma. They were there for months, supposed to be patients. They took advantage of their money and were able to pay their way.

Then at a certain stage they were sent to our camp at Peel. When we went there first there were 800-odd. But nearly every day two or three people were being released. My house used to have 48 chaps in it and I was down to about 30-odd. So here they asked me as house leader, 'There are two men coming to-morrow morning. Could you take …?' I said, 'Oh, yes, yes.' So here I brought them to my house and put them in a room together and that's when I became very friendly with them. But after quite a few weeks this Rowland became pally with the German boys. He became very pally with a chap called Willie—we called him Von Stranz, whose father owned a laundry in Peebles: Strange, Laundries. So Rowland asked me, 'Do you mind, Joe …?' I says, 'Oh, no, no, no. Naturally, make yourself at home. Do what you like.' So here he went to Von Stranz's house in the camp.

Von Stranz was an interesting fellow. I understand he used to be in the German Olympic boxing team. Both Rowland and Von Stranz were on the committee in the camp that organised what we called Olympic Games. I remember being annoyed with them because they started a sort of ball game that the Germans played a lot—I think it might have been volleyball—but we never did. Well, without our permission they got it put into the daily or weekly newsletter sent out by the camp leader. By the way, in charge of the newsletter was the assistant camp leader Quinton Joyce, brother of William Joyce, Lord Haw Haw. I knew Quinton very well: a very, very nice chap.[294]

Now there was another chap in the camp who wouldn't tell us his real name but used the name Estoban. He was the only fellow in the camp that I know of that was in the Spanish Civil War. I think he was Scots but he may have been English. And he went to Spain—I'm sure he was on the Fascist side. Now Tiny Rowland was in charge of our camp canteen and he and Estoban had a quarrel about something. And this stupid ass Estoban challenged him to a fight. Now Tiny Rowland's a six-footer, very well built. Estoban was five feet four or five, but a tough guy. I remember Tiny Rowland coming to me in the camp hospital, wanting to protect his knuckles. I says, 'Well, there are no boxing gloves or anything. Wear a pair of ordinary gloves.' So here he got a pair of gloves and had a fight with this fellow behind the canteen. Estoban went rushing at him, fell to the ground, up and at him again. He did this quite a few times. And of course Tiny Rowland, very white faced, serious, tense, you know, but cool as a cucumber, played with Estoban like anything. He was much superior to Estoban physically and from all points of view. Estoban in the end had to give in.

Tiny Rowland was not a boaster or a brag, he was a gem of a man. He was so nice and gentlemanly he would never show off. I think his name on the camp register was Tiny Rowland but he and Von Stranz told me his real name was Von Fuhrhop. He said he had two brothers who were serving in the German army. After the war he came to visit me once in Edinburgh.

I was in the Peel camp on the Isle of Man almost three years, from the spring of 1941. Every year I was there English boys used to get sent to Brixton Prison in London for a few days so they could go before a tribunal again looking into their cases. So after a couple of years I says, 'Here what the hang's this? These Englishmen go—but what about us Scots?' So I wrote in making an application that we get sent to Saughton Prison for a tribunal: 'If the English get it, why not the Scots?' So here permission was granted but the week beforehand we were told, 'Oh, no, you've to go to Brixton.' We were annoyed it was not Saughton because we were hoping it was a week's holiday there and we might get a visit from the family.

By this time, by the way, my brother Gerry and Victor Crolla had applied to go to an Italian camp but not me. Anglo-Italians were allowed to go to Italian camps if they wanted. So my brother Gerry and Victor and quite a few Italians—we'll say about a quarter to a third of them—said, 'Oh, let's go!' But they were going not because they were Italians but because it was a change of camp. They were fed up with the camp at Peel. So they went to this other camp on the Isle of Man at Ramsey. I would say that was 1943. We went to Douglas once a year to have friendly football matches where we could play Italians. There were two Italian camps in Douglas. We went there and played and then they came to us, home and away. Eleven players got to go and there was one busload with, say, thirty in the bus. The other twenty or so had their names put in the hat and got to travel with the footballers. So we met some real Italians—we called them real Italians, you see—from Edinburgh and Glasgow, when these matches were played. I met a few of my uncles in Douglas. You know, they went pushing away out: 'Oh, it's my nephew. Can I go and say hullo?' The soldiers let them, they were not too strict because they knew they were not going to try and escape.

Well, as I said, I went to Brixton Prison for this tribunal after Victor Crolla and my brother Gerry had gone to Ramsey camp. Another chap from my camp and me went to Brixton and we were in there for about a fortnight or so. Here we're in benediction in the Prison one day and with this hymn *Tantum ergo* we're accustomed to a certain tune. Here there's an air raid going on. You could hear the planes dropping bombs. Well, when they struck up the tune for *Tantum ergo* it was the tune for *Deutschland über alles*. So I remember this other fellow looking at me: 'What's that? I know that tune.' And then they suddenly started singing and the words fitted in. But afterwards we said, 'Fancy playing the tune *Deutschland über alles* with the German planes overhead.' Imagine that.[295]

When I was in Brixton Prison Captain Ramsay, an MP for down in the Borders, was in there. The British Union of Fascists chaps at Peel had told me: 'Tell him we're all right.' So when I got there I said, 'Can you point out Captain Ramsay?' So here he was pointed out to me. So we blethered. He was asking me what like things were in the camp at Peel, and I was asking him what things were like in Brixton. So after about half a dozen mornings he said to me, 'By the way, do you think it's curious me always picking you out right away to talk with you?' I says, 'I'd not thought of it but now that you mention it, right enough. You've come to me immediately I come out and speak to me.' He says, 'Oh, it's great to hear the Edinburgh accent again. I haven't heard it for a long time. How beautiful it is to hear the Edinburgh accent.' He says, 'You know, I am a Covenanter.' I says, 'What the ...?' I thought he was a wee bit ... , you see. 'Oh, he says, 'I'm a Covenanter.' 'Oh,' I says. I knew that was something to do with religion, you know, anti-royalists or something like that. But I remember me thinking, 'He must be a funny guy this, at this time of life speaking about being a Covenanter.' I had several conversations with him but he never said anything about Hitler or Mussolini. It was just about Edinburgh.[296]

Well, eventually, I got out of internment a few days before Christmas 1943. We went from the Isle of Man to the railway station in Liverpool and then we were told we were free. That was the first inkling I had, that morning. And I remember me saying, 'Oh, I'm frightened. What do you say to people when you go back home?' I was frightened that people would think I was a spy or something. They said, 'It's quite all right. Just tell them you've been on secret service.' 'What's that?' 'Nobody'll ask any questions. But if they do tell them you can't speak. Just say to them, "I've been on special secret service and I'm not allowed to talk about it."' What had happened was my in-laws to be in Glasgow had contacted a Labour baillie there who wrote in to London about my case. And my in-laws are under the impression that this baillie's letter got me released. I don't know if that's true or not.

So when I came back I remember arriving at the Caley Station in Edinburgh. I had two or three bars of chocolate and here was a lady porter. I'd never seen a lady porter before. The lady insisted on carrying my case to the taxi, you see. And I gave her a bar of chocolate for a tip. Oh, and she was pleased. She gave me a kiss. I says, 'Fancy giving me a kiss for a bar of chocolate!' Remember, I had not met women for years. So I got home in time for Christmas 1943.

On the Monday I was told to report to the Labour Exchange at Tollcross. So I went up there and here the fellow says, 'Well, you have to report next week to the rubber mill at Fountainbridge'. I says, 'Here, have a heart. I've been away for three and a half years.' He says, 'Enough of your nonsense. You report next Monday to the North British Rubber Mill or you're in for it.' I says, 'What do you mean "in for it"?' He says, 'You'll be sent to prison, that'll be it.' I says, 'Oh!' And of course I'm annoyed and such a loud voice I've got, I says: 'Any more of your nonsense and I'll tell you—send me back to prison!' I says, 'In case you don't know it,' I says, 'I feel at home in prison. I've been in prison for a long time. Here I'm lost. In prison I'm at home. Enough of your nonsense or I'll tell you—put me back in prison!' Anyhow I told him I had duodenal ulcers. I had had an operation for duodenal ulcers before the war, in 1935. I was perfect after that. But they couldn't put me to work in the rubber mill because I was a genuine medical case. So I took over my own business again—the Orchard Confectionery Company, wholesale confectioners, in Eyre Place.

I had to build up the business again from scratch. I was able to do that fairly quickly. There were a few—I'd say about two or three people—refused to deal with me because of me being Italian or being in prison. I remember one person in Seafield Road, Portobello, had not paid her account. So I went down to see her. I says, 'We were such friends ... What the hang ...?' Oh, wwww ... : cold as anything, 'No, no, no, no, I want nothing more to do with you.' I would say that happened maybe with only two cases. A few of them said, 'It's quite all right, Mr Pia, we understand.' Most of them knew me from before the war. They knew that I was, we'll say, a harmless chap. So there was no hostility whatever.

There was one supplier who stopped our supplies. And I wrote to the manufacturer. He was their agent for Scotland. And here he came and he says, 'I admit I was wrong but I was so bitter against Italy that I cut you off.' I says, 'By the way, I'm not Italy. It wasn't me that declared war. I mean, what had I to do with it?' He says, 'I admit that but I was so bitter and so annoyed with Italy I cut off your supplies.' So I resumed my business and remained in the wholesale confectionery business until I retired when I was 72. I had a long working life but I enjoyed it. And I had to give up because of my eyesight.

Well, looking back on my wartime experience there's no bitterness. I recognise in a war more innocent people suffer than guilty people get caught. Churchill had to—I mean, hearing about Franco and his Fifth Column, anyhow he was frightened so he grabbed everybody possible and put them inside and then sifted them out. I wouldn't be surprised if a few guilty ones did get sifted out while the big majority who were not guilty were kept in. But maybe a few of us were guilty, maybe a few, I don't know.

Since the war nobody's ever shown the least animosity towards me. And I would say that that was the experience of other people in the Italian community in Edinburgh. I've not heard any Italian saying that anybody's cast up anything to them. You see, the British are quite easy going people, I think. Of course, being of full Italian blood but fully British educated and brought up here I'm a wee bit international. Good and bad—it's got nothing at all to do with nation.

None of the Italian community have suffered through the war. No permanent damage whatsoever. I've not heard of one member of the Italian community leaving Edinburgh or Scotland after the war because they felt disgusted. And, remember, I have supplied most of them with confectionery so I'm a good judge of them. I would have heard the talk, because I'm mixing with the whole lot often. I'm sure there's no resentment. By the way, there are a few resent how their shops were smashed up when Italy declared war in 1940. But they don't blame Britain. They blame the ragamuffins that did it. They consider it was the bad element out looting. It was not true patriotism or anti-Italianism. It was—pinch what you can: hooligans and looters, but nothing national about it.

NOTES

1   Industrial schools, regulated by the Industrial Schools Act of 1854 and controlled after 1860 by the Home Department, were intended for vagrant and homeless waifs, to prevent them sliding into crime. Before 1893 they were residential but an Act of that year brought the English system of day industrial schools into Scotland. James Scotland, *The History of Scottish Education* (London, 1969), Vol. 2, 94

2   Coconut Tam (died 1894) was a well known diminutive street vendor in Edinburgh, Sinn Fein—'Ourselves' or 'Ourselves alone', founded in 1905 as a political party by Arthur Griffith, a Dublin printer, to pursue a policy of non-co-operation with the British authorities rather than action through the Westminister parliament in the tradition of the Irish National Party, or violent revolution, in the Fenian or Irish Republican Brotherhood tradition. Griffith's views were also distinct from those of the Irish socialists, led by James Connolly. Sinn Fein's policy was that the Irish MPs should withdraw from Westminster and set up an Irish government in Dublin that would take over the administration of the country, from which it was expected the British would peacefully withdraw. The winning of Ireland's political freedom, which Griffith seems to have believed would be established on the basis of a kind of partnership with Britain modelled on that between Austria and Hungary in the then Austrian Empire, would then be followed by a great economic expansion that would industrialise Ireland. It seems likely that not all the signs of Irish nationalism Peter Corstorphine recalls were those of members of Sinn Fein. See, e.g., J C Beckett, *The Making of Modern Ireland, 1603-1923* (London, 1969), 415-16, 420

4   R B Haldane (1856-1928), Viscount from 1911, Secretary of State for War, 1905-12, in 1906 replaced service pay (an award for good conduct and length of service) by proficiency pay to be awarded to soldiers who had a third-class certificate of education and fulfilled specific requirements of military efficiency. The standard of a third-class certificate was about that normally reached by children aged nine in elementary schools. See Edward M Speirs, *Haldane: an Army Reformer* (Edinburgh, 1980), 148

5   These may have been Eurasians

6   King George V, who 'believed that his own presence in India as King-Emperor would do much to revive and consolidate the loyalty of the Indian masses', visited India from 2 December 1911 to 10 January 1912 and held a Durbar or public audience at Delhi on 12 December at which Indian princes did homage to him. He also visited Calcutta and went on a shooting expedition in Nepal. H Nicolson, *George V* (London, 1952), 165-73

7   Peter Corstorphine was in the 2nd Battalion of the Black Watch, which had been abroad since the beginning of the Boer War in 1899, and in India since 1902. Stationed in 1914 at Bareilly in northern India, the 2nd Bn left there for France on 3

September and embarked at Karachi on the SS *Elephanta* on 21 September. 'So keen were the men to reach France that many volunteered to act as extra hands in the stokehold and actually did so all the way up the Red Sea.' The Bn disembarked at Marseilles on 12 October, remained there a week, then entrained for Orleans, where the Bareilly Brigade of the 7th Meerut Division, of which the Bn was part, was concentrating and completing its equipment. The Bn left Orleans on 26 October, detrained at Lillers near Bethune in the Pas de Calais, marched immediately up to the front line and with the other battalions of the Bareilly Brigade took over the extreme right of the British line—'within shouting distance' of the left of the French line 'because the trenches were by no means continuous'. Major General A G Wauchope, *A History of the Black* Watch *(Royal Highlanders) in the Great War, 1914-1918* (London, 1925), Vol. 1, 161–6

8   The 8th Battalion of the Black Watch arrived in France on 10 May 1915 and went into the front line for the first time on 1 July 1915. The Bn was part of the 26th (Highland) Brigade of the 9th (Scottish) Division, one of the first Divisions formed from the New Armies or 'Kitchener's Army' raised in response to Kitchener's appeal in August 1914 for volunteers to supplement the Regular and Territorial armies. The London Scottish lst Bn (Territorial Army) arrived in France on 16 September 1914, 'the first chosen from the whole Territorial Force to go to the front'. It arrived in the front line at Ypres on 30 October 1914. The 8th Battalion of the Royal Scots, in which Bill Hanlan and James Marchbank (above, pp 12-27) were serving, was 'the first of the Scottish Territorial units to be employed on active service' and arrived in France on 5 November 1914. J Ewing, *The History of the 9th (Scottish) Division, 1914-1919* (London 1921), 12, 15; Lt Col. J H Lindsay *The London Scottish in the Great War* (London, 1925), 22–3; J Ewing, *The Royal Scots, 1914-1919* (Edinburgh, 1925), Vol. I, 83

9   The battle of Neuve Chapelle, ten miles north of Lens, began on 10 March 1915 when, after a 35 minute bombardment, four divisions under General Haig attacked on a two-mile front. Fighting continued until the night of 12 March, by which time the British artillery ran short of ammuntion, the Germans had counter-attacked, and for a gain of 1,000 yards deep and 2,000 yards wide British casualties were 544 officers and 11,108 men. German casualties were about the same. The Second Battle of Ypres began on 22 April 1915 with the first (chlorine) gas attack (by the Germans on French troops) of the war. When the battle ended almost five weeks later on 31 May, British losses were 59, 275, German at least 47,000, J E Edmonds, *A Short History of World War I* (Oxford, 1951), 89–92

10   This may be a reference to the German onslaught from 21 February 1916 on the French army at Verdun, a battle which continued until the end of 1916 at a cost of 700,000 casualties. Alistair Horne, *The Price of Glory: Verdun, 1916* (Harmondsworth, 1964), 327

11   In March 1918 the 8th Bn of the Black Watch was in the area Gouzeaucourt-Etricourt-Manancourt, about 8 miles north east of Peronne and, after the German offensive began, at Guinchy, about 8 miles west of its earlier positions. It may be that 'Simcay' was Guinchy. See Wauchope, op. cit., Vol. 3, 50

12   The cans were to give warning of Germans advancing through the wire

13   Peter Corstorphine died at the age of 95, four years after recording these recollections in 1983

14   Maconochie rations supplied to the troops were named after the company, Maconochie Bros Ltd of London, that provided them, and whose managing director, Archibald

Maconochie, had been MP for East Aberdeen, 1900-06

15 Statistics published by the War Office of death sentences passed by courts martial from the outbreak of the Great War until the end of March 1920 showed that in those five and a half years 3,080 men had been condemned to death and 346 of them (11.23 per cent) had been executed. Of the 346, 266 were executed while serving in France and Belgium, the other 24 were in other theatres of war. Of the 346, 266 were shot for desertion, 37 for murder, 18 for cowardice, 7 for quitting their posts, 6 for striking or violence, 5 for disobedience, 3 for mutiny, and 2 each for sleeping on post or casting away arms. *Statistics of the Military Effort of the British Empire During the Great War. Part XXIII—Discipline* (London, 1922), quoted in A Babington, *For the Sake of Example: Capital Courts Martial 1914-18, the Truth* (London, 1983), 189

16 Under the Treaty of Versailles, 1919, German territory west of the Rhine, and bridge-heads across it, were to be occupied by Allied troops for up to fifteen years as a guarantee that Germany would carry out the terms of the Treaty. Cologne was in the area occupied by British troops. Occupation was due to end in three five-year phases and Cologne was the first area to be evacuated, between December 1925 and the end of January 1926. Bill Hanlan died in April 1983 at the age of 89, a month after recording these recollections

17 The battle of Aubers Ridge on 9 May 1915 was part of the British contribution to the beginning then of a major French offensive in Artois. In return for gaining 'two small lodgements' in the German trench-line, the British attack (again marked by shortage of heavy shells and many defective fuses) was broken off after twelve hours of fighting and British casualties of at least 11,000 men. Edmonds, op. cit., 94-5

18 See above, note 9. Chlorine gas released from canisters seems first to have been used by the British in September 1915 at Loos. The Germans were first to use phosgene gas in December 1915 at Ypres, and mustard gas there in summer 1917. The Germans had experimented with gas in October 1914 at Neuve Chapelle and in January 1915 in Poland. Edmonds, op. cit., 140, 144, 302; B H Liddell Hart, *History of the First World War* (London, 1973), 195, 243, 261-2, 428

19 The battle of Festubert, 15-27 May 1915, was a sequel to that at Aubers Ridge (see above, note 17), six miles to the north-east, and resulted in a British advance of three-quarters of a mile on a width of 2½ miles, at a cost of over 16,000 casualties. The battle of Loos, the British contribution to the Third Battle of Artois, took place from 21 to 28 September 1915 and for small gains made in the Geman trench-line cost the British over 48,000 casualties. Edmonds, op. cit., 96, 140-3

20 British casualties in the battle of the Somme, from 1 July to mid-November 1916, totalled 450,000. The inscription on the huge memorial at Thiepval refers to 75,000 British dead in the battle who have no known grave. British, French and German casualties in this battle totalled about 1,200,000. See, e.g., A H Farrar-Hockley, *The Somme* (London, 1966), 253

21 The Clyde Workers' Committee, formed in 1915 as a local rank and file organisation of delegates from several industries, included leading shop stewards such as William Gallacher. The Committee emerged as leader of the rank and file opposition to the Munitions Act (see below, note 36) because of the failure of union executives and local officials effectively to oppose it

22 *John Bull*, founded in 1906 as a weekly penny paper by Horatio Bottomley (1860-1933), fraudulent financier and jingo journalist

23 Harry McShane (1891-1988), engineer, member of the British Socialist Party, a Clyde

shop steward, a close associate of John Maclean until after the 1914-18 War, a member of the Communist Party, 1922-54, a principal leader in Scotland in the inter-war years of the Unemployed Workers' Movement. John Maclean (1879-1923), leading Clydeside revolutionary. Independent Labour Party, founded 1893, parliamentary socialist in ideology, reached a crisis in its relations with the Labour Party (founded 1900) and disaffiliated from it in 1932

24 Without conscription (see note 47 below) and having suffered heavy casualties in the Regular, Territorial and New or Kitchener's armies, the government in 1915 took two main steps to find recruits and reinforcements. One was the passing in July of the National Registration Act, under which every man and woman aged between 15 and 65 was registered. The names and other details of all the registered men aged between 18 and 41 were passed to the army recruiting offices so that they could be canvassed and pressed to enlist. A second step towards conscription was taken by the Derby Scheme, launched after Lord Derby became Director-General of Recruiting on 11 October. Under this scheme men could still enlist to serve immediately but others could attest to join up, if called on, by groups according to age and whether they were married or single. The government then declared that unless most single men came in under the Derby Scheme, compulsory service in the forces would be introduced for them before voluntarily attested married men were called up. By 15 December over two million men attested but only a quarter of a million for immediate service. So the government then introduced the first conscription or Military Service Act in January 1916. Edmonds, op. cit., 23-4

25 *Forward* 1906-60, an independent labour weekly founded and for long edited by Thomas Johnston (1881-1965), Labour MP, 1922-31 and 1935-45, Secretary of State for Scotland, 1941-5. *Labour Leader*, founded 1894, official organ of the Independent Labour Party, continued from 1923 as *New Leader* and later as *Socialist Leader*

26 J Holland Rose (1855-1942), Reader in Modern History, 1911-19 and Professor of Naval History, 1919-33, at Cambridge University

27 *Cambridge Magazine*, 1911 (?)—19

28 Bertrand Russell, Earl Russell (1872-1970), philosopher, mathematician, author, Fellow of Trinity College, Cambridge from 1895 until he was deprived of his appointment because of his pacifism in the 1914-18 War, imprisoned 1918. Professor at Peking, 1920-22, had his Fellowship at Trinity College restored in 1944, renounced pacifism in 1939, from 1949 a champion of nuclear disarmament, awarded Nobel Prize for Literature, 1950. *Justice in Wartime* (London, 1916)

29 David Lloyd George (1863-1945), Liberal MP, 1890-1945, opposed the Boer War, Chancellor of the Exchequer, 1908-15, Minister of Munitions, 1915, Secretary for War, 1916, Prime Minister, 1916-22, described (by Hitler) as 'the man who won the war' of 1914-18. Major Richard Lloyd George (the 2nd Earl) (1889-1968) fought in the 1914-18 and 1939-45 wars and was author of *Lloyd George* (London, 1960), a biography of his father

30 The British Socialist Party was formed in 1911-12 from the Social Democratic Federation (1881/4-1911) and some branches of the Independent Labour Party. In 1920 the BSP united with a section of the Socialist Labour Party (formed in 1903 as a breakaway from the Social Democratic Federation) and some other socialist groups to form the Communist Party of Great Britain

31 John Wheatley (1869-1930), an Independent Labour Party leader, Labour MP for Glasgow Shettleston, 1922-30, Minister of Health, 1924. Emanuel Shinwell (1884-1986), a leader of Glasgow Trades Council from 1911, Labour MP, 1922-4, 1928-31,

1935-70, Parliamentary Secretary for Mines, 1924, 1930-31, Minister of Fuel and Power, 1945-7, Secretary for War, 1947-50, Minister of Defence, 1950-1, life peer from 1970. Patrick J Dollan (1885-1963), miner, journalist, imprisoned as a conscientious objector in the 1914-18 War, a leader of the Independent Labour Party in Scotland, then from 1933 of the Scottish Socialist Party, Lord Provost of Glasgow, 1930-41, knighted 1941

32   James M Messer, a leading Clyde shop steward, secretary of the Clyde Workers' Committee, and one of the stewards deported by the government from the Clyde in 1916-17

33   William Gallacher (1881-1965), British Socialist Party, a leader of the shop stewards' movement and from 1920 of the Communist Party of Great Britain, MP for West Fife, 1935-50

34   During summer 1910 several local disputes took place among boilermakers of the Clyde and Tyne. The shipyard employers, claiming that the workers in these disputes had failed to observe the terms of the shipyard agreement of 1909, declared a national lock-out of all members of the Boilermakers' Society in the federated shipyards from 3 September. After the government had intervened and both sides accepted an amended agreement that included new provisions for the settlement of differences, the lock-out ended on 14 December. The terms of the agreement were a significant victory for the Boilermakers' Society. J E Mortimer, *History of the Boilermakers' Society*, Vol. 2, 1906-1939 (London, 1982), 34-8; G D H Cole, *A Short History of the British Working-class Movement* (London, 1948), 320

35   The success of the Irish Transport and General Workers' Union, under the leadership of James Larkin, supported by James Connolly, led employers from August 1913—especially W M Murphy, owner of the Dublin tramways and of several newspapers and other businesses—to smash the Union by dismissing its members from their jobs. The Union responded by strike action, and the employers by lock-outs. Although British trade union leaders prevented a sympathetic strike taking place in other parts of the United Kingdom in support of the Irish workers, donations of money and shiploads of food were sent to the Dublin workers by workers in Britain. The dispute lasted until early 1914—'a drawn battle'. Cole, op. cit., 344-8. James Larkin, (1876-1947), Irish labour leader, founder, 1908, and organiser of the Irish Transport & General Workers' Union, deported from the United States of America in 1923 for 'anarchistic activities', later a member of the Irish parliament. James Connolly (1868-1916), born in Edinburgh of Irish parents, founder, 1896, of the Irish Socialist Republican Party, a leader of the American Socialist Labor Party, an organiser for the Industrial Workers of the World, executed by the British authorities for his part in the 1916 Easter Rising in Dublin

36   The Munitions Act (5 & 6 Geo. 5. ch. 54), was passed in July 1915, a month after the formation of the Ministry of Munitions headed by Lloyd George. The Act made strikes and lock-outs on war work illegal and arbitration compulsory. It gave statutory recognition to a scheme for war munitions volunteers that had originated on the Tyne and Clyde. Under the statutory scheme 100,000 engineers volunteered within a couple of months of the passing of the Act to work wherever the government chose to send them—thus easing the more acute shortages of skilled labour in munitions work. The Act enabled the Ministry of Munitions to declare any workshop engaged on munitions work a 'controlled establishment' where all restrictive practices were suspended by law and wages and workshop discipline and also profits were under the

control of the Ministry. The other major feature of the Act, which made it particularly unpopular with workers, was that it prohibitied from any employment any worker who had left his previous job within the preceding six weeks without receiving a certificate from his employer that he had left with the latter's consent (though an Amendment Act passed In January 1916 removed some of the worst practices of employers in that respect, e.g., by forbidding them to dismiss a worker without giving him a certificate, or using the system of leaving certificates to blacklist militants). At a time when military conscription had not yet been imposed in Britain (see below, note 47), the Munitions Act was 'the nearest approximation that could be devised ... to the ideal [on the part of the government] of compulsory national service'. James Hinton, *The First Shop Stewards' Movement* (London, 1973), 29-36

37 Thomas Alexander Fyfe (1852-1928), Sheriff Substitute of Lanarkshire at Glasgow, 1906-28

38 Barbettes—fixed circular mountings carrying the revolving turrets in warships

39 Lord Balfour of Burleigh (1849-1921), Conservative Secretary for Scotland, 1895-1903, chairman of Committee on Commercial and Industrial Policy after the War, 1916-17. Sir Lynden Macassey (1876-1963), engineer, KC, chairman of various government committees and tribunals on labour and wages, 1914-16, Director of shipyard labour, Admiralty, 1917-18, member of War Cabinet committee on labour, 1917-18, and of women in industry, 1918-19. The more dictatorial treatment of workers by employers with the passage of the Munitions Act in July 1915 was exemplified not least at the Fairfield shipyard at Govan on the Clyde. There on 26 August the strike by 430 shipwrights (including Charlie McPherson) against the dismissal of the two men for 'loafing' led to fines of £10 each upon 26 of the strikers imposed by Sheriff Fyfe. The strikers returned to work next day but some of those fined said they would go to prison rather than pay the fines. A meeting of shop stewards held on 2 October, amid growing agitation over the case, demanded the repeal of the Munitions Act and it was from this meeting that within a few weeks there emerged the Clyde Workers' Committee (see above, note 21). The three shipwrights (including Charlie McPherson) who continued to refuse to pay the fines were imprisoned on 6 October. Preparations immediately began among Fairfield's and other workers to take strike action from 17 October in protest unless the three were released. The government, desperate to avoid a stoppage of work, was forced to appoint a Commission of Inquiry, one of whose members was Lynden Macassey. He seems to have arranged, directly or indirectly, notices in the press that the three had been released though in fact they had not; but this false report succeeded in postponing the strike for some days. The Commission of Inquiry issued a preliminary report on 21 October that they had no power to release the three men. Trade union officials now intervened and demanded the release of the three men and on 27 October an arrangement was made with the government by which union officials were secretly to pay the fines and Lloyd George as Minister of Munitions to release the men. Meantime, on 25 October Robert Bridges, an engineers' shop steward at Weir's of Cathcart, supported by 300 engineers, forced the withdrawal of a charge against him under the Munitions Act. This victory led to the establishment a few days later of the Clyde Workers' Committee. See Hinton, op. cit., 114-19

40 Mrs Mary Barbour (d. 1958), Labour Party activist, feminist, founder of Govan Women's Housing Association, wife of an engineer at Fairfield's shipyard, later a councillor and first woman baillie in Glasgow, played a leading part in Clyde housing struggles and

rent strikes during and after the 1914-18 War. J Melling, *Rent Strikes: Peoples' Struggle for Housing in West Scotland,1890-1916* (Edinburgh, 1983), 32. l08, 128

41 The rent strikes—by about 25,000 tenants by October 1915—began on the Clyde in the spring of that year and culminated in a strike on 18 November by workers in Dalmuir, Fairfield's, Stephen's and other shipyards and factories over the summons to court of a Dalmuir yard engineer and 17 other tenants from whose wages landlords were attempting to have rents deducted. The strike was followed by the passing in November 1915 of the Rent Restriction Act, which froze rents at the level they had been on the outbreak of the war, and only allowed an increase up to 40 percent if repairs were carried out. Harry McShane and Joan Smith, *Harry McShane, No Mean Fighter* (London, 1978), 75-6

42 John Heenan, Glasgow ILP town councillor, 1918-21 and 1933-6, Hunger Marcher. Andrew McBride, a Gorbals grocer, ILP activist, pioneering housing reformer, formed in 1913 the Housing Committee of the Glasgow Labour Party, Labour town councillor

43 David Kirkwood (1872-1955), Clyde shop steward in the 1914-18 War, a leading figure in the ILP, from which he resigned after its disaffiliation from the Labour Party in 1932, MP for Dumbarton Burghs, 1922-51, accepted a peerage as Baron Kirkwood of Bearsden

44 Tom Bell (1882-1944), editor of *The Socialist*, 1902-22, organ of the Socialist Labour Party, later a leader of the Communist Party

45 Daniel De Leon (1852-1914), a leader of the American Socialist Labor Party and a founder in 1905 of the Industrial Workers of the World

46 Major Bonnar believed this objector was Emanuel Shinwell (see above, note 31), but Shinwell in his autobiography *Conflict without Malice*, (London, 1955), 53, says he was never a conscientious objector

47 The Military Service Acts (5 & 6 Geo. 5, ch. 104, of January 1916 and 6 & 7 Geo. 5, ch. 15, of May 1916), establishing conscription, provided for exemption on several grounds, including 'a conscientious objection to the undertaking of combatant service', provided a local tribunal, set up in each local registration district, and granted a certificate recognising the objection. Appeal Tribunals and a Central Tribunal were also established under the Acts. The first Act conscripted, or deemed enlisted, all unmarried men or childless widowers aged 18 to 41. The second Act extended conscription to married men. A further measure in April 1918 raised the maximum age to 50 and extended (but did not actually apply) conscription to Ireland

48 Sir James D Marwick (1826-1908), Town Clerk of Edinburgh, 1860-73, and of Glasgow, 1873-1903

49 Mary Slessor (1848-1915), born in Dundee, worked in a factory there, became a missionary in the United Presbyterian Church and worked for many years in Calabar, Nigeria

50 Elizabeth Barrett (1806-1861), poet, denounced the employment of children in factories, married the poet Robert Browning in 1846

51 Though the Liberals took office in December 1905 when the Conservative ministry led by A J Balfour resigned, the general election that confirmed them in office was held in January 1906, when they won a landslide victory, winning 377 seats, a majority of 84 over all other parties combined. William Morrison (1893-1961), awarded the Military Cross in 1915, Conservative MP for Cirencester and Tewkesbury, 1929-59, government minister, 1935-45, Speaker of the House of Commons 1951-9, created Viscount

Dunrosil, 1959, Governor General of Australia, 1959-61

52　*Tribune*, a Liberal daily paper, 1906-08. *New Age*, 1894-1938, 'A Weekly Record of Christian Culture, Social Service, and Literary Life'. *Christian Commonwealth*, 1881-1919, continued as *New Commonwealth*, 1919-22. Alfred Richard Orage (1873-1934), teacher, journalist, author, editor, *New Age*, 1907-22. Rev. Reginald J Campbell (1867-1956), Congregationalist then Anglican clergyman, Chancellor of Chichester Cathedral, prolific author of religious and other works

53　Edward Grey (1862-1933), Viscount Grey of Fallodon, Liberal MP for Berwick-on-Tweed, 1885-1916, Secretary for Foreign Affairs, 1905-16. In his time at the Foreign Office Britain moved closer to the Dual Alliance of France and Russia through, e.g., the secret general staff talks with France from 1905 and the naval agreement of 1912, and the Entente of 1907 with Tsarist Russia. Edmund Dene Morel (1873-1924), author, journalist, founded the Congo Reform Association, 1904, vice-president of the Anti-Slavery Society, a founder and Secretary of the Union of Democratic Control, Liberal candidate, Birkenhead, 1912-14 (resigned at outbreak of the war), Labour MP, Dundee, 1922-4. Arthur Ponsonby (1871-1946), Lord Ponsonby, educated at Eton and Oxford, private secretary to Henry Campbell-Bannerman, 1906-08, Liberal MP, Stirling Burghs, 1908-18, opposed Sir Edward Grey's foreign policy on the grounds that it was anti-German and pro-Russian, opposed Britain's entry into the war in 1914, established the Union of Democratic Control with C P Trevelyan and E D Morel, Ramsay MacDonald, Norman Angell and others, supported the making of a negotiated peace; Labour MP for Sheffield from 1922, under-secretary, Foreign Office, 1924, and for the Dominions, 1929-30, Chancellor of the Duchy of Lancaster, 1930-31, leader of the Labour Party in the House of Lords, 1931-5, member of the Parliamentary Pacifist Group from 1936, resigned from Labour Party, 1940, supported an end to the Second World War by negotiation

54　Professor Sir Richard Lodge (1855-1936), Professor of Modern History at Glasgow University, 1894-99, then at Edinburgh, 1899-1933. Laurance J Saunders, Professor of Constitutional Law, Edinburgh University, author of *Scottish Democracy 1815-1840* (Edinburgh, 1950). Francis Hood (1895-1971), Professor of Political Theory and Institutions, Durham University, 1946-55, First Class Honours in History and Kirkpatrick Scholar, Edinburgh University, 1916, lecturer in Economic History at Durham, 1922-40, Reader in History there, 1940-5

55　The Union of Democratic Control was formed in autumn 1914 to urge a negotiated peace, clarify the fundamental principles that must underly the final terms of peace, and press for an end to secret diplomacy and for the democratic control of foreign policy

56　Sir Charles P Trevelyan (1870-1958), Liberal MP from 1899, Parliamentary Secretary, Board of Education, 1908-14, when he resigned because of his opposition to war, President of the Board of Education, 1924 and 1929-31

57　Arthur Woodburn (1890-1978), Secretary, Edinburgh Labour College till 1932, then of Scottish Labour College till 1939, President, National Council of Labour Colleges, 1937-64; Scottish Secretary, Labour Party, 1932-9, MP for Clackmannan and East Stirling, 1939-70, Secretary of State for Scotland, 1947-50

58　Dr John C MacCallum, graduate in Arts and Medicine from Edinburgh University, winner of a scholarship for the best graduate in surgery for his year, played as a forward in all 27 Scotland rugby international teams except one, from March 1905 to March

1912 (five times as captain), sent as a conscientious objector under the Home Office Scheme to work in appalling conditions at a factory at Broxburn, West Lothian, where fertiliser was made from the bones and carcases of animals. John W Graham, *Conscription and Conscience, a History 1916-1919* (London, 1921), 240-1

59   Siegfried Sassoon (1886-1967), infantry officer decorated for bravery, a leading war poet, wounded in the battle of Arras, 1917, and while convalescing in Britain became increasingly convinced the war was being prolonged by the refusal of the Allies to publish their war aims. He issued a statement to that effect and was sent to Craiglockhart war hospital, Edinburgh, and officially described as suffering from shell shock. See Sassoon's own account of his experiences in his *Memoirs of an Infantry Officer* (London, 1932), 205-88. Hugh R L (Dick) Sheppard (1880-1937), Church of England clergyman vicar of St Martin-in-the-Fields, 1914-27, Dean of Canterbury, 1929-31, Canon of St Paul's Cathedral,1934-7, a committed pacifist, founder, 1934, of the Peace Pledge Union. The Union, whose members signed a pledge on a postcard which they sent to Sheppard and which said: 'I renounce war and never again will I support or sanction another, and I will do all in my power to persuade others to do the same' had 100,000 members by the middle of 1936 and appealed for a similar number of women members. C L Mowat, *Britain Between the Wars 1918-1940* (London, 1962), 538. Charles E Raven (1885-1964). The Fellowship of Reconciliation was a union, formed in December 1914, of Christian pacifists of all denominations and which reached its decisions by prayer. It had 8,000 members by 1918

60   Clifford Allen (1889-1939), later Lord Allen of Hurtwood, general manager, *Daily Citizen*, 1911-15, chairman, No-Conscription Fellowship, 1914-18, three times imprisoned as a conscientious objector, 1916-17, treasurer and chairman of the Independent Labour Party, 1922-6, director of the *Daily Herald*, 1925-30. Fenner Brockway (1888-1988), journalist, pacifist, imprisoned as a conscientious objector, 1916-19, secretary, 1917, No-Conscription Fellowship, ILP MP, 1929-31, organising secretary ILP, 1922-3, political secretary,1923-8 and 1933-46, chairman 1931-33, Labour MP, 1950-64, life peer from 1964. John Cliffford (1836-1923), a leading non–conformist Liberal opposed the Education Act, 1902, a pastor at Paddington, London, 1858-1915. Lord Hugh Cecil (1869-1956), son of the 3rd Marquis of Salisbury, Conservative MP, served in the Royal Flying Corps, 1915

61   Charles Cornelius Maconochie (1852-1930), KC, Sheriff of the Lothians and Peebles, 1904-18. George Jeffreys (1648-89), English judge, Chief Justice of King's Bench, 1683-89, sentenced in the 'Bloody Assize' after the battle of Sedgemoor in 1685 hundreds of the defeated followers of the Duke of Monmouth to be hanged, transported, whipped or fined. Robert MacQueen, Lord Braxfield, (1722-1799) Scots judge, who sentenced the 'political martyrs' of 1793-4, including Thomas Muir, to transportation to the penal settlements in Australia

62   Edward Walton (1860-1922), President, Royal Scottish Society of Painters in Water Colours

63   Black maria—a police or prison van

64   Sir Thomas Hunter (1850-1919), Town Clerk of Edinburgh, 1895-1918. Peter Hume Brown (1850-1918), from 1901 Professor of Scottish History at Edinburgh University, Scottish Historiographer Royal from 1908

65   John Crawford Guy (1861-1928), Sheriff Substitute of Lothians and Peebles, 1904-21

66   Prince Peter Kropotkin (1842-1921), imprisoned in 1872 as an anarchist in Russia and again from 1883-6 in France, he settled in England until the Revolution of 1917,

when he returned to Russia

67 Gilbert Murray (1866-1957), born in Australia, Professor of Greek at Glasgow University, 1889, and at Oxford from 1908, author, Liberal, President of the League of Nations Union, 1923-38

68 Sir George Younger (1851-1931), Unionist MP for Ayr Burghs, 1906-22, chairman, George Younger & Son Ltd, chairman, Unionist Party, 1916-23, treasurer, 1923-9

69 Alfred Harmsworth (1865-1922), Lord Northcliffe, newspaper proprietor, founded the *Daily Mail* in 1896 and several other newspapers and magazines, from 1908 proprietor of *The Times*, director in 1918 of British war propaganda

70 The Representation of the People Act, 1918, thus disqualified conscientious objectors from voting in parliamentary or local elections

71 Sir James Frederick Rees (1883-1967), Principal of University College of South Wales and Monmouthshire, 1929-49, lecturer (later Reader) in Economic History, Edinburgh University, 1913-25, Vice-Chancellor of the University of Wales, 1935-7 and 1944-6, head of department of Economic History, Edinburgh University, 1956-8

72 The Very Reverend Lord George MacLeod of Fuinary (1895-1991) won the MC and Croix de Guerre in the 1914-18 War, Church of Scotland minister, founder of the Iona Community, Moderator of the General Assembly, 1957-8

73 Sir Robert Blatchford (1851-1943), pseud. Numquam, successively soldier, clerk, writer, founded the weekly *Clarion* in 1891, it continued until 1934, in its two last years retitled *New Clarion. Merrie England* (London, 1894)

74 Clarion Cycling Clubs were formed around the *Clarion* weekly labour paper

75 There were about 3,300 conscientious objectors in the Non-Combatant Corps. Graham, op. cit., 348

76 The Scottish Labour College was formed in 1916 as a development of classes run or inspired by the Clydeside revolutionary John Maclean during the previous decade. Until 1920, when it ran classes for a year or two for full-time students in Glasgow, the College was a movement of workers' educational groups there and elsewhere in Scotland, not a building. See Nan Milton, *John Maclean* (London, 1973), passim.

77 John S Clarke (1885-1959), writer, lion-tamer, member of the Socialist Labour Party, later Labour MP for Glasgow Maryhill, 1929-31

78 Though Home Rule for Scotland was part of Liberal Party policy from the later 19th century the Party leadership did little to push it forward. Some Liberal supporters of Home Rule therefore formed in 1900 the Young Scots Society to agitate the issue but the Young Scots became less active after the Liberal government was formed in 1905-06. H J Hanham, *Scottish Nationalism* (London, 1969), 94-5

79 Sixty conscientious objectors were sent to France in May and June 1916 by the military authorities. At the front the objectors could be shot for refusing to obey army orders. This was the intention of the army authorities, despite the terms of the Act of 1916 imposing conscription, and the undertakings of government ministers that men would not be shot for refusing on grounds of conscience to become soldiers. The first batch of seventeen conscientious objectors was sent to France on 7 May and other batches followed. One batch was marched off from Kinmel Park barracks, Abergele, to the *Dead March* played by the military band. In France four conscientious objectors were sentenced to Field Punishment No. 1—tied or handcuffed for two hours a day to a wheel or a gun carriage. Of these sixty objectors sent to France, 34 were paraded in front of the regiment and had death sentences pronounced on them—sentences that were then commuted by the army authorities to ten years' penal servitude each. Only

the vigilance and intervention of the No-Conscription Fellowship and other supporters ensured these men were returned from France and other conscientious objectors
were not sent there. Some government ministers denied all knowledge of what was
happening; Asquith, the Prime Minister, genuinely did not know and when he did
find out what was happening forbade the military authorities to carry out the executions
without the knowledge of the Cabinet. Graham, op. cit., 110-35

80 Graham, op. cit., 136-54, illustrates the brutality with which some conscientious objectors were treated by the military authorities. In the House of Commons in May
1916 Philip Snowden, ILP MP, described how, for example, at Preston barracks COs
were beaten with sticks, handcuffed, kicked across the barrack yard, indecently assaulted when undressed, and subjected to filthy language. One objector was handcuffed to a metal bar with his arms above his head for forty minutes, and had to stand
on tiptoe to release the pressure on his wrists. James Brightmore, sentenced as a
conscientious objector to 28 days' detention at Cleethorpes in June 1917, found that
the confinement (as he wrote on a cigarette packet smuggled out to his family) 'was in
a pit which started at the surface at 3 feet by 2 and tapered off to 2 ft 6 inches by 15
inches. Water was struck but they continued until it was 10 feet deep. The bottom is
full of water and I have to stand on two strips of wood all day long just above the water
line. There is no room to walk about, and sitting is impossible. The sun beats down,
and through the long day there are only walls of clay to look at. Already I am half mad.'
Brightmore's account was published in the *Manchester Guardian* on 30 June 1917 and
within forty minutes of the paper reaching Cleethorpes camp he was taken out of the
hole after eleven days' confinement in it. The hole was hastily filled up and other
attempts made to conceal the incidents. A government minister questioned in the
Commons gave 'shamelessly misleading information' about the case. Eventually a major
held responsible for Brightmore's treatment was dismissed from the army.

81 Rajani Palme Dutt (1896-1974), a graduate of Oxford University, imprisoned in the
1914-18 War for refusing to serve in the forces, a founder member of the Communist
Party of Great Britain, founder, 1921, and first editor of *Labour Monthly*, lived in
Brussels for several years from 1924 because of a breakdown in his health, member of
the Central Committee of the Communist Party, 1922-65, and vice-chairman for
twenty years until his retirement in 1965

82 Miss Joan M Fry, a Quaker chaplain, not permitted as a woman to visit civil prisons,
was allowed to visit military camps and detention barracks where conscientious objectors
were held. Graham, op. cit., 134, 167

83 Margery Fry, (1874-1958), daughter of Sir Edward Fry, (see below, note 87), librar-
ian, Somerville College, Oxford, 1898-1904, worked with Quakers' War Victims
Relief Mission in France, 1915-17, Principal of Somerville College, 1926-31, Hon.
Secretary, Howard League for Penal Reform, 1919-26

84 *Plebs*, organ 1909-21 of the Plebs League, then of the National Council of Labour
Colleges, incorporated, 1969, into the *Trade Unionist*

85 Ireland (then entirely in the United Kingdom) had been excluded from the universal
conscription imposed by the Military Service Acts, 1916, and though another Act
passed in spring 1918 empowered the government to extend conscription to Ireland
by order in council, opposition there was so powerful that conscription was not in fact
applied

86 At the Work Centre at Knutsford in Cheshire an extensive riot took place on two
successive evenings. 'The riot had every appearance of being organised.' The police

did nothing to protect the conscientious objectors from a crowd that 'occupied the streets around the Centre and knocked down and kicked and broke the heads and tore the clothes and smashed the bicycles of the men as they came in'. Eighteen conscientious objectors were treated in hospital on the first night and the number of casualties would have been much higher if the agent at the Centre had not sent out warnings to COs approaching the town to keep away and if sympathetic townspeople had not taken them into their homes. The riot, 'the culmination of growing friction between the COs and hooligans of the town', led to the arrest of ten young men. The judge virtually admonished them by binding them over in their own recognizances to keep the peace for six months. He added that he hoped the COs, who were 'unwelcome visitors', would be sent away. Graham, op. cit., 248-9

87   Sir Edward Fry (1827-1918), QC, international jurist, Judge of High Court, Chancery Division, 1877-83, Lord Justice of Appeal, 1883-92, judge, Permanent Court of Arbitration, The Hague, 1900-12

88   Miss Beauchamp was harassed by the police for her part in the publication of *The Tribunal*, weekly paper, 1916-20, of the No-Conscription Fellowship, and was twice sentenced to imprisonment—for a month and 21 days respectively. Graham, op. cit., 199-203

89   Of the total of about 16,000 conscientious objectors in the 1914-18 War, some 1,500 were Absolutists who refused to accept any compromise in their position of being wholly opposed to the war, including refusing to undertake non-combatant work which nonetheless in their view contributed directly or indirectly to the war effort. These men remained in prison when other conscientious objectors, like Dr Dott, J P M Millar and W H Marwick were released from close confinement under the Home Office Scheme to do so-called 'Work of National Importance'. Graham, op. cit, 212-20, 349-50

90   Bill Deans, who died in August 1966 aged 80, had also been imprisoned as a conscientious objector in Ayr Gaol. He was a founder member in 1920 of the Communist Party and remained a member throughout his life. I am grateful to my friend Jim Mair of Newmilns for further information about Bill Deans, some of it contained in *Historical Aspects of Newmilns* (Darvell, 1990), 76-7, including the fact that Deans before the end of the 1914-18 War was sent to work on afforestation in Galloway, where 'he immediately set to work to organise the forestry workers'

91   C H Norman (1886- ?) was a leading figure in the No-Conscription Fellowship and, until his resignation from it in 1921, the Independent Labour Party. When 100 conscientious objectors at Dartmoor went on strike for a day in protest against the death on 6 February 1918 of one of their number through neglect by the authorities to treat him for diabetes (almost certainly the case Dr Dott refers to here), the Home Office arrested C H Norman and another CO. Norman was kept in Exeter prison till the end of the war. Graham, op. cit., 317-18

92   The February (or March—the Russian calendar was ten days behind that of Western Europe) Revolution in 1917 resulted in the formation of a Provisional Government (provisional until the adoption of a state constitution), in which Alexander Kerensky (1881-1970) was successively Justice, War and (from July to October/November) Prime Minister

93   Noman McOmish Dott (1897-1971). CBE, FRSE, MB, ChB, FRCS (Ed.), Professor Emeritus, began as an apprentice joiner and engineer before embarking on a long and distinguished career as a surgeon

94   The battle of the Marne 6-9 September 1914, was decisive in ending the rapid German advance till then on the Western front and in leading to years of relatively static trench warfare

95   Four German cruisers shelled Scarborough and Hartlepool for forty minutes on the morning of 15 December 1914, killing about forty civilians, including women and children, and injuring 400. If William Murray was convalescing then in Scarborough it could not have been as a result of being wounded at the battle of Loos, since that took place nine months later in September 1915 (see above, note 19). It may be either that he was convalescing at Scarborough in December 1914, having been wounded at Loos nine months before the battle there took place; or that he was not at Scarborouph until late 1915-early 1916, having been wounded at the battle of Loos, and has confused the German naval bombardment with the time of his own presence; or possibly he has confused the German naval bombardment also of Lowestoft and Yarmouth, further down the east coast, on 25 April 1916, when he may still have been at Scarborough convalescing after the battle of Loos. For the German naval bombardments, see Nicolson, op. cit., 257, and Edmonds, op. cit., 80, 162

96   The battle of Arras was a British contribution to the major French offensive led by General Nivelle on the river Aisne in April 1917, which proved disastrous and led to extensive mutinies in the French army. The battle of Arras, 9 April to 20 May, resulted in a gain of five miles across a twenty-mile front, at a cost of about 160,000 British and 150,000 German casualties. The battle of Cambrai, 20 November to 5 December 1917, in which the British attack was spearheaded by the first major use of tanks and was without the usual preliminary artillery bombardment, led to the ringing of church bells in London in the belief victory in the war was in sight. But initial advances were soon reversed by German counter-attacks and ground gained by British troops was about equal to that lost to the Germans. Casualties on each side were about 45,000. Edmonds, op. cit., 217-38, 267-72; Liddell Hart, op. cit., 407-16, 435-48

97   Sir Harry Lauder (1870-1950), flaxmill boy, miner, Scots comic singer. Captain John Lauder, born 1893, his only son, was in the 8th Argyll and Sutherland Highlanders and was killed in action on 28 December 1916. Lauder received the War Office telegram informing him of his son's death on New Year's Day 1917, while he was appearing in the review *Three Cheers* at the Shaftesbury Theatre in London. He travelled immediately to his home in Dunoon to comfort his wife and then returned three days later to continue his show in London. 'When he reached the theatre, a letter was handed to him by special messenger. It had come from a fellow-officer who was with his son when he was killed. The Captain, he told him, had died with great gallantry, calling out the words: "Carry on!". Captain Lauder is buried at Ovillers, on the Albert-Peronne road. A monument to him, erected by his parents, stands on the Dunoon-Strachur road in Glen Branter, the estate owned by Sir Harry Lauder until after the 1914-18 War. Gordon Irving, *Great Scot! The Life of Sir Harry Lauder* (London, 1968), 88-91, 94, 109, 117, 145

98   The battle of Passchendaele or Third Ypres, 31 July to 10 November 1917, in which men drowned in the sea of mud and water-filled shellholes that covered the battlefield, 'achieved little except loss'. British casualties totalled 245,000 and German probably at least as many. Edmonds, op. cit., 239-52; Liddell Hart, op. cit., 423-34

99   The brothers Frank (1911-52) and Hugh O'Donnell, who played first for Wellesley Juniors then Celtic and Preston North End, both played for Scotland in the 1930s

100   Withdrawing the fires from the pumps that kept the pits from flooding meant stopping

coal production

101 The Mineworkers' Reform Union of Fife, Kinross and Clackmannan was formed in January 1923 after a long conflict within the Fife, Kinross and Clackmannan Miners' Association (known as the 'old' or county union on or 'Adamson's union') between the more democratic and militant miners on the one hand and on the other William Adamson (1863-1936), the general secretary, 1908-28, and his supporters

102 The United Mineworkers of Scotland (UMS), 1929-36, was a left-wing, militant union in rivalry with the federal National Union of Scottish Mine Workers, 1914-45. The main strength of the UMS lay among the miners of Lanarkshire and Fife. The National Unemployed Workers' Movement (NUWM) was founded in 1921, though until 1929 it was titled National Unemployed Workers' Committee Movement (NUWCM)

103 David Proudfoot (1892-1958), militant Fife miner, general secretary, 1931, United Mineworkers of Scotland, from which he then resigned and, simultaneously, from the Communist Party, though he remained a Marxist until his death. He was chairman, Methil Co-operative Society for twenty years from 1934 and a Labour councillor on Methil and Buckhaven Town Council, 1945-51

104 Sir John Gilmour (1876-1940), Secretary of State for Scotland, 1924-9, Minister for Agriculture, 1931-2, Home Secretary, 1932-5, Unionist MP, East Renfrewshire, 1910-18, Pollok, 1918-40. William Murray is mistaken in saying that Sir John, whose home was in Leven and who was a vice-lieutenant for Fife, was Secretary of State for Scotland at the time of the musical in Letham Glen in 1931

105 Bud Flanagan (Robert Weinthrop, originally Chaim Reuben Weintrop) (1896-1968); Chesney Allen (1894-1982). They became two of the seven British comedians who from the 1930s to the 1960s formed the 'Crazy Gang'

106 This interview with Hugh McIntyre took place in August 1984, so the shrapnel had been in his back almost seventy years

107 In mid-1922 the highest percentage of unemployed people at any Scottish labour exchange waa registered at Alexandria, by which time the number had increased five-fold since the end of 1919 (from 600 to 3,000, out of a total population of 21,618 in the Vale of Leven). Stuart Macintyre, *Little Moscows* (London, 1980), 93-4

108 The first Scots contingent on the National Hunger March to London set out in fact in mid-October 1922, reinforcements on 1 December. See, e.g., *Glasgow Herald*, 17 October and 2 December 1922,

109 The first Scottish Hunger March to Edinburgh, organised by the National Unemployed Workers' Movement, took place in September 1928, the second National March to London in January-February 1929

110 'Unemployed training' by the government for the unemployed had begun in the mid-1920s, apart from training among partly disabled ex-servicemen after the 1914-18 War. By the late 1930s five types of training or instruction were being provided or funded by the Ministry of Labour. One of these was the residential Instructional Centres, of which there were about twenty, taking 20,000 unemployed men each year. The purpose of these Centres was 'not to teach a trade but to cater for men of the labourer type. They were agencies of physical and moral rehabilitation, giving men a twelve weeks' course of fairly hard work, good feeding and mild discipline'. The 'fairly hard work' was mainly afforestation in remote places, such as Glen Branter in Argyllshire, opened as a Centre in August 1933. R C Davison, *British Unemployment Policy* (London, 1938), 113-22. It was these residential Instructional Centres that roused

351

the opposition of the National Unemployed Workers' Movement, which saw them as 'slave camps' comparable with those in Nazi Germany. The Centres, whose remoteness cut off the unemployed sent there from contact with their families, subjected them to a military-like regime of sleeping in dormitory huts, parading for work each morning, roll-calls, lights-out, rarely granted time-off permissions, and heavy manual labour in afforestation, road-making, trench-digging, sewerage etc., for which no wages were paid but only three or four shillings 'weekly allowance'. It was said that the Home Secretary Sir John Gilmour had described these residential Centres, 'by a slip of the tongue' in 1934 as concentration camps. Of the total intake of 83,000 volunteers into these Centres throughout Britain in the four years 1935-8, only 12,000 found employment afterwards. At Glen Branter there were also complaints by the unemployed men about a local policeman McInnes, known as Strachur Dan, who, it was alleged, beat up men at the camp. Wal Hannington, *Ten Lean Years* (London, 1940), 124, 180-205; Scottish Record Office, DD 10/252; *Scotsman*, 29 November 1938

111   Wal Hannington (1896-1966), a toolmaker by trade, a founder in 1921 of the National Unemployed Workers' Movement and its national organiser throughout its existence. J T Walton Newbold (1888-1943), Communist MP for Motherwell, 1922-3, resigned from the Communist Party, 1924, apparently because he disapproved of its attitude to the Labour Party and the then Labour government. Newbold joined the so-called National Labour Party in 1931 and supported Winston Churchill in the 1935 general election

112   Allan Campbell was a member of a deputation from the unemployed led by Harry McShane that met Bonar Law as MP for Glasgow Central in the city on 23 December 1922 after he had refused as Prime Minister to meet the National Hunger Marchers in London. *Glasgow Herald*, 26 December 1922

113   Alex Moffat (1904-67), militant miner, Fife County Councillor, 1929-45, President, Scottish Area, National Union of Mineworkers, 1961-7. John McArthur (1899-1982), militant miner, full-time student under John Maclean at the Scottish Labour College, 1920-1, full-time official, National Union of Mineworkers, 1946-64

114   Bob Stewart (1877-1973), son of an Angus farm worker, a Prohibitionist in his early years, leading Scottish organiser, 1921, and acting general secretary, 1925, of the Communist Party of Great Britain

115   Edwin Scrymgeour (1866-1947), Prohibition MP for Dundee, 1922-31. Winston Churchill (1874-1965), MP for Oldham, 1900-06 (from 1900 to 1904 Conservative; from 1904-08 Liberal), Liberal MP, North West Manchester, 1906-08, Dundee, 1908-22, Conservative MP, Epping, 1924-45, Woodford, 1945-64. At the three elections, 1924, 1929 and 1931, when he stood as Communist candidate in Dundee, Stewart won 8,340, 6,160 and 10,264 votes respectively, compared with 29,193, 50,073, and 32,239 for Scrymgeour. F W S Craig, *British Parliamentary Election Results 1918-1949* (Glasgow, 1969), 577

116   The restrictions imposed by the Trade Disputes Act, 1927, made joint electoral and industrial bodies (and the titles Trades and Labour Councils) less common. In the 1920s and '30s there was also a continuing, and generally successful, attempt by the TUC to diminish the influence of Communists in the trades councils, which culminated in the so-called 'Black Circular' from the TUC General Council in 1934 which advised trade unions to exclude Communists from positions of responsibility within them, and made exclusion of Communist delegates obligatory on trades councils if they wanted to keep formal recognition by the TUC. There were similar tendencies at

work in Scotland, e.g., in 1928-9 the Scottish TUC decided to disaffiliate all trades councils affiliated to the Communist-dominated Minority movement and Edinburgh trades council expelled all delegates who were Communist Party members or supporters. In the same period the Labour Party, while refusing from 1920 to permit the Communist Party to affiliate to it, changed its rules in 1925 to make individual members of the Communist Party ineligible for membership of the Labour Party. See e.g., H Pelling, *A History of British Trade Unionism* (London, 1963), 201; A Clinton, *The Trade Union Rank and File: Trades Councils in Britain, 1900-40* (Manchester, 1977), 138-56

117 Dan O'Hare (1887-1956), a toolmaker dismissed in the 1911 strike at Singer's factory, Clydebank, afterwards a greengrocer, Communist councillor of Dumbarton County from 1925. Archibald Peters later left Vale of Leven because he could not find employment there as an engineer. John Black, an engineer, became politically inactive after 1925 and did not stand for re-election. Macintyre, op. cit, 95, 99, 182; I MacDougall, *Voices from the Hunger Marches* Vol.1 (Edinburgh, 1990), 200

118 Sir Alfred Mond (1868-1930), a founder of Imperial Chemical Industries in 1926, Liberal MP, 1906-28, Minister of Health, 1921-2, joined the Conservative Party in 1926, became Baron Melchett, 1928. The 'Mond Scale' issued by the Ministry of Health at the beginning of 1922 was the first officially sanctioned scale of Poor Law relief and was drawn up under the terms of the Local Authorities (Financial Provisions) Act, which Mond as Minister had hurried through Parliament in late autumn, 1921

119 Hugh McIntyre died at the age of 89 in 1986, two years after he had recorded these recollections

120 The formation of International Brigades of foreign volunteers to assist the Republic against the military and right-wing rebellion was considered by the Spanish Communist Party within two or three weeks of the outbreak of the rebellion in July 1936, then by the Executive Committee of the Communist International and by Stalin. The Spanish Republican government formally authorised the formation of the International Brigades in October. Six International Brigades, about 35,000 men in aggregate, were formed in the course of the war, on a basis of language spoken: XIth (German). XIIth (Italian), XIIIth (Eastern European). XIVth (French), XVth (English), 129th (Central European). A seventh Brigade, the 150th (Central European), existed for a time in 1937

121 Tom Mann (1856-1941). Ernest Thaelmann (1886-1944), Geman Communist Party leader murdered by the Nazis

122 General Francisco Franco (1892-1975), Chief of Staff of the Spanish army, 1935-6, dismissed as Governor of the Canary Islands by the Popular Front government in 1936, became leader of the military and right-wing rebellion against the Republic and from its defeat in 1939 dictator of Spain

123 Phil Gillan (1912-1993) recounted his experiences in the Spanish War in I MacDougall, *Voices from the Spanish Civil War* (Edinburgh,1986), 13-19

124 John Cornford (1915-1936) and Ralph Fox (1900-1936) were killed in action at Cordoba on 28 December 1936. Felicia Browne was killed in Aragon on 25 August 1936, the first British volunteer to be killed in the war. Hans Beimler, a Communist former Deputy in the Reichstag, who had escaped from Dachau concentration camp, was killed in the fighting at Madrid on 12 December 1936

125 General Gonzalo Queipo de Llano (1875-1951). A huge radio transmitter he used for

his broadcasts was a gift in December 1936 from Nazi Germany. Hugh Thomas *The Spanish Civil War* (Harmondsworth, 3rd ed. 1977), 520

126   John Lochore had been a paid canvasser for the *Sunday Express* in 1935-6. See MacDougall, *Hunger Marches*, Vol II, op, cit., 317-18

127   The agreement on non-intervention in the Spanish war was reached in August 1936, within six weeks of its outbreak, by Britain, France, Germany, Italy, Portugal, the Soviet Union, and some other states. Non-intervention, a policy inspired by the British government, proved a dangerous farce. Fascist Italy and Nazi Germany continued to pour in supplies and armed forces to support Franco. The governments of Britain and France (where in 1937 Baldwin was succeeded by Chamberlain and Blum by Chautemps and, in the following year, Daladier), apparently moved by fear of being drawn into the Spanish war in case it developed into a general European conflict, but particularly in the case of the British government because of an unwillingness to do anything that might help the Spanish Republic, which they regarded as 'Red', followed a policy that contributed to the eventual defeat of the Republic, the creation of a fascist state in Spain and hence the removal of a friendly one from France's southern border, and to the strengthening of Hitler's conviction that the two Western Powers would not act decisively to oppose the expansion of Nazi Germany. Non-intervention deprived the legitimate Republican government of Spain of its right under international law to buy arms from abroad for its defence. The Soviet Union declared in October 1936 that unless violations of non-intervention by the Fascist Powers ceased it would send assistance to Republican Spain—and did so, as did to a much lesser extent the Mexican government

128   J R Campbell (1894-1969), wounded and decorated in the 1914-18 War, a leading member of the Communist Party of Great Britain, principal figure in the Campbell Case, 1924, editor of *The Worker, Workers' Weekly* and *Daily Worker*

129   The battle of Jarama was begun on 6 February 1937 by the Nationalist or Fascist forces in order to cut the Madrid-Valencia road southeast of Madrid, surround and seize the city. The Republicans suffered 25,000 casualties, including many members of the International Brigades, the Nationalists about 20,000. Paul Preston, *The Spanish Civil War* (London, 1986), 101-02

130   Frank Ryan (1902-1944), a member of the Irish Republican Army in in the Anglo-Irish War, 1918-20, had fought with the Anti-Treaty forces in the Irish Civil War, 1922-3, and was leader of the first group of volunteers from the Communist Party of Ireland to arrive in Spain in December 1936 to fight for its Republic. Taken prisoner by Franco's forces in 1938 Ryan spent the rest of his life in captivity, first in Spain then in Nazi Germany. His remains were reburied in Ireland in 1979

131   Jack London (1876-1916), American novelist, author of, e.g., *The Call of the Wild, White Fang,* and *The Iron Heel.* Upton-Sinclair (1878-1968), American novelist, author of, e.g., *The Jungle, King Coal, Dragon's Teeth*

132   John Lochore was a seaman from about 1929 to 1931 and again in 1934-5, when he visited Spain twice. The revolutionary uprising by left-wing groups and miners in Asturias in northern Spain in October 1934 was brutally suppressed by General Franco, and contributed to the coming two years later of the Spanish civil war

133   CNT (Confederacion Nacional del Trabajo)—the revolutionary trade union movement of the Anarchists or Anarcho-Syndicalists; FAI (Federacion Anarquista Iberica)—Spanish Anarchist Federation; JSO (Juventudes Socialistas Unificados)—the Socialist-Communist Youth; POUM (Partido Obrero de Unificacion Marxista)—the Workers'

Party of Marxist Unity. The black banners denoted anarchists, the red socialists or communists

134 The battle of Brunete, a few miles west of Madrid, from 6 to 25 July 1937, was a Republican offensive that gained a little territory but failed in its aim of cutting off the Nationalists besieging Madrid. In this battle the Nazi German Condor Legion used the Messerschmitt ME 109 for the first time and also practised on a small scale aspects of tank warfare the Germans developed in the Second World War. Thomas, op. cit., 710-17

135 Flynn was killed at Cordoba in April 1937. Bill Alexander, *British Volunteers for Liberty. Spain 1936-39* (London, 1982), 267

136 Nathan, a brave, competent and highly respected officer, had served in the British army first as a sergeant-major during the 1914-18 War, later as an officer in the Guards. He arrived in Spain in December 1936 and was successively a company and battalion commander, then a major and Chief of Staff of the XVth International Brigade before the battle of Brunete, in which he was mortally wounded by aerial bombing. During his service in the British army he had been in Ireland, and it has been claimed he was attached to the Black and Tans and was responsible for the murder of two leading Irish nationalists in 1921. Thomas, op. cit., 490 and n., 713 and n; J Delperrié de Bayac, *Les Brigades internationales* (Paris, 1968), 99; Alexander, op. cit., 36-129 passim. Jock Cunningham (whom Alexander, op. cit., says came from Coatbridge) had arrived in Spain in early autumn 1936, fought in earlier battles in defence of Madrid before Jarama, became commander of the British Battalion after Jarama, but after the battle of Brunete left Spain and the Communist Party following dissensions among the leaders of the British Battalion. Alexander, op. cit., 59, 131; Thomas, op. cit., 723

137 David Springhall, a leading London communist, was political commissar of the British Battalion at the beginning of 1937 and then in February became Assistant Commissar of the XVth Brigade. T H Wintringham (1898-1949) had served with the Flying Corps and RAF in France in the 1914-18 War and was commander of the British Battalion of the XVth International Brigade in February 1937. Wounded at Jarama he later became a brigade staff officer but was again wounded and was invalided home in November 1937. He helped found Osterley Park Training School for the Home Guard in 1940 and was author of *English Captain* (London, 1939) and other books mainly on war. McCartney, a left-wing journalist and author of *Walls Have Mouths: a Record of Ten Years' Penal Servitude* (London, 1936), was wounded in a firearm accident early in 1937 when he was commander of the British Battalion and had to return to Britain. Compton Mackenzie (1883-1972), novelist and writer, served in the Dardanelles in the 1914-18 War and became director of the Aegean Intelligence Service in Syria. Alexander, op. cit., 38, 45, 91; MacDougall, *Voices from the Spanish Civil War*, op. cit., 99, 148, 336; *Chambers' Biographical Dictionary* (Edinburgh, 1990), 942

138 Francisco Largo Caballero (1869-1946), Spanish Socialist and trade union leader, Prime Minister of the Republican goverrment, September 1936 to May 1937. About 16,000 men, many of them civilians and instructors but including the Condor Legion of 5,000 tank, artillery, and aircraft men, were sent to Spain to help Franco by Nazi Germany, as were about 200 tanks and 600 aircraft. About 75,000 troops, 150 tanks and 650 aircraft were sent by Fascist Italy. Thomas, op. cit., 977-8

139 Buenaventura Durruti (1896-1936), Spanish Anarchist leader, killed during the defence of Madrid in November 1936. Juan Modesto (1906-1969), Communist militia leader, commander of the Communist 5th Regiment in the Republican army and later

of the 5th Corps. General Enrique Lister, commander for a time of the Communist 5th Regiment. General Walter (pseud. of Karol Swierczewski) (1897-1947), a Pole who had fought in the Soviet Red Army, commander of the 35th Division in Spain. General José Miaja (1878-1958), the leading general in the defence of Madrid in 1936

140 J Douglas and James Rae were both from Glasgow. Alexander, op. cit., 266, 273. Clem Beckett (1906-1936), born near Oldham, a blacksmith, joined the Young Communist League, 1924, became from 1927 a speedway rider, formed the Dirt Track Riders' Association, killed 12 February 1937 at Jarama

141 Christopher St John Sprigg, *nom de plume* Christopher Caudwell, (1900-1937) had written seven detective stories, five books on aviation and three on philosophy and economics, including *Illusion and Reality* (London, 1937) and *Studies in a Dying Culture* (London, 1938) which presented a Marxist theory of art. Thomas, op. cit., 593

142 J B S Haldane (1892-1964), educated at Eton and Oxford, Professor of Genetics at London University, 1933-37, and of Biometry at University College, London, 1937-57, chairman, editorial board, *Daily Worker*, 1940-9, left the Communist Party in 1956, emigrated to India and held academic appointments there

143 David John Jones, 'Potato' Jones, (1873-1965), was part-owner and captain of a Cardiff cargo steamer, and also later brought 800 refugees out of Republican Spain and in 1940 ferried British troops back from Dunkirk. Hywel Francis, *Miners Against Fascism. Wales and the Spanish Civil War* (London, 1984), 124, 137

144 Dolores Ibarruri, 'La Pasionaria' (1895-1989), orator and perhaps best known leader of the Spanish Communist Party, wife of an Asturian miner, imprisoned several times for her political activities, a member of the Cortes or parliament before the Civil War and president, Spanish Communist Party, for many years after it, she seemed to many to personify Spanish resistance to fascism. After the Civil War she went into prolonged exile in the Soviet Union

145 George Aitken, a Communist Party organiser and Scots engineer who had served in the 1914-18 War, one of five British Battalion, XVth Brigade, leaders among whom sharp differences of opinion had taken place, sent back to Britain after the battle of Brunete, July 1937, and did not return to Spain. Alexander, op. cit., 67, 74, 130-1. Judith Cook, *Apprentices of Freedom* (London, 1979) 97-8.

146 John Lochore may be mistaken here and 'Vidal' was Vittorio Vidali (pseud. Carlos Contreras) an Italian communist, one of the leaders of the 5th Regiment in the Republican army, and inspector general at the battle of Guadalajara, March 1937. Thomas, op. cit., 323, 599

147 Thomas, op. cit., 982, considers that the Soviet Union supplied the Spanish Republic during the Civil War with about 900 tanks, 1,550 pieces of artillery, 300 armoured cars, 15,000 machine guns, 30,000 automatic rifles, 15,000 mortars, 500,000 rifles, 8,000 lorries, 4 million artillery shells, 1,000 million cartridges and 1,500 tons of gunpowder. David MacKenzie, an Edinburgh medical student who had gone to Spain to fight for the Republic in October 1936, told a public meeting at Coatbridge on 6 January 1937 that the Soviet Union had supplied the Republicans with 'arms the Allied armies had left behind in their hurry to leave the USSR in 1921'. *Glasgow Herald*, 7 January 1937

148 There were two American battalions, the Lincoln and the Washington, in the XVth International Brigade. Two-thirds of the Canadian Mackenzie-Papineau Battalion in the same brigade were Americans. Thomas, op. cit., 723

149 At least 75,000 Moors or Moroccan volunteers enrolled in Franco's forces during the

war. Thomas, op. cit., 980

150 Jack Sylvester is among those killed at Jarama listed in Alexander, op. cit., 275

151 Peter Kerrigan (1899-1977), a Glasgow engineer, member of the Executive Committee of the Communist Party of Great Britain, 1927-9 and 1931-65, successively Scottish Secretary, National Organiser and Industrial Organiser of the Communist Party. Kerrigan was in Spain with the International Brigade until soon after the battle of Jarama in February 1937. Alexander, op. cit., 101

152 Paul Robeson (1898-1976), concert singer and actor. Harry Pollitt (1890-1960), General Secretary, 1929-56, and chairman, 1956-60, of the Communist Party of Great Britain. Ernest Hemingway (1899-1961), American novelist, in Spain as a journalist during the Civil War, author of *For Whom the Bell Tolls* (1940), a novel about the Spanish War

153 George Brown (1906-1937), born in Ireland, moved as a child to Manchester where he became an active trade unionist, an organiser of the unemployed, and Manchester organiser of the Communist Party. He was a company political commissar with the XVth Brigade when he was killed at Brunete in July 1937. Walter Tapsell was circulation manager of the *Daily Worker*, leader of the Young Communist League, commissar of the British Battalion of the International Brigade, and was killed in fighting at Calaceite in April 1938. Alexander, op. cit., 35. 74, 121, 159, 275; Michael O'Riordan *Connolly Column* (Dublin, 1979), 84

154 Santiago Carillo (1915-) General Secretary of the Juventudes Socialistas Unificades, joined the Communist Party, November, 1936, later Secretary General of the Party for many years, exiled after the Civil War, elected a member of the Spanish Parliament, 1982-6. Ronald Fraser, *Blood of Spain* (Harmondsworth, 1981), 263, 496

155 Stephen Spender (1909-95), writer, poet and critic, a supporter of the Spanish Republic, author of *Poems for Spain* (1939) among many other works, a fireman in the London blitz in the 1939-45 war, co-editor of the magazines *Horizon* and *Encounter*, Professor of English at University College, London, 1970-77. Spender went to Spain in spring 1937 successfully to plead for the life of his former secretary, who, disillusioned, had tried to leave the International Brigades and was in danger of being executed. Thomas, op. cit., 608. The POUM (Partido Obrero de Unificacion Marxista, or Workers' Party of Marxist Unity) had been formed in February 1936 following a breakaway five years earlier by its leaders Andreu Nin, Joaquin Maurin and others from the Spanish Communist Party. The POUM was the smallest of the four left-wing parties in the Popular Front electoral alliance that had won the general election in Spain in February 1936 and against whose government the Nationalists or Fascists rebelled in July that year. The POUM, most of whose supporters were in Catalonia, was regarded as Trotskyist by the Communists, though Trotsky himself criticised Nin (his former secretary) for (among other shortcomings) adopting a 'timid and semi-Menshevik' attitude. In May 1937 the growing tensions between the POUM, critical of Stalin and of alliance with middle class Spanish Republican parties and believing that the war would not be won unless the revolution triumphed, and the communist-dominated PSUC (Catalan Socialist Unity Party), and also between the latter and the anarchists, resulted in several days of street fighting in Barcelona, in which 500 were killed and 1,000 wounded. The events of those days in May sharply illustrated the divisions on the Republican side in the Civil War, led to the fall of the government headed by the Spanish Socialist Largo Caballero, the suppression of the POUM and the murder in prison of their leader Nin, and also to a decline in the influence of the

anarchists. I Deutscher, *The Prophet Outcast: Trotsky, 1929-40* (London, 1963), 388; for the complexities of the crisis see, e.g., R Carr, *Spain 1808-1975* (London, 1982), 666-7; Fraser, op. cit., 340-5, 378-82, 561-2; Thomas, op. cit., 523, 646-65, 701-09; and George Orwell, *Homage to Catalonia* (London, 1938), chapters 9-14

156 The Nationalists or Fascists, supported by 10,000 Italian Black Shirt troops, captured Malaga on 8 February 1937. Several thousand Republican sympathisers were executed. Refugees from Malaga fleeing along the coast road to Almeria suffered the fate John Lochore describes. Nazi German planes bombed Guernica in the Basque country on 26 April 1937 and killed about 1,000 people. Thomas, op. cit., 562-7, 625

157 John Lochore had been organiser of the ILP Guild of Youth in 1933-4. Smillie, grandson of the miners' leader of the same name, died in Spain in 1937 in circumstances considered mysterious by Thomas, op. cit., 706

158 John McNair, a biographer of the ILP leader James Maxton, had been Organising Secretary of the ILP in the mid-1920s. He worked for many years in France as a merchant but again became an ILP official in 1936 and spent a year in Spain from the outbreak of the Civil War, from which he returned with Eric and Eileen Blair in 1937. Fenner Brockway, *Inside the Left* (London, 1942), 294-5. George Orwell (*nom de plume* of Eric Blair) (1903-1950), educated at Eton, served in the police in Burma in the 1920s, became a writer, fought and was wounded in the Spanish War, his experiences in which he published as *Homage to Catalonia* (London, 1938)

159 The *North Anglia*, a former German naval vessel, scuttled at Scapa Flow at the end of the 1914-18 War, was the ship on which John Lochore had served as a young seaman on a voyage to South America in 1929. MacDougall, *Hunger Marches*, Vol. 2. op.cit., 311-14

160 John Gollan (1911-1977), General Secretary, 1956-76, Communist Party of Great Britain. Ted Willis (1918-1992), later Lord Willis, writer, playwright, television and film scriptwriter, novelist

161 Poland had made two ten-year pacts of non-aggression: one with the Soviet Union on 25 January 1932, the other with Nazi Germany on 26 January 1934. The Nazi-Soviet Non-Aggression Pact of 23 August 1939 included a top secret agreement between those two states to divide the whole of Eastern Europe into spheres of influence. Under this Finland, Estonia and Latvia were to lie in the Soviet sphere, Lithuania and Vilna in the German, and a partition of Poland was foreshadowed between Nazi Germany and the Soviet Union. This pact, which appeared to reverse the previous Soviet policy of opposing fascism, nazism and their aggression, was partly a result of the Munich Agreement of 1938 (the conference leading to which the Soviet Union and the immediate victim Czechoslovakia had not been invited to attend). Munich and its aftermath in 1938-9, along with earlier failures or refusals by the Western Powers (as in the Spanish War) to stop Fascist aggression, encouraged Stalin to seek an agreement with Nazi Germany. The Nazi-Soviet Non-Aggression Pact gave a green light to Hitler to attack Poland within the week, by committing each of the two signatories to remain neutral if the other became involved in war. By allowing Nazi Germany to expand eastward at the expense of Poland, Stalin appears to have believed that the Pact won him more time to prepare for eventual war with Hitler. Once the collapse of Poland under the German-led onslaught was certain, Stalin ordered the Red Army, under the secret terms of his Pact with Hitler, to occupy eastern Poland, where most of the population were Ukranians or Byelorussians. Red Army garrisons were established more or less simultaneously in Estonia, Latvia and Lithuania, and the Soviet

Union went to war with Finland on 30 November 1939. In Poland the Polish army continued to resist the German invasion until 6 October. Norman Davies, *Heart of Europe: a Short History of Poland* (Oxford, 1986) 65, 126; I Deutscher, *Stalin* (Oxford, 1949), 428-444; A Bullock, *Hitler, a Study in Tyranny* (London, 1952), 479-92

162   NKVD—People's Commissariat of Internal Affairs, earlier titled Cheka, then GPU, and later KGB

163   Wladyslaw Sikorski (1881-1943), Polish general and politician, Prime Minister, 1922-3, War Minister, 1923-5, Prime Minister from September 1939 of the Polish government in exile, killed in an aircrash, 1943. The Nazi invasion of the Soviet Union ended the Nazi-Soviet Non-Aggression Pact, and diplomatic relations between the Soviet Union and the Polish Government in exile in London were established on 30 July and a military convention signed on 12 August 1941. The Soviet government agreed to form a Polish army in the Soviet Union, grant an amnesty to all Polish internees and annul the provisions of the Nazi-Soviet Pact concerning Poland. But the Polish-Soviet frontier remained unsettled and a bone of contention. Davies, op. cit., 70, 75-6; Deutscher, *Stalin,* op. cit., 476-7

164   Lithuania (whose Grand Duchy was a very much larger area, stretching south as far as the Black Sea, than the present state) and Poland were united for 400 years until the Partition of Poland by Austria, Prussia and Russia in 1773-95. Jozef Pilsudski (1867-1935), Polish soldier and politician, born in Vilno in Russian Poland, sent to Siberia in 1887 for five years for supporting Polish independence, leader of the Polish Socialist Party, fought in the 1914-18 War at first for Austria, later imprisoned in Germany, President, Polish Republic from 1918, as Marshal in the Polish army he led it in the Russo-Polish war of 1920, overthrew the Polish government, 1926, and remained dictator of Poland until his death

165   Partitioned in 1773-95 between Russia, Prussia and Austria, Poland ceased to exist in the latter year as a state until it was reconstituted at the end of the 1914-18 War. About half of 18th century Poland (the eastern half) was annexed by Tsarist Russia

166   The Russo-Polish War, 1919-20, was marked in May 1920 by the advance into the Ukraine and the seizure of Kiev by the Polish army under Marshal Pilsudski. The Poles were soon driven back into Poland by the Red Army. The prospect then arose of carrying the Bolshevik Revolution into Europe 'on the bayonets of the Red Army'. Lenin and Stalin favoured this course, Trotsky opposed it. The Red Army invaded Poland, reached Warsaw but was then driven back by the Poles. See, e.g., Deutscher, op. cit., 214-17

167   Joachim von Ribbentrop (1893-1946), Foreign Minister of Nazi Germany, 1938-45, executed by the Allies after the Nuremberg Trials. V M Molotov (1890-1986), Soviet Foreign Mininter, 1939-56. The Pact was the Nazi-Soviet Non-Aggression Pact of August, 1939

168   Vladimir Mayakovsky (1894-1930), born in Georgia, became a leading poet and playwright, supported the Revolution but became very critical of Stalinist bureaucracy. He committed suicide in 1930

169   The last king of Poland had been forced to abdicate at the third Partition in 1795

170   See above, note 163

171   The murderous horrors of the Kolyma labour camps in north eastern Siberia are described by Alexander Solzhenitsyn in *The Gulag Archipelago* (London, 1975), Vol. 2 127-34. Of the estimated two million Polish civilians deported to Siberia, Arctic Russia or Kazakhstan in 1939-40, at least half were dead within a year of their arrest by the

Soviet authorities. Davies, op. cit., 67

172   Although foundations for the Polish underground Resistance were laid in September
1939, its military and civilian branches began to function widely only from the end of
1942. The Polish Home Army, the largest trained and armed forces, numbered about
400,000 by 1944; there was also a much smaller and rival Communist group, the
People's Guard. In the countryside huge areas were controlled by the partisans, and
the German occupation forces were subjected increasingly to ambushes, sabotage and
derailments of trains. The civilian branch of the Resistance proved extremely skilful in
issuing propaganda, holding educational classes, supplying ration cards, painting slo-
gans on walls, passing military intelligence to London, and even succeeded in placing
underground agents in concentration camps such as Auschwitz. By 1944 the Polish
Resistance was the largest in Europe. The defeat and retreat of the German invaders in
the Soviet Union and the approach of the Red Army toward Warsaw—regarded by
non-Communist Poles (a big majority of the population) as a mixed blessing—along
with the bomb attempt on Hitler's life on 20 July, led General Bor-Komarowski,
commander of the Polish Home Army, with an underground force of 150,000 armed
men, to begin on 1 August the Warsaw Rising. Its object was to carry out a Polish
liberation of Warsaw from the Germans. The rising was begun before contact had
been made with the Red Army, to ensure co-ordinated action. The Germans in fact
reinforced their troops in the city and counter-attacked the Red Army, which either
could not or deliberately did not enter Warsaw in time to support the rising: the facts
remain a matter of great controversy. Savage fighting in Warsaw over the two following months resulted in the deaths of over 250,000 civilians, many of them victims of
wholesale massacres by the Germans, enormous losses to the Polish Home Army, and
the virtual razing of Warsaw to the ground. Davies, op, cit., 72–8; Deutscher, op. cit.,
522–3

173   The Yalta conference of 4-11 February 1945 between Stalin, Churchill and Roosevelt
confirmed that the frontier between Poland and the Soviet Union should be more or
less that resulting from the Nazi-Soviet Non-Aggression Pact of 1939, and that a new
provisional government of Poland should be formed from the government in exile in
London and that supported by Stalin in Warsaw. Later that year at the Potsdam
conference of July-August, the Allied leaders moved Poland's western frontier 150
miles to the west, to the rivers Oder and Neisse. Davies, op.cit., 79, 80

174   Hispano-Suiza was a vehicle factory. The French fleet at Toulon was scuttled on 27
Nov. 1942 to prevent it falling into the hands of the Germans. Night and Fog was the
title of a special decree by Hitler in December 1941, that punishment of those 'guilty
of offences against the Reich or against the occupation forces in occupied areas' should
be changed from penal servitude or hard labour for life to the death penalty. As Heinrich
Himmler head (1900-1945) of the S.S. and Gestapo, explained at the time: 'An effective and last deterrent can be achieved only by the death penalty or by taking measures
which will leave the family and the population uncertain as to the fate of the offender.
Deportation to Germany serves this purpose… these measures will have a deterrent
effect because: (a) the prisoners will vanish without leaving a trace; (b) no information
may be given as to their whereabouts or their fate.' Their whereabouts were the
extemination camps. Edward Crankahaw, *Gestapo: Instrument of Tyranny* (London,
1966 ed.), 153-4

175   Savoy until 1860 was part of the kingdom of Sardinia-Piedmont but was ceded then,
along with Nice, by its king to the Second French Empire of Napoleon III as part of

the price for his intervention in the war of 1859 in Italy against·Austria. The cession of Savoy and Nice was confimed by the vote of an overwhelming majority of the population

176 The Beauce is the area around Chartres

177 Henri Pétain (1856-1951), French general who became a national hero by the defence of Verdun in 1916, commander-in-chief from 1917, when he suppressed the widespread mutinies in the French army that year following the disastrous spring offensive by General Nivelle (see above, note 96); Pétain was a marshal of France from 1918, Minister of War in 1934

178 The Croix de Guerre was established in 1915 and was awarded to all ranks of the armed services and subjects of France individually mentioned in despatches, and was awarded also to members of the Allied forces. The ribbon of the medal was green with five equally spaced red stripes and edged in red. The Croix de Feu, founded by Colonel Comte François de La Rocque (1885-1946) was regarded by socialists and communists and others on the Left as fascist or at least semi-fascist or pro-fascist. Along with other right-wing leagues, such as Action Française, the Camelots du Roi and the Jeunesses Patriotes, the Croix de Feu took a leading part in the street demonstrations on 6 February 1934 in Paris against the government, arising from issues raised by the Stavisky affair. In the struggle with police preventing them from forcing their way into the Chamber of Deputies, twelve of the rioters were shot and about sixty wounded. The government of Edouard Daladier, despite winning a vote of confidence, resigned next day. The Confédération Générale du Travail trade union federation called a one-day general strike in protest against the actions of the right-wing leagues. The general strike developed into the first mass anti-fascist demonstration in France and led on to the formation in 1935 of the Popular Front of Socialists, Communists and Radicals, and to the election in 1936 of the Popular Front goverment headed by the Socialist leader Léon Blum. The Popular Front government in 1936 dissolved the Croix de Feu, the Jeunesses Patriotes and other fascist er semi-fascist leagues. De La Rocque and the other leaders of the dissolved Croix de Feu then formed the Parti Social Francais (PSP—French Social Party). The Croix de Feu (which has been described by one historian, David Thomson, as providing 'all the elements of propaganda, private army and mystique which in Gemany, Italy and elsewhere produced Fascist revolutions') or Parti Social Francais claimed in the 1930s a membership of two millions. Colonel de La Rocque himself, along with a large majority of the members of the PSF, at first strongly supported Pétain and the Vichy regime established after the German conquest of France in 1940, but he was deported to Germany in 1943 as an American spy. He returned to France after the Liberation but died soon afterwards. Alexander Werth, *The Destiny of France* (London, 1937), passim; and *France, 1940-55* (London, 1957), 147-8; David Thomson, *Democracy in France since 1870* (Oxford, 1969). 195-6; Jean-Pierre Azéma, *De Munich à La Liberation 1938-44* (Paris, 1979), 222

179 Baccalauréat—French secondary school examination, success in which gives university entrance qualification

180 James Fenimore Cooper (1789-1851), American writer, author of *The Last of the Mohicans* and about fifty other novels. Sir Walter Scott (1771-1832), lawyer, author of a long series of historical novels beginning with *Waverley* (1814). Honoré de Balzac (1799-1850), French novelist, wrote about eighty novels in the series *La Comédie Humaine*

181 The remilitarisation of the Rhineland by Hitler in March 1936 was a breach of the

Treaty of Versailles,1919, but did not result in any action by the French or British governments. It was perhaps the last occasion on which the Second World War could have been averted without serious bloodshed if the Western Powers had acted. Nor was there action by these Powers in the analogous case of the union or Anschluss between Nazi Germany and Austria pushed through by Hitler in March 1938. The Munich Agreement of September 1938 (incidentally warmly approved at the time by Colonel de La Rocque of the Croix de Feu—see Alexander Werth, *The Twilight of France* (London, 1942), 246) between Britain, France, Nazi Germany and Fascist Italy appeared to enable war to be avoided—but at the expense of forcing Czechoslovakia to cede the Sudetenland, the German-speaking part of that country, to Nazi Germany. Six months later Hitler sent his troops into Prague, the Czech capital, and established a 'protectorate' over the provinces of Bohemia and Moravia. Neville Chamberlain (1869-1940) and Edouard Daladier (1884-1970) were the British Conservative and French Radical prime ministers who signed the Munich Agreement. (See also above, note 161)

182   *L'Humanité*—daily newspaper of the French Commmist Party. The paper had been banned by the French government for its headline 'Unity of the French Nation against the Nazi aggressor!' on 26 August 1939. Shortly afterward, on 26 September, the Communist Party and its organisations was dissolved by the French government, and in the following month the seventy Communist deputies or MPs were deprived of their seats and arrested and later tried and sentenced to imprisonment. *L'Humanité* appeared clandestinely (about ten times a month) from the summer of 1939 onward. The Communist Party is said to have regarded it as 'unthinkable' that communists in France should co-operate with the Germans in any way. See Frida Knight, *The French Resistance 1940 to 1944* (London, 1975), 32, 64; Azéma, op. cit., 364-5

183   The Phoney War was the period between the fall of Poland to Nazi Germany in September 1939 and the German offensive on the Western Front in spring 1940. During those months there was no major fighting between Britain and France and Germany, but in fact the leaders of the two former states discussed many plans for an offensive then against Nazi Germany none of which, however, could be carried out because of a lack of resources. The Maginot Line (named after André Maginot, then Minister of War) had been begun in 1929 and was an elaborate underground defence system costing £160,000 million, that was intended to save French lives in any future war with Germany. But the line covered only a part of the French frontier, from Luxembourg to Switzerland. Liddell Hart, *History of the Second World War* (London, 1973), 33; Peter Young, *World War 1939-1945* (London, 1966), 49

184   The German defeat of France in June 1940 was followed by an armistice signed on 22 June, the terms of which included division of the country into an Occupied and an Unoccupied Zone. The zone occupied and administered by the Germans was the northern half of France, including Paris and as far south as Tours and Dijon, plus a broad band of territory on the Atlantic coast right down to the Pyrenees. Alsace and Lorraine were annexed outright to Germany. The remainder of France—the Unoccupied Zone—was controlled by the Vichy goverment headed by Pétain

185   Of the 338,226 men rescued in the 'miracle of Dunkirk' between 26 May and 4 June 1940, 120,000 were French. 'Unfortunately a few thousand of the [French] rearguard were left—and this left sore feelings in France.' Liddell Hart, *Second World War*, op.cit., 79-80; Young, op. cit., 65

186   Pétain, though head of a nominally French state, was not in fact interested in building

up resistance to the Germans but on the contrary collaborated with them in the hope that his Vichy state would become a political partner of Nazi Germany. At his meeting with Hitler on 24 October 1940 at Montoire, Pétain agreed that Vichy and the Axis Powers 'have an identical interest in seeing the defeat of England accomplished as soon as possible. Consequently, the French Government will support, within the limits of its ability, the measures which the Axis Powers may take to this end.' W L Shirer, *The Rise and Fall of the Third Reich* (London, 1970 ed.), 815, quoting the text of the Montoire Agreement.

187 The Légion Française des Combattants (French Legion of Ex-Servicemen) was formed on 29 August 1940 by the Vichy regime and a year later became its only official political party when other parties were suspended, The Milice française, led by Joseph Darnand (1897-1945), was formed in January 1943, a paramilitary body 'of some 45,000 toughs and Fascist fanatics ready to shoot it out with the maquis'. M R D Foot, *Resistance: European Resistance to Nazism 1940-45* (London, 1976), 65 (quoting R O Paxton, *Vichy France* (London, 1972). 298)

188 Charles de Gaulle (1890-1970), fought in the 1914-18 War, on the fall of France in June 1940 went to London to lead the Free French throughout the war, returned to France at the Liberation in 1944 and became head of the provisional government but withdrew from active politics after arousing strong suspicions about his authoritarian tendencies. The crisis in Algeria in 1958 brought him to power again and later that year he became first President of the Fifth Republic created by him and his supporters; and by 1962 Algeria and all other French African colonies had become independent. De Gaulle remained President of the Republic until 1969. Heinz Guderian (1888-1954), German general, tank expert and advocate of blitzkreig warfare, fought in Poland, France and Russia, Chief of the German General Staff, 1944, and commander on the eastern front

189 Hermann Goering (1893-1946), a leading German pilot in the 1914-18 War, joined the Nazi Party in 1922, President of the Reichstag from 1932, deeply implicated in the fire which destroyed it in 1933 and which gave a pretext then for Hitler's establishing a single-party state, founder of the Gestapo (Geheime Staats Polizei, or secret state police), 1933, responsible for the Luftwaffe, made Reichsmarschall, 1940, but his standing later declined. Goering was convicted of war crimes at the Nuremberg Trials in 1945-6 but cheated the hangman by committing suicide

190 Cour-Cheverny is a few miles south of the river Loire, almost midway between Orleans and Tours

191 Maquis meant bush or scrub, hence to take to the maquis was to go underground, to become a member of the Resistance to the German occupation of France

192 The 2nd SS Panzer Division *Das Reich*, moving northward from its bases at Bordeaux and Montauban to oppose the Allied landings in Normandy, massacred at the village of Oradour-sur-Glane near Limoges on 10 June 1944 all 642 villagers, including 240 women and children shot or burned alive in the village church. The *Das Reich* Division, commanded by the SS General Lammerding, who had already established a reputation for murderous cruelty in his treatment of partisans in the Soviet Union, left a swathe of atrocities as it moved north, including 99 hostages hanged at Tulle, 51 hostages shot in the Dordogne, and 54 people massacred at Argenton-sur-Creuse. Azéma, op. cit., 332-3

193 FT.—Francs-Tireurs et Partisans, formed in September 1941, were Communist or Communist-dominated Resistance groups. Henri Michel, *The Shadow War: Resistance*

in Europe 1939-45 (London, 1972), 13, 217-18

194   'Of the Lysander it has been said, as Voltaire said of God, that had it not existed it would have had to be invented.' A small, slow, high-wing monoplane weighing less than five tons, with a radius of 450 miles, carrying up to four passengers it could land and take off over five or six hundred yards of flat grass. Foot, op. cit., 126

195   The Abwehr, German Military Intelligence, was headed by Admiral Wilhelm Canaris (1887-1945), who was implicated in the July 1944 plot to assassinate Hitler and was later murdered by the SS at Oranienburg concentration camp. The Abwehr was then taken over by the SD (Sicherheitsdienst), the SS Security Service under Heinrich Himmler. The favourite method of the Abwehr was to infiltrate double agents into Resistance groups in order to break them up from within and make use of them without their knowledge. Crankshaw, op. cit., 12; Michel, op. cit., 243. 257, 260-1

196   St Cyr-l'École, a few miles from Paris, was the Military College of France until its destruction by bombing in the Second World War

197   Prince Murat's forebear Joachim Murat (1767-1815) was an innkeeper's son who became one of Napoleon Bonaparte's leading generals and King of Naples

198   Many Spanish Republicans fought with the maquis. See e.g., Foot, op. cit., 251. The Atlantic Wall were the fortifications built and the divisions positioned by Hitler to oppose an Allied landing in Western Europe

199   SS—Schutz Staffel (Guard Detachment), formed 1925 as Hitler's personal bodyguard, led from 1929 by Heinrich Himmler. The SS, clad in black uniforms, increased to half a million men, including the Waffen SS (Armed SS). The murderous brutality and ruthlessness of the SS became a byword

200   Women who had slept with Germans had their hair shaved off by the Resistance—see also above p. 274

201   The RPF, founded by General de Gaulle in 1947 as a conservative anti-communist and anti-trade union movement, sought a drastic reform of the constitution of the recently established Fourth Republic. The RPF won almost 40 per cent of the vote in the municipal elections that year in France and control of the municipal councils in almost all the main cities—chiefly at the expense of other right-wing and centre parties. But support for the RPF had declined by the time of the general election to the Chamber of Deputies in 1951, and soon afterward a split took place. De Gaulle did not become President of France until 1958-9 when the Algerian crisis led to the replacement of the Fourth by the Fifth Republic. See, e.g. Alexander Werth, *France 1940-1955* op. cit., 366-78

202   James Annand may be confusing two memories here. Lord Kitchener was drowned on 5 June 1916 when HMS *Hampshire* struck a mine off Orkney while carrying him to Russia. It seems unlikely the school would be in session then in the gloaming

203   Albert Mackie 1904-1985), journalist, editor, 1946-54, Edinburgh *Evening Dispatch,* writer and poet

204   George Ogilvie (1871-1934), as Principal Teacher of English at Broughton Secondary School, 1904-28, he taught and greatly influenced C M Grieve (Hugh MacDiarmid) (1892-1978), Scotland's greatest poet since Robert Burns. Roderick Watson Kerr (1893-1960)

205   Sir Herbert Grierson (1866-1960), Professor of Rhetoric and English Literature, Edinburgh University, 1915-35. Basil Williams (1867-1950), Professor of History, McGill University, Canada, 1921-59 and at Edinburgh, 1925-37

206   Beatrice Webb (1858-1943), social reformer, Fabian socialist, historian

207 Winston Churchill was Lord Rector, Edinburgh University, 1929-32

208 *The Rebel Student* was published from 1923 to (?)1929 by Edinburgh University Labour Party

209 Watson's—George Watson's College, a Merchant Company school

210 Robert Gibson (1886-1965), Lord Gibson, MP for Greenock, 1936-41, chairman, Scottish Land Court, 1941-65

211 See above, note 116

212 Henri Barbusse (1874-1935), French novelist and journalist, fought in the 1914-18 War and wrote as a result *Le Feu* (1916), one of the most widely read novels of the war. After 1919 his writings were mainly political, of a pacifist and socialist character. Barbusse was a contributor to, but not editor of, *Le Monde*, the daily newspaper (which before the 1939-45 war was titled *Le Temps*)

213 The German battleship *Bismarck*, 'the most formidable fighting ship then afloat', sank the British battleship *Hood* near the Denmark Strait off Iceland on 24 May 1941, with the loss of all but three of her crew of 1,419. The *Bismarck*'s fuel tanks were, however, damaged in the encounter with the *Hood*, as were her propeller and rudder in later attacks by British aircraft. After a chase by ships of the Home Fleet, *Bismarck* was sunk in the Western Atlantic on 27 May, with only 110 survivors from her crew of over 2,000 men. Afterwards Nazi Germany relied on submarines, not surface ships, to fight the war in the Atlantic. Captain S W Roskill, *The Navy at War 1939-1945* (London, 1960), 127-38

214 Oerlikon—a light anti-aircraft cannon, named after the suburb of Zürich where it and other armaments are manufactured

215 Vice Admiral Sir Gilbert Stephenson (1878-1972) served in the 1914-18 War, commanded Royal Naval barracks, Portsmouth, 1926-8, general secretary, Navy League, 1932-5, commanded HMS *Western Isles* at Tobermory, 1940-5

216 'Spliced the mainbrace' meant served out grog. drank freely

217 *Candida Casa* (the White House), built at Whithorn, was the church of St Ninian (late 5th century AD), the earliest known Christian leader in Scotland

218 *Weekly Scotsman*, published in Edinburgh, 1860-1967

219 Robert Garioch Sutherland (1909-1981), Scots poet, teacher, and author of *Two Men and a Blanket* (Edinburgh, 1975), his recollections of his experiences as a prisoner of war in the Second World War

220 Norman MacCaig, Scots poet (see above, pp. 282-90). *Sangschaw*, the first book published by C M Grieve (see above, note 204) under his *nom de plume* Hugh MacDiarmid, in 1925. Alan Bold (1943-), author of *MacDiarmid, A Critical Biography* (London, 1988)

221 HMS *Marne*, a destroyer built in 1915 and whose name commemorated the battle of the previous year (see above, note 94), was at the battle of Jutland in 1916 between the British and German fleets off the coast of Denmark, when the British suffered 7,000 casualties and the Germans 3,000. The British fleet lost fourteen warships in the battle, the Germans eleven. The battle was indecisive, though it was seen in Germany as a victory and in Britain as a disappointment. There were no more big battles between the two fleets, both of which became more cautious. But after Jutland the German government put much more emphasis on submarine warfare. Liddell Hart, *First World War*, op. cit., 357-82; Nicolson, op. cit., 279

222 The binder cut the grain harvest and bound it into sheaves which were stooked by hand and later thrashed by a thrashing machine which separated the grain from the straw. Thus the binder was a part-predecessor of the combine harvester

223 The Rome-Berlin Axis was formed by Hitler and Mussolini in 1936, became a full alliance in May 1939 that was joined in September 1940 by Japan, thus creating a Rome-Berlin-Tokyo Axis. These (along with some lesser states such as Hungary and Bulgaria) were the Axis Powers of the Second World War

224 Bromide—potassium or sodium bromide taken as a sedative; a salt or ester of hydrobromic acid

225 Flight Sergeant John Hannah (1921-1947) won the Victoria Cross on 15/16 September 1940 during a raid on Antwerp

226 Some 55,888 officers and other ranks were killed in action or on active service and a further 1,255 died while serving with Bomber Command in the 1939-45 war. The number wounded in action or on active service was 9,162. Of the dead, 47,268 were killed on Bomber Command operations, 8,090 were killed while undertaking non-operational duties and 530 while serving on the ground staff. Of those killed in action or on active service, 38,792 were serving in the Royal Air Force, 9,913 in the Royal Canadian Air Force, 4,037 in the Royal Australian Air Force, 1,676 in the Royal New Zealand Air Force, and 27 in the South African Air Force. Thirty-four belonged to other parts of the British Commonwealth, 928 were Poles, and 481 were from other Allied countries. Most of these casualties were suffered by the relatively small force of aircrew and many have no known grave. The casualties are the best obtainable figures but cannot be regarded as absolutely precise. Nor are the categories entirely clear—for example, not all the Australians in Bomber Command were in the Royal Australian Air Force. Sir Charles Webster and Noble Frankland, *The Strategic Air Offensive against Germany, 1939-1945*, Vol.III, Part 5 (London, 1961), 286-7

227 The cruiser HMS *Coventry* was sunk by German bombers, 14 Sep, 1942, while part of a task force attempting to land troops at the German stronghold of Tobruk in North Africa. Roskill, op. cit., 237-8

228 Sir H Arthur Rose (1875-1937). DL, JP, Hon. LL D, knighted 1919, baronet, 1935, director of various companies, educated Harrow and Trinity College, Cambridge, commanded the 15th Battalion, Royal Scots, 1914-17, DSO and mentioned in despatches, Divisional Food Commissioner, East of Scotland, 1917-18, Food Commissioner for Scotland, 1919-20, chairman, Edinburgh Education, Authority, 1919-20, chairman, General Board of Control for Scotland, 1922-36, Commissioner for Scotland, Special Areas (Development and Improvement) Act, 1934-6

229 The Local Defence Volunteers (LDV) were enrolled from 14 May 1940 and were soon retitled the Home Guard, whose membership by 1943 totalled 1¾ million. Angus Calder, *The People's War* (London, 1969), 121-8, 342

230 Belsen was liberated by British troops on 15 April 1945. 'What was found inside the wire staggered imagination'. As recorded in the British Army Report, 'both inside and outside the wire was a carpet of dead bodies, human excreta, rags and filth'. Peter Padfield, *Himmler* (London, 1990), 582. Bergen-Belsen, ten miles north-west of Celle, Hanover, consisted of two camps. 'In camp No. 1, covering a rectangle one mile by 400 yards, the British troops found 28,000 women, 12,000 men and 13,000 unburied corpses. Another 13,000 died within a few days of liberation. There is absolutely no way of calculating the number of dead who had been buried since the beginning of February 1945, when typhus arrived, but it is at least certain that 40,000 people, the greater part Polish and Hungarian Jews, died in this plague compound, of which every rag and stick had to be destroyed by fire. Camp No. 2 was a camp for privileged Jews, handsomely laid out and containing some good permanent buildings. Camp No. 1

was some distance away and was a hutted camp, originally used for Russian prisoners of war, but which had been expanded by bringing huts from the Jewish camp at Plaszow in Poland during the evacuations of the winter of 1944. Till the last moment efforts were made to keep the flood of arrivals out of Camp No. 2. Thus, though eventually 15,133 people occupied a camp intended for 7,000, there was no typhus and only the beginning of famine in this section. It was far otherwise in Camp No. 1.' Gerald Reitlinger, *The Final Solution. The Attempt to Exterminate the Jews of Europe, 1939-1945* (London, 1953), 466-7

231   WRNS—Women's Royal Naval Service, whose members by 1944 totalled 73,500. Roskill, op. cit., 22

232   The origins of the commandos lay in the formation by the War Office shortly before the war of a research section to study subversion and sabotage. Independent companies drawn mainly from volunteers in the Territorial Army were formed to make amphibious guerrilla attacks against the Germans invading Norway in April 1940. These companies were expanded or reorganised in summer 1940, as a result of an instruction by Churchill to the Chiefs of Staff, to form a series of commandos or self-contained fight units of about 500 men each, and these began to carry out coastal raids on German-occupied France. Charles Messenger, *The Commandos, 1940-46* (London, 1985), 18-42. The raid on the Lofoten Islands, belonging to Norway and lying just inside the Arctic Circle, took place on 4 March 1941. About 500 commandos, along with about fifty Norwegian sailors, escorted by several warships, completely surprised the Germans occupying the islands, destroyed herring and cod liver oil factories that provided materials for the German munitions industry, sank 18,000 tons of enemy shipping, and brought away 315 Lofoten volunteers for the Norwegian forces, 225 German prisoners, and sixty Quislings, at a cost of only one wounded officer who had accidentally shot himself in the thigh. The raid also succeeded in persuading the German authorities to strengthen their garrisons in Norway and in capturing material which gave British code-breakers access to the signals of the German navy for several months and speeded up progress in breaking German codes and cyphers generally. The Lofoten raid strengthened the conclusion that a commando landing must have a strategic, political or economic object. Kenneth Mackesy, *Commando Strike. The Story of Amphibious Raiding in World War II* (London, 1985). 47-51; Messenger, op.cit., 46-8

233   The Lovat Scouts were raised in 1900 as a specialist corps of scouts and snipers from among Scots stalkers and gamekeepers. They fought in the Boer War, the 1914-18 War and in the 1939-45 war, where they were trained as specialist ski troops and in mountain warfare. After 1945 the Lovat Scouts were merged with the Scottish Horse in the Royal Armoured Corps (Territorial Army). Major R Money Barnes and C Kennedy Allen, *The Uniforms and History of the Scottish Regiments* (London, 1960), 311

234   Mohandas K Gandhi (1869-1948), leader of the Indian Home Rule movement, whose method was non-violent non-co-operation. Gandhi, imprisoned several times by the British authorities, was assassinated by a Hindu nationalist a year after India gained its independence

235   The Bengal Famine in 1943 cost about three million lives

236   MTB—motor torpedo-boats

237   OCTU—Officer Cadet Training Unit

238   The atomic bomb was dropped on Hiroshima on 6 August and on Nagasaki on 9 August 1945, killing or injuring about 300,000 people. Japan surrendered on 15 August

239 After heavy fighting, the 2nd Battalion, Royal Scots, surrendered to the Japanese in December 1941. Plany of the men were later sent to Japan as prisoners-of-war on board the *Lisbon Maru* but this vessel was hit, it was thought by a torpedo from an Allied submarine, and the Japanese battened down the holds where the prisoners were held. Though they succeeded in breaking out, about 900 of the prisoners lost their lives, about half of all those on board. Augustus Muir. *The First of Foot. The History of the Royal* Scots (Edinburgh, 1961), 81, 128-30

240 NAAFI—Navy, Army and Air Force Institutes, providing canteens for the Forces

241 James Cagney (1899-1986), American film star who had leading roles in many films about police and gangsters in which he wore a broad-brimmed soft hat

242 The Means Test, introduced in 1931 by the so-called 'National' government headed by Ramsay MacDonald, was loathed by the working class and was a cause of the break-up of families. It was a household means test. Unemployed people applying for subsistence once their insurance benefits were exhausted were subject by the means test to payments assessed on the earnings of all members of their household (sons and daughters, fathers and mothers, brothers and sisters, et al.), as well as savings, pensions, etc. 'Thrift was penalised and improvidence rewarded. Family solidarity was undermined: growing sons were forced to support their parents in a way which frayed the tempers of both generations and might break up the family; sons and daughters would move into lodgings in order not to be "dragged down" by having to support their parents. The test was an encouragement to the tattle-tale and the local blackmailer; to all sorts of unneighbourliness. It stimulated petty tyranny and insolence on the part of Labour Exchange clerks and managers; the weekly visit to the Exchange would bring the sudden, curt announcement by the clerk: "They've knocked you off the dole."' Mowat, op. cit., 470, 483-4

243 Hibernian FC were in the Second Division, Scottish League, in 1931-3

244 Robertson was convicted of the murder of his ex-wife and son and hanged in June 1954

245 *The Iron Heel* (New York, 1907), by Jack London (1876-1916), American socialist and author. Very Rev. Hewlett Johnson (1874-1966), the 'Red' Dean of Canterbury, 1931-63, *The Socialist Sixth of the World* (London, 1939)

246 The Earl of Eglinton (1880-1945). William E Buist, Lord Provost of Dundee, 1932-5

247 The Peace Ballot of 1934-5, conducted by the National Declaration Committee and closely associated with the League of Nations Union, asked five questions in a house-to-house canvass of the population of Britain: (1) Should Britain remain a member of the League of Nations? (2) Are you in favour of an all-round reduction in armaments by international agreement? (3) Are you in favour of an all-round abolition of national military and naval aircraft by international agreement? (4) Should the private manufacture and sale of arms be prohibited by international agreement? (5) Do you consider that, if a nation insists on attacking another, the other nations should combine to compel it to stop by (a) economic and non-military measures? (b) if necessary, military measures ? In an unprecedented number of responses for a private referendum, over 11 million people voted yes to the first question, and about 10 million to the others. To the last question, 5(b), 6,784,368 voted 'yes' and 2,351,981 'no'. Mowat, op, cit., 541-2

248 George Lansbury (1859-1940), Labour MP, 1910-12 and 1922-40, Commissioner of Works, 1929-31, Leader of the Labour Party, 1931-5, resigned the leadership because

as a pacifist he could not support the Party conference's adoption of a policy of sanctions against Mussolini's pending attack on Abyssinia. The brigadier may have been Brigadier General F P Crozier (1879-1937), commandant, 1920-21, of the Auxiliary Division ('Auxies') of the Royal Irish Constabulary in the Anglo-Irish War, who resigned his appointment in February 1921 and urged a truce in the war. Crozier, who had served in the Boer War and the 1914-18 War, and had fought against the Bolsheviks in 1919-20, was author of several books, including *The Men I Killed* (London, 1937)

249   Old Contemptible—soldier in the British army of 1914, which the Kaiser had described as a contemptible little army

250   Joseph F Duncan (1879-1965), General Secretary, 1914-45, Scottish Farm Servants' Union. The union was founded in 1912 and in 1933 amalgamated into the Transport & General Workers' Union, where Scots farm workers were organised in their own section

251   *Manchester Guardian Weekly*, published from 1919, now the *Guardian Weekly*; *Perthshire Advertiser*, published weekly since 1829; *The Bulletin (and Scots Pictorial* from 1923), published daily in Glasgow, 1915-60. The 'local Lockerbie paper' was presumably the *Annandale Herald*, published there weekly since 1862

252   The BBC radio programme 'ITMA' ('It's That Man Again'), with the comedian Tommy Handley (1896-1949), ran from 1939 until his death in 1949. 'The Brains Trust', with Julian Huxley the zoologist, C E M Joad the philosopher, and Commander A B Campbell, retired naval officer, as the three regular members, was another long-running BBC radio programme that began during the war in January 1941 and which within a couple of years had a regular audience of 10 to 12 million listeners. Calder, op. cit., 364-5

253   The buzz bombs were the V1 flying bombs dropped by the Germans on London and the south-east of England in 1944-5, followed by the V2 rockets or guided missiles in the same period, carrying a tonne of high explosive in their warheads

254   UNRRA—United Nations Relief and Rehabilitation Administration

255   Queen Wilhelmina (1880-1962) of the Netherlands

256   Displaced Persons (DPs) were people sent from countries occupied during the war to Nazi Germany to work there as slave labour. There were about 7½ million Displaced Persons in Nazi Germany at the end of the war. In addition there were about 9 million Germans, also sometimes described as Displaced Persons, who had fled from the advancing Red Army and/or were expelled from eastern European countries at the end of the war

257   Marshal Tito (1892-1980), pseudonym of Josip Broz, leader of the Resistance to Nazi German occupation of Yugoslavia, 1941-45, Prime Minister of the Federal Republic of Yugoslavia from 1946, President, 1953-80

258   Wurst—German sausage

259   Aldous Huxley (1894-1963), author of *Brave New World* (1932), *Point Counter Point* (1928), and other works

260   Campaign for Nuclear Disarmament, formed 1958

261   See below, note 278

262   Sir Archibald Black (d.1962), KC, Sheriff of Lanarkshire and of Stirling, Dumbarton and Clackmannan, 1933-7, Procurator for the Church of Scotland, 1936-7, chairman, Conscientious Objectors' Tribunal for South West Scotland, 1939-49

263   Lord Elphinstone (1869-1957), married to Lady Mary Bowes Lyon, daughter of the

Earl of Strathmore, Lord High Commissioner of the Church of Scotland, 1923-4, Captain General of the Royal Company of Archers, 1935-53, chairman, Appellate Tribunal

264 Pacifist Service Units undertook pioneering social work among poor families. Two of the units were based in Liverpool and Manchester, and a third was opened in Stepney in March 1943, but had to close after 18 months through shortage of staff and the disruption caused by Flying Bombs. Denis Hayes, *Challenge of Conscience. The Story of the COs of 1939-1949* (London, 1949), 222-3

265 VE Day—Victory in Europe Day, 8 May 1945

266 For Sir Compton Mackenzie see above, note 137

267 NALGO—National and Local Government Officers' Association

268 Jankers—detention

269 By the end of 1946, 1,050 conscientious objectors had been court-martialled since 1939. Of these 635 had registered as conscientious objectors at the outset, while 415 had first recorded a conscientious objection while in the Forces. The number of times these objectors were court-martialled was: once—716, twice—210, three times—106, four times—15, five times—2, six times—1. Gilbert Lane of Wallington, Surrey, was the only conscientious objector of the Second World War to be court-martialled six times. He was sentenced successively to 28 days' detention, 3 months imprisonment, 6 months' detention, 93 days' imprisonment, 18 months' detention, and 6 months' imprisonment—then he was conditionally registered as a conscientious objector and was discharged from the army. Hayes, op. cit., 112-13, 118

270 At 6 a.m. on 2 July, 1940 the 15,500 ton Blue Star liner *Arandora Star*, on its way to Canada with 1,500 German, Italian and other internees on board, was torpedoed and sunk by a Nazi U-boat off the west coast of Ireland. This was the first news that the British public and relatives of interned 'enemy aliens' had that internees were being sent overseas. Questions in parliament indicated that at least 200 refugees from Nazi Germany and Fascist Italy, as well as some long-standing German, Italian, Austrian and other opponents of fascism or nazism, were among these deportees. The loss of *The Arandora Star* revealed the appalling muddle into which government policy on internment of aliens, including many Jewish, anti-Fascist, and other refugees, in Britain had fallen. See, e.g., F Lafitte, *The Internment of Aliens* (Harmondsworth, 1940), esp. 123-4. See also above, p. 291, 315-17

271 In the first half of July 1940 about 7,700 internees were sent from Britain to Canada and Australia. Lafitte, op. cit., 131. See also above, p. 291, 315-17

272 Easter Road: stadium of Hibernian FC; Tynecastle: stadium of Heart of Midlothian FC

273 There were 422 people born in Italy living in Edinburgh, according to the *Census of Scotland, 1931*, Vol. 1, Part I, *City of Edinburgh* (Edinburgh, 1932), 31

274 Valvona and Crolla were formally established in 1931

275 Tommy was also known as Philip—see p. 332 above

276 At the Armistice Day parade in Edinburgh in 1929 'the rear was brought up by a small band of the Edinburgh Fascisti preceded by a stalwart standard bearer who, because of the wild and tempestuous weather, had some little difficulty in holding aloft the large flag of the Fascist colours.' *Edinburgh Evening News*, 11 November 1929. No other local press reports have been found of Fascist participation in the parade between the mid-1920s and mid-1930s

277 Deadly hostility to trade unionism was a characteristic of fascism. 'Towards the end of

1920, at the moment when Italian trade unionism reached its greatest expansion, there were 2,300,000 trade unionists ... At the end of 1920 the Fascists began methodically to smash the trade unions and the co-operative societies by beating, banishing, or killing their leaders and destroying their property. They made no distinction between Christian Democrats and Socialists, between right-wing and left-wing Socialists, between Socialists and Communists, or between Communists and Anarchists. All the organisations of the working classes, whatever their banner, were marked out for destruction because they were "Bolshevist".' Gaetano Salvemini, *Under the Axe of Fascism* (London, 1936), 17-18. Once Mussolini and the Fascists were established in power in Italy from 1922 the so-called corporations, or corporative system, were 'trade unions' that included both employers and employees. In 1929 Mussolini declared that the former antagonism between capital and labour was at an end and both sides of industry were working together with complete equality of rights and duties: a situtation unique in the world. The fact was that withdrawal of labour in Fascist Italy was a punishable offence. See D Mack Smith, *Mussolini*, (London, 1981). 119-20

278   Intrigue and bribery, aimed at subverting the loyalty of the subordinate Abyssinian chiefs, was carried on by Italian agents before Mussolini invaded Abyssinia in October 1935. The decision to make war on Abyssinia had been taken two years earlier. As Marshal Emilio de Bono (1866-1944), commander-in-chief at the time of the invasion, put it: 'The important thing to understand is this: That from the very outset of the campaign there were signs of the results of this disintegrating political action, and that it deprived our enemy of at least 200,000 men, who either did not take up arms, or who, although enrolled and armed, remained inert.' De Bono, *Anno XIV, The Conquest of an Empire* (London, 1937) p 54. On 30 December 1935 Emperor Haile Selassie of Abyssinia protested to the League of Nations that the Italians were using poison gas in their attacks. In March 1936, taking advantage of European distraction with the Rhineland crisis created by Hitler, 'Mussolini intensified gas attacks and bombing raids, which spared neither Red Cross units nor undefended towns. The effect of the gas was cruel and militarily severe, for the Ethiopian soldiers fought barefoot and suffered terrible burns ... One of the tragedies of the Abyssinian campaign was the suffering of the wounded. The Emperor, in an interview when his usual calm dignity seemed tinged with despair, told Sir Sidney Barton [British Minister at Addis Ababa] that his armies had been demoralised by the use of gas, while the civil population had been bombed. He had been deprived, through the attacks on the Red Cross, of the medical aid organised by foreign sympathisers. After the heaviest fighting in the war, at Ashangi, no medical help at all had been available for large numbers of gassed and wounded.' Earl of Avon (Anthony Eden), *The Eden Memoirs: Facing the Dictators* (London, 1962), 322, 374, 379-80. 'All through March [1936] *The Times* printed accounts of the use of poison gas from their correspondents, and on the 25th they published a telegram from Mr T A Lambie, the distinguished American who was acting as Secretary to the Red Cross organisation in Ethiopia: "The bombing of country villages around Kworam and Waldia, the permanent blinding and maiming of hundreds of helpless women and children, as well as the infliction of similar injuries on soldiers with that most dreadful of all dreadful agencies, yperite, or so-called mustard gas, should cause us to ask ourselves the question—whither?"' G T Garratt, *Mussolini's Roman Empire* (Harmondsworth, 1938), 108-09

279   The beginning of the Second World War in September 1939 seems not to have been expected by Mussolini and his Fascist government until Hitler informed them of his

intentions in August. As a result of his intervention in the Spanish Civil War, 1936-9, Mussolini had become increasingly dependent on Hitler at a time when, as a result of the Abyssinian War and other factors, fascist Italy's relations with Britain and France had deteriorated. In May 1939 the so-called Pact of Steel between Nazi Germany and Italy drew them closer together but on the grounds that it was unprepared for war Italy had remained non-belligerent from September 1939 to June 1940. With the defeat of France the risks of intervention in the war seemed much less; and Mussolini seems to have feared that if he did not enter the war Hitler might wreak vengeance on him as a faithless ally. See Martin Clark, *Modern Italy 1871-1982* (London, 1984), 282-5

280   Within a quarter of an hour of Italy's entry into the war on 10 June, 'a comb-out of the 20,000 Italians estimated to be In the UK was begun,' while in Edinburgh, as in London, Liverpool, Glasgow, Belfast, Manchester, and elsewhere, there was 'an orgy of window-breaking and looting'. Between 20 and 30 shops in Leith Street and Leith Walk in Edinburgh had their windows smashed and their contents scattered about in the roadway, as a crowd variously estimated at from 1,000 to 3,000 went on an anti-Italian rampage. 'Restaurants, ice-cream shops, fish and chip shops, hairdressers' establishments and the premises of a firm of wine-importers had their windows smashed. Expensive plant, such as coffee percolators, tea urns and up to date cooking ranges were damaged. Decorative fittings and tables and chairs were also objects of the crowd's fury ... The police did their best to bring the more hot-headed elements to reason, but they had a more or less impossible job. The wrecking activities seemed to be led by a comparatively small number of irresponsible young men, and the majority of the crowd seemed to be content to stand by and shout and follow on to the next scene of operations. Many expressions of sympathy for the occupants of the shops were heard, as it was known that some of the shopkeepers were Britlsh subjects, and indeed the proprietor of one well known restaurant whose premises were among the most seriously damaged in the city, fought throughout the last war in the ranks of a Scottish regiment. Another man, whose premises were subjected to considerable damage, has two sons at present on active service with the Black Watch, it is believed. The police were far from idle. Nearly 100 arrests were made, but only about 20 of them were detained for interrogation. At some places the policemen had to make use of their batons ... Sporadic outbreaks occurred in other parts of the city. Similar attacks were made in Stockbridge, Dalry, Portobello, the South Side and Abbeyhill, and the window of a shop not many yards from the police headquarters in the High Street was smashed. Many Leith shops were attacked and looted ... The police occupied official Italian premises at Picardy Place in the course of the evening, where burning papers caused a slight outbreak of fire. The Fire Brigade was summoned. The police managed to retrieve a number of documents. During the evening police were engaged in rounding up Italians. At the headquarters there was constant coming and going of motor cars and between 80 and 100 persons were detained. By this forenoon 160 Edinburgh men between the ages of 16 and 70 had been sent to internment camps.' *Edinburgh Evening Dispatch*, 11 June 1940

281   The Defence of the Realm Act had been passed on 8 August 1914 as a wartime measure that gave the government extensive powers to make regulations for 'securing the public safety and the defence of the realm'. In 1935 the Committee of Imperial Defence had set up a secret committee to draft emergency legislation that would be needed if war came. One of the issues raised was that of 'disaffected persons' of British

nationality. It was proposed in 1937 to draft a clause in the projected bill that would enable the government to intern anyone 'whose detention appears to the Secretary of State to be expedient in the interests of the public safety or the Defence of the Realm'. On 24 August 1939, the day after the signing of the Nazi-Soviet Non-Aggression Pact, parliament passed in a day the Emergency Powers Act; and on 1 September, the day of the German invasion of Poland, the government issued its Defence Regulations, not through parliament but by order in council which did not need parliamentary consent. Regulation 18B empowered the Home Secretary to make a detention order 'if satisfied with respect to any particular person that with a view to preventing him acting in a manner prejudicial to the public safety or the Defence of the Realm, it is necessary to do so.' A J P Taylor, *English History 1914-45* (Oxford, 1965), 450; Peter and Leni Gillman, *'Collar the Lot!' How Britain Interned and Expelled its Wartime Refugees* (London, 1980), 119-122

282 Donaldson's Hospital, or school for the deaf and dumb, designed by Playfair, and founded in the mid-19th century by James Donaldson, an Edinburgh bookseller

283 Sir Eduardo Paolozzi (1924-) Professor of Sculpture at Munich, since 1986 Her Majesty's Sculptor in Ordinary for Scotland, sent at the age of 16 for three months to Saughton Prison in 1940, his father, grandfather and uncle were lost on the *Arandora Star*. See interview in *The Times Saturday Review*, 8 September 1990

284 Poole's—Poole's Synod Hall, Castle Terrace, Edinburgh, where there was an indoor shooting range in the basement

285 KOSBs—King's Own Scottish Borderers

286 The place of internment at Huyton near Liverpool was an unfinished housing estate. The houses, which when internees were first put in them in the summer of 1940 had almost no furniture or beds, were supplemented by tents. Lafitte, op. cit.p 105-06,

287 In its first few weeks in summer 1940 as an internment camp there appear to have been four suicides and at least two unsuccessful attempts, at Huyton. One internee, who committed suicide on 2 July, had been in a concentration camp for two years in Nazi Germany or Austria. News of the sinking of the *Arandora Star* on 2 July evidently resulted in two of these suicides. Lafitte, op. cit., 108, 112

288 John Warburton Beckett (1894-1964), journalist and company director, fought in the 1914-18 War, joined the Independent Labour Party, 1917, Labour MP for Gateshead, 1924-9, and Peckham, 1929-31, joined the British Union of Fascists, 1934, and became Director of Publicity, left the BUF later in 1934 and with William Joyce founded the National Socialist League, then in 1939 the British People's Party, arrested 23 May 1940 under Regulation 18B, imprisoned in Brixton and Stafford and interned on the Isle of Man, released 29 Oct, 1943, became a convert to Roman Catholicism, 1952. Biography by Colin Holmes, in J Saville and J Bellamy, *Dictionary of Labour Biography*, Vol. VI (London, 1982), 24-9

289 Rudolf Hess (1894-1987), Hitler's deputy, landed in a plane in Renfrewshire on 10 May 1941, evidently with proposals for a compromise peace between Britain and Nazi Germany. He was a prisoner of war until 1945 then was tried at the Nuremberg War Crimes trials and sentenced to life imprisonment. Galeazzo Ciano (1903-1944), Italian Fascist Foreign Minister, 1936-43, son-in-law of Mussolini. Italo Balbo (1896-1940), politician, aviator, fascist organiser in Ferrara, Minister of Aviation, 1929-33 and Governor of Llbya, regarded as second only to Ciano in succession to Mussolini, commander of Italian forces in North Africa, 1940, shot down and killed by his own anti-aircraft batteries at Tobruk

290   After Mussolini was overthrown by a majority vote in the Grand Council of Fascism in July 1943 and imprisoned, Marshal Badoglio was installed as prime minister and in September 1943 made an armistice with the Anglo-American Allies. The Germans then took over control of central and northern Italy, rescued Mussolini from his imprisonment and restored him to power in their half of Italy. At the meeting of the Grand Council of Fascism in July which overthrew Mussolini, Ciano had voted against him. After Mussolini's restoration, Ciano was tried for treason and shot by the Fascists. There is no evidence that Ciano and other fascist leaders were in the pay of the British government. Mussolini 'sometimes acknowledged quite candidly that they [Ciano and four other Fascist leaders he had executed in January 1944] were not guilty at all'. D Mack Smith, op. cit., 294-303

291   Joe Gloag (1907-1977), Professor, Industrial Administration and Commerce, 1965-72, and Dean of the Faculty of Humanities, 1966-9, at Heriot-Watt University

292   The definitions or equations suggested by Mr Pia beg many questions. Fascism, though varying from country to country in the emphasis it placed on some of its traits, was and remains essentially ultranationalist, racist, anti-democratic, authoritarian, anti-liberal, anti-socialist, anti-trade union, anti-feminist, and ineradicably opposed to internationalism and the brotherhood of man

293   Roland W (Tiny) Rowland (1917-), born as R W Fuhrhop in India, chief executive and managing director, London & Rhodesia Mining and Land Co.

294   William Joyce (1906-1946), born in the United States of Irish parents, his family emigrated from Ireland to England in 1922, member of the British Union of Fascists from 1933, after expulsion from it in 1939, formed the strongly pro-Nazi British National Socialist Party; left England for Germany before the outbreak of war and throughout the war broadcast on the radio from there. Because of his upper class accent he was nicknamed Lord Haw Haw. As he had had a British passport (though falsely acquired) until July 1940, he was convicted of treason after the war and executed

295   *Deutschland über alles*—the German national anthem

296   Captain Archibald H M Ramsay (?-1955), educated at Eton and Sandhurst, severely wounded in the Coldstream Guards, 1916, member of His Majesty's Body Guard for Scotland, 1920-55, Unionist MP for Peebles and South Midlothian 1931-45, detained from 23 May 1940 at Brixton prison under Regulation 18B until released on 26 September 1944, author of *The Nameless War* (1953). Captain Ramsay, who 'believed that a conspiracy of Bolsheviks, Jews and Freemasons was threatening to dominate the world', had founded the Right Club in the 1930s. One of the Right Club's posters put up in London after the war broke out in 1939 declared: 'This is a Jews' war'. P and L Gillman, op. cit.,116, 117, 124-5

Some Further Reading

As well as books mentioned in the notes, the following may be of interest to the general reader:

Frank Williams, *Old Soldiers Never Die* (London, 1964)

Guy Chapman, *A Passionate Prodigality* (London, 1965)

Edmund Blunden, *Undertones of War* (London, 1928)

John Rae, *Conscience and Politics ... 1916-1919* (Oxford, 1970)

F L Carsten, *War against War* (London, 1982)

Gerald Brenan, *The Spanish Labyrinth* (Cambridge, 1960)

John Erickson, *The Road to Stalingrad* (London, 1977)

John Erickson, *The Road to Berlin* (London, 1983)

Maurice Larkin, *France since the Popular Front* (Oxford, 1988)

S Woodburn Kirby and others, *The War against Japan* (London, 1957-69)

John Roberts, *Europe 1880-1945* (London, 1989)

Paul Addison, *The Road to 1945* (London, 1982)

INDEX